FX DERIVATIVES TRADER SCHOOL

The Wiley Trading series features books by traders who have survived the market's ever changing temperament and have prospered—some by reinventing systems, others by getting back to basics. Whether a novice trader, professional, or somewhere in-between, these books will provide the advice and strategies needed to prosper today and well into the future. For more on this series, visit our Web site at www.WileyTrading.com.

Founded in 1807, John Wiley & Sons is the oldest independent publishing company in the United States. With offices in North America, Europe, Australia, and Asia, Wiley is globally committed to developing and marketing print and electronic products and services for our customers' professional and personal knowledge and understanding.

FX DERIVATIVES TRADER SCHOOL

Giles Jewitt

WILEY

Published by John Wiley & Sons, Inc., Hoboken, New Jersey.
Published simultaneously in Canada.

For general information on our other products and services or for technical support, please contact our Customer Care Department within the United States at (800) 762-2974, outside the United States at (317) 572-3993 or fax (317) 572-4002.

Wiley publishes in a variety of print and electronic formats and by print-on-demand. Some material included with standard print versions of this book may not be included in e-books or in print-on-demand. If this book refers to media such as a CD or DVD that is not included in the version you purchased, you may download this material at http://booksupport.wiley.com. For more information about Wiley products, visit www.wiley.com.

Library of Congress Cataloging-in-Publication Data:

ISBN 9781118967454 (Paperback)
ISBN 9781119096610 (ePDF)
ISBN 9781119096474 (ePub)

Cover image: Business World © iStock.com/ktsimage; abstract background © iStock.com/PiexelEmbargo
Cover design: Wiley

Printed in the United States of America
10 9 8 7 6 5 4 3 2 1

For my wife and daughters: Laura, Rosie, and Emily.

CONTENTS

In 2004 I started on an FX derivatives trading desk as a graduate. I wrote down everything I learned: how markets worked, how FX derivatives contracts were risk-managed, how to quote prices, how Greek exposures evolve over time, how different pricing models work, and so on. This book is a summary of that knowledge, filtered through a decade of trading experience across the full range of FX derivatives products.

In 2011 I started sending out monthly "Trader School" e-mails to traders on the desk, covering a wide range of topics. The e-mails were particularly popular with new joiners and support functions because they gave an accessible view of derivatives trading that did not exist elsewhere. This book collects together and expands upon those e-mails.

Part I covers the basics of FX derivatives trading. This is material I wish I'd had access to when originally applying for jobs on derivatives trading desks. Part II investigates the volatility surface and the instruments that are used to define it. Part III covers vanilla FX derivatives trading and shows how the FX derivatives market can be analyzed. Part IV covers exotic FX derivatives trading, starting with the most basic products and slowly increasing the complexity up to advanced volatility and multi-asset products. This material will mostly be useful to junior traders or traders looking to build or refresh their knowledge in a particular area.

Fundamentally, the aim of the book is to explain derivatives trading from first principles in order to develop intuition about derivative risk rather than attempting to be state of the art. Within the text, experienced quant traders will find many statements that are not entirely true, but are true the vast majority of the time. Endlessly caveating each statement would make the text interminable.

Traders can only be successful if they have a good understanding of the framework in which they operate. Importantly though, for derivatives traders this is not the same as fully understanding derivative mathematics. Therefore the mathematics is kept to an accessible "advanced high school" level throughout. Some mathematical rigor is lost as a result of this, but for traders that is a price worth paying.

Also in the interests of clarity, some other important considerations are largely ignored within the analysis, most notably, credit risk (i.e., the risk of a counterparty defaulting on money owed) and interest rates (i.e., how interest rate markets work in practice). Derivative product analysis is the primary concern here and this is cleaner if those issues are ignored or simplified.

Regulations and technology are causing significant changes within the FX derivatives market structure. The most important changes are increasing electronic execution, increasing electronic market data, more visibility on transactions occurring in the market, and less clear distinctions between banks and their clients. These changes will have profound and lasting effects on the market. However, the ideas and techniques explored within the book hold true no matter how the market structure changes.

Finally, and most importantly, if you are a student or new joiner on a derivatives trading desk: *Do the practicals*. I can guarantee that if you complete the practicals, you will hit the ground running when you join a derivatives trading desk. *Do them*. Do them *all*. Do them all *in order*. Do not download the spreadsheets from the companion website unless you are completely stuck. When you're trying to learn something, taking the easy option is never the right thing to do. The practicals require the ability to set up Excel VBA (Visual Basic for Applications) functions and subroutines. If you aren't familiar with this, there is plenty of material online that covers this in detail.

The very best of luck with your studies and careers,

Giles Jewitt, London, 2015.

ACKNOWLEDGMENTS

Thanks are due to
… those who taught me:

Fred Boillereau
Jeff Wang
Mike Killen
Rob Ross
Hossein Zaimi

… those who supported me in writing the book and helped make it happen:

Howard Savery
Caroline Prior
Vincent Craignou
Selene Chong

… all colleagues who helped me with content, especially:

Chris Potter
Charlie Chamberlain
Daniela Asikian
Allen Li

… Marouane Benchekroun and his Quants for the tools I used to produce most of the charts in the book.
… those who looked after my girls and I while the book was completed:

Frances, Tony, Phil, Gerry, Tim, Jod and Mark.

… my family for their support, encouragement and assistance: Mum, Dad, and Anna.

This publication reflects the views of the author only.

This publication is intended to be educational in nature and should be used for information purposes only.

Any opinions expressed herein are given in good faith, but are subject to change without notice.

Any strategies discussed are strictly for illustrative and educational purposes only and are not to be construed as an endorsement, recommendation, or solicitation to buy or sell any financial securities.

All rates and figures used are for illustrative purposes only and do not reflect current market rates.

FX DERIVATIVES TRADER SCHOOL

THE BASICS

Part I lays the foundations for understanding FX derivatives trading. Trading within a financial market, market structure, and the Black-Scholes framework are all covered from first principles. FX derivatives trading risk is then introduced with an initial focus on vanilla options since they are by far the most commonly traded contract.

Introduction to Foreign Exchange

The *foreign exchange (FX) market* is an international marketplace for trading **currencies**. In FX transactions, one currency (sometimes shortened to CCY) is *exchanged* for another. Currencies are denoted with a three-letter code and **currency pairs** are written CCY1/CCY2 where the **exchange rate** for the currency pair is the number of CCY2 it costs to buy one CCY1. Therefore, trading EUR/USD FX involves exchanging amounts of EUR and USD. If the FX rate goes higher, CCY1 is getting relatively stronger against CCY2 since it will cost more CCY2 to buy one CCY1. If the FX rate goes lower, CCY1 is getting relatively weaker against CCY2 because one CCY1 will buy fewer CCY2.

If a currency pair has both elements from the list in Exhibit 1.1, it is described as a *G10 currency pair*.

The most commonly quoted FX rate is the **spot rate**, often just called **spot**. For example, if the EUR/USD spot rate is 1.3105, EUR 1,000,000 would be exchanged for USD 1,310,500. Within a spot transaction the two cash flows actually hit the bank account (*settle*) on the **spot date**, which is usually two business days after the transaction is agreed (called T+2 settlement). However, in some currency pairs, for example, USD/CAD and USD/TRY (Turkish lira), the spot date is only one day after the transaction date (called T+1 settlement).

Another set of commonly traded FX contracts are **forwards**, sometimes called **forward outrights**. Within a forward transaction the cash flows settle on some future date other than the spot date. When rates are quoted on forwards, the **tenor** or **maturity** of the contract must also be specified. For example, if the EUR/USD 1yr (one-year) forward FX rate is 1.3245, by transacting this contract in EUR10m

EXHIBIT 1.1	G10 Currencies		
CCY Code	Full Name	CCY Code	Full Name
AUD	Australian dollar	JPY	Japanese yen
CAD	Canadian dollar	NOK	Norwegian krone
CHF	Swiss franc	NZD	New Zealand dollar
EUR	Euro	SEK	Swedish krona
GBP	Great British pound	USD	United States dollar

(ten million euros) **notional**, each EUR will be exchanged for 1.3245 USD (i.e., EUR10m will be exchanged for USD13.245m in one year's time). In a given currency pair, the spot rate and forward rates are linked by the respective **interest rates** in each currency. By a no-arbitrage argument, delivery to the forward maturity must be equivalent to trading spot and putting the cash balances in each currency into "risk-free" investments until the maturity of the forward. This is explained in more detail in Chapter 5.

Differences between the spot rate and a forward rate are called **swap points** or **forward points**. For example, if EUR/USD spot is 1.3105 and the EUR/USD 1yr forward is 1.3245, the EUR/USD 1yr swap points are 0.0140. In the market, swap points are quoted as a number of **pips**. Pips are the smallest increment in the FX rate usually quoted for a particular currency pair. In EUR/USD, where FX rates are usually quoted to four decimal places, a pip is 0.0001. In USD/JPY, where FX rates are usually only quoted to two decimal places, a pip is 0.01. In the above example, an FX swaps trader would say that EUR/USD 1yr swap points are at 140 ("one-forty").

Pips (sometimes called "points") are also used to describe the magnitude of FX moves (e.g., "EUR/USD has jumped forty pips higher" if the EUR/USD spot rate moves from 1.3105 to 1.3145). Another term used to describe spot moves is **figure**, meaning one hundred pips (e.g., "USD/JPY has dropped a figure" if the USD/JPY spot rate moves from 101.20 to 100.20).

FX swap contracts contain two FX deals in opposite directions (one a buy, the other a sell). Most often one deal is a spot trade and the other deal is a forward trade to a specific maturity. The two trades are called the **legs** of the transaction and the notionals on the two legs of the FX swap are often equal in CCY1 terms (e.g., buy *EUR10m* EUR/USD spot against sell *EUR10m* EUR/USD 1yr forward). FX swaps are quoted in swap point terms (the difference in FX rate) between the two legs. In general, swap points change far less frequency than spot rates in a given currency pair.

A trader takes up a new FX position by buying USD10m USD/CAD spot at a rate of 0.9780. This means buying USD10m and simultaneously selling CAD9.78m. This position is described as "long ten dollar-cad," meaning USD10m has been bought and an equivalent amount of CAD has been sold. If USD10m USD/CAD had been sold at 0.9780 instead, the position is described as "short ten dollar-cad." Note that the long/short refers to the *CCY1* position. The concept of selling something you don't initially own is a strange one in the real world but it quickly becomes normal in financial markets where trading positions can flip often between long (a net bought position) and short (a net sold position).

USD/CAD spot jumps up to 0.9900 after it was bought at 0.9780: The trader is a hero! Time to sell USD/CAD spot and lock in the profit. Selling USD10m USD/CAD spot at 0.9900 results in selling USD10m against buying CAD9.9m. The initial bought USD10m and new sold USD10m cancel out, leaving no net USD position, but the initial sold CAD9.78m and new bought CAD9.9m leave CAD120k profit. This is important: FX transactions and positions are usually quoted in CCY1 terms (e.g., *USD*10m USD/CAD) while the profit and loss (P&L) from the trade is naturally generated in CCY2 terms (e.g., *CAD*120k).

A **long** position in a financial instrument *makes money* if the price of the instrument *rises* and *loses money* if the price of the instrument *falls*. Mathematically, the intraday P&L from a long spot position is:

$$P\&L_{CCY2} = Notional_{CCY1} \cdot (S_T - S_0)$$

where S_0 is the initial spot rate and S_T is the new spot rate.

Exhibit 1.2 shows the P&L from a long spot position. As expected, P&L expressed in CCY2 terms is linear in spot.

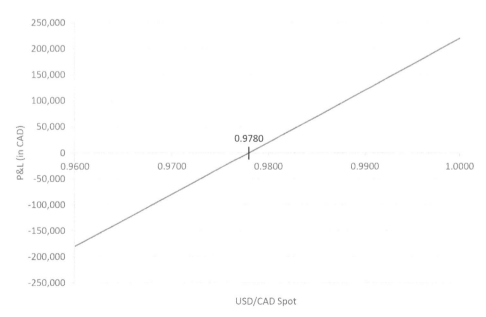

EXHIBIT 1.2   P&L from long USD10m USD/CAD spot at 0.9780

A **short** position in a financial instrument *makes money* if the price of the instrument *falls* and *loses money* if the price of the instrument *rises*. The intraday P&L from a short spot position is also:

$$P\&L_{CCY2} = Notional_{CCY1}.(S_T - S_0)$$

However, the notional will be negative to denote a short position.

Exhibit 1.3 shows the P&L from a short spot position. Again, P&L expressed in CCY2 terms is linear in spot.

If the P&L from these spot deals is brought back into CCY1 terms, the conversion between CCY2 and CCY1 takes place at the prevailing spot rate. Therefore, the CCY1 P&L from a spot position is:

$$P\&L_{CCY1} = Notional_{CCY1}.\frac{(S_T - S_0)}{S_T}$$

At lower spot levels, an amount of CCY2 will be worth relatively more CCY1 (spot lower means CCY2 stronger and CCY1 weaker). At higher spot levels, an amount of CCY2 will be worth relatively fewer CCY1 (spot higher means CCY1 stronger and CCY2 weaker). This effect introduces curvature into the P&L profile as shown in Exhibit 1.4.

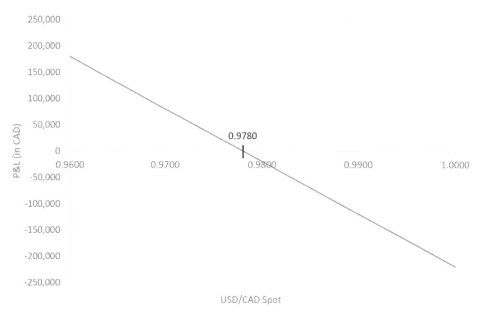

EXHIBIT 1.3   P&L from short USD10m USD/CAD spot at 0.9780

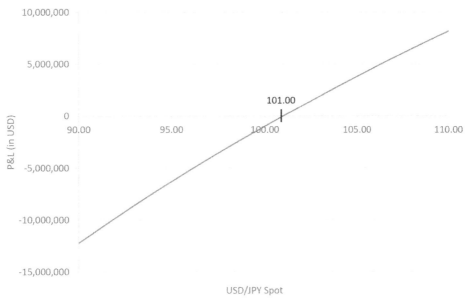

EXHIBIT 1.4 P&L from long USD100m USD/JPY spot at 101.00

▉ Practical Aspects of the FX Market

The international foreign exchange market is enormous, with trillions of dollars' worth of deals transacted each day. The most important international center for FX is London, followed by New York. In Asia, Tokyo, Hong Kong, and Singapore are roughly equally important.

The USD is by far the most frequently traded currency with the majority of FX trades featuring USD as either CCY1 or CCY2. EUR/USD is the most traded currency pair, followed by USD/JPY and then GBP/USD.

FX traders draw a distinction between **major currency pairs**: the most commonly traded currency pairs, usually against the USD, and **cross currency pairs**. For example, EUR/USD and AUD/USD are majors while EUR/AUD is a cross. FX rates in cross pairs are primarily determined by the trading activity in the majors. The FX market is highly efficient so if EUR/USD spot is trading at 1.2000 and AUD/USD spot is trading at 0.8000, EUR/AUD spot will certainly be trading at 1.5000 (1.2/0.8).

Exhibit 1.5 is a mocked-up screen-grab of a market-data tool showing live spot rates in major G10 currency pairs. In practice these rates change (*tick*) many times a second.

Pair	Bid	Offer	Day Low	Day High
EUR/USD	1.3651	1.3652	1.3647	1.3688
GBP/USD	1.6898	1.6899	1.6856	1.6913
USD/CHF	0.8933	0.8934	0.8923	0.8950
AUD/USD	0.9237	0.9238	0.9221	0.9274
NZD/USD	0.8567	0.8568	0.8556	0.8587

EXHIBIT 1.5 Sample G10 spot rates

G10 currency pairs are (mostly) freely floating with no restrictions on their trading. The G10 FX markets are tradable 24 hours a day between Wellington Open (9 A.M. Wellington, New Zealand time) on Monday through to New York Close (5 P.M. New York time) on Friday.

In G10 pairs, the market convention for quoting a currency pair can be deduced from this ordering: EUR > GBP > AUD > NZD > USD > CAD > CHF > NOK > SEK > JPY. For example, the CAD against GBP FX rate is quoted in the market as GBP/CAD. Unfortunately, with market convention rules there are often exceptions. For example, the majority of the market quotes EUR against GBP as EUR/GBP but some U.K. corporates trade in GBP/EUR terms since GBP is their natural notional currency.

Emerging market (EM) countries often have mechanisms in place to control currency flows. For example, some EM currencies have limited spot open hours and some *peg* their currency at a fixed level or maintain it within a trading band by buying and selling spot or by restricting transactions. When trading in an emerging market currency it is vital to learn exactly how the FX market functions in that country. EM majors are quoted as the number of EM currency to buy one USD (i.e., USD/CCY).

In currency pairs with restrictions on spot transactions, **Non-Deliverable Forward (NDF)** contracts are often traded. NDFs settle into a single cash payment (usually in USD) at maturity rather than the two cash flows in a regular FX settlement. The **fix**, a reference FX rate published at a certain time every business day in the appropriate country, is used to determine the settlement payment.

Up-to-date FX rates can be found on the Internet using, for example, Yahoo finance (http://finance.yahoo.com/) or XE.com (http://www.xe.com/).

What Do FX Traders Call Different Currency Pairs?

Nobody on the trading floor calls USD/JPY "*you-ess-dee-jay-pee-why*." Major currency pairs have names that are well established and widely used. Standardized

EXHIBIT 1.6 Selected G10 Currency Pair Names

Currency Pair	Common Name
USD/CAD	"dollar-cad"
USD/JPY	"dollar-yen"
GBP/USD	"cable" (FX prices between London and New York used to be transmitted over a cable on the Atlantic ocean floor.)
EUR/USD	"euro-dollar"
AUD/USD	"aussi-dollar"
NZD/USD	"kiwi-dollar"
EUR/CHF	"euro-swiss" or "the cross"
EUR/NOK	"euro-nock" or "euro-nockie"
EUR/SEK	"euro-stock" or "euro-stockie"

EXHIBIT 1.7 Selected EM Currency Pair Names

Currency Pair	Common Name
USD/HKD	"dollar-honkie"
USD/CNY	"dollar-china"
USD/SGD	"dollar-sing"
USD/MXN	"dollar-mex"
USD/TRY	"dollar-try" or "dollar-turkey"
USD/ZAR	"dollar-rand"
USD/BRL	"dollar-brazil"

language is common in financial markets. It enables quick and accurate communication but it exposes those who are not experienced market participants. For this reason, using the correct market terms is important. See Exhibits 1.6 and 1.7 for common G10 and EM currency pair names.

CHAPTER 2

Introduction to FX Derivatives

The FX market can be split into three main product areas with increasing complexity:

1. Spot: guaranteed currency exchange occurring on the spot date.
2. Swaps / Forwards: guaranteed currency exchange(s) occurring on a specified date(s) in the future.
3. **Derivatives**: contracts whose value is *derived* in some way from a reference FX rate (most often spot). This can be done in many different ways, but the most common FX derivative contracts are **vanilla call options** and **vanilla put options**, which are a *conditional* currency exchange occurring on a specified date in the future.

▣ Vanilla Call and Put Options

Vanilla FX call option contracts give the *right-to-buy* spot on a specific date in the future while vanilla FX put option contracts give the *right-to-sell* spot on a specific date in the future. The term *vanilla* is used because calls and puts are the standard contract in FX derivatives. The vast majority (90%+) of derivative transactions executed by an FX derivatives trading desk are vanilla contracts as opposed to **exotic contracts**. Exotic FX derivatives (covered in Part IV) have additional features (e.g., more complex payoffs, barriers, averages).

To understand how call and put options work, forget FX for the moment and think about buying and selling apples (not Apple Inc. stock, but literally the green round things you eat). Apples currently cost 10p each. I know that I will need to buy

100 apples in one month's time. If I simply wait one month and then buy the apples, perhaps the prevailing price will be 5p and hence I can buy the apples cheaper than they currently are *or* perhaps the price will be 15p and hence more expensive *or* perhaps they will cost 10p, 1p, or 999p. The point is that there is *uncertainty* about how much the apples will cost and this uncertainty makes planning for the future of my fledgling apple juice company more difficult. Call and put options allow this uncertainty to be controlled.

One possible contract that could be purchased to control the risk is a one-month (1mth) call option with a **strike** of 10p and a **notional** of 100 apples. Note the different elements within the contract: the date in the future at which I want to complete the transaction (maturity: one month), the direction (I want to buy apples; therefore, I purchase a call option), the level at which I want to transact (strike: 10p) and the amount I want to transact (notional: 100 apples). After buying this call option, one month hence, at the maturity of the contract, if the price of apples is above the strike (e.g., at 15p) I will **exercise** the call option I bought and buy 100 apples at 10p from the seller (also known as the **writer**) of the option contract. Alternatively, if the price of apples is below the strike (e.g., at 5p), I don't want or need to use my right to buy them at 10p; hence the call option contract **expires**. Instead I will buy 100 apples directly in the market at the lower rate.

Therefore, by buying the call option, the **worst-case purchasing rate** is known; under no circumstances will I need to buy 100 apples in one month at a rate higher than 10p (the strike). This reduction in uncertainty comes at a cost: the **premium** paid upfront to purchase the call option. It is not hard to imagine that the premium of the call option will depend on the details of the contract: How long it lasts, how many apples it covers, the transaction level, plus crucially the **volatility** of the price of apples will be a key factor. The more volatile the price of apples, the more the call option will cost.

Exhibit 2.1 shows the P&L profile from this call option at maturity, presented in familiar hockey-stick diagram terms but without the initial premium included.

At the option maturity, if the price of apples is below the strike (10p), the call option has no value because the underlying can be bought cheaper in the market. If the price of apples is above the strike at maturity, the call option value rises linearly with the value of the underlying.

Mathematically, the P&L at maturity from this call option is:

$$P\&L = Notional \cdot max(S_T - K,\ 0)$$

where *Notional* is expressed in terms of number of apples, S_T is the price of apples at the option maturity, and K is the strike. Often $max(S_T - K,\ 0)$ is written $(S_T - K)^+$.

It is worth noting that the P&L at maturity from the contract depends only on the price of apples at the moment the option contract matures; the path taken to get there is irrelevant.

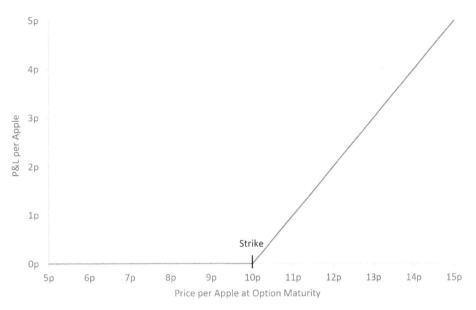

EXHIBIT 2.1   P&L per apple at maturity from call option with 10p strike

Put options are the right-to-sell the underlying. This can be conceptually tricky to grasp at first—*buying* the right to *sell*. Imagine you own a forest of apple trees. You know that by the end of August you will harvest at least 1,000 apples, which you will then want to sell. Again, uncertainty arises from the fact that the future price of apples is unknown. To control this uncertainty, a put option maturing on August 31 could be bought with a notional of 1,000 apples and a strike of 10p.

This time, at the option maturity, if the price of apples is below the strike (e.g., at 5p), the put option will be **exercised** and 1,000 apples will be sold at 10p to the option seller. Alternatively, if the price of apples is above the strike (e.g., at 15p), the put option will **expire** and 1,000 apples can instead be sold in the market at a higher rate.

By buying the put option, the **worst-case selling rate** is known; under no circumstances will I need to sell 1,000 apples at a rate lower than 10p (the strike) at the end of August. The cost of buying this derivative contract will depend on the exact contract details, plus, again, the more volatile the price of apples, the more the option will cost. Exhibit 2.2 shows the P&L profile from this put option at maturity.

Mathematically, the P&L at maturity from this put option is:

$$P\&L = Notional \cdot max(K - S_T, \ 0)$$

Bringing these concepts into FX world, the underlying changes from the price of apples to an FX spot rate. At the option maturity, the prevailing FX spot rate will

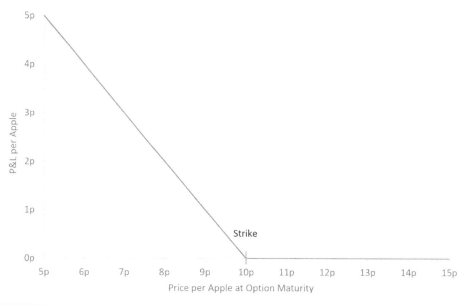

EXHIBIT 2.2   P&L per apple at maturity from put option with 10p strike

be compared to the strike to determine whether a vanilla option will be exercised or expired.

There are actually two main kinds of vanilla option:

1. European vanilla options can be exercised only *at* the option maturity.
2. American vanilla options can be exercised *at any time* before the option maturity.

European vanilla options are the standard product in the FX derivatives market because they are easier to risk manage and mathematically simpler to value. Henceforth, any mention of a *vanilla* option means a European-style contract. American vanilla options are covered in Chapter 27.

The following details are required to describe a vanilla FX option contract:

Currency pair: The spot FX rate in this currency pair is the reference rate against which the value of the vanilla option will be calculated at maturity.

Call or put (call = right-to-buy/put = right-to-sell): FX transactions exchange two currencies: one that is bought and one that is sold. Therefore, a vanilla option in a particular currency pair is simultaneously a right-to-buy one currency and a right-to-sell the other. Therefore, vanilla options are simultaneously a call on CCY1 and a put on CCY2 or vice-versa. Most often only the CCY1 direction is specified when describing the contract, so, for example, a EUR/USD call option is actually a EUR call and a USD put.

Maturity/expiry: The date on which the owner of the option decides whether to exercise their option or let it expire. There is actually a third option to *partially exercise* the option, which is explored in Chapter 9.

Cut: The exact time on the expiry date at which the option matures.

　The two most common cuts in G10 currency pairs are:

- New York (NY): 10 A.M. New York time, which is usually 3 P.M. London time.

- Tokyo (TOK): 3 P.M. Tokyo time, which is 6 A.M. or 7 A.M. London time, depending on the time of year.

Strike: The rate at which the owner of the option has the right to exchange CCY1 and CCY2 at maturity.

Notional: The amount of cash (usually expressed in CCY1 terms) that can be exchanged at maturity. Vanilla option notionals can be converted between CCY1 and CCY2 terms using the strike as shown in Exhibit 2.3 since the strike is the level at which CCY1 and CCY2 are potentially exchanged at maturity.

Mathematically, the P&L at maturity from a long (bought) CCY1 call option is:

$$P\&L_{CCY2} = Notional_{CCY1} \cdot max(S_T - K, \, 0)$$

where S_T is the spot FX rate at the option maturity and K is the strike. The CCY1 call P&L at maturity is the same as a long FX position (to the maturity date, i.e. a forward) above the strike. Exhibit 2.4 shows the P&L at maturity from a long USD/CAD call option (USD call/CAD put).

Likewise, the P&L at maturity from a long (bought) CCY1 put option is:

$$P\&L_{CCY2} = Notional_{CCY1} \cdot max(K - S_T, \, 0)$$

The CCY1 put P&L at maturity is the same as a short FX position below the strike. Exhibit 2.5 shows the P&L at maturity from a long USD/CAD put option (USD put/CAD call).

Exhibit 2.6 shows a USD/JPY vanilla contract in an FX derivatives pricing tool. Traders use systems like this to price vanilla option contracts.

EXHIBIT 2.3　Converting between CCY1 and CCY2 notionals

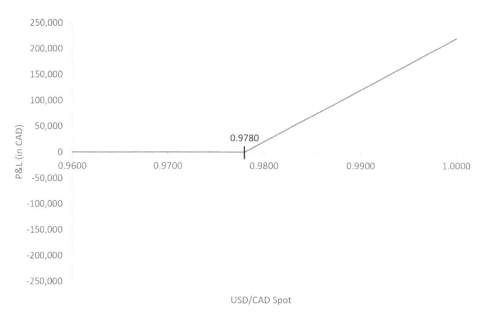

EXHIBIT 2.4   P&L at maturity from long USD10m USD/CAD call option with 0.9780 strike

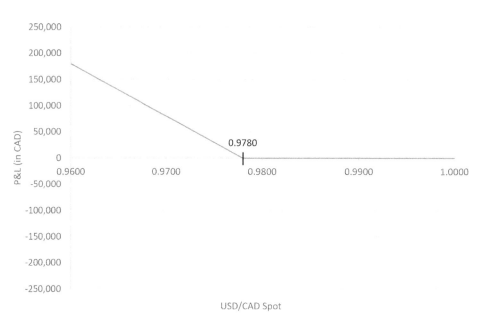

EXHIBIT 2.5   P&L at maturity from long USD10m USD/CAD put option with 0.9780 strike

Contract Details	Leg 1
Currency Pair	USD/JPY
Horizon	Fri 18-Oct-13
Spot Date	Tue 22-Oct-13
Strategy	Vanilla
Call / Put	USD Call / JPY Put
Maturity	1M
Expiry Date	Wed 20-Nov-13
Delivery Date	Fri 22-Nov-13
Cut	NY
Strike	80.00
Notional	USD5m

Market Data	
Spot	79.50
Swap Points	-2.00
Forward	79.48
Deposit (USD)	0.35%
Deposit (JPY)	0.07%
ATM Volatility	7.00%
Pricing Volatility	**7.25 / 7.65%**

Outputs	
Output Currency	USD
Premium	**0.44 / 0.48%**
Price Spread	0.04%

EXHIBIT 2.6   FX derivatives pricing tool showing a USD/JPY vanilla contract

Within the pricing tool, the **horizon** is the current date (i.e., today). On the **expiry date** (Nov. 20, 2013) at 10 A.M. NY time (since the option is priced to NY cut), the owner (buyer) of this European-style vanilla option will contact the writer (seller) of the option to inform them if they want to exercise the option.

If the spot rate at maturity is above the strike (80.00), the option is said to be **in-the-money (ITM)**. In this case the option will be exercised because the option gives its owner the right to transact at a better rate than the spot level. If the option is exercised, on the **delivery date** (Nov. 22, 2013; the delivery date is calculated from the expiry date in the same way that the spot date is calculated from the horizon—see Chapter 10 for more information on tenor calculations), the option owner will get longer USD5m versus shorter JPY400m while the option writer will get the opposite position.

If the spot rate at maturity is below the strike (80.00), the option is said to be **out-of-the-money (OTM)**. The option owner should let the option expire because USD/JPY spot can be bought more cheaply in the market.

Note that for a put option with all other contract details the same, the ITM and OTM sides flip: the ITM side is below the strike and the OTM side is above the strike.

Within the pricing tool, both volatility and premium prices are shown for the contract. Some market participants want prices quoted in volatility terms while others want prices quoted in premium terms. The **Black-Scholes formula** provides the link between volatility and premium. The formula takes as inputs the vanilla option contract details: maturity, option type (call or put), strike, plus market data: current spot, current forward/interest rates to the option maturity. The final input is *volatility* and the Black-Scholes formula can then be used to calculate the *option premium*. In Exhibit 2.6, a *two-way volatility* (explained in Chapter 3) is given and the Black-Scholes formula is used to calculate an equivalent *two-way premium*. It may seem strange that a price would be quoted in volatility terms but this is exactly how the FX derivatives market works. The essence of an FX derivative trader's job is to buy and sell exposure to FX volatility.

Practical Aspects of the FX Derivatives Market

FX derivatives trading volumes are roughly 5% of total foreign exchange trading volumes, equating to hundreds of billions of U.S. dollars' worth of transactions every day. Currency pairs that have higher trading volumes in their spot, forward, and FX swap markets tend to also have higher trading volumes in their FX derivatives markets.

The majority of FX derivatives trading occurs in contracts with maturities of one year and under. However, in some currency pairs long-dated contracts are traded—sometimes out to ten years or even longer.

Vanilla options in G10 currency pairs are usually **physically delivered**, meaning that at maturity, if the option is exercised, an exchange of cash flows (i.e., an FX spot trade) occurs.

In some emerging market currency pairs, vanilla options are **cash settled**, meaning that at maturity a fix is used to determine a settlement amount that is paid as a single (usually USD) cash flow. In G10 currency pairs it is also possible to use a fix to settle derivative contracts but this is less common.

CHAPTER 3

Introduction to Trading

Fundamentally, markets are a mechanism to match buyers and sellers in order to determine the prices of goods and services. Traders interact directly with financial markets, buying and selling in order to manage their deal inventory and change their trading positions.

The process of operating within a financial market is easier to explain using a simple market. Therefore, this chapter uses a market on a single asset, like spot FX or a single equity contract, as the reference. However, the same ideas also apply to more complex markets, including FX derivatives.

Bids and Offers

The building blocks of financial markets are two types of order:

1. *Bid*: a rate at which a price maker is willing to buy
2. *Offer* (also called *Ask*): a rate at which a price maker is willing to sell

Bids and offers need to have a size associated with them. Saying, "I will buy apples for 10p each," is interesting to another market participant but not enough information; will you buy ten apples or a million apples?

There is an important distinction between price makers (also called market makers) and price takers within financial markets. Price makers leave orders in the market. Price takers come into the market and trade on existing orders. If a price taker wants to buy, the contract must be bought at a price maker's offer, and if a price taker wants to sell, the contract must be sold at a price maker's bid. Put another way, the price maker buys at their bid and sells at their offer, while the price taker sells at a price maker's bid and buys at a price maker's offer.

Within the market for a particular financial contract, if a trader wants to buy, there are essentially two ways of doing it:

1. Pay an offer (i.e., buy from someone who is showing an offer).
2. Leave a bid and hope that someone sells to you.

To sell, again, there are two possible methods:

1. Give a bid (i.e., sell to someone who is showing a bid).
2. Leave an offer and hope that someone buys from you.

There are two major differences between these approaches. The first is that trading on existing bids and offers can be executed instantly while leaving orders can take longer and may not happen at all since it requires someone else in the market to trade on your order. Generally, this requires the market to move toward the order level. The second difference is that leaving orders usually results in transacting at a better rate.

A reduced view of the current market is often given, showing only the single best bid and single best offer in a given contract. The best bid is the highest of all current bids (i.e., the most that anyone in the market is willing to pay to buy the contract). The best offer is the lowest of all current offers (i.e., the least that anyone in the market is willing to receive to sell the contract). The best bid and best offer combine to form the tightest **two-way** price in the market (i.e., the price with the tightest bid–offer spread, or put another way, the smallest difference between bid and offer).

Exhibit 3.1 shows a snapshot of an imaginary international apple market, showing bids on the left and offers on the right with shaded backgrounds. This is called the order book, which shows the **depth** in the market (i.e., all current bids and offers in the market) and a size associated with each order. Prior to transacting, this market is anonymous (i.e., it isn't known which market participant has left any particular order) and it often also isn't clear whether an order at a particular level is one order or a collection of multiple orders aggregated together.

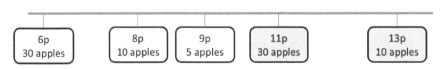

EXHIBIT 3.1 Apple market order book

In this example, the best bid is 9p and the best offer is 11p. Most of the time, the best bid is simply referred to as "the bid" and the best offer is "the offer." Lower bids and higher offers are referred to as being "behind."

For a given contract, offers are (almost) always above bids. However, in some situations, a market will be **choice**, meaning the bid and offer are at the same level. Even rarer, the offer can be below the bid—an **inverted** market. Markets rarely stay genuinely inverted for long, since the market participants showing the inverted bid and offer should be happy to trade with each other and hence restore the normal bid–offer direction. An inverted market often occurs when the relevant market participants *can't* trade with each other for some reason.

Trader X wants to buy 100 apples at 8p and trader Y wants to sell 100 apples at 8p. If trader X and trader Y each know what the other wants to do, they should be happy to trade with each other at 8p. It is therefore vital that both traders know of each other's intentions. For a market to function efficiently, *transparency* and the *flow of information* are key considerations.

Back to our apple order book: As mentioned, selling 10 apples in this market can essentially be done in two ways:

1. *Give the bids.* Five apples can be sold at 9p and five apples can be sold at 8p (so five of the 8p bid would remain). This averages at a rate of 8.5p to sell the apples but the transaction will certainly be completed.
2. *Leave an offer.* The rate of 11p already has an offer there. By "joining" (i.e., showing the same offer) the 11p offer in 10 apples, the size of that offer will go up to 40 apples.

   Note that *if* the 11p offer starts being paid, the original 11p offers will be transacted first. The offer could also be left at a higher level, at 12p or 13p, which would lead to potentially transacting at a better rate (selling higher), but the higher the offer, the lower the chance of transacting and the longer it will take.

In practice, particularly in faster markets, traders work buy or sell orders using a combination of trading on orders and placing orders. If the order was in larger size, the trader might dynamically leave (*place*) and remove (*pull*) orders, depending on how the market is reacting in order to get the best possible transaction level (*fill*).

In the apples example, if the 11p offer were to further increase in size, it is possible that bids would be pulled, or would be moved lower, since traders will see the large size on the offer and conclude that there are a large number of sellers in the market who will push the price lower. For this reason it is sometimes appropriate to transact an order in smaller chunks over time to reduce market impact.

Exchanges offer different order types that give additional control around how a bid or offer is processed. For example, *limit orders* allow buyers to define their maximum purchase price and sellers to define their minimum sale price while *fill-or-kill orders* are either executed immediately in their entirety, or else the order is canceled.

Decisions on how to transact within a certain market are based on an understanding of the relationships between transaction size, probability of transacting, transaction speed, and transaction rate. These factors are often combined into one word: **liquidity**.

Leaving Orders

Bids and offers aren't always left close to the current market. A bid could be left to, for example, buy 100 apples at 5p, with the market currently trading at 10p. In general,

- When an order sells above or buys below the current market level, this is called a **take profit** order. The term "take profit" implies there is an existing position that will make money if the market moves to the order level and the order then closes out the position, hence taking profit, although the original position may not actually exist.

- When an order buys above or sells below the current market level, this is called a **stop loss** order. Again, the term "stop loss" implies there is an existing position that will lose money if the market gets to the order level and the order then closes out the position, hence stopping the loss, although the original position may not actually exist.

Bid–Offer Spread

When a trader makes a two-way price on a contract for a client, the difference between the bid and the offer is called the **bid–offer spread**. Conceptually this spread exists to cover the market maker for the potential risk of holding the position over time if the client trades on either the bid or offer. Bid–offer spread is therefore a function of (amongst other things):

- *Contract volatility*: the more volatile a contract, the wider the bid–offer spread.

- *Average holding period*: the length of time before an offsetting (or approximately offsetting) trade can be found in the market. The longer until an offsetting trade can be found, the wider the bid–offer spread.

Traders also adjust their bid–offer spreads based on risk/reward preference:

- Showing a tighter bid–offer spread (hence a higher bid and a lower offer) increases the chance of the client trading but gives a smaller spread to protect from future price changes.

- Showing a wider bid–offer spread (hence a lower bid and a higher offer) decreases the chance of the client trading but gives a larger spread to protect from future price changes.

Bid and Offer Language

When traders pay offers they say "mine!" (i.e., they're buying it). This is sometimes accompanied with a raised index finger. When traders give bids they say "yours!" (i.e., they're selling it), sometimes accompanied with an index finger pointing down.

If bids in the market are getting "given" or "hit," this is a sign the market is moving lower. If offers in the market are getting "paid" or "lifted," this is a sign that the market is moving higher.

These terms can be confusing until they are used day-to-day, at which point they quickly become second nature.

Market Making

What follows is a simplified example of some market-making activity in our imaginary international apple market. Within this market, traders request prices directly from each other and 1,000 apples have just traded in the market at 10p. Trader B comes to trader A requesting a price in 200 apples. Trader B does not disclose a buying or selling preference so trader A makes the two-way price shown in Exhibit 3.2.

The bid is 9p and the offer is 11p. Therefore, trader A has shown a bid–offer spread of 2p. Trader A is assuming that the midmarket price of apples is still 10p. Hence if trader B transacts on either side of the price, the trade will contain some spread from the midmarket price.

Trader B now has three options:

1. *Buy* 200 apples (or fewer) at 11p (i.e., pay trader A's offer). If trader B buys, trader A sells; hence trader A would have "sold at their offer."
2. *Sell* 200 apples (or fewer) at 9p (i.e., give trader A's bid). If trader B sells, trader A buys; hence trader A would have "bought at their bid."
3. *Pass.* Trader B can decide not to buy at 11p or sell at 9p and therefore can walk away from the transaction. This could happen for many reasons; perhaps better

EXHIBIT 3.2 Trader A two-way price

prices are being shown by other traders in the market (lower offers or higher bids depending on whether trader B is a buyer or a seller) or perhaps trader B has had a change of mind and no longer wants to transact. Trader B does not have to explain to trader A why the price is being passed but it can be useful to know why (called *feedback*): If another trader is, for example, showing better bids, trader A can use that information in their future price making.

Trader B *buys* 200 apples at 11p. Therefore, Trader A has sold 200 apples and Trader A's apples position has gone *shorter* by 200. Although the actual exchange of apples for money may not occur until later, trader A's *exposure* to the price of apples changes as soon as the trade is agreed.

Trader A broadly now has two options:

1. *Warehouse* the risk and "run the position" (i.e., keep the changed exposure to the price of apples).
2. *Close out* the risk by going back into the market and trading to offset the exposure.

Trader A decides to warehouse the risk. Trader C now enters the market and requests a new two-way price in 200 apples from trader A. Here are three different possible scenarios for what happens next:

Scenario 1

Trader A quotes the same two-way price shown in Exhibit 3.3.

This time, trader C *sells* 200 apples at 9p. Hence trader A buys 200 apples, exactly offsetting the first transaction. By showing two-way prices to counterparties with opposite "interests" (buy/sell directions), trader A has managed to *buy low* (at the bid) and *sell high* (at the offer). Overall, trader A's position is back where it started, having earned 200 (contract size) × 2p (spread) = 400p for these two transactions. By market making, the trader has balanced their position (hence reducing risk) while locking in a profit. This scenario illustrates the advantages of being a market maker when counterparties have offsetting interests, called *two-way flow*.

Scenario 2

Due to the initial transaction occurring, trader A believes that the price of apples is rising in the market. Plus trader A is short from the initial transaction and doesn't want to get any shorter. Therefore, trader A makes the price shown in Exhibit 3.4,

EXHIBIT 3.3   Trader A two-way price in scenario 1

EXHIBIT 3.4 Trader A two-way price in scenario 2

with a relatively better (higher) bid to make it more likely that trader C will sell, and a relatively worse (higher) offer to make it less likely that trader C will buy.

Again, trader C has three options:

1. *Buy* 200 apples at 12p.
2. *Sell* 200 apples at 10p.
3. *Pass.*

If trader C is a seller, trader A is hoping that trader C decides 10p is a good price at which to sell. Raising the bid has *increased* the probability of trader C selling but it has *reduced* the amount of spread trader A will capture if trader C does sell.

Trader C was a buyer, but another trader in the market showed a lower offer, so trader C passes trader A's price. Trader A can use this information in future price making. This scenario illustrates how market makers use their *trading position* to influence their price making.

Note how important the flow of information within the market is. Depending on the market structure, the previous trade at 11p may be known by everyone or it may only be known by the traders involved in the transaction. The longer the time between transaction and reporting, the more power market makers have because they are personally involved in more trades and hence have access to better information.

Scenario 3

Once again, trader A does not want an increased short apple exposure so quotes a higher bid and a higher offer as shown in Exhibit 3.5.

Trader C pays the offer: Trader A showed a higher price but again the offer was paid. Trader A goes to the market to get a price in 400 apples to hedge ("get out of" or "offset") the position acquired from the previous two transactions. The rate received back from the market is shown in Exhibit 3.6.

EXHIBIT 3.5 Trader A two-way price in scenario 3

EXHIBIT 3.6 Market two-way price in scenario 3

The price of apples is rising and trader A is stuck with a short position. Trader A certainly does not want to sell even more apples at 12p, and if the position is bought back at 14p, an average loss of 2.5p will be locked in. A substantial part of the market has the same position. As traders go into the market to hedge their positions, the market moves higher, which causes the trader to lose money from the short apple position. This scenario illustrates the *risks* of being a market maker arising from not being in complete control of the trading position.

■ Price Making and Risk Management Overview

Success in price making depends on assimilating information from the market. The more information a trader has about market activity, the more likely it is that they know the current midmarket levels, which in turn increases the chances of successfully servicing clients and capturing spread. When many banks quote on the same contract in competition, to win the trade, the trader needs to show the best price of all traders quoting on the contract, but at the same time they attempt to maximize the spread earned from the midmarket level.

The key to successful risk management is to take positions (long or short) in financial contracts that make money as time passes and the market moves. Traders talk about the market "moving against" them (when losing money) or "moving for" them (when making money). For buy-side market participants (e.g., hedge funds) the risk management process is straightforward: They go into the market and transact only deals that they think will make money based on their analysis. As seen earlier, however, for market makers it is often not their decision to take a position. Rather, positions are generated as a consequence of market-making activities when the trading desk takes on the opposite position to the client when the client transacts.

Key risk management decisions for traders therefore involve **inventory management**, or in other words, deciding when to warehouse risk and when to close it out. Traders make these decisions based on their current reading of the market: direction, liquidity, sentiment, and so on plus trading decisions are also made with reference to risk limits. P&L targets and risk limits should be in line: Greater risk gives the opportunity for greater reward but it does not *guarantee* greater reward, only greater P&L volatility. Risk limits therefore keep P&L volatility to acceptable levels.

Building a Trading Simulator in Excel

This practical demonstrates how simple financial markets work and illustrates the differences between price-taking and price-making roles. Task A sets up a ticking (moving) midmarket price. Task B then introduces a two-way price (bid and offer) around the midmarket and price-taker controls whereby the trader can pay or give the market. Finally, Task C adds the ability for the trader to act as both price taker and price maker. This practical links closely to the material discussed in Chapter 3.

■ Task A: Set Up a Ticking Market Price

The trading simulator has one main VBA subroutine that updates the market price. The Application.OnTime command is used to pause between market ticks.

Step 1: Set Up a Ticking Midmarket Spot

Setting up the framework mainly requires VBA development. User inputs on the sheet are initial spot, time between ticks, and how much spot increments up or down at each tick. Outputs are the current time step and current spot. Control buttons for Go/Pause and Stop are also required:

Trading Simulator

Initial Spot	1.3000	←*Named:* **SpotInitial**
Time Between Ticks (sec)	1	←*Named:* **TickTime**
Spot Increment	0.0010	←*Named:* **SpotIncrement**
Go/Pause	Stop & Reset	
Step		←*Named:* **Step**
Midmarket Spot		←*Named:* **SpotMidMarket**

The input cells should be named as per the screenshot. Naming cells makes development far more flexible than referencing (e.g., cell "A5" from the VBA).

The VBA module should start like this:

```
Option Explicit
Public MarketOn As Boolean
```

The first line forces all variables within the VBA to be declared using Dim statements. This makes the VBA coding more similar to languages like C++ and encourages better programming. The second line defines a global Boolean variable called MarketOn that defines whether the market is currently ticking (MarketOn = True) or not (MarketOn = False).

The GoButton subroutine should run when the Go/Pause button is pressed, flipping the MarketOn variable and initializing the sheet if required:

```
Sub GoButton1()

    'If market is ticking, stop it. If market is not ticking, start it.
    MarketOn = Not MarketOn

    'If market was previously stopped then initialize it
    If Range("Step") = "" Then
        Range("Step") = 0
        Range("SpotMidMarket") = Range("SpotInitial")
    End If

    'Run a market tick
    MarketTick1

End Sub
```

The StopButton subroutine clears the outputs and stops the market if the Stop button is pressed:

```
Sub StopButton1()

    MarketOn = False
    Range("Step").ClearContents
    Range("SpotMidMarket").ClearContents

End Sub
```

The MarketTick subroutine updates the market by moving spot up or down by the "SpotIncrement" amount at random on each market tick. Then a future market tick is scheduled. Note how time is converted from seconds terms into day terms for the OnTime function, plus "_" is used when a code statement goes over more than one line:

```
Sub MarketTick1()

    If (MarketOn) Then
        'Move spot up or down at random
        If (Rnd() > 0.5) Then
            Range("SpotMidMarket") = Range("SpotMidMarket") + _
             Range("SpotIncrement")
        Else
            Range("SpotMidMarket") = Range("SpotMidMarket") - _
             Range("SpotIncrement")
        End If

        'Increment step
        Range("Step") = Range("Step") + 1

        'Schedule a market tick in the future
        Application.OnTime TimeValue(Now() + Range("TickTime") / 24 / _
         60 / 60), "MarketTick1"
    End If

End Sub
```

When the Go/Pause button is first pressed, the market should start ticking with the frequency specified in the cell named "TickTime." Test different inputs to make sure everything is wired up properly. In particular, check that the Go/Pause button works correctly: Pressing the button while spot is ticking should pause it; then pressing again should restart the ticks.

Step 2: Record and Chart Spot

A time series of spot can now be stored on the sheet. Again, this is primarily achieved with VBA development. Columns can be set up to store the step and spot rate, with the upper-left cell of the output named: "DataOutput."

Within the VBA, the MarketTick code needs to be extended to push the data onto the sheet. The .Offset command is used to access the appropriate cell within the sheet:

```
...
If (MarketOn) Then
  'Store data
  Range("DataOutput").Offset(Range("Step"), 0) = Range("Step")
  Range("DataOutput").Offset(Range("Step"), 1) = _
   Range("SpotMidMarket")
...
```

And the StopButton code needs to be extended to clear the stored data:

```
...
'Loop around and clear the spot ticks
Count = 0
While Range("DataOutput").Offset(Count, 0) <> ""
  Range("DataOutput").Offset(Count, 0).ClearContents
  Range("DataOutput").Offset(Count, 1).ClearContents
  Count = Count + 1
Wend
...
```

When the simulator is run, spot ticks should be recorded in the table:

Step	Spot
0	1.3000
1	1.3010
2	1.3000
3	1.2990
4	1.3000
5	1.2990
6	1.2980
7	1.2990
8	1.3000
9	1.2990

Having the ticks stored enables them to be charted. Run the simulator for a few ticks and pause it. Then select cells, starting at the title and running a large number (500ish?) of (currently mostly blank) rows down, including both step and spot columns:

Step	Spot
0	1.3000
1	1.3010
2	1.3000
3	1.2990
4	1.2980
5	1.2990
6	1.2980
7	1.2970
8	1.2980
9	1.2990
10	1.3000
11	1.3010
12	1.3000
13	1.3010

Insert an X-Y Scatter chart with straight lines between points. When the simulator is un-paused, the data should plot with the chart automatically resizing as new data is stored (up to the number of rows originally selected):

Step	Spot
0	1.3000
1	1.3010
2	1.3000
3	1.2990
4	1.2980
5	1.2990
6	1.2980
7	1.2970
8	1.2980
9	1.2990
10	1.3000
11	1.3010
12	1.3000
13	1.3010

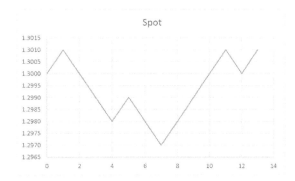

Task B: Set Up a Two-Way Price and Price-Taking Functionality

If price takers want to buy in the market, they must pay the offer. If price takers want to sell in the market, they must give the bid. Within this task, bid and offer prices are set up and the ability to give or pay the market is introduced.

Step 1: Set Up a Two-Way Price

Within the sheet a new bid–offer spread input is required, plus bid and offer rates must be output:

Initial Spot	1.3000	
Time Between Ticks (sec)	1	
Spot Increment	0.0010	
Bid-Offer Spread	0.0030	←Named: **BidOfferSpread**
Go/Pause	Spot & Reset	
Step		
Midmarket Spot		

Bid	Offer

↑Named: **Bid**   ↑Named: **Offer**

These new cells are referenced within the MarketTick VBA subroutine:

```
...
'Calculate bid and offer
Range("Bid") = Range("SpotMidMarket") - Range("BidOfferSpread") / 2
Range("Offer") = Range("SpotMidMarket") + Range("BidOfferSpread") / 2
...
```

New code also needs to be added to the GoButton and StopButton subroutines. Within GoButton, the initial bid and offer need to be set up, and within StopButton, the bid and offer output cells need to be cleared.

Step 2: Set Up Price-Taking Functionality

In order to risk manage, a trader needs to know their *position* and their *P&L*. Within the simulator both position and P&L can be added as outputs and kept updated using VBA code. In addition, at each spot tick, the trader can do one of three actions: nothing, buy (at the market offer), or sell (at the market bid), hence crossing a spread to transact. Controlling these choices could be done in many different ways in Excel but the method implemented here uses Option Buttons from the Form Control menu. These buttons should be grouped so only one of the choices can be selected at a time and the selection is then linked to an output cell that can be referenced within the VBA:

Trader Position		←*Named:* **Position**
Trader P&L		←*Named:* **PnL**
Trader Action		
● No Action	1	←*Named:* **Action**
○ Buy		
○ Sell		

New VBA code needs to update the P&L based on the trader position and the spot move. The trader action then needs to be processed and the position updated if appropriate (and the selection reset back to "Do Nothing"):

```
Sub MarketTick4()

    Dim SpotIncrement As Double

    If (MarketOn) Then
        'Store data
        Range("DataOutput").Offset(Range("Step"), 0) = Range("Step")
        Range("DataOutput").Offset(Range("Step"), 1) = _
         Range("SpotMidMarket")
        Range("DataOutput").Offset(Range("Step"), 2) = Range("Position")
```

```
Range("DataOutput").Offset(Range("Step"), 3) = Range("PnL")

'Calculate spot increment
If (Rnd() > 0.5) Then
    SpotIncrement = Range("SpotIncrement")
Else
    SpotIncrement = -Range("SpotIncrement")
End If

'Update P&L
Range("Pnl") = Range("Pnl") + Range("Position") * SpotIncrement

'Update spot and step
Range("SpotMidMarket") = Range("SpotMidMarket") + SpotIncrement
Range("Step") = Range("Step") + 1

'Calculate bid and offer
Range("Bid") = Range("SpotMidMarket") - _
 Range("BidOfferSpread") / 2
Range("Offer") = Range("SpotMidMarket") + _
 Range("BidOfferSpread") / 2

'Process trader action: Buy
If Range("Action") = 2 Then
    Range("Position") = Range("Position") + 1
    Range("Pnl") = Range("Pnl") - Range("BidOfferSpread") / 2
End If

'Process trader action: Sell
If Range("Action") = 3 Then
    Range("Position") = Range("Position") - 1
    Range("Pnl") = Range("Pnl") - Range("BidOfferSpread") / 2
End If

'Reset the trader action
Range("Action") = 1

'Schedule a market tick in the future
Application.OnTime TimeValue(Now() + _
 Range("TickTime") / 24 / 60 / 60), "MarketTick4"
End If

End Sub
```

Again, new code must also be added to the GoButton and StopButton subroutines to set up and clear the data on the sheet as appropriate.

The P&L and position are now also stored on the sheet and can be displayed in automatically updating charts using the same method as the spot chart:

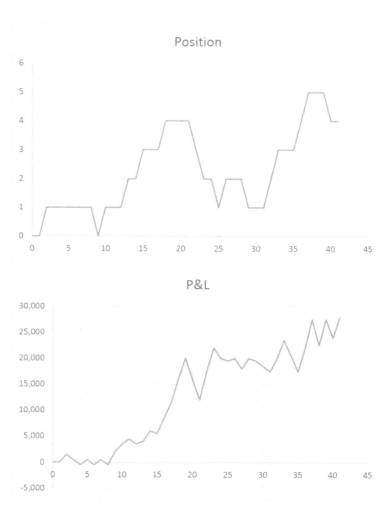

The simulator is now ready to be tested. Check that spot still ticks correctly and the buy/sell controls work as expected. Each time a trade is executed there should be an initial negative P&L impact from spread cross and the trader position should correctly increment up or down. Also, the P&L must update based on market moves.

If everything is happening too quickly, slow it down; five seconds between ticks is fine to start with while the interactions between market, position, and P&L become familiar.

It should become obvious quite quickly that crossing the bid–offer spread to transact makes it difficult to make money within this framework; all transactions result in a negative P&L change so every trade reduces expected P&L. This is an important real-world trading lesson: *Don't over-trade when there is spread cross involved.*

Test different combinations of bid–offer spread and spot increment to observe how their relative size impacts trading behavior and performance.

Task C: Introduce Price-Making Functionality

In practice, traders are sometimes price takers and sometimes price makers. This dynamic is achieved within the simulator by adding price-taking "market participants" to the VBA code. These price takers cause the trader position to change when they trade. Within this simplified framework, when the market participants transact they do so at the market bid and offer rather than at a price made by the trader.

This framework seeks to show how a price-making trader must deal with unpredictable flows. Should the trader wait to see if offsetting deals come in to hedge the existing position? Or should risk be immediately offset? Can the trader pre-position for the flows?

The following new inputs should be added to the sheet:

Initial Spot	1.3000	
Time Between Ticks (sec)	1	
Spot Increment	0.0010	
Bid-Offer Spread	0.0030	
Market Buying Probability	20%	←Named: **MarketBuyProb**
Market Selling Probability	20%	←Named: **MarketSellProb**
Go/Pause	Stop & Reset	
Step		
Midmarket Spot		

Bid	Offer

Trader Position
Trader P&L

Trader Action
⦿ No Action   1
○ Buy
○ Sell

Message
Market Buys
↑Named: **Message**

A random number within the VBA is used to determine whether the other market participants buy or sell. If there is a trade, the position and P&L must be updated accordingly.

```
...
'Process market action
MarketSignal = Rnd()
If MarketSignal < Range("MarketBuyProb") Then
    'Market Buys
    Range("Position") = Range("Position") - 1
    Range("Pnl") = Range("Pnl") + Range("BidOfferSpread") / 2
    Range("Message") = "Market Buys"
ElseIf MarketSignal >= Range("MarketBuyProb") And _
 MarketSignal < Range("MarketBuyProb") + _
 Range("MarketSellProb") Then
    'Market Sells
    Range("Position") = Range("Position") + 1
    Range("Pnl") = Range("Pnl") + Range("BidOfferSpread") / 2
    Range("Message") = "Market Sells"
Else
    'Market No Action
    Range("Message").ClearContents
End If
...
```

When running the simulator with this new functionality, the role of the trader changes. If the probability of the other market participants buying or selling is roughly equal, theoretically the trader should sit and wait for offsetting deals, reducing the position only when it gets too large and the P&L swings are too big. Skewed buy-and-sell preferences and different passive or active trading should be tested.

■ Extensions

The basic framework can be extended in numerous different ways to make it more realistic. Here are some suggestions:

- Add risk limits and P&L targets. Start with the limits and targets in line, then push them out of line to observe how having misaligned risk limits and P&L targets impacts trading performance.

- Evolve the spot rate over time using a volatility-based approach rather than a fixed increment, see Practical H for details.

- Introduce more interesting rules around market participant behavior so, for example, perhaps market participants are more likely to buy if spot goes lower and sell if spot goes higher or vice versa. If the trader knows the rules, managing the flows becomes easier.

- Introduce different sized notionals. In practice, trading in larger size often means trading further away from the current midmarket.

- Most realistic (and most complicated) would be to have the trader manually making prices with the dealt side depending on the relationship between the trader price and the current market bid–offer. For example, if the current two-way market price is 1.3000/1.3030 and the trader shows a 1.3015 offer, if the price taker is a buyer, they should trade with high probability. If the trader shows a 1.3035 offer and the price taker is a buyer, they should only trade with low probability.

CHAPTER 4

FX Derivatives Market Structure

Market structure is a topic that is often skipped over. In practice though, it is vitally important because it defines how clients interact with the trading desk and how the trading desk accesses liquidity to hedge their risk.

In some financial markets all participants access a centralized market or exchange anonymously on the same terms. The FX derivatives market, however, is an over-the-counter (OTC) market, meaning that there is no centralized exchange and a clear distinction exists between banks and their clients. Note that "banks" here refers to large international banks with FX derivatives trading desks.

Fundamentally, bank FX derivatives trading desks transact with clients, aggregate and offset the risk where possible, and close out unwanted residual risk. More specifically:

- Clients come to bank trading desks for prices, often via a sales desk within the bank. Usually the client simultaneously submits the same price request to multiple banks and deals on the best price as per Exhibit 4.1. Traders usually make two-way prices for clients because they do not know for certain whether a client is a buyer or a seller of a particular contract.

- Bank trading desks transact with each other either via the **interbank broker market** or the **direct market** (a price request directly between a trader at one bank and the corresponding trader at another bank). The majority of bank-to-bank transactions occur in the interbank broker market. This structure is shown in Exhibit 4.2.

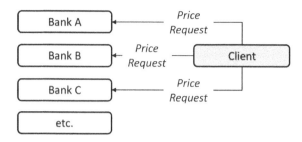

EXHIBIT 4.1 Client requesting prices from banks

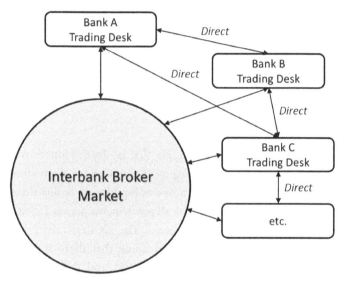

EXHIBIT 4.2 Interbank broker market interactions

Client Types

Many different types of client use FX derivatives for reasons that can generally be classified as hedging, investment, or speculation.

Corporates:

- International companies primarily concerned with managing their FX exposures and funding. For example, consider a car manufacturer with production in Europe but sales in America. This company is exposed to the EUR/USD exchange rate. If unhedged, when EUR/USD goes higher the company will be relatively less successful because the USD received from sales are worth fewer of the EUR needed to pay their workers and build new factories. Likewise, when EUR/USD goes lower the company will be relatively more successful. Fundamentally, the success of the company should depend on their ability to design, manufacture, and sell cars rather than exchange rate fluctuations. Therefore, expected future foreign exchange exposures are hedged—potentially using FX derivatives.

Institutional:

- *Real money*: Professional money managers who use foreign exchange as an asset class. Simply put, they seek to take positions that will generate positive P&L as markets move.

- *Hedge funds*: Professional money managers but typically trade to shorter time horizons than real money.

- *Sovereigns*: Central banks/NGOs (e.g., IMF/World Bank), interested in FX volatility plus potentially manage currency reserves.

Regional Banks:

- Have smaller FX derivatives trading desks or perhaps hold no risk at all and transfer (i.e., "back-to-back") all exposures to larger banks. Regional banks usually trade with international banks as clients in a *nonreciprocal* trading relationship, meaning that the international bank cannot request prices from the regional bank.

Retail:

- Individuals who trade simple FX-linked investment products, for example, *dual currency deposits* (DCDs). Within a DCD the client deposits money in one currency for a fixed term. At the end of the term, the bank has the option to return the money either in the deposited currency or in a second currency. The client has effectively sold a call option on the deposit currency, and the premium earned from selling the option gives the client an enhanced coupon on the deposit.

■ Bank FX Derivatives Trading Desk Structure

FX derivatives trading desks usually deliver follow-the-sun coverage to clients from three global centers, normally London, New York, and one in Asia-Pacific. Traders within the three centers are in constant communication and they aim to provide the best possible client service in terms of pricing consistency between centers, speed, and bid–offer spread.

On the trading desk in each center there are various roles. In practice these roles often overlap and what is presented in Exhibit 4.3 is enormously simplified.

Traders are responsible for keeping desk pricing in line with the market. They make prices for clients and risk manage desk trading positions. In addition they

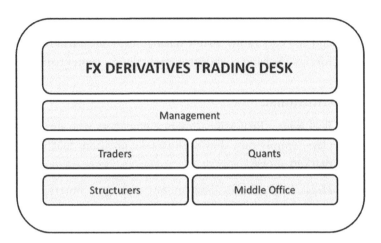

EXHIBIT 4.3   Roles on an FX derivatives trading desk

perform various other tasks that assist with their pricing or risk management, for example, market analysis and trade idea generation.

Traders are usually responsible for risk managing G10 or emerging market (EM) **currency blocks**. Related currency pairs are put together into a currency block, so, for example, the CAD block might actually contain AUD/CAD, CAD/CHF, CAD/NOK, CAD/SEK, EUR/CAD, GBP/CAD, NZD/CAD, and USD/CAD, although the majority of the risk will likely be in USD/CAD and possibly EUR/CAD. The main book-runner for a particular currency block usually sits in the most appropriate center; for example, the AUD block will normally be run out of Asia-Pacific while the Latam (Latin America) block will normally be run out of New York.

Structurers work with sales and relationship managers to understand clients' FX hedging and investment requirements. They design and construct solutions and work with traders to price more complex products. Structurers also educate sales on new derivative products offered by the trading desk.

Quants (quantitative analysts) are usually PhD-level mathematicians who develop and implement the pricing and analysis models and tools used by the trading desk.

Middle office ensure trading positions are correct and that new deals hit the trading positions quickly and accurately. In essence they are responsible for keeping desk risk management running smoothly.

Interacting with Sales Desks

FX Derivatives trading desks are, in a sense, product manufacturers. They create products for clients but it is the sales desks and relationship managers within the bank who are primarily responsible for the client relationships. The interactions between the trading and sales desks are not dwelt upon but collaboration is crucial for the overall success of the business.

Sales desks build relationships with clients by seeking to understand the clients' business and specifically their FX requirements. They provide clients with good information about what is happening in market with the aim that the trading desk is given the chance to quote on any FX contracts that the client wants to transact.

The trading desk assists the sales desk by providing them with good information about the market, coming up with relevant trade ideas, and offering quick, competitive prices in order to help build the client relationship.

Interacting with Support Functions

Trading desks do not operate in isolation; they require support from many other departments within the bank. For example, there are separate teams that do all of the following:

- Ensure the trading desk complies with their regulatory requirements.

- Monitor bank credit exposures to different counterparties across different asset classes.

- Produce official trading desk P&Ls.

- Ensure the trading desk complies with its international tax obligations.

- Deal with recruitment, contracts, and training.

- Build and maintain the desk technology infrastructure.

- Monitor trading risk to ensure risk limits are not broken.

- Ensure the trading desk has booked deals correctly and confirms deals with counterparties.

- Monitor desk pricing versus independent market sources.

- Ensure the trading desk is offering a valid range of products that can be properly priced and risk managed.

- Validate the pricing models (see Chapter 19) used by the trading desk.

Trading Internally

FX derivatives trading desks generally transact internally (i.e., within the bank) with the trading desks of other asset classes in order to hedge non-FX derivatives risk. FX spots, forwards, swaps, NDFs, interest rate products, and cash borrowing and lending will all be traded regularly by an FX derivatives trading desk.

Other departments within the bank come to the FX derivatives trading desk for advice, pricing, and execution on FX derivatives transactions. Sometimes these are for speculation. For example, a trader on the FX spot desk may wish to buy a short-dated vanilla FX option. More often, they are linked to an underlying client transaction. For example, an M&A transaction or trade finance deal may have a structured FX component that the FX derivatives trading desk will price and ultimately risk manage.

■ Tips for a Trading Internship

When you first start on the trading desk, don't race through any learning material you're given: It isn't a race. Developing a good understanding of the material is far more important than showing off that you've read a 40-page document in an afternoon. On the other hand, don't just sit there waiting to be told what to do; ask junior traders for assistance in getting training material if it isn't given to you.

If you're given rubbish jobs to do, just get on and do them; put the team first. Everyone went through the same thing; getting coffees and lunches for traders gives you exposure to them. By doing this they will start to get to know you and will be more likely to help you learn.

Get the right balance between project work and learning about trading. Sitting there the whole time just doing your project is folly (and one to which I fell prey during an internship in 2001). You are there to learn what the trading job involves and whether it is a career you would like to pursue. Speak to people and make connections. At the end of the internship a range of people on the desk will be asked what they thought of you; no impression is almost as bad as a negative impression.

Go and sit with the different parts of the trading desk (structuring, middle office, quants), other teams within the same asset class (sales desks and trading desks), and other asset classes (interest rates, equities, credit). The more you understand about different roles on the trading floor, the better.

Always be on the desk over economic releases and major option expiries. This is when market activity is most likely to occur and it is important to see how traders react to this.

■ Tips for a Junior Trader

Don't be sloppy. This is the worst possible trait for a junior trader. Be precise when describing your position, book trades properly the first time, and be able to explain your P&L and position accurately at all times.

Learn to be aware of multiple things at once: Brokers are shouting, spot traders across the room are shouting, spot is moving, and your boss is asking you a question. This is a difficult skill but it is one that must be learned. Traders become experts at flipping from chatting about sports or the weather to quickly reacting to something that has occurred in the market. If you're sitting and talking with traders, always keep half an eye on the market because you can be sure they are.

Don't get gripped watching spot moving up and down at the expense of all other work. Learn to be aware of spot without staring at it. In practice, traders view their trading positions and pick approximate spot levels where they will hedge ahead of time.

Don't panic under pressure; stay calm and keep your thoughts clear. If you lose your nerve, you might as well not be there.

Don't be lazy: If something looks wrong in the position, investigate and find what is wrong; don't assume problems will fix themselves.

Never exaggerate or bluff. Experienced traders will pick up on bluffs in picoseconds and will delight in taking you apart for it. Saying, "I don't know, let me find out," is usually acceptable. Lying is never acceptable. Also, describe market moves in terms of what has actually happened and try to avoid hyperbole (e.g., "it's going insane" or "it's getting completely destroyed" when implied volatility moves 0.2%).

Don't be afraid to admit you've made a mistake. Everyone makes mistakes. Fix it, learn from it, and make sure it doesn't happen again. Obviously, however, repeated similar mistakes can be harmful to career progression.

Learn how to round exposures and P&Ls when describing them. Traders usually only care about their deltas to the nearest one million or five million, depending on how much risk is being run, so, if asked for a delta exposure, "long ten million, three hundred and twenty-one thousand, five hundred and seven U.S. dollars" is too much information when "long ten bucks" gets the required information over.

Judging market liquidity is a skill that is acquired over time. Knowing where to price a large client trade by estimating how the market will absorb the risk if it is recycled must be experienced to be learned.

Follow as many different financial markets as you can, not just your own. Know where ten-year USD rates, the Nikkei, the Vix, and so forth are all trading. The best traders have a view on the whole market and see the connections between the different parts.

Understand what kind of trading desk you are on and how it makes its money. What were the annual P&Ls of the desk for the last five years and what is the split of that P&L between client trades and position taking? How much of a presence does the trading desk have in the interbank broker market and the direct market? Who are the main client groups (corporate, institutional, etc.) of the desk and what kind of trades do these clients like to transact?

Learn the official desk P&L currency and how the P&L conversion from the natural P&L currency per currency pair into the desk P&L currency is handled. Does this effect create a trading exposure which needs to be managed?

Always have an opinion about the market and a plan for your trading position. Always know and be able to justify your current position. The justification can be made in many different ways, but if you can't justify why you have a position, you

A> USDJPY PLS
B> HIHIHIHI
A> USDJPY 25TH AUG 103 NY IN 75M PLS
B> 4.9 / 5.5%
A> BUY PLS
B> SURE 102.50 SPOT OKAY?
A> AGREED -1 SWAP 0.15% USD DEPO 0.185 USD% 40 DELTA OKAY?
B> AGREED THANKS FOR THE DEAL BIBIBI
A> THX BIBI

EXHIBIT 4.4   Interbank direct call from July 23, 2014

shouldn't have it. Trading positions could be taken as a result of, for example, market analysis (see Chapter 17), client flows, or market positioning.

■ FX Derivatives Interbank Direct Market

FX derivatives traders at different banks can contact each other directly to request prices on simple vanilla contracts. The process is straightforward: Trader A calls bank B via a recorded messaging system and requests a price on a vanilla contract. Trader B picks up the request (because they are currently trading that currency pair) and makes a price on the contract in implied volatility terms. Trader A then has a short amount of time (approximately up to 20 seconds) to deal (hence *crossing* trader B's spread) or pass on the price. After an implied volatility price is dealt on, the traders agree the market data (spot, forward, deposit rate) and option premium between themselves and the deal must then be booked into both risk management systems.

Exhibit 4.4 shows a typical direct call between traders A and B. Note the assumptions made within the call, which enables efficient communication.

Trader A has requested a price in USD75m of 103.00 USD Call/JPY Put with August 25, 2014 NY cut expiry. Within direct calls, notional is always quoted in CCY1 terms; if a year is not specified, the next occurrence of the date is assumed and the out-of-the-money side, in this case a USD call, is always dealt (this is explained in Chapter 7).

Traders have a choice between calling direct or using the interbank broker market. Therefore, the decision to call direct is usually made because it compels the other trader to make a price with none of the safety provided by the broker market. This decision might be made because the trader wants to transact in large size and may need to trade with multiple banks at once in a way that would not be possible through the broker market, or perhaps the market is volatile and there is currently limited liquidity available in the broker market.

There is a well-established etiquette within the direct market: Traders don't call each other too often and most trading desks rarely reject a price request. Also, once a contract has been in the broker market and a price has been made, it is not usual to receive a direct call on the same contract. Most importantly, if the price received is far from what was expected, the price making trader should be given an opportunity to check their rate to avoid bigger problems later when a mistake is discovered.

Direct relationships between traders work best when they call each other with similar frequency on similar-size contracts. Mutually beneficial direct relationships exist but there is always a tension involved that arises from the price making process. When quoting a direct call, the trader thinks, "Why are they calling on this contract?" There is often a catch; otherwise, the contract could be worked in the interbank broker market and probably transacted closer to midmarket. Direct calls are dangerous because they can expose traders who aren't following the market closely enough.

◼ FX Derivatives Interbank Broker Market

The interbank broker market is a crucial part of the FX derivatives market structure since it is where the vast majority of bank-to-bank FX derivative transactions occur. This section explains in detail how the broker market works.

In the FX derivatives market there are currently four main interbank brokerage firms. Each broker *shop* has global teams of FX derivatives brokers who between them speak to the FX derivatives traders at all the banks in the market in a structure shown in Exhibit 4.5.

Brokers are split by currency block (e.g., G10 majors/G10 crosses/Asia EM, etc.) and also by option type (e.g., short-date vanillas/long-date vanillas/exotics).

Communication between broker and trader has traditionally been done either by voice over recorded fixed telephone lines or via recorded text messaging systems. Over time, communication is moving away from free-form text messaging toward standardized electronic messaging.

Market instruments at market tenors are often quoted in the interbank broker market but *specific* contracts make up a large part of the market, too. Specifics are nonstandard vanilla contracts. For example: July 23 1.3250 NY in EUR/USD or 6mth 102.00 TOK in USD/JPY are both specific contracts.

The trader at bank A wants to transact a specific vanilla contract and requests a price from their broker at one of the interbank brokerages. This is called trader A's *interest*, which broker A is *working* as shown in Exhibit 4.6. Brokers are usually working multiple interests for different traders simultaneously. Note that the trader does not have to disclose a contract size at this stage; it may help the broker if the trader reveals that the interest is in large size, but initially a standard "market size"

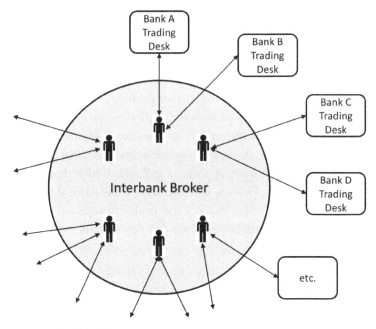

EXHIBIT 4.5   Interbank broker structure

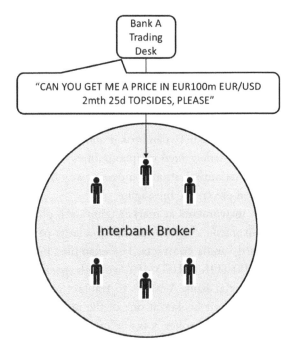

EXHIBIT 4.6   Trader A requesting a price from their broker

would be assumed. In major G10 currency pairs, market size is roughly USD30m to USD50m in normal market conditions. In cross G10 currency pairs and EM currency pairs, market size is smaller.

Broker A tells the other brokers at their shop about the interest and the brokers go to the relevant traders at all the banks in the market requesting a price as shown in Exhibit 4.7.

The traders price the contract in their pricing tools and when ready they return their prices, quoted in implied volatility terms:

- Bank B: no price

- Bank C: 6.75 / 7.25%

- Bank D: no price

- Bank E: 6.6 / 7.1%

In trader A's pricing tool, the mid-value of this vanilla contract is 7.0% implied volatility.

Note that traders are not compelled to make a price and there are many possible reasons why they might choose not to. Perhaps they are busy pricing another contract for a client, perhaps they are remarking their curves, or talking to their boss, or perhaps they are off the desk getting lunch.

The importance of the trader/broker relationship should be starting to become apparent. If a broker and trader have a good relationship, the trader is both more

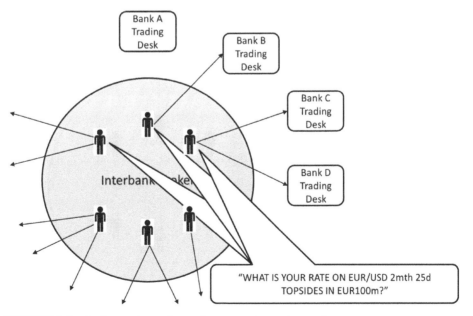

EXHIBIT 4.7 Brokers going to the market requesting a price on the contract

likely to request a price from a particular broker (remember there are four different shops to choose from), and more likely to make prices for the broker.

The relative power of the specific broker within their firm is also important. To get the most rates (prices) possible back from the market, and hence maximize the chance of getting a tight composite rate, broker A must get the other brokers to push their traders for rates. In some instances this will mean bothering a trader who does not want to make a rate. Again, relationships are vital for managing this.

The best composite rate between the two prices made is 6.75/7.1%: bid from bank C and offer from bank E. The broker goes back to trader A with this rate but does not disclose which bank is the bid or the offer. This process is shown in Exhibit 4.8.

Trader A now has five options:

1. Pay the offer.
2. Show a bid.
3. Give the bid.
4. Show an offer.
5. Pass.

If trader A is a buyer (called a *buying interest*), options 1, 2, and 5 are valid choices. If trader A is a seller (called a *selling interest*), options 3, 4, and 5 are valid choices.

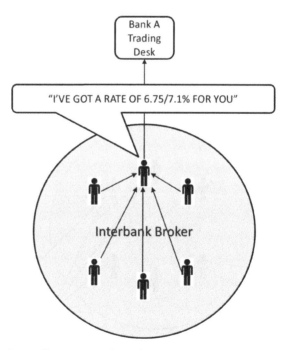

EXHIBIT 4.8 Brokers collecting prices from the market and reporting the best rate back to trader A

If trader A pays the offer or gives the bid immediately, the trade is done and the process is complete. However, in FX derivatives the interbank broker market normally works slower than that. Traders usually make a relatively wide initial rate even if they have a preference to buy or sell the contract; they wait to see whether the interest is a buyer or a seller before showing their own hand.

Therefore, in normal markets, transacting on the "opening rate" is rare. It is far more likely that trader A will show a "counter" (i.e., a bid or offer) to start a process that will result in transacting at a better level. However, in volatile or illiquid markets, where the brokers may struggle to get any rates at all, a trader may have no option but to trade on an opening rate and hence cross the full spread.

Trader A is a seller of the contract and shows a 7.0% offer. The process now becomes a negotiation between trader A and trader C only (since trader C showed the best bid) via their respective brokers as per Exhibit 4.9.

The broker goes back to trader C only and shows them the 7.0% offer (this would be described as a "seven-oh top"). Trader C then has three main options:

1. Keep the 6.75% bid at the same level ("stuck on the bid").
2. Show a higher ("better") bid.
3. Remove ("pull"/"ref"/"refer") the bid. Orders aren't usually pulled unless something has fundamentally changed in the market (i.e., spot has moved sharply) since the order was placed.

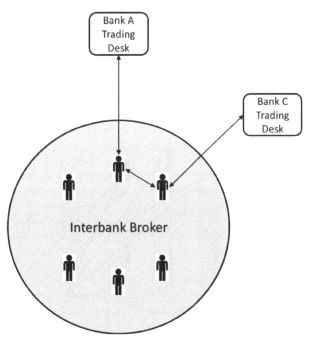

EXHIBIT 4.9 The interest negotiating with the trader who made the best price

Trader A is then told what trader C has chosen to do and similarly can either show a better offer or be stuck, assuming trader A doesn't want to walk away at this point.

This process goes back and forth between traders A and C via their brokers until either the prevailing bid is given or offer is paid and hence they transact, or both traders are "stuck" at different levels. As the price gets closer to being traded, the broker will start to discuss the potential size of the transaction to make sure that enough size exists on the bid or offer for the interest to trade in the required notional.

When both sides are stuck, the broker will ask both traders if they are happy to "show it out," which means letting all traders in the market see the two-way price with the aim of further tightening the rate, which at this point is 6.9/7.0%.

Showing the rate out is a risk for trader A since another trader may decide that 6.9% is a good bid to hit and "give it ahead of the interest." Therefore, the trader's judgment about the current state of the market is vital: Have there been more buyers or sellers of similar contracts in the market recently?

Exhibit 4.10 shows how the brokers show the rate out to the market.

Trader D, who had previously not made a rate, is alerted to this tight price and realizes that buying the contract fits their position. Trader D therefore pays trader A's 7.0% offer but only in EUR50m. Trader A has managed to sell half their full amount at their midmarket rate. The brokers inform everyone in the market about the transaction, without mentioning the names of any of the counterparties involved, known as "printing" the trade. This is shown in Exhibit 4.11.

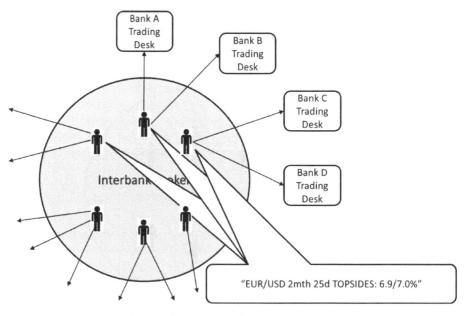

EXHIBIT 4.10   Brokers showing the rate out to the market

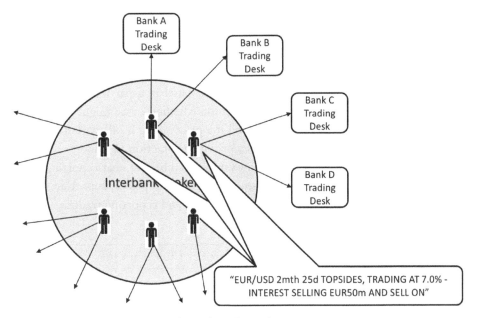

EXHIBIT 4.11   Brokers printing the trade to the market

The level at which this transaction was completed is important information for traders in the market. Even if they have been paying little attention up to this point, traders should price up the contract in their own pricing tools. If the contract is priced differently to the trading level, traders must judge whether their volatility surface needs tweaking or trading the contract represents an opportunity to buy below the midmarket level or sell above.

The information that the contract is "sell on" is also important. That there are no more buyers in the market is a sign that the price of similar contracts is falling in the market. Likewise, if traders have more of a contract to buy, with no sellers found, the brokers report the contract as "bid on" and this is a sign that the market for similar contracts is rising. If the interest managed to trade their full size, the broker would report that the interest has been "taken out."

The brokers continue to match buyers and sellers at the trading level until they are sure that everyone in the market is aware of the trade. Once there are no more interested parties, the contract dies.

The final step in the process is to agree contract details. Vanilla deals are quoted and traded in implied volatility terms but a cash premium is required when booking the deal. Therefore, the traders agree midmarket levels for spot, forward to maturity, and deposit rate (see Chapter 10) to maturity, which is then turned into a spot or forward premium using the Black-Scholes formula. Note that a forward premium (i.e., a premium paid at the delivery date rather than the spot date) will not depend on the deposit rate.

At no point during this entire process were brokers required to have opinions about the "correct" price on the interest, or any knowledge about foreign exchange, derivatives contracts, or anything except the evolution of the price of the contract. However, good brokers have all this knowledge, plus they know which traders in the market are likely to be interested in a particular contract based on recent behavior. They also have a feel for whether a rate might be paid or given ahead of the interest if shown out, and if a price made is off-market (i.e., the price is away from the correct level), they provide protection to traders.

The sidebar provides an example of a broker chat reporting market activity to a trader. Note the combination of requesting prices, reporting live prices (including the interest direction, e.g., "buyer"), and reporting trades.

Example Broker Chat from July 23, 2014

07:24:37 AUD 04 Sep 0.8875P pls
07:33:47 1yr aud trades 9.0
07:38:34 AUD/JPY 23 May 97.00C pls
07:40:29 AUD 04 Sep 0.8875 9.05/9.3 buyer
07:50:10 AUD 04 Sep 0.8875 9.05/9.2 buyer
07:55:44 CHF/JPY 16th May 116.10C 6.25/6.65 seller
07:56:00 JPY O/N 103P vs 103.25P pls
08:07:27 JPY 05 Jun 104P pls
08:20:10 CAD/JPY 12 May TK Cut 93.50 pls
08:21:55 JPY O/N 102.25C vs Tue 102.00C 50 per pls
08:43:50 tues yen 102 8.25 seller outright
08:23:25 JPY O/N 102.25C vs Tue 102.00C trades 12.0/8.3
09:33:03 JPY 1Y 115.00P pls
09:51:52 JPY Tue 103.85P 8.75/9.25 buyer
09:51:52 JPY Tue 103.85P paid 9.25
10:04:01 JPY 1Y 115.00P 9.25/9.45 seller

Brokers are paid commission on the notional (size) of trades they transact. Brokerage rates (often just called "bro" on the trading desk) are quoted in dollar-per-dollar terms, meaning the level of commission in U.S. dollar terms for each USD1m of notional transacted. It is important that traders know the brokerage rates in different broking shops for their currency pairs since that should (at least partially) determine which broker to place an interest with. In general, the more liquid the currency pair, the lower the brokerage rates.

There is an enormous amount of flexibility within this transaction structure. Brokers can work an interest in many different ways. For example, a broker can "build size" at a particular level (i.e., get USD200m on a particular bid for the interest to give all in one go) or they can work an interest more quickly or slowly to get the best fill possible. However, this flexibility inevitably means that part of the broker's skill sometimes involves manipulating the trader's impression of the market in order to get them to trade. Sales 101: Create a sense of urgency:

- "If I show this out, I'm sure it will get paid ahead of you. You should pay it yourself."

- "The guy is pretty shaky on his bid—I think he's about to ref it. You should give it."

In general, the more traders put in, the more they get out of the broker market. By making prices (i.e., being a good liquidity provider), brokers will work harder to get better fills on the trader's interests. Traders who follow the broker market closely (and therefore know the prevailing market sentiment for different types of contract) and have their own pricing up-to-date maximize their chances of transacting at good levels.

CHAPTER 5

The Black-Scholes Framework

Derivatives products have been traded in one form or another for centuries, but the development of the Black-Scholes model in the 1970s enabled financial derivatives markets to flourish by enabling volatility to be consistently priced.

Financial mathematics books generally give the derivation of the Black-Scholes formula and list the reasons why the assumptions underpinning it aren't correct in practice. Traders don't need to know how to derive the Black-Scholes formula from scratch. However, it is vital that they understand the *features* of the Black-Scholes framework since it is the foundation for all derivatives valuation.

■ Black-Scholes Stochastic Differential Equation (SDE)

The Black-Scholes framework assumes that the price of the underlying (i.e., the FX spot rate) follows a geometric Brownian motion. The Black-Scholes stochastic differential equation (SDE) is:

$$\frac{dS_t}{S_t} = (rCCY2 - rCCY1)dt + \sigma dW_t$$

where S_t is the price of the underlying (spot) at time t, dS_t is the change in underlying at time t, $rCCY1$ and $rCCY2$ are continuously compounded (see Chapter 10) CCY1 and CCY2 interest rates respectively, σ is the volatility of the underlying's returns, generally just called "volatility," and W_t is a Brownian motion. Sometimes, $rCCY1$

is called the *foreign* interest rate and $rCCY2$ the *domestic* interest rate because, as seen in Chapters 1 and 2, P&L on standard FX contracts is naturally generated in CCY2 terms.

The left-hand side of the SDE represents *relative changes* in the underlying (often called "returns"). Relative changes are used within the model because as the underlying gets smaller (closer to zero), changes get smaller in absolute terms. Therefore, spot in the model can never hit zero, as in real life for FX (note that an equity underlying *could* go to zero).

The right-hand side of the SDE has two parts:

1. *Drift* from the interest rate differential
2. *Uncertainty* from the volatility of the underlying

Drift

Drift is a predictable, deterministic component that depends on the interest rate differential and the time passed:

$$(rCCY2 - rCCY1)dt$$

The drift gives the no-arbitrage expected future value of spot (i.e., the forward). Forward rates for different maturities in the future define the **forward path**.

If $\sigma = 0$ (i.e., no volatility), then:

$$\frac{dS_t}{S_t} = (rCCY2 - rCCY1)dt$$

which is solved by:

$$F_T = S_0 e^{(rCCY2-rCCY1).T}$$

Plus recall from Chapter 1 that:

$$F_T = S_0 + SwapPoints_T$$

where F_T is the forward to time T and S_0 is current spot plus note the outrageous variable change from S (spot) to F (forward).

This is important: *Zero volatility does not mean that spot is static; it means that spot perfectly follows the forward path.*

Under Black-Scholes assumptions, the forward path is based on current spot and constant interest rates:

■ If CCY1 and CCY2 interest rates are equal, the forward path will equal spot.

■ If CCY2 interest rates are higher than CCY1 interest rates, the forward path moves higher as T increases. This is called *positive drift*.

- If CCY1 interest rates are higher than CCY2 interest rates, the forward path moves lower as T increases. This is called *negative drift*.

Within this simplified framework, at a given maturity, either the forward plus one interest rate can be used to calculate the other interest rate or two interest rates can be used to calculate the forward. All issues regarding credit risk and basis risk are ignored within this analysis.

For example: $rCCY1 = 0\%$ and $rCCY2 = 10\%$. CCY2 interest rates are higher than CCY1 interest rates and therefore there is positive drift. At shorter time-scales the forward path looks linear as shown in Exhibit 5.1.

Pushing the maturity out to ten years, the exponential nature of the function reveals itself in Exhibit 5.2.

This is important when pricing long-dated options. Exhibit 5.3 shows the USD/TRY forward path generated using constant rates to the 10yr tenor under Black-Scholes versus a market forward path generated using different interest rate instruments at different maturities.

When pricing vanilla options or any product where the payoff depends only on the spot at maturity, the forward path within the model isn't a concern so long as the forward to maturity is correct. However, the forward path is an important consideration when pricing **path-dependent options**, that is, options where the payoff depends not just on spot at expiry, but on the *path* that spot takes to get there. Many exotic options are path dependent. Consider an exotic derivative product in USD/TRY that will expire if spot ever trades above 2.5000. Using constant

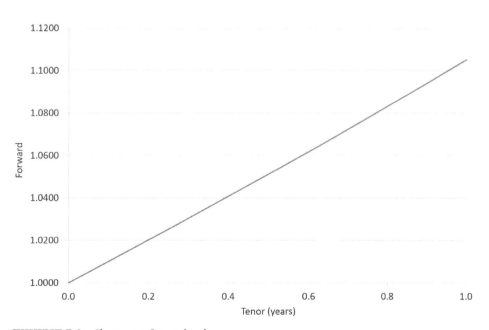

EXHIBIT 5.1 Short-term forward path

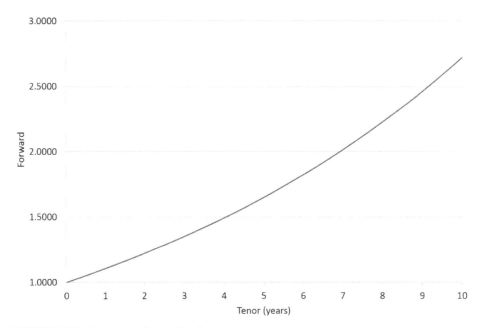

EXHIBIT 5.2   Long-term forward path

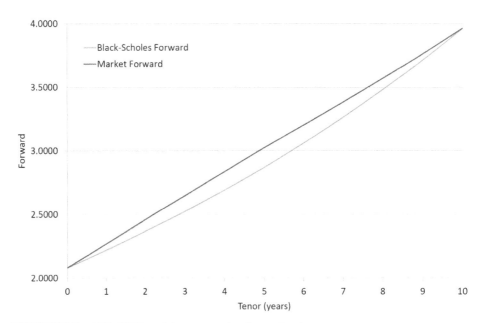

EXHIBIT 5.3   USD/TRY model versus market forward path

interest rates under Black-Scholes will generate different trading exposures than using the full market interest rate curve. Issues like this are therefore very important in practice.

Within the SDE, using full interest rate curves is equivalent to making the interest rates functions of time:

$$\frac{dS_t}{S_t} = (rCCY2(t) - rCCY1(t))dt + \sigma dW_t$$

Uncertainty

The uncertainty term in the SDE is driven by a Wiener process W_t (also called *Brownian motion*). A Wiener process is a continuous stochastic process with stationary independent increments. Translating:

- "Continuous" means "its path doesn't jump."

- "Stochastic" means "it moves."

- "Stationary" means "its probability distribution does not change over time."

- "Independent increments" means "each change does not depend on any previous changes."

Changes in W are random with this distribution:

$$(W_{t+\varepsilon} - W_t) \sim N(0, \varepsilon)$$

In words, the change in W from time *now* to time $(now + \varepsilon)$ is normally distributed with mean 0 and variance ε (i.e., standard deviation $\sqrt{\varepsilon}$).

The fact that the Black-Scholes SDE is driven by a normally distributed process explains why bell-curve shapes appears repeatedly within the Black-Scholes framework.

A discrete realization of W can be plotted in Excel using code shown in Exhibit 5.4 and a sample realization is plotted in Exhibit 5.5.

	A	B	C	D	E	F	G
1							
2		ε	0.003968	← *Named:* **eta** =1/252			
3							
4		Step	W(t)				
5		0	0				
6		1	0.04637	=C5+NORMSINV(RAND())*SQRT(eta)			
7		2	0.222032	=C6+NORMSINV(RAND())*SQRT(eta)			
8		3	0.258739	=C7+NORMSINV(RAND())*SQRT(eta)			
9		4	0.170459	etc...			
10		5	0.164376				

EXHIBIT 5.4   Excel setup for generating a realization of a Wiener process

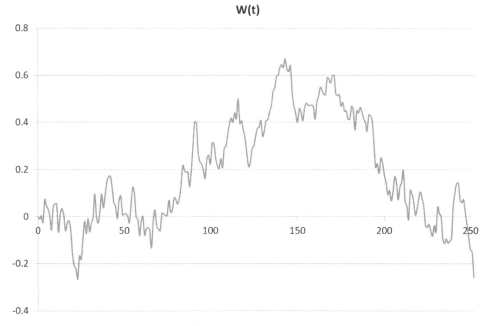

EXHIBIT 5.5   A sample realization of a Wiener process

Within the Black-Scholes SDE, the Wiener process W_t is multiplied by the volatility, meaning that, as expected, higher volatility causes spot to move more:

$$\frac{dS_t}{S_t} = (rCCY2 - rCCY1)dt + \sigma dW_t$$

Solving the Black-Scholes SDE

The Black-Scholes SDE is solved using the magic of Itō Calculus:

$$ln\left(\frac{S_T}{S_0}\right) = \int_0^T \left(rCCY2 - rCCY1 - \frac{\sigma^2}{2}\right) dt + \int_0^T \sigma dW_t$$

$$= \left(rCCY2 - rCCY1 - \frac{\sigma^2}{2}\right) T + \int_0^T \sigma dW_t$$

$$= \left(rCCY2 - rCCY1 - \frac{\sigma^2}{2}\right) T + \sigma W_T$$

The key points to note are that we've moved from regular-space into log-space and the drift has been adjusted by the Itō correction term: $-\frac{\sigma^2}{2}$.

Furthermore, this term: σW_T is normally distributed with mean 0 and variance $\sigma^2 T$ (i.e., standard deviation $\sigma\sqrt{T}$). This is important because it shows how volatility and time to expiry are linked within the distribution. Ignoring the adjusted drift, multiplying time to expiry by four changes the terminal spot distribution in the same way as doubling ($\sqrt{4} = 2$) the implied volatility.

The previous formula shows that the adjusted forward drift is the central reference point of the future log-spot distribution, which at each point is normally distributed with a wider and wider distribution over time due to increasing variance. This is shown in Exhibit 5.6.

Because we're now in log-space, spot *log returns* are normally distributed. This is why log returns are always used within the realized spot volatility calculations in Chapter 17.

Understanding log-normality is important because it impacts distributions and Greek profiles particularly at higher volatility or longer maturity. For example, plotting the terminal spot distribution for 1mth EUR/USD at 8% volatility gives the standard-looking bell-shaped curve in Exhibit 5.7.

However, if volatility is raised to 30% and maturity is increased to five years, the shape of the distribution changes dramatically and the log-normality becomes apparent in Exhibit 5.8.

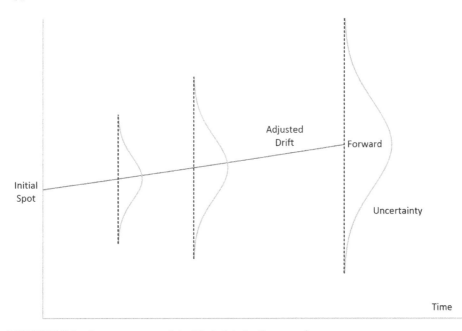

EXHIBIT 5.6 Representation of the Black-Scholes framework

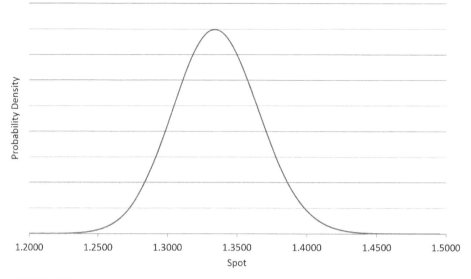

EXHIBIT 5.7 Terminal spot distribution at short tenor and low volatility

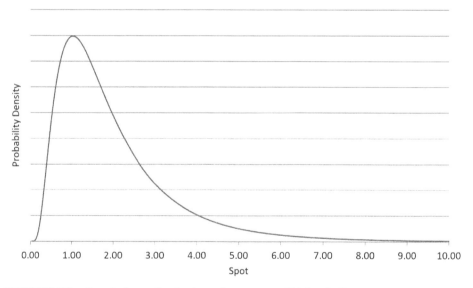

EXHIBIT 5.8 Terminal spot distribution at long tenor and high volatility

In a log-normal world, a spot move from 1.0 to 0.5 (log return = −0.693) is equal and opposite to a spot move from 1.0 to 2.0 (log return = +0.693). Hence log-normal distributions have a longer tail on the topside in regular spot space and never go below zero.

EXHIBIT 5.9	Sample Implied Volatility Term Structure
Tenor	**Implied Volatility**
1mth	5.0%
2mth	6.0%
3mth	7.0%
6mth	10.0%
1yr	15.0%

By taking exponentials, the SDE solution gives this analytic solution for S at time t:

$$S_t = S_0 e^{\left(rCCY2 - rCCY1 - \frac{\sigma^2}{2}\right)t + \sigma W_t}$$

The Black-Scholes formula uses constant volatility. This must be changed to the full ATM term structure when pricing path-dependent options. Within the SDE, this is equivalent to making volatility a function of time:

$$\frac{dS_t}{S_t} = (rCCY2 - rCCY1)dt + \sigma(t)dW_t$$

Consider the sharply upward-sloping implied volatility term structure in Exhibit 5.9.

Two realizations of S can be generated using the same W, one using flat volatility and the other using the implied volatility term structure. This is shown in Exhibit 5.10. Using the term structure of implied volatility leads to lower volatility at shorter tenors and higher volatility at longer tenors.

Within this basic Black-Scholes framework, there is only a single volatility. However, in practice, vanilla options with different maturities and strikes have different implied volatilities. In a given currency pair, the implied volatility for a given strike and expiry date is determined by the volatility surface for that pair. This idea is explored in Chapter 7.

◼ Calculating Option Values Using Terminal Spot Distributions

Terminal spot distributions can be used to price vanilla options or any other derivative product where the payoff depends only on spot at the option maturity. The value of the option can be obtained by integrating the option payoff at maturity against the terminal spot distribution as shown in Exhibit 5.11. Intuitively, this calculation multiplies the probability of spot ending up at each point by the option payoff at that spot level. This technique is implemented in Practical B.

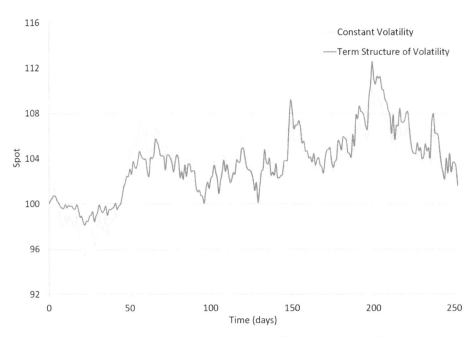

EXHIBIT 5.10   Realizations of a Wiener process using different implied volatility term structures

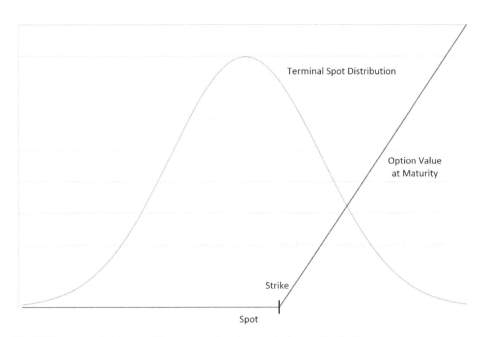

EXHIBIT 5.11   Valuing vanilla options using the terminal spot distribution

The Black-Scholes Formula

Finally, we arrive at the **Black-Scholes formula** itself, which gives prices for European vanilla calls and puts. The **Garman and Kohlhagen** (1983) formula is the FX-specific extension to the Black-Scholes formula that uses interest rates in both currencies:

$$Price_{call} = P_{call} = Se^{-rCCY1.T} N(d_1) - Ke^{-rCCY2.T} N(d_2)$$

$$Price_{put} = P_{put} = Ke^{-rCCY2.T} N(-d_2) - Se^{-rCCY1.T} N(-d_1)$$

where

$$d_1 = \frac{\ln\left(\frac{S}{K}\right) + \left(rCCY2 - rCCY1 + \frac{1}{2}\sigma^2\right).T}{\sigma\sqrt{T}}$$

$$d_2 = d_1 - \sigma\sqrt{T} = \frac{\ln\left(\frac{S}{K}\right) + \left(rCCY2 - rCCY1 - \frac{1}{2}\sigma^2\right).T}{\sigma\sqrt{T}}$$

These formulas are implemented in Practical C.

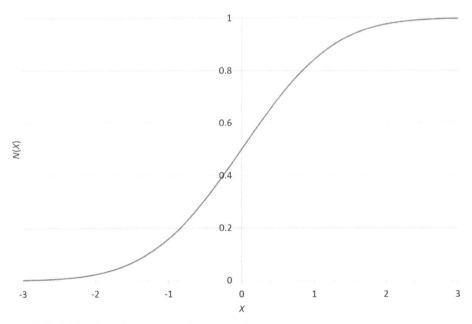

EXHIBIT 5.12 Cumulative normal distribution function

The key to the derivation of the Black-Scholes formula is the assumption that option value can be continuously delta hedged at no cost. This removes all sources of risk except for volatility. The main driver behind the formula is $N(X)$, the cumulative normal distribution function, which gives the probability that a normally distributed variable with mean 0 and standard deviation 1 will have a value less than or equal to X. Exhibit 5.12 shows a graph of the cumulative normal distribution function.

Even though the assumptions underpinning the Black-Scholes framework do not hold in practice, that isn't a day-to-day concern for traders. The main way in which the Black-Scholes formula itself is used is as a method of going between volatility pricing and premium pricing. It is instructive to note that the simplicity of the Black-Scholes framework is one of the key reasons why it is still in use decades after it was developed. Another reason is its extendibility; all the pricing models discussed in Chapter 19 extend Black-Scholes by relaxing different assumptions within the framework.

Building a Numerical Integration Option Pricer in Excel

When an option payoff depends only on the spot rate at the maturity of the contract (e.g., European vanilla options) the price of the option can be calculated using the terminal spot distribution and the option payoff.

■ Task A: Set Up the Terminal Spot Distribution

Step 1: Set Up the Future Spots

First, future spot levels must be generated using a log-normal distribution. The inputs to the function are:

- Spot (S): the current exchange rate in a given currency pair

- Interest rates ($rCCY1$ and $rCCY2$): continuously compounded risk-free interest rates in CCY1 and CCY2 of the currency pair

- Time to expiry (T): the time between the horizon date and expiry date measured in years

- Volatility (σ): the volatility of the spot log returns

Within log-normal world:

$$Expected\ Return\ (\mu) = \left(rCCY2 - rCCY1 - \frac{\sigma^2}{2} \right).T$$

$$Standard\ Deviation = \sigma \sqrt{T}$$

For a given return of X standard deviations:

$$Return\ Level = \mu + X\ .\ Standard\ Deviation$$

$$Spot\ Level = S\ .\ e^{Return\ Level}$$

This framework can be set up in an Excel sheet:

Numerical Integration Option Pricer

Market Data Inputs

Spot	1.3360	←Named: **Spot**
Time to Maturity (years)	1.00	←Named: **T**
CCY1 Interest Rate	0.05%	←Named: **rCCY1**
CCY2 Interest Rate	0.02%	←Named: **rCCY2**
Volatility (σ)	8.00%	←Named: **vol**

Calculated Values

Expected Return (μ)	-0.35%	←Named: **ExpectedReturn**
		=(rCCY2-rCCY1-0.5*vol^2)*T
Standard Deviation ($\sigma\sqrt{T}$)	8.00%	←Named: **StandardDeviation**
		=vol*SQRT(T)

Under a normal distribution, a range from −5 to +5 standard deviations covers almost all possible theoretical returns. Starting with 0.1 steps, go from −5 to +5 standard deviations and calculate the return level and corresponding spot level for each standard deviation value:

	E	F	G	H	I	J	K
1							
2	**X**	**Return Level**	**Spot Level**		**Return Level**		
3	-5.0	-40.35%	0.8924		=ExpectedReturn+E3*StandardDeviation		
4	-4.9	-39.55%	0.8996		**Spot Level**		
5	-4.8	-38.75%	0.9068		=Spot*EXP(F3)		
6	-4.7	-37.95%	0.9141				
7	-4.6	-37.15%	0.9214				

Step 2: Calculate the Probability Density

The probability density function gives the relative likelihood of a random variable falling within a particular range of values. In Excel, =NORMSDIST(X) gives the cumulative normal distribution function, which is the probability of a normally distributed random variable with mean 0 and standard deviation 1 being *at or below* the input level X. Therefore, the probability of being between two levels (i.e., the probability density) can be calculated by taking the difference between two cumulative probabilities:

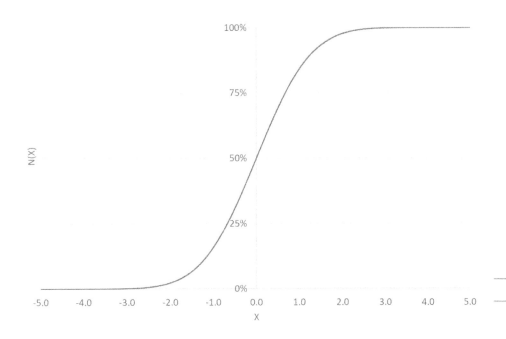

	E	F	G	H	I	J	K
1							
2	X	Return Level	Spot Level	Cumulative Prob.	Prob. Density		e.g., Cumulative Probability H3
3	-5.0	-40.35%	0.8924	0.00%	0.00%		=NORMSDIST(E3)
4	-4.9	-39.55%	0.8996	0.00%	0.00%		
5	-4.8	-38.75%	0.9068	0.00%	0.00%		e.g., Probability Density I3
6	-4.7	-37.95%	0.9141	0.00%	0.00%		=(H4-H3)
7	-4.6	-37.15%	0.9214	0.00%	0.00%		
8	-4.5	-36.35%	0.9288	0.00%	0.00%		

Note how the data in the rows is lined up; the probability density in a given row gives the probability of spot ending up between that spot level and the spot level in the row below.

The probability density can be plotted against spot to visualize the terminal spot distribution:

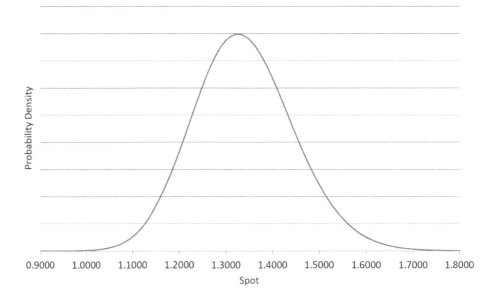

The implementation can be tested by changing the market data and observing how the terminal spot distribution changes. As explained in Chapter 5:

- Shorter maturity or lower volatility should lead to a tighter distribution.

- Longer maturity or higher volatility should lead to a wider distribution.

- Higher CCY2 interest rates or lower CCY1 interest rates should shift the distribution higher via the forward moving higher.

- Higher CCY1 interest rates or lower CCY2 interest rates should shift the distribution lower via the forward moving lower.

Task B: Set Up the Option Payoff and Calculate the Option Price

The option payoff can now be added into the framework. This numerical integration method can be used to price any payoff that only depends on spot at maturity, no matter how complicated, but the most obvious examples are:

- Long forward: $S_T - K$

- Short forward: $K - S_T$

- Vanilla call option: $max(S_T - K, 0)$

- Vanilla put option: $max(K - S_T, 0)$

Remember that these payoffs all return values in CCY2 per CCY1 (i.e., CCY2 pips) terms.

In Excel, add a new "option payoff" column and calculate the payoff at each spot level. To price a vanilla call option, the strike must be inputted:

Payoff Inputs

Strike	1.3600	←Named: **Strike**

Then the option payoff at maturity can be calculated at each spot level:

	E	F	G	H	I	J	K	L
1								
2	X	Return Level	Spot Level	Cumulative Prob.	Prob. Density	Option Payoff (CCY2 pips)		
3	-5.0	-40.35%	0.8924	0.00%	0.00%	0.0000	=MAX(G3-Strike,0)	
4	-4.9	-39.55%	0.8996	0.00%	0.00%	0.0000	=MAX(G4-Strike,0)	
5	-4.8	-38.75%	0.9068	0.00%	0.00%	0.0000	...	
6	-4.7	-37.95%	0.9141	0.00%	0.00%	0.0000		

Within the numerical integration, multiply the probability of spot falling between two spot levels at maturity by the average payoff at maturity between two spot levels:

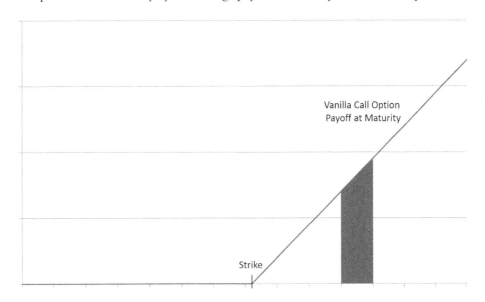

Vanilla Call Option
Payoff at Maturity

Strike

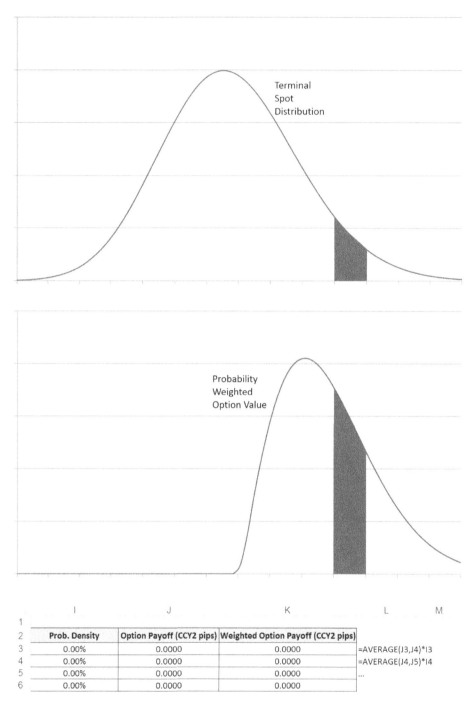

	Prob. Density	Option Payoff (CCY2 pips)	Weighted Option Payoff (CCY2 pips)		
3	0.00%	0.0000	0.0000	=AVERAGE(J3,J4)*I3	
4	0.00%	0.0000	0.0000	=AVERAGE(J4,J5)*I4	
5	0.00%	0.0000	0.0000	...	
6	0.00%	0.0000	0.0000		

Probability-weighted option values are then summed to get the overall option value at maturity. The CCY2 pips option value must then be present valued (see Chapter 10) using the discount factor ($e^{-rCCY2.T}$) and converted into CCY1% by dividing by current spot:

Call Payoff Output	↓Named: **FutValOptionValue**	
Future Valued Option Value (CCY2 pips)	0.0320	=SUM(K3:K102)
	↓Named: **OptionValuePips**	
Present Valued Option Value (CCY2 pips)	0.0320	=EXP(-rCCY2*T)*FutValOptionValue
Present Valued Option Value (CCY1%)	**2.39%**	=OptionValuePips/Spot

■ Testing

Finally, the pricer can be tested:

Test 1: A forward payoff struck *at the forward* should give (approximately) zero value:

Market Data Inputs

Spot	100.00
Time to Maturity (years)	1.00
CCY1 Interest Rate	5.00%
CCY2 Interest Rate	0.00%
Volatility (σ)	10.00%

Derived Values

Expected Return (μ)	-5.50%
Standard Deviation ($\sigma\sqrt{T}$)	10.00%

Forward Payoff Inputs

Strike	95.1229	=Spot*EXP((rCCY2-rCCY1)*T)

Forward Payoff Output

Future-Valued Payoff Value (CCY2 pips)	0.0016
Payoff Value (CCY2 pips)	0.0016
Payoff Value (CCY1%)	**0.0016%**

Test 2: A vanilla CCY1 call option with $S = K = 100$, $rCCY1 = rCCY2 = 0\%$, and $T = 1.0$ should have a value very slightly under 4.00 CCY1%:

Market Data Inputs

Spot	100.00
Time to Maturity (years)	1.00
CCY1 Interest Rate	0.00%
CCY2 Interest Rate	0.00%
Volatility (σ)	10.00%

Derived Values

Expected Return (μ)	-0.50%
Standard Deviation ($\sigma\sqrt{T}$)	10.00%

Call Payoff Inputs

Strike	100.0000

Call Payoff Output

Future Valued Option Value (CCY2 pips)	3.9969
Option Value (CCY2 pips)	3.9969
Option Value (CCY1%)	**3.9969%**

CHAPTER 6

Vanilla FX Derivatives Greeks

It is time to start some derivative analysis. The aim of this chapter is to introduce the basic Greek exposures on European vanilla options. This is stylized Black-Scholes analysis with zero interest rates throughout; hence the forward rate is always equal to the spot rate and discounting considerations can be ignored. The charts within this chapter can be generated in Excel after completing Practical C.

■ Option Value

A vanilla call option gives the right, but not the obligation, at maturity to buy spot (i.e., buy CCY1 versus sell CCY2) at the strike in the agreed notional. Exhibit 6.1 shows the value at maturity of a long (bought) vanilla call option over different spot levels. This value at maturity is often described as the option *payoff*.

For a short (sold) vanilla call option, the value at maturity is reflected in the spot-axis resulting in an increasingly negative value above the strike, as shown in Exhibit 6.2. As expected, a long position plus short position in the same contract results in zero value over all spots (i.e., no position).

The initial option premium is sometimes added into these diagrams, as per Exhibit 6.3. Adding the premium into the payoff is appropriate if the plan is to transact the option and then hold it isolated until maturity (see the section on breakevens in Chapter 17). However, in delta hedged trading portfolios, many options are risk managed together. Therefore, it is *changes* in option value caused by

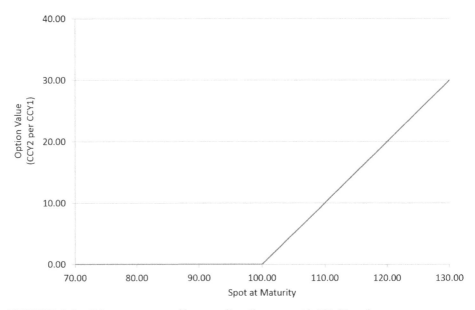

EXHIBIT 6.1   Value at maturity of long vanilla call option with 100.00 strike

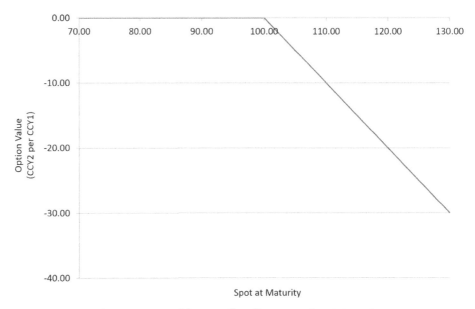

EXHIBIT 6.2   Value at maturity of short vanilla call option with 100.00 strike

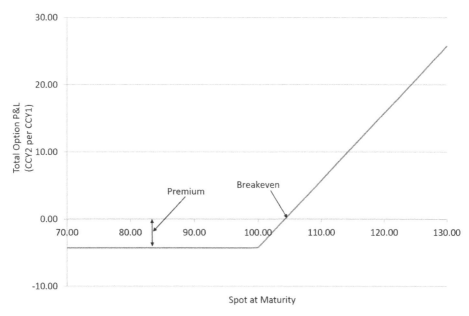

EXHIBIT 6.3   Total P&L at maturity (including initial premium) of long vanilla call option with 100.00 strike

changes in the market data that are most important, called the *exposures*. This analysis is slightly cleaner if premium is omitted.

A vanilla put option gives the right, but not the obligation, at maturity to sell spot (i.e., sell CCY1 versus buy CCY2) at the strike in the agreed notional. Exhibit 6.4 shows the value at maturity of a long vanilla put option over different spots.

Again, a short vanilla put option has a value at maturity that is reflected in the spot-axis. This results in increasingly negative value below the strike, as shown in Exhibit 6.5.

So far, so straightforward. Now see how the long vanilla call option value changes *prior to maturity* in Exhibit 6.6. Call option value prior to maturity is *convex* in spot, implying a positive second derivative (i.e., positive **gamma**, discussed later in this chapter).

The value of a vanilla option can be decomposed into **intrinsic value** plus **time value**:

- Intrinsic value is the option payoff at maturity.

- Time value is the value expected to be generated from the remaining **optionality** in the contract.

Optionality is the ability of the contract to transact spot (e.g., buy spot for a call option), *or not*, depending on the spot level at maturity. In the value at maturity charts, optionality is represented by the change in angle at the strike.

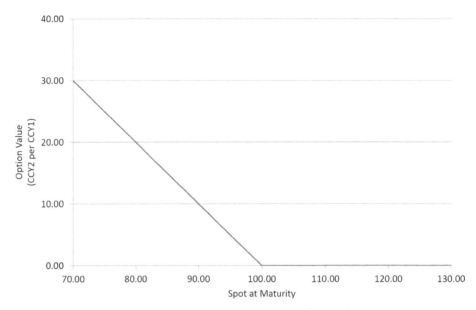

EXHIBIT 6.4 Value at maturity of long vanilla put option with 100.00 strike

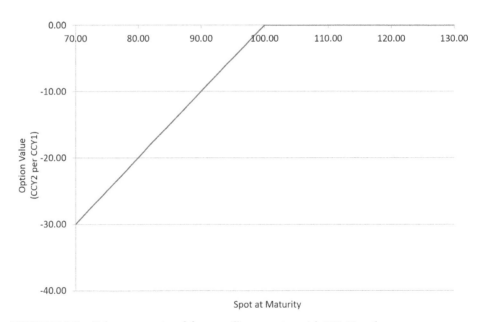

EXHIBIT 6.5 Value at maturity of short vanilla put option with 100.00 strike

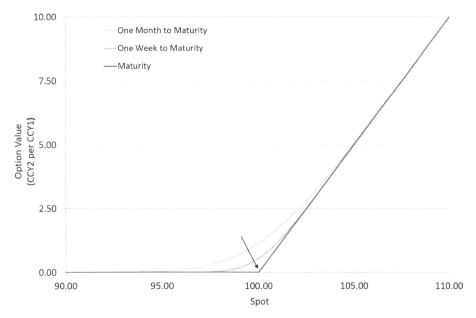

EXHIBIT 6.6   Value of long vanilla call option with 100.00 strike and 10% volatility

If the forward to maturity is far above or below the strike, the optionality has minimal value since there is little chance of spot going through the strike before maturity. Therefore, option value converges to intrinsic value away from the strike on both sides. Maximum time value occurs when the forward to maturity is equal to the strike; here the optionality is most valuable, as shown in Exhibit 6.7.

Looking at call option value at *higher volatility* in Exhibit 6.8 shows how higher volatility leads to higher time value as the distribution widens. Intuitively, if spot is more volatile, it will have more chances to go through the strike.

Therefore, the value of a vanilla option can give information about how much optionality there is within a particular contract. For low-premium vanilla options, there must be minimal intrinsic value and minimal time value on the contract. For high-premium vanilla options, there may be high intrinsic value, high time value, or both.

Within the value charts, the strike of the option is fixed and spot is being changed. If strike were being changed instead for a fixed spot, the diagram would be approximately reflected in the strike level. For example, if the strike moves higher on a call option, the premium decreases because the payoff above the strike is being moved further away from the forward to maturity.

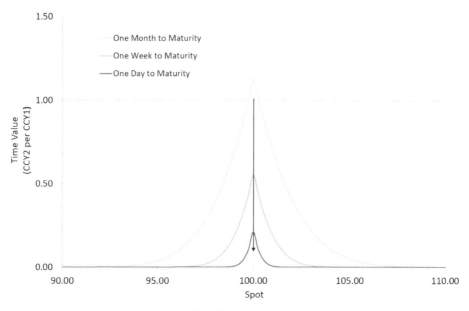

EXHIBIT 6.7 Time value of long vanilla call option with 100.00 strike and 10% volatility

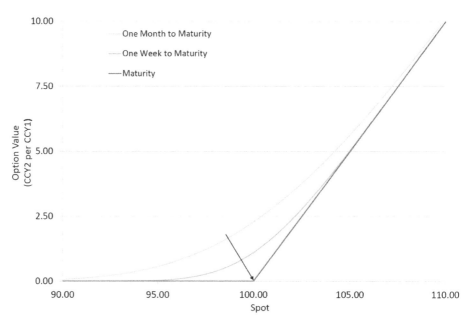

EXHIBIT 6.8 Value of long vanilla call option with 100.00 strike and 20% volatility

■ Delta

Taking the first derivative of option value with respect to spot gives one of the most important Greeks: **delta**, sometimes called **spot delta** for clarity. In symbols:

$$Delta\ (\Delta) = \frac{\partial P}{\partial S}$$

where P is option price and S is the spot rate. Note that traders sometimes say they are, e.g., "long spot" to mean "long exposure to spot" (i.e., long delta). In practice, delta is quoted either as a % of the notional amount, or as a cash amount in the notional currency where:

$$\Delta_{Cash} = \Delta_{\%} \times Notional$$

It is important to appreciate that forward delta can also be calculated, but this distinction will be overlooked for now:

$$Forward\ Delta\ (\Delta_F) = \frac{\partial P}{\partial F}$$

where F is the forward rate to the option maturity.

Delta is the exposure of the option value to the spot rate. The delta amount for a given option is therefore the equivalent spot notional that must be transacted (in the opposite delta direction) in order for the option plus the spot hedge to be **delta neutral** (i.e., zero delta exposure).

For a given option, delta can either be quoted in % terms or cash terms. For example, if an AUD/USD call has 25% spot delta and AUD40m of the contract is bought, AUD10m AUD/USD spot must be sold "on the hedge" in order to leave delta in the trading position unchanged. If the AUD/USD call was sold instead, spot must be bought on the hedge.

When a position is delta neutral, no P&L change results from spot moving higher or lower. However, this only works for small moves in spot if the second derivative (gamma) is non-zero.

Exhibit 6.9 shows the delta of a long vanilla call option with a 100.00 strike. This delta can be calculated by taking the *gradient* of the call option value profile chart from Exhibit 6.6.

At maturity, there is a discontinuity in delta from 0% below the strike to 100% above caused by either expiring the option below the strike (hence having no position) or exercising the option above the strike (hence buying spot in the full notional amount). Prior to maturity, the delta still goes from 0% to 100% but the change occurs over a wider spot range. Notice that the delta at all maturities is

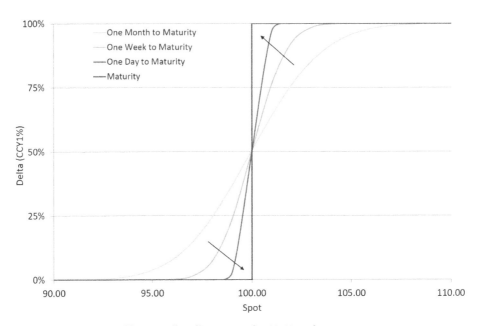

EXHIBIT 6.9 Delta of long vanilla call option with 100.00 strike

around 50% when spot (or more accurately, the forward to maturity) is equal to the strike.

Intuitively, it shouldn't be a surprise that a long call option position has a positive delta since the value of the call option increases with spot higher, the same as a long spot position.

Delta can also be (approximately) thought of as the % chance of ending up in-the-money (ITM) at maturity. Call options with strikes close to spot (the forward) have a delta of approximately 50% (i.e., a 50/50 chance of ending up ITM at maturity). As spot goes lower, the call option delta reduces as does the chance of ending up in-the-money.

Exhibit 6.10 shows the option value of a long vanilla put option with a 100.00 strike.

Again, taking the first derivative of this option value with respect to spot gives delta. The delta of the option value from Exhibit 6.10 is shown in Exhibit 6.11. Intuitively, put options have negative delta because put option value increases with spot lower, the same as a short spot position.

For example, if an AUD/USD put option has −10% spot delta and AUD80m of the contract is bought, AUD8m AUD/USD spot must be bought on the hedge in order to leave delta in the trading position unchanged. If the option was sold instead, spot must be sold on the hedge.

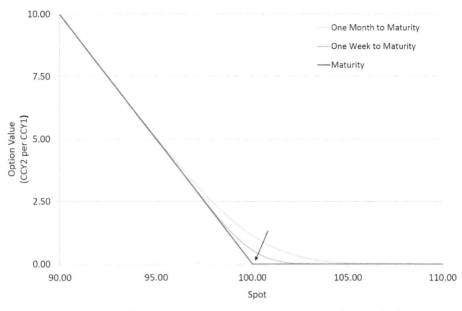

EXHIBIT 6.10   Value of long vanilla put option with 100.00 strike and 10% volatility

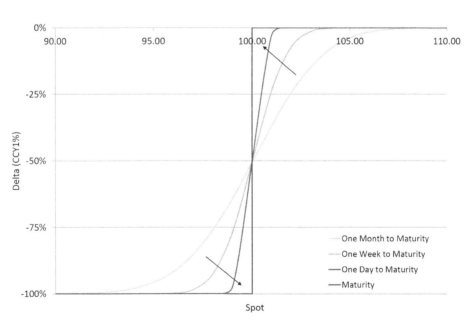

EXHIBIT 6.11   Delta of long vanilla put option with 100.00 strike

Put options with strikes close to the forward have a delta of approximately −50% (i.e., 50/50 chance of ending up ITM), and as spot goes lower, the put delta increases negatively. In practice, when traders describe deltas they often leave off the %, so a "twenty-five delta call" actually has a 25% delta. Plus, when describing put options, the negative sign is often omitted, so a "ten delta put" actually has a −10% delta.

The call delta and put delta profiles in Exhibits 6.9 and 6.11 are identical except that the put option delta is 100% lower than the call option delta over all spot values. Put another way, a call option can be converted into a put option simply by selling a notional amount of forward to maturity. In hockey-stick diagram world, a long call option (shown in Exhibit 6.12) plus a short forward with the same strike, maturity, and notional (shown in Exhibit 6.13) gives a long put option (shown in Exhibit 6.14).

This is a powerful result called **put–call parity**. In words, a vanilla option can be changed from a call into a put (or a put changed into a call) by trading the forward in the same strike, maturity, and notional:

- Long call + short forward = long put
- Long put + long forward = long call

Additionally, a forward can be constructed from a call option and a put option with all other contract details the same. This is called a **synthetic forward**:

- Long call + short put = long synthetic forward
- Short call + long put = short synthetic forward

Consider the formula for a long synthetic forward. At maturity, if spot is above the strike, the long call will be exercised (and the short put expired) and spot will be bought at the strike. If spot is below the strike, the short put will be exercised (and the long call expired) and spot will be bought at the strike. No matter where spot ends up at maturity, spot is bought at the strike—exactly the same as owning the forward contract.

One consequence of this is that since the forward has no optionality, *delta hedged calls and delta hedged puts with the same maturity and strike have the same Greek exposures*. For this reason traders don't usually think in terms of calls or puts once the option is in their trading book; they talk only in terms of *strikes* and *notionals* (e.g., "I've got a 1.3250 strike in EUR50m" rather than "I've got a 1.3250 put in EUR50m").

Another consequence of put–call parity is that *call options and put options with the same maturity and strike must always be valued at the same implied volatility*; otherwise, arbitrage would be possible via trading the forward. This also explains why approaching the trading desk and asking "who does calls and who does puts?" would be met with wide eyes.

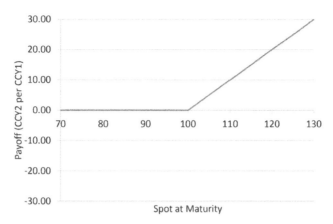

EXHIBIT 6.12   Value at maturity of long call option

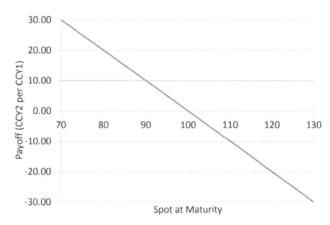

EXHIBIT 6.13   Value at maturity of short forward

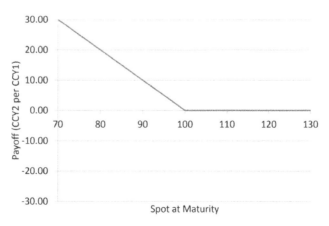

EXHIBIT 6.14   Value at maturity of long put option

Gamma

Taking the first derivative of delta (or the second derivative of option price) with respect to spot gives another important Greek: **gamma**. In symbols:

$$Gamma\ (\Gamma) = \frac{\partial \Delta}{\partial S} = \frac{\partial^2 P}{\partial S^2}$$

In practice, gamma is quoted either as a % of the notional amount, or as a cash amount in the notional currency where:

$$\Gamma_{Cash} = \Gamma_{\%} \times Notional$$

Gamma describes how delta changes with spot and is therefore a measure of how stable delta is as spot moves. Due to put–call parity, call and put options with the same strike and maturity have the same gamma profile, shown in Exhibit 6.15. This gamma can be calculated by taking the gradient of either the call option delta profile from Exhibit 6.9 or the put option delta profile from Exhibit 6.11.

As time moves toward the option maturity, gamma increases and concentrates around the strike. Gamma *at* maturity is not shown on the graph because the discontinuity in delta cannot be neatly differentiated. As discussed previously, gamma can be seen in the *curvature* of the option value versus spot charts. At longer maturities, when there is a wider spot distribution, delta changes slowly as spot moves, hence low gamma. At shorter maturities, when there is a tighter spot distribution, delta changes quickly as spot moves, hence high gamma.

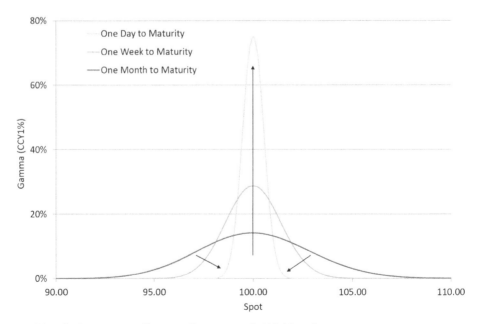

EXHIBIT 6.15 Gamma of long vanilla option with 100.00 strike

Long positions in vanilla options always have long gamma exposure because time value leads to a convex option value versus spot relationship. Likewise, short positions in vanilla options always have short gamma exposure. For a given vanilla option, peak gamma occurs at the strike because this is the point at which optionality is maximized.

Vega

Taking the first derivative of option value with respect to implied volatility gives a third important Greek: **vega**. In symbols:

$$Vega\ (\upsilon) = \frac{\partial P}{\partial \sigma}$$

In practice, vega is usually quoted either as a % of the notional amount, or as a cash amount in the notional currency where:

$$\upsilon_{Cash} = \upsilon_\% \times Notional$$

Note that traders describe their position as, e.g., "long vol" to mean "long exposure to implied volatility" (i.e., long vega).

Exhibit 6.16 shows how the vega profile of a long vanilla option position changes over time. Again, due to put–call parity, since forward contracts have no exposure

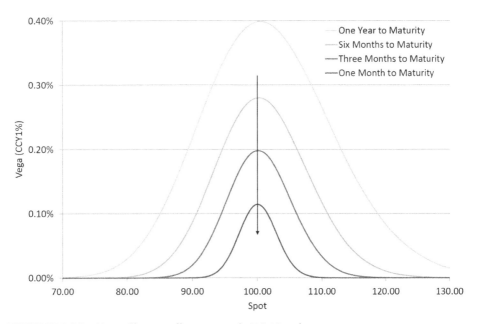

EXHIBIT 6.16   Vega of long vanilla option with 100.00 strike

to implied volatility, call and put options with the same strike and maturity have the same vega profile. The peak vega on a vanilla option reduces over time. Intuitively, vega increases at longer maturities because there is more time for a change in implied volatility to impact the payoff.

For a given vanilla option, peak vega (like gamma) occurs at the strike where optionality and time value is maximized. Far away from the optionality the option is either like a forward (if deep in-the-money) or like no position (if deep out-of-the-money). In either of these cases, changing volatility has minimal impact on option value.

Long vanilla options always have long vega exposure. Intuitively this is because higher volatility widens the distribution and therefore brings larger positive payoffs into play, hence increasing the option value. Likewise, short vanilla options always have short vega exposure.

■ Summary

When trading FX derivatives, the majority of trading P&L is generated from the three Greek exposures introduced in this chapter: delta, gamma, and vega.

Most often, vanilla options are booked into a trader's position *with the appropriate delta hedge* so new deals cause no net change to the delta exposure within the position, only the vega and gamma exposures are impacted. Buying delta hedged vanilla options results in longer vega and gamma exposures. Selling delta hedged vanilla options results in shorter vega and gamma exposures.

Gamma and vega both come from the optionality within the derivative contract and both are therefore maximized at the strike for vanilla options. A trading position with a long vega exposure will make money if implied volatility rises and lose money if implied volatility falls while gamma impacts how delta moves with spot. Trading long and short gamma positions is covered in Chapter 9.

Long-dated vanilla options have relatively higher vega and lower gamma exposures while short-dated vanilla options have relatively higher gamma and lower vega exposures. Therefore, the main risk on a given vanilla option changes over time from mainly vega risk to mainly gamma risk. The inflection point between the two types of risk occurs around two-month maturity.

Building a Black-Scholes Option Pricer in Excel

Building a Black-Scholes vanilla option pricing tool is one of the best ways to develop an understanding of derivatives pricing. Manipulating inputs and observing the impact on vanilla option prices is far more productive than looking at formulas in a book. This practical links closely to the material developed in Chapter 5.

Task A: Set Up a Simple Black-Scholes Options Pricer

Step 1: Set Up Spot/Rates/Time to Expiry

The first inputs to the pricer are:

- Spot (S): the current exchange rate in a given currency pair
- Interest rates ($rCCY1$ and $rCCY2$): continuously compounded risk free interest rates in CCY1 and CCY2 of the currency pair
- Time to expiry (T): the time between the horizon date and expiry date measured in years

The first output is the forward to maturity T:

$$F_T = Se^{(rCCY2 - rCCY1) \cdot T}$$

Inputs

Spot	1.3650	←Named: **Spot**
CCY1 Interest Rate	1.00%	←Named: **rCCY1**
CCY2 Interest Rate	0.40%	←Named: **rCCY2**
Time to Maturity (years)	1.00	←Named: **T**

Outputs

Forward	1.3568	=Spot*EXP((rCCY2-rCCY1)*T)

Test to see how changing the inputs impacts the forward and note what happens when $rCCY1 = rCCY2$.

Step 2: Set Up Vanilla Option Pricing

European vanilla option payoffs are calculated using spot at maturity (S_T) and the strike (K):

- $Payoff_{call} = max(S_T - K, 0)$

- $Payoff_{put} = max(K - S_T, 0)$

As described in Chapter 5, the Garman and Kohlhagen formula calculates FX European vanilla option prices in CCY2 per CCY1 (i.e., CCY2 pips) terms:

- $Price_{call} = Se^{-rCCY1 \cdot T} N(d_1) - Ke^{-rCCY2 \cdot T} N(d_2)$

- $Price_{put} = Ke^{-rCCY2 \cdot T} N(-d_2) - Se^{-rCCY1 \cdot T} N(-d_1)$

where

$$d_1 = \frac{\ln\left(\frac{S}{K}\right) + \left(rCCY2 - rCCY1 + \frac{\sigma^2}{2}\right) \cdot T}{\sigma\sqrt{T}}$$

$$d_2 = \frac{\ln\left(\frac{S}{K}\right) + \left(rCCY2 - rCCY1 - \frac{\sigma^2}{2}\right) \cdot T}{\sigma\sqrt{T}} = d_1 - \sigma\sqrt{T}$$

And σ is the volatility of the spot log returns.
Useful Excel functions are:

- =LN(X) for natural log

- =SQRT(X) for square root

- =EXP(X) for exponential

- =NORMSDIST(X) for the cumulative normal distribution function $N(X)$

Test that if $S = K = 1.0$, $T = 1.0$, $\sigma = 10\%$, and $rCCY1 = rCCY2 = 0\%$, the option price is very slightly under 0.04 pips (0.0399 pips):

Inputs

Spot	1.0000	
CCY1 Interest Rate	0.00%	
CCY2 Interest Rate	0.00%	
Time to Maturity (years)	1.00	
Strike	1.0000	←Named: **K**
Implied Volatility (σ)	10.00%	←Named: **vol**

Working

d1	0.05	=(LN(Spot/K)+(rCCY2-rCCY1+0.5*vol^2)*T)/(vol*SQRT(T))
d2	-0.05	=d_1-vol*SQRT(T)
N(d1)	0.519938806	=NORMSDIST(d_1)
N(d2)	0.480061194	=NORMSDIST(d_2)
N(-d1)	0.480061194	=NORMSDIST(-d_1)
N(-d2)	0.519938806	=NORMSDIST(-d_2)

Outputs

Forward	1.0000	
European Vanilla Call (CCY2 pips)	0.0399	=(Spot*EXP(-rCCY1*T)*Nd_1-K*EXP(-rCCY2*T)*Nd_2)
European Vanilla Put (CCY2 pips)	0.0399	=(K*EXP(-rCCY2*T)*Nminusd_2-Spot*EXP(-rCCY1*T)*Nminusd_1)

Once the pricing is correct, flex each parameter and work through a logical argument of how the parameter change impacts call and put vanilla option pricing. Consider the relative positioning of forward and strike, how time to maturity and implied volatility impact the terminal spot distribution, and discounting of the payoff from maturity back to the horizon (see Chapter 10).

Example 1: For a 100.00 strike call option, if the strike is moved higher, the call option price reduces because the forward is further away from the payoff. The equivalent put option will increase in value:

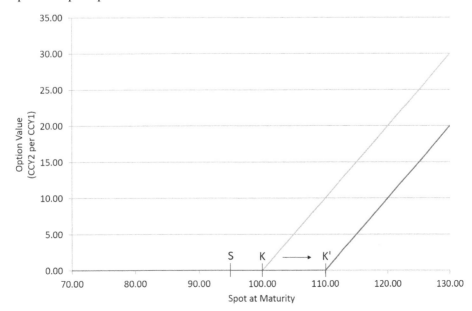

Example 2: For a 1.2500 strike call option, if implied volatility moves higher or time to expiry increases, both call and put option prices increase because the spot distribution moves wider, hence bringing larger payoffs into play:

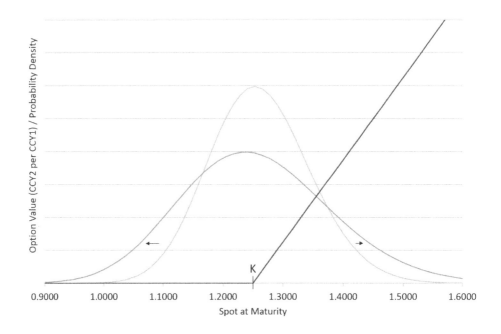

Example 3: If CCY1 and CCY2 interest rates both move higher to the same level, the forward will be unchanged but both call and put option prices decrease due to increased discounting.

Step 3: Add in Option Notional and Convert to CCY1 Payoff

Option notionals are usually quoted in CCY1 terms and option prices are naturally generated in CCY2 pips (CCY2 per CCY1) terms. Given a CCY1 option notional, the **cash price** in CCY1 can therefore be calculated. This is useful because it gives the numbers a real-world feel. As in Practical B:

■ To convert an option price from CCY2 pips terms into CCY2 cash terms, multiply by the CCY1 notional.

- To convert an option price from CCY2 cash terms into CCY1 cash terms, divide by current spot.

Inputs

Spot	1.3650	
CCY1 Interest Rate	1.00%	
CCY2 Interest Rate	2.00%	
Time to Maturity (years)	1.00	
Notional (CCY1)	10,000,000	←Named: **N**
Strike	1.3800	
Implied Volatility (σ)	10.00%	

Working

d1	0.040709295
d2	-0.059290705
N(d1)	0.516236174
N(d2)	0.476360282
N(-d1)	0.483763826
N(-d2)	0.523639718

Outputs

Forward	1.3787	
European Vanilla Call (CCY2 pips)	0.0533	←Named: **CallPriceCCY2Pips**
European Vanilla Put (CCY2 pips)	0.0545	←Named: **PutPriceCCY2Pips**
European Vanilla Call (CCY2 cash)	532,906	=N*CallPriceCCY2Pips
European Vanilla Put (CCY2 cash)	545,468	=N*PutPriceCCY2Pips

European Vanilla Call (CCY1%)	3.90%	←Named: **CallPriceCCY1Pct**	=CallPriceCCY2Pips/Spot
European Vanilla Put (CCY1%)	4.00%	←Named: **PutPriceCCY1Pct**	=PutPriceCCY2Pips/Spot
European Vanilla Call (CCY1 cash)	390,407	=N*CallPriceCCY1Pct	
European Vanilla Put (CCY1 cash)	399,610	=N*PutPriceCCY1Pct	

Step 4: Investigate Put–Call Parity

In payoff terms, put–call parity is often stated as, for example, long call + short put = long forward. However, in terms of *pricing*:

$$Price_{call} - Price_{put} = F - K$$

Therefore, if the strike is set equal to the forward, the call price and the put price should be equal. This can be checked within the pricing tool:

Inputs

Spot	1.3650	
CCY1 Interest Rate	1.00%	
CCY2 Interest Rate	2.00%	
Time to Maturity (years)	1.00	
Notional (CCY1)	10,000,000	
Strike	1.3787	=Forward
Implied Volatility (σ)	10.00%	

Working

d1	0.05
d2	-0.05
N(d1)	0.519938806
N(d2)	0.480061194
N(-d1)	0.480061194
N(-d2)	0.519938806

Outputs

Forward	1.3787
European Vanilla Call (CCY2 pips)	0.0539
European Vanilla Put (CCY2 pips)	0.0539
European Vanilla Call (CCY2 cash)	538,913
European Vanilla Put (CCY2 cash)	538,913

European Vanilla Call (CCY1%)	3.95%
European Vanilla Put (CCY1%)	3.95%
European Vanilla Call (CCY1 cash)	394,808
European Vanilla Put (CCY1 cash)	394,808

When the strike is moved away from the forward, a subtlety reveals itself: Option prices are present valued, whereas the P&L from the forward versus strike difference is realized in the future. The $(F - K)$ value therefore needs to be present valued using the CCY2 discount factor ($e^{-rCCY2.T}$):

Put-Call Parity Check

Call less Put	-0.0012561	=CallPriceCCY2Pips-PutPriceCCY2Pips
Forward less Strike	-0.0012561	=EXP(-rCCY2*T)*(Forward-K)

■ Task B: Set Up a VBA Pricing Function

A lot of additional flexibility becomes possible if the pricing calculation is done within a VBA function rather than using functions constructed in the cells of the Excel sheet. The VBA pricing function should take the following inputs:

```
Public Function OptionPrice(isCall As Boolean, S As Double, K As Double, _
 T As Double, rCCY1 As Double, rCCY2 As Double, v As Double) As Double
```

Helpfully, Excel VBA uses slightly different function names:

- Log(X) is the VBA equivalent of =LN(X)

- Sqr(X) is the VBA equivalent of =SQRT(X)

- Exp(X) is the VBA equivalent of =EXP(X)

- Application.WorkbookFunction.NormSDist(X) is used to access the cumulative normal distribution function.

An explicit check for zero or negative implied volatility or time to maturity should also be included because they would cause the function to throw an error. Instead, set them to a small positive value (e.g., 10^{-10}), which will make the formula return the payoff at maturity.

The VBA option pricing function should look like this:

```
'Garman and Kohlhagen Currency Option Pricing in CCY2 Pips
Public Function OptionPrice(isCall As Boolean, S As Double, K As Double, _
 T As Double, rCCY1 As Double, rCCY2 As Double, v As Double) As Double

    Dim d1 As Double, d2 As Double

    If (T >= 0) Then T = 0.0000000001
    If (v >= 0) Then v = 0.0000000001

    d1 = (Log(S / K) + (rCCY2 - rCCY1 + v ^ 2 / 2) * T) / (v * Sqr(T))
    d2 = d1 - v * Sqr(T)

    If isCall Then
        OptionPrice = (S * Exp(-rCCY1 * T) * _
        Application.WorksheetFunction.NormSDist(d1) - K * _
        Exp(-rCCY2 * T) * Application.WorksheetFunction.NormSDist(d2))
    Else
        OptionPrice = (K * Exp(-rCCY2 * T) * _
        Application.WorksheetFunction.NormSDist(-d2) - S * _
        Exp(-rCCY1 * T) * Application.WorksheetFunction.NormSDist(-d1))
    End If

End Function
```

Call the function from the cell alongside the existing functions to test that both calculations give the same results:

VBA Working

isCall	TRUE	=IF(Payoff="Call",TRUE,FALSE)

Outputs

Forward	1.3787
European Vanilla Call (CCY2 pips)	**0.053290621**
European Vanilla Put (CCY2 pips)	0.0545
European Vanilla Call (CCY2 cash)	532,906
European Vanilla Put (CCY2 cash)	545,468

European Vanilla Call (CCY1%)	3.90%
European Vanilla Put (CCY1%)	4.00%
European Vanilla Call (CCY1 cash)	390,407
European Vanilla Put (CCY1 cash)	399,610

VBA Outputs

Option Price	**0.053290621**	=OptionPrice(isCall,Spot,Strike,T,rCCY1,rCCY2,vol)

■ Task C: Generate First-Order Greeks

Greek exposures are the sensitivity of an option price to changes in market parameters. As explored in Chapter 6, the most important first-order Greeks are **delta** and **vega**.

Delta (Δ) is the change in option value for a change in spot:

$$\Delta_{call} = \frac{\partial P_{call}}{\partial S} = e^{-rCCY1.T} N(d_1)$$

$$\Delta_{put} = \frac{\partial P_{put}}{\partial S} = e^{-rCCY1.T}[N(d_1) - 1]$$

Vega (v) is the change in option value for a change in implied volatility:

$$v_{call} = v_{put} = \frac{\partial P_{call}}{\partial \sigma} = \frac{\partial P_{put}}{\partial \sigma} = Se^{-rCCY1.T}n(d_1)\sqrt{T}$$

where $n(X)$ is the standard normal density function. In Excel this is accessed using =NORMDIST(X, 0, 1, FALSE).

For these first-order Greeks, the Black-Scholes formula can be directly differentiated to generate the formulas. This is called a **closed-form** approach. The same exposures can also be calculated using a **finite difference** approach, which involves manually flexing a parameter (e.g., spot or volatility) a small amount up and down and taking the ratio of the change in price over the change in parameter to calculate the exposure.

In general, the closed-form approach is faster but it is not always available, particularly when pricing exotic contracts. The finite difference approach is slower but it can be applied generically to calculate any exposure for any contract.

Within the pricer both methods can be implemented for comparison. Closed-form exposures can be calculated on the sheet surface but the finite difference approach is easier in VBA. New VBA functions for calculating delta and vega must take additional *spot flex* and *vol flex* parameters respectively. The smaller these parameter flexes, the more accurate the outputs, unless the flex is smaller than the accuracy of the variables themselves within the VBA.

Greek exposures have standard market quotation conventions:

▪ Delta is quoted as a % of the CCY1 notional.

▪ Vega is often quoted in CCY1 terms (i.e., divide the function result by spot) and quoted as a % of CCY1 notional for a 1% move in implied volatility (i.e., divide the Black-Scholes vega by 100 to get it into standard market terms).

Once both functions have been implemented in the VBA, check that the values exactly match and investigate the impact of changing the flex size. Start with a 10^{-6} flex but test what happens to the outputs as flex size is increased and decreased.

The VBA code for the finite difference exposures should look like this:

```
'Finite Difference Option Delta in CCY1%
Public Function OptionDelta(isCall As Boolean, S As Double, K _
 As Double, T As Double, rCCY1 As Double, rCCY2 As Double, v As Double, _
 S_Flex As Double) As Double

    Dim OptionPriceUp As Double, OptionPriceDw As Double

    OptionPriceUp = OptionPrice(isCall, S + S_Flex, K, T, rCCY1, rCCY2, v)
    OptionPriceDw = OptionPrice(isCall, S - S_Flex, K, T, rCCY1, rCCY2, v)

    OptionDelta = (OptionPriceUp - OptionPriceDw) / (S_Flex * 2)

End Function

'Finite Difference Option Vega in CCY1%
Public Function OptionVega(isCall As Boolean, S As Double, K As Double, _
 T As Double, rCCY1 As Double, rCCY2 As Double, v As Double, _
 Vol_Flex As Double) As Double

    Dim OptionPriceUp As Double, OptionPriceDw As Double

    OptionPriceUp = OptionPrice(isCall, S, K, T, rCCY1, rCCY2, _
      v + Vol_Flex)
    OptionPriceDw = OptionPrice(isCall, S, K, T, rCCY1, rCCY2, _
      v - Vol_Flex)

    OptionVega = 0.01 * ((OptionPriceUp - OptionPriceDw) / _
      (Vol_Flex * 2)) / S

End Function
```

VBA Inputs

Option Type	Call	(Call or Put)
Spot Flex	0.000001	←Named: *SpotFlex*
Vol Flex	0.000001	←Named: *VolFlex*

VBA Working

isCall	TRUE

Sheet Outputs

Forward	1.3926
European Vanilla Call (CCY2 pips)	0.0446
European Vanilla Put (CCY2 pips)	0.0323
European Vanilla Call (CCY2 cash)	445,783
European Vanilla Put (CCY2 cash)	323,140

European Vanilla Call (CCY1%)	3.27%
European Vanilla Put (CCY1%)	2.37%
European Vanilla Call (CCY1 cash)	326,581
European Vanilla Put (CCY1 cash)	236,732

Call Delta (CCY1%)	56.217389%
Put Delta (CCY1%)	-43.283859%
Vega (CCY1%)	0.276955%

VBA Outputs

Option Price (CCY2 pips)	0.0446	=OptionPrice(isCall,Spot,Strike,T,rCCY1,rCCY2,vol)
Option Delta (CCY1%)	56.217389%	=OptionDelta(isCall,Spot,Strike,T,rCCY1,rCCY2,vol,SpotFlex)
Option Vega (CCY1%)	0.276955%	=OptionVega(isCall,Spot,Strike,T,rCCY1,rCCY2,vol,VolFlex)

Test that if $S = K = 1.0$, $T = 1.0$, $\sigma = 10\%$, and $rCCY1 = rCCY2 = 0\%$, the option delta is close to 50%, and vega is a shade under 0.40%.

■ Task D: Plot Exposures

The price, delta, and vega VBA functions that have been developed can be used to generate tables and charts of option prices or Greeks over different spots, interest rates, implied volatility levels, or time to expiry. These profiles are key to risk managing a portfolio of vanilla options:

C24			f_x	=OptionDelta(isCall,B24,Strike,T,rCCY1,rCCY2,vol,SpotFlex)	
	A	B	C	D	E	F

	Spot	Option Delta (CCY1%)		Spot	Option Vega (CCY1%)
21					
22	1.0000	0.00%		1.0000	0.000%
23	1.0250	0.01%		1.0250	0.000%
24	1.0500	0.02%		1.0500	0.001%
25	1.0750	0.07%		1.0750	0.002%
26	1.1000	0.19%		1.1000	0.004%
27	1.1250	0.50%		1.1250	0.010%

Interesting exposures to plot are:

- *Delta versus spot*: The gradient of this chart gives gamma, plus try extreme *rCCY1* and *rCCY2* values.

- *Vega versus spot*: Note the location of the vega peak, plus try extreme *rCCY1* and *rCCY2* values.

- *Vega versus time to expiry*: Look at the formula for vega and confirm the relationship.

- *Option value versus volatility*: Try this for strikes close to spot and strikes further away from spot.

CHAPTER 7

Vanilla FX Derivatives Pricing

This chapter introduces two primary responsibilities of a vanilla FX derivatives trader: maintaining volatility surfaces and quoting vanilla price requests.

▓ Maintaining Volatility Surfaces

In some financial markets, all relevant market prices can be observed *directly* in the market. However, in OTC (over-the-counter) derivatives markets, prices are very often requested for contracts that have *not* been directly observed in the market. This flexibility is a key advantage of the OTC market structure.

To quote consistent vanilla option prices for any expiry date and strike, traders keep a **volatility surface** updated in each currency pair. Exhibit 7.1 shows a three-dimensional representation of the volatility surface in one currency pair.

The volatility surface can be split into two components: the **ATM (at-the-money) curve** and the **volatility smile**.

ATM Curve

ATM contracts are the backbone of the volatility surface; they define the *term structure* of implied volatility. ATM contracts are vanilla contracts quoted to a specific maturity and they have a strike near (or at) the forward to the same maturity.

ATM contracts are the most important price reference points within the FX derivatives market. In the interbank broker market ATM contracts are often quoted in a **run** of prices at the **market tenors**, the most liquid expiry dates within the

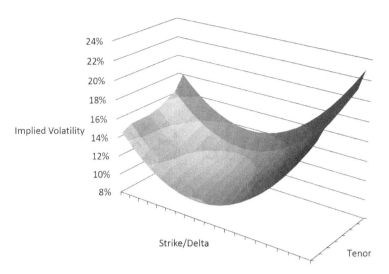

EXHIBIT 7.1   Example volatility surface

EUR/USD (NY Cut)		
Tenor	*ATM Volatility*	
O/N	4.00	5.75
1W	6.75	7.15
2W	6.50	7.20
1M	6.65	6.90
2M	6.90	7.10
3M	6.80	7.05
6M	7.40	7.60
1Y	8.10	8.25
2Y	8.60	8.90

EXHIBIT 7.2   Example ATM run

market. For example, Exhibit 7.2 gives a run of ATM prices at market tenors: O/N (overnight, i.e., tomorrow), 1wk (one week), 2wk, 1mth (one month), 2mth, 3mth, 6mth, 1yr (one year), and 2yr.

The run shows the best bid and best offer that the broker currently has for the ATM contract at each tenor. These are *tradable* rates that have been made (*contributed*) by other banks. Therefore, in Exhibit 7.2, the EUR/USD 1mth ATM NY cut two-way implied volatility price is 6.65/6.9%: The contract will cost 6.9% volatility to buy while selling it will earn 6.65% volatility.

When traders talk, ATM implied volatility is often spoken about in terms of its "vol base," meaning the approximate level of implied volatility in that currency pair. The "handle" is a similar term (e.g., "EUR/USD vol trades off a six handle" means the implied volatility in EUR/USD is 6-point-something-%). When written down, traders often use, for example, 6^1 to mean 6.1% implied volatility.

It is important to understand how this structure based around *fixed market tenors* works in practice. As the horizon date changes, the expiry date for each market tenor changes accordingly (the methodology for calculating tenor expiry dates is given in Chapter 10 and implemented in Practical D). Therefore, the contracts liquidly quoted in the market today have different expiry dates from those quoted yesterday or those quoted tomorrow. Plus as spot (and hence the forward outright) moves, the strike of the ATM contract changes too. This is the nature of an OTC market: Contracts are not standardized, although note that strikes are often rounded to the nearest five or ten pips so the ATM strike does not exactly change pip for pip as spot moves.

ATM implied volatilities at different tenors are plotted in a curve in Exhibit 7.3.

ATM curves are described as *upward sloping* if back-end (e.g., 1yr) ATM volatility is higher than front-end (e.g., 1mth) ATM volatility and as *downward sloping* if front-end ATM volatility is higher than back-end ATM volatility. In quiet markets, back-end ATM volatility tends to be higher than front-end ATM volatility. In stressed market conditions, ATM curves can become "inverted," with higher front-end volatility.

In general, ATM curves move in an orderly manner: Single tenors rarely move in isolation and changes in the ATM curve are often characterized as either parallel or weighted shifts.

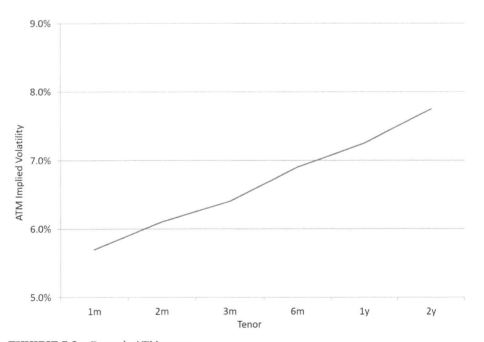

EXHIBIT 7.3 Example ATM curve

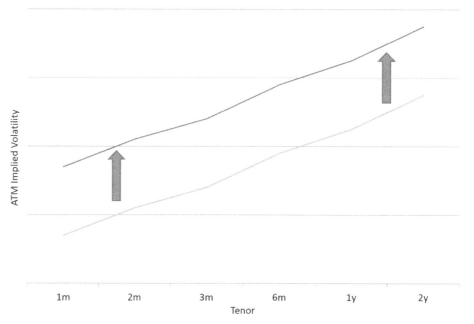

EXHIBIT 7.4 Parallel ATM curve shift

Within a **parallel** ATM shift, the ATM volatility at all maturities moves the same amount up or down as demonstrated in Exhibit 7.4.

Within a **weighted** ATM shift, ATM volatility at near maturities moves more than ATM volatility at far maturities as demonstrated in Exhibit 7.5.

Volatility Smile

The **volatility smile** defines how strikes away from the ATM strike are priced relative to the ATM implied volatility at a given tenor. Slicing through the volatility surface at a particular maturity produces a volatility smile as shown in Exhibit 7.6.

In the interbank broker market, the **butterfly** and **risk reversal** contracts are the instruments used to describe the volatility smile:

- The butterfly contract describes the **wings** of the volatility smile (i.e., how steep the sides of the volatility smile are).

- The risk reversal contract describes the **skew** of the volatility smile (i.e., how tilted the volatility smile is).

Butterfly and risk reversal contracts are quoted at market tenors like the ATM curve. In equity derivatives, lower strikes tend to have higher implied volatility than higher strikes at a given maturity because equities tend to rally slowly and

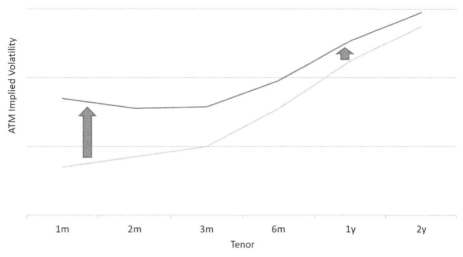

EXHIBIT 7.5 Weighted ATM curve shift

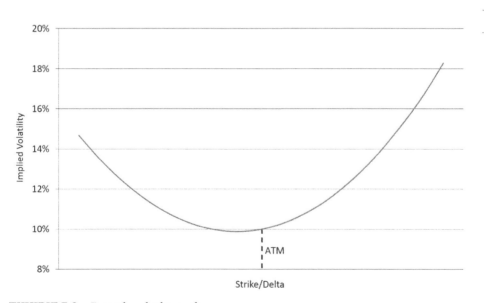

EXHIBIT 7.6 Example volatility smile

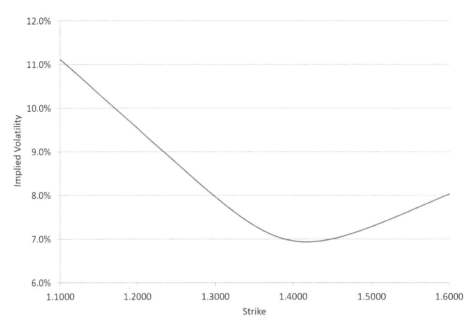

EXHIBIT 7.7   Example downward-sloping volatility smile

drop quickly, but in FX different currency pairs have differently shaped volatility smiles. Some volatility smiles are tilted such that downside strikes have higher implied volatility than topside strikes (e.g., 1yr EUR/USD in July 2014) as shown in Exhibit 7.7.

Some volatility smiles are tilted such that topside strikes have higher volatility than downside strikes (e.g., 6mth USD/ZAR [South African Rand] in July 2014) as shown in Exhibit 7.8.

Some volatility smiles are symmetric and/or have low volatility (e.g., 1mth USD/HKD in July 2014) as shown in Exhibit 7.9.

Some volatility smiles are highly skewed and/or have high volatility (e.g., 1yr AUD/JPY at the height of the 2008 financial crisis) as shown in Exhibit 7.10.

Volatility smiles have higher implied volatility on the "weaker" side of spot (i.e., the direction in which spot is more likely to jump or generally will be more volatile). For example, in major emerging market currency pairs quoted as USD/CCY, the main risk is a sharp EM currency devaluation that causes spot to jump higher. For this reason, USD versus EM currency pair volatility smiles are usually tilted so topside strikes cost more in implied volatility terms than downside strikes (see, e.g., the USD/ZAR example in Exhibit 7.8).

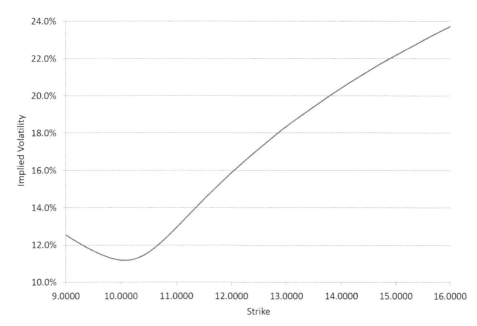

EXHIBIT 7.8 Example upward-sloping volatility smile

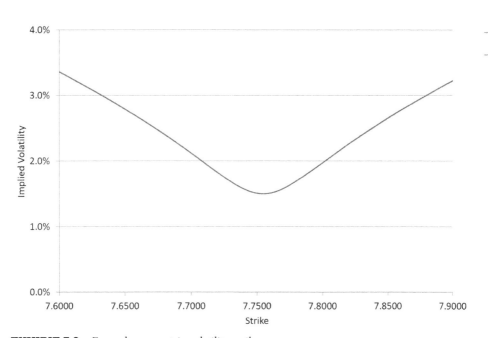

EXHIBIT 7.9 Example symmetric volatility smile

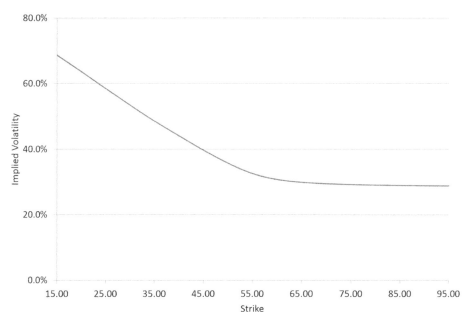

EXHIBIT 7.10   Example extreme volatility smile

Updating the Volatility Surface

Traders watch for new volatility market information in the currency pairs for which they are responsible. The primary source for this information is the interbank broker market.

When a new *price* appears or a *trade* occurs in the broker market, the trader compares that volatility level with the midmarket volatility generated by the desk volatility surface for the same contract. If differences are observed, either the trader updates the volatility surface inputs such that the midmarket volatility hits the market price or the trader may conclude that the price/trade represents a trading opportunity.

Example 1: The USD/CAD 1mth ATM contract two-way price is quoted at 4.8/5.0%. In the trader's volatility surface the current 1mth ATM is marked at 5.0%. The trader takes this as a signal that implied volatility at shorter tenors is reducing and therefore the near end of the ATM curve must be moved lower as shown in Exhibit 7.11.

Example 2: A vanilla trade occurs in the market which suggests that the market is pricing topside strikes at higher implied volatility than before. The volatility smile at the same tenor as the trade is shown in Exhibit 7.12.

The volatility smile at this tenor must be updated to hit this trading level but there are different ways in which this can be achieved. For example:

- The ATM can be moved higher, hence moving the entire volatility smile higher as shown in Exhibit 7.13.

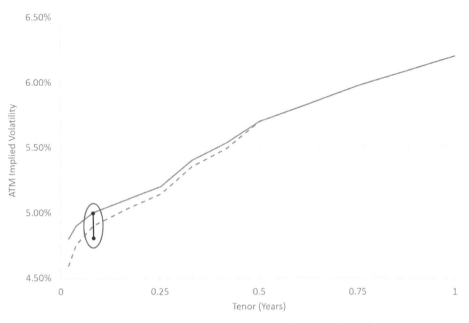

EXHIBIT 7.11   Changing the ATM curve to match new volatility market information

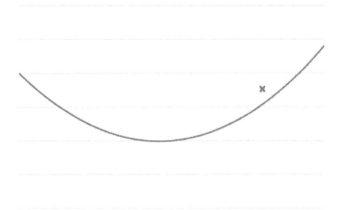

EXHIBIT 7.12   Existing volatility smile plus new volatility market information

■ The wings of the volatility smile can be moved higher (i.e., strikes away from the ATM are priced relatively higher than the ATM) as shown in Exhibit 7.14.

■ The skew of the volatility smile can be moved more "for the topside" (i.e., the volatility smile is tilted such that strikes above the ATM are priced higher while strikes below the ATM are priced lower). Note that the ATM stays unchanged in Exhibit 7.15.

The trader chooses between these three possibilities (or maybe a combination of them) when updating the volatility smile. As mentioned, single tenors within the

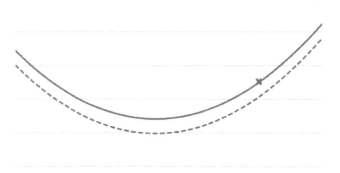

EXHIBIT 7.13   Changing the ATM to match new volatility market information

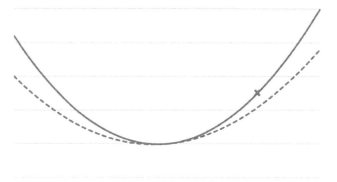

EXHIBIT 7.14   Changing the wings of the volatility smile to match new volatility market information

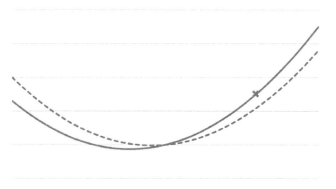

EXHIBIT 7.15   Changing the skew of the volatility smile to match new volatility market information

volatility surface rarely move in isolation so the volatility smile is usually updated over multiple tenors at once. By observing many prices and trades in the market, the trader determines how best to update the entire volatility surface.

Vanilla Bid–Offer Spreads

The volatility surface generates a *midmarket* implied volatility. A bid–offer spread is then applied around the mid-rate to give a *two-way price*. The bid–offer spread for a particular vanilla contract changes depending on its maturity and the proximity of the strike to the ATM.

In practice, standard market bid–offer spreads are observed in the interbank market. Bid–offer spreads for ATM contracts at market tenors in liquid G10 pairs under "normal" market conditions often look similar to Exhibit 7.16. Simple interpolation can be used to generate bid–offer spreads for expiry dates between tenors. In general there is also a strong relationship between spot bid-offer spread and ATM bid-offer spread because the spot bid-offer spread must be crossed when delta hedging the ATM contract to maturity.

ATM volatility spreads are wide in short-dates, reduce to a minimum from 1mth to 1yr, then go wider again at longer tenors, but why? To get a better intuition, *vega* is used to go from ATM volatility spread to ATM premium spread in Exhibit 7.17.

Recall from Chapter 6 that vega is the first derivative of option value with respect to implied volatility:

$$Vega\ (\upsilon) = \frac{\partial P}{\partial \sigma}$$

Therefore the ATM premium spread at a given tenor is calculated by multiplying the ATM volatility spread by the vega. Note that this calculation assumes that vega is unchanged as implied volatility changes.

Exhibit 7.17 shows that looking at ATM volatility spread alone is misleading when comparing bid–offer spreads at different tenors because shorter maturities have lower vega. In most currency pairs the 1mth ATM is the most liquid ATM

EXHIBIT 7.16 Standard ATM Bid–Offer Volatility Spreads

Tenor	ATM Volatility Spread
O/N	3.0%
1wk	1.0%
2wk	0.6%
1mth to 1yr	0.3%
2yr	0.35%
3yr	0.4%
4yr	0.45%
5yr	0.5%

Tenor	ATM Volatility Spread	Vega (CCY1% 2 d.p.)	ATM Premium Spread (CCY1% 2 d.p.)
O/N	3%	0.02%	0.06%
1wk	1%	0.06%	0.06%
2wk	0.6%	0.08%	0.05%
1mth	**0.3%**	**0.10%**	**0.03%**
2mth	0.3%	0.16%	0.05%
3mth	0.3%	0.20%	0.06%
6mth	0.3%	0.28%	0.08%
1yr	0.3%	0.40%	0.12%
2yr	0.35%	0.56%	0.20%
3yr	0.4%	0.69%	0.28%
4yr	0.45%	0.79%	0.36%
5yr	0.5%	0.87%	0.44%

contract and it therefore has the tightest bid–offer premium spread. Bid–offer spreads in less liquid currency pairs will be wider than those shown in Exhibit 7.17, and the most liquid currency pairs will be tighter, but the relative shape of the bid–offer spread curve is fairly consistent across currency pairs.

For strikes away from the ATM at a given maturity, consider two possible methods of generating the bid–offer spread:

1. Constant premium spread
2. Constant volatility spread

At a given maturity, the maximum vega exposure occurs on ATM strikes. Strikes away from the ATM have lower vega as shown in Exhibit 7.18.

A 1yr ATM option has 0.40% vega so a 0.25% ATM bid–offer volatility spread equates to a 0.10% bid–offer premium spread. If all strikes at the 1yr tenor had the same *premium bid–offer spread*, wing strikes would have a wider bid–offer volatility spread due to lower vega as shown in Exhibit 7.19.

If all strikes at the 1yr tenor had the same *volatility bid–offer spread*, wing strikes would have a tighter bid–offer premium spread due to lower vega as shown in Exhibit 7.20.

In practice, for strikes away from the ATM in liquid currency pairs, the bid–offer spread widens in volatility terms, but not as much as constant premium spread. For example, if the 1yr ATM has 0.25% volatility spread and 0.10% premium spread, a 1yr 10 delta vanilla option might have 0.35% volatility spread and hence 0.06% premium spread.

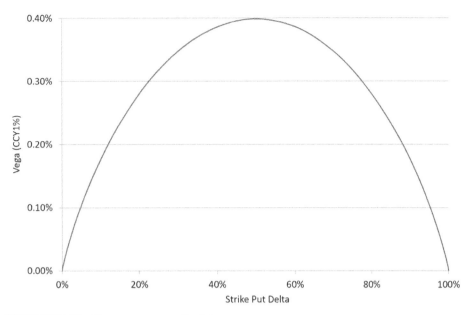

EXHIBIT 7.18   Vega versus put strike delta

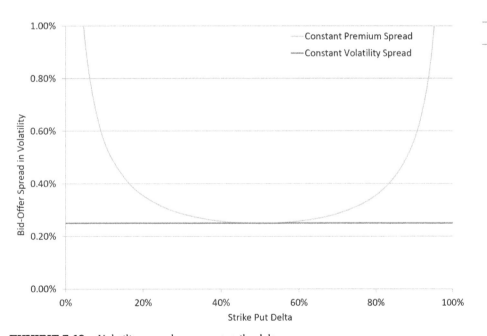

EXHIBIT 7.19   Volatility spread versus put strike delta

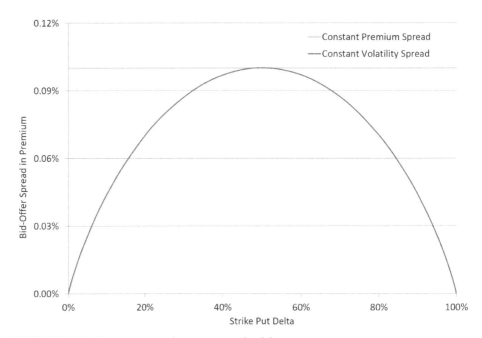

EXHIBIT 7.20 Premium spread versus put strike delta

■ Vanilla Price Making

When price making vanilla FX derivatives, traders adjust their prices based on market sentiment, plus contracts can either be transacted delta hedged or live.

Price Making Overview

When a new vanilla price request is received, the FX derivatives trader views the contract in their desk pricing tool. The price shown in the tool takes the midmarket volatility from the desk volatility surface and applies a default bid–offer spread.

For example, a client requests a GBP/USD 2mth 1.6800 GBP call in GBP20m. The default mid on the contract is 6.45% and the system two-way price is 6.25/6.65%. This is called a *neutral rate* because neither the bid nor the offer has been improved.

The task of the trader is then to go from the default system rate to a rate they are happy to quote. One of the main factors within the adjustment is the *position preference* of the trader. As described in Chapter 3, price making is performed with reference to the current trading position. If a trader aims to change their position (for example, by selling vega, buying gamma, or buying options with topside strikes), these preferences are reflected within price making.

The other important factor within vanilla option price making is *market sentiment*. There are two types of market sentiment: structural and temporary:

Structural market sentiment involves market-wide preferences to, for example, buy very low-premium options on the high side of the volatility smile or buy options near the ATM on the low side of the volatility smile. These effects usually apply over and above the default modeling of the volatility surface and therefore need to be adjusted for within price making.

Temporary market sentiment is the current market preference for various types of contract—that is, is the market currently neutral, bid (the market prefers to buy), or offered (the market prefers to sell) for specific event dates? short-dates? back-dates? skew? wings? For example, suppose the 1mth ATM is 7.5/7.7% but it last traded at 7.6% and was *bid on* at the time. If there is then a new client price request in something *similar* to 1mth ATM (i.e., a contract with a similar expiry date and similar strike for which the 1mth ATM would be a reasonable hedge), it is appropriate to show a better bid on the contract. If the default system two-way rate on the new contract is 8.0/8.25%, an appropriate quoted rate might be 8.1/8.25%.

Market sentiment is most easily judged by observing the interbank broker market. Traders learn how the normal transaction process for different vanilla contracts works. For example, the implied volatility rate on an ATM contract will start relatively wide—12.45/12.75%—and over time it will tighten up as better bids and offers are shown—12.55/12.7% ... 12.6/12.7% ... 12.6/12.65%—before eventually trading somewhere within the original rate. This process usually takes around 30 minutes but it can take anything from a few minutes to a few hours.

The trading level and the speed of transaction are linked and they give information about the current market sentiment:

- If traders can wait to transact and want to deal at the best possible level, they will work slowly toward a midmarket trading level.

- If traders need to transact quickly, they will usually need to cross a larger spread from midmarket.

At the extreme, if the opening bid is hit straightaway, that constitutes a strong sell signal, and if the opening offer is paid straightaway, that constitutes a strong buy signal.

Market sentiment should be reflected within price making because it makes risk easier to recycle and enables better (tighter) prices to be quoted for clients. Occasionally prices will be quoted with either a *midmarket bid* (i.e., the bid shown is equal to the system midmarket) or a *midmarket offer* (i.e., the offer shown is equal to the system midmarket).

Transacting Delta Hedged or Live

Vanilla FX derivative price requests are either quoted in *volatility* or *premium* terms. FX derivatives traders typically quote prices in volatility terms because this makes the price making process easier. For a vanilla contract with a fixed maturity and strike, each time the spot rate (and therefore the forward) changes, the option premium changes (although the premium is usually rounded so this reduces the impact). However, the implied volatility quoted for a given contract can stay stable for longer, perhaps up to a few minutes in normal market conditions.

Vanilla price requests that are quoted in volatility terms are traded **delta hedged.** The Black-Scholes formula is used to calculate option premium and option delta, then a spot or forward hedge is transacted at the same rate at which the deal was priced. The interbank broker market and institutional clients who trade FX volatility typically transact in this manner.

Vanilla price requests that are quoted in premium terms are traded **live** (i.e., without a delta hedge). When a client trades live, the appropriate spot or forward deal must be transacted in the market in order to make the package delta neutral for the FX derivatives trader's position. Corporate clients who want to hedge future FX flows or institutional clients who plan to hold a trade in isolation until maturity typically transact in this manner. Either a salesperson or (increasingly) a machine deals with updating the price as spot moves and then hedges the delta when the client trades.

If the client trades live, the delta must be hedged *as* the deal is transacted. In this case the two-way premium is calculated using not only a two-way implied volatility but also two-way spot and forward rates, since that spread must be crossed in the market when the trade is delta hedged.

For long-dated options, using the correct two-way forward within pricing is particularly important since a substantial amount of the total premium bid–offer spread can come from the forward spread. Exhibit 7.21 shows the same vanilla option twice in a pricing tool: Leg 1 has choiced market data; appropriate if the counterparty is going to transact delta hedged with a forward hedge. Leg 2 has spread market data; appropriate if the counterparty is going to transact live (i.e., without a delta hedge).

Market Conventions

It is important that traders know the market conventions in the currency pairs they trade. For example, different ATM contracts are traded in different currency pairs:

- In all G10 (and some EM) currency pairs, the ATM contract is traded as a straddle (i.e., a call and a put with the same maturity and strike; ATM straddles are covered in more detail in Chapter 8).

- In other EM pairs, the ATM contract is traded as a single ATMF (at-the-money-forward) vanilla option with the strike equal to the forward, plus a forward hedge.

- The final ATM contract is ATMS (at-the-money-spot), which is a single vanilla option with the strike equal to current spot.

When trading vanilla options with strikes away from the ATM, the market convention is to always trade the out-of-the-money side (i.e., trade the call or put, whichever has the *lower absolute delta*). Therefore, if a vanilla option has a strike above the ATM, it will be traded as a CCY1 call/CCY2 put. If the strike is below the ATM, it will be traded as a CCY1 put/CCY2 call. Traded contracts are shown in Exhibit 7.22.

This is important because, although the Greeks on a delta hedged call and a delta hedged put are the same (due to put–call parity), the out-of-the-money direction has a smaller premium and a smaller expected payoff at maturity and hence has less credit

Contract Details	Leg 1	Leg 2
Currency Pair	AUD/USD	AUD/USD
Horizon	Thu 25-Sep-2014	Thu 25-Sep-2014
Spot Date	Mon 29-Sep-2014	Mon 29-Sep-2014
Strategy	Vanilla	Vanilla
Call/Put	AUD Call/USD Put	AUD Call/USD Put
Maturity	5Y	5Y
Expiry Date	Thu 26-Sep-2019	Thu 26-Sep-2019
Delivery Date	Mon 30-Sep-2019	Mon 30-Sep-2019
Cut	NY	NY
Strike	0.9000	0.9000
Notional Currency	AUD	AUD

Market Data		
Spot	0.8790/0.8795	0.8795
Swap Points	-700/-680	-690
Forward	0.8090/0.8115	0.8105
Deposit (AUD)	3.60/3.70%	3.65%
Deposit (USD)	1.95%	1.95%
ATM Volatility	10.45%	10.45%
Pricing Volatility	9.10/10.45%	9.10/10.45%

Outputs		
Output Currency	AUD	AUD
Mid Price	3.45/4.45%	3.50/4.40%

EXHIBIT 7.21 Vanilla option pricing with and without delta hedge

EXHIBIT 7.22 Traded vanilla option contracts

risk than the in-the-money direction. Traders should be careful when in-the-money options are requested by clients: Why wouldn't the conventional side be traded? Some banks tried to sell deep-in-the-money options as a mechanism to earn badly needed cash during the 2008 financial crisis. Although it isn't covered within this book, when trading FX derivatives contracts it is vital that the interest rates used correctly reflect the counterparty credit risk and this is particularly important for high premium in-the-money options.

When quoting in volatility terms, prices are usually rounded to the nearest 0.05% in shorter tenors and 0.025% in longer tenors, with the inflection point usually around the 2mth tenor. This rounding keeps volatility price making clean and ensures that prices quoted in volatility terms can be updated less frequently. When quoting in CCY1% premium terms, prices are usually rounded to the nearest quarter (0.0025%) or half (0.005%) a **basis point** (0.01%). A basis point is a key concept in derivatives pricing; it is always equal to a hundredth of one percent of the notional.

CHAPTER 8

Vanilla FX Derivatives Structures

Vanilla options can be combined to create different payoffs. Some of these combinations are so common that the resultant structures have standardized names that are requested by clients or quoted in the interbank broker market.

For an FX derivatives trader, it is most important to understand how these combinations of long and short vanilla options impact the exposures in the trading position. Within this chapter, vega is the primary focus. If structures are traded to shorter maturities, the most important exposure will be gamma. As observed in Chapter 6; for vanilla options, gamma profiles and vega profiles have similar shapes but they evolve differently over time.

■ Straddle

A straddle contains two vanilla options with identical contract details (same currency pair, buy/sell direction, notional, expiry, strike, and cut) except that one is a call and the other is a put.

Exhibit 8.1 shows the value at maturity of a long USD/JPY 100.00 straddle in notional N per leg:

- Leg 1: Buy USD call/JPY put with strike 100.00 in notional N.

- Leg 2: Buy USD put/JPY call with strike 100.00 in notional N.

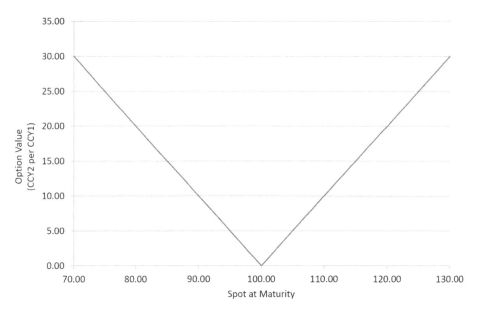

EXHIBIT 8.1 Value at maturity of long 100.00 straddle

Straddle Price Making

Thanks to put–call parity, making a volatility price for a straddle is the same as making a volatility price for a single vanilla option in the combined notional with the same expiry, strike, and cut. A single two-way volatility quote is made and, if dealt, that volatility is used to determine the premiums on both legs.

Zero-Delta ATM Straddles

By far the most commonly traded straddle contracts are **zero-delta straddles**: a straddle with its strike set such that $\Delta_{call} = -\Delta_{put}$ and therefore $\Delta_{straddle} = 0$. In all G10 and some EM currency pairs, the ATM contract is traded as a zero-delta straddle. Therefore, buying a 1mth ATM contract in EUR/USD actually means transacting a call and put, which forms a straddle.

Zero-Delta Straddle Strike Placement

The zero-delta straddle strike is positioned close to the forward for the same maturity but they are not exactly the same. Recall from Chapter 5 that the forward is derived from spot and interest rates:

$$F_T = Se^{(rCCY2 - rCCY1).T}$$

where F_T is the forward to time T (measured in years), S is the spot, and $rCCY1$ and $rCCY2$ are continuously compounded interest rates (see Chapter 10) to time T in CCY1 and CCY2 respectively.

Dipping briefly into Black-Scholes mathematics:

$$\Delta_{call} = \frac{\partial P_{call}}{\partial S} = e^{-rCCY1.T} N(d_1)$$

$$\Delta_{put} = \frac{\partial P_{put}}{\partial S} = e^{-rCCY1.T} [N(d_1) - 1]$$

where $N(x)$ is the cumulative normal distribution function and σ is volatility.

$$d_1 = \frac{\ln\left(\frac{S}{K}\right) + \left(rCCY2 - rCCY1 + \frac{1}{2}\sigma^2\right).T}{\sigma\sqrt{T}}$$

At the zero-delta straddle strike (K), $\Delta_{call} = -\Delta_{put}$. Therefore:

$$e^{-rCCY1.T} N(d_1) = -e^{-rCCY1.T}[N(d1) - 1]$$

$$N(d_1) = -[N(d1) - 1]$$

$$N(d_1) = \frac{1}{2}$$

Recalling the shape of cumulative normal distribution function from Chapter 5, if $N(d_1) = \frac{1}{2}$, then $d_1 = 0$. So

$$\frac{\ln\left(\frac{S}{K}\right) + \left(rCCY2 - rCCY1 + \frac{1}{2}\sigma^2\right).T}{\sigma\sqrt{T}} = 0$$

$$\left(rCCY2 - rCCY1 + \frac{1}{2}\sigma^2\right).T = -\ln\left(\frac{S}{K}\right)$$

$$e^{\left(rCCY2-rCCY1+\frac{1}{2}\sigma^2\right).T} = \frac{K}{S}$$

$$K = Se^{\left(rCCY2-rCCY1+\frac{1}{2}\sigma^2\right).T}$$

Therefore, the zero-delta straddle strike is *higher* than the forward due to the adjustment $+\frac{1}{2}\sigma^2 T$, which is linked to the Itō correction within the Black-Scholes framework (see Chapter 5).

Unfortunately, this is not quite the end of the story. The above is standard Black-Scholes mathematics, which assumes the premium is paid in CCY2. In, for example,

EUR/USD (USD premium), this is the case; but in, for example, USD/JPY (USD premium), the market convention is to pay premium in CCY1.

In CCY1 premium pairs (see Chapter 14 for more details on premium adjusted delta):

$$\Delta_{call} = \frac{\partial P_{call}}{\partial S} = e^{-rCCY1.T} N(d_1) - \frac{P_{call}}{S}$$

$$\Delta_{put} = \frac{\partial P_{put}}{\partial S} = e^{-rCCY1.T}[N(d_1) - 1] - \frac{P_{put}}{S}$$

which works through as:

$$K = Se^{\left(rCCY2 - rCCY1 - \frac{1}{2}\sigma^2\right).T}$$

Therefore, when the premium is paid in CCY1, the zero-delta straddle strike is *lower* than the forward due to the adjustment: $-\frac{1}{2}\sigma^2 T$.

In both cases, the difference between the forward and the ATM zero-delta straddle strike increases as volatility and time to expiry get larger.

Straddle Trading Exposures

Exhibit 8.2 shows the vega profile of a straddle. It is identical to the vega profile of a single vanilla with the same (combined) notional, strike, and maturity. As expected, the vega peak occurs at the strike.

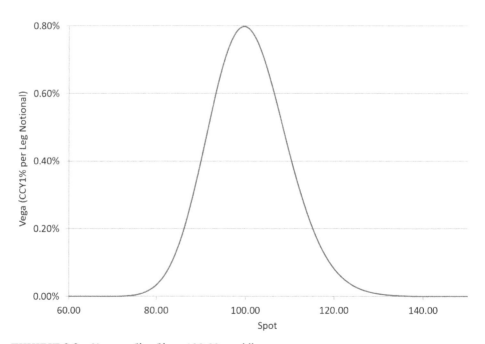

EXHIBIT 8.2 Vega profile of long 100.00 straddle

Strangle

A strangle is like a straddle except that the call and put have *different strikes*. Both strikes are placed out-of-the-money and therefore the call strike is always higher than the put strike.

Exhibit 8.3 shows the value at maturity of a long USD/JPY 90/110 strangle in notional N per leg:

- Leg 1: Buy USD call/JPY put with strike 110.00 in notional N.

- Leg 2: Buy USD put/JPY call with strike 90.00 in notional N.

Strangles are often quoted for a given delta. For example, a 25 delta strangle is constructed with strikes such that call delta = 25% and put delta = (−)25%.

Strangle Price Making

When making a price on a strangle, a *single* two-way volatility is quoted. If dealt, that volatility is used to determine the premiums on both legs. The bid–offer spread quoted on a strangle in volatility terms will usually be wider than the ATM spread to the same maturity because strikes away from the ATM have less vega (see Chapter 7).

A strangle containing strikes K_1 and K_2 has (approximate) implied volatility:

$$\sigma_{strangle} = \frac{\sigma_1 v_1 + \sigma_2 v_2}{v_1 + v_2}$$

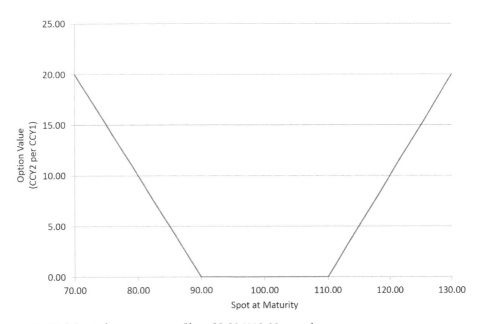

EXHIBIT 8.3   Value at maturity of long 90.00/110.00 strangle

where strike K_1 has implied volatility σ_1 and vega υ_1 while strike K_2 has implied volatility σ_2 and vega υ_2. Therefore, if the strangle contains equal delta call and put strikes with roughly equal vega, the strangle volatility will be close to the *average* of the two individual strike volatilities.

Strangle Trading Exposures

The vega profile of a strangle is similar to the vega profile of a straddle with the same maturity and notional per leg except that the strangle vega profile is wider because the strikes are spread out away from the ATM. At lower deltas the vega profile of the strangle has two distinct peaks from the two strikes as shown in Exhibit 8.4.

■ Butterfly (Fly)

The butterfly contract is a combination of a straddle and a strangle:

- Long butterfly = long strangle + short straddle
- Short butterfly = short strangle + long straddle

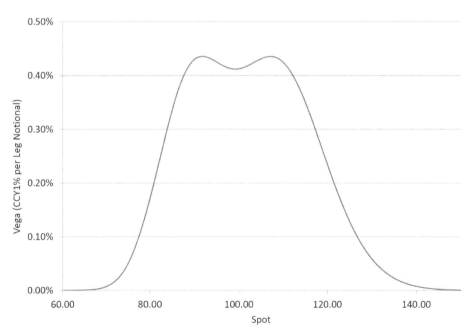

EXHIBIT 8.4 Vega profile of long 90.00/110.00 strangle

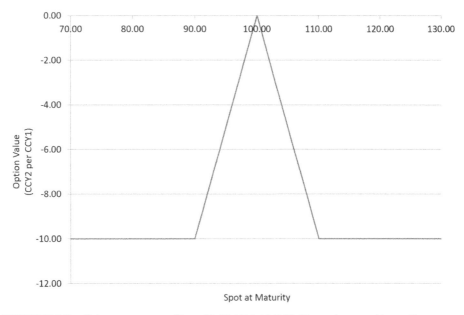

EXHIBIT 8.5   Value at maturity of long 90.00/100.00/110.00 equal notional butterfly

Buying the butterfly means buying the strangle, or put another way, buying the wings. Exhibit 8.5 shows the value at maturity of a long USD/JPY 90.00/100.00/110.00 *equal notional* butterfly:

- Leg 1: Buy USD put/JPY call with strike 90.00 in notional N.

- Leg 2: Sell USD put/JPY call with strike 100.00 in notional N.

- Leg 3: Sell USD call/JPY put with strike 100.00 in notional N.

- Leg 4: Buy USD call/JPY put with strike 110.00 in notional N.

Legs 1 and 4 form a long strangle and legs 2 and 3 form a short straddle. The contract is called a butterfly because its value at maturity looks like a butterfly if you really squint.

In the interbank broker market, the **broker fly** contract is the most commonly traded butterfly contract. A broker fly has equal notional strangle strikes and the notional on the ATM straddle is set such that the package is initially vega-neutral. Broker fly contracts are quoted for a given delta *but* the strikes for a given delta are generated using a different calculation. The broker fly product is examined in far more detail in Chapter 12.

Butterfly Price Making

In the interbank market, prices on broker fly contracts are quoted as the volatility differential between the strangle strikes and the ATM strikes. Plus the contract is quoted such that the *butterfly notional* is the *strangle notional*.

The broker fly has zero vega and minimal gamma by construction. Therefore, it is quoted significantly tighter than the strangle component in isolation. A bid–offer spread less than half the strangle bid–offer spread will often be shown.

Butterfly Trading Exposures

A long butterfly position is often flat ATM vega by construction and long vega in the wings from the long strangle strikes as shown in Exhibit 8.6.

◼ Risk Reversal (RR)

A risk reversal contains two vanilla options with the same currency pair, notional, expiry, and cut. However, the two legs have different strikes, one is a call and the other is a put, plus one is bought while the other is sold. The contract is called a risk reversal because it transfers optionality between the two strikes.

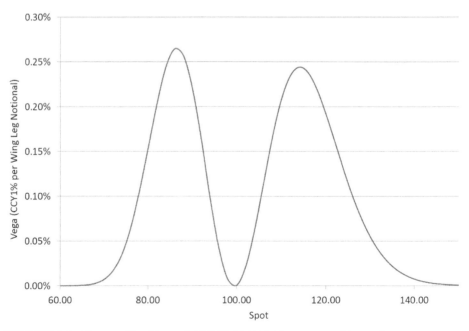

EXHIBIT 8.6 Vega profile of long 90.00/100.00/110.00 vega-neutral butterfly

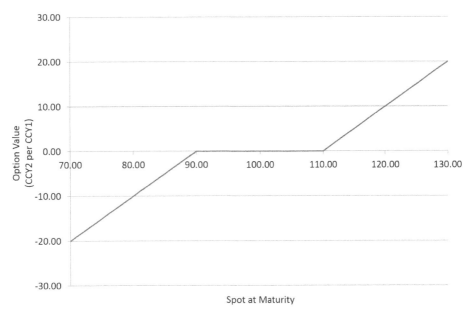

EXHIBIT 8.7   Value at maturity of 90.00/110.00 risk reversal (buying topside)

Exhibit 8.7 shows the value at maturity of a USD/JPY 90/110 risk reversal (buying topside) in notional N per leg:

- Leg 1: Buy USD call/JPY put with strike 110.00 in notional N.

- Leg 2: Sell USD put/JPY call with strike 90.00 in notional N.

Risk reversals are usually quoted to a specific delta. They are constructed using a long call and a short put (or short call and long put) and the delta exposures from the two legs therefore compound (i.e., the delta on both legs is either positive or negative). To calculate the delta hedge on the risk reversal, the delta of the two legs is summed. For example, to delta hedge a 25d risk reversal, containing a long 25d call and a short 25d put, $25\% \times 2 = 50\%$ of the single leg notional of spot must be sold.

Corporates often call risk reversals "collars" when they are used as instruments to hedge future cash flows. A popular structure is a **zero-premium collar**, which caps and floors the P&L from an FX exposure as demonstrated in Exhibit 8.8.

Risk Reversal Price Making

A risk reversal is a **spread** contract. It has two legs: one bought, one sold. There are offsetting gamma and vega exposures between the legs and therefore the product is quoted tighter than the equivalent contract where either both legs are bought or both legs are sold. When quoting a price on spread, rather than quoting tighter two-way prices on both legs, the market convention is to quote one leg with a **choice** price

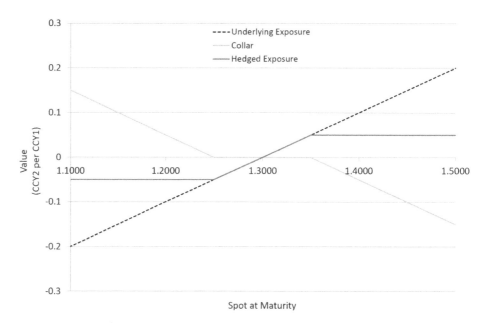

EXHIBIT 8.8 Hedging an FX exposure with a collar (risk reversal)

(i.e., a single volatility at which it is possible to buy or sell, often denoted CH) and the other leg with a **spread** price (i.e., a two-way volatility price). In other words, all the bid–offer spread is put onto one of the legs. Risk reversals are usually quoted with around half the overall bid–offer spread of the equivalent strangle.

For example, USD/BRL 1yr 25d risk reversal:

- Outright 1yr 25d call implied volatility: 14.35 / 14.85%

- Outright 1yr 25d put implied volatility: 10.75 / 11.25%

- 1yr 25d risk reversal implied volatility: 14.35 / 14.85% vs. 11.0% CH

Risk reversals for a given delta are often quoted as an *implied volatility differential* between the two strikes (e.g., 3.35/3.85% in the above USD/BRL example). This is appropriate when the risk reversals strikes have the same delta and hence there is *minimal net vega* on the structure. Once the trade is agreed in volatility differential terms, the volatility on one of the strikes is agreed and that determines the volatility of the other strike; hence both premiums can be calculated. The risk reversal product is examined in far more detail in Chapter 12.

Risk Reversal Trading Exposures

The bought leg in the risk reversal generates a long vega exposure with a peak at the long strike while the sold leg generates a short vega exposure with a (negative) peak at the short strike. This is shown in Exhibit 8.9.

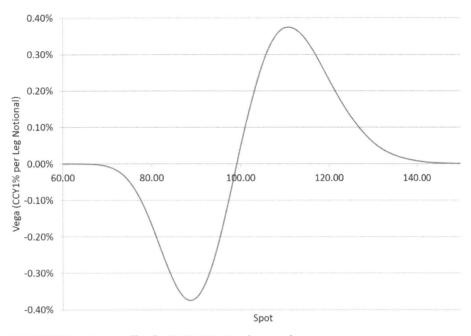

EXHIBIT 8.9   Vega profile of a 90.00/110.00 risk reversal

Leveraged Forward

Recall from Chapter 6 that a synthetic forward is constructed using a long vanilla call and short vanilla put with all other contract details the same.

A leveraged forward is an extension of a synthetic forward in which the two notional amounts are no longer equal. A 200% leveraged forward in which USD/JPY is bought at 100.00 is constructed using two legs with double the notional on the sold leg:

- Leg 1: Buy USD call/JPY put with strike 100.00 in notional N.

- Leg 2: Sell USD put/JPY call with strike 100.00 in notional $2\ N$.

Leveraged forwards can be decomposed into a forward in the matched notional plus a vanilla in the unmatched notional. Since forwards have no optionality, the vega trading risk is equal to a vanilla in the unmatched notional and the implied volatility price will also be equal to the volatility price of the vanilla option in the unmatched notional.

This product is popular with clients hedging FX flows because the underlying can be transacted at a better rate than the forward for zero premium. The better rate is funded by the increased notional on the sell leg.

ATM Calendar Spread

ATM calendar spreads are combinations of two ATM contracts, one bought and one sold (hence a spread), to different maturities. In old-school trading language, calendar spreads are called *horizontal spreads*.

Buying the calendar spread means *buying* the longer date (the "back date" or "far date") and *selling* the shorter date (the "near date"). If the notionals are set such that there is zero net vega on the structure, it becomes a vega-neutral ATM calendar spread.

A long 3mth/6mth equal notional ATM calendar spread is constructed using four legs, assuming the ATM is traded as a straddle:

- Leg 1: Sell 3mth ATM USD call/JPY put in notional N.

- Leg 2: Sell 3mth ATM USD put/JPY call in notional N.

- Leg 3: Buy 6mth ATM USD call/JPY put in notional N.

- Leg 4: Buy 6mth ATM USD put/JPY call in notional N.

Legs 1 and 2 form a short ATM straddle and legs 3 and 4 form a long ATM straddle.

ATM Calendar Spread Price Making

Standard vanilla spread pricing rules apply: A spread (two-way) price is shown on the ATM straddle with more vega and the other ATM straddle is shown choice. Therefore, for ATM calendar spreads the far ATM straddle is spread since vega increases at longer maturities. Calendar spreads usually have substantial offsetting vega risk and are therefore quoted tighter than two ATM contracts in the same direction: Perhaps the standard bid–offer spread will be shown on the far leg, with the near leg quoted choice.

ATM Calendar Spread Trading Exposures

ATM calendar spreads give exposures to the shape of the ATM curve since they contain offsetting vega positions in two tenors. Exhibit 8.10 shows the bucketed vega profile from the long 3mth/6mth vega-neutral ATM calendar spread. This position will make money if the 3mth ATM volatility rises more than the 6mth ATM volatility.

Call/Put Spreads

Vanilla call spreads and vanilla put spreads have two legs in the same notional and to the same maturity, either both calls or both puts. One leg is a buy and the other is a

Tenor	Vega (USDk)
O/N	-
1W	-
2W	-
1M	-
2M	-
3M	-200
6M	200
1Y	-
2Y	-
Total	**-**

EXHIBIT 8.10   Bucketed vega profile from long 3mth/6mth vega-neutral ATM calendar spread

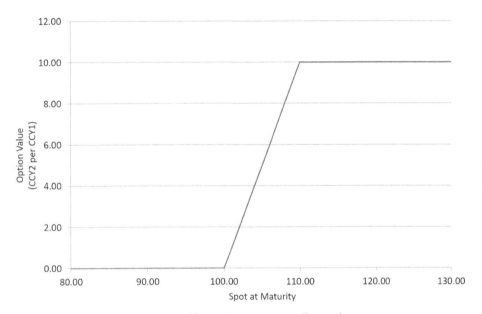

EXHIBIT 8.11   Value at maturity of long 100.00/110.00 call spread

sell; hence the structure is a spread. When buying the call/put spread, the bought leg is always more expensive, and hence further in-the-money than the sold leg.

Exhibit 8.11 shows the value at maturity of a long USD/JPY 100.00/110.00 USD call spread in notional N per leg:

- Leg 1: Buy USD call/JPY put with strike 100.00 in notional N.

- Leg 2: Sell USD call/JPY put with strike 110.00 in notional N.

Buying call/put spreads is popular with institutional clients because they enable a directional view with no possible downside other than the initial premium at a cheaper cost than the outright vanilla. In old-school trading language, call/put spreads are called *vertical spreads*.

If left unhedged until maturity:

■ A long CCY1 call spread pays out if spot is above the lower strike with the payoff capped at the higher strike.

■ A long CCY1 put spread pays out if spot is below the higher strike with the payoff capped at the lower strike.

Call/Put Spread Price Making

The standard vanilla spread quoting rules apply to call spreads and put spreads too: Spread the leg with more vega and choice the other leg. It is interesting to note that once call/put spreads are placed in a delta hedged trading portfolio, the vega exposures are the same as the vega exposures from a risk reversal with the same strikes; the long strike generates a long vega exposure and the short strike generates a short vega exposure.

■ Seagull

A long seagull contract is a long call/put spread *plus* an additional short put/call. It is most often a product sold for zero initial premium to investors who want to hedge an underlying FX exposure.

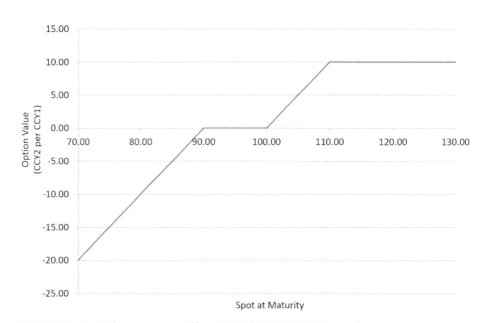

EXHIBIT 8.12   Value at maturity of long 90.00/100.00/110.00 seagull

Exhibit 8.12 shows the value at maturity of a long USD/JPY 90.00/100.00 /110.00 seagull in notional *N* per leg:

- Leg 1: Sell USD put/JPY call with strike 90.00 in notional *N*.

- Leg 2: Buy USD call/JPY put with strike 100.00 in notional *N*.

- Leg 3: Sell USD call/JPY put with strike 110.00 in notional *N*.

Legs 2 and 3 form a long call spread.

Seagull Price Making

On vanilla spreads with more than two legs there are few concrete rules on how to quote prices but generally the price is easier to understand if as many legs as possible are quoted choice. Plus the legs with the most vega should be spread because their price quoted in volatility terms will be the tightest.

CHAPTER 9

Vanilla FX Derivatives Risk Management

F X derivatives trading portfolios contain different types of deal: vanilla options, exotic options, spots, forwards, and so on. To risk manage derivatives positions traders use Greeks; the exposures of the position to market changes. Greeks are calculated on each deal in the portfolio and then aggregated together. For a given market move, some deals in the portfolio will make money or, for example, get longer vega, and others will lose money or get shorter vega: Traders only care about the *net impact* from all deals. For this reason traders primarily describe their positions in terms of long or short positions in aggregated Greek exposures. For example, an FX derivatives trader may describe their position in a given currency pair as "flat delta, short topside gamma, and long vega."

As markets move, positive or negative P&L is generated from different aggregated exposures within the position. The most important exposures are to spot (delta exposure) and ATM volatility (vega exposure). There are also exposures to CCY1 and CCY2 interest rates (rho exposures), exposures to curve moves in these instruments, plus exposures to the shape of the volatility surface. Finally, exposures are not static: Recall the gamma and vega profiles for vanilla options from Chapter 6; exposures change as the market moves or time passes.

For these reasons, trading an FX derivatives position is not straightforward. To simplify analysis, traders often consider similar types of Greeks together:

- *Short-date risk*: delta/gamma/theta

- *ATM risk*: vega/weighted vega/bucketed vega

- *Smile risk*: exposures to the shape of the volatility surface

- *Interest rate risk*: rho/swap points

- *Cross-exposure risk* (e.g., the change in interest rate position when ATM implied volatility changes)

To understand the trading risk in a vanilla derivatives trading position, a trader must investigate all these different types of risk. Fundamentally, though, focusing on higher-order risks while neglecting first-order exposures is obvious folly. The majority of FX derivative trading P&L usually comes from exposures to spot and implied volatility:

- The *short-date position* consists of vanilla options that cause delta to change significantly as spot moves. The resultant delta exposure then causes P&L to change. These exposures mainly come from short-dated vanilla options.

- The *ATM position* consists of vanilla options that generate exposures to the ATM curve. These exposures mainly come from long-dated vanilla options.

■ Trading Gamma

Long vanilla option positions always give long gamma exposures while short vanilla option positions always give short gamma exposures. Exhibit 9.1 recalls how the gamma exposure from a vanilla option increases and concentrates at the strike into maturity. Therefore, the *short-date position* mainly consists of vanilla options expiring within the next month or so with strikes fairly close to current spot. These options generate significant gamma exposures that cause delta and hence P&L to change as spot moves. Traders control these P&L changes by managing their delta and gamma exposures.

One common method of viewing the short-date position is a **spot ladder** that shows P&L, delta, and gamma over a range of spot values. This allows traders to anticipate how their P&L and position will change as spot moves. In particular, traders use spot ladders to determine when to hedge their delta exposures.

The gaps between spot levels in the ladder should be aligned with the spot volatility in the currency pair. The higher the spot volatility, the wider the appropriate spot spacings. Plus, if a pegged or managed currency pair has significant jump risk,

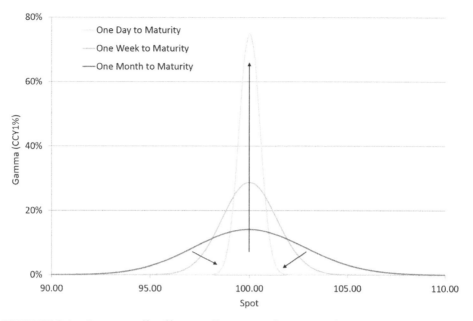

EXHIBIT 9.1   Gamma profile of long vanilla option with 100.00 strike

two ladders—one with tight spacings and one with wide spacings—might be appropriate.

Trading Long Gamma

Exhibit 9.2 shows a EUR/USD spot ladder from a *long* EUR20m 1wk ATM position, with current spot highlighted in the middle of the ladder. Values in this spot ladder are generated assuming market data (apart from spot) remains unchanged and no additional trades are executed as spot moves from its current level. This is a long

EUR/USD	P&L Change (USD)	Delta (EUR)	Gamma (EUR)
1.3328	188,157	9,282,211	1,133,443
1.3262	128,980	8,502,448	2,033,607
1.3196	76,918	7,199,716	3,205,066
1.3130	35,687	5,285,401	4,436,512
1.3065	9,097	2,811,473	5,393,734
1.3000	-	**0.00**	**5,629,367**
1.2935	9,425	-2,827,304	5,400,400
1.2870	36,117	-5,309,527	4,441,749
1.2806	76,873	-7,225,145	3,204,447
1.2742	127,669	-8,523,634	2,027,795
1.2678	184,712	-9,296,817	1,125,729

Daily P&L (USD) | - |

EXHIBIT 9.2   Initial EUR/USD spot ladder with long gamma exposure

vanilla option position and is therefore long gamma. Peak gamma is at current spot because it is an ATM contract. The contract is delta neutral by construction so initial delta is zero.

As spot moves, P&L change occurs faster the further spot moves in either direction. This is characteristic of being long the second derivative (i.e., long gamma). In trading positions, gamma is quoted per 1% move in spot, so, for example, on a 1% spot move higher (from 1.3000 to 1.3130), delta increases by approximately +EUR5.6m (current gamma).

Assume EUR/USD spot rises from 1.3000 to 1.3065, as shown in Exhibit 9.3:

- Spot higher and long gamma $\left(\frac{\partial delta}{\partial spot} \right)$ leads to an increasing long delta position as spot rises.

- Spot higher and long delta $\left(\frac{\partial price}{\partial spot} \right)$ produces *positive P&L change* (i.e., making money, a good thing) as seen in the spot ladder.

The trader now has a decision to make:

1. *Sell spot* in the market to reduce the long EUR2.8m delta exposure, known as "taking profit." Selling EUR2.8m EUR/USD spot will hedge (offset) the delta position back to approximately flat and the delta hedging process can start again. After selling EUR2.8m EUR/USD spot at 1.3065, the position is shown in Exhibit 9.4. Note that the P&L change is now approximately equal for a same-sized up or down move in spot; the position is "balanced."

2. *Do not hedge the delta* (i.e., let the position run). If spot continues higher, the position will make even more money, but if spot retraces back lower, the positive P&L will be lost. If delta is not hedged, the position is not balanced. By allowing a delta position to accumulate the trader has an increased exposure to the future direction of spot.

EUR/USD	P&L Change (USD)	Delta (EUR)	Gamma (EUR)
1.3395	242,426	9,692,767	554,939
1.3328	179,059	9,282,211	1,133,443
1.3262	119,883	8,502,448	2,033,607
1.3196	67,820	7,199,716	3,205,066
1.3130	26,590	5,285,401	4,436,512
1.3065	**-**	**2,811,473**	**5,393,734**
1.3000	-9,097	-14,332	5,656,990
1.2935	420	-2,840,787	5,396,886
1.2870	27,191	-5,320,602	4,435,966
1.2806	68,007	-7,233,124	3,198,182
1.2742	118,844	-8,528,676	2,022,508

Daily P&L (USD)	9,097.47

EXHIBIT 9.3 EUR/USD spot ladder with spot higher

EUR/USD	P&L Change (USD)	Delta (EUR)	Gamma (EUR)
1.3395	150,052	6,892,767	554,939
1.3328	105,345	6,482,211	1,133,443
1.3262	64,735	5,702,448	2,033,607
1.3196	31,147	4,399,716	3,205,066
1.3130	8,299	2,485,401	4,436,512
1.3065	**-**	**11,473**	**5,393,734**
1.3000	9,194	-2,814,332	5,656,990
1.2935	36,911	-5,640,787	5,396,886
1.2870	81,790	-8,120,602	4,435,966
1.2806	140,624	-10,033,124	3,198,182
1.2742	209,389	-11,328,676	2,022,508

Daily P&L (USD) | 9,097.47

EXHIBIT 9.4 EUR/USD spot ladder after rebalancing delta

Now, from the same starting point, assume EUR/USD spot falls from 1.3000 to 1.2935, as shown in Exhibit 9.5:

- Spot lower and long gamma $\left(\frac{\partial delta}{\partial spot}\right)$ leads to an increasing short delta position as spot falls.

- Spot lower and short delta $\left(\frac{\partial price}{\partial spot}\right)$ produces *positive P&L change* again, as seen in the spot ladder.

Once again, spot has moved, a delta position results from the long gamma, and the trader has two choices:

1. *Buy spot* in the market to reduce the delta exposure. Again, this is taking profit but the trader does not have to completely hedge the delta exposure. For example, after buying back just EUR2m EUR/USD spot at 1.2935, the position is shown

EUR/USD	P&L Change (USD)	Delta (EUR)	Gamma (EUR)
1.3262	119,273	8,497,338	2,038,909
1.3196	67,255	7,191,671	3,211,333
1.3130	26,089	5,274,280	4,442,294
1.3065	-419	2,797,970	5,397,263
1.3000	-9,424	-14,332	5,656,990
1.2935	**-**	**-2,827,304**	**5,400,400**
1.2870	26,691	-5,309,527	4,441,749
1.2806	67,448	-7,225,145	3,204,447
1.2742	118,244	-8,523,634	2,027,795
1.2678	175,287	-9,296,817	1,125,729
1.2615	235,673	-9,701,277	548,266

Daily P&L (USD) | 9,425.39

EXHIBIT 9.5 EUR/USD spot ladder with spot lower

EUR/USD	P&L Change (USD)	Delta (EUR)	Gamma (EUR)
1.3262	184,598	10,497,338	2,038,909
1.3196	119,385	9,191,671	3,211,333
1.3130	65,089	7,274,280	4,442,294
1.3065	25,516	4,797,970	5,397,263
1.3000	3,511	1,985,668	5,656,990
1.2935	-	**-827,304**	**5,400,400**
1.2870	13,756	-3,309,527	4,441,749
1.2806	41,642	-5,225,145	3,204,447
1.2742	79,633	-6,523,634	2,027,795
1.2678	123,934	-7,296,817	1,125,729
1.2615	171,642	-7,701,277	548,266

	Daily P&L (USD)	9,425.39

EXHIBIT 9.6   EUR/USD spot ladder after partially rebalancing delta

in Exhibit 9.6. By not buying back the full delta amount, the position is not completely balanced, but it is more balanced than it was.

2. *Do not hedge the delta* (i.e., let the position run). If spot continues lower, the position will make even more money, but if spot retraces back higher, the positive P&L will be lost.

If the delta is initially balanced, long gamma causes a positive P&L change if spot moves either up *or* down, just so long as it moves somewhere. Hedging the delta resulting from a long gamma exposure naturally leads to buying spot when it goes lower and selling spot when it goes higher. *Buying low* and *selling high* locks in P&L over the course of the day in a process known as *trading the gamma*. When leaving orders in the market to trade a long gamma position, *looped take-profit* orders are often used (e.g., sell EUR5m at 1.3130, if done, buy EUR5m at 1.3000, if done, sell EUR5m at 1.3130).

Positions with larger gamma exposures are delta hedged more frequently. In this single option example, if spot stays close to the strike as days pass, the gamma from the vanilla option increases, which will lead to more frequent delta hedging. Then, on the expiry date of the long ATM contract, Exhibit 9.7 shows the trading position with the delta balanced around the strike.

Trading risk is viewed as of a specific horizon date (usually today) and the risk on options that expire on the horizon is viewed *at expiry time*. Therefore, the option is viewed as a *strike*; an *instantaneous delta jump* equal to the option notional rather than gamma exposure. With spot at 1.3001 (above the strike), delta exposure is +EUR10m. With spot at 1.2999 (below the strike), delta exposure is −EUR10m: a EUR20m delta change, the *notional* of the option. Trading this position is similar to trading gamma, except that *all* the delta change occurs at the strike.

EUR/USD	P&L Change (USD)	Delta (EUR)	Gamma (EUR)
1.3339	328,519	10,000,000	-
1.3272	262,158	10,000,000	-
1.3206	196,127	10,000,000	-
1.3140	130,425	10,000,000	-
1.3075	65,050	10,000,000	-
1.3010	**-**	**10,000,000**	**-**
1.2945	48,600	-10,000,000	-
1.2880	113,325	-10,000,000	-
1.2816	177,726	-10,000,000	-
1.2752	241,805	-10,000,000	-
1.2688	305,564	-10,000,000	-

Daily P&L (USD) | - |

EXHIBIT 9.7   EUR/USD spot ladder at maturity

For a **long strike** position:

- If spot goes above the strike, the trader can sell spot in the market to hedge the long delta exposure.

- If spot goes below the strike, the trader can buy spot in the market to hedge the short delta exposure.

Once the delta position is fully hedged back to zero, it is not possible to hedge again until spot goes back through the strike.

In general, P&L volatility from a single vanilla option increases as time to expiry gets shorter if spot remains near the strike. Plus, for a given ATM vanilla option, P&L volatility from trading the strike at expiry tends to be larger than P&L volatility from trading the gamma prior to expiry.

Trading a long gamma position looks easy—buy vanilla options to get long gamma, and if spot moves higher or lower, you make money. Long gamma naturally means spot can be bought low and sold high, hence generating positive P&L. Of course, there is a cost for this and that cost is **theta** $\left(\frac{\partial price}{\partial time} \right)$, also known as **time decay** or just **decay**. For a long gamma position, theta is the *cost* of holding the trading position from one trading day to the next.

If realized volatility is larger than implied volatility there will be more opportunities to delta hedge, which usually results in larger P&L from trading a long gamma exposure than is paid in theta, hence generating positive P&L overall.

If realized volatility is smaller than implied volatility there will be fewer opportunities to delta hedge, which usually results in smaller P&L from trading a long gamma exposure than is paid in theta, hence generating negative P&L overall.

Delta Hedging in Practice

If no delta hedging is performed throughout the trading day (and assuming no P&L from any other source), the daily P&L will be a function of the difference between yesterday's end-of-day spot and today's end-of-day spot (end-of-day market data is the official reference used for P&L generation, limit checking, etc.). Alternatively, if delta hedging were performed continuously (not possible in practice), P&L would be a function of implied volatility and realized volatility (recall from Chapter 5 that this is the essence of the Black-Scholes formula derivation). An FX derivatives trader's main focus, skill, and exposures are to FX volatility. Therefore, option positions are delta hedged frequently throughout the day.

If spot followed a mathematical random walk, the primary factor in determining the optimal delta hedge frequency of a *long gamma* position would be the spot bid–offer spread size. The Euan Sinclair book "*Volatility Trading*" has a good section on this (see Further Reading). In practice, though, decisions on when and how to trade the delta exposure are based on different factors:

- *Spot bid–offer spreads.* The wider the spreads, the less often traders like to delta hedge because they must cross a spread each time they do so. If spot bid–offer spreads are wide, it often makes more sense to leave orders in the spot market rather than transacting directly. Plus, outside the main book-runner's time zone, leaving orders ensures that opportunities to delta hedge are not missed.

- *Expected spot volatility and jumps.* During quieter times, traders may hedge smaller spot moves. But if spot jumps when important economic data is released, traders often let spot run further to take advantage of their positive second derivative.

- *Time of day.* At the start of the trading day, traders tend to let deltas run further in an attempt to generate larger P&Ls, but toward the option expiry they "scalp" (trade the delta) more aggressively.

- *Key levels in the spot market (i.e., rounded spot levels where barriers will be positioned or recent low and high spot levels).* If spot breaks through key levels, this often causes spot to run further and traders may let larger deltas accumulate before hedging.

- *How spot is moving.* If spot is whipping up and down, traders will delta hedge more aggressively, whereas if spot is trending strongly, they may let the delta run further before hedging.

Many derivatives traders love trading spot to manage their delta exposures throughout the day and they believe that they add value by doing this. A friend at another bank reported their boss proclaiming (with a straight face) "trading spot is like playing Mozart" and selling EUR/CHF spot shortly before the Swiss central bank unexpectedly intervened and sent spot over 8% higher. In stable market conditions it is debatable how much value a trader can add, but when unexpected events occur, the ability of a human trader to rapidly process new information in context can be an advantage.

Trading Short Gamma

Exhibit 9.8 shows a EUR/USD spot ladder from a *short* EUR20m 1wk ATM position.

P&L change, delta, and gamma are all equal and opposite (negative) to the long ATM position:

- Spot higher and short gamma leads to an increasing short delta position as spot rises.

- Spot higher and short delta produces *negative P&L change*.

while:

- Spot lower and short gamma leads to an increasing long delta position as spot falls.

- Spot lower and long delta again produces *negative P&L change*.

If spot moves in either direction, the delta change from a short gamma position produces a negative P&L change. The decision for the trader therefore becomes whether to *stop-loss* the delta (i.e., buy high/sell low) or let it run and potentially lose even more at an increasing rate due to the short second derivative. In practice, trading short gamma is often made easier by accepting that at least half the theta earned will be lost through stopping out. Trading with close stop-loss orders helps avoid large negative P&Ls.

A short gamma position *earns* theta but loses money throughout the trading day as spot moves. Again, if the position is delta hedged frequently, the overall P&L generated is primarily a function of implied volatility and realized volatility, but this

EUR/USD	P&L Change (USD)	Delta (EUR)	Gamma (EUR)
1.3328	-188,157	-9,282,211	-1,133,443
1.3262	-128,980	-8,502,448	-2,033,607
1.3196	-76,918	-7,199,716	-3,205,066
1.3130	-35,687	-5,285,401	-4,436,512
1.3065	-9,097	-2,811,473	-5,393,734
1.3000	-	-	**-5,629,367**
1.2935	-9,425	2,827,304	-5,400,400
1.2870	-36,117	5,309,527	-4,441,749
1.2806	-76,873	7,225,145	-3,204,447
1.2742	-127,669	8,523,634	-2,027,795
1.2678	-184,712	9,296,817	-1,125,729

Daily P&L (USD) | - |

EXHIBIT 9.8 Initial EUR/USD spot ladder with short gamma

time the position will generate higher positive P&L if realized volatility is below implied volatility.

Trading the Short-Date Position

Traders investigate their short-date position in order to identify the main trading risks. Exhibit 9.9 shows a spot ladder from an AUD/USD FX derivatives trading position.

The position is long gamma at current spot and to the downside, but short gamma to the topside. This gamma profile implies that at shorter maturities the position is net long downside vanillas and short topside vanillas.

The first thing to check is that the delta and gamma positions tie up:

- Long gamma and spot higher → delta gets longer
- Long gamma and spot lower → delta gets shorter
- Short gamma and spot lower → delta gets longer
- Short gamma and spot higher → delta gets shorter

The position is short gamma to the topside, yet the delta jumps longer as spot goes higher from 0.9177 to 0.9205 as highlighted in Exhibit 9.10. Gamma profiles from vanilla options are smooth. Therefore, there must be a "strike" (i.e., a vanilla option expiring today) in the position causing a delta jump through it. Moreover, it must be a long strike since the delta jumps longer with spot higher.

Details of specific options in the position can be checked using a **trade query** or **strike topography**. A trade query is used to return details of every option in the portfolio as shown in Exhibit 9.11.

Strike topographies display a grid of expiry dates and strikes in one currency pair, making it easier to visualize the positioning of strikes. This is shown in Exhibit 9.12.

AUD/USD	P&L Change (USD)	Delta (AUD)	Gamma (AUD)
0.9288	48,882	1,531,811	-9,589,063
0.9260	40,469	4,415,610	-9,459,303
0.9233	24,357	7,045,015	-7,887,526
0.9205	1,951	8,954,786	-4,722,999
0.9177	-1,510	-308,939	-224,975
0.9150	**0**	**-1,014,115**	**4,736,927**
0.9123	5,509	-3,137,788	9,034,647
0.9095	18,416	-6,306,965	11,653,858
0.9068	40,711	-9,921,215	12,039,969
0.9041	72,630	-13,344,891	10,541,826
0.9014	112,906	-16,121,272	7,929,408

EXHIBIT 9.9 AUD/USD spot ladder

AUD/USD	P&L Change (USD)	Delta (AUD)	Gamma (AUD)
0.9288	48,882	1,531,811	-9,589,063
0.9260	40,469	4,415,610	-9,459,303
0.9233	24,357	7,045,015	-7,887,526
0.9205	1,951	8,954,786	-4,722,999
0.9177	-1,510	-308,939	-224,975
0.9150	**0**	**-1,014,115**	**4,736,927**
0.9123	5,509	-3,137,788	9,034,647
0.9095	18,416	-6,306,965	11,653,858
0.9068	40,711	-9,921,215	12,039,969
0.9041	72,630	-13,344,891	10,541,826
0.9014	112,906	-16,121,272	7,929,408

EXHIBIT 9.10   AUD/USD spot ladder with delta jump highlighted

Trade ID	Currency Pair	Portfolio	Expiry	Direction	Type	Strike	Cut	C/P	CCY1 Notional
41725659	AUD/USD	214	16-Jan-13	B	Vanilla	0.9200	NY	C	10,000,000
42204333	AUD/USD	214	18-Jan-13	B	Vanilla	0.9100	NY	P	50,000,000
42204787	AUD/USD	214	23-Jan-13	S	Vanilla	0.9200	NY	C	50,000,000
42204333	AUD/USD	214	18-Jan-13	B	Vanilla	0.9100	NY	P	50,000,000

EXHIBIT 9.11   AUD/USD trade query

AUD/USD	0.9014	0.9041	0.9068	0.9095	0.9123	**0.9150**	0.9177	0.9205	0.9233	0.9260	0.9288
Wed 16-Jan-13								0.9200 AUD10m			
Thu 17-Jan-13											
Fri 18-Jan-13				0.9100 AUD50m							
Sat 19-Jan-13											
Sun 20-Jan-13											
Mon 21-Jan-13											
Tue 22-Jan-13											
Wed 23-Jan-13								0.9200 -AUD50m			

EXHIBIT 9.12   AUD/USD strike topography

There may be just one option or multiple long/short options at a particular expiry date and strike in the strike topography; only the net notional is displayed. This information plus other missing details (e.g., cut or counterparty) can be obtained by drilling down into a given expiry and strike level.

These views confirm that the position is long AUD10m of 0.9200 strike expiring at NY cut today. This is important information because the delta jump at 0.9200 requires particular attention from the trader. Strikes are closely risk managed due to the delta jumps they generate. The larger the notional, the more attention a strike requires. This long strike will generate negative (paying) theta, but it gives the opportunity to make money back from it by trading delta over the course of the day (before it expires).

In general, the key question for a trader is whether they *like* the short-date position—that is, *will it generate a profit?* If there are aspects of the position that the trader doesn't like, trades should be executed to change the position. However, the *cost* of achieving a preferable position must be taken into account. Very often traders put up with a position they don't particularly like because the liquidity isn't available to get a position they do like at reasonable cost.

Individual traders will assess a short-date position differently but there are several common areas to consider.

P&L Balance

P&L balance involves assessing whether the position generates similar P&L changes for similar-sized up and down spot moves. This, of course, assumes the trader has no strong *opinion* on future spot moves. P&L balance can be checked in the spot ladder.

The P&L and delta positions should tie up:

- Long delta and spot higher → P&L increases

- Long delta and spot lower → P&L decreases

- Short delta and spot lower → P&L increases

- Short delta and spot higher → P&L decreases

Any discrepancies should be investigated; unexpected P&L jumps are most likely caused by exotic risk in the position.

Assuming the trader has no opinion on spot direction, it can be checked that the P&L change on equal-sized up and down spot moves is roughly the same. Traders usually look at a one-day spot move of approximately one-and-a-half standard deviations up and down. In currency pairs with implied volatility somewhere close to 10%, spot moves around 0.75% to 1% are often considered within P&L balance. In practice, though, traders look over a wider spot range, and if there are extreme negative P&Ls at spot levels which might conceivably be reached, it is more important to concentrate on controlling the P&L in those areas rather than on pure spot up/spot down P&L balance.

In the example AUD/USD position, the P&L is roughly balanced, but a bit of additional spot could be bought to balance it better as highlighted in Exhibit 9.13.

To increase the P&L at 0.9233 by USD8k and hence reduce the P&L by USD8k at 0.9068 (the equivalent spot move lower), $8,000/(0.9233 - 0.9150) = \text{AUD960k}$ spot should be bought. Buying spot changes the delta exposure and hence adjusts the P&L profile over spot as shown in Exhibit 9.14.

AUD/USD	P&L Change (USD)	Delta (AUD)	Gamma (AUD)
0.9288	48,882	1,531,811	-9,589,063
0.9260	40,469	4,415,610	-9,459,303
0.9233	24,357	7,045,015	-7,887,526
0.9205	1,951	8,954,786	-4,722,999
0.9177	-1,510	-308,939	-224,975
0.9150	**0**	**-1,014,115**	**4,736,927**
0.9123	5,509	-3,137,788	9,034,647
0.9095	18,416	-6,306,965	11,653,858
0.9068	40,711	-9,921,215	12,039,969
0.9041	72,630	-13,344,891	10,541,826
0.9014	112,906	-16,121,272	7,929,408

EXHIBIT 9.13 AUD/USD spot ladder with P&L balance highlighted

AUD/USD	P&L Change (USD)	Delta (AUD)	Gamma (AUD)
0.9288	62,138	2,491,811	-9,589,063
0.9260	51,057	5,375,610	-9,459,303
0.9233	32,287	8,005,015	-7,887,526
0.9205	7,230	9,914,786	-4,722,999
0.9177	1,125	651,061	-224,975
0.9150	**0**	**-54,115**	**4,736,927**
0.9123	2,873	-2,177,788	9,034,647
0.9095	13,154	-5,346,965	11,653,858
0.9068	32,829	-8,961,215	12,039,969
0.9041	62,137	-12,384,891	10,541,826
0.9014	99,808	-15,161,272	7,929,408

EXHIBIT 9.14 AUD/USD spot ladder with better P&L balance highlighted

In practice, the delta and hence the P&L profile over different spot levels can be adjusted by buying or selling spot but full P&L balance is a multi-dimensional problem. The gamma profile must be considered as well as impacts from ATM volatility and the volatility smile.

Theta

In trading positions, theta is quoted as the cumulative change in value from one trading day to the next for all deals in the position.

If a trading position is mainly long strikes and long gamma, the long option values reduce over time and theta will be negative. The negative theta is roughly the maximum that can be *lost* from the short-date position if the delta is initially balanced since delta hedging the long gamma position will make money back.

If a position is mainly short strikes and short gamma, the short option values reduce over time and theta will be positive. The positive theta is roughly the maximum that can be *made* from the short-date position if the delta is initially balanced since delta hedging the short gamma position will cost money. A trader friend at another bank was once told, "You can have any gamma position you like, so long as you don't pay any theta!"

In Black-Scholes world, gamma and theta are proportional: Higher theta implies higher gamma exposure and hence higher P&L volatility. Put another way, with more positive or negative gamma the trader is more exposed to how spot moves. If a trader decides that theta and hence P&L volatility is too large, short-dated vanilla options should be transacted to reduce the existing gamma position.

It is worth noting here that factors other than gamma can also generate theta, for example, smile decay, roll down the ATM curve, funding cash balances, and so forth. These factors are explored in Chapter 14.

Gamma

The spot ladder shows how the gamma exposure changes at different spot levels. Recall that:

- Long gamma → want spot to move more than implied volatility suggests it will, the more the better.

- Short gamma → want spot to move less than implied volatility suggests it will, the less the better.

Fundamentally, the trader has a decision to make: If the position is long gamma, looking at the spot ladder and the theta paid, will spot move enough to make back the theta from delta hedging? If the position is short gamma, looking at the spot ladder and the theta earned, will spot cause a loss from delta hedging larger than the theta?

Strikes

For options that settle against a cut rather than a fix, at the expiry time of each option in the position, the owner of each option contacts the writer to tell them if they want to exercise the option. The most common cut time in G10 pairs is NY cut and the 20-minute period before NY cut is simply called *expiries* on most trading desks in London and New York.

In practice, from the start of the trading day, bank trading desks contact each other to exercise strikes that are very far from the current spot level. Over the course of the day, the strikes being dealt with get closer and closer to current spot and at some point responsibility passes from middle office to traders.

If spot is very close to a particular strike, communication between the option owner and the option writer will be established shortly beforehand, with the option owner asking to "hold" on the strike. Then as the cut time arrives, the decision to exercise or expire the contract is made based on the prevailing spot level.

This process is usually smooth but it can get dangerous when a trading position has multiple offsetting strikes at the same level. For example, a trader might be short a contract to one bank and long the same contract to a second bank. In order to keep an unchanged delta position the trader must wait for the bank that is long the contract to exercise or expire before they can pass the same decision onto the other bank. Often it is obvious what action should be performed, but if spot is exactly on the strike, this can be a difficult situation to manage. There are stories about traders hiding under the desk and refusing to come out until expiries are finished.

It is also possible for an option to be **partially exercised**. For example, if an option notional is AUD50m, the option owner could partially exercise it in only AUD30m. When this occurs, the new delta exposure within the trading position must be established as quickly as possible. Remaining calm when a partial exercise is requested on a large strike is a rare skill.

After expiries, if there were close strikes, the delta position may need to be rebalanced. For example, if a trading position is long USD100m USD/JPY 105.00 strike, delta may be positioned long USD50m above and short USD50m below the strike. After expiries, when the option has "rolled off," the delta exposure will remain with no protection from the strike and hence the delta must be hedged back to flat by trading spot.

For options that settle against a fix rather than a cut, if the option is in-the-money at expiry, rather than generating a spot FX transaction, the cash-settled option generates a single cash payment. In practice, this means that the delta position from the option disappears and must be replaced with an FX trade which is usually transacted off the same fix as the option settled, hence minimizing risk.

Gamma/Strike Profile

A strike topography can be used to judge how the gamma profile will change over time. Strikes disappear from the position as they expire and options "behind" start to produce more gamma as they move closer to the horizon. Based on this, a trader can judge how their gamma position will evolve. Also, if there are significant option expiries on (what traders call) "good" or "bad" dates in the future, a trader might want to unwind or offset these positions.

So-called "good dates" have events (data releases) on them and spot is therefore expected to move more than usual, for example, days on which employment or GDP data is released. Such events can cause spot to jump as the market adjusts to new information. Traders must therefore know the big events coming up in their currency pairs for the next month at least.

So-called "bad dates" are expected to be quiet and therefore spot is expected to move less than usual, for example, days over Easter or between Christmas and New Year's.

It is easier to risk manage a short-date position that is long good days and short bad days because the position will be long gamma when spot is moving more and short gamma when spot is moving less. However, this must be considered with reference to the price paid to achieve the position. Anyone can buy a Non-Farm Payroll day at 25% volatility or sell a holiday Monday between Christmas and New Year's for 3% volatility, but does that represent good value? Analysis that answers questions like these is introduced in Chapter 17.

Also, some traders are happy to run lots of strike risk (i.e., have lots of open strikes in the book), while others prefer a much cleaner position:

- Many strikes in position → position harder to manage since delta changes more → higher P&L volatility but less spread cross paid away cleaning the position.

- Few strikes in position → position easier to manage since delta changes less → lower P&L volatility but more spread cross paid away to obtain the clean position.

Traders must know the big vanilla options they have in their position, so if there is an opportunity to close out a contract with clients or in the interbank broker market with minimal spread cross (or even spread earned), they can take it. Traders may also show improved prices to clients (called "axes") to close out existing positions.

■ Trading the ATM Position

The ATM position contains exposures to the implied volatilities within the ATM curve. The standard way of assessing the ATM position uses vega and weighted vega exposures. Vega is a position's exposure to *parallel shifts* in the ATM curve. Recall from Chapter 6 that the vega profile on a vanilla option looks like a normal distribution bell-curve, with peak vega at the strike as per Exhibit 9.15.

Buying EUR20m 1yr ATM at 10% implied volatility gives the EUR/USD trading position shown in Exhibit 9.16. Since vega is now the focus of the spot ladder, wider spot spacings are appropriate. Total vega of roughly EUR80k is as expected since a 1yr ATM has 0.40% vega. It is important to remember that vega is proportional to the square root of time (so e.g., the 3mth ATM vega is half the 1yr ATM vega). Traders have these approximate ATM vega reference points in their head: O/N = 0.02%, 1mth = 0.10%, 3mth = 0.20%, 1yr = 0.40%. Therefore, an overnight ATM option costing 10% implied volatility will cost roughly $0.02\% \times 10 = 0.20\%$ in premium terms, although note that this approximation works for ATM options only.

If 1yr ATM implied volatility then rises to 10.5%, the position changes as per Exhibit 9.17.

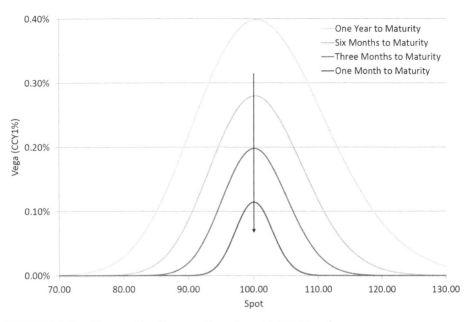

EXHIBIT 9.15 Vega profile of long vanilla option with 100.00 strike

EUR/USD	P&L Change (USD)	Delta (EUR)	Gamma (EUR)	Vega (EUR)
1.5071	1,060,741	8,605,341	267,593	26,815
1.4632	702,992	7,628,744	396,520	39,711
1.4205	405,753	6,247,117	538,387	53,893
1.3792	182,915	4,455,042	669,778	67,026
1.3390	45,726	2,323,725	763,706	76,391
1.3000	-	-	**761,438**	**79,789**
1.2610	46,942	-2,394,104	761,657	76,165
1.2232	179,644	-4,576,507	662,825	66,271
1.1865	382,094	-6,392,052	525,710	52,557
1.1509	635,393	-7,769,436	379,980	37,991
1.1164	921,198	-8,722,450	250,317	25,032

Daily P&L (USD) ___-___

EXHIBIT 9.16 EUR/USD long vega trading position

EUR/USD	P&L Change (USD)	Delta (EUR)	Gamma (EUR)	Vega (EUR)
1.5071	1,030,074	8,421,367	280,162	29,471
1.4632	681,064	7,418,547	400,791	42,138
1.4205	392,797	6,042,695	529,649	55,664
1.3792	177,585	4,298,122	646,544	67,933
1.3390	45,076	2,253,440	729,313	76,594
1.3000	-	**38,635**	**758,610**	**79,788**
1.2610	43,240	-2,245,993	729,548	76,602
1.2232	168,723	-4,349,597	644,039	67,614
1.1865	362,094	-6,132,091	522,685	54,868
1.1509	606,232	-7,521,301	389,924	40,934
1.1164	884,145	-8,517,140	267,407	28,077

Daily P&L (USD) ___51,862.68___

EXHIBIT 9.17 EUR/USD trading position with higher ATM implied volatility

P&L has risen because the position is long vega and implied volatility is higher. Assuming no second-order effects:

$$P\&L_\Delta = \sigma_\Delta \times \upsilon$$

where $P\&L_\Delta$ is P&L change, σ_Δ is implied volatility change, and υ is vega. In the example, P&L change (in USD) = 0.5 (implied volatility change) × EUR79,789 (vega) × 1.3000 (conversion from EUR to USD) = USD51,863.

One way of hedging the long ATM vega exposure would be to sell EUR40m of 3mth ATM, again at 10% implied volatility. This is shown in Exhibit 9.18.

The vega exposure at current spot is roughly flat but importantly the position is not flat in at least three ways:

1. If spot moves higher or lower, the tighter short vega distribution from the 3mth ATM results in a long vega position overall.
2. Since 3mth ATM options have a higher gamma exposure than 1yr ATM options, and double the notional of 3mth has been transacted, the position is overall short gamma.
3. The position is hedged if the ATM curve moves in parallel, but if the curve moves in a nonparallel manner, a P&L change will be generated.

Weighted vega is the exposure to **weighted** changes in the ATM curve. Within a weighted shift, short-dated ATM implied volatilities move more than long-dated ATM implied volatilities. See Chapter 14 for more detail on weighted vega.

Bucketed vega exposures (i.e., the vega exposure at each market tenor) are used to get a fuller view of the ATM position. For vanilla options, the price depends only on the implied volatility to the option maturity. Therefore, *all vega for a particular vanilla option is bucketed at maturity*. If the option expiry is between two market tenors, the vega will be split between them (e.g., the vega from a vanilla option with a 5mth expiry will appear as bucketed exposures in the 3mth and 6mth buckets). Exhibit 9.19 shows the bucketed vega exposures from the AUD/USD position.

The position is short both vega and weighted vega, but it is shorter vega than weighted vega, implying that the main short vega exposures are at longer maturities.

EUR/USD	P&L Change (USD)	Delta (EUR)	Gamma (EUR)	Vega (EUR)
1.5071	-2,017,397	-11,336,261	229,316	25,864
1.4632	-1,504,510	-12,025,713	207,959	35,033
1.4205	-983,502	-12,269,468	-113,324	37,756
1.3792	-496,622	-10,866,826	-911,073	27,950
1.3390	-134,578	-6,641,122	-1,926,667	9,974
1.3000	-	-	**-2,446,896**	**553**
1.2610	-137,737	6,813,856	-1,901,711	10,536
1.2232	-485,193	11,025,358	-852,758	28,944
1.1865	-920,324	12,292,873	-66,311	37,977
1.1509	-1,354,301	11,947,564	221,194	34,081
1.1164	-1,754,487	11,234,289	221,087	24,312

EXHIBIT 9.18 EUR/USD trading position with 3mth vega hedge

Tenor	Vega (AUDk)
O/N	5
1W	20
2W	-40
1M	100
2M	-165
3M	50
6M	190
1Y	-205
2Y	-50
Total Vega	**-95**
Total Weighted Vega	**-31**

EXHIBIT 9.19 AUD/USD bucketed vega profile

If a trader wanted to flatten this position, they should buy back an ATM vanilla in the 1yr tenor since it is the largest single short bucket. AUD25m (=100,000/0.40%) 1yr ATM could be bought back to hedge the vega exposure.

In general, it is not possible to trade implied volatility with the same frequency as spot; there is less liquidity and it is harder to take profit and stop-loss the position. Trading ATM and smile positions is a longer-term endeavor than trading the short-date position. However, the key question for a trader remains whether they *like* the ATM position—*will it generate a profit?* If there are aspects of the position that the trader doesn't like, trades should be executed to change the position.

■ FX Derivatives Trading P&L

If trades are transacted and monitored individually, the total P&L on each trade can be calculated and tracked over time. However, since FX derivatives trading positions contain many (potentially thousands of) trades that are all risk managed together, **mark-to-market** P&L is calculated. This involves periodically recalculating the total mid-value of all contracts in the position. The P&L is then the *change* in total value from some reference point to now. Typically daily (the P&L change since yesterday's end-of-day snapshot), month-to-date, and year-to-date P&Ls are monitored, with traders primarily tracking daily P&L within their risk management.

Throughout the day, P&Ls are updated as trading positions are refreshed with live market data. If new deals are entered into the position, the P&L from the new deal is calculated as the difference between the traded price and the prevailing mid-price within the risk management system.

For example, EUR/USD spot mid is 1.3450. A trader crosses a two-pip spread to sell EUR10m EUR/USD spot at 1.3448. When this trade is entered into a previously empty trading position, the P&L changes by $(1.3448 - 1.3450) \times$ EUR10m $=$ −USD2k: the spread crossed to transact the deal. The trading position now has a short EUR10m delta. If the mid EUR/USD spot then falls to 1.3445 and the trader updates market data within the trading position, the P&L from this deal will rise by USD5k. In practice, there are many deals in FX derivative trading positions, each with their own delta exposures; the net P&L change as spot moves depends on the aggregated delta exposure from all deals.

The same methodology is applied to derivative contracts, with the *premium* additionally considered. For example, AUD/USD 1yr ATM mid is 10.2% implied volatility in the desk volatility surface. Traders say that 1yr ATM is "marked" at 10.2%. A trader buys AUD100m 1yr ATM at 10.2%, sometimes described as trading "at sheets." This deal causes *no P&L change* as it is entered into the risk management system because the deal was transacted at the current midmarket volatility: The long option position has the same mid value as the premium paid for the contract. If the contract had been bought for 10.3% instead, that would generate a negative P&L change of a tenth of the contract vega because the premium paid (calculated at 10.3% implied volatility) would be more than the value of the contract at the midmarket volatility (10.2%).

At the end of each day, a full snapshot of market data is taken: the end-of-day (EOD) data. The official daily P&L for a trading book is then calculated by taking the difference between yesterday's total EOD P&L and today's total EOD P&L where total P&L is calculated by summing the value of all contracts in the trading position using the relevant set of market data.

Finally, it is important to note that official P&Ls additionally take bid–offer spread into account. This is done because there can be differences between a "paper" mid valuation and P&L that could actually be realized. This occurs particularly in less liquid markets. For example, a USD/SGD trading position is long USD500k vega in the 5yr tenor. The 5yr USD/SGD ATM price in the market rises from 16.0/16.5% (16.25% mid) to 16.25/16.75% (16.5% mid). Once this market data is updated within the trading position, the simulation shows a profit of USD125k. However, closing out the position and realizing that profit would only be possible if better bids appear in the market.

■ FX Derivatives Market Language

Here is some common FX derivatives market slang and wisdom:

Phrase	What It Means
"Ones"/"Twos," etc.	1-month ATM implied volatility/2-month ATM implied volatility, etc.
"Double"	0.55% (i.e., "seven double" is 7.55%).
"Flot"	Small.

Phrase	What It Means
"Touch"	The tightest price on a contract shown by the brokers.
"Yard"	One billion.
"Quid"	One million GBP (i.e., "I'm long ten quid cable").
"Buck"	One million USD (i.e., "The notional is fifty bucks").
"Market moving left"	Generally used to describe a price moving lower, specifically used to describe FX swap points moving more negative or less positive.
"Market moving right"	Generally used to describe a price moving higher. Specifically used to describe FX swap points moving less negative or more positive.
"Buy the rumor and sell the fact."	Optionality should be bought when there is uncertainty (around a market event or a political situation) and sold when the uncertainty is removed.
"The first cut is the cheapest."	A reworking of a song lyric to reflect the fact that in the FX derivatives market, expiry cuts that occur earlier in the trading day always have a lower price.
"It's cheap because it's rubbish."	Used as a rebuke to a trading idea that involves buying something very cheap. There is a truth to this, involving the optimal balance between premium and payoff.
"The trend is your friend."	Standard market banter about following a trend.
"Long-and-wrong."	Holding a long position in a financial instrument for which the price is going lower.
"Short-and-caught."	Holding a short position in a financial instrument for which the price is going higher.
"When in trouble, double!"	Dreadful trading advice about doubling exposures in order to make back a negative P&L.
"More sellers than buyers."	A true but unhelpful explanation for the market moving lower.
"More buyers than sellers."	A true but unhelpful explanation for the market moving higher.

CHAPTER 10

Vanilla FX Derivatives Miscellaneous Topics

Several FX derivatives pricing technicalities have thus far been brushed under the carpet. In this chapter, present and future valuing, tenor expiry date calculations, and premium conversions are examined.

Present Valuing and Future Valuing

It is well understood that $10 received today is worth more than $10 received in the future due to the time value of money. The core of the argument is that money received now has interest-earning potential if it is placed on deposit (of course, assuming interest rates are positive).

- **Present valuing** involves bringing a cash value in the future back to its equivalent value at the present day. In derivatives, option values are often calculated at maturity and must then be present valued.

■ **Future valuing** is the opposite operation: taking a cash value today and pushing it to some future date.

The calculation for present and future valuing uses a **discount factors** (df) to a given maturity in the currency in which the cash value in denominated. Discount factors are generally less than 1 and:

$$Value_{present} = df \, . \, Value_{future}$$

Discount factors are calculated from interest rates but the exact calculation depends on how interest compounds on the deposited cash balance. If interest is all paid in one payment at the deposit maturity, the interest rates are called **zero interest rates** and the discount factor is calculated using:

$$df = \frac{1}{(1 + r_0 T)}$$

where T is the time to deposit maturity measured in years and r_0 is a zero interest rate.

If interest is compounded on an *annual basis*, the discount factor is calculated using:

$$df = \frac{1}{(1 + r_A)^T}$$

where r_A is an annually compounded interest rate. The market instrument called **deposits** (also called "depos") follow this convention.

In general, given a regular compounding frequency of m times a year, the discount factor is calculated using:

$$df = \frac{1}{\left(1 + \dfrac{r_m}{m}\right)^{Tm}}$$

where r_m is an interest rate in the given compounding rate.

As m gets larger, in the limit the rate becomes a **continuous compounded interest rate**: the rate used within the Black-Scholes mathematical framework. In this case:

$$df = e^{-rCCY. \, T}$$

where $rCCY$ is a continuously compounded interest rate.

In practice, interest rate curve building and calculations are far more complicated than this. Different interest rate curves are used and they must be bootstrapped together using a variety of quantitative techniques. These methods are important for interest rate traders but they are not day-to-day concerns for most FX derivatives traders.

◼ Market Tenor Calculations

A well-defined logic exists for calculating expiry and delivery dates for market tenors within the FX derivatives market. Four dates are defined:

- *Horizon*: the date on which the trade originates (i.e., today)

- *Spot date*: the date on which the initial transfer of funds (the premium) often takes place and the date on which any spot hedge settles.

- *Expiry date*: the date on which the contract expires and any final transfer of funds is known.

- *Delivery date*: the date on which the final transfer of funds generated from the contract usually takes place and the date on which forward hedges usually settle.

If the final transfer of funds takes place after the natural delivery date, the option is described as **late delivery** (see Chapter 27 for examples of different late delivery vanilla options). All these dates can only ever be weekdays since the FX market is not open over the weekend.

These four dates are summarized on the timeline shown in Exhibit 10.1. This timeline may be different for overnight options since the expiry date can be before the spot date.

The term "business day" is used to describe a day that is not on a weekend and is also not a holiday in either currency within the relevant currency pair. A stylized version of these tenor calculations is implemented in Practical D.

Calculating Spot Dates

The spot date is calculated from the horizon (T). There are two possible cases:

1. If a currency pair has T+1 settlement (e.g., USD/CAD), the spot date is one day after the horizon. In this case, T+1 must be a business day and also not a U.S. holiday. If an unacceptable day is encountered, move one further day into the future and test again.
2. If a currency pair has T+2 settlement, the spot date is two days after the horizon. The calculation of T+2 must be done by considering each currency within the pair separately. For USD there must be one clear working day between the horizon and the spot date and for all non-USD currencies there must be two clear working days between the horizon and the spot date.

EXHIBIT 10.1 Timeline of the four key dates within market tenor calculations

In addition, for most currencies, no money can clear (settle) on U.S. holidays, meaning that the spot date cannot occur on a U.S. holiday even if USD is not a currency within the currency pair.

Calculating Expiry and Delivery Dates

Market tenors for FX option contracts are quoted either as "overnight" or in terms of a number of days, weeks, months, or years. In general, the expiry date can be any weekday even if it is a holiday in one or both of the currencies, except January 1. There are differing conventions for calculating expiry and delivery dates depending on the tenor.

Overnight

For overnight trades, the expiry date is the next weekday after the horizon. The delivery date is then calculated from the expiry date in the same way as the spot date is calculated from the horizon.

Days and Weeks

For a trade with a v *days* tenor, the expiry date is the day v calendar days after the horizon (unless this expiry date is a weekend or January 1, in which case the tenor is invalid) and for a trade with an x *weeks* tenor, the expiry date is $7x$ calendar days after the horizon (unless this expiry date is a weekend or January 1, in which case the tenor is invalid). The delivery date is then calculated from the expiry date in the same way as the spot date is calculated from the horizon.

Months

For a trade with a y *months* tenor, the expiry date is found by first calculating the spot date, and then moving forward y months from the spot date to the delivery date. If the delivery date is a non-business day or a U.S. holiday, move forward until an acceptable delivery date is found. Finally, the expiry date is calculated from the delivery date using an "inverse spot date" operation (i.e., find the expiry date for which the delivery date would be its spot date).

Years

For a trade with a z *years* tenor, the expiry date is found by first calculating the spot date, and then moving forward z years from the spot date to the delivery date. If the delivery date is a non-business day or a U.S. holiday, move forward until an acceptable delivery date is found. Finally, the expiry date is calculated from the delivery date using an "inverse spot date" operation (i.e., find the expiry date for which the delivery date would be its spot date).

Special Cases

There are two special cases involving trades that take place around the end of the month and have a tenor defined in month or year multiples. Defining the *target month* to lie *x* months forward from the spot date month if the tenor is *x months*, for example, if the spot date month is February and the tenor is 3M (three months), the target month is May.

1. If the spot date falls on the last business day of the month in the currency pair, then the delivery date is defined by convention to be the last business day of the target month. For example, assuming all days are business days: If the spot date is April 30, a one-month time to expiry will make the delivery date May 31. This is described as trading "end-end."
2. If the spot date falls before the end of the month but the resultant delivery date is beyond the end of the target month, then the delivery date is defined by convention to be the last business day of the target month. For example, assuming all days are business days: If the spot date is January 30, a *1 month* time to expiry implies a delivery date of February 30; however, this doesn't exist and the expiry date becomes February 28 (in a non-leap year, obviously).

Also, expiry date and delivery date calculations sometimes adjust in different time zones. For example, when trading USD/JPY for Tokyo cut in Asia time, the expiry date may be adjusted to avoid JPY holidays, but once London comes in and starts trading USD/JPY for NY cut, the expiry date will change. Therefore, expiry dates for market tenors can change not only from day to day but within the trading day.

Finally, a quick word for anyone wondering why this section looks similar to the Wikipedia entry on this subject: Documenting this process was one of my first jobs on the trading desk many years ago. Some kind soul obviously took the document and put it up on Wikipedia.

Option Premium Conversions

FX option premiums can be quoted in four ways: CCY1%, CCY2 pips (meaning a number of CCY2 for one CCY1, as spot is quoted), CCY2%, and CCY1 pips (the number of CCY1 for one CCY2).

- % prices have the same notional and premium currency. Example: Notional USD10m, premium 0.40 USD% implies a cash premium of USD40k.

- Pips prices have different notional and premium currencies. Example: Notional USD10m, premium 52 JPY pips implies a cash premium of JPY520m.

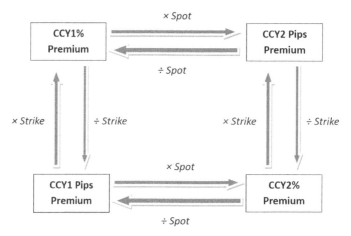

EXHIBIT 10.2   Formulas for converting options premiums

Prices on vanilla FX derivatives are usually quoted in CCY1% or CCY2 pips terms, depending on the market convention in the currency pair. For example, in EUR/JPY the notional will usually be quoted in EUR and the premium will be quoted in EUR terms (i.e., CCY1%) while in EUR/USD the notional will usually be quoted in EUR but the premium will be quoted in USD terms (i.e., CCY2 pips). Pairs where the premium is paid in CCY1 are called left-hand side (LHS) pairs, while pairs where the premium is paid in CCY2 are called right-hand side (RHS) pairs.

When quoting premiums in %, the term **basis point** is often used to mean one-hundredth of a percent (i.e., 0.01%). For example, if the price of a contract is 0.25 EUR%, it might be verbally described as "twenty-five beeps."

Exhibit 10.2 shows how to convert options premiums quoted in different terms. It is important to note that these conversions are only possible if the option contract has a strike.

Generating Tenor Dates in Excel

To build a volatility surface or quote prices based on market tenors, the expiry dates corresponding to each tenor must be calculated. In Excel, dates are internally stored as integers with 0 = Jan 1, 1900, 1 = Jan 2, 1900, and so on. Current dates are therefore over 40,000 (e.g., June 11, 2014 is 41,801). Within VBA code, dates can be represented using variables with type Long.

First, VBA functions are required to:

- Increment a date to the next business day.

- Decrement a date to the previous business day.

Note that these functions don't take holidays into account. The built-in VBA function Weekday is used to check the input day of the week:

```
Function nextBusinessDay(InputDate As Long) As Long

    If Weekday(InputDate) = 7 Then
        'Input Date = Saturday
        nextBusinessDay = InputDate + 2
    ElseIf Weekday(InputDate) = 6 Then
        'Input Date = Friday
        nextBusinessDay = InputDate + 3
    Else
        nextBusinessDay = InputDate + 1
    End If

End Function
```

```
Function previousBusinessDay(InputDate As Long) As Long

    If Weekday(InputDate) = 1 Then
        'Input Date = Sunday
        previousBusinessDay = InputDate - 2
    ElseIf Weekday(InputDate) = 2 Then
        'Input Date = Monday
        previousBusinessDay = InputDate - 3
    Else
        previousBusinessDay = InputDate - 1
    End If

End Function
```

Functions are also required to:

- Calculate the spot date from a horizon date.
- Calculate the horizon date from a spot date.

This can be achieved using VBA functions that increment and decrement a given number of business days. In this code it is assumed that the spot date is always T+2 (i.e., two business days after the horizon):

```
Function businessDayIncrement(InputDate As Long, _
 Increment As Long) As Long

    Dim Count As Long

    businessDayIncrement = InputDate
    For Count = 1 To Increment
        businessDayIncrement = nextBusinessDay(businessDayIncrement)
    Next Count

End Function

Function businessDayDecrement(InputDate As Long, _
 Decrement As Long) As Long

    Dim Count As Long

    businessDayDecrement = InputDate
    For Count = 1 To Decrement
        businessDayDecrement = previousBusinessDay(businessDayDecrement)
    Next Count

End Function

Function getSpotDateFromHorizon(InputDate As Long) As Long

    getSpotDateFromHorizon = businessDayIncrement(InputDate, 2)
```

```
End Function

Function getHorizonFromSpotDate(InputDate As Long) As Long

    getHorizonFromSpotDate = businessDayDecrement(InputDate, 2)

End Function
```

Market tenors can be specified in terms of a number of weeks (e.g., "2W"), months (e.g., "6M") or years (e.g., "5Y"), or the overnight tenor (e.g., "ON"). Therefore, the getExpiryFromTenor function must contain different logic for these different cases using the rules outlined in Chapter 10. The built-in VBA function DateAdd is used to go from spot date to delivery date, and special cases around trading "end-end," and so forth, are all ignored in this code:

```
Function getExpiryFromTenor(Horizon As Long, Tenor As String) As Long

    Dim Count As Long
    Dim SpotDate As Long, DeliveryDate As Long

    If UCase(Tenor) = "ON" Then
        getExpiryFromTenor = nextBusinessDay(Horizon)
    ElseIf Right(UCase(Tenor), 1) = "W" Then
        Count = Left(Tenor, Len(Tenor) - 1)
        getExpiryFromTenor = Horizon + Count * 7
    ElseIf Right(UCase(Tenor), 1) = "M" Then
        Count = Left(Tenor, Len(Tenor) - 1)
        SpotDate = getSpotDateFromHorizon(Horizon)
        DeliveryDate = DateAdd("M", Count, SpotDate)
        getExpiryFromTenor = getHorizonFromSpotDate(DeliveryDate)
    ElseIf Right(UCase(Tenor), 1) = "Y" Then
        Count = Left(Tenor, Len(Tenor) - 1)
        SpotDate = getSpotDateFromHorizon(Horizon)
        DeliveryDate = DateAdd("yyyy", Count, SpotDate)
        getExpiryFromTenor = getHorizonFromSpotDate(DeliveryDate)
    Else
        MsgBox "Invalid Tenor"
        getExpiryFromTenor = -1
    End If

End Function
```

The expiry dates for market tenors can now be set up in an Excel sheet. It is neater to use a subroutine that places expiry dates onto the sheet rather than using functions in the cells.

The horizon must be input and column headers for the tenors and expiry dates must be named TenorRef and ExpiryDateRef respectively. The horizon can be a user input or the Excel function =Today() can be used. It is nice to format date cells so they also show the day of the week. This is achieved by formatting cells with a custom format e.g.: "ddd dd-mmm-yy":

Horizon	Wed 11-Jun-14	←Named: *Horizon*

Populate Expiry Dates

↓Named: *TenorRef*	↓Named: *ExpiryDateRef*
Tenor	**Expiry Date**
ON	
1W	
2W	
1M	
2M	
3M	
6M	
1Y	
2Y	

The following subroutine can be used to populate expiry dates on the sheet:

```
Sub populateExpiryDates()

    Dim Count As Long

    Count = 1
    While Range("TenorRef").Offset(Count, 0) <> ""
        Range("ExpiryDateRef").Offset(Count, 0) = _
         getExpiryFromTenor(Range("Horizon"), _
         Range("TenorRef").Offset(Count, 0))
        Count = Count + 1
    Wend

End Sub
```

Horizon	Wed 11-Jun-14

Populate Expiry Dates

Tenor	Expiry Date
ON	Thu 12-Jun-14
1W	Wed 18-Jun-14
2W	Wed 25-Jun-14
1M	Thu 10-Jul-14
2M	Mon 11-Aug-14
3M	Thu 11-Sep-14
6M	Thu 11-Dec-14
1Y	Thu 11-Jun-15
2Y	Thu 09-Jun-16

PART II

THE VOLATILITY SURFACE

FX derivatives trading desks maintain volatility surfaces in all tradable currency pairs in order to determine the implied volatility for vanilla options with any expiry date and strike. It is therefore important that traders understand details about how volatility surfaces are constructed since it is a vital part of all FX derivatives valuation.

Fundamentally, a volatility surface is constructed along two axes: maturity and strike. The **ATM curve** forms the backbone of the volatility surface along different expiry dates and the **volatility smile** defines the implied volatility for strikes away from the ATM strike. Volatility surface construction is usually split into these two separate considerations.

CHAPTER 11

ATM Curve Construction

ATM curves can be constructed in two steps. First, a core ATM curve is established. Then additional parameters are introduced so the correct ATM implied volatility is generated for all possible expiry dates. Note that within this chapter, some calculations are *approximate*.

■ Variance

The key measure for building ATM curves is

$$variance = \sigma^2 T$$

where σ is the ATM implied volatility to time T (measured in years). For example, the variance of a 3mth ATM option with 12.0% implied volatility is $0.12^2 \times 0.25 = 0.0036$.

Variance can be thought of as a measure of *cumulative spot movement*. It has two powerful properties:

1. Variance over any time period must be nonnegative.
2. Variance is additive (i.e., variance over two days = variance on first day + variance on second day).

Variance can be used to calculate the forward ATM implied volatility (usually called **forward implied volatility** or just "forward vol" by traders) between two dates in the future. Given ATM implied volatility σ_1 to time T_1, ATM implied volatility σ_2 to time T_2, and $T_1 < T_2$:

- Variance from horizon to $T_1 = \sigma_1{}^2 T_1$
- Variance from horizon to $T_2 = \sigma_2{}^2 T_2$

Therefore, variance between T_1 and $T_2 = \sigma_2{}^2 T_2 - \sigma_1{}^2 T_1$ and forward implied volatility between T_1 and $T_2 = \sqrt{\dfrac{\sigma_2{}^2 T_2 - \sigma_1{}^2 T_1}{T_2 - T_1}}$. For example, if the 6mth ATM implied volatility is 10.5% and the 1yr ATM implied volatility is 11.7%, then the forward implied volatility from 6mth to 1yr is $\sqrt{\dfrac{11.7\%^2 \times 1.0 - 10.5\%^2 \times 0.5}{1.0 - 0.5}} =$ 12.8%.

Core ATM Curve Construction

There are two main approaches that can be used to generate core ATM curves:

1. *Input* the ATM curve at the market tenors and *interpolate* to get ATM volatility for expiry dates between the market tenors.
2. Use a *model* to generate the ATM curve and *output* the ATM volatility at the market tenors.

Recall from Part I that the standard market tenors up to two years are: O/N (overnight), 1wk, 2wk, 1mth, 2mth, 3mth, 6mth, 1yr, and 2yr.

Constructing a Core ATM Curve Using Interpolation

Core ATM curves can be constructed using interpolation between market tenors. Exhibit 11.1 shows ATM curve A—an upward-sloping ATM curve defined at market tenors.

For expiry dates between market tenors, first consider **linear volatility** interpolation as shown in Exhibit 11.2. The linear interpolation methodology can be clearly seen between market tenors.

To investigate this interpolation further, variance at each expiry date is calculated in Exhibit 11.3. The variance profile looks reasonable, rising over time as expected.

Exhibit 11.4 shows a new ATM curve B defined at market tenors. ATM implied volatility is 20% at market tenors up to 1yr, and then the next data point is 15% implied volatility at the 2yr tenor.

Interpolating ATM curve B using linear volatility and then calculating the variance at each expiry date gives the profile shown in Exhibit 11.5.

Horizon	Wed 11-Jun-14

Tenor	Expiry Date	ATM Implied Volatility
ON	Thu 12-Jun-14	10.00%
1W	Wed 18-Jun-14	11.00%
2W	Wed 25-Jun-14	12.00%
1M	Thu 10-Jul-14	13.00%
2M	Mon 11-Aug-14	14.00%
3M	Thu 11-Sep-14	15.00%
6M	Thu 11-Dec-14	16.00%
1Y	Thu 11-Jun-15	17.00%
2Y	Thu 09-Jun-16	18.00%

EXHIBIT 11.1 ATM curve A defined at market tenors

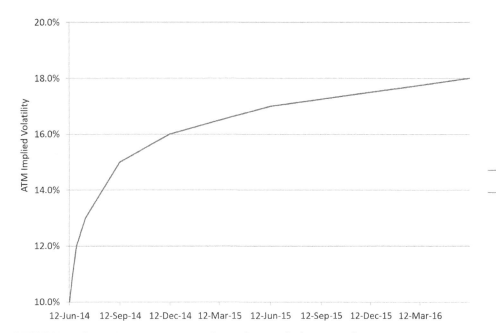

EXHIBIT 11.2 ATM curve A generated using linear volatility interpolation

Calculating *daily variance* (i.e., the change in variance for each expiry date) gives bad news in Exhibit 11.6.

Up to 1yr, implied volatility is constant so variance rises linearly with maturity, but from 1yr to 2yr variance rises and then falls. This sets alarm bells ringing: *Variance must be nonnegative*. Therefore, linear volatility interpolation has failed to build a valid ATM curve from valid inputs (variance to 2yr is larger than variance to 1yr):

- Variance between horizon and 1yr $= 20\%^2 \times 1.0 = 0.04$

- Variance between horizon and 18mth $= 17.5\%^2$ (interpolated) $\times 1.5 = 0.046$

- Variance between horizon and 2yr $= 15\%^2 \times 2.0 = 0.045$

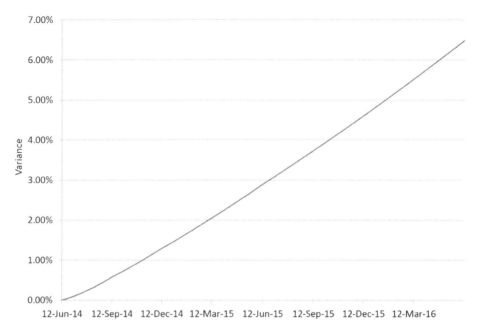

EXHIBIT 11.3 Variance profile for ATM curve A generated using linear volatility interpolation

Horizon	Wed 11-Jun-14

Tenor	Expiry Date	ATM Implied Volatility
ON	Thu 12-Jun-14	20.00%
1W	Wed 18-Jun-14	20.00%
2W	Wed 25-Jun-14	20.00%
1M	Thu 10-Jul-14	20.00%
2M	Mon 11-Aug-14	20.00%
3M	Thu 11-Sep-14	20.00%
6M	Thu 11-Dec-14	20.00%
1Y	Thu 11-Jun-15	20.00%
2Y	Thu 09-Jun-16	15.00%

EXHIBIT 11.4 ATM curve B defined at market tenors

This suggests a new interpolation methodology: **linear variance**. The variance profile resulting from a linear variance interpolation of ATM curve B is shown in Exhibit 11.7.

This variance profile has no negative daily variance and the ATM implied volatility curve shown in Exhibit 11.8 looks good, too.

Going back to ATM curve A, the profile shown in Exhibit 11.9 is generated using a linear variance methodology.

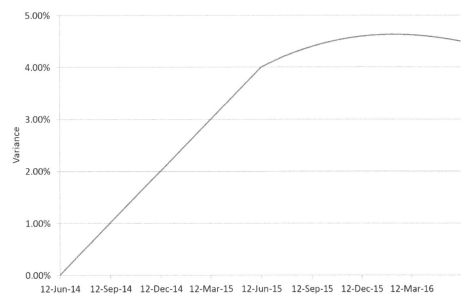

EXHIBIT 11.5   Variance profile for ATM curve B generated using linear volatility interpolation

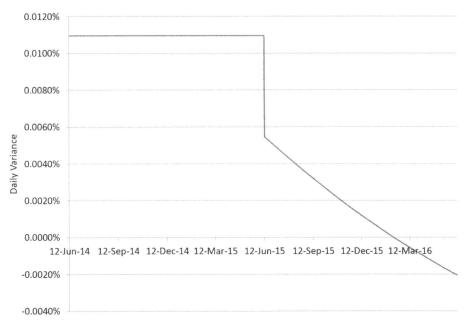

EXHIBIT 11.6   Daily variance profile for ATM curve B generated using linear volatility interpolation

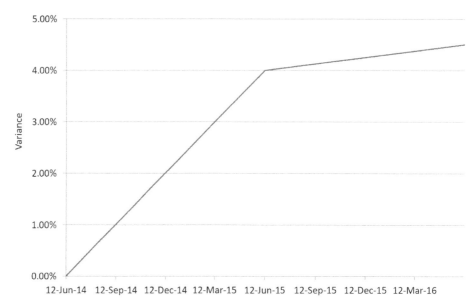

EXHIBIT 11.7   Variance profile for ATM curve B using linear variance interpolation

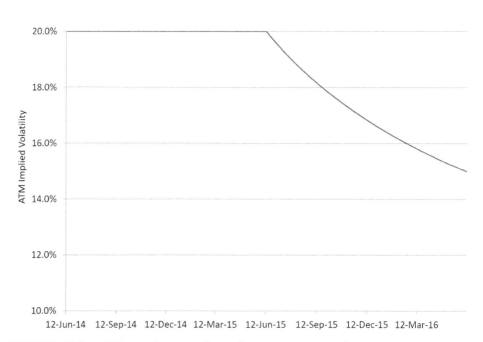

EXHIBIT 11.8   ATM curve B generated using linear variance interpolation

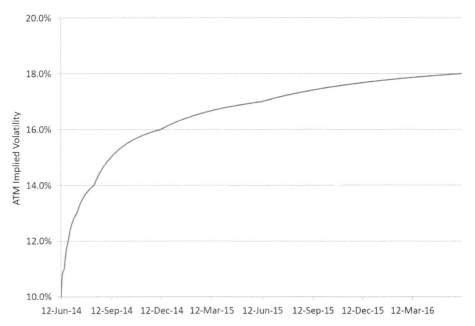

EXHIBIT 11.9   ATM curve A generated using linear variance interpolation

The ATM implied volatility between market tenors in Exhibit 11.9 looks odd. The linear variance methodology generates an ATM implied volatility profile that rises sharply initially and then flattens off between tenors for this upward-sloping ATM curve. Why is this happening? Consider the daily variance profile shown in Exhibit 11.10.

These daily variance patterns are not realistic. Intuitively it does not make sense that daily variance should jump immediately past each market tenor date. Excluding any special factors, why would daily variance one day prior to the 3mth tenor date be significantly different to daily variance one day after the 3mth tenor date? Ideally, the core daily variance function should be smooth.

Comparing these two interpolation methodologies:

1. Linear volatility interpolation often produces intuitively correct ATM curves but does not ensure positive forward variance.
2. Linear variance interpolation produces ATM curves that ensure positive forward variance (given valid inputs) but does not always create intuitively correct ATM curves.

In practice, trading desks use a combination of these approaches to produce intuitive curves with no negative forward variance. ATM curves are generally constructed in variance terms but more sophisticated schemes are used to control how daily variance evolves over time.

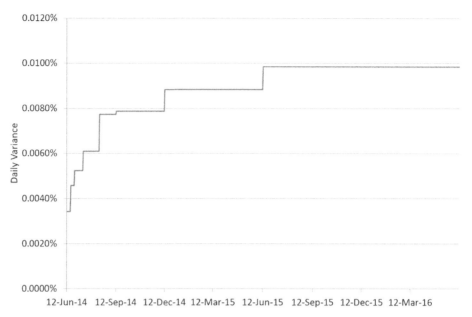

EXHIBIT 11.10 Daily variance profile for ATM curve A generated using linear variance interpolation

Constructing a Core ATM Curve Using a Model

Another possible method of constructing a core ATM curve is to use a model. Many different models are possible but fundamentally the functional form most often involves a *short-term* factor (could be volatility, variance, or daily variance), a *long-term* factor, and a *speed* of moving from short to long.

Here is one possible simple approach (that would never be used in practice because it could generate arbitragable ATM curves):

$$\sigma_t = \sigma_{short} + (\sigma_{long} - \sigma_{short}).(1 - e^{-\lambda T})$$

where σ_{short} and σ_{long} are short-term and long-term ATM volatilities respectively, λ is speed, and T is time to expiry measured in years.

The $(1 - e^{-\lambda T})$ function moves between 0 and 1 as shown in Exhibit 11.11.

Higher λ causes the function to move from 0 to 1 more quickly. This function can be fed with the T's from market tenor expiry dates to calculate ATM implied volatilities as per Exhibit 11.12.

The ATM curve is now an *output* from the model rather than being an input. This approach requires the model parameters to be calibrated to market ATM implied

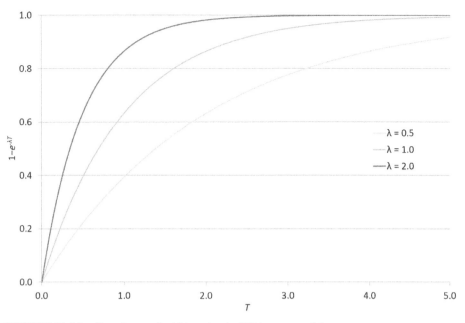

EXHIBIT 11.11   Function used within a simple ATM curve model

Horizon	Wed 11-Jun-14

Tenor	Expiry Date	T	ATM Implied Volatility
ON	Thu 12-Jun-14	0.00274	10.01%
1W	Wed 18-Jun-14	0.01918	10.09%
2W	Wed 25-Jun-14	0.03836	10.19%
1M	Thu 10-Jul-14	0.07945	10.38%
2M	Mon 11-Aug-14	0.16712	10.77%
3M	Thu 11-Sep-14	0.25205	11.11%
6M	Thu 11-Dec-14	0.50137	11.97%
1Y	Thu 11-Jun-15	1.00000	13.16%
2Y	Thu 09-Jun-16	1.99726	14.32%

EXHIBIT 11.12   ATM curve output at market tenors

volatilities. This can be time consuming initially but traders soon learn how the model parameters change as the market ATM curve moves.

Within this approach, *overrides* at market tenors are also required to ensure the system ATM implied volatility hits market mid values. For example, the ATM curve model is set up and all tenors closely match the market except for 2mth ATM, which is 0.1% lower in the market than the model suggests. The trader therefore inputs a −0.1% override at the 2mth tenor. This is useful information because it suggests that the 2mth ATM is relatively cheaper than other tenors.

◼ ATM Curve Construction: Short-Dates

Once the core ATM curve has been constructed, additional parameters or weights are introduced in order to give traders sufficient control over the curve. This control is required because different expiry dates (or even different times within expiry dates) have different expected spot volatility and this information must be incorporated into the ATM curve.

This additional control is mainly important at shorter expiry dates. The following examples demonstrate how the same variance framework can be applied at shorter time scales, as per the diagram in Exhibit 11.13.

Example 1: 1wk (7-day) ATM implied volatility is 12.0%. A 1wk option always contains five weekdays and two weekend days where spot does not move because the market is closed (i.e., zero variance). Assume spot is equally volatile on each weekday (i.e., equal daily variance). What is the 8-day ATM implied volatility?

$$\sigma_{8-day\ ATM} = \sqrt{\frac{variance_{1wk} \cdot \frac{6}{5}}{\left(\frac{8}{365}\right)}} = 12.3\%$$

Example 2: 1wk (7-day) ATM implied volatility is 12.0%. Assume it is known that spot will be completely static during the 8th day (i.e., zero variance). What is the 8-day ATM implied volatility?

$$\sigma_{8-day\ ATM} = \sqrt{\frac{variance_{1wk}}{\left(\frac{8}{365}\right)}} = 11.25\%$$

Due to the properties of variance, this effectively forms a lower bound on the 8-day ATM implied volatility: If the 7-day ATM volatility is 12.0%, the 8-day ATM volatility must be *at least* 11.25%.

Variance and **option premium** are closely linked. If forward drift and discounting are removed from the framework, the vanilla option premium for a specific strike must rise at longer maturities since variance must rise at longer maturities. Otherwise, the ATM curve is arbitrageable.

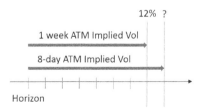

EXHIBIT 11.13 Short-date variance examples framework

In practice, however, with forward drift reintroduced, the situation becomes more complicated. Consider vanilla options on two consecutive expiry dates with the same strike. If the following trading position can be achieved for zero premium, how can a guaranteed profit be generated from these trades?

- Short 7-day call option with strike K

- Long 8-day call option with strike K

If both options are left unhedged until expiry, profitability depends on how spot moves between the two expiry dates. An overall profit will be generated if spot is more in-the-money (ITM) at the second expiry than the first. However, an overall loss will be generated if spot is more ITM at the first expiry than the second. There is no guaranteed profit locked in.

A better strategy would be to sell the second option as the first option expires. This would offer a near-certain nonnegative P&L, but Exhibit 11.14 shows how an extreme forward drift prevents a guaranteed profit. The vanilla call option value at expiry (shown in leg 1) has a higher value than the second vanilla call option (now overnight expiry) due to the large negative forward drift.

Contract Details	Leg 1	Leg 2
Currency Pair	EUR/USD	EUR/USD
Horizon	Mon 13-Oct-2014	Mon 13-Oct-2014
Spot Date	Wed 15-Oct-2014	Wed 15-Oct-2014
Strategy	Vanilla	Vanilla
Call/Put	EUR Call/USD Put	EUR Call/USD Put
Maturity	O/N	O/N
Expiry Date	Mon 13-Oct-2014	Tue 14-Oct-2014
Delivery Date	Wed 15-Oct-2014	Thu 16-Oct-2014
Cut	NY	NY
Strike	1.2000	1.2000
Notional Currency	EUR	EUR

Market Data		
Spot	1.2700	1.2700
Swap Points	0	-35
Forward	1.2700	1.2665
Deposit (EUR)	0.00%	100.00%
Deposit (USD)	0.00%	0.00%
ATM Volatility		10.00%
Pricing Volatility		10.00%

Outputs		
Output Currency	EUR	EUR
Mid Price	5.5125%	5.235%

EXHIBIT 11.14 Impact of forward drift on option prices

ATM CURVE CONSTRUCTION

In practice it is hard to *guarantee* a profit on this trade, particularly once bid–offer spreads are taken into account. However, taking a step back, traders would love to transact this 7-day versus 8-day spread for zero premium. Traders often get carried away describing trades or prices as arbitrages when they really mean "fantastic trading opportunities." As a result, the "arbitrage trading books" on bank derivatives trading desks can occasionally end the year with negative P&L.

Implied Volatility Patterns over the Week

The number of market-open and market-closed days to a specific expiry date has an important impact on the ATM implied volatility. Consider (one-day) overnight ATM volatility compared to the 1wk ATM volatility. Assume each market-open day is equally volatile (i.e., equal daily variance) and no variance over the weekend:

$$variance_{1wk} = variance_{O/N} \times 5$$

$$ATM_{1wk}^{2} \cdot \left(\frac{7}{365} \right) = ATM_{O/N}^{2} \cdot \left(\frac{1}{365} \right) \times 5$$

$$ATM_{1wk} = ATM_{O/N} \times \sqrt{\frac{5}{7}}$$

$$ATM_{1wk} < ATM_{O/N}$$

In words, the (one-day) overnight ATM implied volatility is higher than the 1wk ATM implied volatility because the 1wk expiry date contains two weekend days. This is a commonly observed feature of the FX derivatives market.

The market-open-to-total-days ratio also explains why ATM implied volatility tends to rise for future expiry dates over the working week. For a fixed horizon, a future Monday expiry will almost always have a lower implied volatility than the Friday following it because the Friday has a higher market-open-to-total-days ratio. This ATM saw-toothing, shown in Exhibit 11.15, is commonly observed within the FX derivatives market, although the effect dampens at longer maturities as the market-open-to-total-days ratio stabilizes.

FX Derivatives Market Pricing

Within the FX derivatives market, when using the Black-Scholes formula for pricing, time to expiry (T) is specified in *discrete daily steps*. This is a key feature of the FX derivatives market.

Consider a situation where the current time is 9 A.M. London time on Monday and overnight NY cut ATM implied volatility is 15.0%. The overnight expires tomorrow, so $T = \frac{1}{365}$ and:

$$variance_{O/N} = 0.15^{2} \times \left(\frac{1}{365} \right) = 6.1644 \times 10^{-5}$$

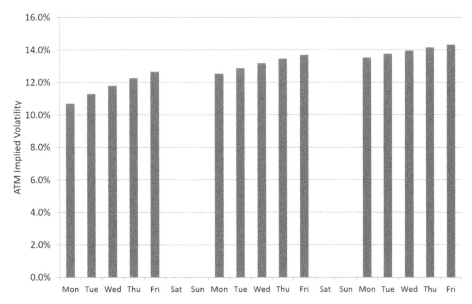

EXHIBIT 11.15   Monday to Friday ATM saw-toothing

This variance can now be split into even smaller time intervals. NY cut is at 10 A.M. New York time, which is (usually) 3 P.M. London time, so this overnight option actually expires in 30 hours. Assuming spot is equally volatile between now and NY cut tomorrow:

$$variance_{hourly} = \frac{6.1644 \times 10^{-5}}{30} = 2.0548 \times 10^{-6}$$

After one hour passes, the remaining variance on the option is:

$$29 \times variance_{hourly} = 5.9589 \times 10^{-6}$$

which implies a new overnight ATM volatility of:

$$\sigma_{O/N\ ATM} = \sqrt{\frac{5.9589 \times 10^{-6}}{\left(\frac{1}{365}\right)}} = 14.75\%$$

Note that T is unchanged within this calculation due to being specified in discrete daily steps. At the start of each trading day, when the overnight option expiry moves forward one trading day, the ATM implied volatility jumps higher due to increased variance. Then over the course of the trading day, the ATM implied volatility gradually moves lower due to reducing variance. Variance (and hence premium) to a fixed expiry date reduces as time passes but because the market uses constant daily T values within the Black-Scholes formula for pricing, implied volatility reduces instead. This effect occurs at all tenors but the impact is only visible in short-dated options, particularly the overnight.

It is interesting to consider that if the market used a more accurate T for pricing, short-dated implied volatility would be more stable throughout the day. However, since spot volatility is *not constant* throughout the day, implied volatility would not be completely static. Therefore, introducing more accuracy into T adds to the complexity of the market for only minimal benefit.

In practice, short-dated implied volatility does tend to drift lower over the course of the day, but spot behavior is also important. If there is a large spot move or spot breaks out of its recent range, implied volatility generally moves higher due to an expectation of increased future spot volatility. Traders with short gamma positions come into the market to hedge their positions and the market implied volatility increases. Alternatively, if spot is static, implied volatility often falls more quickly than its "natural rate" as traders come into the market to reduce long gamma positions where they are struggling to trade their deltas.

If traders believe short-dated implied volatility is falling slower than it should over the course of the day, gamma can be "*rented.*" This involves, for example, buying the overnight ATM at the start of the trading day and then selling the same contract back at the end of the trading day. This technique is only applicable in liquid currency pairs where there is good two-way flow in short-dated vanilla options; otherwise the spread cross involved in the two transactions will kill any value in the trade.

Risk management of FX derivatives positions is also usually performed assuming discrete daily time steps. This is the reason that options expiring on the horizon date generate *delta jumps* through their strike level (as seen in Chapters 7 and 9). It is also the reason that trading positions show all options expiring on the horizon date at their own expiry times. If the trading position has options expiring at different cuts on the expiry date, this is inconsistent, but it keeps the trading risk stable. Traders adjust for this effect within their risk management.

Overnight (O/N) ATM on a Friday

On any weekday apart from Friday, the overnight option expires the following day. However, on Friday, the "overnight" option expires on a Monday; three days later rather than one. Therefore, in a market Black-Scholes pricing world, $T = \dfrac{3}{365}$.

Vega (v) is a function of $\sqrt{T}$:

$$v_{call} = v_{put} = \frac{\partial P}{\partial \sigma} = Se^{-rCCY1.T}n(d_1)\sqrt{T}$$

Therefore (ignoring discounting):

$$v_{1-day\ ATM} \cdot \sqrt{3} = v_{3-day\ ATM}$$

There is no volga $\left(\frac{\partial v}{\partial \sigma} \right)$ on ATM options, so for a given tenor, roughly:

$$Price_{ATM\ call} = Price_{ATM\ put} = v \cdot \sigma_{ATM}$$

Assuming there is no variance over the weekend and each weekday is equally volatile, the O/N ATM contract will have the same *premium* each day and therefore:

$$\sigma_{3-day\ ATM} = \frac{\sigma_{1-day\ ATM}}{\sqrt{3}}$$

In practice this means that the market overnight ATM implied volatility quoted on a Friday cannot be directly compared with the overnight ATM implied volatility quoted on other days. To get the Friday overnight ATM into the same terms it must be multiplied by $\sqrt{3}$. Furthermore, the bid–offer spread shown on a three-day overnight should be tighter in volatility terms in order to show the same premium spread. Again, the level of ATM implied volatility is being impacted by the market-open-to-total-days ratio, or put another way, the ratio of economic time (time adjusted to consider market activity only) to calendar time (see Practical E).

In practice, the market pricing of the overnight ATM contract on a Friday is closely related to the market's *weekend decay* position. The jump from Friday end-of-day to Monday morning covers three days. If this is not correctly adjusted for within risk management systems, theta from Friday to Monday will be artificially large. In a simplified world with no adjustment for this effect, a position that is long the same amount of gamma each day will, on average:

- Make money on Tuesday through to Friday as only (5 / 7) = 71% of the correct theta is paid per day.

- Lose all additional profit the following Monday as (5 / 7) × 3 = 213% of the correct theta is paid from Friday into Monday.

Amazingly, in a sophisticated financial market in the twenty-first century, this effect still produces trading opportunities as short-dated options can become too cheap on Friday as some banks oversell to reduce their weekend theta.

New York Cut versus Tokyo Cut Pricing

In G10 currency pairs the two most common expiry cuts are New York (NY) and Tokyo (TOK). The New York cut versus Tokyo cut ATM volatility differential can be analyzed using the same variance framework:

- TOK cut: 3 P.M. Tokyo time (often 6 A.M. GMT)

- NY cut: 10 A.M. New York time (often 3 P.M. GMT)

That is, NY cut options contain an extra nine hours of optionality.

Therefore, the Tokyo cut ATM implied volatility is always lower ("trades at a discount") than the New York cut ATM implied volatility because both are priced using the same discrete daily T but the Tokyo cut occurs first in the day and therefore has less variance and a lower premium.

Assuming spot is always equally volatile:

$$\frac{variance_{TOK}}{T_{TOK}} = \frac{variance_{NY}}{T_{NY}}$$

$$\frac{\sigma_{TOK}^{2} \cdot T_{market}}{T_{TOK}} = \frac{\sigma_{NY}^{2} \cdot T_{market}}{T_{NY}}$$

$$\sigma_{TOK} = \sigma_{NY} \cdot \sqrt{\frac{T_{TOK}}{T_{NY}}}$$

where T_{market} is the time to expiry measured in years used within the market Black-Scholes pricing framework, T_{TOK} is the real time to expiry to the Tokyo cut and T_{NY} is the real time to expiry to the New York cut.

Therefore, the New York cut versus Tokyo cut volatility differential increases over the course of a given trading day.

At 9 A.M. GMT:

- O/N TOK cut = 6 A.M. GMT the next day = 21 hours

- O/N NY cut = 3 P.M. GMT the next day = 30 hours

$$\sigma_{TOK} = \sigma_{NY} \cdot \sqrt{\frac{21}{30}} = \sigma_{NY} \times 0.84$$

At 5 P.M. GMT:

- O/N TOK cut = 6 A.M. GMT the next day = 13 hours

- O/N NY cut = 3 P.M. GMT the next day = 22 hours

$$\sigma_{TOK} = \sigma_{NY} \cdot \sqrt{\frac{13}{22}} = \sigma_{NY} \times 0.77$$

For maturities past three months, New York and Tokyo cuts will generally be priced at the same implied volatility (assuming no events, etc., on the expiry date). For example, at the three-month tenor, approximately:

$$\sigma_{TOK} = \sigma_{NY} \cdot \sqrt{\frac{2151 \; hours}{2160 \; hours}} = \sigma_{NY} \times 0.998$$

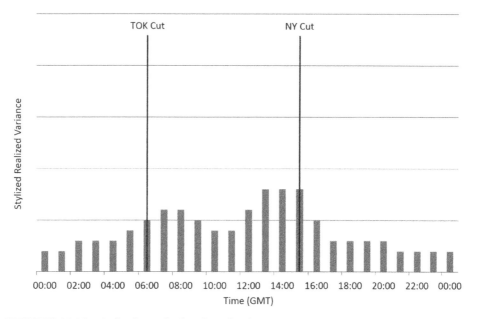

EXHIBIT 11.16 Stylized intraday hourly realized variance

Intraday Variance Patterns

The simplifying assumption that spot is equally volatile throughout the trading day is obviously not correct in practice. In liquid G10 currency pairs, realized variance follows a fairly well-established pattern shown in Exhibit 11.16 in which it:

- Starts low and builds up during Asia trading time

- Peaks around GMT 08:00 as Europe/London come in

- Dips during Europe/London lunch around GMT 11:00

- Picks up again in the afternoon with New York in and reaches day highs around GMT 14:00

- Decreases after GMT 15:00 (NY cut) to the end of the day in the New York afternoon

The intraday variance patterns are different in emerging market currency pairs where trading is concentrated in one region or the spot market opening hours are restricted. Such variance patterns should be taken into account within the option pricing framework for maximum accuracy when pricing options expire at different cut times.

Events and Holidays

Events (economic data releases, election results, etc.) cause spot to move as the market adjusts to new information. Exhibit 11.17 shows the USD/JPY spot reaction to the Non-Farm Payroll data release (an important gauge of U.S. employment usually released on the first Friday on the month) from May 2013, in which spot jumps immediately after the economic data is made public.

Event days are therefore assigned higher variance within the ATM curve, specifically in the period immediately after the data is released. This in turn increases the ATM implied volatility for options expiring on that expiry date (if the cut occurs after the event has been released) and also expiry dates following it. The exact date and time of events is known beforehand and therefore the market ATM curve incorporates this information.

On days containing important data releases, realized spot variance is usually similar or slightly lower than the spot variance on a "normal day" until the data release. Over the data release, realized spot variance increases sharply and then reverts back to the normal day as shown in Exhibit 11.18. On this expiry date, the NY cut contains the additional expected spot variance from the event but the TOK cut does not. This leads to a far larger NY cut versus TOK cut ATM implied volatility differential than usual.

The presence of an event also causes short-dated implied volatility to decay differently over the course of the day. Prior to the event, short-dated ATM implied

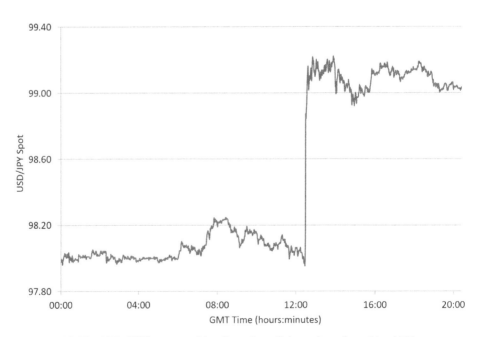

EXHIBIT 11.17 USD/JPY spot over Non-Farm Payroll data release from May 2013

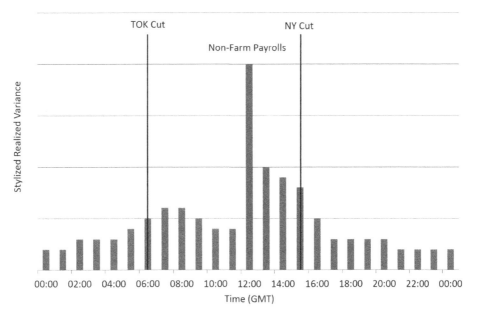

EXHIBIT 11.18   Stylized intraday hourly realized variance on Non-Farm Payroll day

volatility will move lower only slightly but after the event has occurred ATM implied volatility can drop sharply as expected future spot variance reduces.

Events usually occur in a particular currency. For example, European employment data primarily impacts spot in currency pairs that include EUR. However, for the most important events, crosses can also exhibit increased volatility if the majors move in an asynchronous manner. For example; Non-Farm Payrolls impacts USD, but if EUR/USD and AUD/USD are both more volatile but they do not move in a perfectly synchronized manner, EUR/AUD realized volatility also increases.

Public holidays also impact realized volatility and variance. There is often significantly less spot activity in pairs containing the holiday currency simply because there are fewer market participants operating that day. In addition, U.K. and U.S. public holidays are important enough to reduce spot activity across all currency pairs. Therefore, public holiday days in a particular currency have lower variance within the ATM curve.

Weekday Variance Patterns

The FX spot market often exhibits increased realized variance later in the working week, as shown in Exhibit 11.19. This effect occurs partially because there tend to be more data releases later in the week. However, even with the effect of events removed, Mondays are often less volatile than other weekdays.

Like the NY cut versus TOK cut implied volatility differential, the day of the week of a particular expiry date matters more at shorter tenors than at longer

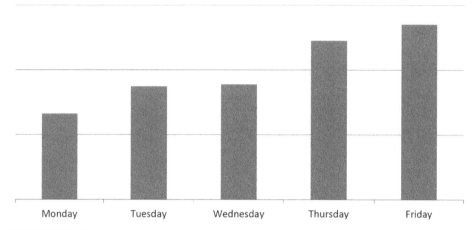

EXHIBIT 11.19   Average daily spot variance for G10 pairs in 2012

tenors. The market often has a preference to buy the next few Friday expiries and sell the next few Monday expiries but the weekday of, for example, the 6mth ATM contract is not a major concern.

Pricing Same-Day Options

Pricing options that expire later today is impossible within the standard market Black-Scholes pricing framework. The number of days is zero; hence T is zero and therefore same-day options cannot be quoted in volatility terms. Recall from Chapter 5 that in the Black-Scholes option pricing formula:

$$d_1 = \frac{\ln\left(\dfrac{S}{K}\right) + \left(rCCY2 - rCCY1 + \dfrac{\sigma^2}{2}\right).T}{\sigma\sqrt{T}}$$

would break because the denominator is zero.

So-called **same-day options** must therefore be quoted in *premium* terms. One way to calculate the premium of a same-day option is to start with an overnight option and use the variance framework to adjust the implied volatility.

Example: At 9 A.M. GMT a client requests a price in a same-day NY cut option. This is shown in Exhibit 11.20.

The O/N NY ATM implied volatility is 12%. Therefore:

$$variance_{O/N\ NY\ Cut} = 0.12^2 \times \left(\frac{1}{365}\right) = 3.945 \times 10^{-5}$$

EXHIBIT 11.20 Pricing a same-day vanilla option

Assuming each hour has equal variance:

$$variance_{Same-day\ NY\ Cut} = \left(\frac{6}{30}\right) \times 3.945 \times 10^{-5} = 7.89 \times 10^{-6}$$

Therefore, the equivalent one day ATM volatility is:

$$\sigma_{1\ day\ ATM} = \sqrt{\frac{7.89 \times 10^{-6}}{\left(\frac{1}{365}\right)}} = 5.3\%$$

This implied volatility can then be used to price an overnight option which gives the same-day option premium. Note that interest rates should be set to zero within the same-day pricing since forward drift and discounting will have no impact.

In general, same-day options are nonstandard and a wider bid–offer spread should be charged. Plus it is vital to take expected intraday variance profiles and events into account. Be suspicious: Why wouldn't the counterparty be happy to wait until the standard option expiry time?

Constructing an ATM Curve in Excel

Within this practical, three methods of constructing an ATM curve are developed. First, an ATM curve is constructed using *interpolation* between market tenors. Then, an ATM curve is constructed using a parameterized *model*. Finally, *weights* are added to a simple ATM curve to demonstrate how ATM curves are maintained by traders in practice. These steps mirror the material developed in Chapter 11.

Task A: Constructing an ATM Curve Using Interpolation

When constructing an ATM curve based on market tenors, the expiry date for each market tenor must first be calculated using functions developed in Practical D. The ATM implied volatility is then manually inputted at each tenor. For the purposes of testing, a simple upward-sloping ATM curve can be used initially:

Horizon	Wed 11-Jun-14	←Named: **Horizon**

Populate Expiry Dates

Tenor	Expiry Date	ATM Implied Volatility
ON	Thu 12-Jun-14	10.00%
1W	Wed 18-Jun-14	11.00%
2W	Wed 25-Jun-14	12.00%
1M	Thu 10-Jul-14	13.00%
2M	Mon 11-Aug-14	14.00%
3M	Thu 11-Sep-14	15.00%
6M	Thu 11-Dec-14	16.00%
1Y	Thu 11-Jun-15	17.00%
2Y	Thu 09-Jun-16	18.00%

↓Named: **ATMVolRef**

Using these inputs, a VBA function can interpolate to give the ATM volatility for any date. This function references the expiry dates and ATM volatilities at market tenors using named cells, with linear interpolation used to generate ATM volatility for expiry dates between tenors:

```
Function getATMVol(QueryDate As Long) As Double

    Dim Count As Long
    Dim TimeLow As Double, TimeHigh As Double
    Dim VolLow As Double, VolHigh As Double

    'Find the relevant Expiry date row (requires the Expiry dates _
     to be ordered)
    Count = 1
    While Range("ExpiryDateRef").Offset(Count, 0) < QueryDate _
     And Range("ExpiryDateRef").Offset(Count, 0) <> ""
        Count = Count + 1
    Wend

    If Range("ExpiryDateRef").Offset(Count, 0) = "" Then
        'Query Date beyond Maximum Expiry Date
        getATMVol = -1
    ElseIf Count = 1 And Range("ExpiryDateRef").Offset(Count, 0) > _
     QueryDate Then
        'Query Date before Minimum Expiry Date
        getATMVol = -1
    ElseIf Range("ExpiryDateRef").Offset(Count, 0) = QueryDate Then
        'Exact Expiry Date Found
        getATMVol = Range("ATMVolRef").Offset(Count, 0)
    Else
        'Interpolate to get ATM Implied Volatility
        TimeLow = (Range("ExpiryDateRef").Offset(Count - 1, 0) - _
         Range("Horizon")) / 365
```

CONSTRUCTING AN ATM CURVE IN EXCEL

```
      TimeHigh = (Range("ExpiryDateRef").Offset(Count, 0) - _
       Range("Horizon")) / 365
      VolLow = Range("ATMVolRef").Offset(Count - 1, 0)
      VolHigh = Range("ATMVolRef").Offset(Count, 0)
      getATMVol = LinearVolatilityInterpolation(TimeLow, TimeHigh, _
       VolLow, VolHigh, (QueryDate - Range("Horizon")) / 365)
    End If

End Function

Function LinearVolatilityInterpolation (TimeLow As Double, _
 TimeHigh As Double, VolLow As Double, VolHigh As Double, _
 QueryTime As Double) As Double

    LinearVarianceInterpolation = VolLow + (VolHigh - VolLow) * _
     (QueryTime - TimeLow) / (TimeHigh - TimeLow)

End Function
```

The getATMVol function can be tested by querying for implied volatility in four different cases:

1. An expiry date before the minimum tenor expiry date
2. An expiry date after the maximum tenor expiry date
3. An expiry date at a tenor expiry date
4. An expiry date between two tenor expiry dates

Query Date	ATM Implied Volatility	
01-Jan-15	16.12%	=getATMVol(QueryDate)

↑Named: **QueryDate**

The ATM volatility for daily expiry dates (starting at the overnight tenor and going for two years) can now be calculated. This subroutine (run by pressing the button) populates the ATM implied volatilities:

```
Sub populateATMImpliedVolatilities()

    Dim Count As Long

    Count = 1
    While Range("ChartExpiryDateRef").Offset(Count, 0) <> ""
        Range("ChartATMVolsRef").Offset(Count, 0) = _
         getATMVol(Range("ChartExpiryDateRef").Offset(Count, 0))
        Count = Count + 1
    Wend

End Sub
```

Interpolate ATM Implied Volatility

↓Named: **ChartExpiryDateRef**	↓Named: **ChartATMVolsRef**
Expiry Date	**ATM Implied Volatility**
12-Jun-14	10.00%
13-Jun-14	10.17%
14-Jun-14	10.33%
15-Jun-14	10.50%
16-Jun-14	10.67%
17-Jun-14	10.83%
18-Jun-14	11.00%

This data can be plotted in a chart:

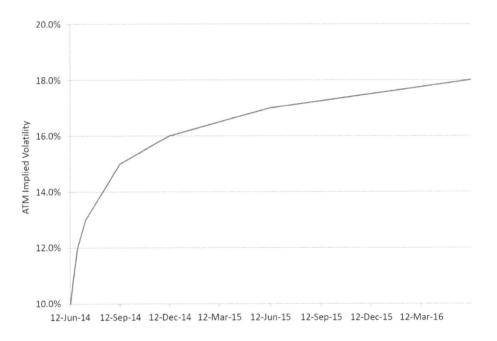

Variance for each expiry date can also be calculated (see Chapter 11) and pushed onto the sheet using this subroutine:

```
Sub populateVariance()

    Dim Count As Long
    Dim T As Double, vol As Double

    Count = 1
    While Range("ChartExpiryDateRef").Offset(Count, 0) <> ""
        T = (Range("ChartExpiryDateRef").Offset(Count, 0) - _
        Range("Horizon")) / 365
```

```
        vol = Range("ChartATMVolsRef").Offset(Count, 0)
        Range("ChartVarianceRef").Offset(Count, 0) = T * vol ^ 2
        Count = Count + 1
    Wend

End Sub
```

Interpolate ATM Implied Volatility	Calculate Variance	

↓*Named: **ChartVarianceRef***

Expiry Date	ATM Implied Volatility	Variance
12-Jun-14	10.00%	0.00%
13-Jun-14	10.17%	0.01%
14-Jun-14	10.33%	0.01%
15-Jun-14	10.50%	0.01%
16-Jun-14	10.67%	0.02%
17-Jun-14	10.83%	0.02%

Finally, linear variance interpolation can be used instead if required:

```
Function LinearVarianceInterpolation(TimeLow As Double, TimeHigh As _
Double, VolLow As Double, VolHigh As Double, QueryTime As Double) As _
Double

    Dim VarianceLow As Double, VarianceHigh As Double, _
     QueryVariance As Double
    VarianceLow = TimeLow * VolLow ^ 2
    VarianceHigh = TimeHigh * VolHigh ^ 2

    QueryVariance = VarianceLow + (VarianceHigh - VarianceLow) * _
     (QueryTime - TimeLow) / (TimeHigh - TimeLow)
    LinearVarianceInterpolation = Sqr(QueryVariance / QueryTime)

End Function
```

■ Task B: Constructing an ATM Curve Using a Model

There are many possible ATM curve models. One of the simplest possible parameterizations introduced in Chapter 11 is:

$$\sigma_T = \sigma_{short} + (\sigma_{long} - \sigma_{short}).(1 - e^{-\lambda T})$$

where σ_T is the ATM implied volatility at time T (measured in years), σ_{short} and σ_{long} are the short- and long-term ATM volatilities respectively, and λ is the speed of reversion from σ_{short} to σ_{long}. This model can be implemented in an Excel sheet, with time displayed in monthly intervals (use 1/12 intervals within this stylized framework):

	A	B	C	D	E	F
3						
4		Short Vol (σ short)	10.0%	←Named: **ShortVol**		
5		Long Vol (σ long)	15.0%	←Named: **LongVol**		
6		Speed (λ)	1.0	←Named: **Speed**		
7						
8		**Time**	**ATM Volatility**			
9		0.08333	10.4%	=ShortVol+(LongVol-ShortVol)*(1-EXP(-Speed*B9))		
10		0.16667	10.8%	=ShortVol+(LongVol-ShortVol)*(1-EXP(-Speed*B10))		
11		0.25000	11.1%	...		
12		0.33333	11.4%			

The output can be plotted in a chart:

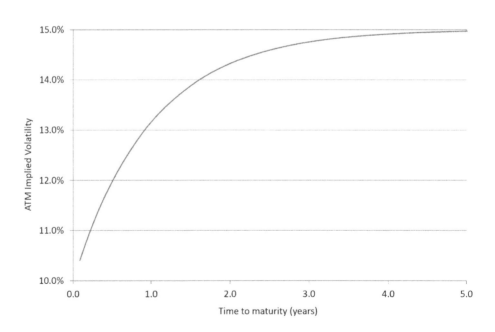

The function can then be attached to the market expiry dates (and their T's) to calculate ATM implied volatility:

ATM Curve Construction

	Horizon		Wed 11-Jun-14		
	Short Vol (σ_{short})		10.0%		
	Long Vol (σ_{long})		15.0%		
	Speed (λ)		1.0		

Populate Expiry Dates

Tenor	Expiry Date	T	ATM Implied Volatility	
ON	Thu 12-Jun-14	0.00274	10.01%	=ShortVol+(LongVol-ShortVol)*(1-EXP(-Speed*D12))
1W	Wed 18-Jun-14	0.01918	10.09%	
2W	Wed 25-Jun-14	0.03836	10.19%	
1M	Thu 10-Jul-14	0.07945	10.38%	
2M	Mon 11-Aug-14	0.16712	10.77%	
3M	Thu 11-Sep-14	0.25205	11.11%	
6M	Thu 11-Dec-14	0.50137	11.97%	
1Y	Thu 11-Jun-15	1.00000	13.16%	
2Y	Thu 09-Jun-16	1.99726	14.32%	

Task C: Adding Weights to an ATM Curve

In practice, traders keep their ATM curves aligned with the market by controlling the expected variance assigned to individual dates. This control is used to, for example, assign low variance to weekends/holiday days and high variance to major event days. One common way this can be achieved is by splitting variance into discrete daily chunks based on the weight assigned to each day.

Within this model, a single flat volatility is used. By introducing a separate row for each date starting one day after the horizon (for at least a year), **calendar time** can therefore be calculated:

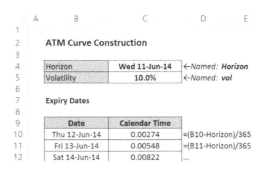

Day weights can now be added. These are defined in a table:

Weekday	Weight
Sunday	1.0
Monday	1.0
Tuesday	1.0
Wednesday	1.0
Thursday	1.0
Friday	1.0
Saturday	1.0

↓Named: **DayWeightRef**

A VBA subroutine can be used to push the day weights onto the expiry dates. Note how the Weekday VBA function is cunningly used to generate the offset reference to the correct cell:

```
Sub populateDayWeights()

    Dim CountExpiryDates As Long

    CountExpiryDates = 1
    While Range("DateRef").Offset(CountExpiryDates, 0) <> ""
        Range("DateRef").Offset(CountExpiryDates, 2) = _
            Range("DayWeightRef").Offset(Weekday(Range("DateRef"). _
            Offset(CountExpiryDates, 0)), 1)
        CountExpiryDates = CountExpiryDates + 1
    Wend

End Sub
```

The day weights up to a given tenor can then be summed and divided by 365 to calculate **economic time**. This calendar time versus economic time technique is used within real ATM curve models. Controlling economic time allows variance to be unevenly distributed over different days or, in more sophisticated models, over different parts of the day. For now, though, set weights of 1 on each day so calendar time and economic time are identical:

Expiry Dates

Populate Day Weights

↓Named: **DateRef**

Date	Calendar Time	Day Weight	Day Weight Sum	Economic Time
Thu 12-Jun-14	0.00274	1.00	1.00	0.00274
Fri 13-Jun-14	0.00548	1.00	2.00	0.00548
Sat 14-Jun-14	0.00822	1.00	3.00	0.00822
Sun 15-Jun-14	0.01096	1.00	4.00	0.01096

When weights are added, total variance to (calendar) time t changes from:

$$var_T = \sigma^2 T$$

into

$$var_T = \sigma^2 \sum_{i=1}^{n} \omega_i dt$$

where $dt = \dfrac{1}{365}$.

	A	B	C	D	E	F	G	H
17								
18		**Expiry Dates**		Populate Day				
19				Weights				
20								
21		Date	Calendar Time	Day Weight	Day Weight Sum	Economic Time	Total Variance	
22		Thu 12-Jun-14	0.00274	1.00	1.00	0.00274	0.000027	=F23*vol^2
23		Fri 13-Jun-14	0.00548	1.00	2.00	0.00548	0.000055	=F24*vol^2
24		Sat 14-Jun-14	0.00822	1.00	3.00	0.00822	0.000082	...
25		Sun 15-Jun-14	0.01096	1.00	4.00	0.01096	0.000110	

ATM volatility is then calculated from total variance using calendar time:

	A	B	C	D	E	F	G	H	I	J
17										
18		**Expiry Dates**		Populate Day						
19				Weights						
20										
21		Date	Calendar Time	Day Weight	Day Weight Sum	Economic Time	Total Variance	ATM Volatility		
22		Thu 12-Jun-14	0.00274	1.00	1.00	0.00274	0.00003	10.00%	=SQRT(G22/C22)	
23		Fri 13-Jun-14	0.00548	1.00	2.00	0.00548	0.00005	10.00%	=SQRT(G22/C22)	
24		Sat 14-Jun-14	0.00822	1.00	3.00	0.00822	0.00008	10.00%	...	
25		Sun 15-Jun-14	0.01096	1.00	4.00	0.01096	0.00011	10.00%		

When plotted with constant day weights of 1, the ATM volatility is flat as expected:

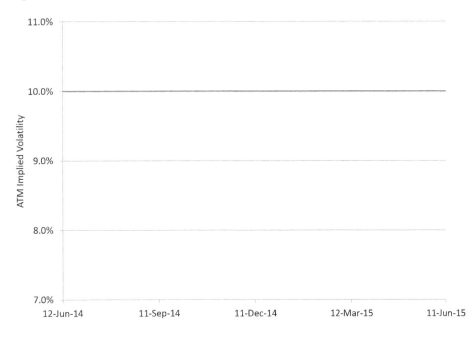

Now comes the magic: Set the weekend day weights to zero, repopulate the expiry date day weights using the populateDayWeights subroutine, and check the graph again:

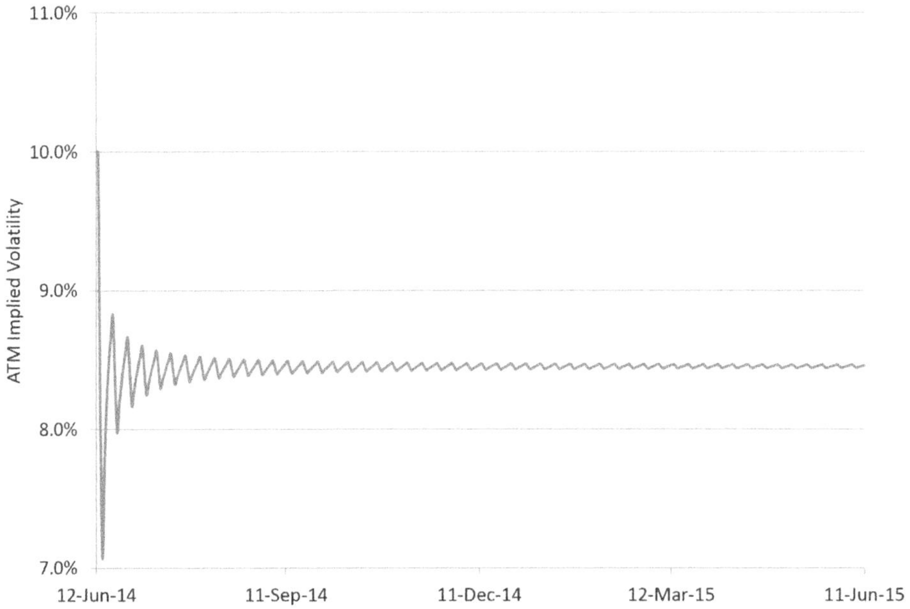

The output now contains the ATM saw-toothing observed in the real FX derivatives market. Look at the data in the sheet:

Expiry Dates

Populate Day Weights

Date	Calendar Time	Day Weight	Day Weight Sum	Economic Time	Total Variance	ATM Volatility
Thu 12-Jun-14	0.00274	1.00	1.00	0.00274	0.00003	10.00%
Fri 13-Jun-14	0.00548	1.00	2.00	0.00548	0.00005	10.00%
Sat 14-Jun-14	0.00822	0.00	2.00	0.00548	0.00005	8.16%
Sun 15-Jun-14	0.01096	0.00	2.00	0.00548	0.00005	7.07%
Mon 16-Jun-14	0.01370	1.00	3.00	0.00822	0.00008	7.75%
Tue 17-Jun-14	0.01644	1.00	4.00	0.01096	0.00011	8.16%
Wed 18-Jun-14	0.01918	1.00	5.00	0.01370	0.00014	8.45%
Thu 19-Jun-14	0.02192	1.00	6.00	0.01644	0.00016	8.66%

In the model, economic time stops over the weekend because the FX market isn't open on Saturday or Sunday. In practice, trading desks usually assign a small but non-zero variance to the weekend because there is a small chance that unexpected news over the weekend will cause spot to move sharply first thing on Monday morning. The reduction in the economic-time-to-calendar-time ratio causes the ATM implied volatility for the Monday expiry to be lower than the Friday preceding it.

In this case, ATM volatility tends toward a value that is lower than the flat volatility input due to the ratio of economic time to calendar time being less than 1. In practice, this effect is adjusted for when there are target volatility levels that must be hit.

Finally, consider how the model is adjusted when there is an event. On Thursday, July 3, 2014, Non-Farm Payrolls (a big USD economic indicator, which normally occurs on the first Friday of the month) is released. Therefore, expected variance on that date is higher and the ATM volatility for that date is correspondingly higher. This is achieved within the model by moving the weight for that date higher:

Expiry Dates		Populate Day Weights				
Date	Calendar Time	Day Weight	Day Weight Sum	Economic Time	Total Variance	ATM Volatility
Fri 27-Jun-14	0.04384	1.00	12.00	0.03288	0.00033	8.66%
Sat 28-Jun-14	0.04658	0.00	12.00	0.03288	0.00033	8.40%
Sun 29-Jun-14	0.04932	0.00	12.00	0.03288	0.00033	8.16%
Mon 30-Jun-14	0.05205	1.00	13.00	0.03562	0.00036	8.27%
Tue 01-Jul-14	0.05479	1.00	14.00	0.03836	0.00038	8.37%
Wed 02-Jul-14	0.05753	1.00	15.00	0.04110	0.00041	8.45%
Thu 03-Jul-14	0.06027	3.00	18.00	0.04932	0.00049	9.05%
Fri 04-Jul-14	0.06301	1.00	19.00	0.05205	0.00052	9.09%
Sat 05-Jul-14	0.06575	0.00	19.00	0.05205	0.00052	8.90%
Sun 06-Jul-14	0.06849	0.00	19.00	0.05205	0.00052	8.72%
Mon 07-Jul-14	0.07123	1.00	20.00	0.05479	0.00055	8.77%

The ATM volatility for the Non-Farm Payroll date itself moves higher plus the increased variance causes subsequent days to move higher, too. This is a real feature observed when building ATM curves: If expected variance for a given date increases, the ATM volatility for that date *and subsequent dates* rises:

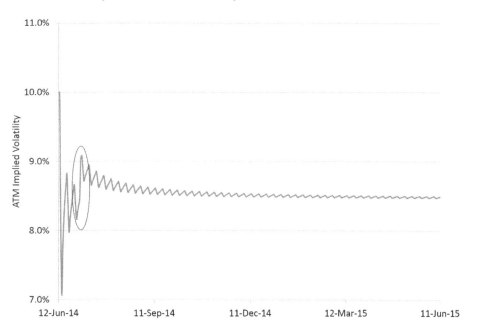

Daily variance can now be calculated by taking the difference in variance between subsequent expiry dates, which in turn can be used to calculate daily ATM volatility. The daily ATM volatility is effectively the implied volatility for a strip of forward overnight ATM contracts. Traders use these forward overnight ATM volatilities to determine whether the ATM curve is overpriced or underpriced over events.

Expiry Dates			Populate Day Weights						
Date	Calendar Time	Day Weight	Day Weight Sum	Economic Time	Total Variance	ATM Volatility	Daily Variance	Daily Volatility
Thu 12-Jun-14	0.00274	1.00	1.00	0.00274	0.00003	10.00%	0.00003	10.00%
Fri 13-Jun-14	0.00548	1.00	2.00	0.00548	0.00005	10.00%	0.00003	10.00%
Sat 14-Jun-14	0.00822	0.00	2.00	0.00548	0.00005	8.16%	0.00000	0.00%
Sun 15-Jun-14	0.01096	0.00	2.00	0.00548	0.00005	7.07%	0.00000	0.00%
Mon 16-Jun-14	0.01370	1.00	3.00	0.00822	0.00008	7.75%	0.00003	10.00%
Tue 17-Jun-14	0.01644	1.00	4.00	0.01096	0.00011	8.16%	0.00003	10.00%
Wed 18-Jun-14	0.01918	1.00	5.00	0.01370	0.00014	8.45%	0.00003	10.00%
Thu 19-Jun-14	0.02192	1.00	6.00	0.01644	0.00016	8.66%	0.00003	10.00%

Vanilla FX derivative traders actively update weights within their ATM curve model to match market prices observed in the interbank broker market, plus future economic release dates are assigned higher weights when release schedules are known. Holiday days in a particular currency are known far in advance, too, and are assigned lower weights to reflect the reduced expected variance.

In practice, trading desks use frameworks similar to this but more granularity is usually included within the model. Exact times of events are often specified, enabling the correct pricing of different cuts within the same day. Trading desks also require a sophisticated core ATM curve, not just flat volatility. An approach similar to those developed in Task A or Task B in this practical will be usually be taken, with weights added on top in such a way that nonnegative forward variance is guaranteed.

CHAPTER 12

Volatility Smile Market Instruments and Exposures

In the interbank broker market, at each market tenor, three **market instruments** define the volatility smile:

1. *At-the-money (ATM)* contracts define the implied volatility for a specific strike close to (or exactly at, depending on the market conventions for a given currency pair) the forward for the given tenor.
2. *Butterfly (Fly)* contracts define the implied volatility differential between the wings of the volatility smile and the ATM—a measure of the height of the wings of the volatility smile.
3. *Risk reversal (RR)* contracts define the implied volatility differential between strikes above and below the ATM—a measure of how skewed or tilted the volatility smile is.

Butterfly and risk reversal contracts are most often quoted at 25 delta (25d) and 10 delta (10d) strikes. An example run of market instruments at market tenors is shown in Exhibit 12.1.

Exhibit 12.2 shows the relative positioning of different deltas within a stylized volatility smile. Recall that it is the market convention to trade the out-of-the-money side.

Tenor	Expiry Date	ATM	25d Fly	10d Fly	25d RR	10d RR
ON	26-Jun-14	5.50%	0.10%	0.25%	-0.25%	-0.40%
1W	02-Jul-14	4.10%	0.125%	0.30%	-0.25%	-0.40%
2W	09-Jul-14	5.05%	0.125%	0.325%	-0.35%	-0.55%
1M	24-Jul-14	4.625%	0.125%	0.35%	-0.40%	-0.60%
2M	25-Aug-14	4.825%	0.15%	0.45%	-0.50%	-0.85%
3M	25-Sep-14	5.15%	0.15%	0.50%	-0.60%	-0.95%
6M	23-Dec-14	5.625%	0.225%	0.75%	-0.75%	-1.35%
1Y	25-Jun-15	6.30%	0.275%	1.00%	-0.90%	-1.65%
2Y	23-Jun-16	6.90%	0.30%	1.10%	-1.00%	-1.85%

EXHIBIT 12.1 Example EUR/USD market instruments at market tenors

10d Put	25d Put	**ATM**	25d Call	10d Call	(Put / Call
(90d Call)	(75d Call)	**(50d Put and Call)**	(75d Put)	(90d Put)	on CCY1)

EXHIBIT 12.2 Deltas quoted within the volatility smile

The following *approximations* link the ATM, 25d butterfly, and 25d risk reversal instruments with the implied volatilities for the *outright* 25d call and put options at a given tenor:

- $\sigma_{Call25d} = \sigma_{ATM} + \sigma_{Fly25d} + \frac{1}{2}\sigma_{RR25d}$
- $\sigma_{Put25d} = \sigma_{ATM} + \sigma_{Fly25d} - \frac{1}{2}\sigma_{RR25d}$

Therefore:

- $\sigma_{RR25d} = \sigma_{Call25d} - \sigma_{Put25d}$
- $\sigma_{Fly25d} = \frac{(\sigma_{Call25d} + \sigma_{Put25d})}{2} - \sigma_{ATM}$

Exhibit 12.3 shows how these market instruments fit into the volatility smile.

These approximations were generalized into a single formula for any delta by Allan M. Malz in 1997:

$$\sigma_{X\ Delta\ Put} = \sigma_{ATM} + 2\ \sigma_{RR25d}\cdot(X - 50\%) + 16\ \sigma_{Fly25d}\cdot(X - 50\%)^2$$

In words, the ATM represents the central reference point, the butterfly lifts the wings symmetrically higher on both sides, and the risk reversal tilts the smile one way or the other. As mentioned in Chapter 7, put deltas are often quoted without the negative sign. Positive put delta values between 0% and 100% are used in the Malz formula.

If butterfly and risk reversal contracts at all deltas are zero, the volatility smile is flat as shown in Exhibit 12.4, and any strike at that tenor will be assigned the same midmarket implied volatility.

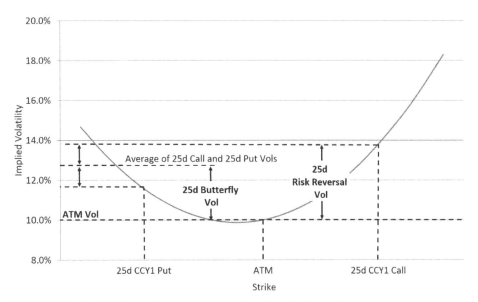

EXHIBIT 12.3   25 delta market instruments within the volatility smile

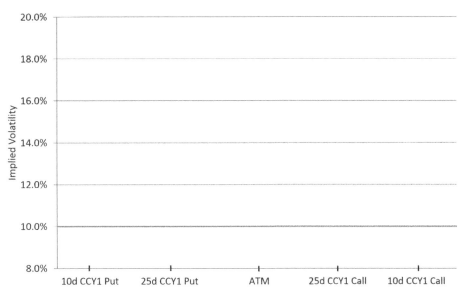

EXHIBIT 12.4   Volatility smile with zero risk reversal and zero butterfly

If the butterfly increases, the wings of the volatility smile rise symmetrically as shown in Exhibit 12.5.

With a positive risk reversal, strikes above the ATM have a higher implied volatility than the equivalent delta strikes below the ATM. This is shown in Exhibit 12.6.

With a negative risk reversal, strikes below the ATM have a higher implied volatility than the equivalent delta strikes above the ATM. This is shown in Exhibit 12.7.

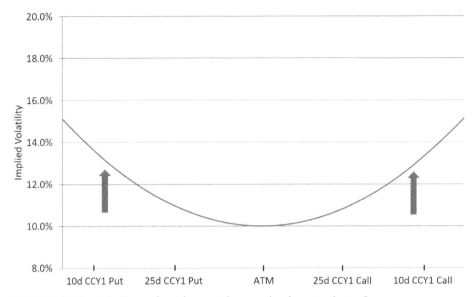

EXHIBIT 12.5   Volatility smile with zero risk reversal and positive butterfly

VOLATILITY SMILE MARKET INSTRUMENTS AND EXPOSURES

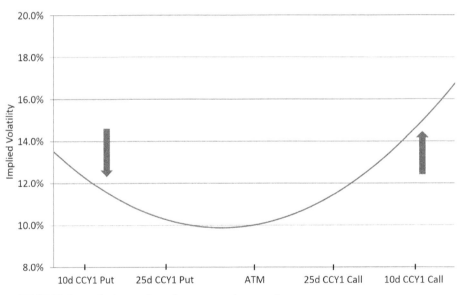

EXHIBIT 12.6   Volatility smile with positive risk reversal

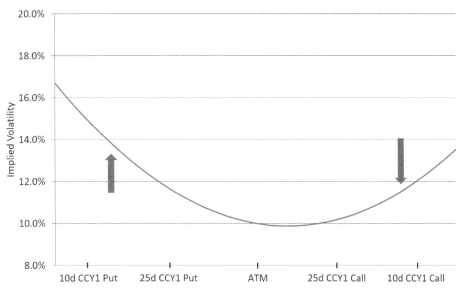

EXHIBIT 12.7 Volatility smile with negative risk reversal

Market Instrument Vega Exposures

The reason for describing the volatility smile with ATM, butterfly, and risk reversal instruments becomes clearer when the implied volatility exposures of the three market instruments are examined. The key implied volatility exposures are:

- *Vega* $\left(\frac{\partial P}{\partial \sigma}\right)$: sensitivity of price to changes in implied volatility.

- *Vanna* $\left(\frac{\partial vega}{\partial spot}\right)$: sensitivity of vega to changes in spot. Vanna can also be thought of as the sensitivity of delta to changes in implied volatility, i.e., $\left(\frac{\partial delta}{\partial \sigma}\right)$ since $\left(\frac{\partial P}{\partial \sigma}\right) / \partial spot = \left(\frac{\partial P}{\partial spot}\right) / \partial \sigma.$

- *Volga* $\left(\frac{\partial vega}{\partial \sigma}\right)$: sensitivity of vega to changes in implied volatility. Volga is the second derivative of price with respect to changes in implied volatility. Therefore, volga is to implied volatility as gamma is to spot and as the volatility of implied volatility rises, the expected P&L from a long volga trading position increases.

ATM Exposures

The vega profile for a long ATM vanilla option has a single peak around current spot. Exhibit 12.8 shows how, at higher volatility, the vega profile is wider since the spot distribution is wider, but vega is unchanged at the initial spot.

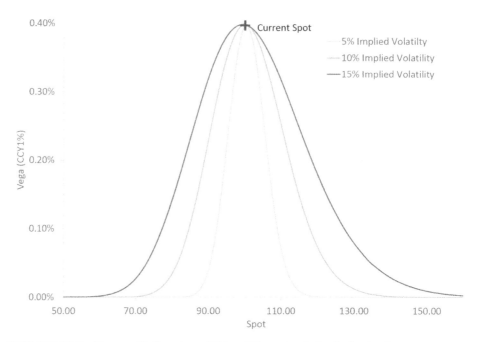

EXHIBIT 12.8 Vega profile from long ATM at different implied volatility levels

Therefore, a long ATM contract at inception has the following exposures:

- Vega: positive exposure

- Vanna (the gradient of the vega/spot chart): no exposure

- Volga (the difference between the vega profiles for different implied volatility levels at the initial spot level): no exposure

Vanna with spot above the strike is negative since vega rises into the (now) downside peak. Vanna with spot below the strike is positive since vega rises into the (now) topside peak. The vanna profile from a long ATM option is shown in Exhibit 12.9.

Recalling the dual interpretation of vanna as $\frac{\partial vega}{\partial spot}$ or $\frac{\partial delta}{\partial \sigma}$, consider an out-of-the-money topside call option (i.e., strike above spot). At current implied volatility the strike has 25% delta. If implied volatility rises, the chance of the strike ending in-the-money at maturity increases as the distribution widens and hence delta rises. Therefore, this option has a long vanna exposure.

Likewise, consider a downside (in-the-money) call strike (i.e., strike below spot). At current implied volatility the strike has 75% delta. If implied volatility rises, the chance of the strike ending in-the-money at maturity decreases as the distribution widens and hence delta falls. Therefore, this option has a short vanna exposure.

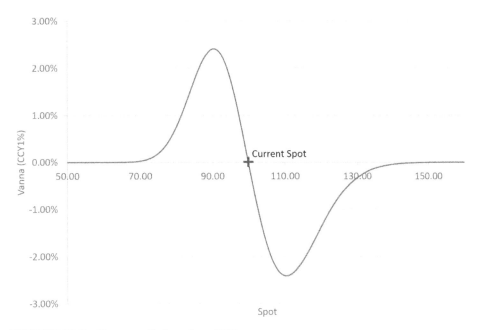

EXHIBIT 12.9   Vanna profile from long ATM

Volga with spot above or below the ATM strike is positive since long wing vanilla options generate positive volga. The volga profile from a long ATM option is shown in Exhibit 12.10.

Risk Reversal Exposures

For a risk reversal contract, again, higher implied volatility moves the vega profile wider but at initial spot the vega exposure is unchanged at zero. This is shown in Exhibit 12.11. It is important to understand that these exposure profiles are generated with fixed strikes, equivalent to calculating the exposures immediately after trading the contract.

In this instance, *buying* the risk reversal means buying the topside strike versus selling the downside strike but in different currency pairs or tenors this may be the other way around. Therefore, a *long* risk reversal position can give either a long or short vanna exposure, depending on whether topside strikes are at higher or lower implied volatility than the equivalent delta downside strikes. If the topside strikes have a higher implied volatility, traders say the risk reversal is "for topside," whereas if downside strikes have a higher implied, traders say the risk reversal is, yes, "for downside." In a currency pair where the risk reversal is for downside, a long risk reversal position initially gives a short vanna position as shown in Exhibit 12.12.

Notice that these vega profiles aren't perfectly rotationally symmetric since vega persists further to the topside. This occurs because the Black-Scholes formula is

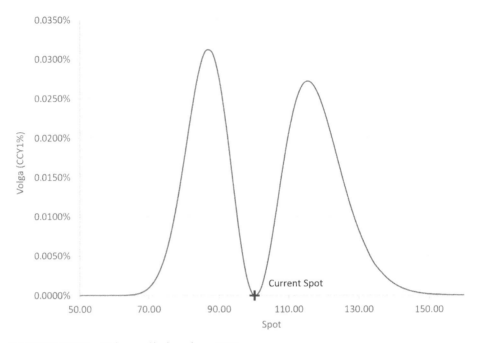

EXHIBIT 12.10   Volga profile from long ATM

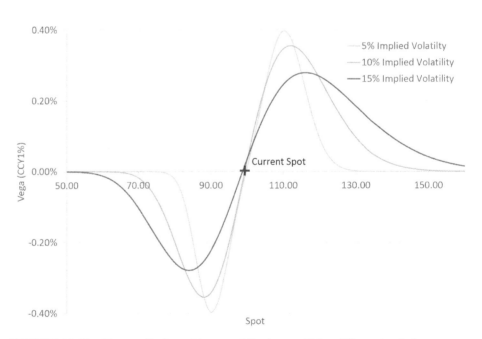

EXHIBIT 12.11   Vega profile from risk reversal (buying topside) at different implied
volatility levels

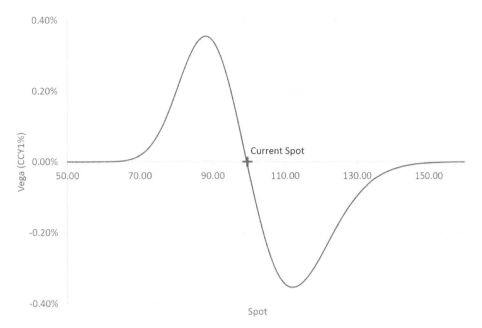

EXHIBIT 12.12 Vega versus spot profile from risk reversal (buying downside)

stated in log-return terms, which causes distances in spot space to compress toward zero. A stylized vega versus spot log-return graph for a risk reversal *is* rotationally symmetric as shown in Exhibit 12.13.

The vanna exposure on a risk reversal does not persist over all spot levels. Rather it is maximized at the initial spot as shown in Exhibit 12.14.

Therefore, a long risk reversal contract at inception has the following exposures:

- Vega: no exposure
- Vanna: positive or negative exposure depending on whether the risk reversal is "for topside" or "for downside" (i.e., whether topside or downside strikes are priced at higher implied volatility within the volatility smile)
- Volga: no exposure

Butterfly Exposures

A long butterfly contract is constructed using a long strangle (long wings) and a short straddle (ATM) with the ATM notional set such that the structure is initially vega-neutral and the call and put legs in the strangle have the same notional and delta. Exhibit 12.15 shows the vega profile from a long butterfly. Again, the butterfly strikes are fixed and hence the chart shows how the vega exposure changes at different implied volatility levels after trading.

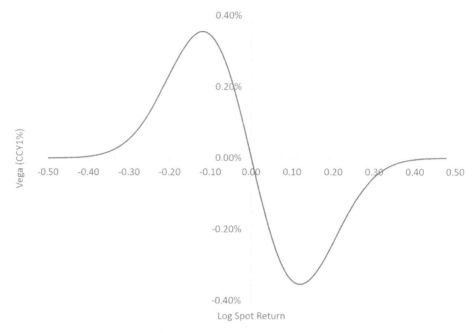

EXHIBIT 12.13   Vega versus log spot profile from risk reversal (buying downside)

VOLATILITY SMILE MARKET INSTRUMENTS AND EXPOSURES

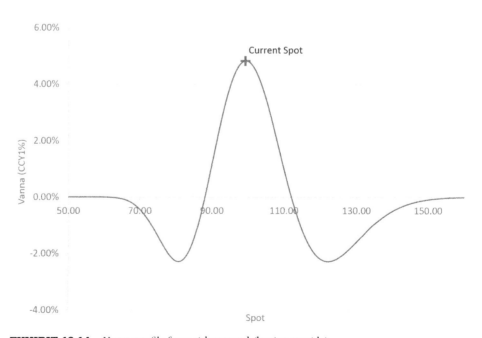

EXHIBIT 12.14   Vanna profile from risk reversal (buying topside)

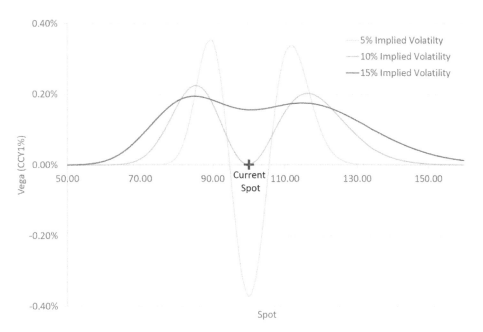

EXHIBIT 12.15 Vega profile from long butterfly at different implied volatility levels

The volga exposure on a butterfly does not persist over all spot levels. Rather it is maximized at the initial spot as shown in Exhibit 12.16.

A long butterfly contract at inception has the following exposures:

■ Vega: no exposure (by construction)

■ Vanna: no exposure

■ Volga: positive exposure

Summary

Within this stylized analysis using a flat volatility smile and ignoring issues like adaption (explained in Chapter 14) and broker fly strike placement (explained later in this chapter), the three different market instruments give the three unique vega exposures at inception shown in Exhibit 12.17.

In practice this means that:

■ ATM contracts are used to trade the *level* of implied volatility because their main exposure at inception is vega $\left(\frac{\partial P}{\partial \sigma} \right)$.

■ Risk reversal contracts are used to trade the spot versus implied volatility relationship because their main exposure at inception is vanna $\left(\frac{\partial vega}{\partial spot} \right)$.

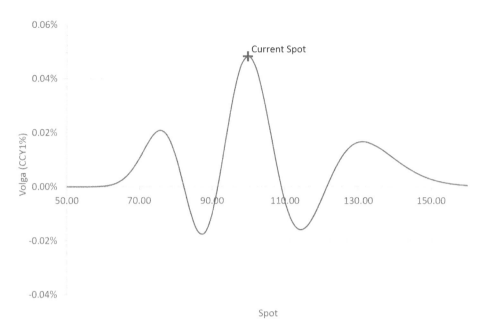

EXHIBIT 12.16 Volga profile from long butterfly

Instrument/Exposure	Vega	Vanna	Volga
ATM	✓	✗	✗
Risk Reversal	✗	✓	✗
Butterfly	✗	✗	✓

EXHIBIT 12.17 Vega exposures from market instruments

- Butterfly contracts are used to trade the volatility of implied volatility because their main exposure at inception is volga $\left(\frac{\partial vega}{\partial \sigma} \right)$.

Finally, it is mildly interesting to observe that the vanna profile of the ATM takes the same shape as the vega profile of the risk reversal while the volga of the ATM takes the same shape as the vega of the butterfly.

■ Risk Reversal Contract

The Black-Scholes formula assumes that the volatility of the underlying is constant. In practice, implied volatility changes depending (amongst other things) on how spot moves. Plus, in the market there is often differing supply and demand for topside or downside optionality, which leads to an asymmetric volatility smile.

The FX derivatives market expresses the amount of **skew** in the volatility smile via the risk reversal contract. Specifically, the risk reversal gives the differential between the call strike implied volatility and the put strike implied volatility for the same tenor and delta.

In the interbank broker market, risk reversals are quoted in positive terms, with the *direction* also quoted. For example, in USD/ZAR, if the 1yr 25d call is priced at 15.5% implied volatility and the 1yr 25d put is priced at 11.25% implied volatility, the 1yr 25d risk reversal would be quoted as "4.25% USD calls over," meaning that the USD call volatility is higher than the USD put volatility. In some currency pairs, it is market convention to quote the risk reversal direction in CCY2 terms. USD/JPY risk reversals are quoted as, for example, "1.4% JPY calls over" if the implied volatility for the downside strike is 1.4% higher than the implied volatility for the topside strike. As noted, *buying* the risk reversal always means *buying* the call or put strike with the higher volatility, and *selling* the other leg.

The delta used to calculate the risk reversal strikes is sometimes spot delta and sometimes forward delta, depending on market convention. Most often, short-dated G10 risk reversals are quoted using spot delta strikes while long-dated G10 and emerging market risk reversals are quoted using forward delta strikes. Whichever delta convention is used to generate the strikes will also be used to delta hedge the transaction if dealt.

When trading a risk reversal, particularly if it is long-dated, it is important to pay attention to exactly which strikes are being transacted. Strikes traded within a risk reversal are the *outright* strikes—the same strikes as if same-tenor and same-delta call or put vanillas are traded in isolation.

If a currency pair had a completely flat volatility smile, the risk reversal strikes would be positioned approximately symmetrically around the ATM strike in log-space. Therefore, the topside strike will be further away from the ATM than the downside strike in regular spot space. At short maturities this effect is small but at longer maturities the impact can be significant.

Additionally, if a currency pair has a large forward drift, at longer maturities the ATM strike will be far from current spot and it is possible that, for example, if the forward drift is large positive, the 35d put strike is positioned close to current spot.

Remembering that out-of-the-money strikes are always traded within a risk reversal contract, the volatility smile also impacts risk reversal strike placement:

- If the implied volatility for a given delta is higher on the smile, the strike moves further away from the ATM; think about the increasing chance of ending up in-the-money at higher volatility.

- If the implied volatility for a given delta is lower on the smile, the strike moves closer to the ATM; think about the decreasing chance of ending up in-the-money at lower volatility.

Finally, market conventions play an important role in risk reversal strike placement. If the premium currency is CCY1 and the ATM is a zero-delta straddle, the ATM strike is lower than the forward (see Chapter 8) and the risk reversal strikes are relatively lower also.

Exhibit 12.18 shows a typical volatility smile in AUD/JPY—a CCY1 premium pair with a large downside risk reversal.

- The AUD call strike is located on a relatively flat part of the smile, so the implied volatility from the relatively lower strike (caused by a CCY1 premium) is not too different.

- The AUD put strike is located on a steeply sloping part of the smile, so the implied volatility from the relatively lower strike (caused by a CCY1 premium) is significantly higher.

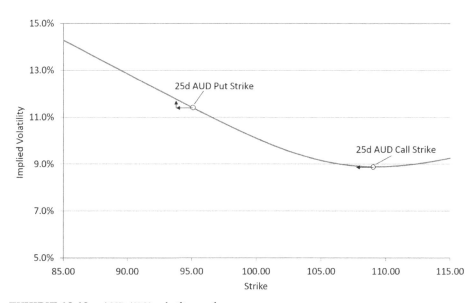

EXHIBIT 12.18 AUD/JPY volatility smile

This effect causes AUD/JPY risk reversal contracts to be valued at higher implied volatility levels and the impact gets larger for long-dated options. In practice this means that care must be taken when assessing the term-structure of long-dated risk reversals or comparing risk reversals between currency pairs with different market conventions.

What Drives the Risk Reversal in the Market?

The risk reversal contract expresses the prevailing market preference for topside versus downside optionality. This preference is a function of market positioning (see Chapter 17) but it also depends on the market's perception of expected spot moves, realized spot volatility, and implied volatility changes.

At shorter tenors the risk reversal is largely driven by expectations of spot moves and realized spot volatility. For example, if shorter tenor risk reversals go more for downside, that may imply the market expects that *if* spot goes lower, spot will be more volatile. Or it may imply that the market expects that there is an increased chance that spot will move lower.

At longer tenors the risk reversal is largely driven by expectations of spot moves and implied volatility changes. For example, if longer tenor risk reversals go more for downside, that may imply that the market expects that *if* spot goes lower, implied volatility will rise more. Or it may imply that the market expects that there is an increased chance that spot will move lower.

The risk reversal contract can be thought of as a measure of the *relative strength* of the two currencies in the currency pair. In a USD versus emerging market currency pair (e.g., USD/TRY or USD/BRL), the risk reversal will invariably be positive because there is a far higher chance of a sharp devaluation of the emerging market currency (i.e., spot jumps higher) than the USD. When spot jumps, implied volatility invariably rises and therefore a long risk reversal position with a long vega exposure to the topside will make money.

This idea of the relative strength of currencies also links to the interest rate differential (i.e., *carry*; see Chapter 17). Usually, the larger the interest rate differential in a given currency pair, the larger the risk reversal. This relationship becomes more important at longer tenors. Buying the higher-yielding currency and selling the low-yielding currency to benefit from the carry and then buying the risk reversal for protection from a blowup is a classic trading strategy in emerging market currency pairs.

Historically, interest rate differentials and risk reversals were highly correlated since low interest rate currencies (e.g., JPY or CHF) implied a more stable country with lower growth potential while high interest rate currencies (e.g., BRL or TRY) implied a country with higher growth potential but more political, social, or economic instability. However, since the 2008 financial crisis most G10

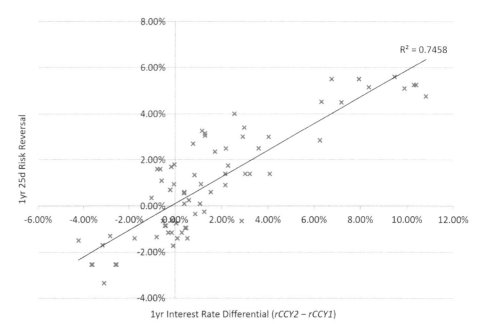

EXHIBIT 12.19 1yr interest rate differential versus 1yr 25d risk reversal scatter plot

currency pairs have low interest rates and the link between carry and risk reversals has weakened, although it remains an important factor. Exhibit 12.19 shows the relationship between 1yr interest rates and 1yr 25 delta risk reversals in 70 of the most liquid currency pairs as of October 1, 2014.

Trading the Risk Reversal

In the same way that realized volatility is often lower than implied volatility (see Chapter 17 for details), **realized skew** is often less than **implied skew** (i.e., it costs more to buy and hold the risk reversal position than can be made back from trading the spot versus implied volatility relationship). This implies that there is a risk premium associated with holding a long risk reversal position, which makes sense since the risk reversal offers protection from the most likely extreme market moves. When spot breaks out of recent trading ranges there is often a risk reversal overvaluation as the risk premium increases, particularly at longer tenors.

For risk reversals, as for all other financial instruments, traders must be careful not to fall into the trap of believing that the status quo will prevail indefinitely. Exhibit 12.20 shows a chart of USD/JPY 1yr 25 delta risk reversals over ten years with trader comments at various points.

In the interbank broker market, the risk reversal is traded in terms of the volatility differential between the two strikes. After a transaction is agreed, the actual implied volatilities must be agreed. For example, two banks could agree to transact an

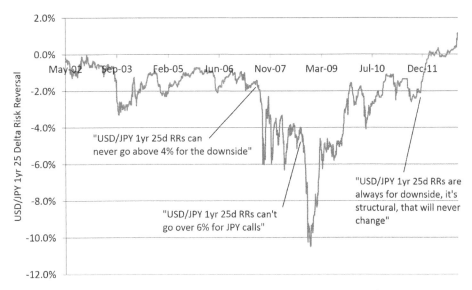

EXHIBIT 12.20 USD/JPY 1yr 25d risk reversals from May 2002 to November 2012

AUD/USD 1yr 25d RR at 2.6% AUD puts over, but then the risk reversal buying bank wants 11.6% on the AUD put (and therefore 9.0% on the AUD call) while the RR selling bank wants 11.4% on the AUD put. This disagreement occurs for two reasons:

1. *Strike placement.* The call and put strikes are backed out of an inverted Black-Scholes formula. For the risk reversal *buying* bank, the higher the agreed implied volatilities, the further away from the ATM both risk reversal strikes are positioned. The higher volatility side of the volatility smile is steeper than the lower volatility side. Therefore, by pushing the strikes further away from the ATM, the risk reversal buying bank gets a long strike which is marked even higher (i.e., better) on the volatility smile.

2. *Adapted vega* (explained in Chapter 14). Buying a risk reversal results in a short adapted vega exposure. Therefore, the risk reversal buying bank wants the highest implied volatilities possible so they get short adapted vega from the highest possible level. Likewise, the risk reversal selling bank wants the lowest implied volatilities possible so they get long adapted vega from the lowest possible level.

Traders must check the proposed market data and only agree to trade at correct implied volatility levels. There will be occasions where transacting the risk reversal is more important than these second-order effects but traders should always calculate the P&L difference from mid implied volatility levels so they know how much additional "spread" the transaction is costing.

Finally, traders use their short-dated risk reversal exposures to manage their delta positions. For example, in a currency pair with a risk reversal for topside, if a trader is long short-dated risk reversal and spot jumps higher, even if the trader has not seen any implied volatility prices in the market it is clear that implied volatility will be higher. Due to the long vanna $\left(\frac{\partial delta}{\partial \sigma}\right)$ exposure from the risk reversal the trader knows that their position will be longer delta. Assuming USD is CCY1, if vanna is long USD20m and implied volatility is approximately 1% higher, delta will be USD20m longer and additional delta can be sold at the higher spot. In effect, the long risk reversal position creates delta changes equivalent to being long gamma.

25d versus 10d Risk Reversal Contracts

Exhibit 12.21 shows vega profiles from 25d and 10d risk reversals.

The wider positioning of the strikes within the 10 delta risk reversal causes the vega peaks to be positioned further away from the ATM and the peak vega exposures to be larger since the vega offsets less when the strikes are further apart.

The risk reversal quotes at different deltas are linked. Investigating these relationships is useful for understanding the volatility smile. In many pairs, only 25d risk reversals are regularly quoted in the interbank broker market. The relationships between risk reversals at different deltas are called **risk reversal multipliers**. In almost all currency pairs, at lower delta the risk reversal quote increases, as shown in Exhibit 12.22.

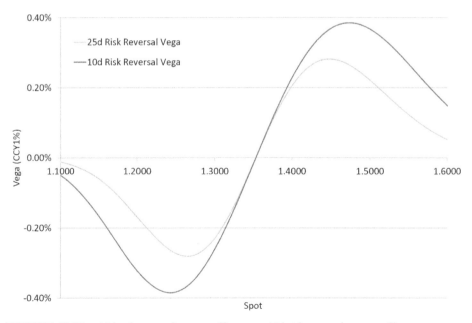

EXHIBIT 12.21   25d risk reversal vega profile versus 10d risk reversal vega profile

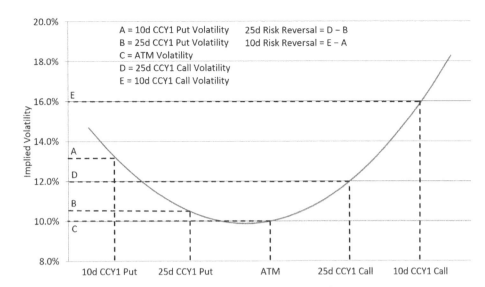

EXHIBIT 12.22   25d and 10d risk reversals on the volatility smile

Within the Malz volatility smile formula, substituting 10% put delta and 10% call delta into the formula gives:

- $\sigma_{10\%\ Delta\ Put} = \sigma_{ATM} - 0.8\ \sigma_{RR25d} + 2.56\ \sigma_{Fly25d}$

- $\sigma_{10\%\ Delta\ Call} = \sigma_{90\%\ Delta\ Put} = \sigma_{ATM} + 0.8\ \sigma_{RR25d} + 2.56\ \sigma_{Fly25d}$

Therefore:

- $\sigma_{RR10d} = \sigma_{Call10d} - \sigma_{Put10d} = 1.6\ \sigma_{RR25d}$

This 25d/10d multiplier of 1.6 is a touch lower than values typically observed in the market for liquid currency pairs where the value is usually around 1.8. Risk reversal multipliers are usually fairly stable in liquid currency pairs.

Another method for calculating risk reversal multipliers is to assume that the cost of vanna remains constant. This method is back-of-the-envelope, old-school, and circular, but it gives some intuition as to how risk reversal contracts at different deltas are linked. Exhibit 12.23 shows vega for AUD/USD 1yr outright strikes and vanna for AUD/USD 1yr long risk reversals over a range of deltas (AUD puts over hence short vanna).

The 1yr AUD/USD 25d risk reversal is −2.5%. Therefore, this risk reversal contract "costs" approximately 2.5% volatility × 0.31% vega = 0.775 AUD% more to buy in premium terms than if the risk reversal was 0%.

The 1yr AUD/USD 25d RR has −4.2% vanna while the 1yr AUD/USD 10d RR has −4.1% vanna. If the premium cost of vanna is constant, the 10d RR should cost (4.1/4.2 =) 0.975 of the 25d RR in premium terms. If the 10d RR costs (0.775% × 0.975 =) 0.755% in premium terms, that equates to a 10d risk reversal quote of

Strike	Vega (AUD%)	Vanna (AUD%)
ATM	0.40%	0.00%
35 Delta	0.36%	-2.70%
30 Delta	0.34%	-3.60%
25 Delta	0.31%	-4.20%
20 Delta	0.28%	-4.55%
15 Delta	0.23%	-4.55%
10 Delta	0.17%	-4.10%

EXHIBIT 12.23   AUD/USD 1yr outright strike vega and 1yr long risk reversal vanna

RR Strikes	RR Multiplier (Versus 25d RR)
35 Delta	0.55
30 Delta	0.78
25 Delta	1.00
20 Delta	1.20
15 Delta	1.46
10 Delta	1.78

EXHIBIT 12.24   AUD/USD 1yr risk reversal multipliers

(0.755%/0.17% vega =) −4.45%, which is (−4.45%/−2.5% =) 1.775× the 25d risk reversal.

For 1yr AUD/USD, the above methodology gives risk reversal multipliers shown in Exhibit 12.24. These multipliers are close to values often observed in the market.

Cross Risk Reversals

Given 25d risk reversals in EUR/USD and USD/JPY, how can the 25d risk reversal in EUR/JPY be calculated?

In some cases, cross risk reversals can be calculated as a fixed offset to the risk reversal in one of the major pairs. This methodology is suitable if there is clearly a dominant currency within the pair that will contribute the vast majority of the skew. For example, EUR/HKD risk reversals can be generated off EUR/USD risk reversals since USD/HKD is a managed currency pair with low implied volatility.

A **copula** approach, in its most simple form, takes probability densities (see Chapter 13 for more information on probability density functions) generated by the major volatility smiles at a given tenor and builds a cross volatility smile assuming a static correlation between the major pair spots. In some cases this works well but in others it fails to produce a smile close to the market. A more effective variation uses the copula to generate *changes* in the cross risk reversal rather than generating the absolute level.

Another possible approach is to look at a system of risk reversals in many currencies against each other, imply a relative "strength" parameter for each currency, and then use this to generate cross risk reversals (taking the level of the ATM into account each time). Alternatively, the realized historic spot versus volatility relationship can be used to imply a cross risk reversal using a regression-style calculation.

Cross risk reversals are a tricky area and this section barely scratches the surface. Different banks take different approaches but flexibility is important; finding a single method that works for all crosses all the time is very difficult.

■ Butterfly Contract

The Black-Scholes formula assumes constant volatility. In practice, volatility (both implied and realized) itself is volatile. This causes wing vanilla options to be often priced at higher implied volatility than the ATM due to the volga (second derivative of implied volatility) they contain.

The FX derivatives market expresses the height of the wings of the volatility smile via the butterfly contract, quoted as the average of the same-delta call strike implied volatility and put strike implied volatility less the ATM volatility at a given tenor.

Strike placement is very important within the butterfly contract. The butterfly contract that is quoted and traded in the interbank broker market is called the **broker fly**. The strikes within the 25d broker fly are *not* the outright 25d call and 25d put strikes. Therefore, the strikes within the same-tenor and same-delta risk reversal and broker fly are different. The butterfly constructed using the outright 25d call and 25d put strikes is sometimes called a **strike fly** but this instrument is rarely traded in practice.

The broker fly is a messy concept, but put as simply as possible:

> *The broker fly is the implied volatility at which the premium of the call and the put generated and priced using the ATM + broker fly volatility is equal to the premium of the same strikes on the full volatility smile.*

This statement can be broken down into two parts:

Part 1: The ATM + broker fly volatility is used to generate the call and put strikes within the broker fly. Crucially, this means the risk reversal/skew is **not** taken into account within broker fly strike placement.

Example: In EUR/USD, spot is 1.2600, the 1yr forward is 1.2660, the 1yr ATM strike is 1.2740, and the 1yr ATM implied volatility is 11.5%:

- Outright 25d call strike = 1.3690 (10.80% volatility)

- Outright 25d put strike = 1.1695 (13.15% volatility)

  If the 25d broker fly volatility is +0.40%:

- Broker fly 25d call strike = 1.3810. The 25d broker fly call strike is further away from the ATM strike than the outright 25d call strike since it is generated using

11.9% volatility (11.5% ATM volatility + 0.4% broker fly volatility) rather than 10.8% volatility on the smile.

- Broker fly 25d put strike = 1.1775. The 25d broker fly put strike is closer to the ATM strike than the outright 25d put strike since it is generated using 11.9% volatility rather than 13.15% volatility on the smile.

In general, on the higher side of the volatility smile, the strike within the broker fly will be closer to the ATM than the same delta outright strike since broker fly strike volatility will be lower than the smile strike volatility. While on the lower side of the volatility smile, the strike within the broker fly will be further away from the ATM than the same delta outright strike since broker fly strike volatility will be higher than the smile strike volatility. Exhibit 12.25 gives a diagram showing broker fly strike placement.

Particularly at long-dated maturities or in high skew currency pairs the difference between outright strikes and broker fly strikes can be large.

Example: In AUD/JPY, spot is 80.25, the 5yr forward is 63.85, the 5yr ATM strike is 58.20, and the 5yr ATM implied volatility is 19.25%:

- Outright 25d put strike = 46.05 (22.55% volatility)

- Outright 25d call strike = 79.10 (14.15% volatility)

- Broker fly 25d put strike = 49.60 (30% forward delta on the smile)

- Broker fly 25d call strike = 82.80 (20% forward delta on the smile)

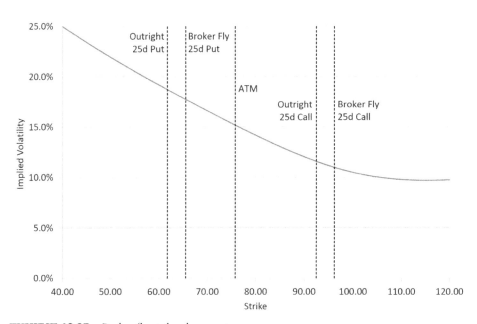

EXHIBIT 12.25 Broker fly strike placement

Part 2: The combined premium of the call and put options priced using the ATM + broker fly volatility is equal to their combined premium priced using the full volatility smile. Exhibit 12.26 shows this in a pricing tool.

The broker fly strikes are generated in leg 1 and inputted in legs 2 and 3. Look at the premiums: The cost of the strangle (the call plus the put) at ATM + broker fly volatility is the same as the cost of the call using the full smile plus the cost of put on the full smile (8.49% = 5.65% + 2.84%).

Some long-dated AUD/JPY volatility surface instruments are shown in Exhibit 12.27. The ATM and RR are both rising at longer tenors but the 25d broker flies are going more negative. This is a counterintuitive result because a higher ATM and larger skew is intuitively linked with higher wings within the volatility smile. In fact, the broker fly goes more negative because the *broker fly contract contains vanna exposure* when valued on the smile caused by the strike positioning.

In a CCY1 premium pair a long broker fly contains long vanna exposure because the CCY1 premium pulls all strikes lower. This makes the long topside strike

Contract Details	Leg 1	Leg 2	Leg 3
Currency Pair	EUR/USD	EUR/USD	EUR/USD
Horizon	Mon 03-Sep-12	Mon 03-Sep-12	Mon 03-Sep-12
Spot Date	Wed 05-Sep-12	Wed 05-Sep-12	Wed 05-Sep-12
Strategy	25d Strangle	Vanilla	Vanilla
Call/Put	N/A	EUR Put/USD Call	EUR Call/USD Put
Maturity	5Y	5Y	5Y
Expiry Date	Fri 01-Sep-17	Fri 01-Sep-17	Fri 01-Sep-17
Delivery Date	Tue 05-Sep-17	Tue 05-Sep-17	Tue 05-Sep-17
Cut	NY	NY	NY
Strikes	1.1060/1.6240	1.1060	1.6240
Notional Currency	EUR	EUR	EUR

Market Data			
Spot	1.2600	1.2600	1.2600
Swap Points	270	270	270
Forward	1.2870	1.2870	1.2870
Deposit (EUR)	0.35%	0.35%	0.35%
Deposit (USD)	0.80%	0.80%	0.80%
ATM Volatility	12.40%	12.40%	12.40%
Pricing Volatility	12.75%	13.85%	11.55%

Outputs			
Output Currency	EUR	EUR	EUR
Premium	8.49%	5.65%	2.84%

EXHIBIT 12.26 Pricing tool showing broker fly premiums

EXHIBIT 12.27 AUD/JPY Volatility Surface Instruments

Tenor	ATM	25d RR	25d Fly
1yr	15.3%	−5.7%	+0.1%
2yr	16.6%	−7.2%	**−0.5%**
3yr	17.0%	−7.8%	**−1.0%**
4yr	18.3%	−8.1%	**−1.5%**
5yr	19.25%	−8.4%	**−2.0%**

relatively closer and the long downside strike relatively further away, resulting in long vanna.

In a CCY2 premium pair, if the risk reversal is for topside, a long broker fly contains short vanna exposure, whereas if the risk reversal is for downside, a long broker fly contains long vanna exposure.

These vanna exposures significantly impact the volatility price of the broker fly contract in CCY1 premium currency pairs. If the risk reversal is for topside, the broker fly quote will be pulled higher due to the long vanna (long risk reversal exposure). If the risk reversal is for downside, the broker fly quote will be pulled lower due to the long vanna (short risk reversal exposure), as in the above AUD/JPY case.

What Drives the Butterfly in the Market?

The butterfly contract expresses the prevailing market preference for wing optionality compared with ATM optionality. This preference is a function of market positioning (see Chapter 17) but it also depends on the market's perception of expected realized and implied volatility changes.

At shorter tenors the butterfly reflects the prevailing market preference for wing gamma (i.e., gamma away from current spot) while at longer tenors the butterfly is largely driven by market expectations of how volatile implied volatility will be, plus it also reflects the prevailing market preference for wing vega.

In emerging market currency pairs, traders buy the butterfly contract as protection from sharp moves in spot and implied volatility. The cost/benefit of holding a long butterfly position is compared with the cost/benefit of holding a long risk reversal position or holding a long gamma position.

Trading the Butterfly

In the interbank market, butterfly contracts are not traded as frequently as risk reversal contracts. Butterfly contracts in a given currency pair might not trade for a few days at a time. However, traders update the wing parameters within their volatility surface more frequently in order to match implied volatility prices or trading levels on specific contracts.

25d versus 10d Butterfly Contracts

Exhibits 12.28 and 12.29 give the vega and volga profiles for 25d and 10d butterflies.

As shown in Exhibit 12.28, both 10d and 25d butterfly contracts give sharp changes in vega away from current spot. The 10d flies have over double the peak vega in the wings versus the 25d flies for *equal wing notional*, plus a wider distribution. The 25d butterflies can therefore be traded in large size without significantly impacting the trading position. Within 25d broker butterflies in CCY1 premium pairs the strikes can be positioned so closely together that they can generate large localized vanna exposures. Believe me, I found this out the hard way.

Exhibit 12.29 shows how the long volga at current spot goes flat and then short as spot moves away from the current level in the wings and how 10d flies give a wider (better) volga distribution than 25d flies. Within a butterfly contract, the maximum volga exposure occurs at current spot. Therefore, if the aim of the trader is to get longer volga at higher or lower spot levels, the butterfly (particularly the 25d butterfly) is not necessarily the best contract to trade.

Finally, it is worth noting that the broker fly strike placement prevents the existence of stable 25d/10d butterfly multiples in most currency pairs.

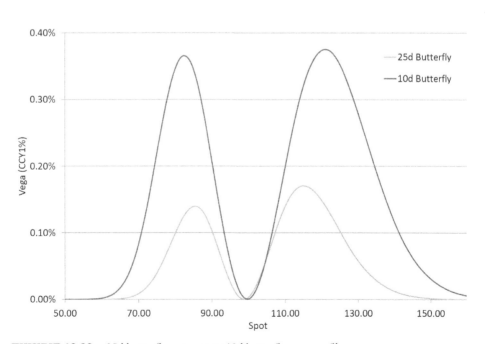

EXHIBIT 12.28 25d butterfly vega versus 10d butterfly vega profiles

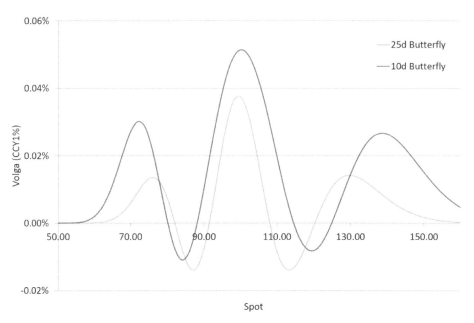

EXHIBIT 12.29   25d butterfly volga versus 10d butterfly volga profiles

■ Volatility Smile Risk Management

When trading an FX derivatives position it is important to understand how the vega exposure will be impacted as spot and implied volatility changes, and also the exposures to the smile instruments themselves. The smile position is therefore monitored using two sets of exposures:

1. Vanna $\left(\frac{\partial vega}{\partial spot} \right)$ and volga $\left(\frac{\partial vega}{\partial \sigma} \right)$ explain how the vega position changes as spot and implied volatility changes.
2. Rega $\left(\frac{\partial P}{\partial RR} \right)$ and sega $\left(\frac{\partial P}{\partial Fly} \right)$ explain how P&L changes as the risk reversal and butterfly prices change. Both rega and sega are quoted to whichever delta contracts are used to build the volatility surface. For example, if only 25 delta risk reversals are used to build the volatility smile, only 25 delta rega is meaningful. That rega represents the P&L generated from revaluing all contracts in the position using a volatility surface with changed 25 delta risk reversal contracts.

Vanna is usually quoted as change in vega for a change in spot, or, recalling the dual interpretation of vanna, the change in delta for a 1% change in ATM implied volatility. Therefore, if a trading position is long USD1m vanna, if spot moves 1% higher, vega will get longer by USD10k. Or, if ATM implied volatility moves 1% higher (i.e., from 8% to 9%), delta will get longer by USD1m.

Volga is usually quoted as a change in vega for a 1% move in ATM implied volatility. Therefore, if a trading position is short USD250k volga, if implied volatility rises by 0.1%, vega will get shorter by USD25k. As mentioned, volga is a second derivative like gamma. A long volga exposure therefore means that vega can be sold when implied volatility rises and bought when implied volatility falls.

Rega is usually quoted as the sensitivity to a 1% change in the volatility price of the risk reversal instrument. Therefore, if a trading position is long USD150k of 25 delta rega, if the 25d risk reversal moves from +0.8% to +1.0%, a P&L change of +USD30k will be generated.

Sega is usually quoted as the sensitivity to a 1% change in the volatility price of the butterfly instrument. Therefore, if a trading position is long USD100k of 25 delta sega, if the 25d butterfly moves lower by 0.1%, a P&L change of –USD10k will be generated.

Like other exposures, within a trading position; vanna, volga, rega, and sega will not be static; they will change as spot or ATM implied volatility moves, so all have their own higher-order derivatives (e.g., $\frac{\partial vanna}{\partial spot}$ or $\frac{\partial rega}{\partial \sigma}$, etc.). However, when analyzing derivatives trading positions it is often better to view, for example, vanna exposures within a spot ladder or implied volatility ladder rather than considering higher-order sensitivities at current spot only.

For reference, the rega on a risk reversal is approximately the average of the two absolute strike vegas while the sega on a butterfly is approximately the sum of the two wing strike vega exposures. In addition, a 25d topside strike in isolation will have a 25d rega approximately equal to *half* of its vega since, for example, a +0.1% change in the risk reversal will roughly move the implied volatility for the 25d call strike up by 0.05% and the implied volatility for the 25d put strike down by 0.05%.

The quotation conventions used for these smile exposures will differ from trading desk to trading desk. Plus, although rega and sega here are specifically the sensitivities to the market risk reversal and butterfly instruments, they can more generally be thought of as the sensitivities to the parameters that control the skew and wings within the volatility surface construction.

Risk reversal contracts have vanna and rega exposures while butterfly contracts mainly have volga and sega exposures. It is therefore natural to assume that trading positions that have vanna exposures also have corresponding rega exposures and trading positions that have long volga exposures also have long sega exposures. However, when trading a portfolio of vanilla options in high-skew pairs or when trading exotic contracts the links between vanna and rega and between volga and sega can break down. For example, a trading position might be flat volga but long sega. Therefore, traders must monitor all these exposures within their risk management.

■ Volatility Smile Construction Methods

The Malz volatility smile formula shows how it is possible to construct a volatility smile directly from the market instruments but in practice the process is far more complicated. As with the ATM curve, the volatility smile can be either an input or an output.

Some trading desks express the volatility smile using the market instruments directly in a process that must adjust for market conventions and strike placement issues. Within this approach, since only 25 and 10 delta market instruments are liquid, if market instruments are used to build the volatility surface, volatilities are defined only between 10 delta puts on the downside and 10 delta calls on the topside. Implied volatilities beyond the 10 delta strikes must either be controlled using extrapolation or generated automatically using a model like Stochastic Volatility Inspired (SVI)-see Gatheral's book in Further Reading for more information.

Other trading desks use models such as Hagan, Kumar, Lesniewski, and Woodward's SABR model, with traders updating the parameters of the model such that the market instruments output by the model at market tenors match the market.

In addition, the volatility smile must be interpolated between tenors. Trading desks develop their own methods for this, interpolating in e.g., delta terms, strike terms, or model parameter terms.

Other asset classes express volatility surfaces in different ways. In interest rate derivatives, the SABR model has become the market standard while in equity derivatives, implied volatility is quoted at different percentage distances from the current stock price. It is important to understand that there is nothing about the FX derivatives market that makes the ATM, risk reversal, and butterfly approach the only possible way of representing the volatility smile. It is a market convention that has developed and become the standard over time, but other parameterizations would be equally valid.

Constructing a Volatility Smile in Excel

Constructing a volatility smile using the Malz smile model builds understanding of the volatility surface market instruments. The Black-Scholes framework can then be used to calculate strikes for different deltas to show how the market instruments impact strike placement within the volatility smile.

■ Task A: Set Up the Malz Smile Model

Recall the Malz formula for implied volatility at a given (positive) delta put from Chapter 12:

$$\sigma_{X\ Delta\ Put} = \sigma_{ATM} + 2\ \sigma_{RR25d} \cdot (X - 50\%) + 16\ \sigma_{Fly25d} \cdot (X - 50\%)^2$$

This formula can be coded up in Excel:

Smile Inputs

ATM	10.0%	←Named: **ATM**
25d RR	2.0%	←Named: **RR**
25d Fly	3.0%	←Named: **Fly**

Put Delta	75%	←Named: **PutDelta**
Call Delta	25%	=1-PutDelta
Implied Vol	**14.0%**	=ATM+2*RR*(PutDelta-50%)+16*Fly*(PutDelta-50%)^2

Check that $\sigma_{50\% \; Delta \; Put} = \sigma_{ATM}$ and the 25% put delta and 25% call delta (75% put delta) implied volatility matches up with the standard approximations:

- $\sigma_{Call25d} = \sigma_{ATM} + \sigma_{Fly25d} + \frac{1}{2}\sigma_{RR25d}$

- $\sigma_{Put25d} = \sigma_{ATM} + \sigma_{Fly25d} - \frac{1}{2}\sigma_{RR25d}$

Task B: Plot Implied Volatility versus Delta and Investigate Parameters

The function output can be extended to generate a full volatility smile from 0% to 100% delta:

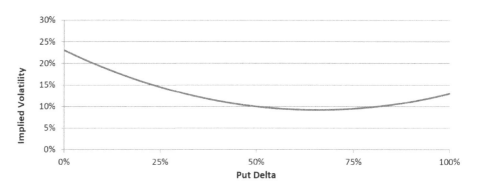

Smile Inputs

ATM	10.0%
25d RR	2.0%
25d Fly	3.0%

Put Delta	0%	5%	10%	15%	20%	25%	30%	35%	40%
Call Delta	100%	95%	90%	85%	80%	75%	70%	65%	60%
Implied Vol	20.0%	17.9%	16.1%	14.5%	13.1%	12.0%	11.1%	10.5%	10.1%

The volatility smile can then be plotted:

Smile Inputs

ATM	10.0%
25d RR	-5.0%
25d Fly	2.0%

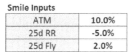

Check that the volatility smile updates as expected when the ATM, risk reversal, and butterfly prices change. This becomes easier if the volatility smile chart is placed next to the inputs on the same Excel sheet, and the low and high values of the implied volatility axis in the chart are fixed rather than automatically rescaling.

Task C: Use Black-Scholes to Get Strike from Delta

The Black-Scholes framework can be used to get the equivalent strike for a given delta. Recall that:

$$\Delta_{call} = \frac{\partial P_{call}}{\partial S} = e^{-rCCY1.T}N(d_1)$$

$$\Delta_{put} = \frac{\partial P_{put}}{\partial S} = e^{-rCCY1.T}[N(d_1) - 1]$$

where S is spot, K is strike, $rCCY1$ and $rCCY2$ are continuously compounded interest rates in CCY1 and CCY2, T is time to expiry (in years), σ is implied volatility, $N(X)$ is the cumulative normal distribution function, and $d_1 = \frac{\ln\left(\frac{S}{K}\right) + \left(rCCY2 - rCCY1 + \frac{\sigma^2}{2}\right).T}{\sigma\sqrt{T}}$.

The formula for Δ_{put} can be inverted to get the strike from the put delta:

$$K = \frac{S}{e^{N^{-1}(e^{rCCY1.T}\Delta_{put}+1).\sigma\sqrt{T} - \left(rCCY2 - rCCY1 + \frac{\sigma^2}{2}\right).T}}$$

where $N^{-1}(X)$ is the inverse cumulative normal distribution function.

These functions can be implemented first on the Excel sheet using =NORMSDIST(X) for $N(X)$ and =NORMSINV(X) for $N^{-1}(X)$. A strike input is used to generate the put delta, which is itself then used to generate a strike output. If the strike input and output are equal as other inputs change, this confirms that the formulas are correctly implemented:

Market Data Inputs

Spot	100.00	←Named: *Spot*
Strike Input	90.00	←Named: *Strike*
CCY1 Interest Rate	0.0%	←Named: *rCCY1*
CCY2 Interest Rate	0.0%	←Named: *rCCY2*
Time to Maturity (years)	1.00	←Named: *T*
Implied Volatility (σ)	10.0%	←Named: *Vol*

Delta	-13.5%	=EXP(-rCCY1*T)*(NORMSDIST((LN(Spot/StrikeInput)+(rCCY2-rCCY1+0.5*Vol^2)*T)/Vol*SQRT(T))-1)
Strike Output	90.00	=Spot/EXP(NORMSINV(EXP(-rCCY1*T)*Delta+1)*Vol*SQRT(T)-(rCCY2-rCCY1+0.5*Vol^2)*T)

Note that the put delta used within Black-Scholes formulas is its true (negative) value rather than the positive quoted put delta.

Task D: Switch to VBA Functions and Plot Implied Volatility versus Strike

These functions are long and messy in the sheet but they are much neater as VBA functions. The Malz smile volatility function is simple:

```
Function MalzSmileVol(ATM As Double, RR25d As Double, Fly25d As _
  Double, PutDelta As Double) As Double

    MalzSmileVol = ATM + 2 * RR25d * (PutDelta - 0.5) + 16 * _
    Fly25d * (PutDelta - 0.5) ^ 2

End Function
```

The put delta from strike VBA function uses the cumulative normal distribution worksheet function:

```
Function PutDeltaFromStrike(S As Double, K As Double, rCCY1 As _
  Double, rCCY2 As Double, T As Double, v As Double) As Double

    Dim d1 As Double

    d1 = (Log(S / K) + (rCCY2 - rCCY1 + v ^ 2 / 2) * T) / (v * Sqr(T))

    PutDeltaFromStrike = Exp(-rCCY1 * T) * _
      (Application.WorksheetFunction.NormSDist(d1) - 1)

End Function
```

The strike from put delta VBA function accesses the inverse cumulative normal distribution worksheet function. The calculation is split into three parts to make it easier to follow and debug:

```
Function StrikeFromPutDelta(S As Double, PutDelta As Double, rCCY1 As _
  Double, rCCY2 As Double, T As Double, v As Double) As Double

    Dim part1 As Double, part2 As Double, part3 As Double

    part1 = Exp(rCCY1 * T) * PutDelta + 1
    part2 = v * Sqr(T)
    part3 = (rCCY2 - rCCY1 + 0.5 * v ^ 2) * T

    StrikeFromPutDelta = S / Exp(Application.WorksheetFunction _
      .NormSInv(part1) * part2 - part3)

End Function
```

Again, the VBA functions can be tested by placing them alongside the existing Excel functions:

Smile Inputs

ATM	10.0%
25d RR	2.0%
25d Fly	3.0%

	Excel	VBA
Put Delta	25%	
Call Delta	75%	
Implied Vol	12.00%	12.00%

Market Data Inputs

Spot	100.00
Strike Input	90.00
CCY1 Interest Rate	0.0%
CCY2 Interest Rate	0.0%
Time to Maturity (years)	1.00
Implied Volatility (σ)	10.0%

	Excel	VBA
Put Delta	-13.4882%	-13.4882%
Strike Output	90.00	90.00

Once matches are confirmed, the VBA functions can be combined to plot implied volatility versus delta and implied volatility versus strike.

It is not possible to find strikes for 0 or 100 delta options, so replace 0% delta with, for example, 0.01% and replace 100% delta with, for example, 99.99%:

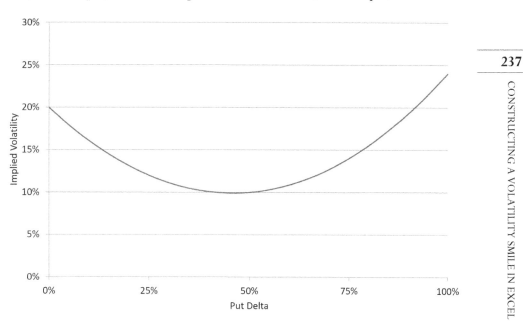

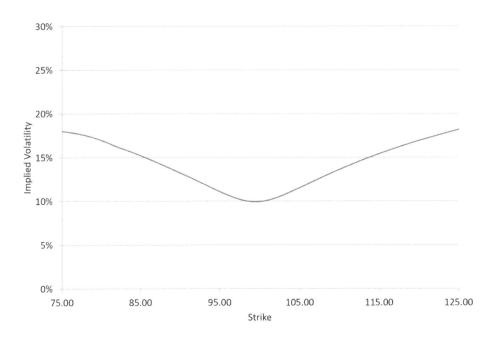

▪ Task E: Investigate Volatility Smile Strike Placement

In practice, the most important strikes at a given tenor are 10 delta and 25 delta puts and calls, plus the ATM. In the Malz framework these strikes are equivalent to these put deltas: 10d, 25d, 50d, 75d, 90d. Using the functions developed, strike placement within the volatility smile can be investigated, remembering to use the negative delta to calculate the strike. With no volatility smile, the strikes for these deltas are roughly equally spaced, with relatively slightly larger differences for topside strikes due to the log-normality of the terminal spot distribution:

Market Data Inputs

Spot	100.00
CCY1 Interest Rate	0.0%
CCY2 Interest Rate	0.0%
Time to Maturity (years)	1.00

Smile Inputs

ATM	10.0%
25d RR	0.0%
25d Fly	0.0%

Put Delta	10%	25%	50%	75%	90%
Implied Vol	10.00%	10.00%	10.00%	10.00%	10.00%
Strike	88.41	93.95	100.50	107.51	114.24
Strike Difference from ATM	-12.09	-6.56	0.00	7.01	13.74

Reducing implied volatility or time to maturity causes the terminal distribution to tighten and hence the strikes are positioned closer to the ATM:

Market Data Inputs	
Spot	100.00
CCY1 Interest Rate	0.0%
CCY2 Interest Rate	0.0%
Time to Maturity (years)	0.25

Smile Inputs	
ATM	10.0%
25d RR	0.0%
25d Fly	0.0%

Put Delta	10%	25%	50%	75%	90%
Implied Vol	10.00%	10.00%	10.00%	10.00%	10.00%
Strike	93.91	96.80	100.13	103.56	106.75
Strike Difference from ATM	-6.21	-3.32	0.00	3.43	6.63

Increasing implied volatility or time to maturity causes the terminal distribution to widen and hence the strikes are positioned further from the ATM:

Market Data Inputs	
Spot	100.00
CCY1 Interest Rate	0.0%
CCY2 Interest Rate	0.0%
Time to Maturity (years)	1.00

Smile Inputs	
ATM	20.0%
25d RR	0.0%
25d Fly	0.0%

Put Delta	10%	25%	50%	75%	90%
Implied Vol	20.00%	20.00%	20.00%	20.00%	20.00%
Strike	78.95	89.15	102.02	116.75	131.83
Strike Difference from ATM	-23.07	-12.87	0.00	14.73	29.81

Increasing the butterfly causes the strikes to move further from the ATM, with a larger impact at lower delta strikes due to the higher implied volatility:

Market Data Inputs	
Spot	100.00
CCY1 Interest Rate	0.0%
CCY2 Interest Rate	0.0%
Time to Maturity (years)	1.00

Smile Inputs	
ATM	10.0%
25d RR	0.0%
25d Fly	5.0%

Put Delta	10%	25%	50%	75%	90%
Implied Vol	22.80%	15.00%	10.00%	15.00%	22.80%
Strike	76.63	91.40	100.50	111.90	137.46
Strike Difference from ATM	-23.87	-9.10	0.00	11.40	36.96

Changing the risk reversal moves the strikes for a given delta further away from the ATM on the high side of the volatility smile and closer to the ATM on the low side of the volatility smile:

Market Data Inputs		Smile Inputs	
Spot	100.00	ATM	10.0%
CCY1 Interest Rate	0.0%	25d RR	5.0%
CCY2 Interest Rate	0.0%	25d Fly	0.0%
Time to Maturity (years)	1.00		

Put Delta	10%	25%	50%	75%	90%
Implied Vol	6.00%	7.50%	10.00%	12.50%	14.00%
Strike	92.77	95.33	100.50	109.65	120.83
Strike Difference from ATM	-7.74	-5.17	0.00	9.15	20.33

Moving CCY1 interest rates higher or CCY2 interest rates lower causes the forward to move lower and hence the whole volatility smile moves lower:

Market Data Inputs		Smile Inputs	
Spot	100.00	ATM	10.0%
CCY1 Interest Rate	10.0%	25d RR	0.0%
CCY2 Interest Rate	0.0%	25d Fly	0.0%
Time to Maturity (years)	1.00		

Put Delta	10%	25%	50%	75%	90%
Implied Vol	10.00%	10.00%	10.00%	10.00%	10.00%
Strike	80.46	85.69	92.15	100.00	117.38
Strike Difference from ATM	-11.68	-6.45	0.00	7.85	25.23

Moving CCY2 interest rates higher or CCY1 interest rates lower has the opposite effect.

CHAPTER 13

Probability Density Functions

A volatility smile at a given maturity can be converted into an equivalent probability density function (pdf). The probability density function contains useful information because integrating an area under the curve gives the likelihood of spot being within the given range at maturity.

Starting with the simplest case, Exhibit 13.1 shows a 1yr volatility smile with 10% volatility for all strikes (i.e., pure Black-Scholes world).

This volatility smile generates the standard log-normal bell-shaped pdf shown in Exhibit 13.2. The method of generating pdfs from option prices is explored in Practical G.

Exhibit 13.3 shows implied volatility rising to 15% for all strikes. Increased volatility widens the distribution and the pdf extends out on both sides as shown in Exhibit 13.4.

The area under the pdf represents a probability space. Therefore the total area under the pdf is always equal to 1 and the pdf function can never go negative. If the pdf does go negative, that indicates a potentially arbitrageable volatility surface. This can manifest itself in many different ways within pricing or risk management systems, most visibly via incorrect implied volatility or unstable gamma exposures.

Exhibit 13.5 shows how the volatility smile changes when positive wings are added.

As shown in Exhibit 13.6, higher wings in the volatility smile causes the pdf to rise in the wings (often called "fat tails") and rise around the ATM but fall in between,

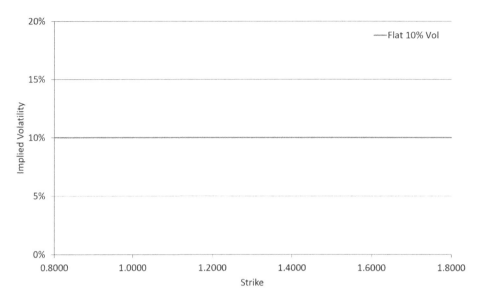

EXHIBIT 13.1   Volatility smile with flat 10% implied volatility

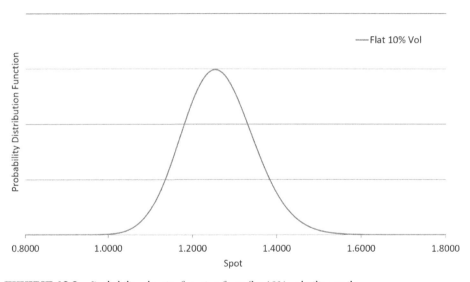

EXHIBIT 13.2   Probability density function from flat 10% volatility smile

although the total area under the pdf must remain unchanged. Distributions with this shape are known as **leptokurtotic** and they are often observed in financial markets.

Adding positive or negative skew causes the volatility smile to tilt one way or the other, as shown in Exhibit 13.7. The skew also causes the pdf to tilt. On the higher volatility side, the pdf stretches further as expected since the higher volatility causes

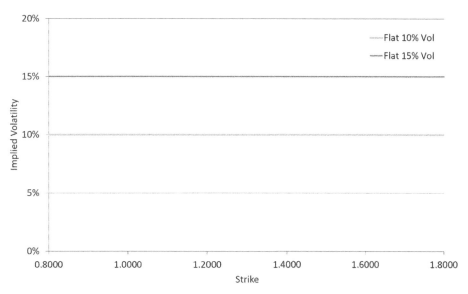

EXHIBIT 13.3   Volatility smiles with flat 10% and flat 15% implied volatility

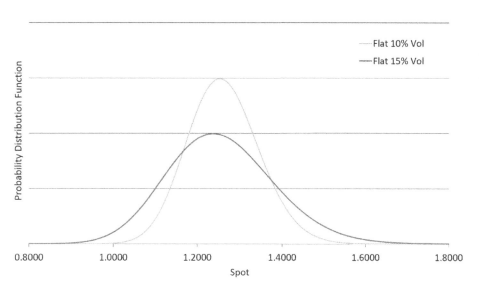

EXHIBIT 13.4   Probability density functions from flat 10% and flat 15% volatility smiles

the distribution to widen but the peak of the pdf moves the opposite direction. This occurs because the no-arbitrage condition ensures that the forward is the expected future value of spot. Therefore, if probability mass moves into the wings on one side of the smile due to higher volatility, the center of the probability mass must shift the other way. This is shown in Exhibit 13.8.

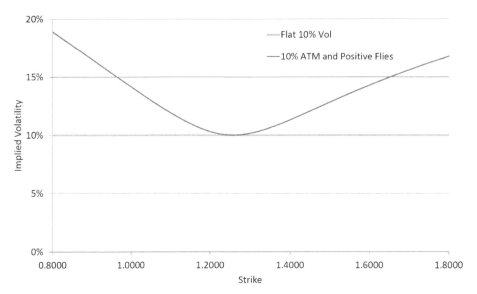

EXHIBIT 13.5 Volatility smiles with flat 10% and positive wing implied volatility

PROBABILITY DENSITY FUNCTIONS

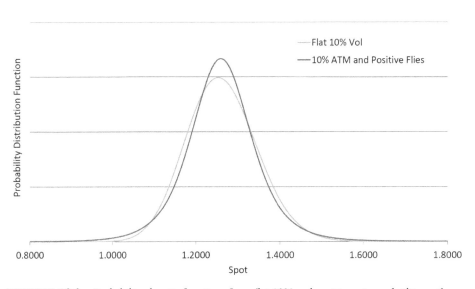

EXHIBIT 13.6 Probability density functions from flat 10% and positive wing volatility smiles

■ Fat-Tailed Distributions

The existence of fat-tailed distributions (i.e., excess kurtosis versus the normal distribution) in financial markets is a well-known phenomenon. Exhibit 13.9 shows the realized distribution of ten years of daily log-returns in USD/JPY spot versus the theoretical normal distribution with the same volatility.

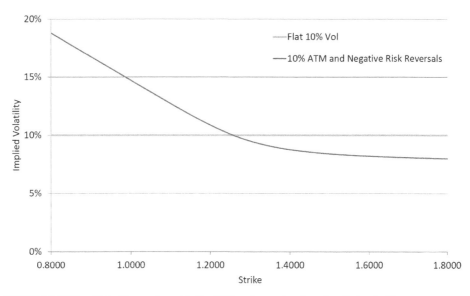

EXHIBIT 13.7 Volatility smiles with flat 10% and negative skew implied volatility

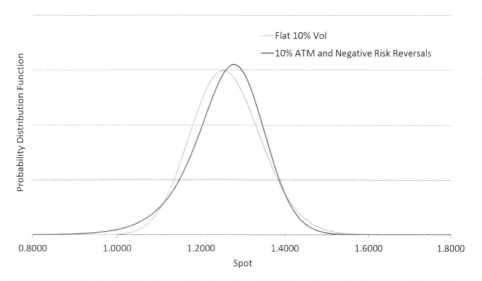

EXHIBIT 13.8 Probability density functions from flat 10% and negative skew volatility smiles

The difference around the peak is easy to see, but to see the wings more clearly a change to a log-scale for frequency is required as in Exhibit 13.10. Within this sample, the largest down moves occurred roughly ten million times more frequently than a normal distribution would suggest.

Fat tails in the spot distribution can be most easily explained by **volatility of volatility** (in freely floating currency pairs) or **spot jumps** (in emerging market

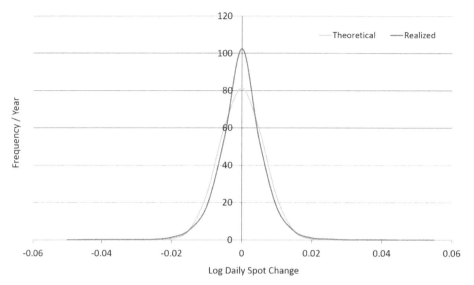

EXHIBIT 13.9 USD/JPY realized versus theoretical log daily change distribution (2003 to 2013)

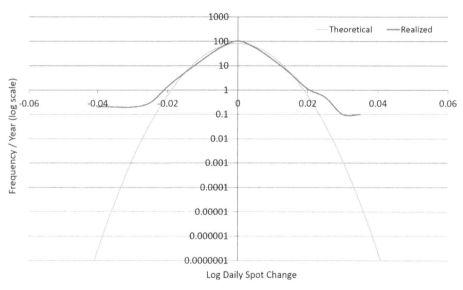

EXHIBIT 13.10 USD/JPY realized versus theoretical log daily change distribution (2003 to 2013/log scale)

or pegged/managed currency pairs). The reality is usually a combination of these two effects but for simplicity they tend to be applied in isolation within financial models (see Chapter 19).

To understand how volatility of volatility generates fatter tails within the spot distribution, consider a simple model where the spot diffusion has an equal chance of

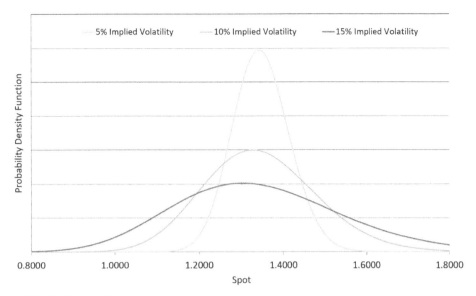

EXHIBIT 13.11   Three-state volatility model pdfs

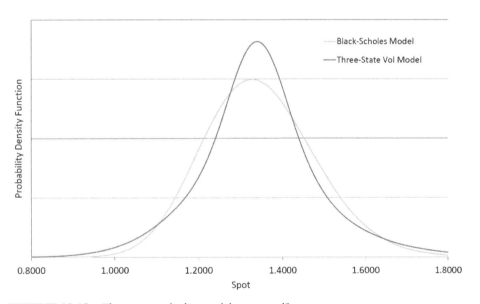

EXHIBIT 13.12   Three-state volatility model average pdf

having 5%, 10%, or 15% volatility. The three separate probability density functions are shown in Exhibit 13.11.

The probability density function of the three-state model is an equal combination of the three states. Therefore, Exhibit 13.12 shows how averaging the pdfs gives a fat-tailed pdf compared to a static 10% volatility distribution. The low-volatility state contributes the higher peak while the high-volatility state contributes the fatter tails.

The presence of spot jumps has a similar impact, pushing probability mass into the wings if a jump occurs and keeping it around current spot if a jump does not occur. As volatility of volatility increases or jumps increase in magnitude or frequency, the wings of the volatility smile move higher and the pdf gets fatter tails. See Chapter 19 for more details on FX derivatives pricing models.

■ Confidence Intervals

Probability density functions can also be used to generate confidence interval charts, which are an interesting way of visualizing how the volatility smile suggests spot may move in the future. For given probability intervals (e.g., 50% or 90%), the probability density function is queried for the appropriate spot levels. Exhibit 13.13 shows an example confidence interval chart in GBP/USD. The volatility surface suggests that, for example, there is a 50% chance of spot being within the 50% confidence interval bounds. Note how the bounds stretch further to the downside due to the downside skew in the GBP/USD volatility surface.

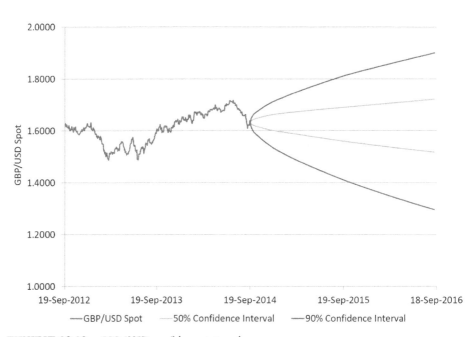

EXHIBIT 13.13   GBP/USD confidence intervals

Limitations of Volatility Smile Parameterization

Within FX derivatives trading desks, volatility smiles are expressed using a limited number of parameters. On some trading desks the five market instruments—ATM, 25d RR, 10d RR, 25d Fly, 10d Fly—are used; on others, perhaps just one ATM parameter, one wing parameter, and one skew parameter are used. In liquid currency pairs these reduced-form parameterizations work well and they allow a lot of information to be expressed in an efficient manner.

However, there are instances where these parameterizations cause problems. Exhibit 13.14 shows EUR/CHF spot from 2011 and 2012.

In mid-2011, EUR/CHF was freely floating and the EUR/CHF market instruments at June 1, 2011 were as per Exhibit 13.15.

The corresponding volatility smile and probability density function for 1yr EUR/CHF are shown in Exhibit 13.16. As expected, the higher implied volatility

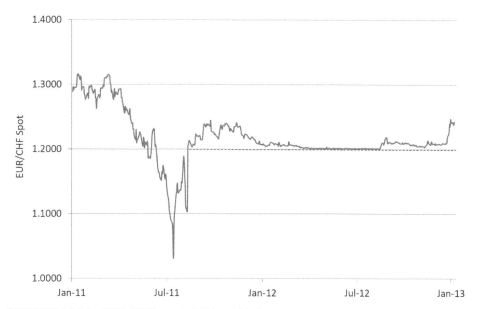

EXHIBIT 13.14   EUR/CHF spot in 2011 and 2012

EXHIBIT 13.15	EUR/CHF 1mth and 1yr Market Instruments at June 1, 2011				
Tenor	ATM	25d RR	10d RR	25d Fly	10d Fly
1mth	11.15%	−1.75%	−2.65%	0.25%	0.70%
1yr	12.10%	−3.45%	−6.05%	0.40%	1.85%

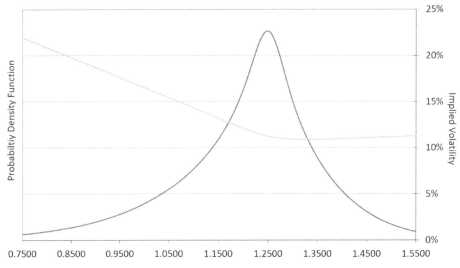

EXHIBIT 13.16 EUR/CHF 1yr implied volatility smile and pdf at June 1, 2011

for downside strikes (i.e., negative risk reversal) causes the probability density function to stretch more to the downside.

A series of interventions and announcements from late 2011 onward saw the Swiss central bank establish a floor in the spot market at 1.2000, which they actively defended (i.e., they bought EUR/CHF spot in the market in order to prevent it going below 1.2000) until early 2015.

While the floor was actively defended, what should the probability density function look like? In a vastly simplified world there are two scenarios that could potentially have played out:

1. The central bank successfully defends the 1.2000 level; spot floats freely above this level but cannot go any lower.
2. The central bank decides to change its policy, at which point spot could have a big adjustment lower.

Given these scenarios, the pdf would intuitively be expected to look like Exhibit 13.17. The most likely spot position in one year is close to, but above, the intervention level. Plus, the downside of the pdf has a longer tail, because if the intervention level was removed, there is significant risk of spot jumping lower, as happened in practice.

Exhibit 13.18 shows the market instruments one year later. The pdf derived from these quotes is overlaid onto the intuition in Exhibit 13.19.

When constructing volatility surfaces using a limited parameter set, only certain types of volatility smile can be generated. This means that only certain types of

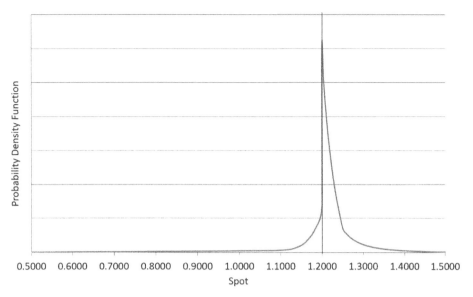

EXHIBIT 13.17   EUR/CHF 1yr intuitive pdf

EXHIBIT 13.18	**EUR/CHF 1mth and 1yr Market Instruments at June 1, 2012**				
Tenor	**ATM**	**25d RR**	**10d RR**	**25d Fly**	**10d Fly**
1mth	2.00%	−0.70%	−1.40%	1.15%	3.75%
1yr	6.70%	−4.60%	−9.65%	1.80%	6.10%

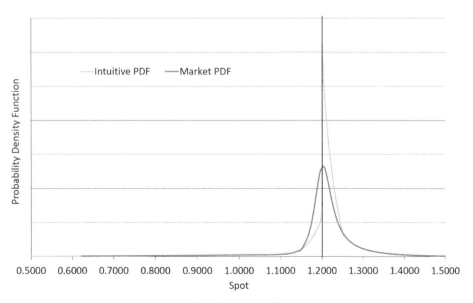

EXHIBIT 13.19   EUR/CHF 1yr actual and intuitive pdfs at June 1, 2012

unimodal (i.e., single peaked) probability density function can be generated, which presents a problem in currency pairs with more complex spot dynamics. In currency pairs where there is a peg, floor, intervention level, or similar, a more complex pdf would often better fit reality. Ideally the volatility surface construction should take into account the fact that spot ending just inside an intervention level is significantly more likely than spot ending just beyond an intervention level but there is no way to include this information within standard parameterizations.

The typical warning sign of this issue is that market instruments hit the correct market values but the implied volatility for individual strikes around key spot levels does not match the market, or vice versa.

Generating a Probability Density Function from Option Prices in Excel

This practical introduces a method of generating a probability density function from a volatility smile by numerically differentiating vanilla option prices twice with respect to the strike. The code reuses volatility smile functions developed in Practical F and vanilla options pricing functions developed in Practical C. Probability density functions are explored in detail within Chapter 13.

First, volatility smile inputs and market data must be defined within the Excel sheet. Then a range of delta values is established, from 0.1% to 99.9% in tight steps of 0.1%:

Market Data Inputs

Spot	100.00	←*Named:* **Spot**
CCY1 Interest Rate	0.0%	←*Named:* **rCCY1**
CCY2 Interest Rate	0.0%	←*Named:* **rCCY2**
Time to Maturity (years)	1.00	←*Named:* **T**

Populate Smile

Volatility Smile Inputs

ATM	10.0%	←*Named:* **ATM**
25d RR	0.0%	←*Named:* **RR25d**
25d Fly	2.0%	←*Named:* **Fly25d**

↓ *Named:* **VolatilitySmileRef**

Put Delta	Implied Vol	Strike
0.10%		
0.20%		
0.30%		
0.40%		
0.50%		
0.60%		
0.70%		

The implied volatility and strike must be calculated for each delta value. Due to the amount of data on the sheet it is better to use a VBA subroutine to calculate the values and place them on the sheet surface. The MalzSmileVol and StrikeFromPutDelta functions from Practical F can being used. Note that StrikeFromPutDelta takes a negative put delta value as input:

```
Sub populateSmileStrikesAndVols()

    Dim InputPutDelta As Double
    Dim ImpliedVol As Double
    Dim DeltaCount As Long

    DeltaCount = 1
    While Range("VolatilitySmileRef").Offset(DeltaCount, 0) <> ""
        InputPutDelta = Range("VolatilitySmileRef").Offset(DeltaCount, 0)
        ImpliedVol = MalzSmileVol(Range("ATM"), Range("RR25d"), _
         Range("Fly25d"), InputPutDelta)
        Range("VolatilitySmileRef").Offset(DeltaCount, 1) = ImpliedVol
        Range("VolatilitySmileRef").Offset(DeltaCount, 2) = _
         StrikeFromPutDelta(Range("Spot"), -InputPutDelta, _
         Range("rCCY1"), Range("rCCY2"), Range("T"), ImpliedVol)
        DeltaCount = DeltaCount + 1
    Wend

End Sub
```

GENERATING A PROBABILITY DENSITY FUNCTION

Next, in a new column, define equally spaced strikes for calculating the probability density function (pdf):

↓ Named: **StrikeRef**

Strike	Implied Vol	Put Price (CCY2 pips)
70.00	17.5%	0.1108
70.50	17.4%	0.1220
71.00	17.4%	0.1340
71.50	17.3%	0.1469
72.00	17.3%	0.1606
72.50	17.2%	0.1752
73.00	17.1%	0.1908

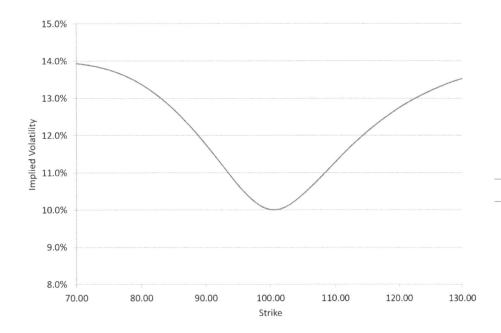

A VBA function is used to calculate the implied volatility and equivalent option price at each strike level. It is okay to use linear interpolation to generate the implied volatility since delta has small increments. The OptionPrice function from Practical C is reused:

```
Sub populatePDFImpliedVolsAndPrices()

    Dim PDFStrikeCount As Long, SmileDeltaCount As Long
```

```
Dim LowStrike As Double, HighStrike As Double
Dim LowVol As Double, HighVol As Double

Dim InputStrike As Double, ImpliedVol As Double

PDFStrikeCount = 1
While Range("StrikeRef").Offset(PDFStrikeCount, 0) <> ""
    InputStrike = Range("StrikeRef").Offset(PDFStrikeCount, 0)
    ImpliedVol = -1
    SmileDeltaCount = 1
    While Range("VolatilitySmileRef").Offset(SmileDeltaCount + 1, 0) _
     <> ""
        LowVol = Range("VolatilitySmileRef").Offset(SmileDeltaCount, 1)
        HighVol = Range("VolatilitySmileRef").Offset(SmileDeltaCount _
         + 1, 1)
        LowStrike = Range("VolatilitySmileRef") _
         .Offset(SmileDeltaCount, 2)
        HighStrike = Range("VolatilitySmileRef") _
         .Offset(SmileDeltaCount + 1, 2)

        'Linear Interpolation to get Implied Vol
        If (InputStrike > LowStrike) And (InputStrike _
         < HighStrike) Then
            ImpliedVol = LowVol + (HighVol - LowVol) * (InputStrike - _
             LowStrike) / (HighStrike - LowStrike)
        End If

        SmileDeltaCount = SmileDeltaCount + 1
    Wend

    Range("StrikeRef").Offset(PDFStrikeCount, 1) = ImpliedVol
    Range("StrikeRef").Offset(PDFStrikeCount, 2) = _
     OptionPrice(False, Range("Spot"), InputStrike, Range("T"), _
     Range("rCCY1"), Range("rCCY2"), ImpliedVol)

    PDFStrikeCount = PDFStrikeCount + 1
Wend

End Sub
```

The probability density can now be calculated by finding the second derivative of price with respect to strike on the sheet:

	Strike	Implied Vol	Put Price (CCY2 pips)	dStrike =F17-F16	dPrice =H17-H16	dPrice/dStrike =J17/I17	d (dPrice/dStrike) =K18-K17	↓ Probability Density d (dPrice/dStrike) /dStrike =L18/I18
13								
14								
15								
16	70.00	13.9%	0.0193					
17	70.50	13.9%	0.0226	0.50	0.0033	0.0066		
18	71.00	13.9%	0.0263	0.50	0.0037	0.0075	0.0009	0.0018
19	71.50	13.9%	0.0306	0.50	0.0042	0.0085	0.0010	0.0020
20	72.00	13.9%	0.0354	0.50	0.0048	0.0096	0.0011	0.0022

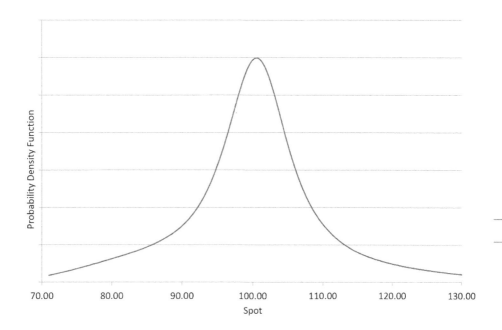

Note that the probability density (second derivative of option value with respect to strike) takes a similar shape to that of gamma (second derivative of option value with respect to spot).

Probability density functions can then be compared by copying the output values. When making changes to the volatility smile or market data inputs, remember to rerun both VBA subroutines in order to correctly set up the calculation.

Flat volatility smile versus long wings volatility smile:

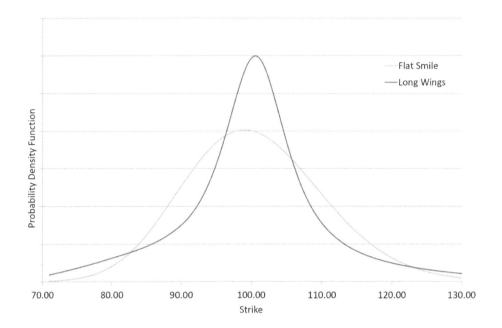

Flat volatility smile versus long topside risk reversal volatility smile:

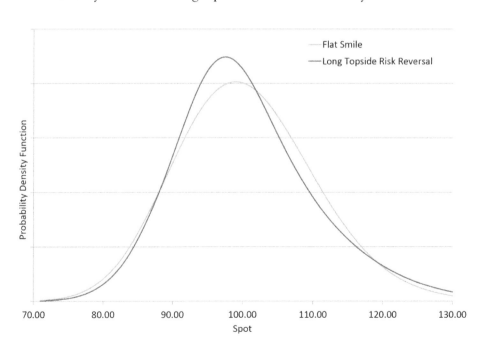

Finally, as discussed in Chapter 13, the area under the probability density function should equal one since it represents a probability mass. This can be checked by multiplying the average pdf between strikes by the change in strike at each strike level and summing the total. This indicates how accurate the output is. If the strike spacings are tight enough, the total probability value should be between 0.99 and 1.01.

PART III

VANILLA FX DERIVATIVES TRADING

The material up to this point has been developed within a stylized framework. This is important because the increased clarity makes learning easier. However, it is now time to confront some of the real-world issues faced by vanilla FX derivatives traders.

CHAPTER 14

Vanilla FX Derivatives Trading Exposures

In Part I, Greek exposures were examined within a stylized framework. In practice, even the simplest Greek exposures have additional layers of complexity that must be understood by FX derivatives traders within their risk management.

▎ Delta

Delta (Δ) is one of the most important exposures to a derivatives trader—the sensitivity of price to a change in the underlying. It is a simple concept but there are many possible variations in exactly what the delta exposure represents.

Spot Delta versus Forward Delta

Apologies if this is obvious, but the spot delta on a spot deal is 100% of the notional. Therefore, buying GBP50m GBP/USD spot results in longer GBP50m GBP/USD spot delta exposure within the trading position. For this reason, FX spot traders talk only in terms of net long or short positions, rather than their exposures. The forward delta on a forward outright contract is 100% of the notional. Selling USD100m of 1yr USD/CAD forward outright results in a shorter USD100m USD/CAD 1yr forward delta exposure within the trading position.

Delta exposures can be present valued or future valued like cash flows. Therefore, on a specific trade:

$$\Delta = \Delta_F \cdot df$$

where df is the discount factor in the delta currency to the forward maturity, Δ is the spot delta, and Δ_F is the forward delta. When interest rates in the delta currency are positive (as they usually are), the discount factor is below 1 and $|\Delta| < |\Delta_F|$. For example, buying AUD50m of AUD/USD 5yr forward outright has a spot delta exposure of approximately AUD42m when the 5yr AUD discount factor is around 0.84. This means that, for example, when AUD100m of spot versus AUD100m of forward is traded in an equal notional FX swap, a residual spot delta exposure remains.

Spot delta is the delta exposure most often used within FX derivatives risk management because spot is most often used to hedge delta, particularly in G10 currency pairs. When this is the case, exposures to interest rates and swap points must be additionally monitored.

Delta Quoting Conventions

Traders most often quote option delta in CCY1% or CCY1 cash terms with CCY1 determined by market convention for that currency pair. Spot and forward deals are generally traded in CCY1 terms, so when the option delta is also given in CCY1 terms the hedge amount and direction are immediately clear. For example, an option has *long* CCY1 delta exposure: *Sell* spot on the hedge. Quoting delta in CCY2 terms can cause mistakes. For example, if the delta on a GBP/USD option is quoted as *short* USD16m, the delta hedge at current spot would be to *sell* GBP10m GBP/USD.

To convert CCY1% spot delta to CCY2% spot delta the following formula is used:

$$\Delta_{CCY1\%} = -\Delta_{CCY2\%} \cdot \frac{S}{K}$$

where S is spot and K is the strike. Note that when $S = K$, the delta is unchanged between CCY1% and CCY2% terms.

To convert CCY1% forward delta to CCY2% forward delta the following formula is used:

$$\Delta_{F\ CCY1\%} = -\Delta_{F\ CCY2\%} \cdot \frac{F}{K}$$

where F is the forward.

The negative signs are present within these formulas because CCY1 is bought while CCY2 is sold, or vice versa within an FX transaction.

CCY1 versus CCY2 Premium Delta

The standard delta profile for a long vanilla call option goes from 0% (with spot far below the strike) to +100% (with spot far above the strike), hitting +50% around the ATM, as shown in Exhibit 14.1.

This analysis assumes that the option premium is paid in CCY2 (the domestic currency). If the option premium is paid in CCY1 (the foreign currency), the delta exposure changes.

In USD/JPY, consider a long USD call option with JPY as the natural P&L currency but premium paid in USD by market convention. When buying this option, an additional *short USD delta* exposure is generated since USD are paid out in the premium.

In general:

$$\Delta_{CCY1\ Premium} = \Delta_{CCY2\ Premium} - Premium$$

where delta and premium are quoted in the same terms.

The intuition that the inclusion of premium moves delta shorter is as follows:

- At lower spot, the USD premium will be relatively cheaper to pay in JPY (domestic) terms.

- At higher spot, the USD premium will be relatively more expensive to pay in JPY (domestic) terms.

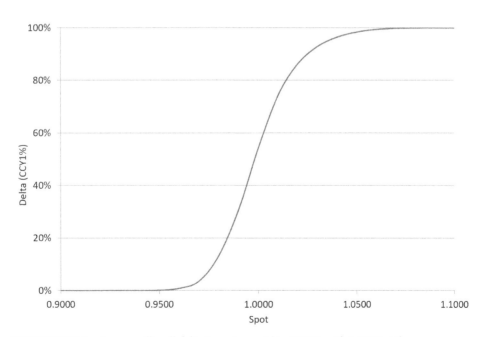

EXHIBIT 14.1   Long vanilla call delta (premium paid in CCY2) with 1.0000 strike

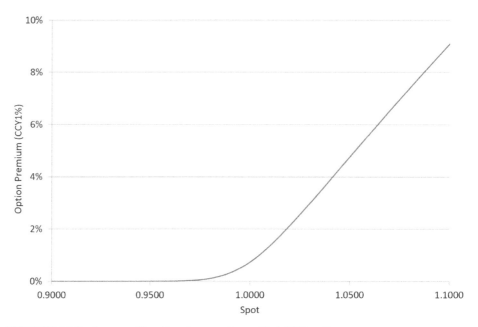

EXHIBIT 14.2 Long vanilla call option premium with 1.0000 strike

The long call CCY1% option premium profile is shown in Exhibit 14.2. The delta adjustment will be particularly large when the option is deep in-the-money and therefore has a large premium. This is shown in Exhibit 14.3. At longer tenors this effect can cause the delta of ATM options to be far away from the stylized 50%.

For a long put option, the stylized delta profile goes from –100% (with spot far below the strike) to 0% (with spot far above the strike). Again, a CCY1 premium causes an additional short delta, which this time has a larger impact with spot in-the-money to the downside as shown in Exhibit 14.4.

The premium currency in a particular currency pair is determined by market convention. If the currency pair contains USD, then the premium currency will be USD. Other G10 currencies can be approximately ordered: EUR > GBP > AUD > NZD > CAD > CHF > NOK > SEK > JPY.

In G10 versus emerging market currency pairs, the premium is usually paid in the G10 currency.

Delta Bleed

Greek exposures within derivatives trading positions do not stay constant over time. Traders therefore investigate how exposures change (bleed) over the next few trading days. Specifically, traders roll the horizon date forward near the end of the

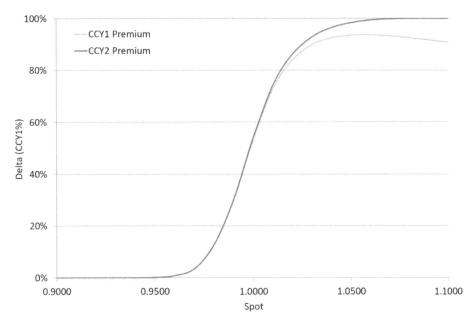

EXHIBIT 14.3 Long vanilla call option delta (premium paid in CCY1 or CCY2) with
1.0000 strike

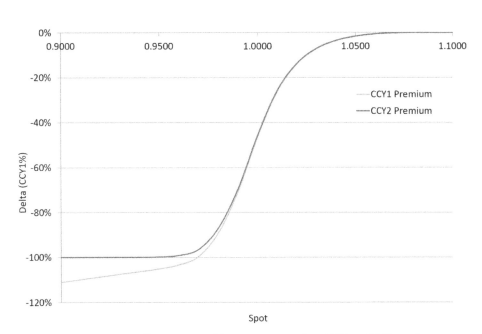

EXHIBIT 14.4 Long vanilla put option delta (premium paid in CCY1 or CCY2) with
1.0000 strike

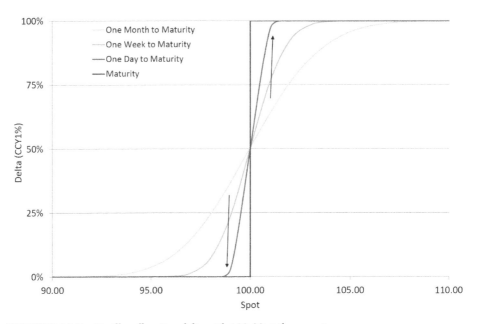

EXHIBIT 14.5 Vanilla call option delta with 100.00 strike over time

day to see how their position will look on the next trading day. This allows them to assess position bleed, particularly **delta bleed**.

Exhibit 14.5 shows how delta on a vanilla call option changes over time. Prior to the expiry date there are three possible cases for the relative positioning of spot and the strike of a long vanilla call option:

- For an out-of-the-money (OTM) spot (i.e., spot below strike), delta bleeds shorter.

- For an at-the-money (ATM) spot (i.e., spot close to the strike), delta remains roughly unchanged over time.

- For an in-the-money (ITM) spot (i.e., spot above strike), delta bleeds longer.

    Example: EUR/USD spot: 1.3650.

- 7-day 1.3750 EUR call/USD put: 31% delta

- 6-day 1.3750 EUR call/USD put: 29% delta (i.e., -2% delta bleed)

Intuitively this makes sense when delta is thought of as the chance of ending up in-the-money at maturity. Lower time to maturity gives spot less time to move through the strike. Therefore:

- For an OTM option, as time to expiry shortens, the probability of ending up ITM at maturity (and hence the delta) reduces.

- For an ATM option, as time to expiry shortens, the probability of ending up ITM at maturity (and hence the delta) remains roughly unchanged at approximately 50%.

- For an ITM option, as time to expiry shortens, the probability of ending up ITM at maturity (and hence the delta) increases.

For a long put option the ITM versus OTM side is switched (e.g., spot below the strike is OTM for a call but ITM for a put) but additionally, put deltas are negative so the delta bleed on call options and put options ends up being equivalent, as expected due to put–call parity.

Example: EUR/USD spot: 1.3650.

- 7-day 1.3750 EUR put/USD call: −69% delta

- 6-day 1.3750 EUR put/USD call: −71% delta (i.e., −2% delta bleed)

The delta bleed for a particular strike increases as the expiry date approaches with the most dramatic delta bleed occurring into the expiry date itself. On vanilla options with large notionals, traders pay close attention to these delta changes.

Consider a long call option:

- On the day before maturity, if spot is slightly above the strike, delta will be approximately +50%. On the expiry date itself and with spot unchanged delta will be +100% above the strike. Therefore, delta bleed will be +50% of the option notional.

- On the day before maturity, if spot is slightly below the strike, delta will be approximately +50%. On the expiry date itself and with spot unchanged delta will be 0% below the strike. Therefore, delta bleed will be −50% of the option notional.

Generally, delta bleed *assists* traders with their risk management:

- If the trading position is mainly long downside or short topside vanilla options, delta will bleed longer.

- If the trading position is mainly long topside or short downside vanilla options, delta will bleed shorter.

In each of these scenarios, the delta bleed matches a natural risk management preference to run delta into short gamma areas (i.e., running long delta if short topside gamma) and to run delta away from long gamma areas (i.e., running long delta if long downside gamma). Delta bleed therefore often helps to produce a balanced P&L profile.

■ Gamma and Theta

As discussed in Chapter 9, buying vanilla options produces long gamma exposures, which costs theta over time. Selling vanilla options produces short gamma exposures, which earns theta over time.

Gamma (Γ) is the rate at which delta changes as spot moves and in risk management tools it is usually quoted for a 1% move in spot.

Theta (θ) is the rate at which price changes over time and in risk management tools it is usually quoted as the P&L from a *one-day shift* forward in the horizon date. It therefore represents the net cost (negative theta) or net benefit (positive theta) from holding the trading position for one full trading day. This seems clear enough but it is important that traders know what assumptions are used within the calculation. For example, what happens to the implied volatility and interest rate curves as the horizon date rolls forward?

In practice, cumulative position value changes with time in two different ways. First, when the horizon is rolled forward, there is a P&L jump (i.e., theta). This P&L jump will be particularly large for slightly out-of-the-money vanilla options expiring on the new horizon date. Second, throughout the day, implied volatility moving lower at shorter maturities is an additional source of value change (as per Chapter 11).

Under Black-Scholes, gamma and theta are linked by this formula:

$$\theta = -\frac{1}{2}\Gamma \sigma^2 S^2$$

where σ is volatility and S is spot. The negative sign exists because, for example, long (positive) gamma causes paying (negative) theta.

Looking at the formula, gamma and (negative) theta are proportional ($\Gamma \propto -\theta$). This makes intuitive sense because, e.g., long gamma gives the ability to make money out of spot moves and the more delta changes as spot moves, the more money can be made from delta hedging. Put another way, more theta must be paid for the privilege of more long gamma.

Since gamma and theta are proportional, the theta profile shown in Exhibit 14.6 takes an identical shape to the corresponding gamma profile; rising into the strike at maturity.

The next thing to note from the gamma-theta formula is that for the same amount of gamma, higher volatility (σ) causes theta to rise negatively. Intuitively, vanilla options have higher premium at higher implied volatility and therefore they have more value to decay away.

Additionally, for the same amount of theta, higher volatility causes lower gamma. To understand why, consider the delta profile: If volatility is low, there will be a big delta change over a given spot change, whereas if volatility is high, there will

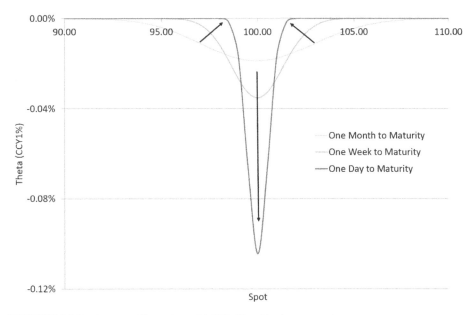

EXHIBIT 14.6 Long vanilla option with 100.00 strike theta over time

be a much smaller delta change over the same fixed spot change. During the 2008 financial crisis, buying 1mth AUD/JPY ATM at 50% volatility gave 3% gamma while buying 1mth USD/HKD ATM today at 0.25% volatility gives 490% gamma.

Traders actively track the gamma/theta ratio in their trading positions. Within the Black-Scholes framework, theta simply pays for gamma, but in practice theta comes from different aspects of the trading position.

ATM Curve and Volatility Smile Roll Theta

Over time, options roll down the ATM curve as an option maturity goes from, for example, 365 days to 364 days, and so on. If the ATM curve is upward sloping (i.e., 1yr ATM higher than 1mth ATM), this effect causes additional theta to be paid on long vanilla option positions (and additional theta to be earned on short vanilla option positions) as the ATM implied volatility drops over time as the expiry date moves closer to the horizon. If the ATM curve is downward sloping (e.g., 1yr ATM lower than 1mth ATM), the opposite effect occurs. The more steeply sloped the ATM curve, the larger the impact. Exhibit 14.7 demonstrates the ATM curve roll process.

In practice, this effect occurs within the entire volatility surface as all strikes roll to closer maturities.

Forward Roll Theta

With everything else fixed constant, but the horizon shifted forward by one day, the forward outright to a fixed expiry date drifts toward spot. For a given option this is

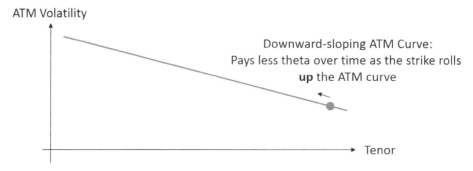

ATM Volatility

Downward-sloping ATM Curve:
Pays less theta over time as the strike rolls
up the ATM curve

Tenor

EXHIBIT 14.7   ATM curve roll

similar to a free spot move equal to the one-day swap points. The P&L impact from this is only a small part of the total option theta, but in high interest rate differential currency pairs it can be important.

Cash Balance Theta

Consider what happens when spot deals in a derivatives trading position settle at maturity. Long AUD10m 0.9500 AUD/USD spot settles into long AUD10m and short USD9.5m on the spot date. Cash balances from settled spot or forward deals, option premiums, or other cash payments accumulate in a trading position over time. These cash balances can be managed by putting long cash balances on deposit, hence earning interest on the cash and borrowing to offset short cash balances, hence paying interest on the cash. Alternatively, FX swaps can be traded, usually against the USD, to push cash balances into the future. It is important that traders know how to monitor these cash balances in their position and understand how they are managed day-to-day.

Smile Gamma

One aspect of a trading position with a significant impact on the gamma/theta ratio is the *smile position*. Owning options high on the volatility smile results in a lower gamma/theta ratio due to the higher implied volatility (recall the gamma-theta formula). This can be thought of as one of the costs of holding a long smile position. In high-skew currency pairs, long smile positions are expensive to hold over time.

Vanilla traders sometimes look at their gamma exposure calculated from vanilla options valued using the ATM curve (called *ATM gamma*) and compare it to the gamma exposure calculated from options valued using the full volatility surface. The difference is the **smile gamma effect**; the amount of gamma coming from the smile:

- If the trading position is mainly long vanilla options priced at higher implied volatility and/or short vanilla options priced at lower implied volatility on the smile, the net smile gamma effect will be negative.

- If the trading position is mainly long vanilla options priced at lower implied volatility and/or short vanilla options priced at higher implied volatility on the smile, the net smile gamma effect will be positive.

A common issue for risk managers is a low gamma/theta ratio within their trading position. To fix this issue, traders search for options in their position with large negative smile gamma effect. It is worth noting that in currency pairs where the smile is high compared to the volatility base, this approach can overlook options that have very low premiums priced using the ATM volatility (e.g., up to 0.02%) but higher premiums priced using the smile volatility (e.g., 0.10% to 0.20%). These options have almost no smile gamma effect (they contain little gamma of any kind because they are low delta), yet long positions in them can contribute significant negative theta.

P&L Distributions from Long Gamma or Short Gamma

On a given trading day in a stylized Black-Scholes world, the maximum P&L that can be *lost* from a long gamma trading position (ignoring P&L from vega, rho, new deals, etc.) is theta while more (potentially much more) can be made if spot is highly volatile. Exhibit 14.8 shows the P&L distribution from a long gamma position; it contains many small losses and few large gains, although the expectation of the distribution is zero.

Similarly, the most P&L that can be *made* from a short gamma trading position is theta while (much) more can be lost if spot is highly volatile. Exhibit 14.9 shows

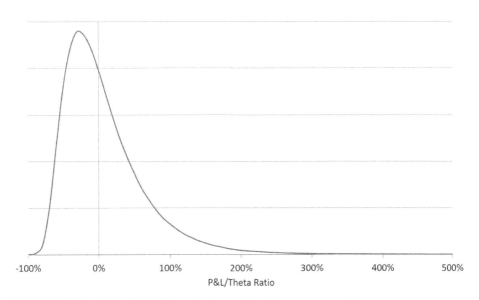

P&L/Theta Ratio

EXHIBIT 14.8   Stylized P&L/theta distribution from long gamma position

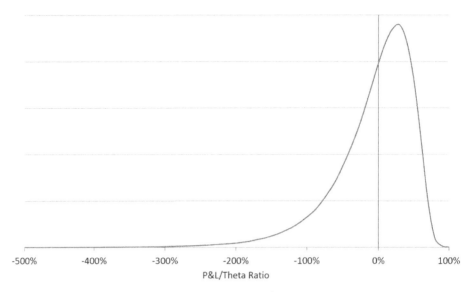

P&L/Theta Ratio

EXHIBIT 14.9   Stylized P&L/theta distribution from short gamma position

the P&L distribution from a short gamma position: It contains many small gains and few large losses, although, again, the expectation of the distribution is zero.

Preference for a long or short gamma P&L distribution impacts how risk managers position their trading books. Some traders prefer to trade long gamma positions while others prefer to trade short gamma positions. In a job interview, though, the correct answer is obviously that you are equally happy trading with whichever gamma position gives the best risk/reward at the time.

■ Vega and Weighted Vega

The most important exposure on most derivatives contracts is vega. Like delta, vega discounts in the currency it is expressed, so while stylized vega generally changes proportionally to the square root of time, in practice discounting can have a large effect at longer maturities. It is therefore not safe to assume that vega on ATM contracts always increases at longer maturities. For example, Exhibit 14.10 shows long-dated AUD/JPY ATM vega.

Traders most often view vega exposures in CCY1 terms, but sometimes vega will be viewed in CCY2 if that is the P&L currency. For example, in EUR/USD, a vega exposure quoted in USD may be preferred.

A standard vega calculation assumes the ATM curve moves in parallel. A **weighted vega** calculation assumes the ATM curve moves proportional to $\frac{1}{\sqrt{t}}$. If the ATM curve moves in a weighted manner, it is therefore expected that, for

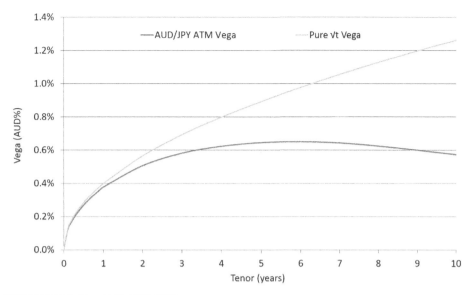

EXHIBIT 14.10   AUD/JPY ATM vega

example, the 3mth ATM moves twice as much as the 1yr ATM. This links to vega exposures where 3mth ATM vega is half that of the 1yr ATM.

The weighted vega calculation folds all exposures into a single reference pillar (usually 1mth or 3mth depending on which tenor is most liquid in a particular currency pair). For example, a 3mth weighted vega of USD400k implies that the full vega exposure in the position is equivalent to a vega exposure of USD400k *in the 3mth tenor*. It is therefore important to know which reference pillar the weighted vega calculation uses.

The following formula is used to convert vega (v) at time t into weighted vega ($v_{weighted}$) at the weighted reference time $t_{weighted}$.

$$v_{weighted} = \sqrt{\frac{t_{weighted}}{t}} \cdot v$$

Exhibit 14.11 gives vega multipliers for converting bucketed vega at market tenors into 1mth weighted vega. The same methodology can also be used to calculate weighted vega on each option individually.

If the ATM curve is moving in a parallel manner, *vega* will most accurately predict P&L changes caused by changes to the ATM curve, whereas if the ATM curve is moving in a weighted manner, *weighted vega* will most accurately predict P&L changes caused by changes to the ATM curve. Most often, the ATM curve moves in *neither* a parallel nor weighted manner but some combination of the two. Traders therefore view both measures within their risk management and assess how the ATM curve is currently moving when deciding which exposure to pay closest attention to.

EXHIBIT 14.11 Weighted Vega Multipliers (1mth reference)

Tenor	t (years)	$\sqrt{t}$	Weighted Vega Multipliers (1mth reference)
O/N	0.00274	0.052342	5.515
1wk	0.01923	0.138675	2.082
2wk	0.03846	0.196116	1.472
1mth	0.08333	0.288675	1.000
2mth	0.16667	0.408248	0.707
3mth	0.25000	0.500000	0.577
6mth	0.50000	0.707107	0.408
9mth	0.75000	0.866025	0.333
1yr	1.00000	1.000000	0.289
2yr	2.00000	1.414214	0.204
5yr	5.00000	2.236068	0.129

■ Adapted Greeks

Greek exposures for vanilla options can be calculated using a **sticky strike** or a **sticky delta** methodology.

Under sticky strike, the implied volatility for a given expiry date and *strike* stays constant as the forward moves. Standard Black-Scholes Greeks are calculated assuming a sticky strike methodology since only one constant volatility is used within the Black-Scholes framework.

Under sticky delta, the implied volatility for a given expiry date and *delta* stays constant as the forward moves. These so-called **adapted Greeks** are calculated assuming a sticky delta methodology.

It is important that traders understand the differences between standard exposures and adapted exposures so they can risk manage using the correct exposures given prevailing market behavior.

Throughout this analysis, *Black-Scholes delta* refers to the delta calculated under Black-Scholes using the smile volatility and it is easiest to think of the delta on a long vanilla call option when following these logical arguments.

Adapted Delta

Consider a finite difference spot delta calculation in which spot is flexed up and down a small amount and the resultant premium change is divided by the spot flex to calculate delta. In the standard Black-Scholes delta calculation, the implied volatility at which the vanilla is valued remains constant but in an adapted delta calculation the implied volatility for the fixed strike changes as spot flexes up and down: This is the **adaption**.

Adapted delta is such a well-accepted concept within the FX derivatives market that in some emerging market currency pairs, risk reversals are traded in the interbank broker market with an adapted delta forward hedge.

In symbols:

$$\Delta_{Black-Scholes} = \frac{\partial P(S)}{\partial S}$$

$$\Delta_{Adapted} = \frac{dP(S, \ \sigma(S))}{dS} = \frac{\partial P}{\partial S} + \frac{\partial P}{\partial \sigma}.\frac{d\sigma}{dS} = \Delta_{Black-Scholes} + v.\frac{d\sigma}{dS}$$

The formula for adapted delta comes from the chain rule. In words, adapted delta is equal to Black-Scholes delta plus vega (v) multiplied by the change in implied volatility for a change in spot. To understand this $\frac{d\sigma}{dS}$ quantity, consider a finite difference delta calculation within a volatility smile with the risk reversal *for downside* shown in Exhibit 14.12.

Within the volatility smile:

■ When spot is flexed *up*, the whole volatility smile moves higher with the flex and the fixed strike rolls up to a *higher* implied volatility. This makes the vanilla option premium relatively higher.

■ When spot is flexed *down*, the whole volatility smile moves lower with the flex and the fixed strike rolls down to a *lower* implied volatility. This makes the vanilla option premium relatively lower.

Therefore, $\frac{d\sigma}{dS}$ is positive.

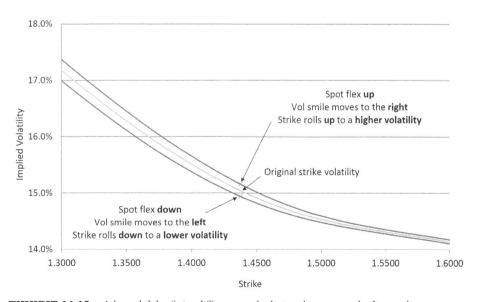

EXHIBIT 14.12 Adapted delta finite difference calculation shown on volatility smile

Looking back at the adapted delta formula, vega (v) for a long vanilla option is always positive. Therefore, the direction of the adapted delta versus Black-Scholes delta difference comes from the $\frac{d\sigma}{dS}$ quantity. The whole volatility smile moves with spot under the adaption:

■ If implied volatility increases at lower strikes, the implied volatility for a fixed strike will rise as spot rises and $\frac{d\sigma}{dS}$ will be positive (as in the previous example).

■ If implied volatility increases at higher strikes, the implied volatility for a fixed strike will fall as spot rises and $\frac{d\sigma}{dS}$ will be negative.

In addition, vega decreases away from the strike so Black-Scholes delta versus adapted delta differences reduce to zero in the wings.

Therefore, in a currency pair with relatively higher skew and lower wings:

■ If the risk reversal is for *topside*, adapted delta is usually *shorter* than Black-Scholes delta.

■ If the risk reversal is for *downside*, adapted delta is usually *longer* than Black-Scholes delta.

In a currency pair with relatively higher wings and lower skew, adapted delta versus Black-Scholes delta differences change sharply over different spot levels around the ATM. Exhibit 14.13 shows a symmetric volatility smile with zero skew and positive wings.

When an ATM contract is traded, the implied volatility will be at the lowest point of the volatility smile, technically called "at the bottom of the bucket."

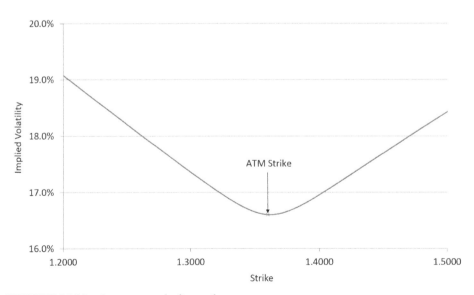

EXHIBIT 14.13   Symmetric volatility smile

If spot moves higher, the volatility smile at the fixed strike becomes locally sloped higher to the downside, hence $\frac{d\sigma}{dS}$ is positive and:

$$\Delta_{Adapted} > \Delta_{Black-Scholes}$$

If spot moves lower, the volatility smile at the fixed strike becomes locally sloping up to the topside, hence $\frac{d\sigma}{dS}$ is negative and:

$$\Delta_{Adapted} < \Delta_{Black-Scholes}$$

Adapted Gamma

Adapted gamma takes into account how a fixed strike rolls around the volatility smile in exactly the same way as adapted delta does. The important measure from a risk management perspective is the **gamma adaption effect**—the difference between adapted gamma and Black-Scholes gamma.

Consider a symmetric volatility smile with no skew but positive wings. The adapted gamma argument is visualized in Exhibit 14.14.

As described in the previous section on adapted delta, for a strike that is initially ATM:

- Spot flexed higher → fixed strike becomes downside → $\Delta_{Adapted} > \Delta_{Black-Scholes}$
- Spot flexed lower → fixed strike becomes topside → $\Delta_{Adapted} < \Delta_{Black-Scholes}$

Therefore, under adaption, delta moves more for both up and down spot flexes. Hence around the ATM point there is *positive* gamma adaption effect and the

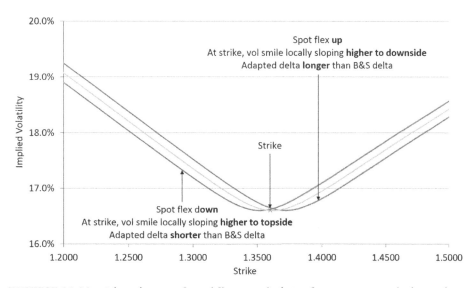

EXHIBIT 14.14   Adapted gamma finite difference calculation for a symmetric volatility smile

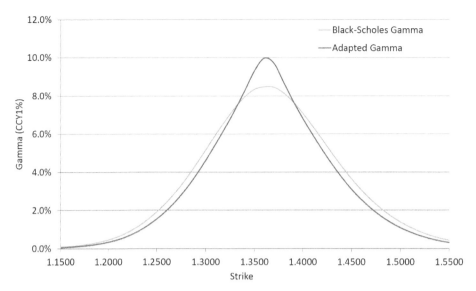

EXHIBIT 14.15 Adapted gamma versus Black-Scholes gamma in a symmetric volatility smile

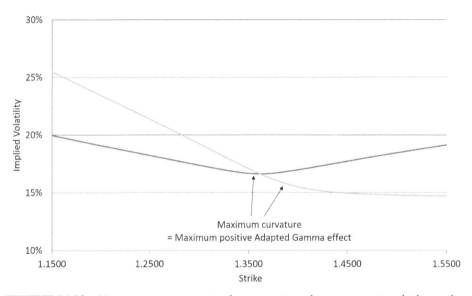

EXHIBIT 14.16 Maximum curvature points for symmetric and non-symmetric volatility smiles

effect is larger the more pronounced the wings of the smile. Exhibit 14.15 shows Black-Scholes gamma and adapted gamma for an ATM strike within a symmetric volatility smile.

The largest positive gamma adaption effect occurs at the point of maximum curvature in the volatility smile (i.e., maximum $\frac{d^2\sigma}{dS^2}$). When a skew component

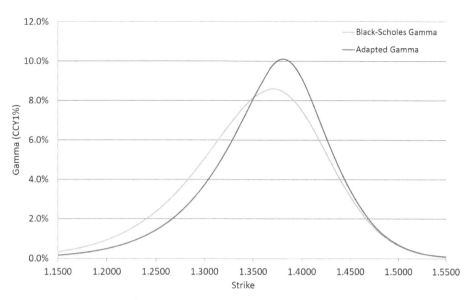

EXHIBIT 14.17 Adapted gamma versus Black-Scholes gamma profiles for a non-symmetric volatility smile

is added into the volatility smile, this point of maximum curvature moves to the lower volatility side of the volatility smile. In Exhibit 14.16, the risk reversal is for downside and the point of maximum curvature has moved to the topside.

This results in the gamma profiles shown in Exhibit 14.17, which in turn results in the gamma adaption effect profile shown in Exhibit 14.18.

In general, the gamma adaption effect follows these rules of thumb:

- Strikes on the high side of the volatility smile usually have a *negative* gamma adaption effect.

- Strikes on the low side of the volatility smile usually have a *positive* gamma adaption effect.

Therefore, buying vanillas high on the volatility smile (i.e., at an implied volatility above the ATM) results in a worse gamma/theta ratio under adaption than under Black-Scholes. *In extremis* it is possible for a trading position to be *short* adapted gamma yet *paying* theta—a difficult situation to risk manage.

Adapted Vega

Vega (v) is the exposure to ATM volatility changes. Consider a finite difference vega calculation in which ATM implied volatility is flexed up and down a small amount and the resultant premium change is divided by the ATM flex to calculate vega. In the standard Black-Scholes vega calculation the implied volatility at which a vanilla

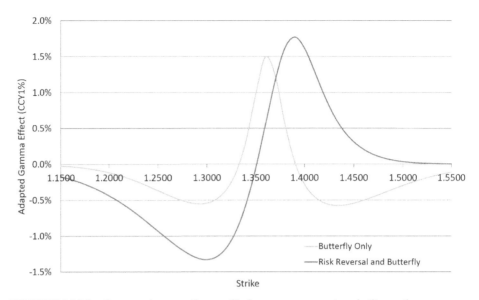

EXHIBIT 14.18   Gamma adaption effect profile for a non-symmetric volatility smile

is priced changes exactly as much as the ATM flex but in an adapted vega calculation the implied volatility changes differently because the whole volatility curve rebuilds under the adaption.

When the ATM is flexed higher, the strikes for a specific delta move away from the ATM. This pushes the whole volatility smile wider and causes the implied volatility for a specific strike to rise less on the high side of the smile. This effect is shown in Exhibit 14.19.

Therefore, strikes on the high side of the volatility smile have $v_{Adapted} < v_{Black-Scholes}$ and strikes on the low side of the volatility smile have $v_{Adapted} > v_{Black-Scholes}$. Traders observe this effect most frequently when a bought risk reversal contract gives a short adapted vega exposure and a sold risk reversal contract gives a long adapted vega exposure.

Risk Managing with Adapted Greeks

A trader has done some analysis and concludes that 1yr USD/JPY risk reversals are too high. Therefore they go into the market and sell USD100m/leg of 1yr 25d risk reversal. In USD/JPY the risk reversal is for downside so selling the risk reversal involves selling the downside strike versus buying the topside strike. The risk reversal is delta hedged by selling USD50m of USD/JPY 1yr forward. This results in the trading position shown in Exhibit 14.20. The exposures in Exhibit 14.20 are calculated using the standard Black-Scholes methodology that assumes volatility for a given strike stays unchanged as spot moves (i.e., sticky strike).

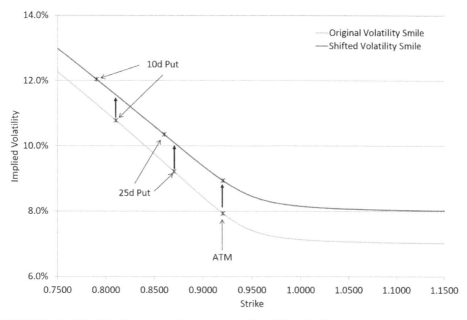

EXHIBIT 14.19   Volatility smile adjustment at higher ATM volatility

USD/JPY	P&L Change (USD)	Delta (USD)	Gamma (USD)	Vega (USD)
116.58	2,834,782	36,382,477	1,834,940	150,114
113.54	1,806,624	32,707,504	2,444,849	182,744
110.50	875,257	26,554,805	3,122,341	211,548
107.46	185,515	17,433,223	3,442,592	211,455
104.42	-119,800	7,056,247	2,728,312	148,375
101.38	-	**175,555**	**692,797**	**16,217**
98.33	287,975	1,722,526	-1,853,292	-136,078
95.29	290,955	11,668,370	-3,576,380	-239,513
92.25	-258,190	25,241,657	-3,708,416	-250,840
89.21	-1,388,173	36,638,252	-2,781,588	-201,084
86.17	-2,887,062	44,833,891	-1,771,521	-137,062

EXHIBIT 14.20   Spot ladder from selling USD/JPY 1yr risk reversal (Black-Scholes exposures)

However, the P&Ls within Exhibit 14.20 are generated by changing spot to each level in the ladder, rebuilding the volatility smile using the new spot level as the reference point, and revaluing all the options within the portfolio. This is equivalent to a sticky delta methodology and therefore the delta exposures and P&L change do not tie in between different spot levels within the spot ladder. For example, delta is roughly flat at 101.38 and yet there is significant positive P&L at 98.33 and significant negative P&L at 104.42.

Put another way, if the method used to calculate P&L within the spot ladder and the method used to calculate the exposures within the ladder are not aligned, delta exposures and P&L changes will not be aligned.

USD/JPY	P&L Change (USD)	Delta (USD)	Gamma (USD)	Vega (USD)
116.58	2,834,782	40,129,976	1,076,353	119,024
113.54	1,806,624	37,249,157	1,995,306	161,485
110.50	875,257	30,514,174	3,770,450	215,015
107.46	185,515	18,003,437	5,383,001	245,376
104.42	-119,800	2,973,223	5,490,513	201,361
101.38	**-**	**-9,381,917**	**1,998,537**	**43,285**
98.33	287,975	-6,688,560	-3,491,865	-149,308
95.29	290,955	7,354,156	-5,410,616	-265,644
92.25	-258,190	26,420,817	-5,095,665	-253,564
89.21	-1,388,173	39,386,742	-2,240,424	-177,100
86.17	-2,887,062	46,475,717	-1,168,101	-115,891

EXHIBIT 14.21   Spot ladder from selling USD/JPY 1yr risk reversal (adapted exposures)

If adapted exposures are displayed in the spot ladder instead as in Exhibit 14.21, delta at 101.38 spot is shorter and P&L changes are aligned with the delta exposures.

When a spot ladder is constructed as per Exhibit 14.21, volatility surface changes need to be additionally considered. This risk reversal trade therefore will be risk managed based on how implied volatility for the two strikes in the risk reversal is expected to change as spot moves:

- If the implied volatility surface inputs are not changing as spot moves, adapted exposures should be used. Under adaption, the trading position looks too short delta and some spot or forward could be bought back to balance the delta position better.

- If the implied volatility surface inputs are changing as spot moves such that the implied volatility for the transacted strikes remains (roughly) constant, the Black-Scholes exposures should be used and the delta position looks balanced.

Holding the short risk reversal position will cause the trading book to earn money over time if everything stays static as the short smile value decays positively. However, as spot moves, ATM implied volatility changes will probably cost money since in a currency pair with downside risk reversal:

- Spot lower → ATM implied volatility higher while the position gets shorter vega.

- Spot higher → ATM implied volatility lower while the position gets longer vega.

Traders often have a choice whether to risk manage vanilla positions using Black-Scholes exposures or adapted exposures. For risk management it is best to view both exposures and judge how the market is currently trading:

- If the volatility surface is not changing as spot moves, adapted exposures should be used.

- If the volatility surface changes and particularly the ATM changes as suggested by the volatility smile as spot moves, Black-Scholes exposures should be used.

In practice, for small spot moves the volatility surface often remains unchanged (i.e., use adapted exposures), but for larger spot moves the volatility surface often reacts such that the implied volatility for specific strikes remains constant (i.e., use Black-Scholes exposures). The speed of spot moves also matters, since implied volatility reacts more if spot moves more quickly. In some sense, the volatility surface therefore contains information about expected speed of spot moves higher or lower.

Zeta

The zeta of a vanilla option is the premium difference between the value of the option priced using the smile volatility less its value priced using the ATM volatility. Zeta therefore quantifies the value in the option which is due to the volatility smile.

The zeta for a vanilla option is approximately (ignoring second-order effects) vega multiplied by the smile volatility less ATM volatility difference. Therefore:

- $\sigma_{Smile} > \sigma_{ATM} \rightarrow$ positive zeta

- $\sigma_{Smile} < \sigma_{ATM} \rightarrow$ negative zeta

In AUD/JPY, the risk reversal is for downside as shown in Exhibit 14.22.

The equivalent zeta curve shown in Exhibit 14.23 reflects this. Of course, the zeta for an ATM strike is zero.

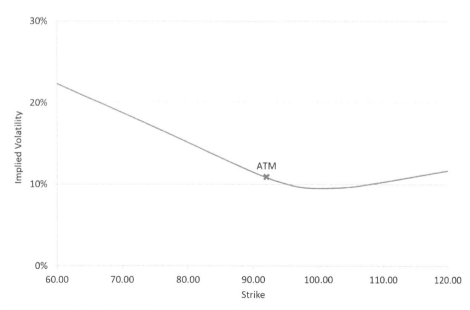

EXHIBIT 14.22 AUD/JPY 1yr volatility smile

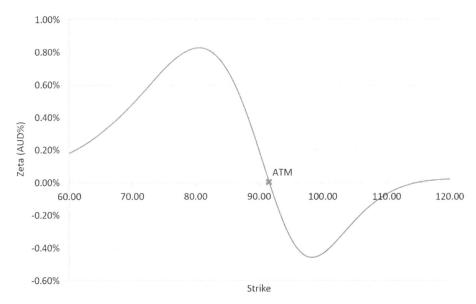

EXHIBIT 14.23 AUD/JPY 1yr zeta profile

In high-skew currency pairs:

- The high point of the zeta curve is often located around the 15d point on the high side of the smile. Being high on the zeta curve causes options to decay more quickly because of their additional value due to the smile.

- The low point of the zeta curve is often located around the 35d point on the low side of the smile.

It is important that traders know approximately where these points are in strike and delta terms because market participants often try to sell vanilla options around the most expensive point on the volatility smile and buy vanilla options around the cheapest point on the volatility smile.

Another popular strategy in high-skew currency pairs is to sell 15 delta vanilla options and buy 2 delta vanilla options, both on the high side of the smile. The idea behind this strategy is as follows:

- If spot doesn't move, the short 15d option decays (positively) more quickly than the long 2d option since the 2d option has a far lower premium.

- If spot blows up to the high side of the volatility smile, the 2d option relatively picks up in value far more than the 15d option as the ATM and risk reversals contracts increase sharply in price.

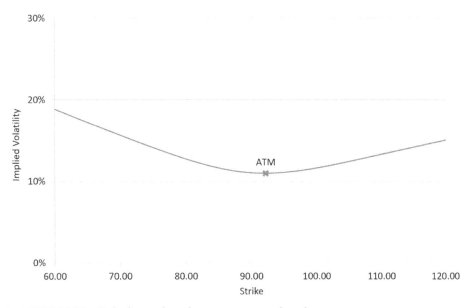

EXHIBIT 14.24 Volatility smile with positive wings and no skew

Unfortunately, the market does not make implementing this strategy easy: Offers on very low delta options on the high side of the risk reversal are often well above their theoretical midmarket (see Chapter 15).

Finally, in a currency pair with no risk reversal, the volatility smile is symmetric and the implied volatility never goes below the ATM as shown in Exhibit 14.24.

This results in the zeta profile shown in Exhibit 14.25, which is roughly symmetric and always positive.

Interest Rate Risk (Rho)

Within standard Black-Scholes mathematics, rho1 (ρ_1) and rho2 (ρ_2) are sensitivities to changes in the CCY1 and CCY2 continuously compounded risk-free interest rates respectively. In FX derivatives there are always two rho values to consider: one for each currency in the currency pair. Rho is most often quoted in per basis point (pbp) terms—the P&L change for a 0.01% change in interest rates.

The following analysis examines rho exposures for vanilla contracts using stylized Black-Scholes analysis where premiums and hence subtleties around the P&L currency are ignored.

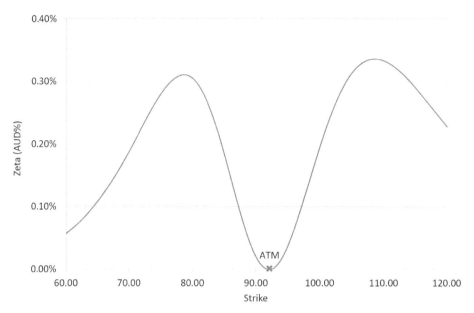

EXHIBIT 14.25 Zeta profile for volatility smile with positive wings and no skew

Future Cash and Forwards

Very generally, long-dated contracts have more interest rate risk than short-dated contracts. Future cash payments generate negative rho exposure linearly proportional to notional and tenor. In per basis point terms:

$$\rho_{Cash} \approx -0.01\% \,.Notional\,.\,T$$

where *Notional* is future cash notional and *T* is the time (in years) to the future cash delivery date. The negative sign in the formula indicates that, for example, USD must be sold forward to get longer USD rho. This can be confusing because when USD cash is *held*, higher return is generated with higher USD rates. The difference comes from holding the cash position versus taking delivery of a fixed cash amount in the future.

The same formula can be applied to forward contracts by considering each currency separately. For example, buying EUR100m EUR/USD 1yr forward at 1.3100 generates short EUR10k pbp EUR rho and long USD13.1k pbp USD rho.

Long Vanilla Call Option

The per basis point rho exposure on a long vanilla call option prior to maturity is shown in Exhibit 14.26:

- If the forward to expiry is far below the strike, the long CCY1 call vanilla has no payoff, no risk, and no rho exposures.

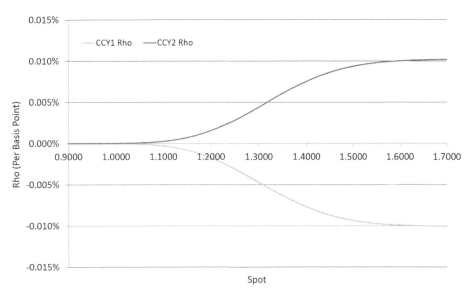

EXHIBIT 14.26   Long 1yr call option with 1.3100 strike rho

- If the forward to expiry is far above the strike, the long CCY1 call vanilla payoff behaves like a long forward and hence generates negative CCY1 rho and positive CCY2 rho exposures.

The rho exposure on a vanilla option contract is linked to its forward delta exposure. Exhibit 14.27 shows how a long 1yr CCY1 call vanilla has a long forward delta that produces short CCY1 rho and long CCY2 rho:

- *At 0% forward delta*: Per basis point rho is 0%.

- *Around the ATM*: Per basis point rho is 0.005%.

- *At 100% forward delta*: Per basis point rho is 0.01%.

Therefore:

$$\rho_{CCY1\ Call} \approx -0.01\% \,.\Delta_F\,.Notional\,.\,T$$

and

$$\rho_{ATM\ CCY1\ Call} \approx -0.01\% \,.\frac{1}{2}.Notional\,.T$$

where Δ_F is the forward delta expressed in notional currency %.

As noted, longer tenor options have higher rho exposure. Therefore, over time the rho exposures on a vanilla reduce as shown in Exhibit 14.28.

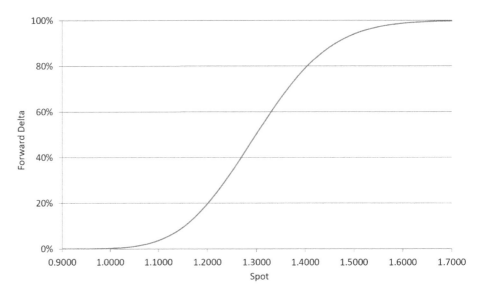

EXHIBIT 14.27 Long 1yr call option with 1.3100 strike forward delta

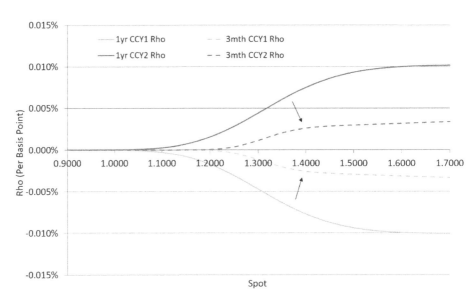

EXHIBIT 14.28 Long 1yr call option with 1.3100 strike rho over time

Long Vanilla Put Option

There are no surprises with the rho for a long vanilla put option. Prior to maturity, if the forward to expiry is far above the strike, the CCY1 put vanilla has no payoff and no risk. If the forward to expiry is far below the strike, the long CCY1 put vanilla is essentially a short forward position and hence generates long CCY1 rho and short CCY2 rho. These rho profiles are shown in Exhibit 14.29.

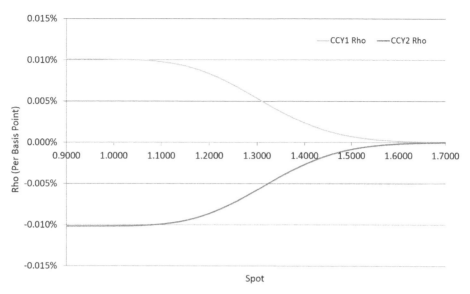

EXHIBIT 14.29   Long 1yr put option with 1.3100 strike rho

Long ATM Straddle

Combining long CCY1 call and CCY1 put vanillas with the same ATM strike and maturity gives a long ATM straddle position:

■ With a lower forward to maturity, forward delta gets shorter, CCY1 rho gets longer, and CCY2 rho gets shorter.

■ With a higher forward to maturity, forward delta gets longer, CCY1 rho gets shorter, and CCY2 rho gets longer.

The crossing point occurs around the ATM as shown in Exhibit 14.30. It is instructive to note that the same rho exposures as Exhibit 14.30 are generated by this straddle, a forward-hedged CCY1 call option or a forward-hedged CCY1 put vanilla option.

In general, if there is a negative correlation between spot and CCY1 interest rates or a positive correlation between spot and CCY2 interest rates, buying an ATM straddle results in a desirable trading position.

Exhibit 14.31 shows how the ATM straddle rho exposures change with implied volatility:

■ At higher implied volatility, the rho exposures stretch out as the distribution widens.

■ At lower implied volatility, the rho exposures compress as the distribution tightens.

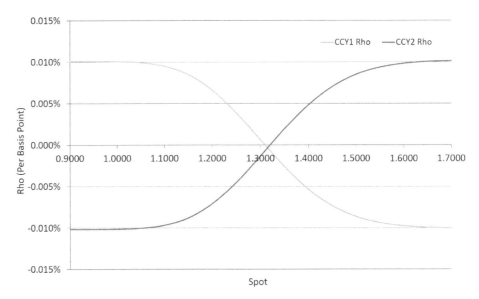

EXHIBIT 14.30 Long 1yr ATM straddle with 1.3100 strike rho

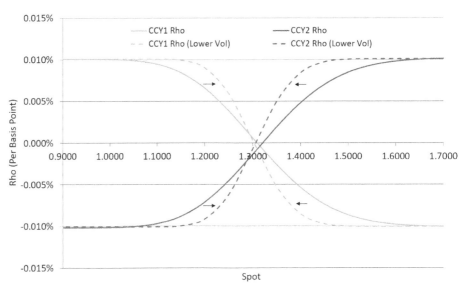

EXHIBIT 14.31 Long 1yr ATM straddle with 1.3100 strike rho at different implied volatility levels

Finally, changing interest rates with a fixed spot impacts the forward and this feeds through to the rho exposures on an ATM straddle:

- CCY1 rates higher → forward lower → longer CCY1 rho

- CCY2 rates higher → forward higher → longer CCY2 rho

Hence a long ATM straddle position contains *long interest rate gamma*, although this effect only becomes significant at longer tenors.

CHAPTER 15

Vanilla FX Derivatives Trading Topics

The following topics highlight common situations that FX derivatives traders come across when risk managing their positions.

■ Understanding the FX Derivatives Market

Traders must learn the characteristics of the markets in which they are operating. Every market is different and this guides how traders interact with the market and how positions are risk managed. Within foreign exchange there are enormous differences between the spot, forward, and derivatives markets in different G10 and emerging market currency pairs.

Speed

G10 spot markets "tick" (change) many times a second. They are very fast, simple (in the sense that the market consists of a single contract per currency pair) markets in which high-frequency algorithmic trading plays a large (and increasing) role.

The OTC FX derivatives market moves more slowly than the FX spot market for several reasons:

- *Contract range*. Vanilla option contracts have two main additional dimensions: maturity and strike. There is therefore a very wide range of different possible contracts that can be traded.

- *Quoting implied volatility*. In the interbank broker market and for most institutional clients, prices are quoted in rounded implied volatility terms. This rounding causes volatility prices to be stickier at a given level.

- *Quoting structure*. For the majority of transactions, vanilla option trades are agreed in implied volatility terms and then prevailing market data is used to generate full contract details. This process of generating and agreeing contract details after trading makes it more appropriate for larger size to be transacted at a given implied volatility level rather than multiple smaller tickets at different levels.

Size

Within FX derivatives, different instruments in different currency pairs trade in different standard transaction sizes. For example, in EUR/USD 1mth ATM (the most liquid currency pair, tenor, and instrument), buying EUR30m will not move the market or be of much interest to other traders; but in, for example, USD/VND (Vietnamese Dong), a USD30m transaction in any tenor would be enormous.

It is important that traders know standard market sizes and therefore how relatively large or small a contract is, This impacts the way a trader interacts with the market. For example, if a trader knows they have to buy EUR750m EUR/CHF O/N ATM (large size), they may not reveal their full size initially in the interbank broker market because that may scare other traders away. On the flipside, a trader who wants to sell USD15m 1mth ATM USD/JPY to clean their position may decide to run the risk rather than transacting because that contract is so small that it makes the bank and the trader look like small-fry in the eyes of other banks. This shouldn't matter, but it does: The reputation of the bank and the individual trader within an OTC market is important.

Liquidity

Liquidity is an enormously important consideration: Liquidity, speed, size, and bid–offer spread are all closely linked. The more liquid a contract, the larger the size that can usually be transacted without moving the market and the tighter the bid–offer spread. Put simply, liquidity enables traders to smoothly enter and exit trading positions at minimal cost. For this to be the case there must be good sized bids and offers tight around the midmarket level.

Liquidity does not stay constant within a given market; it changes as market conditions change. In general:

- Lower market volatility often leads to increased liquidity over time as traders become comfortable with the trading levels and require less spread to cover subsequent market moves. This leads to increased trading size and tighter bid–offer spreads.

- Higher market volatility often leads to decreased liquidity as traders require more spread to cover subsequent market moves and remain within their risk tolerance. This leads to decreased trading size and wider bid–offer spreads.

The manner of market moves is also important: Large jumps in the price level, and hence increased uncertainty, normally lead to a larger reduction in liquidity. The level of the market also has an impact. For example, spot moving and breaking new highs or lows will often lead to reduced liquidity while spot moving the same distance back into the middle of a well-established range may lead to increased liquidity.

Liquidity can also be impacted by the amount of pain the market is collectively experiencing. If traders are losing money, they are less likely to provide liquidity to each other. This can be a nasty self-reinforcing cycle for the market as a whole.

Judging liquidity within a market is a vital trading skill. In general, it is dangerous to assume that the current market liquidity will always prevail. Every trader has experienced correct positioning being undone by a lack of liquidity preventing exiting the position at the optimal moment.

In FX derivatives, one of the most striking liquidity reductions occurred in USD/KRW during 2008. Prior to 2008, USD/KRW FX was stable and implied volatility was creeping lower toward 3%. The market had become very accustomed to the trading levels and many market participants were happy to sell volatility because the underlying was so static—1mth ATM was quoted (e.g., 2.95/3.05% in USD30m. Then the FX market jumped sharply higher and ATM-implied volatility exploded to around 100% in a matter of weeks. Liquidity vanished and bid–offer spreads widened enormously—1mth ATM was now quoted, e.g., 60/120% in USD10m. The market liquidity situation had changed completely and performing any transactions within the market cost huge amounts of bid–offer spread. USD/KRW spot and implied volatility over this period is shown in Exhibit 15.1. It is at these moments that the best traders already have the right position (long gamma and long wing vega), or they are able to quickly appreciate that an extreme market event is occurring and aggressively seek to obtain the right position before liquidity reduces too much.

Another important issue is that liquidity is often not symmetric around the midmarket level. Most FX derivatives traders will be happier to buy vanilla options expiring on important event dates (i.e., an expiry date on which a large spot move may occur) than sell them, so the size that can be transacted at the bid will be larger

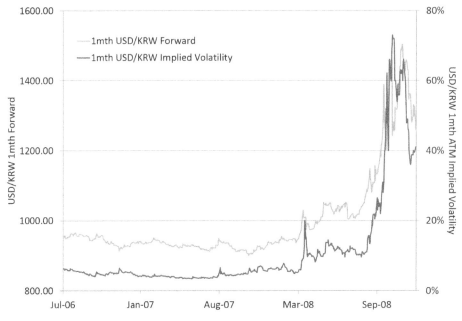

EXHIBIT 15.1 USD/KRW spot and implied volatility from 2006 to 2009

than the size that can be transacted at the offer. Traders adjust for this within their price making when quoting price requests in larger size.

■ Trading the Overnight

A trader thinks spot will slowly rise higher over the course of the next day. How can this opinion be best expressed by trading vanilla options? An initial answer might be to buy an overnight call option with a topside strike. This doesn't sound unreasonable since call options pay out if spot moves higher.

If the long call option is traded live (without delta hedge), the total P&L at maturity is given by the standard hockey-stick P&L diagram (including the initial premium) shown in Exhibit 15.2.

To make money from this trade, it is not enough for spot to move higher to the strike; it must move far enough *through* the strike to also cover the initial premium.

What if the option is delta hedged rather than being traded live? Assuming no other trades are in the position, the initial delta hedged trading position is shown in Exhibit 15.3.

AUD/USD spot is 0.9150 and AUD50m of O/N 0.9200 has been purchased; notice that the gamma peak is to the topside. Intraday the gamma can be traded but the trader's idea was that spot would rise, rather than whipping up and down. If

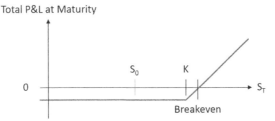

Total P&L at Maturity

Breakeven

EXHIBIT 15.2 P&L from buying topside call option

Horizon	July 14, 2014

AUD/USD	P&L Change (USD)	Delta (AUD)	Gamma (AUD)
0.9288	320,237	40,730,570	6,966,749
0.9260	211,435	37,216,724	16,984,543
0.9233	117,627	30,124,217	29,844,457
0.9205	48,777	19,716,799	37,818,882
0.9177	10,570	8,612,919	34,501,702
0.9150	**0**	**-2,103**	**22,704,866**
0.9123	7,752	-4,871,342	10,737,612
0.9095	24,381	-6,861,088	3,653,591
0.9068	44,118	-7,451,006	894,304
0.9041	64,613	-7,577,824	157,411
0.9014	85,202	-7,597,579	19,918

Daily P&L (USD)	-

EXHIBIT 15.3 Inception trading position from buying O/N topside call option

spot remains static until the end of the day, the next morning the trading position is as per Exhibit 15.4.

The horizon is now equal to the expiry date of the option and the option is out-of-the-money at current spot. Therefore, both option value and option delta are zero within the risk management system. The theta paid (negative USD18.5k P&L) is the loss in option value from the previous day to today. The delta has bled shorter due to the change from long delta on the previous day to zero delta today. If the trader still thinks that spot will rise, the short delta should be hedged back to flat by buying spot. Then (again) the only chance to make any money out of this position is for spot to move through the strike. If no spot is bought back, the worst thing that can happen is that spot rises up to the strike, but not through it. In market-speak, spot ending up at a strike at expiry is called being "pinned."

It turns out that if the trader's view is that spot will rise slowly—sometimes called "grinding higher"—buying a wing vanilla option in that direction is a bad

Horizon	July 15, 2014

AUD/USD	P&L Change (USD)	Delta (AUD)	Gamma (AUD)
0.9288	335,442	42,400,000	-
0.9260	217,651	42,400,000	-
0.9233	100,213	42,400,000	-
0.9205	-16,875	42,400,000	-
0.9177	-20,862	-7,600,000	-
0.9150	-	-7,600,000	**-**
0.9123	20,862	-7,600,000	-
0.9095	41,661	-7,600,000	-
0.9068	62,398	-7,600,000	-
0.9041	83,073	-7,600,000	-
0.9014	103,686	-7,600,000	-

Daily P&L (USD)	-18,487

EXHIBIT 15.4   Trading position from long topside call option on expiry date

Horizon	July 14, 2014

AUD/USD	P&L Change (USD)	Delta (AUD)	Gamma (AUD)
0.9288	-218,060	-33,330,570	-6,966,749
0.9260	-129,817	-29,816,724	-16,984,543
0.9233	-56,505	-22,724,217	-29,844,457
0.9205	-8,090	-12,316,799	-37,818,882
0.9177	9,743	-1,212,919	-34,501,702
0.9150	-	7,402,103	-22,704,866
0.9123	-28,065	12,271,342	-10,737,612
0.9095	-64,946	14,261,088	-3,653,591
0.9068	-104,874	14,851,006	-894,304
0.9041	-145,500	14,977,824	-157,411
0.9014	-186,159	14,997,579	-19,918

Daily P&L (USD)	-

EXHIBIT 15.5   Inception trading position from selling topside call option and buying spot

trade. A far better trade is to *sell* the overnight topside option and *buy* spot, which results in the initial position shown in Exhibit 15.5.

The position with the horizon rolled forward is shown in Exhibit 15.6. Theta is earned and more profit is made if spot grinds higher, exactly fitting the trader's view.

Exhibit 15.7 shows the P&L profiles from buying spot only versus buying spot *and* selling the topside vanilla option. Selling the option earns theta but causes a potential sharp decline in P&L if spot goes above the short strike. Selling a strike

Horizon	July 15, 2014

AUD/USD	P&L Change (USD)	Delta (AUD)	Gamma (AUD)
0.9288	-233,266	-35,000,000	-
0.9260	-136,033	-35,000,000	-
0.9233	-39,091	-35,000,000	-
0.9205	57,562	-35,000,000	-
0.9177	41,175	15,000,000	-
0.9150	-	15,000,000	-
0.9123	-41,175	15,000,000	-
0.9095	-82,226	15,000,000	-
0.9068	-123,155	15,000,000	-
0.9041	-163,960	15,000,000	-
0.9014	-204,643	15,000,000	-

Daily P&L (USD)	18,486.58

EXHIBIT 15.6   Trading position from short topside call option and long delta on expiry date

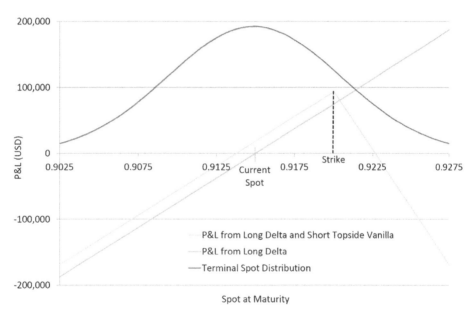

EXHIBIT 15.7   P&L profiles from different trading strategies

closer to current spot would result in more theta earned but the P&L decline to the topside would happen at closer spot levels. Strike positioning is therefore a risk/reward balance based on a trader's expectations of where/how spot will move. Selling strikes close to current spot increases the median P&L but it increases P&L volatility and introduces larger negative P&L scenarios.

■ Gartman's Rules of Trading

Dennis Gartman (of "Gartman Letter" fame) publishes an updated list of trading rules every year. These rules contain a great deal of trading common sense. I strongly advise searching for the full list on the Internet. In my opinion the most important are:

■ Never, under any circumstances, add to a losing position—ever! Adding to losing position will lead to ruin.

■ Trade like a mercenary soldier. We must fight on the winning side and be willing to change sides readily when one side has gained the upper hand. *He is talking here about not getting too attached to, for example, a long vega or short vega position; be willing to actively flip positions.*

■ Mental Capital trumps Real Capital. Of the two types of capital, the mental is the more important and expensive of the two. Holding losing positions costs measurable sums of actual capital, but it costs immeasurable sums of mental capital. *The emotions that result from a run of big losses and the emotional swings that result from market moves are key reasons why trading is such a difficult job.*

■ The objective is not to buy low and sell high, but to buy high and to sell higher. We can never know what price is "low." Nor can we know what price is "high."

■ Trading runs in cycles: some good; most bad. Trade large and aggressively when trading well; trade small and modestly when trading poorly. In "good times," even errors are profitable; in "bad times," even the most well-researched trades go awry. This is the nature of trading; accept it.

■ Keep your technical systems simple. Complicated systems breed confusion; simplicity breeds elegance.

■ The hard trade is the right trade: If it is easy to sell, don't; and if it is easy to buy, don't. Do the trade that is hard to do and that which the crowd finds objectionable. *In FX derivatives, an example of this is selling strikes with expiries on important event days (e.g., Non-Farm Payrolls) to reduce vega or gamma exposures. If there is a loss to take, take it on the chin by doing the right trades; trying to avoid the loss only prolongs the agony.*

■ There is never just one cockroach! The lesson of most markets is that bad news usually follows bad.

■ All these rules are meant to be broken—but only very infrequently. Genius comes in knowing how and when to break these rules.

■ Vega Positioning

In USD/TRY the risk reversal is for topside, spot is at 2.1200, and the 1yr forward is at 2.2900. A USD/TRY FX derivatives trader wants a trading position that generates positive P&L if implied volatility goes significantly higher. Therefore, 1yr ATM (2.2800 strike) is bought at 9.0% implied volatility in order to get long vega. However, this causes significant theta (paying) so to mitigate this a gamma-neutral notional of 3mth ATM is sold. This results in the trading position shown in Exhibit 15.8.

The trader is proved correct; implied volatility does jump *but* this occurs as USD/TRY spot moves sharply higher due to a sudden TRY devaluation.

Over the course of a few days, USD/TRY spot jumps to 2.3000, the 1yr ATM implied volatility jumps from 9% to 18%, and the 1yr 25d risk reversal goes from +5% to +15%. The trader makes a profit from the long wing gamma as spot moves but the implied volatility for the purchased 2.2800 strike only moves from 9% to 14% due to the increased topside skew. The strike has become downside and is now marked at a lower implied volatility than the ATM, as shown in Exhibit 15.9.

Money has been made from the vega position but not as much as could have been made from owning an option with a higher strike. During most major market moves, the biggest P&L is generated from wing options on the high side of the volatility smile. This is a key reason why the skew of the volatility smile exists in the first place; options that may pick up more sharply in value on a spot jump trade at higher levels of implied volatility.

ATM implied volatility is unlikely to jump higher if spot is static or range-bound. In addition, the supply of optionality into the market (from, e.g., corporate FX hedging, DCDs) means that if spot stays within a range, ATM implied volatility often drifts lower over time.

USD/TRY	P&L Change (USD)	Delta (USD)	Gamma (USD)	Vega (USD)
2.4577	2,354,594	43,358,466	2,990,751	307,966
2.3861	1,274,075	32,790,132	4,110,128	453,311
2.3166	520,097	19,786,812	4,482,310	595,231
2.2491	129,216	7,844,848	3,324,371	693,790
2.1836	13,012	1,247,550	1,112,544	735,225
2.1200	-	246,596	-49,690	748,560
2.0564	-656	-878,492	1,206,172	757,306
1.9947	121,657	-8,321,378	3,649,295	732,830
1.9349	581,360	-21,864,913	4,934,686	639,350
1.8768	1,506,155	-36,603,053	4,515,565	491,355
1.8205	2,878,672	-48,542,765	3,274,585	335,029

EXHIBIT 15.8 Trading position from buying 1yr ATM and selling a gamma-neutral amount of 3mth ATM

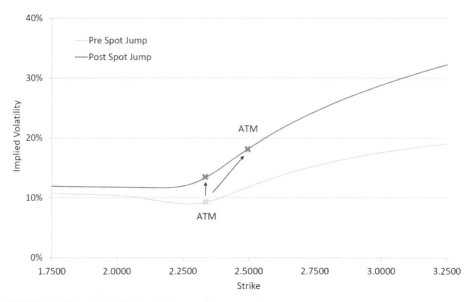

EXHIBIT 15.9 USD/TRY volatility smile pre– and post–spot jump

When positioning an FX derivatives trading portfolio, traders consider spot and implied volatility moves together. For example, if spot moves lower or higher, how will the ATM change? How will the skew change? How will the wings change? More generally, flattening a large FX derivatives trading position is never a matter of simply flattening all the current Greek exposures to zero. It is vital to also examine how exposures change as spot, interest rates, and implied volatility move.

This is one of the toughest aspects of OTC FX derivatives trading relative to exchange trading or FX spot trading; *positions cannot be easily closed down*. The majority of FX derivatives deals are warehoused and since exact offsets for deals are rarely found it can take months or even years of concerted effort to completely close out an FX derivatives trading position.

Short-Date Trading: Long ATM versus Short Wings

In liquid G10 markets one popular strategy in the short-dates is to set up the position long ATM versus short wings. An example of such a trading position is shown in Exhibit 15.10.

The position is *long gamma* around the ATM and *short gamma* with spot higher or lower. From a balanced starting delta, if spot moves up and down within a fairly tight range, the gamma can be traded. Plus, less theta is paid overall for the gamma

AUD/USD	P&L Change (AUD)	Delta (AUD)	Gamma (AUD)
0.9732	303,514	203,669	-439,124
0.9636	300,126	1,367,363	-2,236,098
0.9541	272,418	5,346,163	-5,792,570
0.9446	189,803	11,588,356	-5,200,576
0.9353	65,225	11,771,616	6,108,779
0.9260	**-**	**-29,467**	**14,890,872**
0.9167	69,386	-12,090,150	6,447,645
0.9076	201,563	-11,938,276	-5,246,471
0.8985	291,675	-5,478,941	-5,965,022
0.8895	325,881	-1,381,476	-2,294,934
0.8806	335,570	-200,978	-443,825

EXHIBIT 15.10 Trading position from long ATM and short wings

because short wing vanillas usually decay (positively) relatively more quickly than long ATM vanillas decay (negatively).

One trader I know has implemented this strategy repeatedly in liquid G10 pairs for almost 20 years. He trades the gamma as spot moves in the long gamma area, and if spot moves into a short gamma area, he aggressively makes prices in the brokers to get the position back to long ATM versus short wings again at minimal cost. The simplest ideas are often the most effective when well executed.

This strategy ties in with the fat-tailed distributions observed in the spot market. Traders like selling short-dated wings in liquid currency pairs because long periods of time can pass between spot moves large enough to cause significant negative P&L.

■ Client Option Orders

Rather than transacting directly, clients sometimes leave option orders, which are transactions provisional on certain market conditions being met. There are three main types of option order:

1. *Spot firm* (i.e., transact if spot reaches a certain level). This involves the FX derivatives trading desk transacting a delta hedge at a specified spot level and the client trading the option structure live. Since the implied volatility when spot is at the order level cannot be known with certainty, the premium of the option structure cannot be guaranteed.

2. *Premium firm* (i.e., transact if the premium of the structure reaches a certain level). This involves the FX derivatives trading desk transacting a hedge at the prevailing market rate when the structure premium hits the target level and the client trading the option structure live. Since future levels of the implied volatility and spot cannot be known, this requires the option structure premium

to be periodically (ideally continuously) recalculated and checked against the target level.

3. *Volatility firm* (i.e., transact an option structure if the implied volatility for the structure reaches a certain level). This involves the client trading a simple vanilla option structure delta hedged with the FX derivatives trading desk.

Note that it is not possible for an option order to be both spot firm and premium firm without the trading desk taking some risk.

Pricing spot firm client option orders off a spot reference away from the current level (off-market spot) must be done with care. What assumptions is the pricing tool making about the volatility surface at the new spot reference? Looking at the volatility smile, will the level of ATM volatility likely be higher or lower than the current level if spot moves to the reference level?

Occasionally, clients want to deal option structures with a delta exchange at an *off-market* spot level. In this situation, the current spot should be used to price the contract, then the structure premium must be adjusted for the P&L from the delta hedge at current spot versus the delta hedge at the off-market delta exchange level. Plus, check it is valid that the client is using an off-market spot.

Finally, clients sometimes leave *OCO* (one cancels others) orders incorporating multiple sub-orders. When one of the sub-orders is transacted, the others are canceled. The same terminology is used when the client requests multiple prices but requests prices OCO, which means that the trader quotes rates on all the contracts but only one can be traded.

■ Quoting Vanilla Spreads

As seen in Chapter 8, a price request is called a *spread* if it has multiple legs with *offsetting* gamma or vega risk between the legs. Therefore, within a vanilla spread some legs are bought and some legs are sold since a long vanilla is always long vega and long gamma.

Spreads are quoted tighter than equivalent price requests where risks compound, but to be quoted as a spread, the request must have *significant* offsetting gamma or vega risk. For example, O/N ATM (e.g., 100% gamma and 0.02% vega) against 3mth ATM (15% gamma and 0.20% vega) in equal notionals is *not* a spread. In this instance, two-way prices would be quoted on both legs with no tightening.

The most common spread variant has two vanilla legs—one a buy, the other a sell—but it isn't known which way around the client wants to transact. Usually, a two-leg spread request will be quoted with the leg with most vega (hence the most risk) **spread** (i.e., bid and offer at different levels) and the other leg **choice**, sometimes denoted CH (i.e., bid and offer at the same level).

For example, a vanilla spread request might be 1mth 1.3500 versus 2mth 1.3500 NY Cut. The midmarket implied volatility for the 1mth 1.3500 is 6.95% and for the 2mth 1.3500 is 7.05%. A trader might therefore quote a neutral (i.e., no better bid or better offer) rate of 6.95% CH versus 6.95%/7.15%. The price taker then pays or gives the 2mth (the spread leg) with the 1mth traded in the opposite direction.

It is worth briefly noting that there are occasions where spreading the leg with the smaller vega is more appropriate. For example, when quoting an O/N versus three-day spread, the price of the O/N could be well known in the market as 10/13% and it would be more natural to quote 10/13% (or similar) versus a choiced three-day mid implied volatility.

In the interbank broker market, vanilla spreads are quoted in **volatility differential** terms. A broker has a price on 1mth ATM versus 2mth ATM:

- If the price made is 6.95% CH versus 7.00%/7.20%, the price would be quoted as "0.05/0.25%, 2mth over."

- If the price made is 6.95% CH versus 6.95%/7.15%, the price would be quoted as "flat/0.2%, 2mth over."

- If the price made is 6.95% CH versus 6.90%/7.10%, the price would be quoted as "0.05/0.15% around favoring 2mth." In this case the price is −0.05/0.15%; "around" means one side of the price is negative and the other is positive. The "favored" side has the higher mid volatility.

If the broker is trading a 1mth versus 2mth ATM spread at 7.6% versus 8.0%, they might say they are "buying twos, selling ones, paying 0.4%."

Once a contract has been traded in differential terms, the *exact* implied volatilities have to be agreed between the two traders. If there is a net vega exposure on the deal, the trader who gets long vega from the spread will try to set a relatively low volatility on both legs while the trader who gets short vega from the spread will try to set a relatively high volatility on both legs.

If a trader cannot trade a spread as a package, they may try to "leg into" the spread. This means trading one leg of the spread at a time (i.e., trading the 1mth ATM first and then the 2mth ATM later with a different counterparty). The downside to this approach is that additional bid–offer spread must usually be paid plus before the spread has been fully transacted the trading position has additional risk.

■ Trading Long-Dated FX Derivatives

In most major currency pairs there is only good liquidity for maturities out to five years in the interbank broker market. However, there are currency pairs, particularly involving JPY, in which options can be traded out to 30 years or even longer. Following are some high-level suggestions when trading a long-dated FX derivatives position.

- Understand **market positioning**. This is important in less liquid markets generally but it is particularly important in the long-dated FX derivatives markets. Clients tend to trade a limited range of products, which leaves market-making banks with similar positions. Therefore, a detailed understanding of the risks on standard products is absolutely essential. For example, traders must get a sense of what will happen to the market vega position if ten-year USD interest rates rise 0.25%.

- Understand **market liquidity**. Engage with the interbank broker market and actively make prices in order to understand the limits of the liquidity, the standard price skews caused by the market positioning, and how liquidity reduces in stretched markets.

- Learn **market conventions**. For example, the ATM contract in G10 pairs goes from being traded as a zero-delta straddle to being an at-the-money forward strike plus forward hedge past the ten-year maturity. This impacts relative strike placement, which causes ATM curves to jump when the convention changes.

- A deep understanding of the **interest rate markets** is not absolutely necessary if mainly trading short-dated vanilla FX derivatives because these contracts have minimal rho exposures and the spot is usually close to the forward. However, in long-dated FX derivatives markets understanding different interest rate instruments and their pricing and liquidity is vital.

Trading long-dated FX derivatives positions is often a matter of trying to balance the position as well as possible: running delta against vega against smile against rates exposures such that the P&Ls from the different elements offset as the market moves. Understanding the relationships between these elements in the position is therefore vital. Often risk managers trade around a high-level view; for example, USD interest rates will rise and implied volatility will fall. This approach often works better in practice than attempting to keep the P&L flat. **Scenario analysis** also helps; positions are stressed with different market data scenarios in order to identify the main danger scenarios.

◼ Trading Pegged Currency Pairs

Unique risk management challenges are presented when a currency pair is pegged or managed in some way by the country's central bank. This most often happens in emerging market currencies and there are many variations on the methods used to control the currency. Following are some high-level suggestions for trading FX derivatives in pegged currency pairs.

- When trading a pegged currency pair it is good to understand the exact mechanisms used to control it, the context of why these measures were put in place originally, and the history of how the mechanisms evolved over time. This is important because these decisions are often linked to political factors that must be monitored for potential changes in approach.

- From a risk management perspective often spot is curtailed but the forward or NDF can move freely outside the band or range. The consequence of this is that interest rates become driven by the forward rather than being a reflection of the future value of money in the two currencies. Also, the volatility of the forward is often far higher than the volatility of spot.

- Pegged currency pairs typically have very low implied volatility (e.g., below 1%). This causes large gamma exposures and it often makes sense to track the cost of certain benchmark options (i.e., a 1yr option with the strike at the intervention level) in premium terms rather than implied volatility terms.

- For currency pairs with very low volatility but relatively high skew or wings, the standard volatility surface building methodologies sometimes struggle to construct valid volatility surfaces. Bank trading desks expend enormous amounts of quant brainpower on generating valid arbitrage-free volatility surfaces in pegged currency pairs. Traders learn the warning signs that the volatility surface is close to breaking, often via unstable Greek exposures.

- Care must be taken when trading exotic contracts in pegged or managed currency pairs. In terms of pricing, market prices for exotic contracts can be far from model prices generated (see Part IV). Within risk management, the biggest danger is extreme gamma exposures from barriers close to expiry.

- A key consideration within pegged/managed currency pair risk management is preparation for a large spot revaluation. This is especially important considering the reduction in liquidity that will likely occur once spot jumps. Risk management often involves simulating 2%, 5%, 10%, 20% spot revaluations and checking the P&Ls over these scenarios. Controlling these P&Ls is inevitably a balance: Holding a position for which the P&L is positive for all of these spot jumps will certainly cost money over time.

Positive Vanilla Spreads

One popular risk management technique is to place positive vanilla spreads within the trading position. In essence this involves placing long vanillas *in front of* (i.e.,

AUD/USD	P&L Change (AUD)	Delta (AUD)	Gamma (AUD)
0.9494	-	-	-
0.9447	-	-	-
0.9400	-	-	-
0.9353	-	-	-
0.9306	-	-	-
0.9260	-	-	-
0.9214	-	-	-
0.9168	-80,375	100,000,000	-
0.9122	-583,292	100,000,000	-
0.9076	-1,088,735	100,000,000	-
0.9031	-1,596,719	100,000,000	-

EXHIBIT 15.11   Trading position containing short downside wing strike

AUD/USD	P&L Change (AUD)	Delta (AUD)	Gamma (AUD)
0.9494	-	-	-
0.9447	-	-	-
0.9400	-	-	-
0.9353	-	-	-
0.9306	-	-	-
0.9260	-	-	-
0.9214	61,322	-50,000,000	-
0.9168	232,511	50,000,000	-
0.9122	-17,577	50,000,000	-
0.9076	-268,922	50,000,000	-
0.9031	-521,529	50,000,000	-

EXHIBIT 15.12   Trading position containing short downside wing strike and a long strike in front

closer to current spot than) short vanillas so P&L goes positive and then negative as spot moves through the two strikes.

For example, Exhibit 15.11 shows a trading position that is short AUD100m of downside wing strike.

The danger is that spot drops sharply through the strike. One method of hedging this risk would be to buy back the same strike for the same expiry date. However, a potentially preferable approach is to buy a smaller amount of a closer strike. Exhibit 15.12 shows the effect of buying AUD50m of long strike in front of the short strike, hence smoothing the P&L profile.

Profit is made through the long strike, which then provides P&L protection if spot continues through the short strike.

■ Writing-Off Vanilla Risk

Writing-off is a powerful risk management technique. The idea is that very low-value vanillas options are removed from the main trading book at zero premium live (i.e., no delta hedge) and placed in a separate trading book (sometimes called the *write-off book*). From there the options are usually left until maturity as lottery tickets that may pay out if spot moves through the strike prior to maturity. If only a few of these lottery tickets pay out over the course of the year, they can generate sizable profits. Note that because long option positions are moved live at no cost the write-off book can never have negative P&L.

For example, a trading portfolio is long a low premium and low delta topside vanilla option in large notional. If spot rises sharply, the value of the vanilla will pick up, but crucially the long gamma and negative theta will also increase. The trader expects it will be difficult to make back the theta from trading the long gamma with a higher spot. Therefore, the option is sold from the main trading book to a dedicated write-off book at zero premium. This causes a loss in the main trading book equal to the prevailing value of the vanilla option. From here the main trading book is risk managed as normal without the removed vanilla. Importantly, the risk from the write-off book must not be incorporated into the main book risk.

- If spot does not go up to the strike prior to the option maturity, the (low) option premium has been lost.

- If spot moves up to the strike prior to the option maturity, the option can be sold back into the main book, again at zero premium. This generates a profit in the main trading book that can be used to risk manage the position (close it out?), resulting in positive P&L.

- If spot moves through the strike close to the option maturity, the full P&L can be realized at the option expiry.

It is also possible to write-off long vanilla strike spreads with the same expiry date. This can be used to clean up strike risk in the portfolio that would otherwise cost money in the form of spread cross to close out in the interbank broker market or would cause increased P&L volatility.

The writing-off technique works best when traders are engaged with their position:

- When spot moves significantly higher, downside strikes should be investigated and very low premium options can be written off.

- When spot moves significantly lower, topside strikes should be investigated and very low premium options can be written off.

- When implied volatility falls, both downside and topside strikes should be investigated.

Writing-off changes the P&L distribution of the trading book by paying small amounts of P&L (the premiums) for the (low) chance of making big returns. It works particularly well in currency pairs where spot has a tendency to jump or trend strongly, which brings written-off strikes into play.

Vanilla Pin Risk

Being pinned on a large long strike is a nightmare for vanilla FX derivatives traders. This involves being long an option with its strike fairly close to current spot and hence paying sizable theta into the expiry date. The delta bleeds away from the strike and spot then dribbles toward the strike such that delta can never be traded. The only way to salvage something from this situation is to unwind the delta bleed and run delta into the strike (i.e., run long delta if long the topside strike). This may be applicable if the strike is known to be in the market in large size and hence spot may gravitate toward it. For the equal and opposite reasons, being pinned on a large short strike can generate large positive P&L.

The best situation for a trader with long strikes in the book is for the strike to be too far away from spot to have paid much theta for it; then a large spot move takes spot through the strike and generates significant profits.

Low Delta Vanilla Options

The volatility smile is well defined and reasonably liquid in the market for strikes between 10 delta puts on the downside and 10 delta calls on the topside. Outside those levels vanilla options have little vega and for very low delta strikes it often makes more sense to quote prices on them in *premium terms* rather than *implied volatility terms*, particularly at shorter tenors.

Example: the system mid premium for a EUR/USD 1wk 1.3665 EUR call/USD put vanilla option with spot at 1.3530 is approximately 0.01 EUR% (one basis point) off an implied volatility of 4.1%. Delta is around 4% as shown in Exhibit 15.13.

The trader wants to show a 0.025% premium bid–offer spread on the contract but they cannot spread it symmetrically (since the bid cannot go below zero) so instead they want to show 0.005/0.03 EUR%. In implied volatility terms this is 3.75%/5.4%, but the trader could also quote the premium price directly: The delta is so small that the rounded premium will not change as spot moves within a reasonable range.

Market participants often do not like to sell very low premium wing vanilla options since there is very little premium earned compared to the potential negative P&L that may result if spot jumps through the strike. This results in lopsided liquidity at the bid and offer levels for these contracts. It is usually possible to sell a large amount at or near to the system midmarket. However, to buy them, a price relatively far above the system midmarket will usually need to be paid. More

Contract Details	Leg 1
Currency Pair	EUR/USD
Horizon	Mon 21-Jul-14
Spot Date	Wed 23-Jul-14
Strategy	Vanilla
Call/Put	EUR Call/USD Put
Maturity	1W
Expiry Date	Mon 28-Jul-14
Delivery Date	Wed 30-Jul-14
Cut	NY
Strikes	1.3665
Notional Currency	EUR

Market Data	
Spot	1.3530
Swap Points	0
Forward	1.3530
Deposit (EUR)	0.00%
Deposit (USD)	0.00%
ATM Volatility	4.10%
Pricing Volatility	**4.10%**

Outputs	
Output Currency	EUR
Premium	**0.01%**

EXHIBIT 15.13 Pricing tool showing low delta 1wk EUR/USD vanilla option

generally, most traders dislike doing trades where the potential downside is far larger than the potential upside (the premium), sometimes called **leverage**.

Another important factor is how the volatility base determines the range of vanilla options that can be traded in the interbank market. This is particularly relevant in emerging market currency pairs. When implied volatility is low, the range of options that can be liquidly traded in the interbank market is constrained to strikes fairly close to current spot. If the main risk is that spot suddenly jumps a long way, it is hard to transact suitable options to adequately hedge vega risk at the post-jump spot level because even vanilla options that were quite low delta to start with can become deep in-the-money after the spot jump.

Agreeing Broker Market Data

Within the interbank broker market, once a transaction is agreed in volatility terms the remaining inputs to the Black-Scholes formula must be agreed in order to calculate the option premium.

If a trader gets long gamma from the transaction, they naturally want the spot reference to be as far from the current midmarket level as possible. On booking the deal, spot effectively jumps from the agreed hedge level to the current market spot. If a trader gets short gamma from the deal, they will want the spot reference exactly at the current market spot.

Likewise, if a trader gets long volga from the transaction, they naturally want the implied volatility reference to be as far from current midmarket level as possible. On booking the deal, implied volatility effectively jumps from the agreed hedge level to the current market level. If a trader gets short volga from the deal, they will want the volatility reference exactly at the current market level.

True midmarket data is usually easy to obtain, so this issue rarely causes problems because there can be little debate about which market data to use, but it is important for traders to understand that this issue exists. Do not assume that fair market data will always be suggested: Most market participants are extremely smart and are constantly looking for ways in which to gain an edge, no matter how small.

CHAPTER 16

ATM Volatility and Correlation

Correlation is an important measure within FX derivatives. The ATM volatility and correlation framework is often used to calculate ATM volatility in cross-currency pairs. Dephased vega exposures are also calculated within the same framework.

ATM Volatility Triangles

In trigonometry, the cosine rule relates the lengths of sides of a triangle to the cosine of one of its angles as shown in Exhibit 16.1. If the length between point A and point B is denoted AB, the cosine rule states that:

$$BC^2 = AB^2 + AC^2 - (2 . AB . AC . \cos x)$$

The cosine rule can also be applied to ATM implied volatility in three currency pairs at the same tenor as shown in Exhibit 16.2. The distance between EUR and USD represents EUR/USD ATM volatility; the longer the length, the higher the ATM volatility. The angle θ is the inverse cosine ($\cos^{-1}$) of the correlation (ρ) between spot log returns in EUR/USD and GBP/USD. Going forward, ρ is described as the *correlation between* the *major currency pairs* (EUR/USD and GBP/USD in this example) and the output pair (EUR/GBP) is called the *cross-currency pair*. Beware of the overlap in symbols between correlation and rho exposure (see Chapter 14); the correct meaning should be obvious from the context.

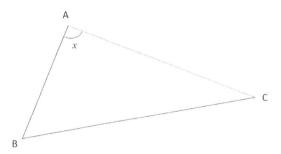

EXHIBIT 16.1 Cosine rule triangle

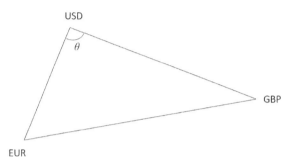

EXHIBIT 16.2 ATM implied volatility triangle

A proof that this transformation from trigonometry to ATM volatility is valid can be found in Iain J. Clarke's book, *Foreign Exchange Option Pricing: A Practitioners Guide* (John Wiley & Sons, 1st Edition, 2010).

The cosine rule for ATM volatilities is therefore, for example,

$$\sigma_{EURGBP}{}^2 = \sigma_{EURUSD}{}^2 + \sigma_{GBPUSD}{}^2 - (2\,\sigma_{EURUSD} \cdot \sigma_{GBPUSD} \cdot \rho)$$

Rearranging:

$$\rho = \frac{\sigma_{EURUSD}{}^2 + \sigma_{GBPUSD}{}^2 - \sigma_{EURGBP}{}^2}{2\,\sigma_{EURUSD} \cdot \sigma_{GBPUSD}}$$

These formulas can be used to calculate the ATM volatility in cross-currency pairs where a limited number of contracts are traded in the interbank broker market. The framework can also be used to calculate an implied correlation from three ATM volatilities.

Example: Calculating 1mth AUD/CAD ATM:

- $\sigma_{AUDUSD\ 1mth\ ATM} = 6.30\%$

- $\sigma_{USDCAD\ 1mth\ ATM} = 4.25\%$

- $\rho_{AUDUSD\ USDCAD\ 1mth} = -50\%$

Therefore:

$$\sigma_{AUDCAD\ 1mth\ ATM} = \sqrt{6.30\%^2 + 4.25\%^2 - (2 \times 6.30\% \times 4.25\% \times 50\%)}$$
$$= 5.55\%$$

Note that the *negative correlation* is used in the formula to take the currency pair quotation order into account. The formula takes correlation between AUD/USD and CAD/USD (the common currency as CCY2 in both cases). However, since the market quotes AUD/USD and USD/CAD, the negative of the correlation is used.

When correlation is an input to the formula, it is often not straightforward to determine what value to use. The implied correlation between tenors is often fairly consistent so interbank broker prices in the cross-currency at other tenors could be used to calculate it. If market prices are not available, traders often assess the historical spot correlation using different sample windows, and then take an average adjusted for any strong recent trend in the data as per Exhibit 16.3.

If correlation is more unstable, this implies that a wider bid–offer spread should be applied in the cross-currency pair.

The triangle representation of implied ATM volatilities explains the link between cross volatility and correlation. If the correlation between major pairs is 0%, the angle within the triangle is 90 degrees ($\cos^{-1} 0 = 90°$). This is shown in Exhibit 16.4. Note that the cosine rule reduces to Pythagoras's Theorem in this case.

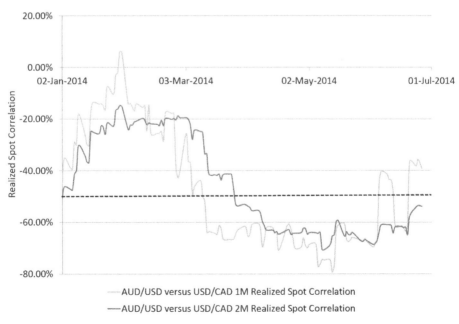

—AUD/USD versus USD/CAD 1M Realized Spot Correlation
—AUD/USD versus USD/CAD 2M Realized Spot Correlation

EXHIBIT 16.3 Realized AUD/USD versus USD/CAD historical spot correlation

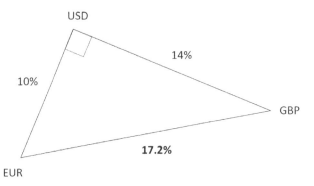

EXHIBIT 16.4   ATM implied volatility with zero correlation

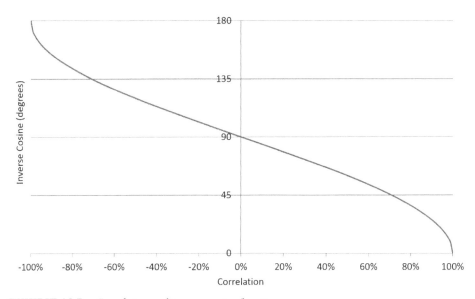

EXHIBIT 16.5   Correlation and inverse cosine function

As the correlation between major pairs goes higher, the angle within the implied volatility triangle tightens as per Exhibit 16.5.

As the angle tightens, with the major lengths remaining constant, the cross-currency ATM volatility (EUR/GBP) reduces as shown in Exhibit 16.6.

If the correlation is 100%, the angle is 0 degrees and the lines will be on top of each other as shown in Exhibit 16.7. Put another way, when EUR/USD and GBP/USD spots move perfectly together the cross-currency pair EUR/GBP will be static.

If EUR/USD and GBP/USD ATM volatilities are not equal but their correlation is 100%, the cross-volatility formula breaks due to square-rooting a negative value. In effect, ATM implied volatility levels create bounds on the correlation.

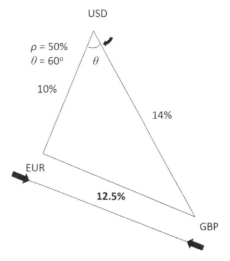

EXHIBIT 16.6 ATM implied volatility triangle with correlation above zero

EXHIBIT 16.7 ATM implied volatility triangle with 100% correlation

As the correlation between major pairs goes lower, the angle widens and the major lengths stay constant; hence the cross-ATM volatility increases as shown in Exhibit 16.8.

If the correlation between major pairs is −100%, the angle is 180 degrees and the cross ATM volatility is the sum of the two major ATM volatilities since −100% correlation implies EUR/USD and GBP/USD spots move in perfectly opposite directions as shown in Exhibit 16.9.

If EUR/USD ATM volatility is 10% and GBP/USD ATM volatility is 10%, the relationship between correlation and cross volatility is shown in Exhibit 16.10.

This is a key result: *Correlation and cross volatility move in opposite directions*:

■ Higher correlation between major pairs → tighter angle in ATM volatility triangle → lower cross volatility

■ Lower correlation between major pairs → wider angle in ATM volatility triangle → higher cross volatility

In practice, this framework is often used to generate ATM curves in cross-currency pairs using the ATM curves in the two major currency pairs and a term structure of

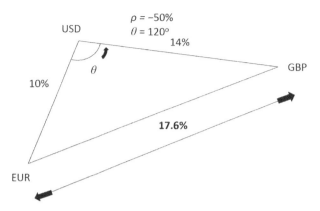

EXHIBIT 16.8 ATM implied volatility triangle with correlation below zero

EXHIBIT 16.9 ATM implied volatility triangle with –100% correlation

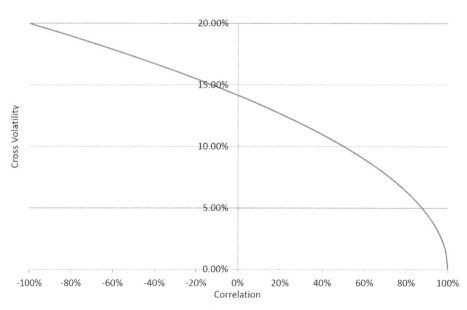

EXHIBIT 16.10 Cross-currency ATM volatility versus correlation profile

implied correlation maintained by traders. Within this framework it is important to correctly adjust for events. For example, if EUR/USD and AUD/USD ATM at the same tenor are both raised due to an important USD event, the EUR/AUD ATM should disregard the effect of the USD event.

▓ Dephased Vega

The same ATM volatility triangle framework can be also used to calculate dephased vega exposures. *Dephasing* is a term from physics that roughly means "shifting an exposure into its core constituents."

For example, the vega on a EUR/AUD contract can be split into equivalent EUR/USD and AUD/USD vega exposures plus an exposure to the EUR/USD versus AUD/USD correlation. This transformation is particularly useful in less liquid cross-currency pairs or when risk in many currency pairs is being considered simultaneously. Usually the cross pair is split into two USD pairs but this is not always the case; for example, USD/PLN would most naturally be split into EUR/USD and EUR/PLN.

Within the dephasing calculation, the system of ATM volatilities and correlations is kept constant except for one element, which is flexed. Given two major currency pairs, CCY1/CCY2 and CCY1/CCY3, and a vega exposure in the cross currency pair: CCY2/CCY3, as shown in Exhibit 16.11:

- $\sigma_{CCY1CCY2}$ only is flexed a small amount and the impact on $\sigma_{CCY2CCY3}$ is calculated; that is, one major ATM volatility is flexed and its impact on the cross-ATM volatility is measured using: $dephased\_vega_{CCY1CCY2} = vega_{CCY2CCY3} \cdot \dfrac{\partial \sigma_{CCY2CCY3}}{\partial \sigma_{CCY1CCY2}}$. The magnitude of $dephased\_vega_{CCY1CCY2}$ therefore depends on the correlation between pairs CCY1/CCY2 and CCY2/CCY3. The higher the correlation, the more CCY2/CCY3 cross vega will dephase into CCY1/CCY2 vega.

- $\sigma_{CCY1CCY3}$ only is flexed a small amount and the impact on $\sigma_{CCY2CCY3}$ calculated; that is, the other major ATM volatility is flexed and its impact on the cross-ATM volatility is measured using $dephased\_vega_{CCY1CCY3} = vega_{CCY2CCY3} \cdot \dfrac{\partial \sigma_{CCY2CCY3}}{\partial \sigma_{CCY1CCY3}}$. The magnitude of $dephased\_vega_{CCY1CCY3}$ therefore depends on the correlation between pairs CCY1/CCY3 and CCY2/CCY3. The higher the correlation, the more CCY2/CCY3 cross vega will dephase into CCY1/CCY3 vega.

- The sensitivity to changes in correlation ρ is also calculated. The major ATM implied volatilities ($\sigma_{CCY1CCY2}$ and $\sigma_{CCY1CCY3}$) are held constant and hence the dephased correlation causes a change in the cross-ATM volatility ($\sigma_{CCY2CCY3}$) only, which changes contract values.

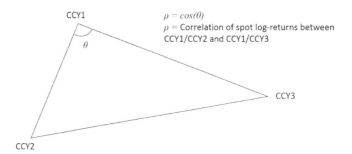

$\rho = cos(\theta)$
ρ = Correlation of spot log-returns between CCY1/CCY2 and CCY1/CCY3

EXHIBIT 16.11   ATM implied volatility triangle

EXHIBIT 16.12   1yr ATM implied volatility triangle containing EUR, USD, and CNH

Vega	EUR Vega
EUR/CNH	32,276
Dephased Vega	**EUR Vega**
EUR/USD	30,779
USD/CNH	15,676

EXHIBIT 16.13   Dephased vegas from a 1yr EUR/CNH vega exposure

Example: Consider 1yr EUR, USD, and CNH ATM volatility. USD/CNH has a low ATM volatility and the correlation between EUR/USD and USD/CNH is small negative. Therefore, EUR/CNH has an ATM volatility similar to EUR/USD as shown in an ATM volatility triangle in Exhibit 16.12.

The sharpness of the angle at θ' shows the high correlation (95%) between EUR/USD and EUR/CNH. Therefore, the majority of EUR/CNH vega will dephase into EUR/USD rather than USD/CNH as shown in Exhibit 16.13. Note that the dephased vegas do not necessarily sum to equal the cross vega.

■ Managing Cross-Currency Positions

It is important that traders understand how to manage exposures in cross-currency pairs. Sometimes, exposures are moved directly into more liquid currency pairs. For example, in the above EUR/USD/CNH example, the EUR/CNH Greek exposures might be viewed *as* EUR/USD exposures, in effect assuming that USD/CNH doesn't move (a fairly reasonable assumption given the low implied volatility in USD/CNH).

When managing cross-currency positions, traders often transact delta hedges and then split the risk into two separate currency pairs. For example, if the JPY trader is long EUR/JPY delta and short CHF/JPY delta, they may sell EUR/CHF spot and split it into short EUR/JPY and long CHF/JPY spot trades, with offsetting JPY amounts.

Gamma positions in cross-currency pairs produce deltas that are often hedged in the major currency pairs for convenience or due to larger spot bid–offer spreads in cross-currency pairs. Consider a long EUR/CAD gamma position. If EUR/USD spot moves higher in isolation, EUR/CAD gets pulled higher and EUR/CAD gets longer delta from the long gamma. This is equivalent to getting longer EUR/USD delta and longer USD/CAD delta so spot can be sold in both major currency pairs to rebalance the deltas.

If USD/CAD goes higher in isolation, again, EUR/CAD gets pulled higher and EUR/CAD gets longer delta from the long gamma. This is equivalent to getting longer EUR/USD delta and longer USD/CAD delta so spot can be sold in both major currency pairs to rebalance the delta.

Risk managing cross-gamma positions becomes a multidimensional problem when the exposures are moved into the major currency pairs. Continuing the EUR/CAD example, the USD/CAD delta is no longer driven only by USD/CAD spot; it now also depends on EUR/USD spot. Therefore, it is no longer sufficient to view, e.g., USD/CAD delta as a single number. It should be ideally viewed as a two-dimensional grid for changes in both EUR/USD spot and USD/CAD spot. This is very similar to how multi-asset exotic contracts are risk managed (see Chapter 30).

CHAPTER 17

FX Derivatives Market Analysis

Traders analyze the FX derivatives market in order to identify relatively cheap and expensive aspects of the volatility surface. This analysis is then used to position trading books and generate trade ideas for clients. The FX derivatives market has many moving parts and there are a correspondingly large number of ways in which it can be investigated.

Calculating Breakevens

The simplest FX derivatives analysis involves combining a short-dated vanilla option payoff with its premium to calculate its **breakeven**. Assuming the option is left unhedged until maturity, if spot moves beyond the breakeven point, the trade will make money. This breakeven point can be compared with expectations of spot movement to determine whether the option is cheap or expensive.

For a single vanilla option, the premium (expressed in CCY2 pips) is added onto (for a call option) or taken away from (for a put option) the strike level to determine the breakeven. For example, if current USD/JPY spot is 95.00 and the premium on a 3mth 100.00 USD call/JPY put option is 400 JPY pips, the breakeven on the option is 104.00. This is shown in Exhibit 17.1.

As the strike is moved higher, the premium decreases but the breakeven moves further away, as shown in Exhibit 17.2.

For a short-dated ATM straddle, the breakeven is calculated by summing the call and put premiums. The breakeven is now two-sided and symmetric, as per Exhibit 17.3.

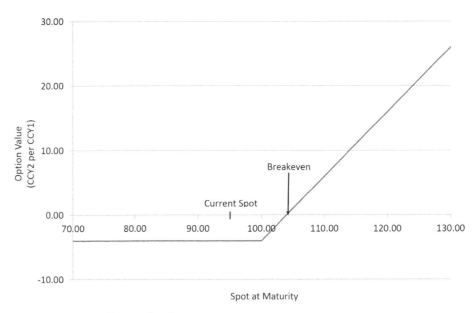

EXHIBIT 17.1   Call option breakeven

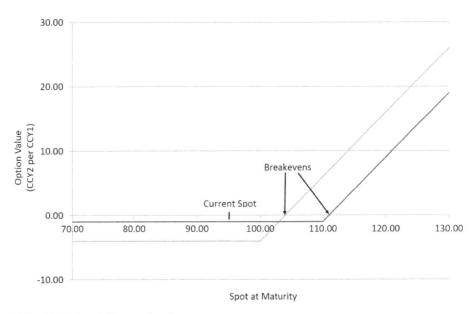

EXHIBIT 17.2   Call option breakevens

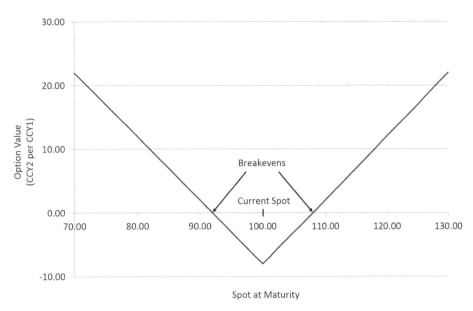

EXHIBIT 17.3 ATM straddle option breakeven

Typical trader analysis compares the historic *range* of spot in, for example, the last week versus the *breakeven* on a 1wk ATM straddle. However, care must be taken because these measures are not directly comparable. For example, spot may well establish a range larger than a 60-pips breakeven, but if it moves, for example, 80 pips up and then 80 pips down, unless the delta has been hedged perfectly (not likely), money will still be lost from buying the straddle. As a rough rule of thumb, spot usually needs to establish a range approximately double the breakeven for positive P&L overall to be generated from buying a short-dated ATM contract.

Breakeven analysis is particularly popular when the expiry date covers a major economic event. The one-day breakeven over the event can be calculated from the forward overnight volatility (i.e., the overnight ATM option expiring after the event). This value can be compared with historic spot moves caused by the event.

◼ Implied versus Realized Analysis

The most popular FX derivatives market analysis compares implied volatility with realized volatility. The central idea is that if implied volatility is higher than realized volatility, vanilla options should be sold and if implied volatility is lower than realized volatility, vanilla options should be bought. This is simple analysis but it can be effective if applied with an understanding of its limitations.

Implied volatility is at the core of the FX derivatives market. Within analysis the ATM implied volatility at a market tenor (e.g., 1mth, 2mth, etc.) is usually used because these reference contracts are directly quoted in the market. Using the implied volatility for another strike (e.g., the forward) or a non-market tenor expiry would require the entire volatility surface to be constructed—additional complication for only minimal benefit.

Realized (historic) spot volatility is calculated from spot samples. The required measure is the annualized volatility of the sample log returns.

Implied volatility and realized volatility are linked but they are *not always directly comparable* for a number of reasons. First, implied volatility is forward looking; it gives the pricing for option contracts expiring in the future. Realized volatility is backward looking; it is calculated using historic spot samples. This is shown in Exhibit 17.4.

Second, both volatility measures are impacted by events and holidays. Event days (i.e., days on which significant economic data is released) usually have increased volatility and holiday days usually have reduced volatility. Implied volatility and realized volatility are best compared when they mean the same thing; assessing the value in events themselves is another problem.

For example, comparing 1mth ATM implied volatility with 1mth realized volatility in early January will usually show a higher implied volatility because Christmas and New Year's holidays dampen realized volatility. In this case, implied volatility above realized volatility is not a signal that implied volatility is expensive. This situation is shown in Exhibit 17.5.

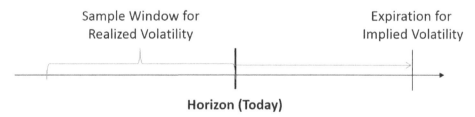

EXHIBIT 17.4   Realized volatility versus implied volatility

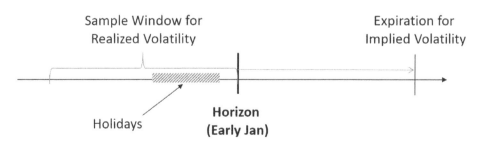

EXHIBIT 17.5   Realized volatility versus implied volatility in early January

Therefore, when analyzing volatility at shorter tenors (approximately sub-3mth) the effect of events and holidays should ideally be removed. Core (excluding events) realized volatility can be calculated by removing log returns at or immediately after major events. Core implied volatility can be calculated by removing the additional variance attributed to major events. At longer tenors, event and holiday day effects can be ignored because they will not significantly bias the analysis.

Sample frequency and *sample time* also significantly impact the realized volatility calculation. Exhibit 17.6 shows one month of market AUD/USD spot trades plus two daily snapshots, one taken at 3 P.M. and the other at 5 P.M. Note the gaps in data over the weekends, the outlier samples in the high-frequency data, and how much information is being ignored if only daily samples are used.

Using the data from Exhibit 17.6:

- Realized volatility calculated using 3 P.M. samples = 7.9%

- Realized volatility calculated using 5 P.M. samples = 7.6%

- Realized volatility calculated using minute samples = 10.5%

In general, using a small number of samples causes realized volatility to be biased low.

Using higher frequency samples gives better results up to a point but realized volatility does not necessarily converge as sampling frequency increases. So-called "tick data" contains *all* spot market activity on a given trading venue but noise in the

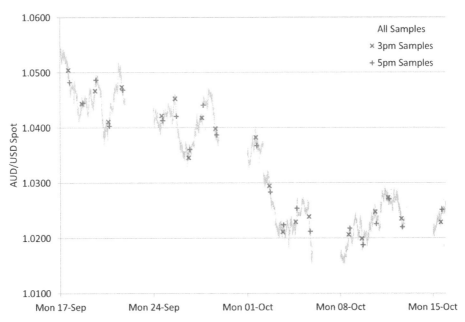

EXHIBIT 17.6   High-frequency AUD/USD spot trades

data can cause realized volatility calculated using a full set of tick data to be biased high. Therefore, tick data is often filtered before being used to calculate realized volatility, or the result is adjusted afterward.

It is important to take into account what the spot samples represent; is it trade data or is the data derived from a market bid and offer? Fundamentally, the point of the calculation is to measure volatility that can be traded, so, for example, if the bid–offer spread widens, that should not result in increased realized volatility.

In general, sample frequency should be aligned with calculation tenor. Using high-frequency data to calculate 5yr realized volatility is unnecessary and using daily data to calculate 1wk realized volatility will not contain enough samples for the result to be meaningful. In general, there is no truly "correct" realized volatility for a given period of market spot action. It is most important to ensure that a sensible and consistent methodology is used throughout the analysis.

Care must also be taken when using implied volatility at longer tenors (past two years) because ATM strike versus forward differences introduce a possible source of error into the analysis.

Example: AUD/JPY ATM versus ATMF (at-the-money-forward) implied volatility:

- AUD/JPY spot: 95.90

- 5yr ATM strike: 73.85

- 5yr ATM implied volatility: 15.35%

- 5yr forward: 78.30 (almost five figures above the ATM strike)

- 5yr ATMF implied volatility: 14.30% (more than 1% below the ATM volatility)

When analyzing longer tenors it is often preferable to use the implied volatility of the forward strike because the positioning of the ATM strike is impacted by market conventions. Alternatively, a convention-free long-term volatility parameter from a volatility surface model or pricing model could be used.

Calculating Realized Spot Volatility

The standard sample realized volatility calculation is:

$$\sigma_{Realized} = \sqrt{\frac{\sum (X_i - \overline{X})^2}{N - 1}}$$

where N is the number of log returns in the sample, X_i are log returns $= ln\left(\dfrac{S_i}{S_{i-1}}\right)$, and $\overline{X}$ is the mean of the X_i. This function can be accessed in Excel using =STDEV or =STDEV.S.

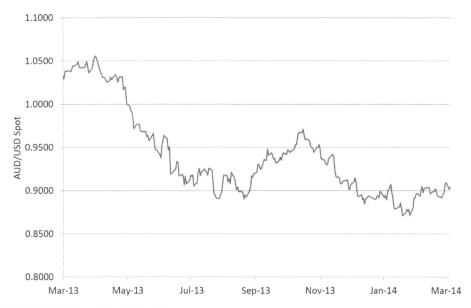

EXHIBIT 17.7 AUD/USD daily spot samples

To calculate the annualized volatility, multiply $\sigma_{Realized}$ by $\sqrt{N_{year}}$ where N_{year} is the number of samples per year.

Example: Calculating AUD/USD realized spot volatility using daily samples:

- Get daily sampled spot data (shown in Exhibit 17.7).

- Calculate log returns (shown in Exhibit 17.8).

- Calculate the standard sample realized volatility of the log returns using the above formula.

- Calculate annualized realized volatility. Data is sampled daily so the realized volatility must be multiplied by $\sqrt{252}$. Going forward, the term *realized volatility* is taken to mean annualized realized volatility.

Assessing *trends* in realized volatility is also important when comparing realized volatility with implied volatility. Set up a rolling calculation window and calculate a realized volatility time series using the samples within the window. In Exhibit 17.9 the realized spot volatility is calculated using a rolling 6mth calculation window.

Notes on Calculating Realized Spot Volatility

Note 1: The number of trading days in a year in the United States is usually 252, and this is the factor most often used to annualize daily sampled realized volatility whether there are exactly 252 trading days in a given currency or not.

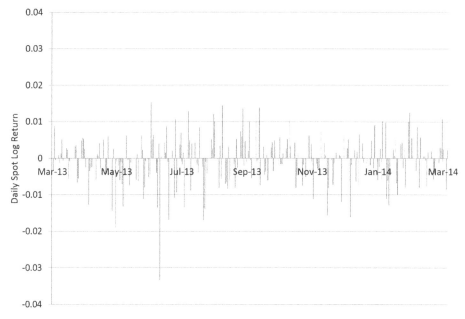

EXHIBIT 17.8 AUD/USD daily spot log returns

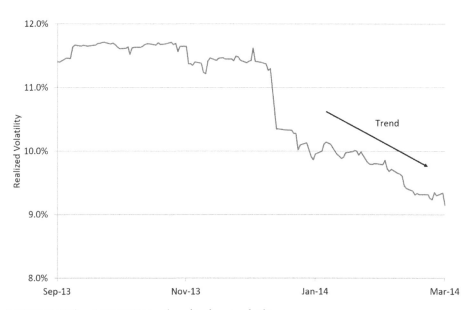

EXHIBIT 17.9 AUD/USD 6mth realized spot volatility

Note 2: It sometimes makes sense to remove the mean term from the realized volatility calculation because it can introduce noise into the calculation, that is,

$$\sigma_{Realized} = \sqrt{\frac{\sum (X_i)^2}{N-1}}$$

Tradable volatility depends mainly on spot changes rather than whether the market is trending (hence a larger mean term exists in the calculation). Consider that a spot steadily rising the same amount (in log-space) each day will have zero daily realized volatility when calculated with the standard method. However, that spot action is certainly not equivalent to a static spot within a trading position.

Note 3: To keep things simple, enough data samples should be used to ensure that issues around biased versus unbiased calculations can be ignored. As a very rough rule of thumb, aim for at least 50 data samples within the realized volatility calculation.

Exponentially Weighted Moving Average (EWMA) Volatility

The standard realized volatility calculation does not behave well when there are extreme jumps within the data: Standard realized volatility drops sharply as the jump data point exits the back of the sample window. This feature makes it difficult to compare standard realized volatility with implied volatility when the data contains jumps. A rolling realized volatility calculation that clearly shows the entrance and exit of an extreme jump into the sample window is given in Exhibit 17.10.

Therefore, **Exponentially Weighted Moving Average (EWMA)** volatility can be used instead. Within EWMA, weights are attached to each log return in the sample with the most recent samples weighted most highly and weights decreasing exponentially on older samples based on a λ parameter ($0 < \lambda < 1$). The weights for historic parameters for different λ parameters are shown in Exhibit 17.11.

Higher λ is therefore equivalent to using a larger sample window. A groundbreaking J.P. Morgan RiskMetrics paper from 1996 which is available on the internet shows that using $\lambda = 0.97$ is roughly equivalent (1% tolerance) to using 151 samples.

The EWMA calculation builds up over all available samples, not a specific sample window. Therefore, for example, "0.97 EWMA realized volatility" is calculated rather than, for example, "6mth EWMA realized volatility," although EWMA volatility still needs to be annualized in the same way as standard realized volatility.

$$\sigma_{EWMA,1} = \sqrt{(1-\lambda)X_1^2}$$
$$\sigma_{EWMA,i} = \sqrt{(1-\lambda)X_i^2 + \lambda\sigma_{EWMA,i-1}^2}$$

Under EWMA, the impact of the extreme spot jump decays away exponentially over time as per Exhibit 17.12.

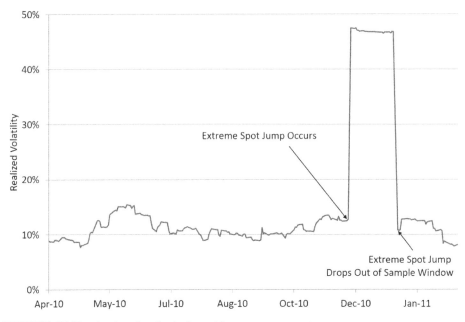

EXHIBIT 17.10   1mth realized volatility with an extreme spot jump

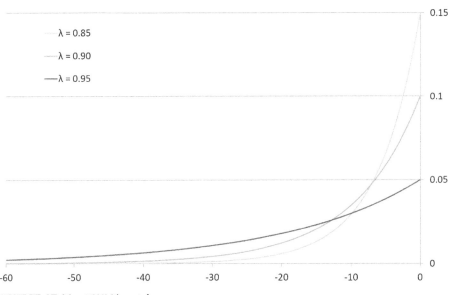

EXHIBIT 17.11   EWMA weights

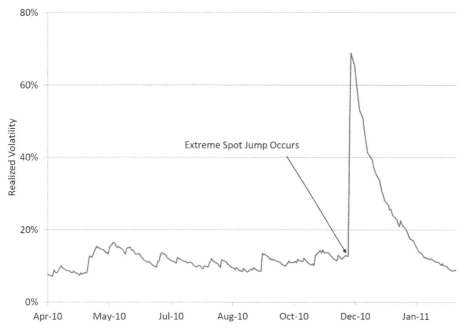

EXHIBIT 17.12 0.97 EWMA realized volatility with an extreme spot jump

This measure of realized volatility looks intuitively better, but if the extreme event is truly an outlier, perhaps it would be better to exclude it completely from the analysis. Plus, although the exponential decay function seems reasonable, there is no certainty that it is the right way to model the market "forgetting" extreme events.

Finally, the choice of λ can make a big difference to the output. Once again, there is no "correct" λ, although values between 0.90 and 0.99 are most commonly used in practice. The choice of λ must be made with reference to the sample frequency and the approximate number of samples which should have significance within the EWMA calculation.

Realized Spot Volatility versus Realized Forward Volatility

A European vanilla option has delta exposure (along with all other Greeks) to the option expiry; i.e., a 1yr vanilla option should ideally be delta hedged with a 1yr forward. In practice this means that if delta hedging was performed to the option maturity throughout its life, forward deltas to closer and closer maturities should be traded with each day that passes. This suggests that the realized volatility calculation should be adjusted in a similar manner, using different expiry dates. However, this requires substantial additional calculation for minimal benefit so this adjustment is rarely applied in practice.

However, when analyzing long-dated maturities, the realized volatility of the forward outright to a fixed tenor is often calculated. Realized volatility analysis now becomes two-dimensional; forward tenor and sample window can both be varied.

Example: Calculating AUD/USD realized 5yr forward outright volatility from daily samples. The realized volatility of the forward outright is calculated in the same way as the realized volatility of spot:

- Collect daily sampled 5yr forward outright data (shown in Exhibit 17.13).

- Calculate log returns.

- Calculate annualized volatility based on sample frequency.

- Use a rolling calculation window to generate a time series of implied volatility. In Exhibit 17.14, the spot and 5yr forward outright realized volatility is calculated over a rolling 6mth calculation window.

Realized spot volatility versus realized forward volatility differences are driven by:

- Spot versus interest rate correlation

- Interest rate volatility

Recall that in continuous time space:

$$F_T = S.e^{(rCCY2 - rCCY1).T}$$

EXHIBIT 17.13 AUD/USD daily spot and 5yr forward outright samples

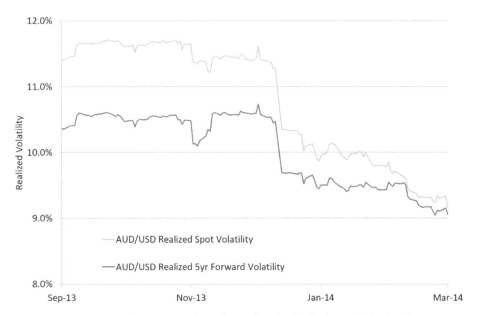

EXHIBIT 17.14 AUD/USD spot and 5yr forward realized volatility with 6mth rolling calculation window

And **swap points** define the difference between spot (S) and forward to time T (F_T):

$$F_T = S + SwapPoints_T$$

This framework is shown in Exhibit 17.15.

If CCY1 interest rates fall or CCY2 interest rates rise, swap points go more positive. If spot is static, the forward moves higher as shown in Exhibit 17.16.

If CCY1 interest rates rise or CCY2 interest rates fall, swap points go more negative. If spot is static, the forward moves lower as shown in Exhibit 17.17.

Therefore:

- Negative correlation between spot and CCY1 interest rates or positive correlation between spot and CCY2 interest rates → as spot moves higher or lower the forward moves more in the same direction → realized forward volatility will be higher than realized spot volatility.

- Positive correlation between spot and CCY1 interest rates or negative correlation between spot and CCY2 interest rates → as spot moves higher or lower the forward moves less in the same direction → realized forward volatility will be lower than realized spot volatility.

Plus, if interest rate volatility is zero, realized forward volatility is equal to realized spot volatility, whereas if interest rates are volatile (with no significant correlation effect), then realized forward volatility will be higher than realized spot volatility.

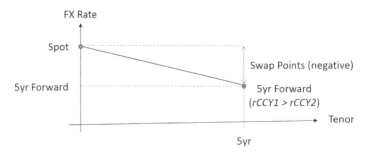

EXHIBIT 17.15   Spot and 5yr forward framework

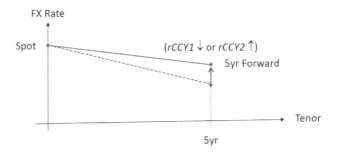

EXHIBIT 17.16   Spot and 5yr forward framework with a higher forward

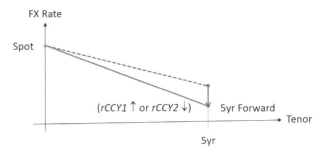

EXHIBIT 17.17   Spot and 5yr forward framework with a lower forward

Calculating Realized Spot versus Interest Rate Correlations

Correlation is a measure of the strength of relationship between two variables. **Pearson's coefficient** ρ is the standard measure of realized correlation:

$$\rho_{X,Y} = \frac{cov(X, Y)}{\sigma_X \sigma_Y}$$

where $cov(X, Y) = \dfrac{\sum_i (X_i - \overline{X})(Y_i - \overline{Y})}{N}$ is the covariance between X and Y, σ_X is the realized volatility of X, $\overline{X}$ is the mean of the X_i, and N is the number of data samples. This function can be accessed in Excel using =CORREL.

Correlation calculated using a small number of samples can be extremely unstable as shown in Exhibit 17.18. As with realized volatility, the calculation window should be linked to the sample frequency; short time-scale correlations should be calculated using high-frequency data plus sample times must be synchronized; that is, both variables should be sampled at exactly the same time.

Example: Calculating spot versus interest rate correlation using daily samples:

■ Get daily sampled spot and interest rate data (shown in Exhibit 17.19).

It is not always straightforward to determine which interest rate data to use within analysis; different interest rate instruments are traded at different maturities. In liquid G10 currency pairs at shorter tenors, OIS, libor, deposits, and futures are traded, whereas at longer tenors, interest rate swaps are often the most liquid instrument. In other currencies, interest rate markets are less liquid than forwards, so, for example, a USD rates curve plus the forward can be used to imply interest rates in the other currency. These issues can usually be ignored within FX derivatives market analysis providing a consistent measure of interest rates is used. Whether

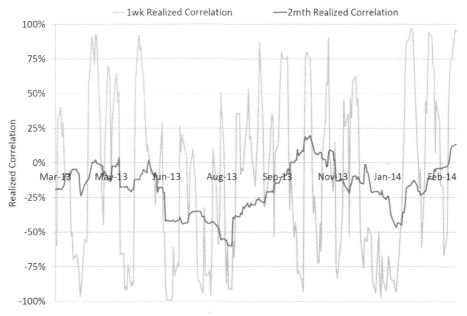

EXHIBIT 17.18   AUD/USD versus USD/JPY spot correlation

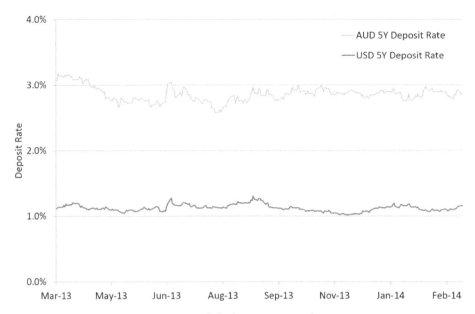

EXHIBIT 17.19 AUD versus USD 5yr daily deposit rate samples

the product is a swap, a deposit, or a future becomes inconsequential so long as the rate reacts appropriately as market interest rates change.

In this analysis, full interest rates curves were generated using different instruments; then the "5yr interest rate" is calculated in deposit rate terms, even though that contract is never actually quoted in the market.

- Take log returns or returns as appropriate. For interest rates, since they can go negative, it is arguably better to use returns rather than log returns within the calculation (i.e., $X_i = r_i - r_{i-1}$ where r_i is the ith interest rate sample).

- Calculate the correlation between spot log returns and interest rate returns.

- Calculate a realized correlation time series using a rolling sample window.

Exhibit 17.20 shows that within the data there is no strong correlation between AUD interest rates and AUD/USD spot, but a persistent negative correlation between USD interest rates and AUD/USD spot.

In this case, the negative correlation between USD (CCY2) interest rates and AUD/USD spot causes forward volatility to be lower than spot volatility.

Increasing interest rates in a particular currency often results in that currency becoming relatively stronger in the spot market because (unless there are major problems with the country) a currency with higher yield is more desirable to own. Therefore, there is often a positive realized correlation between CCY1 interest rates and spot and a negative realized correlation between CCY2 interest rates and spot (as seen in the AUD/USD example above). However, such changes impact the

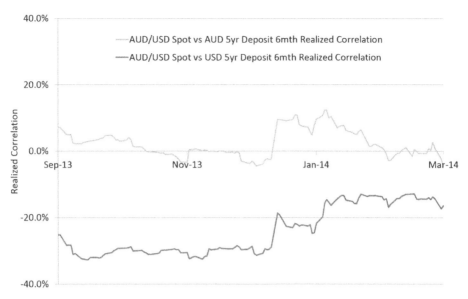

EXHIBIT 17.20   AUD/USD spot versus interest rate correlation

forward in the opposite direction and lead to forward volatility below spot volatility: spot higher as CCY1 interest rates higher → swap points more negative → forward moves less than spot.

The realized volatility of the interest rates themselves can also be calculated and this is shown in Exhibit 17.21. Interest rate volatility reduces over the same period as the realized forward outright volatility versus realized spot volatility difference narrows, as shown in Exhibit 17.14.

It is also possible to calculate EWMA correlation. The calculation is analogous to EWMA volatility:

$$\rho_{EWMA,X,Y,i} = \frac{cov_i}{\sigma_{X,EWMA,i} \; \sigma_{Y,EWMA,i}}$$

where:

$$cov_1 = (1 - \lambda).X_1.Y_1$$
$$cov_i = (1 - \lambda).X_i.Y_i + \lambda cov_{i-1}$$

Trading Implied Volatility

There are two main ways to trade implied volatility:

1. Buy or sell an ATM contract and lock in the implied volatility versus realized volatility difference by delta hedging the gamma exposure on the contract. This is most appropriate at shorter tenors where the main exposure on ATM contracts is

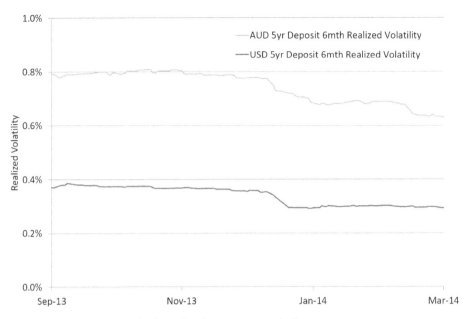

EXHIBIT 17.21   AUD and USD realized interest rate volatility

gamma rather than vega. For this analysis, *absolute levels* of implied volatility are compared with *absolute levels* of realized spot volatility in a similar tenor, ideally adjusted for the impact of economic data releases and holidays. For example, if a 1mth ATM contract can be bought for 8.0% implied volatility and spot consistently realizes 10.0% through to the option maturity, delta hedging the contract will be expected to generate a profit overall.

The frequency of delta hedging is also an important consideration. Within this analysis, the realized volatility versus implied volatility difference is most important and therefore delta should be hedged as often as possible. However, over-trading the delta in a currency pair with a wide bid–offer spread on the underlying can produce negative expected P&L.

Clients sometimes like to trade implied volatility versus realized spot volatility differences with a **volatility swap**—a forward contract on realized volatility over an agreed period usually using daily spot samples. This is attractive because no delta hedging is required and the exposures remain roughly ATM as spot moves, although bid–offer spreads on volatility swaps are wider than the spread on equivalent ATM contracts. See Chapter 31 for more details.

2. Buy or sell an ATM contract and then later unwind the trade at better implied volatility levels. This is most appropriate at longer tenors where the main exposure on ATM contracts is vega rather than gamma. For example, if a 1yr ATM contract can be bought at 8.0% implied volatility and then sold back at 9.0% implied volatility

that will (almost certainly) generate a profit. For this analysis it is most appropriate to investigate *trends* in implied volatility and realized volatility since the two measures often trend in the same direction. Consider the spread between implied volatility and realized volatility and look for lags in the data: Are realized volatility changes driving implied volatility changes or vice versa?

When trading ATM contracts, although the initial exposures are primarily gamma and vega, the exposures change as time passes or the market moves. For example, on short-dated vanilla options, as time passes the gamma exposure on short-date contracts increases if spot stays around the strike or reduces if spot moves away from the strike. Therefore, the realized P&L from trading a delta hedged ATM contract is not simply a function of realized volatility versus implied volatility; it is also path dependent.

After trading a long-dated ATM contract, if spot moves, the traded strike is no longer ATM and therefore the implied volatility for the strike becomes a function of the full volatility surface. When this happens the P&L from the trade is no longer simply a function of vega and implied ATM volatility change. Put another way, long-dated ATM options are *not* contracts for difference on implied volatility.

Clients sometimes like to trade implied volatility using a **forward volatility agreement** (**FVA**). This is a pure exposure to forward implied volatility between two dates in the future and therefore requires no delta hedging prior to the first date. See Chapter 31 for more details.

Many of the techniques covered in this chapter work best as relative value tools. Running analysis over multiple currency pairs and tenors can identify outliers that might work as trade ideas although the bid–offer spread on the ATM should always be taken into account. Looking at theoretical midmarket implied volatility levels in obscure crosses often suggests interesting trading opportunities but the spread cross involved in actually executing the trade always needs to be considered.

Finally, many studies conclude that there is a persistent trend that short-dated implied volatility is too expensive. In academic circles this is called the *volatility risk premium*. One of the key reasons for this risk premium is the preference of traders for the P&L profile from long gamma (many small losses versus few large gains) over the P&L profile from short gamma (many small gains versus few large losses) from a job preservation perspective, particularly on expiry dates when important economic data is released.

Trading Implied Correlation

To trade implied correlation using ATM instruments, a volatility triangle can be constructed as per Exhibit 17.22.

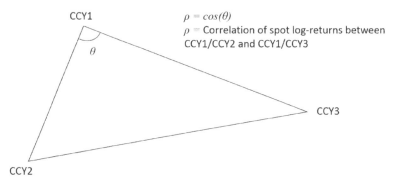

$\rho = cos(\theta)$
$\rho =$ Correlation of spot log-returns between CCY1/CCY2 and CCY1/CCY3

CCY1

θ

CCY3

CCY2

EXHIBIT 17.22 ATM volatility triangle for trading correlation

Recall from Chapter 16 that to go *long implied correlation* between CCY1/CCY2 and CCY1/CCY3: Buy the majors and sell the cross, that is,

- Buy CCY1/CCY3 and CCY1/CCY2 ATM contracts.

- Sell a CCY2/CCY3 ATM contract.

To go short implied correlation between CCY1/CCY2 and CCY1/CCY3: Sell the majors and buy the cross, that is,

- Sell CCY1/CCY3 and CCY1/CCY2 ATM contracts.

- Buy a CCY2/CCY3 ATM contract.

The notionals on the ATM contracts should be set such that there is zero initial dephased vega (see Chapter 16) in the major currency pairs to ensure a clean initial implied correlation exposure. As with trading implied volatility, the position can be either delta hedged to generate a P&L based on implied correlation versus realized correlation, or unwound later at a different level of implied correlation. Again though, issues involving exposures changing over time apply, plus transacting all three legs in the volatility triangle may cost a significant amount of spread cross.

Clients sometimes trade implied correlation versus realized correlation differences using a **correlation swap**—a forward contract on realized correlation using daily samples over an agreed period.

Realized Volatility Convexity

A final point to be aware of when comparing implied volatility with realized volatility is that *expected P&L is not linear in realized volatility*. Under stylized Black-Scholes assumptions it can be shown that expected P&L from trading a constant long gamma position is proportional to realized volatility *squared* based on the following equation:

$$E[P\&L_\Gamma] = -\theta.\left(\frac{\sigma_{Realized}}{\sigma_{Implied}}\right)^2$$

where $P\&L_\Gamma$ is the P&L from gamma trading and θ is theta.

If $\sigma_{Realized} = \sigma_{Implied}$, the expected P&L from gamma trading will exactly offset the theta paid. But when long gamma, more money is made trading gamma if realized volatility outperforms implied volatility than is lost if realized volatility underperforms implied volatility by the same amount. In other words, there is **realized volatility convexity**. The practical consequence of this is that implied volatility should be higher than realized volatility for it to be fair value. This effect is another cause of the *volatility risk premium* (discussed in the Trading Implied Volatility section above).

Exhibit 17.23 shows simulation results demonstrating how P&L from gamma trading changes with realized volatility and hedging interval:

- $E[P\&L_\Gamma]$ is proportional to realized volatility squared as per the above formula (i.e., the chart is quadratic, not linear).

- As hedging interval increases, P&L volatility increases. When a very tight hedging interval is applied the P&L volatility is small (this is the essence of the standard Black-Scholes formula derivation).

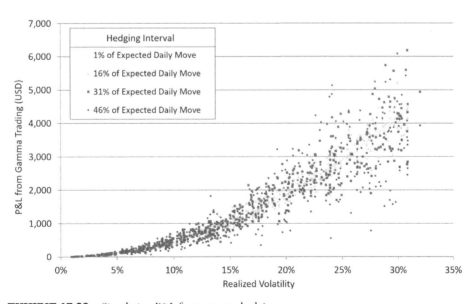

EXHIBIT 17.23   Simulation P&L from gamma hedging

■ Market Instrument Analysis

As well as being linked to the FX spot, forward, and interest rate markets, FX derivatives market instruments can be also assessed against their own history.

ATM Curve

Implied volatility often mean reverts, and **volatility cones** are a common method of visualizing how the current ATM curve looks versus its history. The lowest and highest implied volatility observed in each tenor over a given period is shown, plus the current level is highlighted. An example volatility cone is shown in Exhibit 17.24.

The idea is, if implied volatility mean reverts (i.e., tends to move back toward its long-run average over time) and it is currently toward the high or low end of the cone, it is more likely to move back toward the middle. This is fine, however, it is vital to consider *why* the current ATM curve is toward the extreme top or bottom of its historic range. If spot is stuck in a well-established range and realized volatility is still below implied volatility, the ATM curve *should* be near the bottom of its historical range.

Implied volatility mean reverts because the magnitude of the flows in a given currency pair can be fairly consistent over time and hence similar realized volatility is generated. For traders, the key moments are *regime changes*, when the level of a financial instrument completely changes from its historical level. For example, during the financial crisis in 2008, implied volatility in most currency pairs jumped

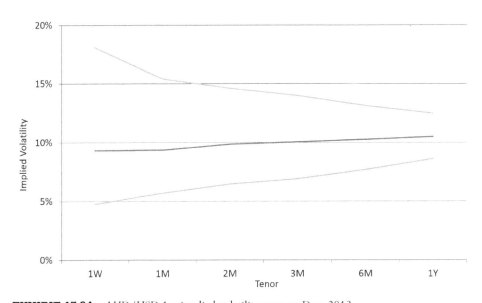

EXHIBIT 17.24   AUD/USD 1yr implied volatility cone on Dec. 2013

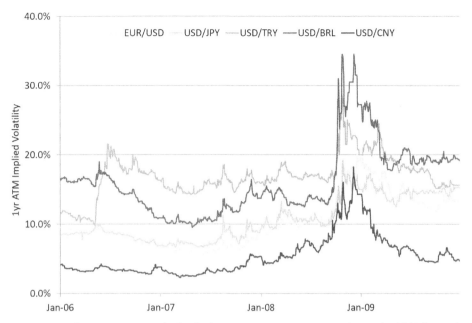

EXHIBIT 17.25 1yr ATM implied volatility in various currency pairs during the 2008 financial crisis

significantly higher, as shown in Exhibit 17.25 caused by sharp movements in spots and forwards plus increased uncertainty as shown in Exhibit 17.25.

When trading the ATM curve, it is also important to remember that, in practice, ATM implied volatility usually falls slower than it rises. If spot is range-bound, ATM implied volatility will tend to slowly drift lower over time, but if spot breaks out of its range, ATM implied volatility often jumps higher.

ATM Curve: Slope

If the ATM curve is sharply upward or downward sloping, calendar spread trades may be attractive. For example:

- AUD/USD 3mth ATM implied volatility = 8.2%

- AUD/USD 6mth ATM implied volatility = 11.5%

This implies a 3mth in 3mth forward implied volatility (see the calculation in Chapter 11) of 14.05%—much larger than the current 3mth ATM implied volatility. Therefore, buying 3mth ATM against selling 6mth ATM may be a good trading opportunity. The spread could be transacted with either initially vega-neutral notionals (to reduce P&L volatility from parallel moves in the ATM curve) or initially gamma-neutral notionals (to reduce the P&L volatility caused by spot moves). The trade will make a profit if the ATM curve "flattens" (i.e., the 3mth versus 6mth spread decreases).

The slope of the ATM curve can be assessed over time to identify levels significantly different from history. It is also interesting to compare ATM curve shapes in similar currency pairs. If there is an outlier, perhaps this implies a trading opportunity.

At longer tenors, ATM implied volatility becomes relatively more impacted by interest rate volatility and relatively less impacted by spot volatility:

■ If longer-dated realized forward volatility is higher than shorter-dated realized forward volatility, the ATM curve will more likely be upward sloping at longer tenors.

■ If longer-dated realized forward volatility is lower than shorter-dated realized forward volatility, the ATM curve will more likely be downward sloping at longer tenors.

Comparing realized spot volatility versus realized forward differences with the shape of the long-dated ATM curve may imply trading opportunities. As usual, though, care must be taken with market conventions.

ATM Curve: Seasonality

In currency pairs where there are significant amounts of corporate FX hedging, ATM volatility around the 1yr tenor can exhibit seasonality as corporates tend to hedge at either the start of the calendar year or at the start or end of their accounting year.

The majority of corporate hedge structures net sell vega and this flow into the market can cause implied volatility to consistently move lower at certain times of the year.

Volatility Smile: Skew

Using time series data, the current skew in the volatility smile can be compared with history using either market risk reversals or skew parameters from a volatility surface model. *If* the skew of the volatility smile mean reverts, then a quote toward the upper or lower historical limits will more likely move back toward the average. An example of this is shown in Exhibit 17.26.

Within this analysis it must be remembered that some currency pairs have persistent positive or negative skew due to client flow, particularly at longer tenors. Plus the risk reversal is often proportional to the ATM so the risk reversal/ATM ratio is often a cleaner measure of skew to use. It can also be interesting to compare ATM changes with risk reversal changes because the two instruments often move together.

Analyzing Value: Skew

In currency pairs where spot and volatility surface moves cause a long risk reversal position to make a profit, traders say the skew is "performing." Traders seek to

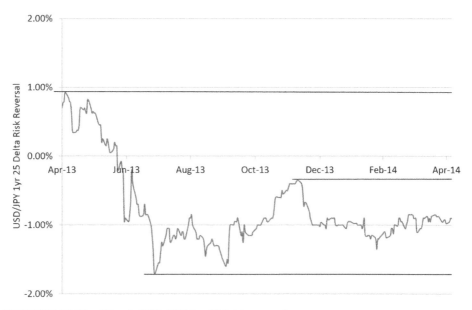

EXHIBIT 17.26   Historic USD/JPY 1yr 25d risk reversals

buy skew in currency pairs where it is performing and sell skew in currency pairs where it is not.

One possible skew analysis technique compares market risk reversal quotes with the realized spot versus volatility relationship. This ties in with the fact that the main exposure in the risk reversal contract is vanna $\left(\frac{\partial vega}{\partial spot} \right)$ as seen in Chapter 12.

A first idea might be to look at the *correlation* between spot log returns and ATM implied volatility log returns. However, using correlation is not appropriate because it is important to quantify *how much* spot and ATM implied volatility are moving together, not just *how* they are moving together. Therefore, the spot versus implied volatility relationship can be modeled using the *covariance* of spot log returns with implied volatility log returns.

As an aside, *correlation* (ρ) is dimensionless; it expresses how two variables (X and Y) move together: $\rho = 1$ or $\rho = -1$ implies perfect linear dependence while *covariance* $(= \rho . \sigma_X . \sigma_Y)$ additionally reflects how much the variables are moving. For example, if implied volatility moves up 0.01% for every pip that spot moves up and implied volatility moves down 0.01% for every pip that spot moves down, the correlation between absolute spot changes and absolute volatility changes will be +100%. Now, if implied volatility moves up 0.02% for every pip that spot moves up and implied volatility moves down 0.02% for every pip that spot moves down, the correlation between absolute spot changes and absolute volatility changes will still be +100%. However, the covariance in the second instance will be larger than that of the first.

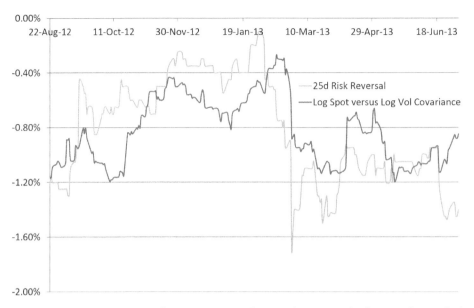

EXHIBIT 17.27   Time series of EUR/USD 2M risk reversal versus 30-day log spot/log implied volatility changes covariance

Assuming the 25 delta or 10 delta market risk reversal is proportional to the realized covariance of log spot changes versus log implied volatility changes, these time series can be plotted and compared in order to perceive value. This is demonstrated in Exhibit 17.27.

This analysis works best at mid tenors (1mth to 6mth) but there are plenty of issues to consider. Most obviously the risk reversal contract is forward looking while the realized covariance is calculated from historical data. Plus strong incorrect trading signals will be generated if there are regime shifts, if there is intervention in the spot market, or if spot is pegged or managed. As with all this historic analysis, trading signals must be considered rather than being blindly followed. It is interesting to run both 10 delta and 25 delta risk reversals through the same analysis to see how they compare in order to identify relatively cheap or expensive 10 delta or 25 delta risk reversals in different currency pairs.

Volatility Smile: Wings

Using time series data, the current wings of the volatility smile can be compared with history. The market butterfly instrument can be used but due to the broker butterfly conventions in high-skew currency pairs the wings versus market butterfly relationship can break down as shown in Chapter 12. Exhibit 17.28 shows AUD/JPY market instruments on January 1, 2008, and January 1, 2009, while Exhibit 17.29 shows the outright 10d and 25d and ATM strikes on the AUD/JPY volatility smiles for the same two dates.

Horizon	Tenor	ATM	25 RR	10 RR	25 Fly	10 Fly
01-Jan-08	1Y	15.60%	-5.00%	-10.00%	**0.25%**	3.00%
01-Jan-09	1Y	27.90%	-10.55%	-21.10%	**0.20%**	5.20%

EXHIBIT 17.28 Historic AUD/JPY market instruments

Horizon	Tenor	10d Put	25d Put	ATM	25d Call	10d Call	Average of 25d Strikes Less ATM	Average of 10d Strikes Less ATM
01-Jan-08	1Y	23.71%	18.72%	15.60%	13.72%	13.71%	0.62%	3.11%
01-Jan-09	1Y	44.60%	34.46%	27.90%	23.91%	23.50%	1.29%	6.15%

EXHIBIT 17.29 Historic AUD/JPY key strikes on the volatility smile

Between January 1, 2008, and January 1, 2009, the 1yr 25d broker butterfly went lower from +0.25% to +0.2% although the wings of the volatility smile are far higher on the later date.

Therefore, rather than using the market butterfly instrument within analysis, a convention-free volatility-of-volatility parameter from a volatility surface model could be used to quantify the wings of the volatility smile. Alternatively, the 10d strike fly (e.g., the average of the 10 delta call and 10 delta put implied volatility less the ATM implied volatility) could be used.

Again, *if* the wings of the volatility smile mean revert, then a quote toward the upper or lower historical limits will more likely move back toward the average.

Analyzing Value: Wings

In currency pairs where volatility surface moves cause a long butterfly position to make a profit, traders say the wings are "performing." Traders seek to buy wings in currency pairs where they are performing and sell wings in currency pairs where they are not.

One possible wing analysis technique uses the exposures of a long butterfly contract to compare the P&L generated from the volga $\left(\dfrac{\partial vega}{\partial \sigma} \right)$ based on historic ATM implied volatility moves with the theta paid to hold the butterfly contract over time.

The theta from a broker fly contract comes mainly from volga but there are also contributions from gamma and vanna. The gamma exposure can be hedged with a shorter-dated (1wk?) ATM contract and the vanna exposure can be hedged with a risk reversal contract.

By hedging away the other elements, the theta from *volga only* can be determined. The amount that implied volatility must move per day in order to make back the theta can therefore be calculated. Within this analysis, recall that volga is the second derivative of price with respect to implied volatility and therefore broker fly P&L is not linear in implied volatility, as shown in Exhibit 17.30.

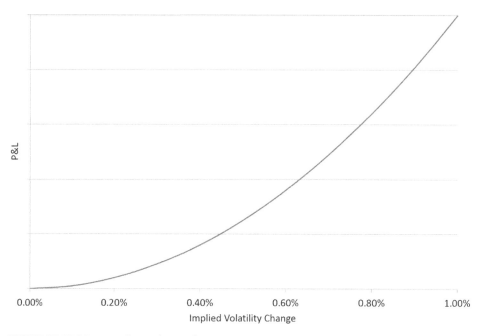

EXHIBIT 17.30 P&L from a long volga position

The breakeven daily implied volatility change can then be compared with historic daily implied volatility changes but this is rough-and-ready analysis with plenty of issues to be aware of. Most obviously the butterfly contract is forward looking while the realized daily implied volatility moves are calculated from historical data. Plus volga from the butterfly is assumed to stay constant over its life, and using daily data underestimates the realized volatility of implied volatility. In addition, relatively large ATM bid-offer spreads means that, in practice, implied volatility must move further than the midmarket level in order for the value to be captured in practice. Again, this analysis is most effective when applied over different currency pairs, tenors, and deltas to identify relative value trading opportunities.

Discussion on Historical Analysis

Comparing a current market quote with its history is a common analysis technique. One standardized way of quantifying this uses a **Z-score**, which is a measure of how many standard deviations from the average the most recent sample is:

$$Z\text{-}score = \frac{X_T - \overline{X}}{\sigma_X}$$

where X_T is the most recent sample, $\overline{X}$ is the sample mean, and σ_X is the sample volatility.

For any mean reverting variable, a negative Z-score is a buy signal and a positive Z-score is a sell signal. If the variable is normally distributed, Z-scores beyond approximately -2.5 and $+2.5$ are significant.

Again, this analysis fails during regime changes when the level of a financial instrument completely changes from its historical level. Regime changes will often generate strong false trading signals with any systematic analysis. As always, results should be considered carefully before being acted on.

Looking only at recent history is another common issue. Even if value is to be gauged using only quite recent history, it is instructive to check a longer time horizon to determine the historic bounds of the sample. Fundamentally, using historical data as a reference for what the future will look like is sensible and convenient but keep in mind that the future may look very different indeed.

Volatility Smile: Sticky Strike Analysis

Within **sticky strike analysis** the implied volatility for a specific expiry date and strike is tracked over time. For example, if it is currently January 2015, the implied volatility for a September-23 2015 1.3050 strike can be calculated today, one week ago, two weeks ago, three weeks ago, and so on, using full sets of historic market data. If the implied volatility was stable and then deviates, this may represent a trading opportunity. This analysis is essentially a more sophisticated version of the ATM implied volatility cone and again it relies on implied volatility mean reverting but on a per-expiry and -strike basis rather than in the ATM contract itself at a given tenor. This analysis is appropriate at longer tenors where the main exposure on the trade is vega and the analysis tends to work better in high-skew currency pairs.

Another way to analyze sticky-strikeness is with a scatter chart of historic ATM implied volatility versus spot. Spot higher or lower and ATM volatility higher or lower should tie in with the direction (positive or negative) of the risk reversal in the market. For example, USD/JPY usually has a negative risk reversal, implying higher implied volatility with lower spot. This spot versus ATM implied volatility relationship was very strong during 2007 and 2008 as shown in the scatter plot in Exhibit 17.31.

Market Positioning

Understanding how to interpret market positioning is a key skill that traders acquire. In simple terms, determining market positioning involves observing how market participants react to market changes.

Market participants' vega positions impact the FX implied volatility market. Since interbank flow is mostly zero-sum risk transfer it is *client trades* that generate the net market position. For example, if spot moves sharply and implied volatility stays around the same levels when it would normally be expected to rise, it can be concluded that the market is *long vega* around current spot because there are fewer

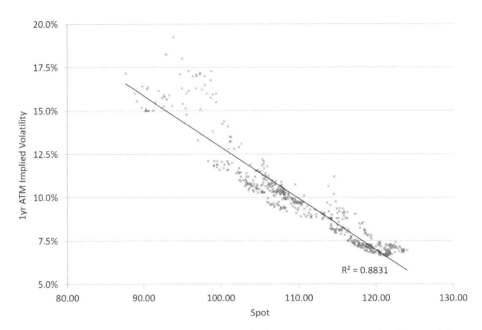

EXHIBIT 17.31 USD/JPY 1yr ATM implied volatility versus spot scatter plot showing daily samples from 2007 and 2008

market participants buying vega since they are already long. Remember that market vega positioning will change as spot moves.

Market participants' gamma positions impact the FX spot and markets via market participants' delta hedging. If market participants are long gamma in a certain spot region, increased taking profit when delta hedging may cause spot to remain range-bound. If the market is short gamma in a certain spot region, increased stop-loss orders may cause spot to be more volatile. When key spot levels (i.e., round numbered spot values) trade for the first time in recent history, American barriers are often knocked, which can dramatically change the market gamma positioning (see Chapters 23 and 24).

The maximum gamma from vanilla options comes from strikes close to maturity and the spot market often gravitates toward existing strikes with large notionals, called "market strikes." It is therefore useful to know the big strikes expiring in the market over the next week or so. This information can be sourced from the interbank broker market plus increasing data on expiries is becoming available as a consequence of new market regulations.

■ Carry Trades

The essence of a successful carry trade is to make money if "nothing happens" (i.e., the market does not significantly move). The classic FX carry trade is driven by the interest rate differentials in a given currency pair—buying the higher yielding currency and selling the lower yielding currency. This can be executed simply by trading the forward. For example, AUD/USD currently has one of the largest interest rate differentials in the universe of G10 currency pairs (although it is a small differential by historical standards). If AUD/USD spot is 0.9400, the 1yr AUD interest rate is 3%, and the 1yr USD interest rate is 0.5%, then AUD/USD 1yr forward will be approximately 0.9170. By buying the 1yr forward at 0.9170 and holding it to maturity, if AUD/USD spot at maturity is *above* 0.9170, money will be made from the strategy.

Another carry trade variation is achieved within a trading position by holding long cash balances in higher yielding currencies versus holding short cash balances in lower yielding currencies. As described, cash balances generate income based on their yield and the net money earned from the long and short cash balances can also be thought of as carry. Interest rate differential carry trades are particularly popular in currency pairs that contain one high-yielding emerging markets currency and one low-yielding G10 currency.

In quiet markets carry trade positions build over time; but if there is a market shock, the positions can rapidly unwind as everyone exits the same trade at the same time. The longer the carry trade builds up, the more dramatic the unwinding when it occurs. Exhibit 17.32 shows AUD/USD spot from 2006 to 2009. Part of this spot rise was due to increasing carry trade positioning. Each time investors went long AUD versus short USD within carry trades, at maturity they had gained not only from the interest rate differential but also the currency appreciation.

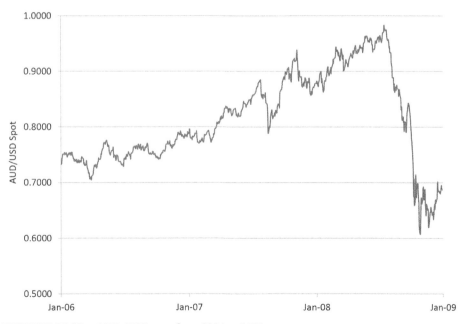

EXHIBIT 17.32 AUD/USD spot from 2006 to 2009

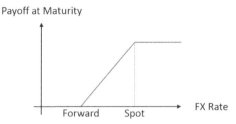

EXHIBIT 17.33 Call spread carry trade

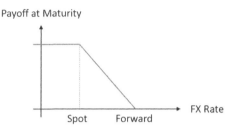

EXHIBIT 17.34 Put spread carry trade

This strategy worked really well until it went spectacularly wrong. The P&L distribution from carry trades is that of many small gains versus few large losses although academic studies often conclude that there is a long-term bias that gives carry trades a positive expected P&L. In practice, though, losses incurred in 2008 would cause any systematic trading strategies based on a pure carry trade methodology (buy the high-yielding currencies versus sell the low-yielding currencies) to be permanently shut down.

The link between interest rate differentials and the risk reversal is partly driven by carry trade positioning, which can unwind rapidly and cause a big increase in implied volatility to the high side of the risk reversal. Therefore FX carry trades are particularly popular in currency pairs with relatively high interest rate differentials but low implied volatility.

A multitude of variations on the carry trade theme are possible. In vanilla FX derivatives there can be carry strategies based on the ATM curve, the volatility smile, the interest rate differential, or combinations of all three. The common factor is that all carry strategies decay positively, providing the market stays static.

One simple FX derivatives carry trade involves trading a vanilla ATM spot versus ATM forward spread. This can be either a put spread or a call spread, depending on whether the forward is above or below spot. The two cases are shown in Exhibits 17.33 and 17.34.

Again, the idea is that the spread will pay out if spot remains at its current level. This strategy can be analyzed as a ratio of the cost of the spread over the potential maximum payoff. Ratios over 2.5 are often thought of as interesting. This carry trade is a function of the forward drift and the volatility smile.

PART IV

EXOTIC FX DERIVATIVES

When an FX derivative contract contains additional features above and beyond the basic vanilla option it becomes an **exotic** FX derivative contract. There are a staggering range of features that can be added: barriers, averages, variable notionals, payoffs returned in a third currency, and so on. Exotic options can also be combined to form popular structures used to hedge FX exposures.

Clients like trading exotic options because they can reflect more precise market views. For example, introducing a barrier that causes the contract to expire if a specified spot level ever trades can make a vanilla option payoff significantly cheaper. By adding a downside knock-out barrier to a vanilla call option the market view expressed by the trade (in isolation) evolves from "spot will be higher at maturity" to "spot will be higher at maturity without having first gone below the barrier level."

As shown previously, the market price for vanilla options is determined using the volatility surface. Exotic options are priced differently because they cannot be successfully priced using a single adjusted volatility. Instead, a reference price for the exotic contract is generated using the Black-Scholes framework and an *adjustment* is then calculated. The adjustment takes into account the volatility smile plus other factors not included in the Black-Scholes framework. Pricing models (covered in Chapter 19) are usually used to generate this adjustment.

Exotic options are often more difficult to risk manage than vanilla options. The Greek exposures from exotic options evolve differently and can get large particularly near barrier levels.

Within Part IV, exotic FX derivatives pricing is outlined and then popular classes of pricing models and a wide range of exotic products are introduced. For each product the key trading risks are explored and the pricing and risk management of the product is explained with reference to Greek profiles and pricing models. The aim of this approach is that by explaining trading risks from first principles, risk management rules can be applied generically to any exotic product, no matter how complicated.

CHAPTER 18

Exotic FX Derivatives Pricing

Vanilla option contracts are priced using a volatility surface that returns a midmarket implied volatility for a specific maturity and strike. A bid–offer spread is then applied around the mid-rate to get a two-way price quoted in *implied volatility* terms. Exotic option pricing works differently. Exotic contracts cannot be priced directly off a volatility surface because they have additional parameters (e.g., barrier levels) and therefore a more generic approach is required.

Exotic option contracts are priced in *premium* terms and the pricing is anchored by **Theoretical Value (TV)**—the CCY1% value of the exotic contract under Black-Scholes assumptions, specifically:

- A single, static volatility

- A single, static interest rate in each currency

- No relationship between spot, volatility, and interest rates

The ATM volatility to the final expiry date is used for calculating TV on exotic contracts. This volatility is often taken directly from the desk volatility surface. When calculating TV on an exotic contract it is vital that the correct ATM volatility is used. In practice this means the exotic trader checking the validity of the desk ATM curve with the appropriate vanilla trader or with interbank brokers prior to pricing.

After calculating TV, the market price is then quoted as an adjustment to TV that takes into account all relevant factors not included within the Black-Scholes framework. This is called the **TV adjustment**. It is quoted in CCY1% premium terms such that:

$$TV \ + \ TV \ Adjustment \ = \ Midmarket \ Price$$

A bid–offer spread is then applied around the midmarket price to obtain a two-way market price quoted in CCY1% of notional terms.

The main factor within the TV adjustment is usually the volatility smile. If a vanilla option were priced under this exotics framework, the TV would be the vanilla price calculated using the ATM volatility and the TV adjustment would be the *zeta* of the vanilla option (see Chapter 14 for details). This is shown in Exhibit 18.1.

Many exotic options contracts have exposures to the whole ATM curve up to the option maturity, not just to the ATM volatility at the option maturity itself. In this case the value of the ATM curve term structure must be included in the TV adjustment.

Some exotic options contracts have significant exposures to interest rate term structure, interest rate gamma, or spot versus interest rate correlation, none of which are accounted for within the Black-Scholes framework. In this case the value of these effects must be included in the TV adjustment.

Traders generate TV adjustments on exotic contracts using pricing models developed by quants. Pricing models are extensions of the Black-Scholes framework with additional parameters that are calibrated such that, for example, vanilla options priced using the model match prices generated by the volatility surface. These calibrated models are then used to price exotic contracts. A selection of popular pricing models and their various dynamics are introduced in Chapter 19.

By understanding the main trading risks on an exotic contract, traders use the most suitable pricing model to obtain a midmarket price. Traders must also recognize when pricing models will not capture significant risks on a contract and in these situations pricing will need to be manually adjusted.

Throughout this section, if not specified otherwise, Greek exposures are TV Greeks (i.e., exposures calculated using the Black-Scholes framework). This keeps

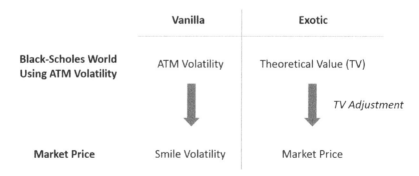

EXHIBIT 18.1 Vanilla and exotic pricing methodologies

the profiles clean but in practice traders often use Greeks generated by pricing models since these exposures better reflect expected changes in P&L as the market moves.

Exotic Pricing Example

Here are some exotic contract details quoted on a chat between a trader and an interbank exotics broker on July 30, 2013: *3mth 30 oct-1 nov 13 tky/0.8100 aud/usd ot/spot 0.9080/tv 5.35% vol 11.4/del A$2.1/−55/0.30/A$1-2 vh.*

Translating, that is:

- *Contract type*: one-touch (*ot*): A one-touch contract pays out cash at maturity if the barrier level trades prior to maturity.

- *Currency pair*: AUD/USD (*aud/usd*).

- *Expiry*: 3mth, and the exact dates are specified for clarity: expiry date: October 30, 2013/delivery date: November 1, 2013 (*3mth 30 oct-1 nov 13*).

- *Cut*: Tokyo (*tky*).

- *One-touch barrier level*: 0.8100.

- *Notional*: AUD1m to AUD2m (*A$1-2*).

This is enough information to enter the contract details into a pricing tool as shown in Exhibit 18.2.

Reference AUD/USD market data is also given:

- *Spot*: 0.9080 (*spot 0.9080*)

- *3mth swap points*: −55/USD deposit rate: 0.30% (*−55/0.30*)

- *3mth ATM volatility*: 11.4% (*vol 11.4*)

Contract Details	Leg 1
Currency Pair	AUD/USD
Horizon	Tue 30-Jul-13
Spot Date	Thu 01-Aug-13
Strategy	One Touch
Up/Down Barrier	Down
Maturity	3M
Expiry Date	Wed 30-Oct-13
Delivery Date	Fri 01-Nov-13
Cut	TOK
Barrier	0.8100
Notional Currency	AUD

EXHIBIT 18.2 One-touch option contract details

Market Data	Leg 1
Spot	0.9080
Swap Points	-55
Forward	0.9025
Deposit (AUD)	2.75%
Deposit (USD)	0.30%
ATM Volatility	11.40%

EXHIBIT 18.3   One-touch option market data

Outputs	Leg 1
Output Currency	AUD
TV	5.35%
TV Adjustment	+4.95%
Mid Price	11.30%
Price Spread	2.50%
Price	9.05/11.55%
Delta	-214%

EXHIBIT 18.4   One-touch option pricing outputs

This market data should be close to mid values observed in the market at the time of pricing. Exhibit 18.3 shows the market data in the pricing tool and Exhibit 18.4 shows the pricing tool outputs.

Under Black-Scholes, market data to a given expiry date is fully defined using spot, forward, one interest rate, and the volatility. Therefore, these exotic contract details could be priced by *any trading desk* in the market using the supplied market data and the same TV would be generated.

By entering the trade details and market data, the resultant TV can be checked against a reference. This TV matching helps confirm that the correct contract is being priced. Given the extra parameters within exotic contracts this additional safety is important. TV matching on exotic contracts occurs when trading in the interbank broker market plus some institutional clients also use it.

Going back to the example trade, the TV shown in the pricing tool is 5.35 AUD%, which matches the broker details (*tv 5.35%*). The delta in the pricing tool is 214AUD% which also matches the broker details (*del A$2.1*). Once the TV has been matched, the trader quotes a price in the form of a two-way TV adjustment. The key questions are therefore: What does the TV adjustment represent, and how is it calculated?

■ Pricing the Volatility Smile

The primary element within the TV adjustment is usually the volatility smile. Therefore, the first step in understanding exotic pricing is knowing how to estimate the impact of the volatility smile for a given contract.

Starting from first principles, exotic contracts with "good" features compared to the Black-Scholes model will cost more than TV to buy (a positive TV adjustment) and exotic contracts with "bad" features compared to the Black-Scholes model will cost less than TV to buy (a negative TV adjustment).

In the context of the volatility smile, long smile exposures (i.e., long-skew or long-wing exposures) are "good" features while short smile exposures (i.e., short-skew or short-wing exposures) are "bad" features. Therefore, the exotic contract is assessed to determine whether it has long smile exposures, in which case it will have a positive TV adjustment and will "trade over TV," or it has short smile exposures, in which case it will have a negative TV adjustment and will "trade under TV."

Just as the volatility smile can be split into the wings and the skew (as described in Chapter 12), exposures to the volatility smile can be split into the same two elements: exposure to the wings of the smile and exposure to the skew of the smile. A vega versus spot profile of an exotic contract is a simple method for assessing smile exposures and hence whether a contract will trade over or under TV.

Pricing the Skew

In a currency pair with a topside risk reversal, the vega profile of a long risk reversal position gets longer to the topside and shorter to the downside as shown in Exhibit 18.5.

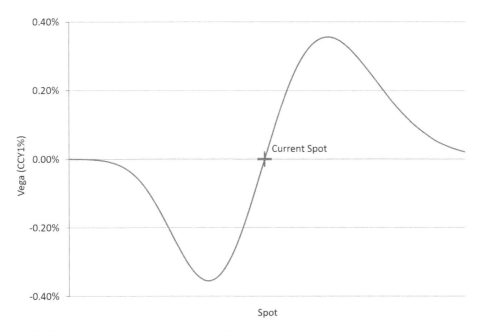

EXHIBIT 18.5   Long risk reversal vega profile

The zeta on the long topside strike within this risk reversal will be positive and greater than the zeta of the short downside strike, which may well be negative. Therefore, net zeta on this risk reversal is positive. By definition, buying a risk reversal results in a long smile position.

Example: Long Risk Reversal Zeta

Tenor: 1yr
Spot: 90.00
Forward: 89.50
Downside 25d put strike: 82.95
Downside strike ATM volatility = 15.10%/premium = 2.80 CCY1%
Downside strike smile volatility = 11.60%/premium = 1.70 CCY1%
Downside strike zeta = −1.10 CCY1%
Topside 25d call strike: 101.95
Topside strike ATM volatility = 15.10%/premium = 1.75 CCY1%
Topside strike smile volatility = 19.40%/premium = 3.10 CCY1%
Topside strike zeta = +1.35 CCY1%
In this currency pair, long 25d risk reversal is long topside strike and short downside strike.
Long 25d risk reversal zeta = +1.35% − −1.10% = +2.45 CCY1%

A similar methodology can also be applied to exotic contracts. In a currency pair with the risk reversal for topside, if the vega exposure on an exotic contract gets longer to the topside and shorter to the downside, the exotic is said to be "long risk reversal" or "long skew." In the same currency pair, if the vega gets longer to the downside and shorter to the topside, the exotic is said to be "short risk reversal" or "short skew."

More generally, if the vega exposure on an exotic contract gets longer on the higher side of the volatility smile, the exotic is said to be "long risk reversal." If the vega gets longer on the lower side of the volatility smile, the exotic is said to be "short risk reversal."

Exhibit 18.6 shows the vega versus spot profile from a long 1yr 130.00 one-touch contract. As stated previously, a one-touch contract pays out a fixed amount of cash at maturity providing spot has touched the barrier level throughout the life of the option. When calculating a TV adjustment on a single exotic contract, a *long position in the option is assumed*.

Intuitively, the long one-touch option is long vega because higher spot volatility makes the barrier knock, and hence the payout, more likely. With spot at 90.00, the one-touch vega profile in Exhibit 18.6 is "long risk reversal" because vega gets

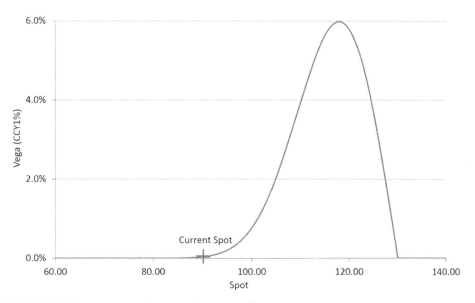

EXHIBIT 18.6 Long topside one-touch vega profile

longer to the topside and shorter to the downside, exactly like a long risk reversal position in this currency pair with topside skew.

Therefore, in this example, with spot at 90.00 and a risk reversal for topside, the one-touch will trade *over TV* (i.e., it will have a positive TV adjustment).

Example: Topside One-Touch

Tenor: 1yr
Spot: 90.00
Forward: 89.50
One-touch up barrier: 130.00
ATM volatility: 15.1%
TV: 2.0 CCY1%
TV adjustment: **+6.5 CCY1%**
One-touch midmarket price: 8.5 CCY1%

Buying this one-touch contract makes a trading position longer topside vega. To hedge this vega exposure, vanilla options with topside strikes must be sold. These topside vanilla options trade at a higher implied volatility than the ATM due to the risk reversal being for topside. Selling vanilla options at a higher volatility than the ATM earns zeta. Therefore, the exotic must cost more than TV: If it were possible to buy the one-touch under TV and then sell topside vanilla options on the hedge over TV, this would be a (very weak) form of arbitrage.

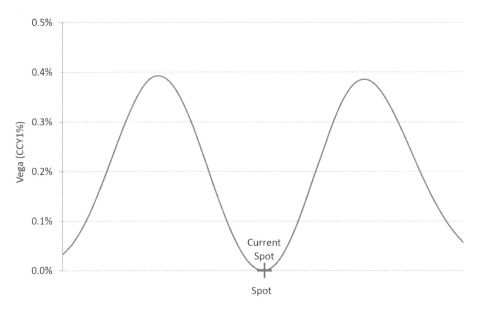

EXHIBIT 18.7 Long butterfly vega profile

When hedging the one-touch contract with vanilla options, the smile value of the vanilla hedge should be approximately equal (but negative) to the smile value of the exotic option. For example, if the one-touch contract was bought in USD1m at a TV adjustment of +USD6.5%, that implies +USD65k of smile value has been purchased. On the vanilla hedge, a similar amount of smile value should be sold.

Pricing the Wings

The wing exposure of the exotic contract must also be considered within pricing. This can be done using the butterfly contract. The vega on a long butterfly contract gets longer to both the topside and downside, as shown in Exhibit 18.7.

Ignoring broker fly complications, volatility smiles have positive wings and the sum of the zetas on the topside and downside same-delta strikes within the butterfly will be positive.

By definition, buying a butterfly results in a long smile position that, if priced within the exotics framework, would have a positive TV adjustment.

Example: Long Broker Butterfly Zeta

Tenor: 1yr
Spot: 90.00
Forward: 89.50

Downside 25d call broker butterfly strike: 82.95

Downside strike ATM volatility $= 15.10\%/$premium $= 2.15$ CCY1%

Downside strike smile volatility $= 11.05\%/$premium $= 1.05$ CCY1%

Downside strike zeta $= -1.10$ CCY1%

Topside 25d call broker butterfly strike: 99.20

Topside strike ATM volatility $= 15.10\%/$premium $= 2.35$ CCY1%

Topside strike smile volatility $= 18.65\%/$premium $= 3.60$ CCY1%

Topside strike zeta $= +1.25$ CCY1%

Long 25d butterfly is long topside strike and long downside strike.

Note that the ATM strikes within the butterfly are ignored when assessing the zeta because ATM contracts have zero zeta.

Long 25d broker butterfly zeta $= -1.10\% + 1.25\% = +0.15$ CCY1%

Assuming the exotic contract is vega hedged (which a butterfly is by construction), if the vega gets longer in the wings (i.e., away from current spot), the exotic is said to be "long wings" or "long fly." If the exotic vega gets shorter in the wings, the exotic is said to be "short wings" or "short fly."

Exhibit 18.8 shows the vega versus spot profile from a long 1yr 80.00/100.00 double-no-touch (DNT). A double-no-touch contract pays out cash at maturity providing spot hasn't touched either of the two barrier levels throughout the life of the option. Therefore, the long double-no-touch contract is short vega; lower spot volatility makes it more likely that spot stays within the range to get the payout.

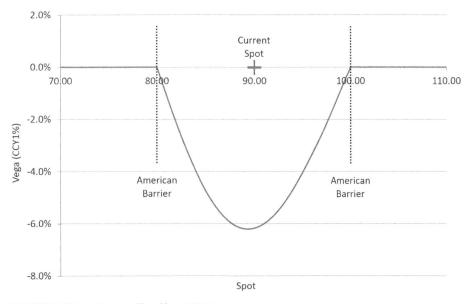

EXHIBIT 18.8   Vega profile of long DNT

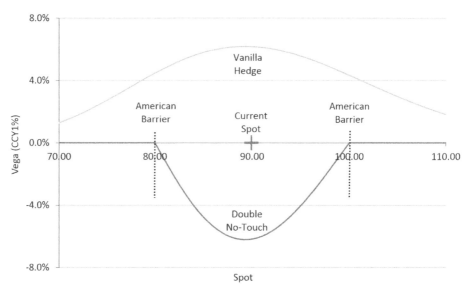

EXHIBIT 18.9 Vega profiles of long DNT and ATM vega hedge

It is hard to judge from Exhibit 18.8 whether the double-no-touch contract is long wings or short wings. Hedging the vega at current spot with an ATM option gives more clarity. This is valid since hedging with the ATM does not affect the smile position of the exotic contract plus hedge.

Exhibit 18.9 shows the vega versus spot profiles from a long 1yr 80.00/100.00 double-no-touch and its ATM vega hedge separately while Exhibit 18.10 shows the aggregate vega profile from the double-no-touch *plus* the ATM vega hedge.

With spot at 90.00, the double-no-touch is said to be "long wings" since the vega hedged long double-no-touch gets longer vega in the wings, exactly like a long butterfly position.

Therefore, in this example, with spot at 90.00, the double-no-touch will trade *over TV*, i.e., it will have a positive TV adjustment.

Example: Double-No-Touch

Tenor: 1yr
Double-no-touch barriers: 80.00/100.00
Spot: 90.00
Forward: 89.50
ATM volatility: 15.10%
TV: 12.75 CCY1%
TV adjustment: **+8.0 CCY1%**
Double-no-touch midmarket price: 20.75 CCY1%

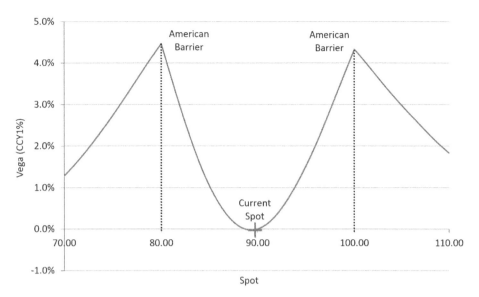

EXHIBIT 18.10   Aggregate vega profile of long DNT plus ATM vega hedge

Buying this double-no-touch contract with vega hedge makes the position longer vega to both the downside and topside. To hedge this wing vega exposure, topside and downside wing vanilla options must be sold. On average, wing vanilla options trade at a higher implied volatility than the ATM due to the shape of the volatility smile. Selling vanilla options at a higher volatility earns zeta. Therefore, the exotic must cost more than TV because buying it allows vanillas that trade higher than TV to be sold on the hedge. If it were possible to buy the double-no-touch under TV and then sell wing vanilla options on the hedge over TV, again, this would be a form of arbitrage.

As in the risk reversal case, when hedging the double-no-touch contract with vanilla options, the smile value of the vanilla hedge should be approximately equal (but negative) to the smile value of the exotic option.

Summary

For a given exotic contract, the TV adjustment from the volatility smile can be split into two separate effects: skew and wings. Exposure to the skew of the volatility smile is primarily assessed with reference to the risk reversal contract at the same maturity. Exposure to the wings of the volatility smile is primarily assessed with reference to the butterfly contract at the same maturity. The two examples given in this section neatly separate the two effects but most exotic option contracts have both exposures, which must be combined within the TV adjustment.

■ VVV Pricing Example: Part 1

VVV (vega/volga/vanna) pricing formalizes this approach. Second-order vega Greeks are used to measure the exposure the exotic contract has to the skew and wings of the volatility smile:

■ Vanna $\left(\frac{\partial vega}{\partial spot}\right)$ gives the exposure of the exotic contract to the *skew* of the volatility smile.

■ Volga $\left(\frac{\partial vega}{\partial \sigma}\right)$ gives the exposure of the exotic contract to the *wings* of the volatility smile.

VVV is a heuristic rather than a model. One possible implementation replicates the vega, volga, and vanna exposures in the exotic contract using ATM, 25d call, and 25d put vanilla options to the same maturity as the exotic. The TV adjustment of the exotic is estimated by calculating the cost of the vanilla replication "on the smile" (i.e., its cumulative zeta) and weighting this cost by the stopping time (explained later in this chapter) of the exotic contract.

This methodology can be applied to the example broker AUD/USD 3mth one-touch with 0.8100 barrier contract that was introduced earlier in the chapter. In AUD/USD the risk reversal is for downside and the one-touch has a downside barrier also. Exhibit 18.11 shows the AUD/USD 3mth volatility smile on the deal horizon while Exhibit 18.12 shows the vega profile from the one-touch option.

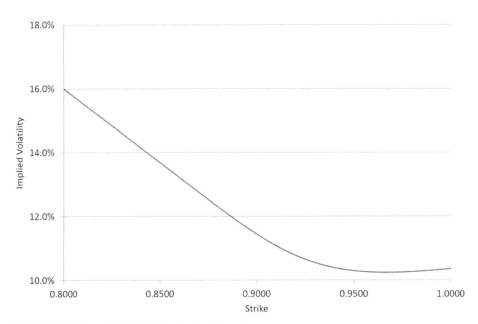

EXHIBIT 18.11 AUD/USD 3mth volatility smile

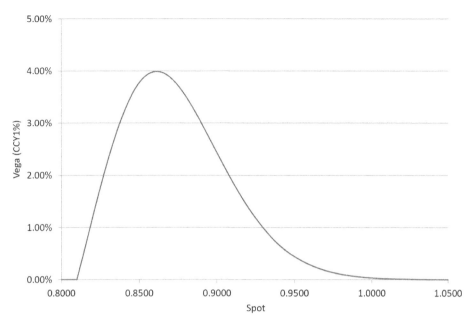

EXHIBIT 18.12 Vega profile of long AUD/USD downside one-touch contract

Under Black-Scholes, and with all exposures quoted in AUD% terms, the long one-touch contract has:

- Vega: 1.99%
- Vanna: −47.1%
- Volga: 0.29%

The signs of these exposures should not be a surprise: Vega is long because higher spot volatility increases the chance of the barrier touching, vanna is negative because vega gets longer to the downside at current spot, and volga is positive because vega overall gets longer in the wings.

The AUD/USD 3mth 25d call vanilla has a 0.9360 strike and:

- Vega: 0.165%
- Vanna: 1.95%
- Volga: 0.006%

The AUD/USD 3mth 25d put vanilla has a 0.8660 strike and:

- Vega: 0.115%
- Vanna: −1.85%
- Volga: 0.007%

The vega component can be ignored since it does not impact the smile exposures. What remains is a system of two linear equations with two unknowns—the notionals of the topside and downside vanilla options respectively, n_{call} and n_{put}:

$$n_{call} \cdot 1.95\% + n_{put} \cdot -1.85\% = -47.1\%$$
$$n_{call} \cdot 0.006\% + n_{put} \cdot 0.007\% = 0.29\%$$

which solves to give:

$$n_{call} = 5.8$$
$$n_{put} = 31.6$$

Therefore, the vega profile from the one-touch can be approximately replicated by buying 31.6× the one-touch notional of 25d downside vanilla options and 5.8× the one-touch notional of 25d topside vanilla options. Therefore, if AUD2m of this one-touch contract were bought, approximately AUD60m of 25d put options and AUD10m of 25d call option could be sold to hedge the vega profile.

On the smile, the 3mth 25d topside vanilla is marked at 10.45% implied volatility, which equates to –0.14 AUD% zeta (recall that the ATM volatility is 11.4%), and the 25d downside vanilla is marked at 12.95% implied volatility, which equates to +0.25 AUD% zeta. Therefore, the replication has a cost on the smile equal to $5.8 \times -0.14\% + 31.6 \times +0.25\% = +7.1$ AUD%. The positive TV adjustment implies that the one-touch option has long smile exposures, as expected since vega gets longer to the downside and the risk reversal in AUD/USD is also for downside.

The final step in the VVV methodology is to weight this cost by the stopping time of the contract.

Stopping Time

Stopping time (also known as *first exit time* or *expected life*) is the expected length of time an exotic option will stay alive. This is useful information about the risk on the trade and it is an important measure within exotic option pricing and risk management.

Stopping time takes a value between 0% and 100%, expressed as a percent of the life of the option. Therefore, if the stopping time of an exotic option is 50%, the option is expected to live for half of its life. The stopping time of a European vanilla option is 100% since the option always lives right up to expiry.

The most common reason an exotic option might not live through to expiry is that it contains continuously monitored barriers (called *American barriers*). If spot is close to an American barrier, stopping time is low. If spot is far from the barrier, stopping time is high. Higher volatility reduces the stopping time since barriers are more likely to trigger earlier. Exhibit 18.13 shows how the stopping time reduces (expected barrier knock sooner) as volatility increases.

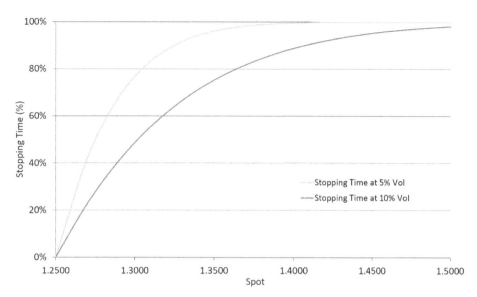

EXHIBIT 18.13 Stopping time of a EUR/USD 1yr 1.2500 American barrier at different implied volatility levels

It is important to appreciate that stopping time doesn't depend on the option payoff, only the relative positioning of barriers within the contract.

Stopping time on American barrier options is conceptually similar to the valuation of a *no-touch* contract (see Chapter 23) that pays out a fixed amount of cash at maturity if barrier levels *do not touch* prior to expiry. However, the no-touch value will be lower than stopping time because if the barrier trades prior to expiry, the no-touch has zero value where realized stopping time is non-zero. Exhibit 18.14 compares stopping time with the TV of an equivalent no-touch contract.

Stopping time is also an important measure for target redemption options (see Chapter 28) where the option expires based on a target.

When stopping time is displayed in a pricing tool it is important to understand what methodology is used to calculate it: Is a single ATM volatility to expiry, the full ATM curve but no smile or the full volatility surface used? Are single interest rates used or is the full interest term structure used?

■ VVV Pricing Example: Part 2

Back to the VVV pricing example: The stopping time of the example AUD/USD 3mth 0.8100 one-touch contract is 98.6%—very close to 100% since the barrier is far from current spot (given its maturity). Applying this weighting to the cumulative zeta from the replication has minimal impact: TV Adjustment = +7.1 AUD% × 98.6% = +7.0 AUD%. This VVV TV adjustment is fairly close to the market TV adjustment of +5.35%, although given the market bid–offer spread for this contract

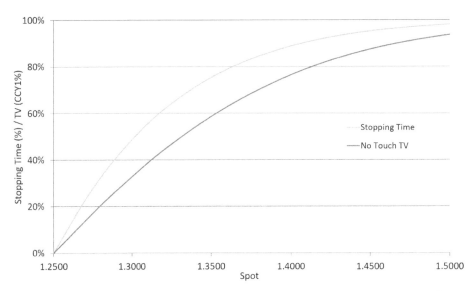

EXHIBIT 18.14 Stopping time versus no-touch TV of a 1yr 1.2500 EUR/USD American barrier

would be around 2.0%, the VVV TV adjustment is not accurate enough to be used in practice.

The advantages of VVV are that it is very quick to calculate and it gives intuition about the risks on the trade: By analyzing vanna and volga exposures it is possible to judge whether an exotic is long or short skew and long or short wings at current spot. Also, VVV suggests an appropriate vanilla hedging strategy. In the AUD/USD one-touch example, the majority of the smile risk can be hedged by selling 30× the one-touch notional of 25d downside vanilla options.

However, VVV prices do not consistently match the market because only exposures at current spot are used within the price and the fact that exposures change over time or at different spot levels is ignored. Other problems include valuation jumps near barriers, and if the skew within the volatility smile is large, it is possible to generate VVV TV adjustments larger negatively than TV itself. Historically, much effort was put into applying fixes to the VVV methodology to adjust for its deficiencies. For example, different delta vanilla options were used within the replication, more advanced exposures (e.g., $\frac{\partial vanna}{\partial spot}$) were added, or different weightings or floors and caps were used. However, for exotic option pricing, most FX derivative trading desks have now moved to using pricing models calibrated to the whole volatility surface rather than a VVV-based approach.

Finally, note that this is stylized analysis. Issues regarding differing vanna exposures from ATM contracts with different premium currencies and TV exposure versus smile exposure inconsistencies have been brushed under the carpet; for most traders these aren't important concerns.

■ Path Dependence

A key feature of exotic options is their **path dependence**. Path dependence means that the exotic option payoff is affected by the *path* that spot takes over the life of the option. Vanilla options are path independent because their payoff depends only on the spot level *at* the option expiry. Although note that when a vanilla option is delta hedged infrequently within a trading portfolio, the P&L from the option *and delta hedges* is highly path dependent. Within exotic contracts, the presence of barriers, averages, or targets makes the option path dependent.

For pricing and risk management the consequence of path dependence is that the full ATM curve and interest rate curve must be used to value options and these factors must be included within the TV adjustment. Alternatively, some bank trading desks use two TV values: an ATM TV and a term structure TV.

This is worth restating to be as clear as possible: Trading desks use forward curves, interest rate curves, and the volatility surface for valuing derivative contracts. For a vanilla option, only the forward, interest rate, and implied volatility for the specific strike and expiry date is used for pricing. For a path-dependent exotic option, the *entire* interest rate term structure and volatility surface (up to the option maturity) must be incorporated into the pricing, hence a different pricing methodology is required.

Traders learn which exotic option contracts have significant path dependence. For example, consider a window barrier option (see Chapter 26) with a knock-out barrier that is only active for the first month of the trade. If the ATM curve is upward sloping (short-date ATM volatility lower than long-date ATM volatility), the single volatility TV calculation will *overestimate* the chance of the window barrier knocking.

CHAPTER 19

FX Derivatives Pricing Models

FX derivatives trading desks use pricing models to value exotic contracts. Pricing models extend the Black-Scholes framework by adding new elements into the model dynamics. Different pricing models have different spot, volatility, and interest rate dynamics, which in turn generates different prices on exotic contracts. When using any pricing model it is vital to understand the model dynamic and how this dynamic impacts pricing.

Exhibit 19.1 shows the high-level connections between vanilla options, exotic options, probability density functions, and exotic pricing models.

Exotic pricing models are split into two main categories:

1. **Smile models** incorporate the volatility surface. All smile models are calibrated to the volatility surface, plus some smile models have additional calibration to exotic contracts. Common smile models are stochastic volatility, local volatility, mixed volatility, and jump diffusion. Smile models often have static or deterministic interest rates.
2. **Interest rate models** incorporate stochastic (i.e., randomly moving) interest rates in order to correctly value the effects of interest rate volatility and spot versus interest rate correlation. These effects are particularly important on long-dated contracts. Interest rate models often have static or deterministic volatility of the underlying's returns.

Models exist that combine both the volatility surface and stochastic interest rates but it is important to understand that more features within a model does not necessarily make it better. The more complex a model, the harder it is to keep

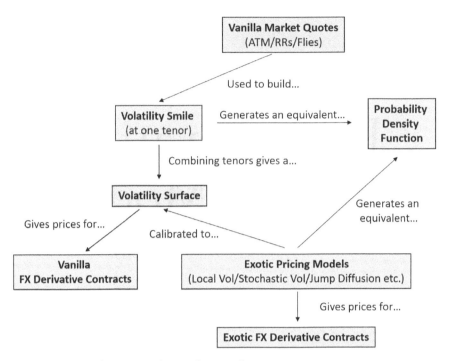

EXHIBIT 19.1   FX derivatives valuation framework

it correctly calibrated and the longer it takes to generate a price. Speed is very important within pricing and risk management. Prices on exotic contracts need to be made for clients quickly and risk managing an FX derivatives position involves periodically revaluing all deals in the portfolio. If it takes five hours to generate the exposures for a trading portfolio, risk management becomes extremely challenging when the market moves sharply.

In practice, traders match the main features of the exotic contract with the dynamic of the pricing model, choosing the simplest pricing model available that gives minimal difference between the model price and the market price.

When assessing pricing models, traders compare model prices with interbank exotic broker market prices. They therefore learn which types of exotic option contracts match market prices under different pricing models. By risk managing using exposures generated by different pricing models, traders discover whether the exposures from the model allow them to successfully hedge their exposures over time and lock-in P&L.

It can be instructive to price the same exotic contract with multiple different pricing models. The range of prices generated by the models can be thought of as a measure of the model risk within the contract. On more complex products, or simply as a sense check, traders sometimes also perform a manual risk analysis: As shown in Chapter 18, a vega versus spot profile can be used to estimate whether the TV adjustment from the volatility smile should be positive or negative.

■ Stochastic Volatility Models

Within stochastic volatility models (sometimes shortened to "stoch vol models"), volatility has its own process. There are many different stochastic volatility models but one of the original and best known is the Heston model from 1993 because it has intuitive parameters that mirror the risk reversal and butterfly instruments and a closed-form expression for vanilla options. The stochastic differential equations (SDE) of the Heston model are:

$$\frac{dS_t}{S_t} = (rCCY2 - rCCY1)dt + \sqrt{v_t}dW_{1,t}$$

$$dv_t = \lambda(\alpha - v_t)dt + \beta\sqrt{v_t}(\rho \, dW_{1,t} + \sqrt{(1 - \rho^2)} \, dW_{2,t})$$

The first line of the model is identical to Black-Scholes except that volatility has been replaced with the square root of a variance term (v_t). The process for variance includes parameters for long-run variance (α), the speed of mean reversion (λ), volatility of instantaneous variance (β), although this parameter is often referred to as the "vol-of-vol," and the correlation (ρ) is applied to the two independent Wiener processes $W_{1,t}$ and $W_{2,t}$. The first Wiener process drives spot and the two together drive variance. The Ornstein-Uhlenbeck (OU) model and Exponential Ornstein-Uhlenbeck and SABR models are other commonly used stochastic volatility models. Within the Exponential Ornstein-Uhlenbeck model, volatility cannot go to zero, which is an issue within the Heston model.

Pure stochastic volatility models do not depend on the level of spot; an equivalent volatility surface will be generated no matter the initial spot. Therefore, stochastic volatility models can be thought of as *sticky delta* models (see Chapter 14).

The parameters within the model are calibrated such that the vanilla volatility surface is (approximately) reproduced within the model. For example, if the initial and long run volatility is set to 10%, with zero vol-of-vol and correlation, the volatility smile produced by the model is a flat 10% as shown in Exhibit 19.2.

If the vol-of-vol parameter (β) is increased, the wings of the volatility smile move higher as shown in Exhibit 19.3. Note that in this instance, the ATM level increases too, unlike the standard volatility smile construction.

If the correlation parameter (ρ) is increased, the volatility smile tilts such that topside strikes have higher implied volatility than same delta downside strikes as shown in Exhibit 19.4. This is equivalent to a larger topside skew within the volatility smile.

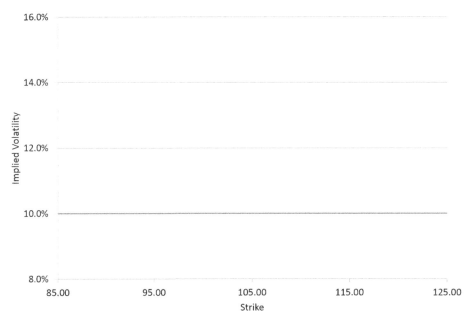

EXHIBIT 19.2 Volatility smile from Heston model with zero vol-of-vol and correlation parameters

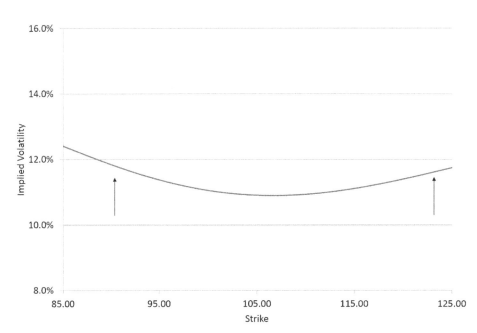

EXHIBIT 19.3 Volatility smile from Heston model with zero correlation parameter and positive vol-of-vol parameters

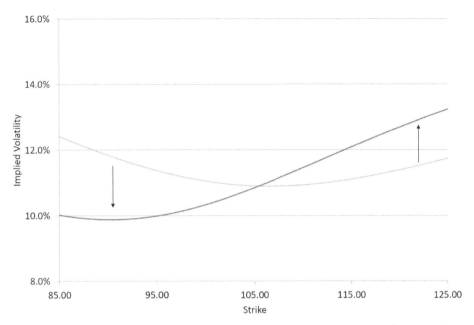

EXHIBIT 19.4 Volatility smile from Heston model with positive correlation and vol-of-vol parameters

Parameter calibration within the stochastic volatility model is an automatic process that uses vanilla option prices. This is why closed-form expressions or accurate approximations for vanilla option prices under a given pricing model are so important; it enables the model to be calibrated quickly. In practice, there are often multiple different parameter sets that generate near-identical volatility surfaces. When using any model with calibrated parameters it is important that traders observe the parameters over time and ensure they are stable and respond sensibly to changes in the volatility surface; that is, changes in the skew of the volatility surface should be mainly reflected by changes in the correlation parameter (ρ).

These Heston parameters can attempt to match a volatility smile at a single tenor but in order to match the entire volatility surface, parameters must change over time. In other words, the variance parameters within the SDE become functions of time:

$$dv_t = \lambda(t)(\alpha - v_t)dt + \beta(t)\sqrt{v_t}(\rho(t)\,dW_{1,t} + \sqrt{(1 - \rho(t)^2)}\,dW_{2,t})$$

When calibrating models with parameter sets that are functions of time, the parameters should evolve smoothly rather than jumping around.

In practice, in order to successfully calibrate to vanilla contracts, stochastic volatility models often have a higher volatility of implied volatility than is observed in the market. Put another way, *volatility convexity is overvalued by stochastic volatility models.* For this reason, stochastic volatility models do not consistently match prices in the interbank broker exotics market, particularly for contracts with significant convexity, like double-no-touch options, for which the stochastic volatility model price will be too high. The same effect also causes forward smiles to be overvalued.

In addition, under stochastic volatility models the skew within the volatility smile can get overwhelmed by the volatility mean reversion, plus some stochastic volatility models can struggle to have enough vol-of-vol at short maturities to produce the correct volatility smile.

◼ Local Volatility Models

The local volatility model was developed in the mid-1990s by superstar quant Bruno Dupire. The key to the model is that volatility, rather than being constant, is a deterministic function of spot and time. Therefore, the Black-Scholes stochastic differential equation is extended to:

$$\frac{dS_t}{S_t} = (rCCY2 - rCCY1)dt + \sigma(S_t, t)dW_t$$

A local volatility surface is generated within the model using the full volatility surface. The local volatility surface can be thought of as a grid of forward volatilities spanning out in time as shown in Exhibit 19.5. Implied volatility and local volatility smiles at one tenor in USD/JPY (a currency pair with a small downside risk reversal currently) and USD/BRL (a currency pair with a large topside risk reversal currently) are shown in Exhibits 19.6 and 19.7 respectively.

The local volatility model is neither a sticky strike nor a sticky delta model, although it is more sticky strike than sticky delta. The *local* volatility depends on

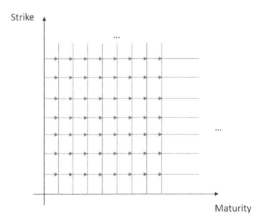

EXHIBIT 19.5   Local volatility surface construction

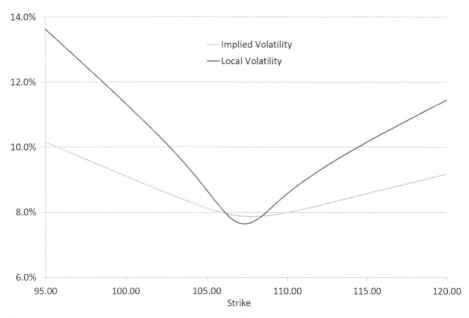

EXHIBIT 19.6   USD/JPY implied volatility and local volatility smiles

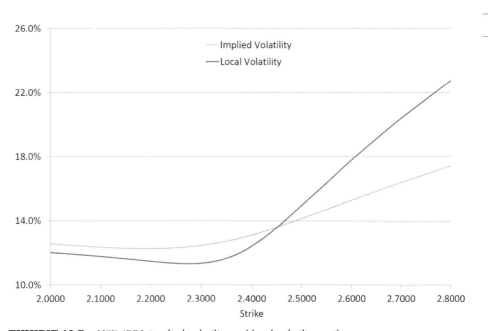

EXHIBIT 19.7   USD/BRL implied volatility and local volatility smiles

the level of spot but that does not necessarily imply that the implied volatility for a specific strike is fixed as spot moves.

The Dupire local volatility model has no parameters to calibrate and the model is quick to setup and price. Plus, if the vanilla volatility surface contains either strike spread arbitrage (call options with increasing value at higher strikes) or calendar spread arbitrage (options with decreasing value at longer maturity), the model will be unstable due to undefined local volatility. This feature can be used to identify potential problems with the volatility surface.

Another possible approach is to build the local volatility surface using a defined functional form. This approach has the advantage of guaranteeing an arbitrage-free volatility surface but it is slower because the parameters within the functional form must be calibrated.

Because vanilla options are correctly priced within the model and no time consuming calibration is required, the Dupire local volatility model is a good pricing model to use for exotic contracts with no/minimal path dependence.

The main problem with local volatility models is that the volatility of implied volatility generated from the local volatility function is lower than reality. Put another way, *volatility convexity is undervalued by local volatility models*. For this reason, local volatility models do not consistently match prices in the interbank broker exotics market, particularly for contracts with significant convexity, like double-no-touch options, for which the local volatility model will be too low.

Another feature of the model is that forward smile can be undervalued, again, caused by low volatility of implied volatility. This can be checked by querying for the 1yr in 1yr forward volatility smile from the model. In most currency pairs this forward volatility smile under local volatility will have significantly lower wings and skew than the current 1yr volatility smile. Also, since volatility is a deterministic function within local volatility models it should not be used to price forward volatility agreements or forward start options (see Chapter 31), where option value depends primarily on the random nature of implied volatility.

In summary, local volatility models are stable, quick, and give fairly accurate valuations and exposures, particularly for options with minimal path dependence. However, for contracts with significant convexity or forward skew exposures, local volatility often gives inaccurate prices.

■ Mixed Volatility Models

Mixed volatility models (sometimes called *stochastic local volatility* models) are, as it sounds, a combination of a stochastic volatility model (which overvalues volatility convexity) and a local volatility model (which undervalues volatility convexity).

There are many different ways in which the stochastic and local volatility models can be combined. One possible approach would be to extend a Heston stochastic volatility model with a local volatility component ($\hat{\sigma}$) plus a mixing weight (ξ):

$$\frac{dS_t}{S_t} = (rCCY2 - rCCY1)dt + \sqrt{v_t}\hat{\sigma}(S_t, t)dW_{1,t}$$

$$dv_t = \lambda(t)(\alpha - v_t)dt + \xi(t)\beta(t)\sqrt{v_t}\left(\rho(t)\ dW_{1,t} + \sqrt{(1 - \rho(t)^2)}\ dW_{2,t}\right)$$

Mixing weights define how much stochastic volatility is applied at each tenor. Conceptually, the stochastic volatility model can be calibrated first and the local volatility component can then be used to ensure that the correct vanilla surface is generated after the stochastic volatility component is weighted by the mixing weight. Within this formulation, a mixing weight of 0% implies full local volatility and a mixing weight of 100% implies full stochastic volatility.

The behavior of the model can be driven by a single mixing weight or a term structure of mixing weights set by traders to match exotic contracts in the interbank market. Alternatively, the model could be calibrated directly to prices of exotic contracts. In general, if convexity is being more highly valued in the market than the model, the model price will be lower than the market price for exotic contracts with significant volga exposures. In this case, mixing weights should be moved higher to increase the stochastic volatility element within the mixed volatility model. In obscure pairs with few quotes on interbank broker exotics, mixing weights in similar, more liquid currency pairs can be used.

Variations on the mixed volatility model are used by the vast majority of FX derivatives trading desks to price exotic contracts out to two-year maturities in most currency pairs. It is so successful that development of new single asset pricing models on bank FX derivatives trading desks has virtually stopped.

Jump Diffusion Models

There is a lot of evidence of jumps in the history of financial markets. One of the original jump diffusion models is the Merton model from 1976, which extends the Black-Scholes SDE by adding a jump term:

$$\frac{dS_t}{S_t} = (rCCY2 - rCCY1 - \lambda\kappa)dt + \sigma dW_t + (\mathbf{y_t} - 1)dN_t$$

where N_t is a poisson process with intensity λ and $(y_t - 1)$ is log-normally distributed with mean κ. Note that the introduction of jumps also requires an additional correction to the drift.

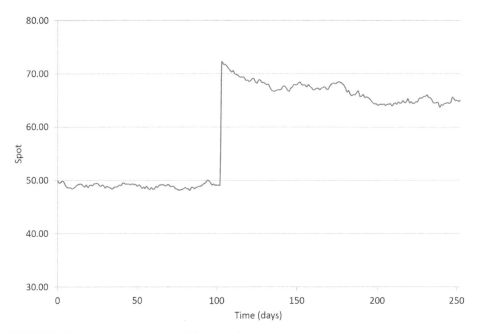

EXHIBIT 19.8 Sample Merton model spot path

Spot paths like Exhibit 19.8 are generated from a Merton model, with the probability and size of up or down jumps generating the wings and skew in the volatility surface.

Merton is a popular model because it has a semi-closed-form expression for vanilla options, hence allowing for quick calibration, and like Heston, it has intuitive parameters that mirror the skew and wings of the volatility surface. Jump diffusion models can generate a wide range of volatility smiles but their pricing doesn't consistently match exotics prices observed in the interbank market for liquid currency pairs. Jump models work best in managed or pegged currency pairs where the model dynamic best matches the real market dynamic. Jump models can also be used to, for example, imply an expected probability and size of spot jump from the volatility smile. By comparing this with their intuition traders can identify relative value in the volatility surface.

Stochastic Interest Rate Models

The smile models reviewed in this chapter all have interest rates that are static or deterministic (i.e., they move in a predetermined manner). In practice, interest rates have a volatility of their own and they can move in a correlated manner with spot. Stochastic interest rate models extend the Black-Scholes SDE by introducing processes for the two interest rates (or perhaps their spread). For example, if the so-called "short rates" are being modeled:

$$\frac{dS_t}{S_t} = (rCCY2_t - rCCY1_t)dt + \sigma dW_t$$

$$drCCY1_t = a_1(t)dt + b_1 dW_{1,t}$$

$$drCCY2_t = a_2(t)dt + b_2 dW_{2,t}$$

The effect of stochastic interest rates is particularly important on long-dated (approximately past two-year) exotic contracts. When a contract has a large sensitivity to interest rates, the effect of stochastic interest rates must be quantified and included within the TV adjustment.

Finally, it is important to note that generating TV adjustments with a smile model and an interest rate model separately and then summing the adjustments is not always a valid approach. The smile and interest rates may well interact with each other. Local volatility is often added into stochastic interest rate models in order to value the volatility surface in a manner which requires no additional parameters to be calibrated.

CHAPTER 20

Exotic FX Derivatives Product Classification

Exotic products are typically split into different *generations*, indicating how long the product has been traded in the market. When reviewing the exotic product classification it is important to understand that risk management does not get more complicated for higher-generation options. In fact, the opposite is often true as features like averages, accruing notionals, or targets can reduce risk management complexity. In general, exotic products which are conceptually simple are often harder to risk manage while exotic products which are conceptually more involved are often easier to risk manage.

The following list of exotic FX derivative product types is by no means exhaustive; it primarily aims to introduce the main exotic option types. Exotic features can be combined and extended in many different ways. Over time, different products and structures come in and out of fashion, plus new structures are developed by innovative trading and structuring desks to meet client requirements.

First-Generation Exotics

First-generation exotic products are the fundamental building blocks of exotic risk. The two primary exotic features are *European barriers* and *American barriers*. European digitals and touch options are the simplest exotic contracts, followed by European and American barrier options.

European Digital Options

European digital options payout cash if spot is above (CCY1 digital call) or below (CCY1 digital put) the digital level at maturity. If it happens, the cash payment actually occurs on the delivery date.

European digital example: EUR/USD 1yr 1.3000 EUR digital call in EUR1m payout. Digital options are quoted as a % of the payout, so if the offer is 25.0 EUR%, the contract will cost EUR250k. Like vanillas, it is most common to trade the out-of-the-money side so European digital prices will rarely be above 50%.

European digital options are known by various other names, including *binary options, cash-or-nothing options*, or *digital bets*. They are covered in Chapter 21.

Touch Options

Touch options, also called *rebates* or *American digitals*, generate a cash payout at maturity if spot ever touched (one-touch) or never touched (no-touch) specified barrier levels. The barriers within touch options are called **American** or **continuous** because they are active throughout the life of the option.

If the touch option has a single barrier, it is called a **one-touch** (OT) or a **no-touch** (NT). If it has two barriers, it is called a **double-one-touch** (DOT) or a **double-no-touch** (DNT), plus double-no-touch options are also known as **ranges**. Within double barrier touch options, at inception, one barrier must be above spot and one barrier must be below.

Standard touch options pay out on the delivery date. There are also **instant touch options,** which instead pay out two business days (value spot) after the barrier is hit. The market convention is to trade single barrier touches as one-touch options with payout at maturity and two barrier touches as double-no-touch options.

One-touch example: EUR/USD 1yr 1.3000 one-touch with USD1m payout. Like European digitals, touch options are quoted as a % of the payout, so if the price is 10.5 USD%, the contract will cost USD105k.

Touch options are covered in Chapter 23.

Barrier Options

Barrier options pay off like a vanilla option at maturity. Additionally, they have barriers that can knock the option out (i.e., expire it) or knock the option in (i.e., enable the payoff). There are two main types of barrier: European and American.

European Barrier Options

European barriers are only applicable *at the option maturity*. European barrier levels must therefore be positioned in-the-money versus the payoff; otherwise they have no impact.

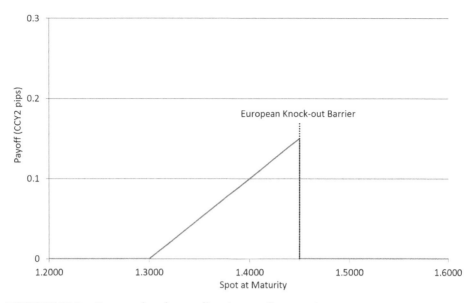

EXHIBIT 20.1   European knock-out call option payoff at maturity

European knock-out example: EUR/USD 1yr 1.3000 EUR call/USD put **European knock-out** (EKO) 1.4500. If spot at maturity is *below* 1.4500, the payoff of this option will be the same as a EUR call/USD put vanilla option with the same strike. However, if spot at maturity is *above* 1.4500, the EKO will have no payoff because spot is through the knock-out barrier. This is shown in Exhibit 20.1.

European knock-in example: EUR/USD 1yr 1.3000 EUR call/USD put **European knock-in** (EKI) 1.4500. If spot at maturity is *below* 1.4500, the option will have no payoff because spot is not through the knock-in barrier. However, if spot at maturity is *above* 1.4500, the payoff of the option will be the same as a EUR call/USD put vanilla option with the same strike. This is shown in Exhibit 20.2.

European barrier options are covered in Chapter 22.

American Barrier Options

American knock-out and knock-in barriers exist *continuously* throughout the life of the option. If spot *ever* trades through the barrier level prior to expiry, the structure either knocks in (comes alive) or knocks out (expires). In the standard variations of the product, barriers within the structure are either all knock-out or all knock-in.

To clarify what is meant by "ever" in the previous paragraph: In liquid G10 currency pairs, for the barrier to have triggered, spot must usually have traded through the barrier level between Monday 9 A.M. Wellington time (sometimes called "market open") and Friday 5 P.M. New York time (sometimes called "market close") in "market size," generally around USD5m. In emerging-market currency pairs, the spot market usually has to be officially open for a barrier knock to

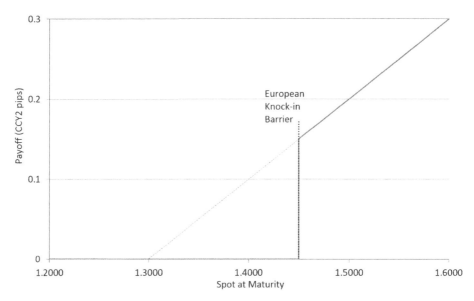

EXHIBIT 20.2 European knock-in call option payoff at maturity

occur. The exact details of what constitutes a barrier knock are described within the confirmation ("confo") documents, plus for each option there is a **barrier determining agent**—one of the option counterparties who makes a fair final decision on whether there has been a barrier knock if a disagreement occurs.

The relative positioning of the strike and barrier within the option determines what an American barrier option is called. If the option has a single American barrier positioned out-of-the-money versus the payoff, the option is a **regular knock-out** or **regular knock-in**. Often the "regular" is dropped and these contracts are simply called **knock-out** (KO) or **knock-in** (KI) options.

Knock-out example: EUR/USD 1yr 1.3000 EUR call/USD put knock-out 1.2000. This option will pay off like a 1.3000 EUR call/USD put vanilla option at maturity unless spot ever trades through (below) 1.2000 during the life of the option, in which case there will be no payoff at maturity. This is shown in Exhibit 20.3.

If the option structure has a single barrier positioned in-the-money versus the payoff, the option is a **reverse knock-out** (RKO) or **reverse knock-in** (RKI).

Reverse knock-out example: EUR/USD 1yr 1.3000 EUR call/USD put reverse knock-out 1.4000. This option will pay off like a 1.3000 EUR call/USD put vanilla option at maturity unless spot ever trades through (above) 1.4000 during the life of the option, in which case there will be no payoff at maturity. This is shown in Exhibit 20.4.

If an option structure has two American barriers, one either side of the inception spot level, it is a **double knock-out** (DKO) or **double knock-in** (DKI).

Double knock-out example: EUR/USD 1yr 1.3000 EUR call/USD put double knock-out 1.2000/1.4000. This option will pay off like a 1.3000 EUR call/USD

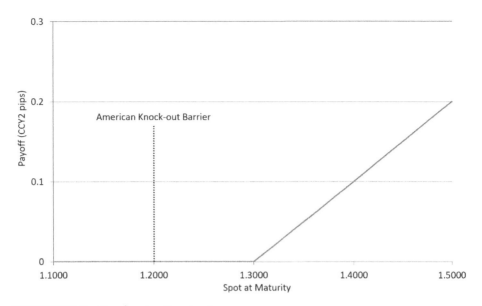

EXHIBIT 20.3   Knock-out option structure

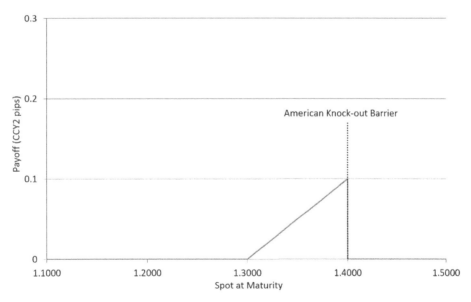

EXHIBIT 20.4   Reverse knock-out option structure

put vanilla option at maturity unless spot ever trades through (below) 1.2000 or (above) 1.4000 during the life of the option, in which case there will be no payoff at maturity. This is shown in Exhibit 20.5.

Payoff, valuation, and exposure charts for options with American barriers assume that barriers have not knocked. However, once spot goes through an American barrier level, exposures change. For a knock-out American barrier, all exposures

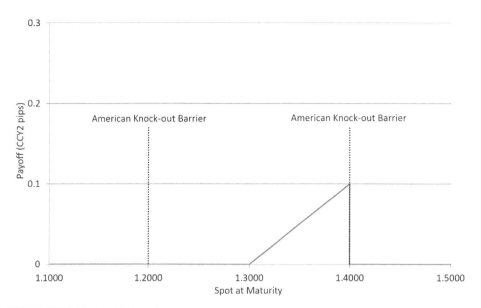

EXHIBIT 20.5 Double knock-out option structure

disappear when the barrier hits, whereas for a knock-in American barrier, the exposures become that of a standard vanilla option.

Different types of American barrier are shown in Chapter 24.

In-the-Money Barrier Options

If a single American barrier is positioned in-the-money versus the payoff and the inception spot is *even further* in-the-money, this is a special case called an **in-the-money (ITM) barrier option**.

In-the-money knock-out example: EUR/USD 1yr 1.1000 EUR call/USD put ITM knock-out 1.2000 with spot at 1.3000. This option will pay off like a 1.1000 EUR call/USD put vanilla option at maturity unless spot ever trades through (below) 1.2000 during the life of the option, in which case there will be no payoff at maturity. This is shown in Exhibit 20.6.

If the strike and barrier are at the same level, the option is called a **strike-out** (for a knock-out barrier) or **strike-in** (for a knock-in barrier). The trading risks on ITM barrier options are different from regular American barriers. In the ITM knock-out case spot can never go through the strike and hence the strike produces no optionality.

Transatlantic Barrier Options

Transatlantic barrier options have a vanilla payoff at maturity plus one American barrier and one European barrier (hence the name). Both barriers can be separately either knock-out or knock-in but the most common configuration has a knock-in European barrier and a knock-out American barrier.

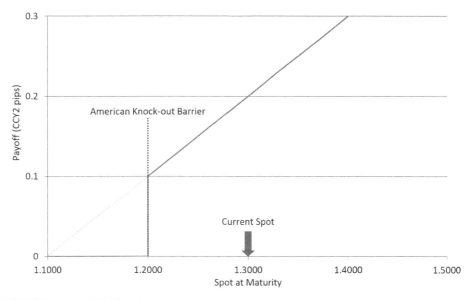

EXHIBIT 20.6 ITM knock-out option structure

Transatlantic example: EUR/USD 1yr 1.3000 EUR call/USD put European knock-in 1.4500/American knock-out 1.2500. This option will pay off like a 1.3000 EUR call/USD put European knock-in 1.4500 at maturity unless spot ever trades through (below) 1.2500 during the life of the option, in which case there will be no payoff at maturity. This is shown in Exhibit 20.7.

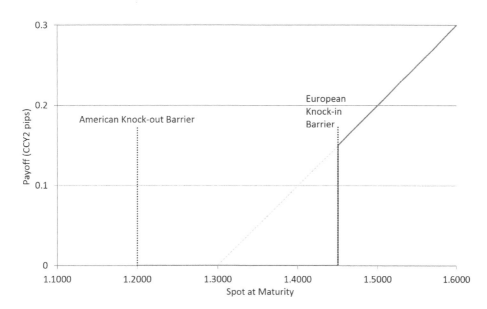

EXHIBIT 20.7 Transatlantic option structure

Within the transatlantic option, the European barrier is always positioned in-the-money versus the payoff (otherwise it has no impact) and the American barrier is usually positioned out-of-the-money versus the payoff.

Knock-in/Knock-out Barrier Options

Knock-in/Knock-out (KIKO) barrier options have a vanilla payoff at maturity plus two American barriers: One barrier is knock-in and the other is knock-out. The subtlety with this product comes from the fact that there are two possible variations:

1. *Knock-out until expiry*. If the knock-in barrier hits first, the option will still knock out if the knock-out barrier level trades later.
2. *Knock-out until knock in*. If the knock-in barrier hits first, the option cannot then be knocked out and therefore the option has a guaranteed payoff at maturity.

Discrete Barrier Options

Discrete barrier options are monitored against a specified (usually daily) fix rather than being continuously monitored against the spot market.

Discrete barrier example: EUR/USD 1yr 1.3000 EUR call/USD put knock-out at 1.4500 on ECB37 fix. The ECB37 fix is sampled daily from the spot market at around 2.15 P.M. Central European time (CET) and then published to a website shortly after.

Discrete barrier monitoring creates additional risk management challenges to standard American or European barriers.

Discrete barriers are covered in Chapter 26.

American Vanilla Options

American vanilla options are identical to standard European vanilla options except that American vanilla options can be exercised by the option buyer *at any time* prior to expiry where European vanilla options can only be exercised by the option buyer *at expiry*.

This early exercise feature is mainly applicable to vanilla options. A client once asked for a price in a reverse knock-out with American exercise: Definitely not a standard product.

American vanilla options are covered in Chapter 27.

Quanto Options

Quanto options have nonstandard payoff currencies. As seen in Part I, the natural vanilla payoff case is CCY1 notional and CCY2 payout. If this becomes a CCY1 notional *and* CCY1 payout, with conversion from CCY2 payout to CCY1 payout using the strike rather than the spot at expiry, this is a **self-quanto** option, covered in Chapter 27. Alternatively, if payout is in CCY3 (i.e., neither CCY1 nor CCY2), this is a **third currency quanto** option, covered in Chapter 30.

Second-Generation Exotics

Second-generation exotics add additional features to forwards, vanilla options, or first-generation exotic products. For example, window barrier options are extensions of American barrier options while accrual, target redemption, and Asian options each extend standard forward or European vanilla payoffs.

Window Barrier Options

Window barrier options exist for some (but not all) of the life of the option. If barrier observation starts at the option inception and goes until some date prior to expiry, the option is a **front window barrier** option. If barrier observation starts at some date after horizon and ends at the option expiry, the option is a **rear window barrier** option. Like American barrier options there are up barrier, down barrier, knock-in, knock-out, and double barrier variations.

Window barrier options are covered in Chapter 26.

Accrual Options

Within accrual options, the option notional is not fixed but rather it accrues (builds up) over the life of the option depending on how spot moves. For example, it could be that each time there is a daily fix where spot lies between 1.2500 and 1.3500 the option notional increases by USD100k, whereas if spot fixes below 1.2500 or above 1.3500 the option notional will not increase.

The most commonly traded option structure involving an accrual feature is the **accrual forward**. At maturity, the client buys or sells the accrued notional at the strike.

Accrual options are covered in Chapter 28.

Target Redemption Options

Within target redemption options, the payoff is generally a strip of forwards or leveraged forwards that knock out if some target is reached. This target can be specified in different ways, for example, cumulative client profit or the number of expiry dates at which the client has profited.

The most common option structure involving a target redemption feature is the **target redemption forward (TARF)**. At each fixing, the client transacts a fixed notional, providing the target has not been reached.

Target redemption options are covered in Chapter 28.

Asian Options

Asian options are also known as **average rate options**. Some aspect of the Asian option payoff depends on an average calculated from spot fixings. There are three common variations:

1. *Average rate option*: spot at maturity is replaced with an average of spot fixings.
2. *Average strike option*: the option strike is replaced with an average of spot fixings.
3. *Double average rate option*: both spot at maturity and the strike are replaced by averages of spot fixes taken over different periods during the life of the option.

Asian options are covered in Chapter 29.

Compound Options

Compound options are an *option on an option*. The owner of the compound option has the opportunity at a first expiry date to buy or sell a specified vanilla option to a second expiry date for a fixed premium. This product is covered in Chapter 31.

Forward Start Options

The contract details (e.g., strike and barrier levels) on **forward start options** are determined from a spot fix at a specified date in the future. For example, after three months a spot fix is used to set the strike of a call option expiring three months later. This product is covered in Chapter 30.

■ Third-Generation Exotics

Third-generation exotics cover multi-asset products, volatility products, and correlation products. These options are often risk managed in separate trading books due to their complexity.

Basket Options

Basket options have a payoff based on a basket spot which is calculated by averaging spot changes across the currency pairs in the basket. At maturity the payoff is a function of the basket spot and a basket strike. This product is covered in Chapter 30.

Best-of/Worst-of Options

Best-of (BO) and **Worst-of** (WO) options pay out either the best (maximum) or worst (minimum) payoff resulting from vanilla options in multiple currency pairs to the same expiry date. The payoff is highly dependent on the correlation between currency pairs. This product is covered in Chapter 30.

Dual Digital Options

Dual digital options have two European digital payoffs in different currency pairs to the same expiry date. If *both* digitals are in-the-money at maturity, the option generates a cash payout. This product is covered in Chapter 30.

Volatility (Vol) and Variance (Var) Swaps

Volatility swaps pay out based on realized spot volatility compared to a "strike" expressed in volatility terms. **Variance swaps** pay out based on realized spot variance compared to a "strike" expressed in variance terms. This product is covered in Chapter 31.

Correlation Swaps

Correlation swaps pay out based on realized spot correlation between two currency pairs compared to a "strike" expressed in correlation terms.

Forward Volatility Agreements (FVA)

Forward volatility agreements pay out based on the future level of implied volatility. For example, a 3mth in 3mth FVA is a trade on the forward ATM implied volatility between the 3mth expiry date and the 6mth expiry date. This product is covered in Chapter 31.

CHAPTER 21

European Digital Options

European digital options are conceptually one of the simplest exotic products; at maturity the option either pays out a fixed cash amount or nothing, depending on whether spot is above or below a specified digital level. However, the risk management of these options, particularly at expiry, can be challenging due to the *binary* nature of the payout (either receive all the cash or none) over a one-pip spot difference.

A European digital call option pays out cash on the delivery date if spot at maturity is at or above the digital level, as shown in Exhibit 21.1. While a European digital put option pays out cash on the delivery date if spot at maturity is below the digital level.

As a technical aside, the European digital call here is defined as paying out *at* the digital level while the European digital put does not. This is not necessarily the case but it is important that European digital put + European digital call = guaranteed payout at maturity. Put another way, transacting both the digital put and digital call with all other details the same should not result in both contracts paying out. In practice these issues are dealt with via the confirmation documents agreed when trading the contract.

European digital options prices are quoted as a percent of the payout amount, with prices generally rounded to the nearest 0.05% for customers or 0.25% in the interbank broker market. For example, a trader might make a rate of 23.5/24.5 USD% on USD/JPY 3mth 100.00 USD European digital call in USD1m payout (also called USD1m *notional*). If the client wishes to buy, they must pay USD245k value

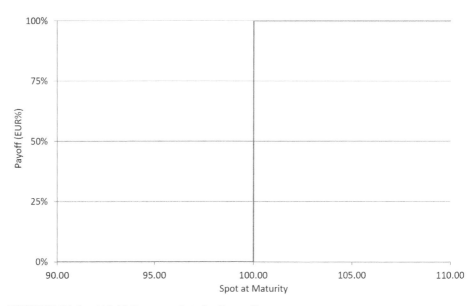

EXHIBIT 21.1   100.00 European digital call payoff at maturity

spot. At expiry, if the spot rate is above 100.00, the client will receive USD1m on the delivery date. Prices cannot be quoted as a percent of the non-payout currency; there is no way to switch between the currencies because the option does not have a strike.

European digital prices are generally between 0% and 100%. If the forward is close to the digital level, the European digital option value will be around 50%. European digital call prices over time are shown in Exhibit 21.2.

■ European Digital Replication

European digital calls can be replicated using tight vanilla call spreads and European digital puts can be replicated using tight vanilla put spreads. The vanilla call spread replication for a 100.00 European digital call is shown in Exhibit 21.3.

The tighter the strikes in the replication, the larger the notional required to replicate the digital payout, as shown in Exhibit 21.4. The tightest replication possible would involve trading a one-pip spread with enormous notionals. However, this isn't possible in practice due to the notionals required, plus strike levels are usually rounded to the nearest five or ten pips, particularly in the interbank market.

The calculation for determining the notionals required within the replication depends on the payout currency of the digital. Recall from Part I that vanilla options naturally generate P&L in the opposite currency to the notional.

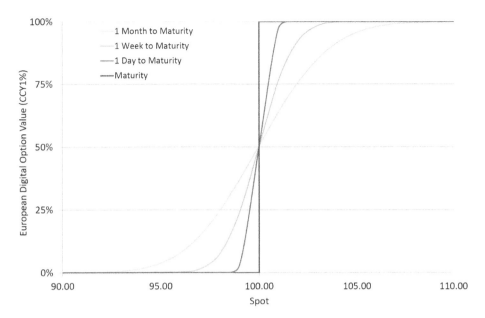

EXHIBIT 21.2 100.00 European digital call value over time

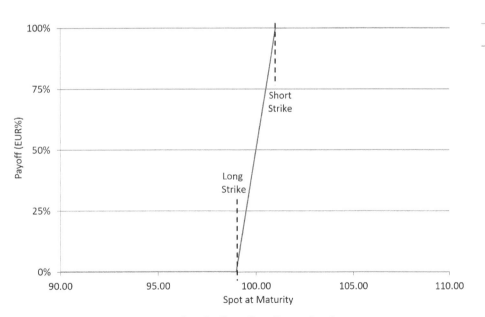

EXHIBIT 21.3 100.00 European digital call vanilla call spread replication

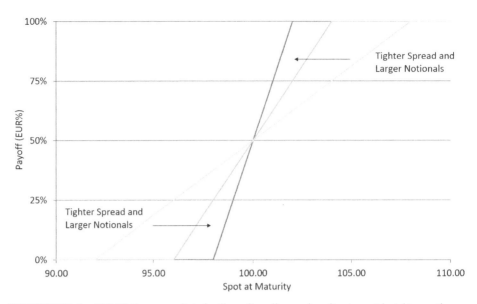

EXHIBIT 21.4   100.00 European digital call vanilla call spread replication with tighter strikes

European Digital with CCY2 Payout Replication

Given a European digital call with *CCY2* payout X at level K, if the call spread replication strikes are long strike K_1 and short strike K_2 (symmetrically positioned around K) with CCY1 notional N, a CCY2 payout of $(K_2 - K_1) \times N$ is generated at K_2. Therefore:

$$X = (K_2 - K_1) \times N$$

that is,

$$N = \frac{X}{K_2 - K_1}$$

As expected, the closer K_2 and K_1 are together (smaller $K_2 - K_1$), the larger the required notional.

Example: Replicating a USD/CNH 1yr 6.1000 USD digital put. A 1yr 6.1250/6.0750 USD vanilla put spread is constructed around the digital level to replicate the payout. The payout of the digital is CNH1m (CCY2) so the USD put spread notional = CNH1m/(6.1250 − 6.0750) = USD20m per leg.

When the digital payout is in CCY2, the replication spread has equal CCY1 notionals but different CCY2 notionals, which in effect generates the payout.

European Digital with CCY1 Payout Replication

Given a European digital call with *CCY1* payout X at level K, since a CCY1 payout is required, a CCY2 notional will naturally be calculated within the replication. Therefore, the strikes must be flipped into reciprocal terms.

If the call spread replication strikes are long strike K_1 and short strike K_2 with CCY1 notional N, a CCY1 payout of $(1/K_1 - 1/K_2) \times N$ is generated at K_2 (the strike order in the calculation gets flipped when the reciprocal is taken). Therefore:

$$X = \left(\frac{1}{K_1} - \frac{1}{K_2} \right).N$$

that is,

$$N = \frac{X}{\left(\dfrac{1}{K_1} - \dfrac{1}{K_2} \right)}$$

Example: Replicating a USD/CNH 1yr 6.1000 USD digital call. A 1yr 6.0750/6.1250 USD call spread can be constructed around the digital to replicate the payout. The payout of the digital is USD1m (CCY1), so the USD put spread notional = USD1m/(1/6.0750 − 1/6.1250) = CNH744.2m per leg.

This time, when the digital payout is in CCY1, the replication spread has equal CCY2 notionals, but different CCY1 notionals.

European Digital Pricing

Prices for European digital options under Black-Scholes can be calculated directly using cumulative normal distribution function $N(X)$. There is a strong link between European digital option prices and the *delta* of the European vanilla option with the same maturity and the vanilla strike set to the digital level.

Under Black-Scholes, the chance of $S \geq K$ at maturity is given by

$$prob(S \geq K) = N(d_2)$$

where S is spot, K is the strike or digital level, $rCCY1$ and $rCCY2$ are continuously compounded interest rates to time T (measured in years), σ is volatility, $N(X)$ is the cumulative normal distribution function, and $d_2 = \dfrac{\ln\left(\frac{S}{K}\right) + \left(rCCY2 - rCCY1 - \frac{\sigma^2}{2}\right).T}{\sigma\sqrt{T}}$.

The CCY2% European digital call price under Black-Scholes discounts this value back to the horizon in the payout currency:

$$P_{CCY2\% \ Digital \ Call} = e^{-rCCY2.T} N(d_2)$$

The CCY1% European digital call price under Black-Scholes is calculated by adjusting from d_2 to d_1 due to a change of numeraire plus the discounting back to the horizon is changed to CCY1 also:

$$P_{CCY1\% \ Digital \ Call} = e^{-rCCY1.T} N(d_1)$$

where $d_1 = \dfrac{\ln\left(\frac{S}{K}\right) + \left(rCCY2 - rCCY1 + \frac{1}{2}\sigma^2\right).t}{\sigma\sqrt{t}}$.

Recall from Practical C that the delta of a European vanilla call option is:

$$\Delta_{call} = \frac{\partial P_{call}}{\partial S} = e^{-rCCY1.T} \, N(d_1)$$

The CCY1% value of a European digital option is equal to the delta of a European vanilla option with the same expiry and strike/digital level (and with payout and quoting conventions aligned). Taking the next derivative with respect to spot implies that the *delta* of a European digital option is the *gamma* of a European vanilla with the same expiry and strike/digital level. These relationships are useful for building understanding of the European digital product but note that they hold under Black-Scholes only and not once the volatility smile is included.

Traders price exotic options by calculating the adjustment from the Black-Scholes theoretical value (TV) to a market price. European digital payoffs depend only on the spot at maturity. Hence they have no path dependence and their TV adjustment comes *only* from the volatility smile. Any well-calibrated volatility smile pricing model could therefore be used to generate a midmarket price for European digital options. Alternatively, the replication strategies examined above are a more direct method of obtaining midmarket prices from the vanilla market:

- If the vanilla options in the replicating spread are priced using the ATM volatility, the replication price approximates the TV of the digital.

- If the vanilla options in the replicating spread are priced on the volatility smile, the replication price approximates the midmarket smile price of the digital.

- The difference between these two values therefore approximates the TV adjustment of the digital. The tighter the replication, the more accurate the valuation.

Therefore, very tight (not practically attainable) vanilla call and put spreads can be constructed within code in order to obtain accurate smile-on mid prices for European digital options.

It is important to note that these "smile-on" digital prices assume the volatility smile at the option maturity matches the market, specifically around the digital level. If this is not the case, for example, in a pegged currency pair, there is no reason to expect that the digital smile-on price will match the market.

The following valuation identities apply to European digital options with the same contract details:

- European digital put TV + European digital call TV = guaranteed payout at maturity.

- European digital put midmarket price + European digital call midmarket price = guaranteed payout at maturity.

This means that the TV adjustment on a European digital call will be equal and negative to the TV adjustment on the equivalent European digital put. Plus taking this a step further, the TV adjustment on a long European digital call option will be the same as the TV adjustment on a short European digital put option with all contract details the same. In the same way that call and put vanilla options are both described as "strikes" within a trading position, European digitals are spoken about in terms of their payout direction and the higher P&L side at maturity.

European Digital Bid–Offer Spread

The vanilla replication of the European digital can also be used to calculate a digital bid–offer spread by multiplying the vanilla option bid–offer spread by the notionals within the replication for strikes set at some fixed width. Alternatively, conservative vanilla spreads can be constructed such that e.g., the full digital payout is generated *at* the barrier level in order to calculate bid or offer prices directly.

In practice, trading desks more often maintain grids of digital bid–offer spreads for different maturities. Bid–offer spreads for European digitals in liquid G10 currency pairs often have a term structure that looks similar to Exhibit 21.5. Less liquid G10 currency pair and EM currency pair digital bid–offer spreads will typically be quoted wider but the relative shape of the bid–offer spread function over different tenors often remains unchanged.

European Digital Greeks

Many of the Greeks arising from European digital options are similar to the exposures on vanilla options. However, risk management becomes significantly more challenging if spot ends up near the digital level at expiry.

EXHIBIT 21.5 Typical EUR/USD European Digital Bid–Offer Spreads

Tenor	Bid–Offer Spread (CCY1%)
O/N	20%
1wk	10%
2wk	7%
1mth	4%
2mth	3%
3mth	2%
6mth	2%
1yr	2%

Vega Risk

The European digital vega profile against spot is identical to a risk reversal vega profile that tightens over time. Recalling the replication strategies introduced previously, this should not be a shock. Notice in Exhibit 21.6 how the peak vega stays approximately constant over time. Thinking about the gamma versus vega relationship on a vanilla option, this implies that gamma will pick up sharply on the European digital option into the option maturity.

European digital options are:

- Short vega (and short gamma) when the forward is on the higher P&L side of the digital barrier: Lower volatility means an increased chance of staying in the higher P&L area.

- Long vega (and long gamma) when the forward is on the lower P&L side of the digital barrier: Higher volatility means an increased chance of moving to the higher P&L area.

Therefore, if the higher P&L scenario is to the topside, the TV adjustment will be in the same direction as the TV adjustment generated from buying strikes below the digital level and selling strikes above the digital level. Alternatively, if the higher P&L scenario is to the downside, the TV adjustment will be in the same direction as the TV adjustment generated from buying strikes above the digital level and selling strikes below the digital level.

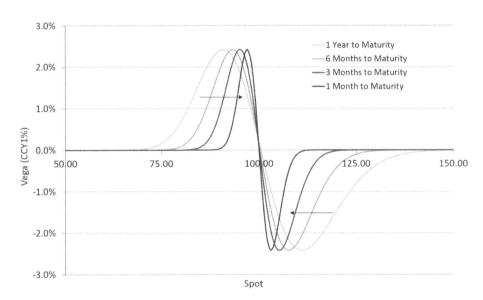

EXHIBIT 21.6   100.00 European digital call vega over time

This implies that the TV adjustment on a European digital option depends on the *slope* of the volatility smile at the digital level to the expiry date. The thought process for traders when asked to price a digital option (with a digital level around current spot) is therefore something like: *It's a digital call so the payoff is to topside, so the vega gets longer to the downside. That's a long/short risk reversal position, so I expect this option to trade over/under TV.*

Exhibit 21.7 shows TV adjustments for a European digital call with different digital levels in a currency pair with a downside risk reversal.

Hedging European digital vega risk with a vanilla spread or risk reversal works well when there is a fair amount of time until expiry (approximately over a month). On the hedge, a vanilla spread to the same expiry as the digital will be transacted; in the positive P&L region for the bank the strike will be bought and in the negative P&L region for the bank the strike will be sold.

The important decision is how wide apart to place the strikes around the digital level and therefore in what notionals to transact the spread. For example, in EUR/USD, if the digital is at 1.4000 in USD1m payout, either a 1.3500/1.4500 spread in EUR10m or a 1.3900/1.4100 spread in EUR50m could be transacted to replicate the size of the payout and therefore the vega profile.

The wider the strikes in the vanilla hedge, the quicker the hedge breaks down. As a rule of thumb, the hedges will stay relevant until they go beyond 25 delta

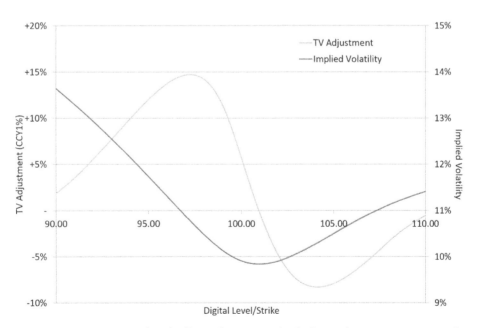

EXHIBIT 21.7 European digital call TV adjustment and volatility smile in a currency pair with a downside risk reversal

strike levels. Therefore, price 1mth 25d call and put options with spot set to the digital level. If the vanilla hedge is set up with the strikes around the 25 delta levels, the hedge will remain relevant approximately until the option has one month until expiry. Traders seek the best balance between transaction costs (larger notionals mean higher cost to establish the hedge) and the length of time the hedge stays valid. Note that if spot moves away from the digital level, the hedge is no longer required.

Gamma and Pin Risk

Gamma (and hence theta) from a European digital increases dramatically toward maturity. The gamma profile for a European digital over time is shown in Exhibit 21.8. This presents risk management challenges if spot is near the digital level near expiry as the gamma and theta exposures can overwhelm the rest of the risk in a trading position. Again, this position is hedged by buying options on the positive P&L side and selling options on the negative P&L side of the digital.

At some point, risk management attention turns from managing vega and gamma exposures to the **pin risk**; The chance of spot ending near the digital level on the expiry date. European digital options generate significant P&L volatility *on* the expiry date if spot is close to the digital level. Overnight into the expiry date the theta from a USD1m 100.00 digital call is shown in Exhibit 21.9.

Consider this theta profile: If spot is around the digital level one day prior to expiry, the value of the digital will be around 50%. Then at expiry, the value of the digital is either 0% or 100% depending on whether spot is in-the-money or out-of-the-money (note the similarities with delta bleed on vanilla options).

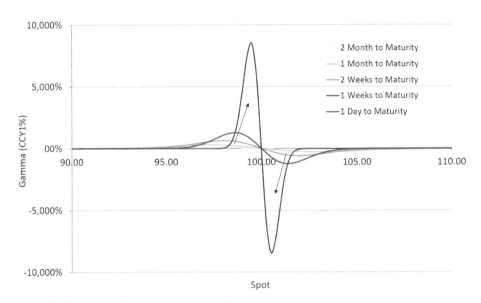

EXHIBIT 21.8   100.00 European digital call gamma over time

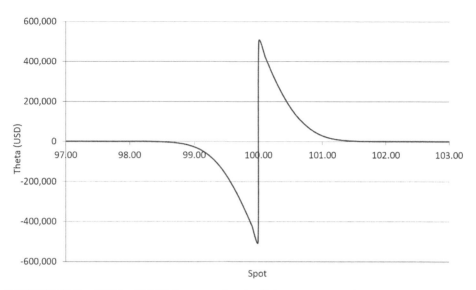

EXHIBIT 21.9 USD1m 100.00 European digital call theta into expiry date

Therefore, the daily theta into the expiry date is at most 50% of the digital value. The practical consequence of this is that, ignoring hedges, the worst-case final-day P&L from a European digital is *half* the payout amount.

When risk managing a European digital at expiry, traders often work to reduce the worst-case final-day negative P&L to an acceptable level. The worst-case P&L scenario most often occurs with spot one pip away through the digital level on the negative P&L side. To hedge this risk, strikes can be sold at or near the digital level (to the same expiry) and this earns additional theta around that level. However, short strikes generate larger negative P&L in the wings, so traders adjust their delta exposure and buy wing strikes until the best possible P&L distribution is achieved.

If spot is on the negative P&L side of the digital coming up to expiry, risk management is difficult. Into the expiry date, theta will be paid and there will be a P&L *gain* equal to the payout through the digital level.

If spot is on the positive P&L side of the digital coming up to expiry, risk management is easier. Into the expiry date, theta will be earned and there will be a P&L *loss* equal to the payout through the digital level. A large delta exposure can therefore be used to generate additional P&L if spot moves toward the digital level (and hence toward the negative P&L side).

In general, it is easier to risk manage a trading position that starts with positive P&L (the theta) but will lose P&L if a certain spot move occurs, rather than a trading position that starts with negative P&L (the theta) but will gain P&L if a certain spot move occurs. Even experienced, well-regarded traders have been known to shout at a spot rate on a screen to encourage it to move.

■ European Digital Range

Another popular European digital product is a European digital range (also called a European digital spread or a bet spread) that has two digital barriers and pays out if spot at maturity is between the barrier levels. The payoff at maturity of a European

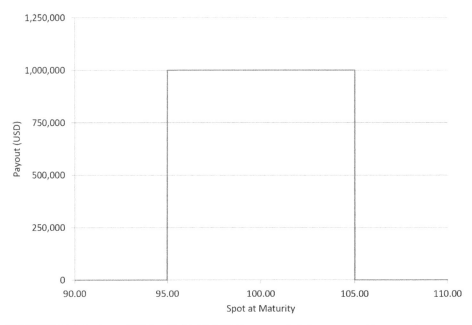

EXHIBIT 21.10   Long USD1m 95.00/105.00 European digital range payoff at maturity

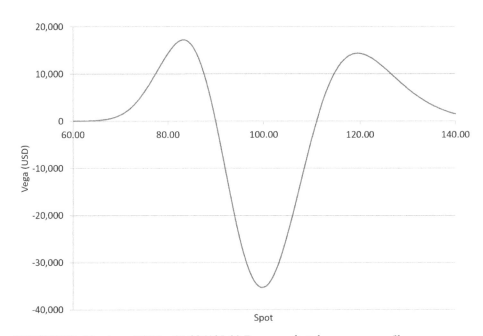

EXHIBIT 21.11   Long USD1m 95.00/105.00 European digital range vega profile

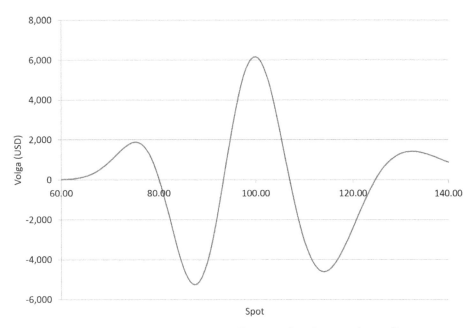

EXHIBIT 21.12   Long USD1m 95.00/105.00 European digital range volga profile

digital range is shown in Exhibit 21.10. This product can be replicated with two European digital calls or two European digital puts: one bought and one sold.

The vega profile of this European digital range is shown in Exhibit 21.11. With spot between the barriers, the option increases in value if implied volatility falls since there will be more chance of spot ending up inside the range, hence short vega. With spot outside the barriers, the option increases in value if implied volatility rises since there will be more chance of spot moving into the range, hence long vega.

This long-wings vega profile implies a long volga and long convexity exposure that is confirmed in Exhibit 21.12. Therefore, European digital ranges often have positive TV adjustments.

European digital ranges can be used to estimate the probability of spot being within a certain range on a given date in the future. For example, it is anticipated that significant risk management challenges will occur if spot is between 1.6250 and 1.6350 at the end of February next year. A European digital range for the expiry date and spot levels in question can be constructed. The price of the contract gives the approximate probability of spot being within that range.

CHAPTER 22

European Barrier Options

European barrier options have a vanilla payoff at expiry plus they also have a single European barrier. For a European knock-out (EKO) barrier option, if spot at maturity is beyond the barrier level, the contract expires worthless despite being in-the-money. The payoff at maturity of a long European knock-out call with 1.3000 strike and 1.4500 European knock-out barrier is shown in Exhibit 22.1. European barriers must be positioned in-the-money, otherwise they have no impact.

European knock-in (EKI) barrier options have a vanilla payoff at expiry *only if* spot at maturity is beyond the barrier level. The payoff at maturity of a long European knock-in call with 1.3000 strike and 1.4500 European knock-in barrier is shown in Exhibit 22.2.

In the European knock-out barrier case, the curtailing of the payoff beyond the barrier can significantly reduce the cost of the European barrier option compared to the equivalent European vanilla option. This is shown in Exhibit 22.3.

Beyond the barrier, the European knock-out contract still has value prior to expiry because there is time remaining for spot to move back inside the barrier. However, as time passes and the probability of such a move occurring reduces, the value of the European knock-out option with spot beyond the barrier level decreases. This is shown in Exhibit 22.4.

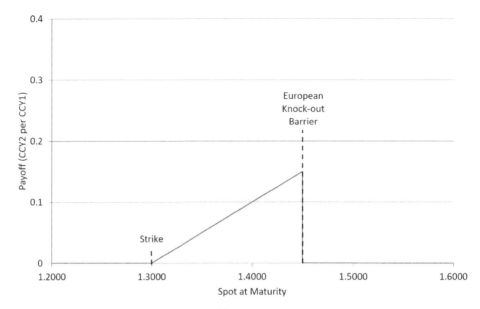

EXHIBIT 22.1   European knock-out payoff at maturity

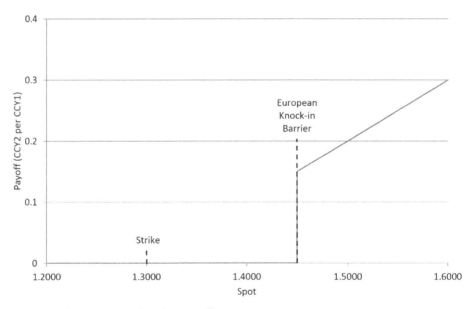

EXHIBIT 22.2   European knock-in payoff at maturity

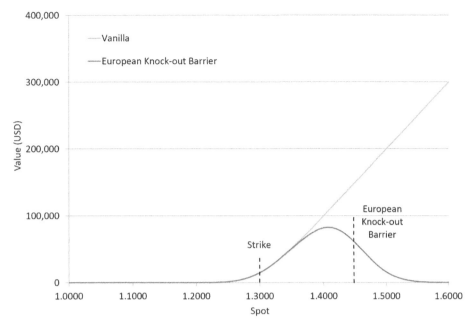

EXHIBIT 22.3   European knock-out barrier versus European vanilla value profiles

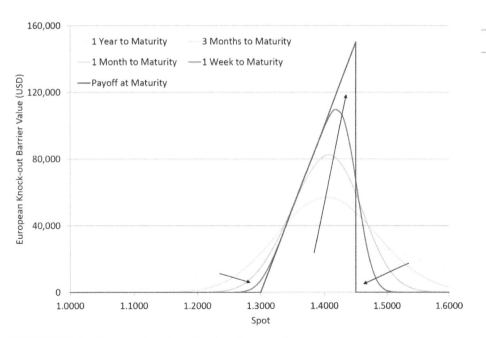

EXHIBIT 22.4   European knock-out barrier value over time

■ European Knock-out Replication

Like European digital options, a European knock-out has no path dependence: The payoff depends only on spot at maturity. Also like European digital options, European barrier options can be replicated using combinations of simpler products.

A long European knock-out call option with notional N, strike K, and barrier B can be perfectly replicated using a long call spread with notionals N and strikes K and B (shown in Exhibit 22.5) plus a short European digital at B (shown in Exhibit 22.6).

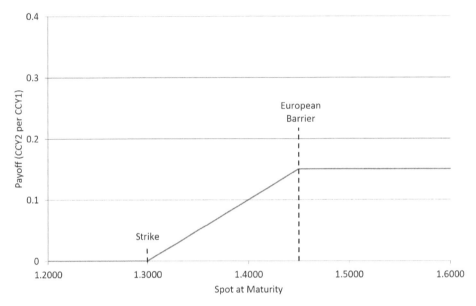

EXHIBIT 22.5   Long vanilla call spread payoff at maturity

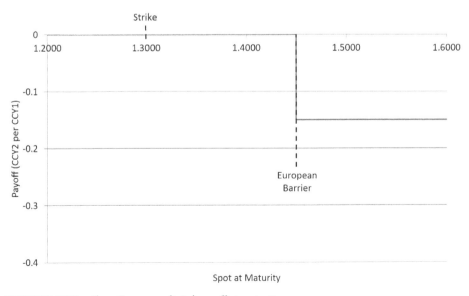

EXHIBIT 22.6   Short European digital payoff at maturity

Note that the digital in Exhibit 22.6 could itself be replicated using vanilla options so a European knock-out can theoretically be replicated using vanilla options only.

Intrinsic Value

The amount of European digital risk in a European barrier option is given by the **intrinsic value**. Intrinsic value measures the payoff at maturity at the barrier level, and therefore how much P&L change occurs at maturity if spot ends up one side of the barrier level or the other. The intrinsic value on a European knock-out barrier option is highlighted in Exhibit 22.7.

Therefore:

$$Intrinsic\ Value_{CCY2} = Notional_{CCY1} \times |Barrier - Strike|$$

$$Intrinsic\ Value_{CCY1} = Notional_{CCY1} \times \frac{|Barrier - Strike|}{Barrier}$$

The CCY2 intrinsic value is divided by the barrier level to get it into CCY1 terms rather than current spot because for the P&L jump to be realized spot must be *at* the barrier level.

$$Intrinsic\ Value_{CCY1\%} = \frac{|Barrier - Strike|}{Barrier}$$

Example: USD/JPY USD100m 1yr 100.00 USD Call/JPY Put European knock-out 120.00. Intrinsic value = $(120 - 100)/120 = $ USD 16.7% = USD 16.7m. There-

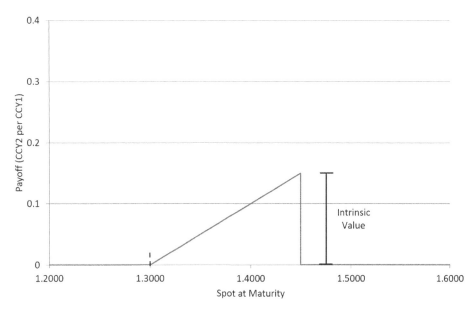

EXHIBIT 22.7   Intrinsic value in a European knock-out barrier option

fore, the European knock-out option contains USD16.7m of European digital risk at 120.00.

Intrinsic value is also called *parity*, *cliff*, or *spike* and it is a key concept that is returned to often within exotic FX derivatives pricing and risk management.

European Knock-in Replication

A long European knock-in call option with notional N, strike K, and barrier B can be perfectly replicated using a long vanilla call option with notional N and strike B (shown in Exhibit 22.8) plus a long European digital at B (shown in Exhibit 22.9).

Again, the notional of the European digital in the replication is the intrinsic value of the European knock-in. Intrinsic value can be determined using the same calculation as the European knock-out case. The intrinsic value on a European knock-in barrier option is highlighted in Exhibit 22.10.

The replications confirm that, as expected, long European knock-in + long European knock-out = long European vanilla since the digital options and vanilla options at the barrier within the replications cancel each other out.

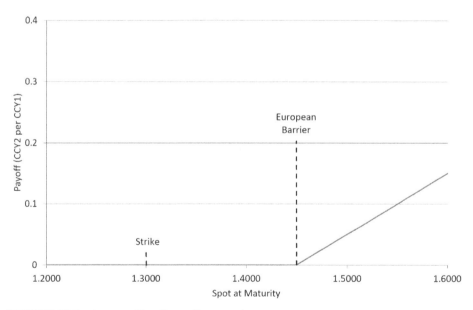

EXHIBIT 22.8   Long vanilla call payoff at maturity

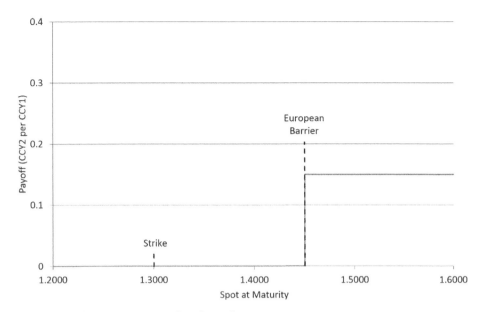

EXHIBIT 22.9 Long European digital payoff at maturity

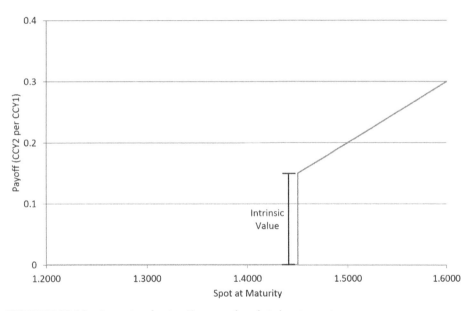

EXHIBIT 22.10 Intrinsic value in a European knock-in barrier option

European Barrier Greeks

European barrier option Greeks exposures can be understood via the replications shown previously.

Vega Risk

If the strike and barrier levels are far enough apart within a European knock-out barrier option, each element can be observed separately within the vega profile as in Exhibit 22.11. At the strike there is a standard vanilla vega profile while the European barrier produces a vanilla spread or risk reversal vega profile.

If the strike and barrier levels are closer together, the vega exposures from the strike and the European barrier merge together as shown in Exhibit 22.12. Also, the proximity of the strike and barrier causes lower option value and vega exposure.

These vega profiles match the intuition of the payoff: With spot beyond the barrier, vega exposure is long because higher volatility increases the chance of spot moving back inside the barrier. If spot is between the strike and the barrier, the contract is conflicted: Higher implied volatility allows the optionality from the strike to be used more but it also increases the chance of spot moving beyond the barrier. Therefore, vega exposures from the contract go both positive and negative between the strike and the barrier.

The European knock-in vega profile also matches the intuition of the payoff. With spot beyond the European barrier level, higher volatility increases the chance of spot moving back inside the barrier and hence, like a European digital, European knock-in barrier options have short vega exposures on the positive P&L side of the barrier level and long vega exposures on the negative P&L side of the barrier level. This is shown in Exhibit 22.13.

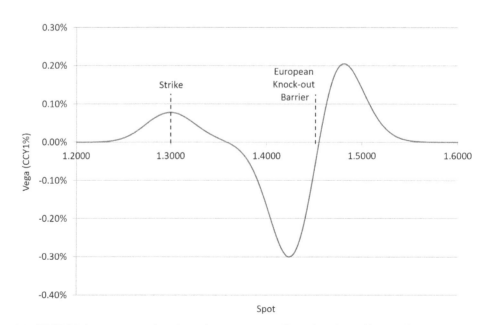

EXHIBIT 22.11   European knock-out barrier vega profile with strike and barrier far apart

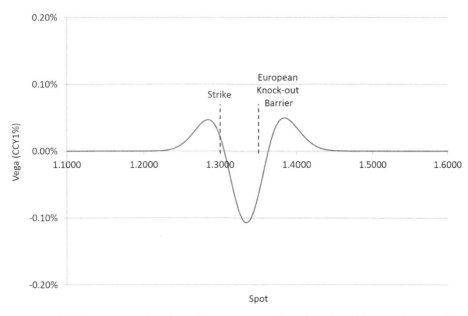

EXHIBIT 22.12   European knock-out barrier vega profile with strike and barrier close together

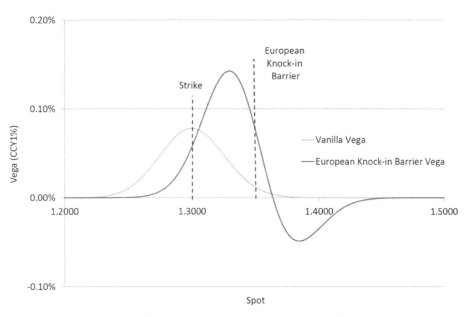

EXHIBIT 22.13   European knock-in barrier versus vanilla vega profiles

Gamma and Pin Risk

Toward expiry, if spot is close to the strike of a European knock-out barrier, the trading risk is simply that of a regular vanilla option and can be risk managed as such. Alternatively, if spot is close to the European barrier, the trading risk is that of a European digital option in size equal to the intrinsic value.

European Barrier Pricing

Like European digitals, prices for European barrier options incorporating the volatility smile can be generated using vanilla option replication. Alternatively, since European barrier value depends only on the terminal spot distribution, any well-calibrated smile pricing model could be used.

European Barrier Bid–Offer Spread

Intrinsic value is also used to calculate the bid–offer spread on European barrier options. As seen from the replication, a European knock-out consists of vanilla spread risk plus European digital risk. The main risk (and hence the wider spread) usually comes from the digital risk at the barrier. Since spot cannot be close to both the barrier and the strike at maturity it is usually only appropriate to take bid–offer spread from the larger of the strike bid-offer and the barrier digital bid-offer.

Therefore, if the bid–offer spread on the digital risk embedded within the European barrier option is 2%, the European barrier bid–offer spread will be approximately 2% multiplied by the intrinsic value.

CHAPTER 23

Touch Options

If FX derivative contracts contain a barrier that is monitored continuously against spot, the barrier is described as **American** or **continuous**. The simplest American barrier products are **touch options**. There are two main kinds of touch option: **One-touch** options pay out a fixed amount of cash on the delivery date if spot trades through a specified barrier level at any time between horizon and expiry. **No-touch** options pay out a fixed amount of cash on the delivery date if spot *does not* trade through a specified barrier level.

Touch options are the American barrier version of European digitals and there are many similarities. Prices on touch options are quoted as a percentage of the payout notional, and like European digitals, prices cannot be quoted in the non-payout currency because there is no strike to switch between notional currencies.

The Greek exposures on touch options can be thought of as being "caused by" the American barrier, just as Greek exposures on vanilla options are "caused by" the strike.

The theoretical value (TV) of a one-touch usually lies between 0% and 100%, as shown in Exhibit 23.1. Note that one-touch TV doesn't *always* lie between 0% and 100% because interest rates could be negative.

It is important to understand that prior to expiry, in a delta hedged trading position, there is no large P&L gain or loss generated from the touch option triggering. As spot nears the barrier, the mark-to-market value of the one-touch option rises (ignoring discounting), e.g., 98% to 99% to 100% (barrier touched), and the trading risks prior to expiry can be hedged using standard Greek exposures.

On the expiry date itself, if risk is viewed in discrete daily steps (see Chapter 11) and the one-touch has not previously triggered, its value is 0%. If it then triggers,

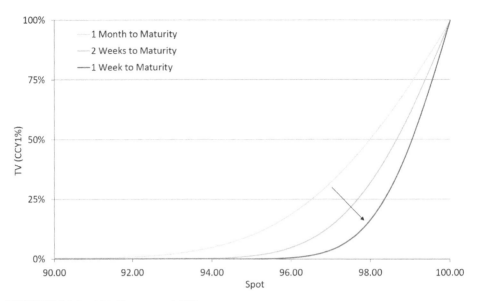

EXHIBIT 23.1   100.00 one-touch TV over time

its value becomes 100%. In trading systems this is shown as an instantaneous P&L jump through the barrier level. This can be a challenging situation to risk manage, particularly if the one-touch notional is large.

Delta Risk

The delta exposure from a one-touch contract will be long into a topside barrier and short into a downside barrier since option value increases with spot closer to the barrier. Delta on a one-touch option over time is shown in Exhibit 23.2.

If spot is *far* from the one-touch barrier, delta bleeds away from the barrier as the sensitivity to changes in spot decreases over time. If spot is *near* the one-touch barrier, the delta bleeds toward the barrier as the sensitivity to changes in spot increases over time. The inflection point between far and near in this context occurs around the spot level at which the one-touch option has 30% TV.

On the expiry date, the one-touch option is viewed as a cash-or-nothing payout with no delta exposure. This potentially causes a large delta bleed away from a long barrier or toward a short barrier. For example, on the day before expiry, an untriggered long topside one-touch option will have a long delta exposure, whereas on the expiry date itself it will have zero delta. Therefore, there will be significant *short* delta bleed into the expiry date.

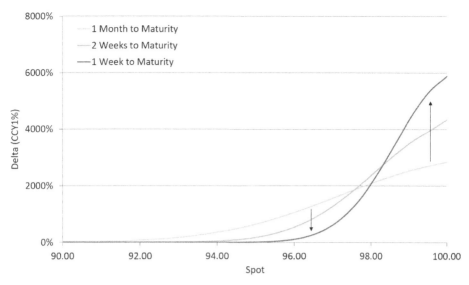

EXHIBIT 23.2 100.00 one-touch delta over time

Vega Risk

One-touch options are generally long vega since if spot volatility increases there is more chance of spot moving and hitting the barrier. Exhibit 23.3 shows how one-touch vega moves toward the barrier over time. The peak vega exposure stays roughly constant and there is no exposure to implied volatility through the barrier because the contract has knocked and is now a guaranteed cash payout at maturity.

Far from the barrier, spot has a very small chance of trading through the barrier level and therefore the sensitivity to implied volatility is low. Similarly, very close to the barrier, spot will almost certainly touch the barrier level so sensitivity to implied volatility is low.

The maximum sensitivity to implied volatility comes at the point where the barrier knock is in the balance. This point moves closer to the barrier over time. As discussed in the delta risk section, the point is located at the spot level for which the TV of the one-touch is around 30%.

The vega exposure on a one-touch can be hedged with a vanilla option since the two vega profiles take similar shapes. However, vega on a vanilla option evolves differently over time. Vanilla vega reduces and drifts toward the strike as shown in Exhibit 23.4.

Therefore, if a one-touch option is hedged with vanilla options, no static vanilla hedge will remain valid for the life of the option. The vanilla vega hedge will either be better now or better later as the exposures evolve.

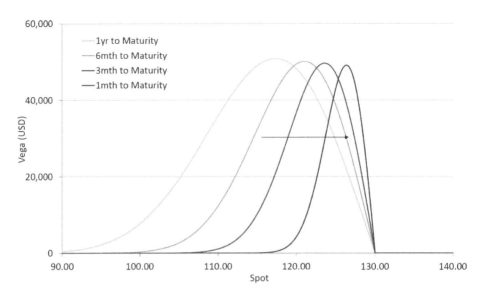

EXHIBIT 23.3 130.00 one-touch vega over time

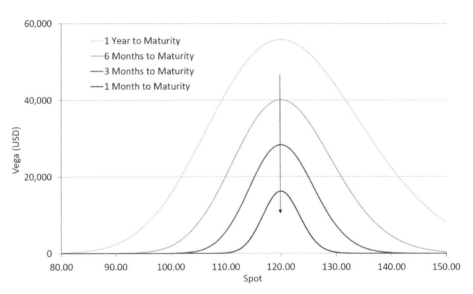

EXHIBIT 23.4 120.00 vanilla vega over time

To minimize rehedging costs it is usually preferable to put a vanilla vega hedge in place that becomes better over time, at least initially. Even then, there can be substantial residual risk, particularly at the barrier, as shown in Exhibit 23.5.

As the vanilla vega dies away, the composite vega position of the one-touch plus the vanilla hedge starts to look more like the one-touch only. At this point, the risk management focus switches to the gamma coming from the barrier rather than the vega.

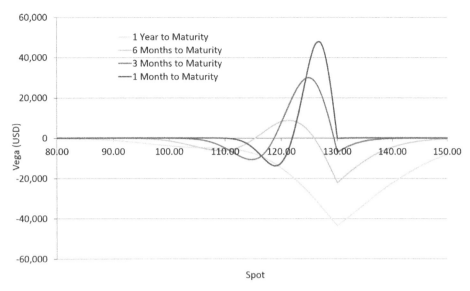

EXHIBIT 23.5 Vega of 130.00 one-touch hedged with 120.00 vanilla in proportions such that vega risk at 6mth tenor is minimized

In addition, when the touch barrier is closer to spot, stopping time will reduce; the option is not expected to live to expiry and therefore vega exposures move to *closer maturities* than the expiry date. It is important to always view bucketed vega Greeks when risk managing contracts with American barriers.

An important subtlety is that one-touch vega, unlike vanilla option vega, is not always positive. In high-interest-rate differential pairs the vega profile shown in Exhibit 23.6 can be generated for a long downside one-touch option.

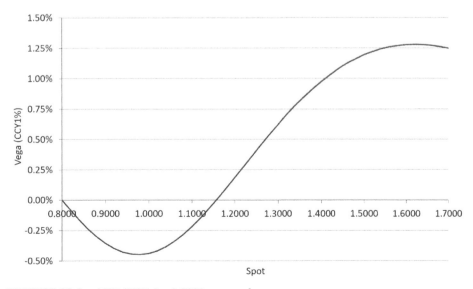

EXHIBIT 23.6 AUD/USD 5yr 0.8000 one-touch vega

This counterintuitive negative vega on a long one-touch option with a downside barrier occurs when CCY1 interest rates are far larger than CCY2 interest rates and therefore swap points are large negative. With spot at, for example, 0.9000, the forward is below the one-touch barrier and therefore the model expects the barrier to be touched with very high probability. If implied volatility rises, spot is likely to diverge further from the forward path and hence is less likely to touch the barrier. This recalls an important feature of the Black-Scholes framework first described in Chapter 5: Zero volatility does not mean the spot is static; it means that spot perfectly follows the forward path. This is relevant particularly in high-interest-rate differential or pegged currency pairs.

Gamma and Pin Risk

One-touch options are generally long gamma and the gamma moves toward the barrier over time and increases sharply into expiry as shown in Exhibit 23.7.

Just as a vanilla option changes from being gamma risk into being strike risk on the expiry date, a one-touch option changes from being gamma risk into being cash-or-nothing P&L risk on the expiry date.

If spot is close to the barrier into the expiry date, the theta will be equal to the remaining value of the one-touch as the value in the risk management system drops from almost 100% to 0%. This theta can be sizeable and therefore the best hedge for a long one-touch into expiry is often to sell vanillas at (or slightly in front of) the barrier level to the same expiry date. This offsets the increased

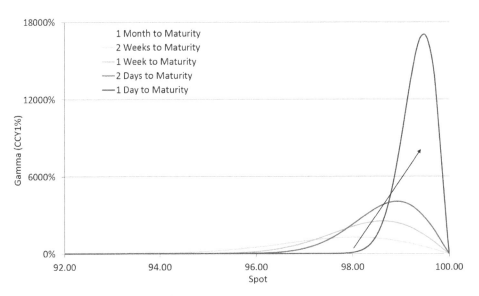

EXHIBIT 23.7   100.00 one-touch gamma over time

gamma risk on the last few days of the option and the theta risk into the last day itself.

Traders often find themselves long one-touch barriers and short vanilla hedges at/near the barrier level to the same expiry date. If the barrier knocks prior to expiry, the exposures from the one-touch disappear and the position is left short optionality from the vanilla hedges. If the position is now too short gamma/vega, the vanilla hedges must be bought back just as spot has broken into a new range and implied volatility has often risen due to increased uncertainty. Therefore, it is often better to increase vanilla hedges over time if possible, rather than putting on the full hedge notional up front.

■ Touch Barrier Delta Gap

If a one-touch barrier knocks prior to expiry, the delta from the option disappears to zero. This potentially causes a delta jump (also known as a delta gap) that must be risk managed.

For example, if a long topside one-touch barrier knocks, the delta from the one-touch jumps from long delta to flat delta (no further exposure to spot) once it knocks. This causes the trading position to get shorter delta. Therefore, spot must be *bought* in order to replace the delta that has been lost. As described in Chapter 3, buying spot when it moves higher is called a *stop-loss* order.

The following rules apply to all American barrier products:

- Long the barrier (i.e., want the barrier to touch) naturally generates a **stop-loss** order.

- Short the barrier (i.e., don't want the barrier to touch) naturally generates a **take-profit** order.

Executing these spot orders can result in "slippage," the risk that the spot market moves against the spot order as it is being executed and hence results in negative P&L. This is particularly a risk for larger-sized spot orders. See Chapter 25 for more information on how large spot orders can cause negative P&L.

In G10 currency pairs, spot orders to hedge barrier delta gaps in the position are usually calculated ahead of time and placed in an order management system so the delta exposure within the trading position remains unchanged as barriers knock. Note that when risk is viewed in discrete daily steps, on the expiry date, when risk becomes cash-or-nothing risk, the delta disappears and hence no delta gap order exists on the expiry date of options with American barriers.

Within risk management systems it is usually possible to view spot ladders assuming delta gap spot orders from American barriers are either executed or not. Traders in G10 currency pairs usually view their trading positions assuming delta gap orders from barriers are executed, but traders in emerging market currency pairs often view their positions assuming no barrier delta gap orders are executed. In all currency pairs, the levels and sizes of delta gaps within trading positions must be calculated and monitored over time.

One-Touch Pricing

For one-touch options, the vega versus TV profile is fairly consistent across tenors and currency pairs, as shown in Exhibit 23.8.

Similarly, volga versus TV and vanna versus TV profiles are fairly consistent across tenors and currency pairs. In practice this means that simply by knowing a few details about a one-touch contract, the TV adjustment can be estimated and sense-checked versus a model price. Exhibit 23.9 shows a typical vanna versus TV profile for a topside one-touch. For a downside barrier one-touch, the vanna profile is simply the negative of Exhibit 23.9.

The vanna in Exhibit 23.9 implies that in terms of skew exposure only, if the risk reversal is in the same direction as the barrier, lower TV one-touches will have a positive TV adjustment and higher TV one-touches will have a negative TV adjustment. Alternatively, if the risk reversal is in the opposite direction to the barrier, lower TV one-touches will have a negative TV adjustment and higher TV one-touches will have a positive TV adjustment.

Exhibit 23.10 shows a typical volga versus TV profile for a topside or downside one-touch.

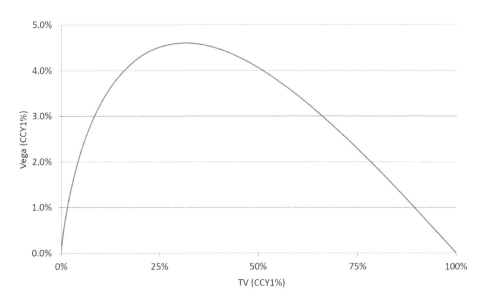

EXHIBIT 23.8   One-touch vega versus TV

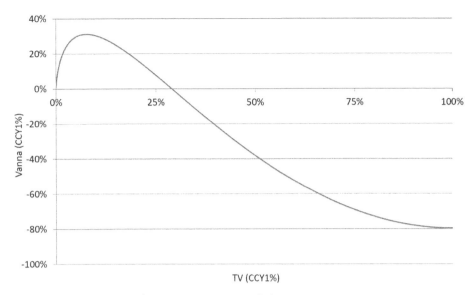

EXHIBIT 23.9 One-touch vanna versus TV (topside barrier)

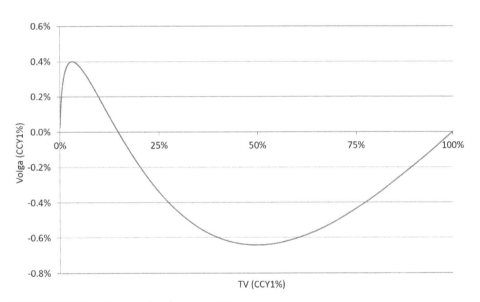

EXHIBIT 23.10 One-touch volga versus TV

This profile implies that in terms of the wing exposure only, lower TV one-touches will have a positive TV adjustment while higher TV one-touches will have a negative TV adjustment.

How these vanna and volga exposures are reflected within a TV adjustment depends on the volatility surface in a particular currency pair.

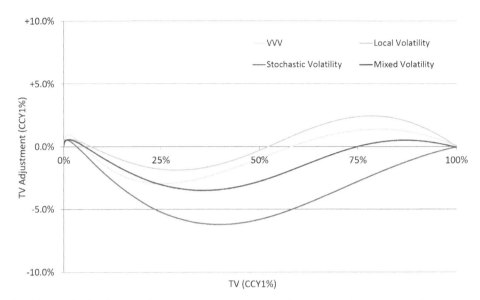

EXHIBIT 23.11 1yr EUR/USD topside one-touch TV adjustment under various smile pricing models

Exhibit 23.11 shows the one-touch TV adjustments generated by various smile pricing models for a 1yr EUR/USD *topside* one-touch with the risk reversal for *downside*.

As predicted by the vanna and volga profiles, TV adjustments on these one-touches are positive for very low TV contracts due to the long volga exposure, then at low TV the TV adjustment goes negative due to the vanna exposure and at high TV the TV adjustment stays negative due to the short volga exposures.

All models except VVV have their most negative adjustment around 40% TV due to the short volga. The mixed volatility model gives prices between the local volatility and stochastic volatility models, as expected. Recall from Chapter 19 that the local volatility model undervalues volatility convexity and the stochastic volatility model overvalues volatility convexity; this can be seen in these results.

Exhibit 23.12 shows the one-touch TV adjustments generated by various pricing models for a 1yr EUR/USD *downside* one-touch with a risk reversal also for *downside*.

As predicted by the vanna and volga profiles, TV adjustments on low TV one-touches are positive due to the vanna and the long volga exposures. TV adjustments on high TV one-touches are negative due to the flipped vanna and the short volga exposures.

Again, the local volatility model undervalues volatility convexity, but values the skew component well. The stochastic volatility model overvalues volatility convexity and undervalues the skew component.

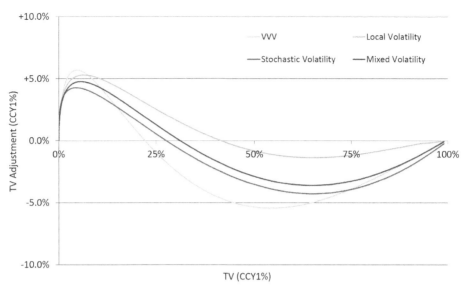

EXHIBIT 23.12 1yr EUR/USD downside one-touch TV adjustment under various smile pricing models

In general, the mixed volatility model gives good pricing for one-touch contracts in liquid currency pairs provided the model is correctly calibrated. There are two main situations in which the mixed volatility model may fail to give prices close to the market:

1. Contracts for which there is a large exposure to interest rates
2. Currency pairs in which there is a spot jump dynamic.

The pricing models examined in this chapter all assume that interest rates are constant and therefore spot volatility ≈ forward volatility. This is obviously not the case in practice (see Chapter 17 for more details). The key point is that American barriers knock out on spot, but are usually priced and valued using the ATM volatility, which is *not* the expected spot volatility. Therefore, when pricing a one-touch:

■ If the volatility of spot is higher than the volatility of the forward, the market value of the one-touch will be higher than the smile model price since spot is more likely to knock the barrier than the model suggests.

■ If the volatility of spot is lower than the volatility of the forward, the market value of the one-touch will be lower than the smile model price since spot is less likely to knock the barrier than the model suggests.

This interest rate impact can be quantified using a stochastic interest rate pricing model. There are two main elements to consider within such a model:

1. *Interest rate volatility*. Higher interest rate volatility increases the forward volatility and hence reduces the market value of one-touch options.

2. *Correlation between spot and interest rates.* As seen in Chapter 17, positive correlation between spot and CCY1 rates or negative correlation between spot and CCY2 rates depresses the volatility of the forward and hence increases the market value of one-touch options. Similarly, positive correlation between spot and CCY2 rates or negative correlation between spot and CCY1 rates increases the volatility of the forward and hence decreases the market value of one-touch options.

This spot volatility versus forward volatility difference is important at longer tenors (approximately beyond 2yr) or in pegged/managed currency pairs. In these cases the impact of stochastic interest rates should always be quantified within pricing.

Finally, it is worth noting that one-touch value is intuitively similar to the probability of the one-touch barrier touching. Specifically, one-touch TV is the discounted, risk-neutral probability of the barrier touching priced under single static volatility and single static interest rates assumptions. Touch options should be priced using pricing models and adjusting for the limitations of the pricing models rather than guessing barrier knock probabilities. However, if the trader's intuition about the barrier knock probability is significantly different from the one-touch valuation, it is important to investigate why this is the case.

One-Touch Bid–Offer Spread

In practice, bid-offer spreads for touch options, like bid-offer spreads for European digitals, are usually generated using grids of bid–offer spreads at different maturities maintained by traders. Since one-touch contracts can knock out prior to expiry, and hence avoid the biggest risk management challenges at expiry, they are often quoted with a tighter bid–offer spread than the equivalent European digital contract, perhaps two-thirds of the width.

One-Touch Variations

Clients often request prices on one-touch options that have subtle variations from the standard one-touch contract.

CCY1 versus CCY2 Payout

One-touch options can pay out either CCY1 or CCY2 cash at maturity. For *topside* one-touch options, a CCY1 payout will have relatively higher valuation than CCY2 payout because CCY1 is relatively worth more with spot higher at the barrier level. Therefore, flipping from CCY1 to CCY2 payout on a topside one-touch will cause the TV% to fall. Exhibit 23.13 shows an example of this.

Contract Details	Leg 1	Leg 2
Currency Pair	USD/JPY	USD/JPY
Horizon	Wed 21-Aug-2013	Wed 21-Aug-2013
Spot Date	Fri 23-Aug-2013	Fri 23-Aug-2013
Strategy	One Touch	One Touch
Maturity	1Y	1Y
Expiry Date	Thu 21-Aug-2014	Thu 21-Aug-2014
Delivery Date	Tue 26-Aug-2014	Tue 26-Aug-2014
Cut	NY	NY
Notional Currency	USD	JPY
Down Barrier		
Up Barrier	120.00	120.00

Market Data		
Spot	99.35	99.35
Swap Points	-35	-35
Forward	99.00	99.00
Deposit (AUD)	0.35%	0.35%
Deposit (USD)	0.00%	0.00%
ATM Volatility	12.50%	12.50%

Outputs		
Output Currency	**USD**	**JPY**
TV	**13.73%**	**11.38%**

EXHIBIT 23.13 CCY1 versus CCY2 one-touch options in pricing tool

Similarly, for *downside* one-touch options, a CCY2 payout will have relatively higher valuation than CCY1 payout because CCY2 is relatively worth more with spot lower. Therefore, flipping from CCY1 to CCY2 payout on a downside one-touch will cause the TV% to rise.

For two-sided touch options that could knock with spot higher *or* lower, there is usually minimal valuation difference between CCY1 payout and CCY2 payout.

Since the standard one-touch pays out at maturity, the effect of discounting must also be taken into account. For a standard one-touch contract, the higher the interest rates in the payout currency, the relatively lower the option value since the payout at maturity must be present valued to the barrier knock date (see Chapter 10).

Pay-at-Maturity versus Pay-at-Touch

Standard one-touch contracts pay at maturity, but clients sometimes request prices on one-touch contracts that pay out *when the barrier touches* (value spot). These are called **pay-at-touch**, or **instant** one-touch options.

When interest rates are positive, the instant one-touch will be more expensive than the standard version because a fixed amount of payout cash will be received sooner (when the barrier knocks) rather than later (at maturity).

For short-dated contracts, this value difference is usually negligible, but for longer expiries there can be a significant price difference, particularly if interest rates in the payout currency are high or if there is a strong correlation between spot and interest rates in the payout currency. For example, if interest rates in the payout currency tend to increase as spot heads higher toward a topside one-touch barrier, the differential between smile model TV adjustment and the market value of the instant one-touch should be higher than the standard version.

■ No-Touch Options

No-touch options pay out a fixed amount of cash at maturity if spot does *not* trade through a specified barrier level at any time between the horizon date and the expiry date.

A long one-touch option plus a long no-touch option with all other contract details the same therefore results in a guaranteed payout at maturity. The Greeks and the TV adjustment on a no-touch contract are the equal and opposite (negative) of the equivalent one-touch option.

The market convention is to trade single-barrier touch contracts as one-touch options and double-barrier touch contracts as no-touch options; therefore, double-no-touch (DNT) options are a standard exotic product in the interbank broker market and with institutional clients.

As seen in Chapter 18, the main exposure on a double-no-touch is usually volga. Intuitively this makes sense; with barriers either side of current spot, pricing depends less on the relationship between spot and implied volatility and more on the volatility of implied volatility.

A long double-no-touch has a short vega exposure since lower volatility gives a greater chance of spot not touching either barrier and hence the payout being generated. The vega profile of a double-no-touch option is shown in Exhibit 23.14.

As time passes (or if the barriers are placed wider apart) the separate vega exposures from each barrier become clear and this is shown in Exhibit 23.15. The vega first increases as the value of the double-no-touch rises; then it starts to split into two separate vega exposures from each barrier over time.

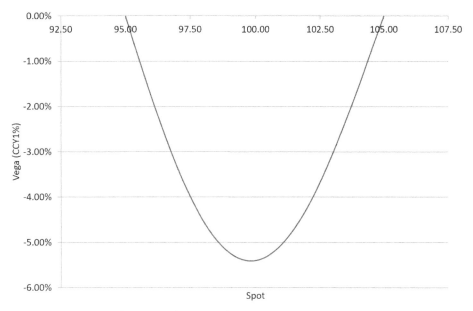

EXHIBIT 23.14   Double-no-touch vega profile

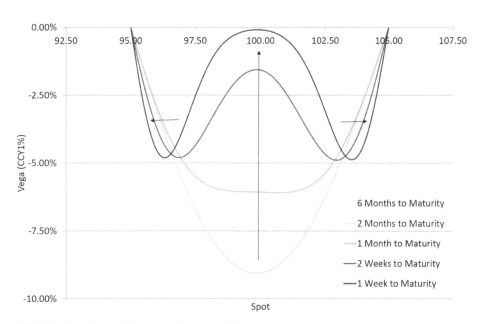

6 Months to Maturity
2 Months to Maturity
1 Month to Maturity
2 Weeks to Maturity
1 Week to Maturity

EXHIBIT 23.15   Double-no-touch vega profile over time

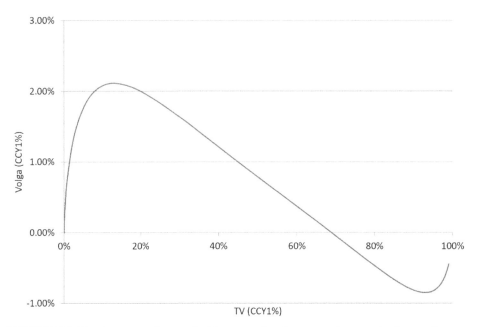

EXHIBIT 23.16 Symmetric-barrier double-no-touch volga against theoretical value profile

Lower TV double-no-touch options are long volga, but higher TV double no-touches can have negative volga. Exhibit 23.16 shows how the volga exposure on a symmetric double-no-touch changes as the barriers widen and hence TV increases.

The bid–offer spread shown on double-barrier touch options is usually similar to the bid–offer spread shown on single-barrier touch options since it is unlikely that traders will encounter risk management issues at both barriers at expiry.

Finally, note that instant versions of no-touch options are not possible: Spot must get to maturity without having triggered the barrier for a no-touch option to pay out.

CHAPTER 24

American Barrier Options

Standard American barrier options are one of the most frequently traded exotic FX derivative contracts. American barrier options have a vanilla payoff at expiry plus they also have a single American-style barrier. There are two main variations: **Regular barrier options** have the American barrier positioned out-of-the-money compared to the option payoff and **reverse barrier options** have the American barrier positioned in-the-money compared to the option payoff. As described in Chapter 20, American barriers are monitored continuously against the spot level in the market.

Regular American Barrier Options

A regular American knock-out (KO) call option structure is shown in Exhibit 24.1. Note that the barrier is positioned out-of-the-money.

Consider a CCY1 call knock-out barrier option with the barrier positioned so far below the strike that there is zero chance of spot hitting the barrier and then ending up back in-the-money at expiry. The pricing and risks of this knock-out option will be identical to the equivalent vanilla option:

- Far barrier knock-out option TV = vanilla priced using ATM volatility
- Far barrier knock-out option vega = vanilla vega
- Far barrier knock-out option TV adjustment = vanilla zeta

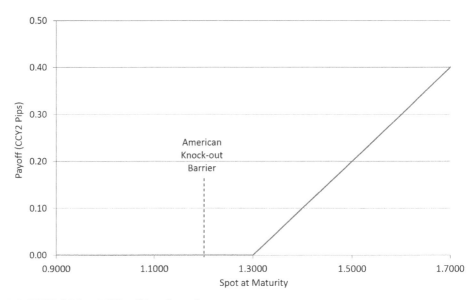

EXHIBIT 24.1 CCY1 call knock-out barrier option structure

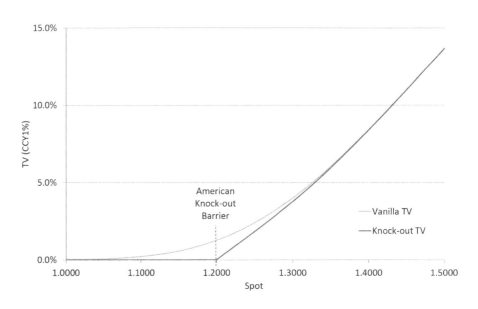

EXHIBIT 24.2 Knock-out barrier and vanilla TV profiles

As Exhibit 24.2 shows, even with a barrier (1.2000) much closer to the strike (1.3000), as spot goes higher, the downside barrier is less likely to be touched and the knock-out TV converges to the vanilla TV. If spot goes down through the barrier, the barrier option knocks out and becomes worthless.

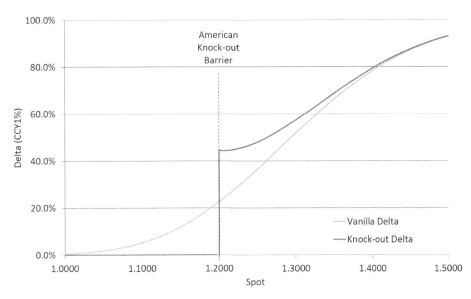

EXHIBIT 24.3   Knock-out barrier and vanilla delta profiles

The delta profile of the knock-out option versus the equivalent vanilla option is shown in Exhibit 24.3.

As spot goes higher, the knock-out delta converges to the vanilla delta. If spot goes down through the barrier, the knock-out barrier has triggered and there is no delta exposure or indeed any other Greek exposures. Therefore, American barrier options have barrier delta gaps like touch options (see Chapter 23).

Exhibit 24.4 shows how the theoretical value of a knock-out barrier option changes as the barrier level changes. As the barrier level moves closer to spot, the knock-out barrier TV reduces because there is an increased chance of the barrier knocking prior to maturity.

Contract details: EUR/USD 1yr 1.3000 EUR call/USD put knock-out option. Spot: 1.3000.

EXHIBIT 24.4   TV of knock-out barrier option with different barrier levels

Barrier Level	Stopping Time	Knock-out Barrier TV (CCY1%)
0.5000	100.00%	3.781%
1.0000	99.94%	3.781%
1.1000	98.18%	3.781%
1.2000	80.52%	3.638%
1.2500	52.38%	2.782%
1.2900	12.85%	0.762%

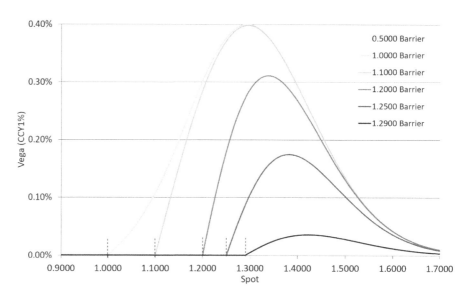

EXHIBIT 24.5 Vega profiles of knock-out barrier option with different barrier levels

Exhibit 24.5 shows the vega profiles for knock-out barrier options with these different barrier levels. As the barrier moves higher, the peak vega also shifts higher and the increasing chance of knocking out causes the premium and the vega exposure to reduce. The closer barrier also causes increased vanna $\left(\frac{\partial vega}{\partial spot}\right)$ exposures at current spot because vega falls sharply into the barrier level.

As mentioned in Chapter 23, when American barriers are close to spot, the option is not expected to live to expiry and therefore vega exposures are to implied volatility at maturities closer than the expiry. Again, it is important to view bucketed Greek exposures when risk managing any option contracts with American barriers.

The volga $\left(\frac{\partial vega}{\partial \sigma}\right)$ profile of a knock-out barrier option changes dramatically as the barrier moves higher, as shown in Exhibit 24.6.

With barriers far from spot (0.50 and 1.00) the knock-out barrier volga profile looks like the vanilla volga profile, as expected. As the knock-out barrier moves closer to spot, volga gets generally less positive and eventually creates an area of negative volga. In general, *regular American knock-out barriers produce negative volga*, which leads to more negative TV adjustments. Intuitively, the reason for this is:

- Volatility higher brings the knock-out barrier relatively closer to spot → option is more likely to knock and less likely to pay out.

- Volatility lower reduces the expected option payout.

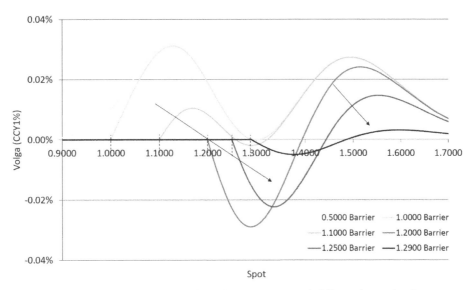

EXHIBIT 24.6   Volga profiles of knock-out barrier option with different barrier levels

It is therefore preferable that implied volatility does not move, hence producing a negative volga exposure.

Regular Knock-in Barrier Options

Knock-out barrier options have a vanilla payoff at expiry providing the American barrier has *not* triggered prior to expiry, whereas knock-in (KI) barrier options have a vanilla payoff at expiry, providing the American barrier *has* triggered prior to expiry.

Providing all contract details (expiry, strike, barrier, cut, and notional) are the same:

- Knock-out barrier + knock-in barrier = vanilla option

It follows that:

- Knock-out TV + knock-in TV = vanilla TV

- Knock-out barrier TV adjustment + knock-in barrier TV adjustment = vanilla zeta

Exhibit 24.7 shows the vega of a knock-in barrier option with a 1.2000 barrier. Note the vega symmetry around the barrier with peak vega at the barrier level. The vega beyond the knock-in barrier must be equal to the vanilla vega.

Looking at the vega profile, it is clear that the knock-in barrier option will be longer volga around 1.3000 spot since vega increases to the downside. This is shown in Exhibit 24.8. Again, note the symmetry around the barrier level.

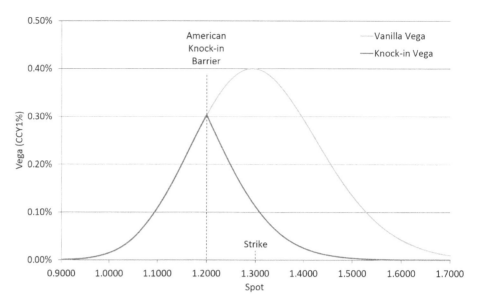

EXHIBIT 24.7   Vega profile of a vanilla option versus a knock-in barrier option with the same strike

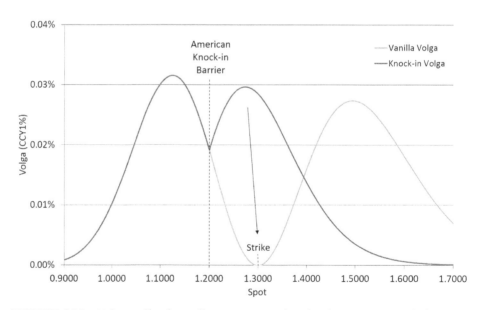

EXHIBIT 24.8   Volga profile of a vanilla option verses a knock-in barrier option with the same strike

Regular Barrier Option Pricing

The main trading risks on knock-out and knock-in options are vega and gamma exposures, which can be hedged with vanilla options. Over time, either the knock-out option triggers or the risk becomes more vanilla as the chance of the barrier triggering decreases. For the knock-in option, the option either triggers and becomes a vanilla option or the risk dies away as the chance of triggering decreases. Regular American barrier options therefore become easier to risk manage over time.

Local volatility pricing models will generate a price above the market price for knock-out options and below the market price for knock-in options due to local volatility undervaluing (short) convexity. A well-calibrated mixed-volatility model will generally give good pricing for knock-out and knock-in options in liquid currency pairs, but as always, the interest rate effect must be additionally quantified on longer-dated trades.

As a quick sense-check for knock-out TV adjustment, it will usually be lower (due to the volga) than vanilla zeta × stopping time (i.e., the cost of the strike on the smile multiplied by the length of time the option will be alive).

In terms of bid–offer spread, knock-outs and knock-ins are generally spread slightly wider than the equivalent vanilla because barrier options have only marginally higher trading risks than the equivalent vanilla options.

Finally, barrier delta gaps must be considered when pricing knock-out and knock-in options. Most often, market participants do not want stop-loss spot orders since they represent a larger P&L risk than take-profit orders. The pricing of regular American barrier options reflects that preference: Knock-out options become relatively more attractive to buy and less attractive to sell, while knock-in options become relatively less attractive to buy and more attractive to sell. This idea is covered in more detail in Chapter 25.

■ Reverse American Barrier Options

Reverse knock-out (RKO) and reverse knock-in (RKI) barrier options have a vanilla payoff at expiry plus a single American barrier that is positioned in-the-money versus the payoff, as shown in Exhibit 24.9.

Reverse barrier options have additional trading risks that arise from the in-the-money barrier. At expiry, a reverse knock-out option goes from being worth the intrinsic value (see Chapter 22) with spot just before the barrier to being worth nothing if spot trades through the barrier level: the same P&L dynamic as a touch option. When the reverse knock-out option is *bought*, one-touch risk is effectively *sold* because P&L changes negatively as spot goes through the barrier level.

Exhibit 24.10 shows the TV profiles of a reverse knock-out barrier option versus the equivalent vanilla option.

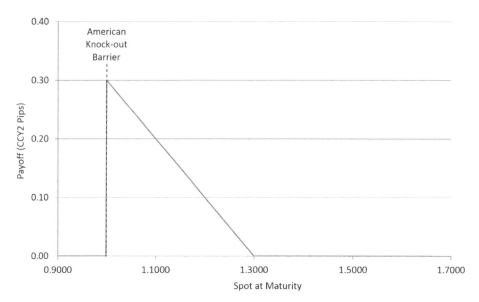

EXHIBIT 24.9 CCY1 put reverse knock-out structure

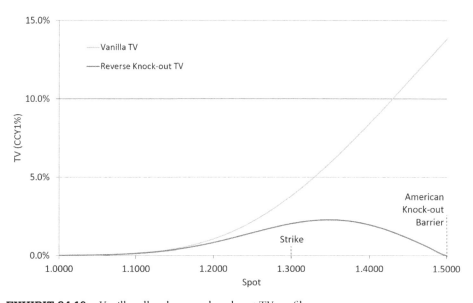

EXHIBIT 24.10 Vanilla call and reverse knock-out TV profiles

The unlimited upside from the vanilla option is curtailed by the in-the-money barrier. For this reason, reverse knock-out options are often significantly cheaper than the equivalent vanilla options and they are therefore an effective way to express the view that spot will move in a certain direction but not very far. For institutional clients, short-dated RKOs are an attractive product: They can be bought cheaply, transacted live (i.e., no delta hedge), and then left until expiry to hopefully generate a payoff.

Traders and clients often compare the value of the reverse knock-out option with the equivalent vanilla option to get a measure of how much discount the barrier provides. Plus they compare the value of a reverse knock-out option with the equivalent European knock-out option to ascertain the value of the "American-ness" of the barrier. Another popular analysis compares the maximum payoff from the option (i.e., spot just inside the knock-out barrier) with the cost. This is sometimes called the **leverage** of the option.

Within a delta hedged options portfolio, reverse knock-out options with large notionals can be challenging to risk manage due to the touch risk at the barrier. As with European barriers (see Chapter 22), the size of the risk at the barrier is the intrinsic value (IV). For example, USD100m of USD/JPY 1mth 95.00 reverse knock-out 98.00 has 100m × (98.00 − 95.00)/98.00 = USD3.06m of touch risk embedded within it.

The trading risk on a long reverse knock-out option can be decomposed into two parts: the long strike and the short one-touch (recall that single barrier touch risk is always traded in the market via a one-touch contract). The vega profile of a reverse knock-out shown in Exhibit 24.11 confirms this.

Specifically, a long reverse knock-out option in notional N with strike K and American knock-out barrier B can be approximately decomposed into these two elements:

1. Long vanilla call in notional N with strike K
2. Short one-touch in payout IV with barrier B

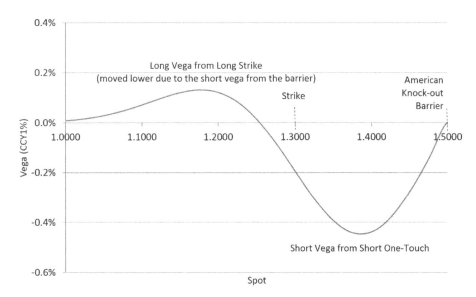

EXHIBIT 24.11 Long 1yr 1.3000 strike/1.5000 barrier CCY1 call reverse knock-out vega profile

A quick sense-check for the reverse knock-out TV adjustment can therefore be obtained by calculating:

$$\textbf{RKO}\ \text{TV Adjustment} = \text{Strike Zeta} \times \text{Stopping Time}$$
$$- \text{Intrinsic Value} \times \text{One-touch TV Adjustment}$$

- The "*Strike Zeta × Stopping Time*" gives the cost of the strike on the smile, weighted by how long the option is likely to exist for.

- The "*Intrinsic Value × One-touch TV Adjustment*" gives the TV adjustment on the one-touch risk at the barrier level. This quantity is subtracted because long a reverse knock-out barrier gives short one-touch risk.

Example: EUR/USD 6mth 1.3500 RKO 1.4500 with spot 1.3430, ATM volatility 8.15% and RKO TV 0.73 EUR%. Working to the nearest basis point in CCY1% terms:

- Strike Zeta from EUR/USD 6mth 1.3500 vanilla = +0.02% (a small value since the strike is close to the ATM)

- Stopping Time = 93%

- Strike Zeta × Stopping Time = 0.02%

- Intrinsic Value = (1.45 − 1.35)/1.45 = 6.9%

- One-touch TV Adjustment = −2.85%

- Intrinsic Value × One-touch TV Adjustment = −0.19%

These results suggest that the majority of the *smile risk* on this reverse knock-out comes from the barrier (-0.19%) rather than the strike (0.02%).

The reverse knock-out TV adjustment approximation of 0.02% − (−0.19%) = +0.21% is close to the mixed volatility model TV adjustment of +0.19%. Exhibit 24.12 shows these options within a pricing tool.

In practice, this means that when pricing a reverse knock-out it is important to know the intrinsic value at the barrier and the equivalent TV of a one-touch at the barrier level. Then, knowing whether the one-touch option trades over or under TV gives quick guidance on whether the reverse knock-out will trade over or under TV in the opposite direction.

Recall that one-touch vega moves toward the barrier over time but does not reduce. An RKO vega exposure shows similar behavior in Exhibit 24.13. At the 1mth expiry, the risk has started noticeably splitting into strike risk and one-touch risk at the barrier. This long strike versus short one-touch risk spread creates a vega profile that is quite similar to a risk reversal. Trading a vanilla spread with strikes at the RKO strike and RKO barrier level to the RKO expiry date is often an effective way to hedge reverse knock-out vega.

Contract Details	Leg 1	Leg 2	Leg 3
Currency Pair	EUR/USD	EUR/USD	EUR/USD
Horizon	Tue 20-Aug-2013	Tue 20-Aug-2013	Tue 20-Aug-2013
Spot Date	Thu 22-Aug-2013	Thu 22-Aug-2013	Thu 22-Aug-2013
Strategy	Reverse Knock-out	Vanilla	One Touch
Call/Put	EUR Call/USD Put	EUR Call/USD Put	
Maturity	6M	6M	6M
Expiry Date	Thu 20-Feb-2014	Thu 20-Feb-2014	Thu 20-Feb-2014
Delivery Date	Mon 24-Feb-2014	Mon 24-Feb-2014	Mon 24-Feb-2014
Cut	NY	NY	NY
Strike	1.3500	1.3500	
Notional Currency	EUR	EUR	EUR
Down Barrier			
Up Barrier	1.4500		1.4500

Market Data			
Spot	1.3430	1.3430	1.3430
Swap Points	10	10	10
Forward	1.3440	1.3440	1.3440
Deposit (GBP)	0.15%	0.15%	0.15%
Deposit (USD)	0.30%	0.30%	0.30%
ATM Volatility	8.150%	8.150%	8.150%
Smile Volatility		7.95%/8.25%	

Outputs			
Output Currency	EUR	EUR	EUR
TV	0.73%		19.55%
TV Adjustment	+0.19%		-2.85%
Mid Price	0.92%	2.06%	16.70%
Expected Life	93.10%		93.10%
Zeta		0.02%	

EXHIBIT 24.12 Reverse knock-out "replication" in pricing tool

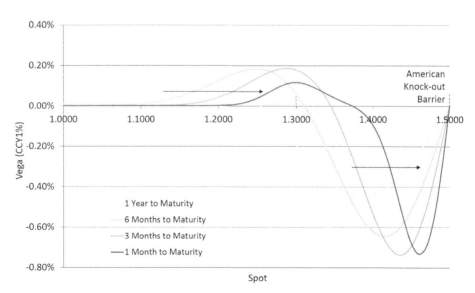

EXHIBIT 24.13 Long 1.3000 strike/1.5000 barrier CCY1 call reverse knock-out vega profile over time

Reverse Knock-in Barrier Options

A familiar pricing identity exists for reverse barrier options. Providing all contract details (expiry, strike, barrier, cut, and notional) are the same:

- Reverse knock-out + reverse knock-in = vanilla

A long reverse knock-in has similar trading risk to a long one-touch at the barrier level, providing the strike and barrier are far enough apart. This is shown in the vega profiles in Exhibit 24.14.

The reverse knock-in and equivalent one-touch vega profiles are very similar in front of the barrier. At the barrier, the reverse knock-in becomes a vanilla so the reverse knock-in and vanilla vega profiles intersect at that point.

Reverse Barrier Option Pricing

From a risk management perspective, the major risks on reverse barrier options are initially vega Greeks, which can be approximately hedged with vanillas. For a reverse knock-out option, the main risk is a strike versus barrier vega spread. The pricing of this risk on the smile will be heavily impacted by the skew in the volatility surface. For a reverse knock-in option, the main vega risk comes from the barrier. Over time, touch risk at the barrier becomes the major risk and this can be hedged like a standard one-touch option.

In freely floating currency pairs, a well-calibrated mixed volatility model will usually give reverse barrier option prices that match the market well, especially

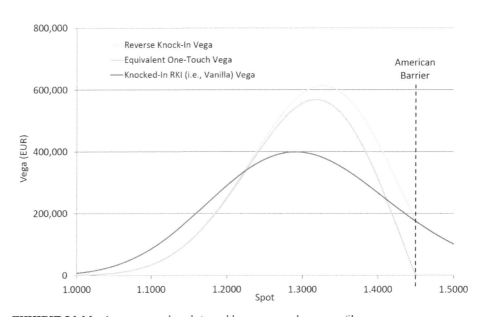

EXHIBIT 24.14 Long reverse knock-in and long one-touch vega profiles

since reverse barrier options are generally quite short-dated hence minimal interest rate risk and have low premium hence low vega exposures.

In terms of bid–offer spread, reverse knock-out and reverse knock-in options usually derive the majority of their spread from their touch risk in the same way that European barrier options derive the majority of the spread from their European digital risk. Exhibit 24.15 shows a reverse knock-in and equivalent one-touch option within a pricing tool. In approximate terms:

Reverse barrier bid–offer spread = intrinsic value × equivalent one-touch bid–offer spread.

However, a reverse knock-out generally has less vega than a one-touch (due to the strike versus barrier risk offset), so the reverse knock-out may be quoted relatively slightly tighter.

Contract Details	Leg 1	Leg 2
Currency Pair	USD/JPY	USD/JPY
Horizon	Tue 20-Aug-2013	Tue 20-Aug-2013
Spot Date	Thu 22-Aug-2013	Thu 22-Aug-2013
Strategy	Reverse Knock-In	One Touch
Call/Put	USD Put/JPY Call	
Maturity	6M	6M
Expiry Date	Thu 20-Feb-2014	Thu 20-Feb-2014
Delivery Date	Mon 24-Feb-2014	Mon 24-Feb-2014
Cut	NY	NY
Strike	95.00	
Notional Currency	USD	USD
Down Barrier	85.00	85.00
Up Barrier		
Market Data		
Spot	97.10	97.10
Swap Points	-10	-10
Forward	97.00	97.00
Deposit (GBP)	0.30%	0.30%
Deposit (USD)	0.05%	0.05%
ATM Volatility	12.20%	12.20%
Outputs		
Output Currency	USD	USD
TV	1.41%	11.90%
TV Adjustment	+0.21%	+1.45%
Mid Price	1.62%	13.35%
Price Spread	0.24%	2.00%

EXHIBIT 24.15   Reverse knock-out and equivalent one-touch option within a pricing tool

One-touch bid–offer spreads are monitored and directly observed in the interbank broker market so exotics traders tend to describe reverse barrier bid-offer spreads in terms of the embedded one-touch bid-offer. Saying "I showed an AUD/USD 6mth RKO 1.5% wide on the one-touch" is far more useful than "I showed an AUD/USD 6mth RKO 0.20% wide."

Finally, traders need to be careful when clients request prices in reverse knock-in options with barriers close to the strike. These options have a virtually identical theoretical value to the vanilla option with no barrier. However, since vanilla = reverse knock-out + reverse knock-in, the equivalent reverse knock-out is very low TV and would often trade higher than a pricing model suggests. Therefore, the reverse knock-in should be priced correspondingly lower.

■ Double American Barrier Options

Double knock-out (DKO) and double knock-in (DKI) barrier options have a vanilla payoff at expiry plus two American barriers: one barrier positioned in-the-money versus the payoff and one positioned out-of-the-money versus the payoff as shown in Exhibit 24.16.

The primary risk on double American barrier options usually comes from the in-the-money barrier. Therefore, similar pricing and spreading methodologies are used for double knock-out options as reverse knock-out options.

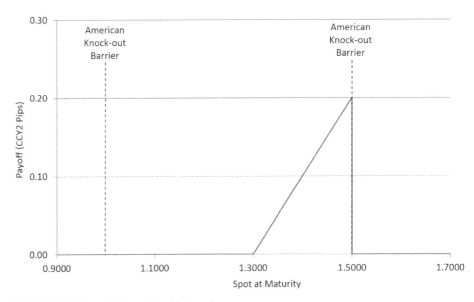

EXHIBIT 24.16 CCY1 call double knock-out structure

Traders often simplify the product in order to identify the most important risks on a double-barrier option. By removing each barrier in turn, a small TV change implies an unimportant barrier and a large TV change implies an important barrier. Therefore, pricing and risk management can be focused around the most appropriate element of the structure.

Finally, the presence of two barriers can sometimes cause double knock-out options to have trading risks initially similar to a double-no-touch, specifically, larger convexity exposures.

Knock-in/Knock-out Option Replication

Knock-in/knock-out (KIKO) options have a vanilla payoff at expiry plus two American barriers: one barrier positioned in-the-money and one positioned out-of-the-money. One of the barriers is knock-out while the other is knock-in. There are two variations of knock-in/knock-out options:

1. Knock-out until expiry
2. Knock-out until knock-in

A long knock-out until expiry KIKO option with knock-in barrier $B1$ ($B1 > K$) and knock-out barrier $B2$ ($B2 < K$) can be replicated with the following standard American barrier options with the same strike, payoff, and notional:

- Long knock-out with barrier $B2$

- Short double knock-out with barriers $B1$ and $B2$

  Thinking through the possible scenarios:

- Spot gets to maturity without having touched either KIKO barrier level: The knock-out and double knock-out payoffs within the replication offset and there is no payout.

- Spot touches the KIKO knock-out barrier level $B2$ first: The knock-out and the double knock-out both expire and there is no payoff at maturity.

- Spot touches the KIKO knock-in barrier level $B1$ first: The short double knock-out expires and only the long knock-out risk remains; the structure has been "knocked in." If spot then touches the KIKO knock-out barrier level $B2$, the knock-out option will expire; otherwise the option has a vanilla payoff at maturity.

Therefore this variation is called "knock-out until expiry." Exhibit 24.17 shows the legs of the replication. Note that this replication works no matter the payoff.

Contract Details	Leg 1	Leg 2	Leg 3
Currency Pair	AUD/USD	AUD/USD	AUD/USD
Horizon	Tue 20-Aug-2013	Tue 20-Aug-2013	Tue 20-Aug-2013
Spot Date	Thu 22-Aug-2013	Thu 22-Aug-2013	Thu 22-Aug-2013
Strategy	KIKO	American Barrier	American Barrier
Call/Put	AUD Call/USD Put	AUD Call/USD Put	AUD Call/USD Put
Maturity	1Y	1Y	1Y
Expiry Date	Thu 21-Aug-2014	Thu 21-Aug-2014	Thu 21-Aug-2014
Delivery Date	Tue 26-Aug-2014	Tue 26-Aug-2014	Tue 26-Aug-2014
Cut	NY	NY	NY
Strike	0.9000	0.9000	0.9000
Notional Currency	AUD	AUD	AUD
Down Barrier Type	Knock-out	Knock-out	Knock-out
Up Barrier Type	Knock-In		Knock-out
Down Barrier	0.8000	0.8000	0.8000
Up Barrier	1.0000		1.0000

Market Data			
Spot	0.9090	0.9090	0.9090
Swap Points	-205	-205	-205
Forward	0.8885	0.8885	0.8885
Deposit (AUD)	2.65%	2.65%	2.65%
Deposit (USD)	0.35%	0.35%	0.35%
ATM Volatility	11.175%	11.175%	11.175%

Outputs			
Output Currency	AUD	AUD	AUD
TV	3.18%	3.74%	0.56%
TV Adjustment	-0.38%	-0.22%	+0.16%
Mid Price	2.80%	3.52%	0.72%

EXHIBIT 24.17   Knock-in/knock-out replication in pricing tool

Strike-out Options

Strike-out options are American knock-out barrier options such that strike = barrier. Consider an AUD/USD 1yr 0.8000 AUD call/USD put with American knock-out barrier at 0.8000. Assume initially that AUD and USD interest rates are zero and hence spot = forward as shown in Exhibit 24.18.

With spot at 0.9000, the TV of this option is simply the intrinsic, that is, (0.9000 − 0.8000)/0.9000 = 11.11%. There is 100% delta, zero vega, and zero gamma over all spots (above the barrier). This trade is equivalent to a long spot position in the notional amount that is closed out once the barrier level trades. The important thing to note is that there is no optionality coming from the strike due to the barrier. Exhibit 24.19 shows this option in a pricing tool.

AUD (CCY1) rates are now increased to 5% and USD (CCY2) rates are kept at 0%. The forward moves to the left (to 0.8571) and the option value drops to 7.31%. Importantly the option value is not equal to the intrinsic any more:

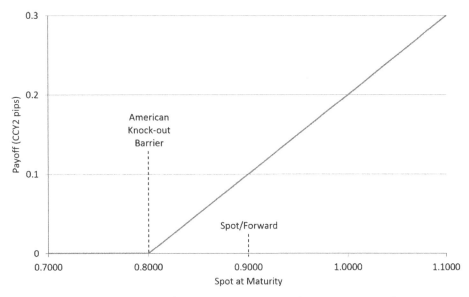

EXHIBIT 24.18 AUD/USD strike-out option structure with 0% AUD rates and 0% USD rates

Contract Details	Leg 1
Currency Pair	AUD/USD
Horizon	Wed 21-Aug-2013
Spot Date	Fri 23-Aug-2013
Strategy	Continuous Barrier
Call/Put	AUD Call/USD Put
Maturity	1Y
Expiry Date	Thu 21-Aug-2014
Delivery Date	Tue 26-Aug-2014
Cut	NY
Strike	0.8000
Notional Currency	AUD
Barrier Type	Knock-out
Down Barrier	0.8000
Up Barrier	

Market Data	
Spot	0.9000
Swap Points	0
Forward	0.9000
Deposit (AUD)	0.00%
Deposit (USD)	0.00%
ATM Volatility	11.50%

Outputs	
Output Currency	**AUD**
TV	**11.11%**
TV Delta	**100.00%**
TV Gamma	**0.00%**
TV Vega	**0.00%**

EXHIBIT 24.19 AUD/USD strike-out option with 0% AUD rates and 0% USD rates

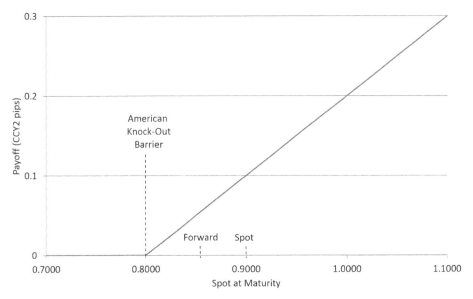

EXHIBIT 24.20 AUD/USD strike-out option payoff with 5% AUD rates and 0% USD rates

$(0.8571 - 0.8000)/0.8571 = 6.66\%$. The option payoff using this new market data is shown in Exhibit 24.20. As shown in the pricing tool in Exhibit 24.21, the option is now long vega, and it only has 80.52% delta, so there must be another mechanism at work. The vega profile of the strike-out with higher CCY1 interest rates is shown in Exhibit 24.22.

Now, AUD (CCY1) rates are put back to 0% and USD (CCY2) rates are increased to 5%. The forward moves to the right (to 0.9465), the option TV increases to 15.07%, delta is 110%, and vega is now short. The option payoff using this new market data is shown in Exhibit 24.23. The strike-out option is shown priced with this new market data in Exhibit 24.24. The vega profile of the strike-out with higher CCY2 interest rates is shown in Exhibit 24.25.

Given there is no optionality coming from the strike, where is this vega exposure coming from? The key element within strike-out options is the **interest rate carry**.

Intuitively, the hedge for this strike-out option is to sell spot now and buy it back if spot trades at or through the barrier. If CCY1 rates are larger than CCY2 rates, holding the short cash position on the hedge will cost money over time. Therefore, ideally spot trades through the barrier level as quickly as possible and hence the hedge can be unwound. This explains why the higher AUD (CCY1) rates case is long vega; higher volatility will increase the probability of knocking out earlier.

Contract Details	Leg 1
Currency Pair	AUD/USD
Horizon	Wed 21-Aug-2013
Spot Date	Fri 23-Aug-2013
Strategy	Continuous Barrier
Call/Put	AUD Call/USD Put
Maturity	1Y
Expiry Date	Thu 21-Aug-2014
Delivery Date	Tue 26-Aug-2014
Cut	NY
Strike	0.8000
Notional Currency	AUD
Barrier Type	Knock-out
Down Barrier	0.8000
Up Barrier	

Market Data	
Spot	0.9000
Swap Points	-429
Forward	0.8571
Deposit (AUD)	5.00%
Deposit (USD)	0.00%
ATM Volatility	11.50%

Outputs	
Output Currency	**AUD**
TV	**7.31%**
TV Delta	**80.50%**
TV Gamma	**1.93%**
TV Vega	**0.13%**

EXHIBIT 24.21   AUD/USD strike-out option with 5% AUD rates and 0% USD rates

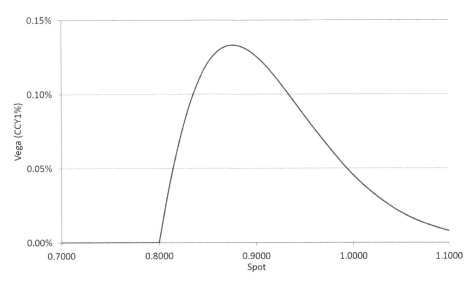

EXHIBIT 24.22   AUD/USD 0.8000 strike-out vega profile (AUD rates = 5%/USD rates = 0%)

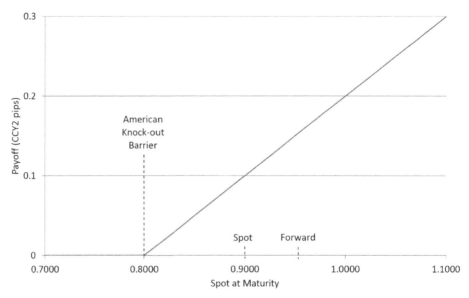

EXHIBIT 24.23 AUD/USD strike-out option payoff with 0% AUD rates and 5% USD rates

Contract Details	Leg 1
Currency Pair	AUD/USD
Horizon	Wed 21-Aug-2013
Spot Date	Fri 23-Aug-2013
Strategy	Continuous Barrier
Call/Put	AUD Call/USD Put
Maturity	1Y
Expiry Date	Thu 21-Aug-2014
Delivery Date	Tue 26-Aug-2014
Cut	NY
Strike	0.8000
Notional Currency	AUD
Barrier Type	Knock-out
Down Barrier	0.8000
Up Barrier	

Market Data	
Spot	0.9000
Swap Points	465
Forward	0.9465
Deposit (AUD)	0.00%
Deposit (USD)	5.00%
ATM Volatility	11.50%

Outputs	
Output Currency	**AUD**
TV	**15.07%**
TV Delta	**109.35%**
TV Gamma	**-2.02%**
TV Vega	**-0.12%**

EXHIBIT 24.24 AUD/USD strike-out option with 0% AUD rates and 5% USD rates

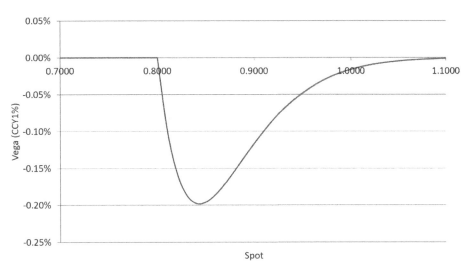

EXHIBIT 24.25   AUD/USD 0.8000 strike-out vega (AUD rates = 0%/USD rates = 5%)

Alternatively, if CCY1 rates are lower than CCY2 rates, holding a short cash position on the hedge will earn money over time. It is therefore preferable that spot trades through the barrier level as late as possible, or ideally not at all. This explains why the higher USD (CCY2) rates case is short vega; again, higher volatility will increase the probability of knocking out earlier.

When pricing and hedging strike-out options, it is important that:

■ *The full interest rate curves are used.* The single interest rate to expiry may be drastically different from the short-dated interest rates, which generate the positive or negative return from holding the spot hedge.

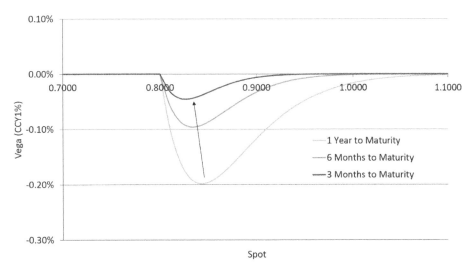

EXHIBIT 24.26   AUD/USD 0.8000 strike-out vega over time (AUD rates = 0%/USD rates = 5%)

- *The full ATM curve is used.* If the ATM curve is steeply upward or downward sloping and the stopping time is short, this could have a significant impact on pricing and Greeks.

- *Spot versus interest rate correlations are taken into account.* Changes in the knock probability versus carry earned on hedge will have a significant impact on the TV adjustment. Over time, the vega decays away linearly with time (since interest rate carry is interest rate differential × time) and moves toward the barrier as shown in Exhibit 24.26. Therefore, any vanilla hedges put on to offset the strike-out vega will need to be rebalanced over time.

CHAPTER 25

Exotic FX Derivatives Trading Topics

The following topics cover common situations that exotic FX derivative traders come across. Issues around risk management and pricing are investigated, along with how exotic derivatives are used within FX hedging and investment strategies.

Exotic Risk Management Overview

Exotic FX derivative contracts are primarily risk managed using the same Greek exposures (delta, gamma, vega, etc.) as vanilla FX derivatives contracts. Therefore, exotic and vanilla FX derivatives in the same currency pair are often risk managed within the same trading position.

When vanilla and exotic contracts are risk managed together it is important that their valuation and Greeks are aligned as closely as possible. Where possible, exactly the same volatility surface (including, e.g., ATM event weights) should be used for all options. If it isn't, risk management becomes more challenging, particularly when exotic risk is hedged with vanilla options close to maturity.

The main additional complication when risk managing exotic FX derivatives comes from *barriers* (both European and American) close to maturity. For exotic FX derivatives traders the key decisions come around how to hedge barrier risk. There are essentially two possible approaches:

1. Hedge with vanilla options.
2. Hedge with exotic options.

In practice, traders use both approaches. Prior to expiry, when the risk on the exotic is mainly vega-based and Greeks evolve fairly smoothly, vanilla hedges can work well. However, coming up to expiry, if the barrier risk is large and spot is fairly close to the barrier level it may be preferable to try and hedge the barrier risk itself rather than transacting increasingly large vanilla hedges.

■ Exotic Bid–Offer Spreading

The bid–offer spread on exotic FX derivative contracts comes from two primary factors: volatility surface exposures and barriers. The most important volatility surface exposure is often vega.

The vega exposure on exotic options can be multiplied by the ATM volatility spread to the deal expiry to obtain the exotic bid–offer spread *from vega*. For example, if a 1yr knock-out barrier option has 0.20 CCY1% vega and the 1yr ATM volatility bid–offer spread is 0.4%, the bid–offer spread from vega on the exotic would be 0.08 CCY1%.

This approach keeps an important link between exotic and vanilla bid–offer spreads, but note that exotic contracts may have zero vega at current spot but significant vega exposures in the wings (for example, a European digital option with digital level at the forward). Bid-offer spread from exposures to the volatility smile could either be quantified using rega and sega exposures or volga and vanna exposures could be used via a VVV-esque methodology (see Chapters 12 and 18).

American and European barrier risk within exotic options must be individually considered in terms of the barrier size (using intrinsic value), the equivalent one-touch bid–offer spread (for American barriers) or European digital bid–offer spread (for European barriers), and the probability of the barrier needing to be risk managed (i.e., less bid-offer spread should be taken on barriers very far from spot).

If the exotic option contains a delta gap at an American barrier, that should also be included in the bid–offer spread. As discussed in Chapter 23, barrier delta gaps can lead to slippage, which increases P&L volatility. Additional spread must therefore be charged to cover this risk, perhaps using expected slippage multiplied by the barrier delta gap size.

Having said all this, traders quickly learn that summing the bid–offer spread from all these different elements of an exotic trade usually results in a bid–offer spread that is wider than can be shown in practice. For this reason, certain elements are often omitted or a scaling factor is applied at the end of the calculation.

For a trader it is most important to understand the exotic bid–offer spreading methodology used by the desk pricing tool, keep any input parameters (e.g., one-touch or European digital spread grids) updated, and work with quants to ensure the spreading methodology remains appropriate as market conditions change.

Exotic Interbank Broker Market

The interbank broker market is the primary source of liquidity in exotic FX derivatives because there is no direct market (i.e., traders do not directly call each other for prices on exotic contracts). In the interbank broker market, it is possible to get prices on almost any exotic contract but the most commonly traded contracts are knock-outs, reverse knock-outs, one-touches, and double-no-touches. Volatility swaps, variance swaps, and correlation swaps are also quoted fairly frequently. The majority of trading in the exotic interbank broker market takes place over chat systems and by voice.

Exotic contracts in the interbank broker market are generally traded **vega hedged**. Within the AUD/USD broker details in Chapter 18, the letters "vh" indicate that the contract is traded with a vega hedge; that is, when trading the exotic option, an appropriate notional of ATM to the option expiry is also transacted (priced at the implied volatility level used to generate the exotic contract TV) such that the initial vega on the transaction is zero. This means that, for small changes in the ATM implied volatility, no significant P&L will be generated in the trading position. Hedging the vega in this way helps isolate the *exotic* (i.e., barrier) risk within the contract.

Some exotic contracts are priced and traded with a **rho hedge**, denoted "rh." This involves trading different notionals of spot and forward contract to delta hedge the trade (rather than *either* a spot hedge *or* forward hedge) such that the initial rho exposure on the transaction is zero. Again, this is done to isolate the exotic risk on the contract. Rho hedges are particularly relevant on long-dated exotic options.

Some exotic contracts are priced and traded with **delta exchange**, denoted "dx." This involves the two counterparties within an American barrier transaction agreeing that when the barrier level hits they will exchange an agreed notional of spot at the barrier level. This agreement reduces the amount of spot both parties need to transact in the market and therefore reduces slippage and P&L volatility. Delta exchange is particularly relevant on exotic options with significant barrier delta gaps.

Structured FX Hedging Strategies

FX derivatives contracts are often combined into strategies that clients use to hedge their FX exposures.

Corporate clients could simply use forward contracts to hedge their future FX flows. However, by using options, particularly exotic FX options, hedging strategies can be customized to closely match the client requirements. In general, clients either want to beat the forward rate, in which case they must accept some additional risk, or are willing to accept a worse rate than the forward in return for some additional potential upside.

There are numerous FX hedging strategies available, many of which are covered in Uwe Wystrup's book: *FX Options and Structured Products* (John Wiley & Sons, 2006). One of the simplest strategies is a **forward extra**. Within a forward extra contract the client has the right, but not the obligation, to buy a currency in the future (at maturity) at the pre-agreed strike providing spot hasn't touched a barrier level. If the barrier level trades at any time, the right becomes an obligation.

A forward extra to buy EUR and sell GBP is constructed using two separate derivatives contracts with equal notionals:

1. Client buys EUR call/GBP put vanilla at 0.8000.
2. Client sells EUR put/GBP call at 0.8000 with a reverse American knock-in barrier at 0.7500.

If spot at maturity is above 0.8000, the client will use their EUR call option to buy EUR/GBP at 0.8000. If spot at maturity is below 0.8000 (and spot has never traded below 0.7500), the client can buy spot in the market at the prevailing rate. If the 0.7500 barrier has knocked, the client will, again, buy spot at 0.8000.

Clients can choose to enter this forward extra strategy rather than entering into a EUR/GBP forward at 0.7900. In this example, the client would be accepting a worst-case hedge rate worse than the forward (0.8000 versus 0.7900) in order to potentially buy the currency at market rate between 0.7500 and 0.8000 if 0.7500 never trades.

The client's short FX exposure is shown in Exhibit 25.1. The payoff of the forward extra strategy is shown in Exhibit 25.2 and the client's FX exposure plus the forward extra strategy are combined in Exhibit 25.3.

The strike and barrier levels within the strategy are often set such that the package is transacted for **zero premium**. Within hedging strategies there is invariably a balance to be struck. In this case the worse (higher) the guaranteed hedge rate, the more the client can benefit from favorable spot movement down to a better (lower) barrier.

Structured forwards often have one bought leg and one sold leg, so the vega risk is partially offset. This EUR/GBP forward extra is net *short vega* for the client and hence *long vega* for the trading desk. This is common; clients often net sell vega within hedging strategies. It is easier for many clients to believe that the current market situation will continue, rather than any particular scenario occuring. Intuitively, the client wants a less volatile spot because this makes it less likely that the right to buy at 0.8000 becomes an obligation (i.e., it is less likely that spot hits the barrier).

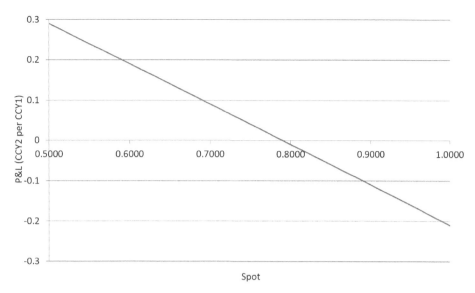

EXHIBIT 25.1 Underlying client FX exposure

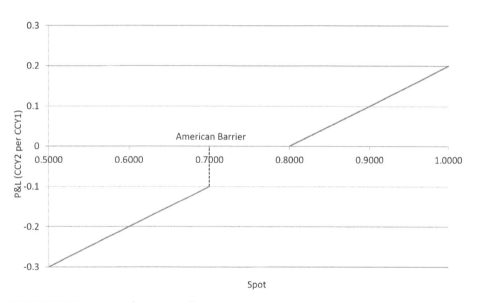

EXHIBIT 25.2 Forward extra payoff

■ FX Derivatives Investment Products

FX derivatives contracts are also often combined into investment products. The simplest investment instrument is a **structured deposit**, in which the client

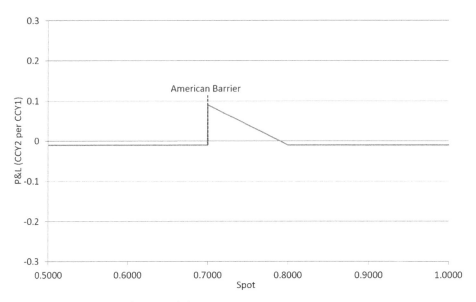

EXHIBIT 25.3 Forward extra and client FX exposure net position

deposits money and rather than receiving a guaranteed coupon based on the money market interest rate, the coupon is instead generated by an embedded FX derivative contract.

When interest rates are high in the deposit currency, it is common for the deposit to be **principal protected**. This involves taking the interest earned on deposit up front and using it to purchase options that may pay out more at maturity. The client cannot lose their investment, although they have forgone the interest they would otherwise have earned. As an increasing amount of principal is put at risk, increasingly large option notionals can be purchased.

For example, a client deposits AUD1m for one year within a structured FX deposit. Within the deposit, the 5% AUD interest rate should earn approximately AUD50k at maturity but this amount is present valued and used to purchase a 1yr European digital option that pays out AUD100k (i.e., approximately 10% coupon on the deposit) if spot at maturity is higher than the initial spot rate.

■ Shadow Barriers

Shadowing barriers is a risk management technique that is conceptually similar to writing-off vanilla risk. It involves moving barrier levels within the trading position in a way that costs a small amount of money but creates large potential windfalls. This technique is also known as *smoothing* or *bending* barriers.

Example: A trading book is long a downside USD/CAD one-touch option in USD1m with a 1.0500 barrier. This barrier can be *shadowed* (i.e., moved) to 1.0450, which will cause a loss in the trading book as the value of the option has reduced. However, if the one-touch has a low value initially, it may not cost much to move the barrier a long way.

To be clear, the barrier on the client transaction is not changed, but for risk management purposes the barrier level has been changed. If this functionality is not available within the risk management system, the same effect can be achieved manually by booking a barrier spread between the main trading book and a shadow barrier trading book. Within the USD/CAD example, the main trading book would sell the 1.0500 barrier and buy the 1.0450 barrier at zero cost. The risk within the shadow barrier trading book should be left untouched until either maturity or if the shadow is unwound.

The 1.0450 one-touch barrier can now be risk managed as usual, but a windfall equal to the barrier notional is generated in the shadow barrier trading book if spot touches the real long 1.0500 barrier but does not touch the 1.0450 shadow barrier. Traders sometimes use part of the initial bid–offer spread cross on exotic transactions to establish shadow barriers at the deal inception, and/or they may shadow barriers further away gradually over time.

Like writing-off vanilla risk, shadow barriers work best when traders are engaged with their position:

- When spot moves significantly higher, distant downside barriers can be shadowed at minimal cost.

- When spot moves significantly lower, distant topside strikes can be shadowed at minimal cost.

- When implied volatility drops, there may be additional opportunities to shadow barriers on both sides.

A similar barrier shifting approach can also be used to generate bid–offer spreads for barrier products by looking at the value change produced by flexing barriers up and down a certain amount. This approach works particularly well in structures containing many different barriers.

Recycling Exotic Risk

Traders on bank trading desks have the ability to access the bank's client base in order to complete transactions at better levels than would be possible within the interbank broker market. For example, a trader may want to sell USD/MXN USD100m 6mth ATM. The current midmarket level is 10.2%, the "support" (i.e., the generic starting rate) two-way volatility in the interbank broker market is 10.0/10.4%, and if the trader sells within the broker market, the expected transaction level is 10.1%.

However, a 10.2% offer for USD100m 6mth ATM could first be shown to clients (usually via the sales desks) who may be interested in purchasing the ATM contract at a midmarket level.

The 8.2% offer is called an **axe:** a special, better-than-usual bid or offer that the trader is showing because they are especially interested in completing the transaction in a specific direction.

The FX derivatives market can often get "one way" (i.e., all market participants simultaneously want to buy or sell the same types of contract). Therefore, showing axes to clients is not always applicable, but when it works it creates a win-win-win situation. The trader transacts at better levels than would probably be possible in the interbank broker market, plus they have not revealed anything about their positioning to the market, the client has transacted the deal at midmarket, and sales have executed a deal, improved their relationship with the client, and potentially earned commission, too.

For vanilla options, the process of axing out prices to offset the client flows is sometimes called *recycling* risk. This must be done with care. For example, generic contracts must often be used rather than the exact strike and maturity originally traded by clients.

Within exotic options, risk can be recycled in more complex ways. For example, if a reverse knock-out option has been *bought* by a client, the trader is left with *long* one-touch risk at the barrier level as described in Chapter 24. This one-touch risk can then be offered out to clients at an improved rate. Alternatively, if the exotic position contains short one-touch options, they could be hedged by selling reverse knock-out options to clients. In the same way, the digital risk on European barrier options can be recycled using European digital options.

■ Why Market Participants Prefer to Sell American Barriers

Buying or *long* the American barrier means that on the barrier deals, positive P&L change results from spot trading through the barrier level. Long barrier positions can be obtained in a number of different ways, e.g., buying a one-touch, selling a double-no-touch, selling a knock-out, selling a reverse knock-out.

Selling or *short* the American barrier means that on the barrier deals, negative P&L change results from spot trading through the barrier level. Likewise, short barrier positions can be obtained by, e.g., selling a one-touch, buying a double-no-touch, buying a knock-out, buying a reverse knock-out.

Importantly this is not the same as the whole trading position making or losing money due to the hedges which are in place. Market participants generally prefer to sell American barriers for a number of reasons:

Spot Dynamic

In some currency pairs, spot often follows a dynamic whereby it usually moves with low volatility but it jumps as economic data is released or other external events occur. This creates a fat-tailed distribution that is reflected within the volatility smile, but importantly it is specifically the spot jump dynamic that leads to a preference to sell American barriers. Selling high TV (i.e., expensive/close) one-touch barriers is an effective strategy when spot follows a jump dynamic. If realized spot volatility is low and the barrier does not trigger, one-touch options can lose value rapidly over time.

This effect is particularly important in pegged or managed currency pairs, where there is often an extreme jump dynamic and traders must be very careful pricing exotic contracts with American barriers. Consider a USD/HKD 1yr 7.7490 one-touch option. USD/HKD spot is currently kept within a 7.7500/7.8500 range by the HKMA (Hong Kong Monetary Authority) so the down barrier is positioned slightly below the lower band. The TV of this one-touch is 92%, but the market price will be far lower.

The same preference is observed in the vanilla market. In liquid currency pairs there is common market preference to sell short-dated wings (i.e., short-dated vanilla options away from current spot).

Delta Gap Orders

As described in Chapter 23, within delta hedged trading portfolios, long American barriers produce a stop-loss spot order and short American barriers produce a take-profit spot order. There is usually a larger chance of losing money from stop-loss orders than take-profit orders. With a stop-loss order, the risk is that spot trades through the barrier and continues before the stop-loss order can be fully executed. The difference between the order level and the execution level is *slippage* and it can cause large negative P&L. Therefore, short American barriers are more attractive than long American barriers.

Example: Long an AUD/USD 1.1000 topside one-touch generates a stop-loss order to buy AUD150m versus USD. Spot trades through the barrier and then even higher before all the spot can be bought in the market. In the end, the order is transacted at an average of 1.1012—a painful loss of USD180k.

Limited Spot Market Open Hours

Consider what happens in emerging market currency pairs with restricted spot market open hours. When the spot market is closed, the NDF market is still active and it is possible to accurately imply a spot rate from the level of the NDF. The NDF market may imply a spot rate at which the American barrier would trigger but the barrier can only officially be knocked once the spot market reopens.

If the NDF implies a spot rate through a topside barrier level but the stop-loss order is not executed, if spot continues higher, the stop-loss spot order might have to be executed far through the barrier level and hence cause a P&L loss when the spot market reopens. If the NDF implies a spot level through the barrier and the stop-loss order is executed by trading an NDF, but the market then retraces below the barrier, the barrier will not have triggered and unwinding the NDF trade will cause a P&L loss.

With stop-loss orders in currency pairs which are not constantly tradable it is possible for traders to be damned if they transact the hedge and damned if they don't—a difficult situation to risk manage. Therefore, in currency pairs with restricted spot market open hours there is a particularly strong market preference to sell American barriers.

Spot Volatility versus Forward Volatility

The ATM curve represents the volatility of the forward (with a changing maturity), but *American barriers knock out on spot*. Therefore, if the forward is significantly more or less volatile than spot, any pricing model that does not have a stochastic interest rate component will not correctly capture the barrier knock probability and therefore structures with American barriers, particularly at longer tenors, will be mispriced.

Horizon	Wed 21-Aug-2013
Currency Pair	USD/JPY
Cut	NY

Tenor	Expiry Date	ATM Volatility
O/N	Thu 22-Aug-2013	17.00%
1W	Wed 28-Aug-2013	11.75%
2W	Wed 04-Sep-2013	11.60%
1M	Thu 19-Sep-2013	13.10%
2M	Mon 21-Oct-2013	12.60%
3M	Thu 21-Nov-2013	12.75%
6M	Thu 20-Feb-2014	12.50%
1Y	Thu 21-Aug-2014	12.45%
2Y	Thu 20-Aug-2015	13.05%
3Y	Fri 19-Aug-2016	14.00%
5Y	Tue 21-Aug-2018	15.50%
7Y	Thu 20-Aug-2020	16.20%
10Y	Mon 21-Aug-2023	17.50%

EXHIBIT 25.4   USD/JPY ATM volatility run

Often the ATM curve rises at longer tenors but that does not imply that the market expects spot to get more volatile over time; rather it means that there is a significant interest rate component that must be taken into account when trading long-dated American barrier options. An example long-dated USD/JPY ATM curve is shown in Exhibit 25.4.

Generally, forward volatility is higher than spot volatility and therefore the market price for one-touch options will be lower than prices generated using a smile pricing model without stochastic interest rates.

CHAPTER 26

Window Barrier and Discrete Barrier Options

Window barrier options are extensions of American barrier options. The difference being that window barriers are active only for a subsection of the life of the option. The two main window barrier variations are **front-window barriers** (barriers active from the horizon until a specified date prior to expiry) and **rear-window barriers** (barriers active from a specified date after the horizon until expiry).

■ Front-Window Barrier Options

Front-window barrier options, also called **early ending** barriers, have a vanilla payoff at expiry plus single (one) or double (two) American barriers that are active from the horizon but cease to be active on the barrier end date. The barrier end date occurs prior to the expiry date and the window barriers are either all knock-out or all knock-in. Exhibit 26.1 shows a typical front-window double knock-out barrier contract.

Within a front-window knock-out barrier option:

- If spot trades at or beyond (touches) a barrier prior to the barrier end date, the whole contract expires.

- If spot does not touch a knock-out barrier prior to the barrier end date, at expiry there is a vanilla payoff.

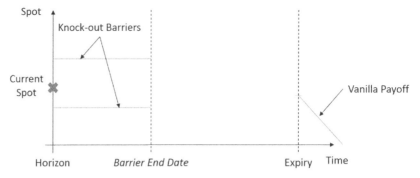

EXHIBIT 26.1 Front-window double knock-out barrier structure

Example: GBP/USD 1yr 1.6000 GBP call/USD put with front-window knock-out barriers for the first month at 1.5500 and 1.6000. With GBP/USD spot at 1.5865, the front window barriers make the contract significantly cheaper; the vanilla is valued at 2.25 GBP% and the window barrier is valued at just 0.25 GBP%. Ignoring smile effects, this suggests that the chance of spot not touching the barriers is only approximately 1 in 9 (the ratio of the prices). Window barrier options are attractive to institutional clients who have a specific market view. In this case, the view is that GBP/USD spot will hold a tight range for the first month before moving higher (if traded live) or before implied volatility increases (if traded delta hedged).

There are two main trading risks on front-window barrier options that can be considered separately:

1. Touch risk from the barrier(s)
2. Payoff risk (e.g., strike risk from the vanilla payoff at expiry)

Front-Window Barrier Risk

If front-window barriers are knock-out, the risk within the barriers is equivalent to *no-touch* risk: "Payment" occurs if the barrier levels don't trade. Alternatively, if the window barriers are knock-in, the risk within the barriers is equivalent to *one-touch* risk: "Payment" occurs if the barrier levels do trade. In this context, "payment" is not a fixed cash amount as it is for a touch option; rather it is the value of the payoff at expiry. The value of the payoff with horizon set to the barrier end date and spot at the barrier level can be thought of as the **intrinsic value** of the barrier. As usual, the intrinsic value gives the notional of touch option that must be transacted in order to hedge the barrier risk. Intrinsic value on front-window barriers is not static, but it is stable enough for the risks to be effectively offset using a static touch option hedge.

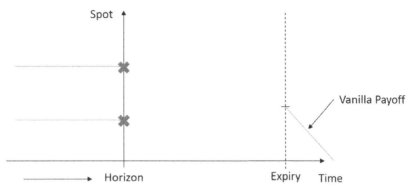

EXHIBIT 26.2 Estimating barrier risk on a front-window barrier option

Intrinsic value can be estimated within a pricing tool by moving the horizon forward to the barrier end date and pricing the payoff at expiry with spot at the barrier levels as shown in Exhibit 26.2. Alternatively, the horizon can be kept constant and the expiry can be moved such that the number of days from horizon to expiry is equal to the number of days from barrier end date to expiry in the original window barrier contract. This second approach ignores forward volatility, forward skew, and forward interest rates but in most instances it will give a reasonable guide to the amount of touch risk contained in the barriers.

Example: AUD50m AUD/USD 1yr 0.9200 AUD call/USD put with a 3mth front-window knock-out up barrier at 0.9300. The 9mth 0.9200 AUD call/USD put vanilla with spot at 0.9300 has a midmarket price of 2.54 AUD%. Therefore, there is approximately (AUD50m × 2.54% =) AUD1.25m of touch risk in the window barrier.

The trading risk from reverse American barriers is maximized at the end of the barrier life where the P&L difference between touching the barrier or not is maximized. The same is true within window barrier structures; the main risk management challenges occur into the barrier end date.

Payoff Risk

The smile value of the option payoff at expiry is given by the zeta of the equivalent vanilla option. In addition, the probability of the option being active at expiry must be taken into account. Ignoring discounting and volatility surface considerations, for front-window knock-out barriers this probability can be approximated by the TV of a no-touch option to the barrier end date. For front-window knock-in barriers this probability can be approximated by the TV of a one-touch option to the barrier end date.

To remove the effect of discounting from calculations like this on longer-dated trades, fix the forward and set the payout currency interest rates to 0%. This results in zero discounting but leaves the forward drift unchanged.

Combining Barrier and Payoff Risks in a TV Adjustment

The smile risk from the barrier and payoff within a front-window barrier option can be combined into an approximate TV adjustment:

$$\text{Front-window barrier TV adjustment} =$$
$$\text{Intrinsic Value } (IV) \times \text{Touch TV adjustment} +$$
$$\text{Probability of payoff occurring} \times \text{Vanilla zeta}$$

For double-barrier front-window barriers, each barrier will have a different intrinsic so the average intrinsic can be substituted into the above formula.

Example: AUD50m AUD/USD 1yr 0.9200 AUD call/USD put with a 3mth front-window up-and-out barrier at 0.9300.

- Intrinsic Value (IV) = 2.54 AUD% (as per the above calculation)

- 3mth no-touch (since knock-out barrier) TV adjustment = +0.85 AUD%

- Probability of payoff occurring (i.e., 3mth 0.9300 no-touch TV) = 38%

- Vanilla zeta = +0.205 AUD%

Therefore, front-window barrier TV adjustment = 2.54% × 0.85% + 38% × 0.205% = +0.10 AUD%. This compares with the mixed volatility model TV adjustment of +0.11 AUD% shown in Exhibit 26.3. Note how the window barrier in leg 3 shows only one ATM volatility to the final expiry but is only one ATM volatility used to calculate TV?

Trading Risks

Front-window barrier options are long vega to the expiry date (from the strike) and either short vega from knock-out barriers or long vega from knock-in barriers to the barrier end date. Because window barriers have important vega exposures to different maturities it is vital that the full ATM term structure is used for pricing window barriers and that vega risks are correctly bucketed within risk management systems.

If the ATM curve is downward sloping (short-dated ATM implied volatility higher than long-dated ATM volatility), front-window barrier options are particularly attractive to clients because adding front-window knock-out barriers significantly reduces the price of the contract.

Contract Details	Leg 1	Leg 2	Leg 3
Currency Pair	AUD/USD	AUD/USD	AUD/USD
Horizon	Mon 24-Mar-2014	Mon 24-Mar-2014	Mon 24-Mar-2014
Spot Date	Wed 26-Mar-2014	Wed 26-Mar-2014	Wed 26-Mar-2014
Strategy	No Touch	Vanilla	Window Barrier
Maturity	3M	1Y	1Y
Expiry Date	Tue 24-Jun-2014	Tue 24-Mar-2015	Tue 24-Mar-2015
Delivery Date	Thu 26-Jun-2014	Thu 26-Mar-2015	Thu 26-Mar-2015
Cut	NY	NY	NY
Strike		0.9200	0.9200
Call/Put		AUD Call/USD Put	AUD Call/USD Put
Notional Currency	AUD	AUD	AUD
Window Type			Knock-out
Barrier Type			Early Ending
Barrier Date			Tue 24-Jun-2014
Down Barrier			
Up Barrier	0.9300		0.9300
Market Data			
Spot	0.9110	0.9110	0.9110
Swap Points	-55	-225	-225
Forward	0.9055	0.8885	0.8885
Deposit (AUD)	2.70%	2.85%	2.85%
Deposit (USD)	0.20%	0.30%	0.30%
ATM Volatility	9.15%	10.05%	10.05%
Smile Volatility		9.50%	
Outputs			
Output Currency	AUD	AUD	AUD
TV	37.85%		0.38%
TV Adjustment	+0.85%		+0.11%
Mid Price	38.70%	2.27%	0.49%
Zeta		0.21%	

EXHIBIT 26.3   Front-window barrier TV adjustment approximation in pricing tool

Example: USD/CAD 1yr 1.1500 USD call/CAD put is 1.85 USD% premium (7.50% implied volatility). Adding 1mth front-window double knock-out barriers at 1.0900 and 1.1300 reduces the price to 0.50 USD% as shown in Exhibit 26.4.

The initial vega exposure from this trade is shown in Exhibit 26.5. As expected, vega looks like a double-no-touch vega profile until the barrier end date. Once the barriers are no longer active the vega will simply be that of a vanilla option to the expiry date.

The most sophisticated pricing model available should be used when pricing window barriers because they are complex products with significant exposures to the forward smile. For a front-window barrier trade, if spot does stay within the range for the first month, at the barrier end date the ATM curve is likely to be lower than was envisaged at the option horizon. When pricing window barrier options it can be important to take this kind of reasoning into account manually since pricing models do not usually account for it.

It is also important to confirm at exactly what time the front window ceases to be active on the barrier end date. Most often the cut from the payoff is used but this is not always the case.

Contract Details	Leg 1	Leg 2	Leg 3
Currency Pair	USD/CAD	USD/CAD	USD/CAD
Horizon	Mon 10-Mar-2014	Mon 10-Mar-2014	Mon 10-Mar-2014
Spot Date	Tue 11-Mar-2014	Tue 11-Mar-2014	Tue 11-Mar-2014
Strategy	Vanilla	Window Barrier	No Touch
Maturity	1Y	1Y	1M
Expiry Date	Tue 10-Mar-2015	Tue 10-Mar-2015	Thu 10-Apr-2014
Delivery Date	Wed 11-Mar-2015	Wed 11-Mar-2015	Fri 11-Apr-2014
Cut	NY	NY	NY
Strike	1.1500	1.1500	
Call/Put	USD Call/CAD Put	USD Call/CAD Put	
Notional Currency	USD	USD	USD
Window Type		Knock-out	
Barrier Type		Early Ending	
Barrier Date		Thu 10-Apr-2014	
Down Barrier		1.0900	1.0900
Up Barrier		1.1300	1.1300
Market Data			
Spot	1.1100	1.1100	1.1100
Swap Points	95	95	10
Forward	1.1195	1.1195	1.1110
Deposit (AUD)	0.30%	0.30%	0.30%
Deposit (USD)	1.15%	1.15%	1.00%
ATM Volatility	7.10%	7.10%	6.95%
Smile Volatility	7.50%		
Outputs			
Output Currency	AUD	AUD	AUD
TV		0.40%	26.75%
TV Adjustment		(+0.10%)	+2.50%
Mid Price	1.85%	0.50%	29.25%

EXHIBIT 26.4   Front-window barrier option in pricing tool

Front-window barrier bid–offer spreads can be calculated by considering the bid–offer spreads from the barrier risk and payoff risk. The two spreads should be combined because both elements may require risk management attention but the payoff spread should be weighted by the probability of the payoff occurring.

Finally, when assessing the stopping time of a window barrier, remember that stopping time is defined in terms of a single value: the expectation, when in reality it has a distribution. For example, if a window barrier option has a one-year expiry and an active barrier for the first month only, the stopping time may be given as, for example, 70% when the option can never actually knock 70% of the way through its life.

■ Rear-Window Barrier Options

Rear-window barrier options, also called **late-starting** barriers, have a vanilla payoff at expiry plus single (one) or double (two) American barriers that are active from the barrier start date to the expiry date. The barrier start date must be after the horizon date but before the expiry date and the barriers must either be all knock-out

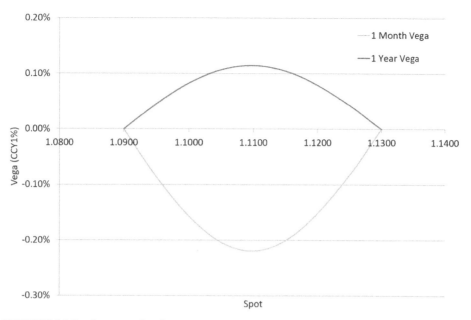

EXHIBIT 26.5 Front-window barrier vega exposure

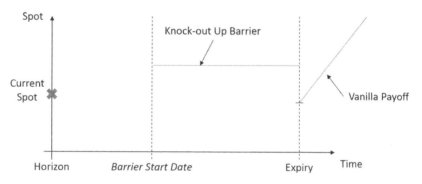

EXHIBIT 26.6 Rear-window up-and-out barrier structure

or all knock-in. The type and direction (e.g., down-and-out/down-and-in, etc.) of rear-window single barriers must always be specified since their direction cannot always be determined from the inception spot level.

Exhibit 26.6 shows a typical rear-window up-and-out barrier call option.

Within a rear-window knock-out barrier option:

- Spot can go through knock-out barrier levels prior to the barrier start date and the trade does not knock out.

- If spot ever goes above the knock-out barrier level between the barrier start date and expiry, the trade expires. Also, if spot is through the barrier level *at* the barrier start date, the trade also expires.

Example: GBP/USD 1yr 1.6000 GBP call/USD put with a rear-window double-knock-out for the last month at 1.5000 and 1.7000. Therefore, if spot trades through (below) 1.5000 or (above) 1.7000 at any point in the month before the expiry date, the option expires. If spot is within the 1.5000/1.7000 range one month prior to expiry, the option becomes a standard double knock-out option. The barriers significantly cheapen the window barrier option (0.59 GBP%) compared to the vanilla (2.26 GBP%) and, plus, it allows for a more sophisticated spot view to be expressed.

To assess the smile risk on a rear-window barrier option, price the payoff with no barrier and ascertain its smile value. Then price European barrier and the American barrier versions, each time noting the TV adjustments:

- If the barrier start date is near the horizon, the risk on the rear-window barrier will be more similar to the equivalent American barrier option.

- If the barrier start date is near the expiry, the risk on the rear-window barrier will be more similar to the equivalent European barrier option and a local volatility model may be sufficient for pricing.

This approach gives good intuition about the risks on rear-window barrier options but it is important to appreciate that the rear-window barrier TV adjustment does not simply move from American barrier TV adjustment to European barrier TV adjustment as the barrier start date goes from horizon to expiry. Also, if the rear-window barrier is through current spot, this approach does not work because the American barrier option variation will have already knocked.

It may also be useful to assess the probability of the rear-window barriers being knocked. One quick way of estimating a barrier-knock probability is to price two vanilla options (CCY1 call for an up barrier and CCY1 put for a down barrier) with the strikes set to the barrier level; one expiry at the window barrier start date and one expiry at the window barrier expiry date. The delta of the vanilla options gives a very rough indication of the barrier-knock probability.

Prior to the barrier start date, the rear window vega profile depends on the barrier characteristics:

- For a knock-out barrier, with spot in front of the barrier the contract will be short vega.

- For a knock-in barrier, with spot in front of the barrier the contract will be long vega.

After the barrier start date, the trading risks and vega profile simply become those generated by the equivalent standard American barrier option. As with front-window barriers, for rear-window barriers the most sophisticated possible pricing model should be used. Rear-window barriers usually have a similar bid–offer spread to the equivalent European or American barriers because the magnitude of their trading risk is similar.

Generic Window Barrier Options

In practice, a window barrier option may contain any number of knock-out or knock-in barriers with different start and end dates. For example, if a sophisticated customer thinks that spot will trend lower in a specific way over time, a product with bespoke barriers could be constructed as per Exhibit 26.7.

To identify which barriers are most important, remove each barrier in turn from the structure and check the impact on TV: Big TV change implies an important barrier. If there are just one or two important barriers, the TV adjustment on the whole structure can be estimated by considering the smile risk on the important barriers in isolation. This is done by multiplying the TV adjustment of the barrier by the probability of the barrier being live at its start date.

Window Barrier Risk Management

Window barrier options have additional trading risks to American barrier options. Specifically, there are increased exposures to the ATM curve, and additional exposures to the forward smile. Therefore, when pricing and risk managing window barrier options it is important to assess exactly which pricing methodology is used. For example:

- Which ATM volatility curve is used to generate TV? Is only the ATM volatility to expiry used (i.e., pure Black-Scholes), are two volatilities used (one to barrier

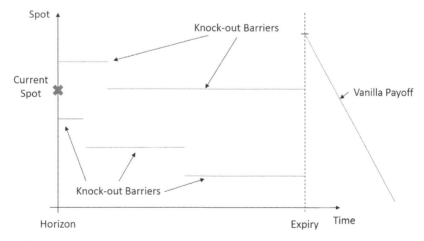

EXHIBIT 26.7   Generic window barrier structure

start/end date and one to expiry), or is the full term structure of ATM volatility used? If only a single ATM volatility to expiry is used, the TV adjustment must take into account the effect of the full ATM volatility curve.

- How are bucketed Greek exposures displayed? Is the vega all bucketed to the option expiry, or is vega bucketed correctly? This is particularly important within risk management.

It is also important to assess what the forward smile looks like within the smile pricing model. Does the forward smile from the barrier start or end date until the expiry look credible with reference to the current volatility surface? If not, that brings the validity of the TV adjustment generated by the model into doubt.

■ Discrete Barrier Options

Discrete barrier options are like American barrier options except that the barrier is monitored against a fix rather than being monitored continuously. Discrete barriers are monitored against a spot fix in the market, usually at regular intervals (i.e., once a day or once a week). If the fix is through the barrier level, the trade will knock. Therefore, it is vital to know the exact methodology used to calculate the fix.

In terms of pricing, discrete monitoring *reduces* the probability of a barrier knock compared with continuous barrier monitoring for the same barrier level. The TV of a discrete knock-out barrier option will therefore be *higher* than the TV of the equivalent American knock-out barrier.

An elegant approximation for adjusting discrete barriers into equivalent continuous barriers was developed by Broadie, Glasserman, and Kou (*A continuity correction for discrete barrier options*, M. Broadie, P. Glasserman, S. Kou, Mathematical Finance, 1997). To price a discrete barrier option, price the continuous barrier version with the barrier level adjusted using these formulas:

$$\text{Barrier below spot: } Barrier_{Continuous} = Barrier_{Discrete}.e^{-\beta\sigma\sqrt{\Delta t}}$$

$$\text{Barrier above spot: } Barrier_{Continuous} = Barrier_{Discrete}.e^{\beta\sigma\sqrt{\Delta t}}$$

where Δt is the time between monitoring events:

$$\beta = \frac{\xi\left(\frac{1}{2}\right)}{2\pi} \approx 0.5826$$

Where ξ is the Riemann Zeta function (... no, me neither ...).

These formulas give good intuition about discrete barriers: A discrete barrier option is equivalent to a continuous barrier option with the barrier placed further away from spot.

Discrete barrier options also present additional risk management challenges. When spot goes through an American barrier level, the resultant barrier delta gap can be hedged in the spot market to leave the delta exposure within the trading position unchanged. However, with a discrete barrier, spot may go through the barrier level in-between fixes. Should the trader hedge the delta gap, or not?

Suppose the trader has a stop-loss order to buy spot at a higher level if a topside discrete barrier knocks out. If spot goes through the barrier level but the trader does *not* buy spot, the spot rate may do one of two things:

1. Continue higher, and when the barrier officially knocks at the fix the trader will have to buy spot at a higher level, hence causing a loss.
2. Reverse back lower below the barrier level prior to the fix, and hence the trader was correct not to buy spot, hence causing no loss or gain.

Alternatively, if the trader *does* buy spot, the spot rate may do one of two things:

1. Reverse back lower below the barrier level prior to the fix and the trader will have to sell the spot out at a lower level when it becomes clear that the barrier will not knock out at the fix, hence causing a loss.
2. Continue higher, and hence the trader was correct to buy spot, hence causing no loss or gain.

This is the same issue as the restricted spot market open hours case discussed in Chapter 25. This additional risk means that discrete barrier options are often quoted wider than the equivalent American barrier options, particularly on larger-sized trades.

Building a Monte Carlo Option Pricer in Excel

The Monte Carlo pricing method is a flexible and powerful technique. Within a basic Monte Carlo pricing framework a simulation is set up that produces random realized option payoffs. The simulation is then run many times and the resultant payoffs are averaged to obtain option valuations.

■ Task A: Set Up the Simulation

For each currency pair within the simulation the following market data is required:

- Spot (S): the current exchange rate in a given currency pair

- Interest rates ($rCCY1$ and $rCCY2$): continuously compounded risk-free interest rates in CCY1 and CCY2 of the currency pair

- Volatility (σ): the volatility of the spot log returns

We start in Black-Scholes world so only a single volatility (no term structure or smile) and single interest rates (no term structure) are specified at this stage.

The simulation contains multiple time steps so the time (measured in years) between steps must be defined. For daily time steps, weekends can be removed and it is usually assumed that there are 252 trading days in the year; hence the time step is $\frac{1}{252}$. As a sense check, at the 252nd step, time should be exactly 1:

Market Data

Currency Pair	EUR/USD	← Named: *Pair*
Initial Spot	1.3850	← Named: *S_Initial*
CCY1 Interest Rate	0.50%	← Named: *rCCY1*
CCY2 Interest Rate	1.00%	← Named: *rCCY2*
Implied Volatility (σ)	6.25%	← Named: *vol*

Monte Carlo

| Time Step (years) | 0.0040 | =1/252 |
| | ↑ Named: **TimeStep** | |

Simulation

Step	Time (years)
0	0
1	0.003968254
2	0.007936508
...	...
250	0.992063492
251	0.996031746
252	1

The following formula is used for calculating the spot evolution between time steps within the simulation:

$$S_{t+1} = S_t e^{\left(rCCY2 - rCCY1 - \frac{1}{2}\sigma^2\right)\Delta t + \sigma\sqrt{\Delta t}\,\varepsilon}$$

where ε is generated in Excel using =NORMSINV(RAND()).

	A	B	C	D	E
11		Simulation			
12		Step	Time (years)	Spot	
13		0	0	1.3850	
14		1	0.003968254	1.3876	=D13*EXP(((rCCY2-rCCY1-0.5*vol^2)*TimeStep)+vol*SQRT(TimeStep)*NORMSINV(RAND()))
15		2	0.007936508	1.3950	=D14*EXP(((rCCY2-rCCY1-0.5*vol^2)*TimeStep)+vol*SQRT(TimeStep)*NORMSINV(RAND()))
16		3	0.011904762	1.4028	...

The spot path generated on the sheet represents one sample of the simulation. Pressing F9 in Excel recalculates the sheet and generates a new sample.

As a check, the realized volatility of the spot path can be calculated. If the simulation is set up properly, the realized volatility should be approximately equal to the volatility input:

	A	B	C	D	E	F	G	H	I	J
10										
11		Simulation								
12		Step	Time (years)	Spot	Log-Return		Standard Deviation of Log Returns		0.003759391	=STDEV(E14:E265)
13		0	0	1.3850			Annualised Volatility		5.968%	=SQRT(252)*I12
14		1	0.003968254	1.3877	0.001921793	=LN(D14/D13)				
15		2	0.007936508	1.3776	-0.007297067	=LN(D15/D14)				
16		3	0.011904762	1.3760	-0.001163165	...				

It is also useful to plot spot against time to judge whether the generated path looks realistic:

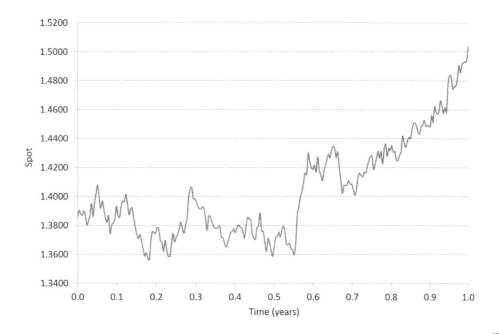

Try flexing market data inputs to see how the spot paths are impacted; test low volatility, high volatility, low interest rate differential, high positive and negative interest rate differential, and different initial spot values.

■ Task B: Set Up a Vanilla Option Payoff and the Monte Carlo Loop

A vanilla option payoff at maturity can now be calculated. First, set up the payoff details and copy the spot and time at maturity from the appropriate simulation step into the payoff calculation area. Recall that vanilla option payoffs are $\max(S_T - K, 0)$ for a CCY1 call and $\max(K - S_T, 0)$ for a CCY1 put.

In addition, the payoff is at maturity and it therefore needs to be present valued back to the horizon to calculate the option value. Payoff P&L is naturally in CCY2 so this is present valued using the CCY2 discount factor $(e^{-r_{CCY2}.T})$. In addition, the CCY2 pips option value at the horizon can be converted into CCY1 terms by dividing by the inception spot.

When the sheet recalculates, the vanilla option payoff should update:

Payoff

Strike	1.4000	← *Named:* **Strike**		
Payoff Direction	1	← *Named:* **PayoffDirection** *(1 = Call / -1 = Put)*		
Spot at Maturity	1.3702	← *Named:* **S_Maturity**	=D266	
Time at Maturity	1.00	← *Named:* **T_Maturity**	=C266	
Vanilla Payoff (CCY1%)	0.00%	← *Named:* **VanillaPayoff**	=EXP(-rCCY2*T_Maturity)*MAX(PayoffDirection*(S_Maturity-Strike),0)/S_Initial	

A reasonable question at this point would be: "If the vanilla payoff only depends on spot at maturity, why are daily time steps required within the Monte Carlo?" Good question, and for a single vanilla payoff, daily time steps are not required; but as the framework is extended to price multiple options with different expiry dates, or for options with path dependence, more frequent time steps will be required and it is easier to set up the simulation properly from the start.

The number of runs (i.e., the number of times the simulation is rerun) now needs to be added as an input. Run count, timing, and the option value should be added as outputs:

Monte Carlo

Time Step (years)	0.0040	
Number of Runs	10,000	← *Named:* **NumberOfRuns**
Run Count		← *Named:* **Count**
Time (seconds)		← *Named:* **MCTimer**
Monte Carlo Vanilla Price (CCY1%)		← *Named:* **MCVanillaPrice**

The Monte Carlo is controlled by a VBA subroutine that does the following:

1. Loads up relevant config.
2. Loops around, recalculating the simulation and collecting the relevant results.
3. Calculates outputs and pushes them back onto the sheet.

The VBA code can be written in fewer than 20 lines:

```
Option Explicit
Option Base 0 'Ensures arrays start at 0

Sub RunMonteCarlo1()

    Dim MCRuns As Long, Count As Long
    Dim TimeStart As Date, TimeEnd As Date
    Dim VanillaPayoffs() As Double

    'Load Settings
    MCRuns = Range("NumberOfRuns")
    ReDim VanillaPayoffs(MCRuns - 1) As Double
    Range("MCTimer") = "Running"

    'Loop
    TimeStart = Now
    Count = 0
    While (Count < MCRuns)
        ActiveSheet.Calculate
```

```
        '(Recalculates the sheet: equivalent to pressing F9)
        Range("Count") = Count + 1
        VanillaPayoffs(Count) = Range("VanillaPayoff")
        Count = Count + 1
    Wend
    TimeEnd = Now

    'Outputs
    Range("MCVanillaPrice") = Application.WorksheetFunction _
      .Average(VanillaPayoffs)
    Range("MCTimer") = (TimeEnd - TimeStart) * 24 * 60 * 60
    '(Conversion of Time from Days into Seconds)
End Sub
```

Before starting the Monte Carlo, ensure that this sheet is the only one loaded into the Excel, so the "Calculate" command does not also cause other sheets to recalculate.

If everything is set up correctly, the subroutine runs the Monte Carlo and on the sheet the run count increments up to the number of runs. When the Monte Carlo is finished, the timing and option price are output:

Monte Carlo

Time Step (years)	0.0040
Number of Runs	10,000
Run Count	10,000
Time (seconds)	70
Monte Carlo Vanilla Price (CCY1%)	**2.21%**

For a vanilla option, the Monte Carlo Black-Scholes price can be compared to a closed-form Black-Scholes price. However, the closed-form price should be calculated in the VBA subroutine and pushed onto the sheet rather than being calculated in the sheet because that would potentially slow down the Monte Carlo. Using the OptionPrice function from Practical C enables this with one additional line of code (don't put it within the loop):

```
'Calculate Closed-form Option Price
Range("CFVanillaPrice") = OptionPrice(Range("PayoffDirection") = 1, _
  Range("S_Initial"), Range("Strike"), Range("T_Maturity"), _
  Range("rCCY1"), Range("rCCY2"), Range("vol")) / Range("S_Initial")
```

Monte Carlo

Time Step (years)	0.0040	
Number of Runs	1,000	
Run Count	1,000	
Time (seconds)	22	
Monte Carlo Vanilla Price (CCY1%)	**2.322%**	
Closed Form Vanilla Price (CCY1%)	**2.210%**	← Named: *CFVanillaPrice*

Due to limitations of the Application.WorksheetFunction.Average function, in earlier versions of Excel a running total variable must be used instead of an array if the number of runs is over 65,000. The advantage of using an array (if possible) is that information about the *distribution* of payoffs can be calculated.

As the number of runs increases, the Monte Carlo outputs get more accurate but the calculation takes longer. Changing the number of runs within an example Monte Carlo generates the following results:

Closed Form Vanilla Price (CCY1%)	2.2103%						

Number of Runs	1,000	2,000	4,000	8,000	16,000	32,000	64,000
Time (seconds)	9	13	26	50	103	204	397
Monte Carlo Vanilla Price (CCY1%)	2.2515%	2.2357%	2.1543%	2.1589%	2.2146%	2.2144%	2.2117%
Difference vs Closed Form Price (CCY1%)	0.0412%	0.0254%	-0.0560%	-0.0514%	0.0042%	0.0040%	0.0014%

Only relatively simple derivative payoffs have closed-form solutions but a key feature of Monte Carlo pricing is that any payoff can be priced.

Task C: Set Up Multiple Payoffs

With only relatively minor tweaks, the Monte Carlo simulation can be expanded to output four option prices at once:

1. European vanilla call
2. European vanilla put
3. European digital call
4. European digital put

To generate European digital prices, the payoff formula must be adjusted to, for example, =IF(FinalSpot > Strike, 1, 0). Plus note that the digital payout must be present valued back to the horizon in the same currency as the payout.

The VBA code also needs to be extended to pick up the four payoffs:

```
Sub RunMonteCarloMultiPayoffs()

    Dim MCRuns As Long, Count As Long
    Dim TimeStart As Date, TimeEnd As Date
    Dim VanillaCallPayoffs() As Double
    Dim VanillaPutPayoffs() As Double
    Dim DigitalCallPayoffs() As Double
    Dim DigitalPutPayoffs() As Double

    'Load Settings
    MCRuns = Range("NumberOfRuns")
    ReDim VanillaCallPayoffs(MCRuns - 1) As Double
    ReDim VanillaPutPayoffs(MCRuns - 1) As Double
    ReDim DigitalCallPayoffs(MCRuns - 1) As Double
    ReDim DigitalPutPayoffs(MCRuns - 1) As Double
    Range("MCTimer") = "Running"
```

```
'Loop
TimeStart = Now
Count = 0
While (Count < MCRuns)
    Calculate
    Range("Count") = Count + 1
    VanillaCallPayoffs(Count) = Range("VanillaCallPayoff")
    VanillaPutPayoffs(Count) = Range("VanillaPutPayoff")
    DigitalCallPayoffs(Count) = Range("DigitalCallPayoff")
    DigitalPutPayoffs(Count) = Range("DigitalPutPayoff")
    Count = Count + 1
Wend
TimeEnd = Now

'Outputs
Range("MCVanillaPriceCall") = _
 Application.WorksheetFunction.Average(VanillaCallPayoffs)
Range("MCVanillaPricePut") = _
 Application.WorksheetFunction.Average(VanillaPutPayoffs)
Range("MCDigitalPriceCall") = _
 Application.WorksheetFunction.Average(DigitalCallPayoffs)
Range("MCDigitalPricePut") = _
 Application.WorksheetFunction.Average(DigitalPutPayoffs)
Range("MCTimer") = (TimeEnd - TimeStart) * 24 * 60 * 60

End Sub
```

The Monte Carlo now takes approximately the same time to calculate four option prices as it took to calculate one:

Payoff

Strike	1.4000	←Named: *Strike*
Spot at Maturity	1.5706	←Named: *S_Maturity*
Time at Maturity	1.00	←Named: *T_Maturity*

Option Type

Vanilla Call (CCY1%)	12.20%	←Named: *VanillaCallPayoff*
Vanilla Put (CCY1%)	0.00%	←Named: *VanillaPutPayoff*
Digital Call (CCY1%)	100%	←Named: *DigitalCallPayoff*
Digital Put (CCY1%)	0%	←Named: *DigitalPutPayoff*

Monte Carlo

Time Step (years)	0.0040	
Number of Runs	1,000	
Run Count	1,000	
Time (seconds)	35	
Vanilla Call Monte Carlo Payoff (CCY1%)	2.0743%	←Named: *MCVanillaPriceCall*
Vanilla Put Monte Carlo Payoff (CCY1%)	2.8015%	←Named: *MCVanillaPricePut*
Digital Call Monte Carlo Payoff (CCY1%)	42.8850%	←Named: *MCDigitalPriceCall*
Digital Put Monte Carlo Payoff (CCY1%)	56.6162%	←Named: *MCDigitalPricePut*

This highlights another key feature of Monte Carlo pricing: Once sample paths have been generated they can be reused to simultaneously price multiple different option payoffs to different expiry dates.

■ Task D: Pricing Barrier Options

European Barrier Options

The payoff from a European barrier option depends only on spot at maturity so European barrier options can be priced in the same Monte Carlo framework using an adjusted payoff calculation:

Payoff

Strike	1.4000	
Payoff Direction	1	(1 = Call / -1 = Put)
European Down and Out Barrier	0.0000	
European Up and Out Barrier	1.5000	
Spot at Maturity	1.4575	
Time at Maturity	1.00	
Vanilla Payoff (CCY1%)	4.11%	=EXP(-rCCY2*T_Maturity)*MAX(PayoffDirection*(S_Maturity-Strike),0)/S_Initial
European Barrier Payoff (CCY1%)	4.11%	=IF(AND(S_Maturity>EuropeanDownBarrier,S_Maturity<EuropeanUpBarrier),VanillaPayoff,0)

Plus the VBA needs to be updated so the Monte Carlo code grabs the European barrier payoff rather than the vanilla payoff.

American Barrier Options

For American knock-out barrier options, if spot ever trades through the barrier level, the product knocks out. Therefore, as a first approximation, at each time step spot can be checked against the barrier levels (0 = no knock / 1 = knock):

	A	B	C	D	E	F	G	H
12								
13		Simulation						
14		Step	Time (years)	Spot	isKnock			
15		0	0	1.3850	0	=IF(OR(D15<AmericanDownBarrier,D15>AmericanUpBarrier),1,0)		
16		1	0.003968254	1.3855	0	=IF(OR(D16<AmericanDownBarrier,D16>AmericanUpBarrier),1,0)		
17		2	0.007936508	1.3770	0	...		
18		3	0.011904762	1.3725	0	...		
19		4	0.015873016	1.3840	0	...		

Then the payoff must be adjusted accordingly:

Payoff

Strike	1.3500	
Payoff Direction	1	(1 = Call / -1 = Put)
American Down and Out Barrier	0.0000	
American Up and Out Barrier	1.4000	
Spot at Maturity	1.5039	
Time at Maturity	1.00	
Vanilla Payoff (CCY1%)	11.00%	
American Barrier Payoff (CCY1%)	0.00%	=IF(SUM(isKnocks)>0,0,VanillaPayoff)

This is clearly not quite right since the barrier is effectively being discretely monitored once a day rather than being continuously monitored. There are many advanced Monte Carlo techniques for solving this problem. One simple approach would be to use tighter time steps but this also increases the Monte Carlo runtime. Another accessible approach would be to use the Broadie, Glasserman, Kou formula for converting a continuous barrier to the equivalent discrete barrier given in Chapter 26.

Once American knock-out barrier options are being successfully priced, American knock-in barrier options can be priced simply by adjusting the payoff formula or using the vanilla price, which can be effectively calculated for free.

Window Barrier Options

Window barriers options, can be implemented within the framework by adding new date inputs and adjusting the isKnock test within the simulation:

Market Data

Currency Pair	EUR/USD	
Horizon	08-May-14	← Named: **Horizon**
Initial Spot	1.3850	
CCY1 Interest Rate	0.50%	
CCY2 Interest Rate	1.00%	
Implied Volatility (σ)	6.25%	

Payoff

Strike	1.4000	
Payoff Direction	1	(1 = Call / -1 = Put)
American Down and Out Barrier	0.0000	
American Up and Out Barrier	1.4000	
Window Barrier Start Date	21-Jul-14	← Named: **BarrierStartDate**
Window Barrier Start Time	0.2027	=(BarrierStartDate-Horizon)/365
Window Barrier End Date	21-Aug-14	← Named: **BarrierEndDate**
Window Barrier End Time	0.2877	=(BarrierEndDate-Horizon)/365
Spot at Maturity	1.4052	
Time at Maturity	1.00	
Vanilla Payoff (CCY1%)	0.37%	
Window Barrier Payoff (CCY1%)	0.00%	=IF(SUMPRODUCT(isKnocks,isBarrierActives)>0,0,VanillaPayoff)

Simulation

	A	B	C	D	E	F	G	H	I
17									
18	Simulation								
19		Step	Time (years)	Spot	isKnock	isBarrierActive			
20		0	0	1.3850	0	0	=IF(AND(C17>BarrierStartTime,C17<BarrierEndTime),1,0)		
21		1	0.003968254	1.3862	0	0	=IF(AND(C18>BarrierStartTime,C18<BarrierEndTime),1,0)		
22		2	0.007936508	1.3846	0	0	...		
23		3	0.011904762	1.3898	0	0	...		
24		4	0.015873016	1.3880	0	0	...		

The flexibility of the Monte Carlo approach should now be starting to become apparent. The process of moving between different barrier types is far easier within Monte Carlo than within closed-form pricing.

Task E: Multi-Asset Simulation

In order to introduce multiple assets into the Monte Carlo framework, correlations between the paths must be defined. This can be done by generating sequences of independent normal random numbers $\varepsilon \sim N(0, 1)$ and then adjusting the sequences to be correlated.

In the two-asset case, start with two uncorrelated ε sequences, X_1 and X_2. Define $Y = \rho X_1 + \sqrt{1 - \rho^2} X_2$. The new sequence Y has a correlation of ρ to the X_1 sequence. Plus briefly note that this formula will enter the realms of the imaginary if $|\rho| > 1$.

This can be set up in the simulation:

Market Data	Asset 1	Asset 2	
Currency Pair	EUR/USD	GBP/USD	
Initial Spot	1.3850	1.6950	
CCY1 Interest Rate	0.50%	2.00%	
CCY2 Interest Rate	1.00%	1.00%	
Implied Volatility (σ)	6.25%	5.00%	
Correlation Between Assets		80.00%	← Named: **Correlation**

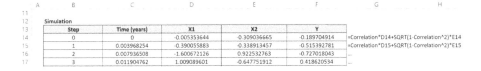

	A	B	C	D	E	F	G	H
11								
12		Simulation						
13		Step	Time (years)	X1	X2	Y		
14		0	0	-0.005353644	-0.309036665	-0.189704914	=Correlation*D14+SQRT(1-Correlation^2)*E14	
15		1	0.003968254	-0.390055883	-0.338913457	-0.515392781	=Correlation*D15+SQRT(1-Correlation^2)*E15	
16		2	0.007936508	-1.600672126	0.922532763	-0.727018043	...	
17		3	0.011904762	1.009089601	-0.647751912	0.418620534	...	

The transformation can be confirmed by plotting X_1 against X_2 in a scatter plot:

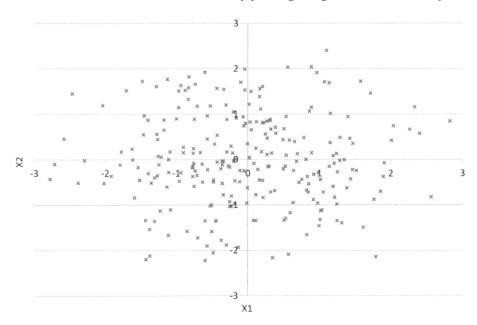

Then plotting X_1 against Y for comparison (80% correlation shown):

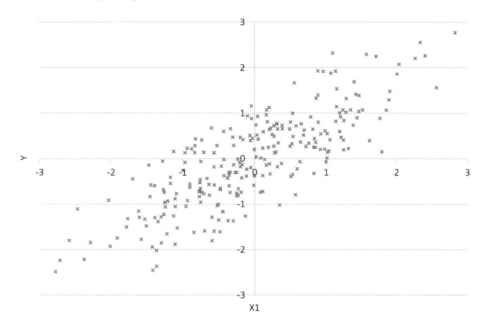

The correlated ε values can be used to drive the spot processes, hence making spot log returns correlated, as required:

Step	Spot 1	Spot 2
0	1.3850	1.6950
1	1.3924	1.6949
2	1.3924	1.6966
3	1.3971	1.6937
4	1.3894	1.6982
5	1.3868	1.6955
6	1.3869	1.7019

Multi-asset option payoffs that depend on both spot levels at maturity can therefore be set up. For example, a dual digital option (introduced in Chapter 30) pays out in the common currency (CCY2 in this case) if both spots are above defined levels:

Payoff

Dual Digital Call Strike 1	1.4000	← Named: *DualDigitalLevel1*
Dual Digital Call Strike 2	1.7000	← Named: *DualDigitalLevel2*
Spot at Maturity 1	1.5398	
Spot at Maturity 2	1.7592	
Time at Maturity	1.00	
Dual Digital Call Payoff (CCY2%)	99.00%	=EXP(-rCCY2*T_Maturity)*IF(AND(S_Maturity>DualDigitalLevel1,S_Maturity2>DualDigitalLevel2),1,0)

To move from a two-asset framework into an N-asset framework, an $N \times N$ correlation matrix must be defined. For example:

Correlation	Asset 1	Asset 2	Asset 3
Asset 1	100%	75%	85%
Asset 2	75%	100%	35%
Asset 3	85%	35%	100%

This correlation matrix is then converted into multipliers for converting non-correlated sequences into correlated sequences using either Cholesky factorization or eigenvector decomposition.

■ Extensions

There are numerous possible extensions to this basic Monte Carlo framework. For example, term structure of volatility and interest rates could be used, the volatility surface could be added, or stochastic interest rates implemented.

The volatility surface would be added using a pricing model. For example, under a stochastic volatility model there would be an additional variance term evolving with spot over time.

In practice, trading desks use either Monte Carlo or partial differential equations (PDEs) to value derivative contracts. In both cases, the challenge for quants is to add the effects of pricing models into the option valuations as efficiently as possible.

CHAPTER 27

Vanilla Variations

With only minor adjustments to the contract details, the trading risks on European vanilla options can be significantly changed. The adjustments discussed in this chapter are late-delivery, American exercise, and self-quanto payoff.

■ Late-Delivery Vanilla Options

Consider the options shown in Exhibit 27.1. Leg 1 is a standard European vanilla option with a 1yr expiry. Leg 2 is identical except that the delivery date is one year after the standard delivery date. For a European vanilla option with the *standard delivery date*, the price of a physically delivered option is the same as the price of a cash-settled option. However, for a late-delivery vanilla option the price difference can get large.

In practice, Exhibit 27.1 doesn't contain enough information to price the late-delivery option because these same contract details could represent three different derivative contracts. When pricing late-delivery options it is important to confirm exactly what payoff is required and understand what methodology the pricing model uses so any necessary additional adjustments can be made.

Late Cash Vanilla Options

The late-delivery vanilla option in Exhibit 27.1 could be a **late cash** vanilla option. At maturity, the option is exercised against a fix. The option is then *cash settled* on the late delivery date (August 18, 2016).

The price difference between the late cash vanilla and the standard European vanilla depends on discounting in the payout currency between the standard delivery

Contract Details	Leg 1	Leg 2
Currency Pair	USD/JPY	USD/JPY
Horizon	Thu 14-Aug-2014	Thu 14-Aug-2014
Spot Date	Mon 18-Aug-2014	Mon 18-Aug-2014
Strategy	Vanilla	?
Call/Put	USD Call/JPY Put	USD Call/JPY Put
Maturity	1Y	1Y
Expiry Date	Fri 14-Aug-2015	Fri 14-Aug-2015
Delivery Date	Tue 18-Aug-2015	Thu 18-Aug-2016
Cut	NY	NY
Strike	103.00	103.00
Notional Currency	USD	USD

EXHIBIT 27.1 Pricing tool showing two vanilla option contracts, one with late delivery

date and the late delivery date. If interest rates in the payout currency are positive, the fixed cash settlement paid further into the future will be worth less and the late cash vanilla option will be cheaper than the regular European vanilla.

The effect of this discounting is included in the pricing tool mid-price shown in Exhibit 27.2. Note the slightly lower price of leg 2 due to small positive USD interest rates.

Prices within Exhibit 27.2 are calculated using a pricing model that assumes interest rates are static, so the effects of stochastic interest rates must be additionally factored in. The most important effect will come from the correlation between spot and payout currency interest rates, which must be considered with reference to the option payoff. This call option pays out more USD with a higher spot. Therefore, if there is a positive correlation between spot and USD interest rates, USD interest rates will likely be higher when the option pays out. This effect will make the market price lower than the static interest rate price generated by the pricing model due to the discounting.

Option on Forwards

The late-delivery vanilla option in Exhibit 27.1 could alternatively be an **option on forward**, meaning a vanilla option that physically delivers into a forward rather than into spot. At maturity, the option is expired or exercised by comparing the strike (103.00) with the prevailing forward outright to the late delivery date (August 18, 2016). If exercised, the option physically delivers into a 103.00 forward that matures on the late delivery date.

The difference in pricing between this variation and the standard European vanilla depends mainly on the swap points between the standard delivery date and the late delivery date.

Contract Details	Leg 1	Leg 2
Currency Pair	USD/JPY	USD/JPY
Horizon	Thu 14-Aug-2014	Thu 14-Aug-2014
Spot Date	Mon 18-Aug-2014	Mon 18-Aug-2014
Strategy	Vanilla	Late Cash Vanilla
Call/Put	USD Call/JPY Put	USD Call/JPY Put
Maturity	1Y	1Y
Expiry Date	Fri 14-Aug-2015	Fri 14-Aug-2015
Delivery Date	Tue 18-Aug-2015	**Thu 18-Aug-2016**
Cut	NY	NY
Strike	103.00	103.00
Notional Currency	USD	USD

Market Data		
Spot	102.50	102.50
Swap Points	-40	-165
Forward	102.10	100.85
Deposit (USD)	0.30%	0.65%
Deposit (JPY)	0.00%	0.00%
ATM Volatility	8.05%	8.05%
Pricing Volatility	**8.05%**	**8.05%**

Outputs		
Output Currency	USD	USD
Mid Price	2.75%	2.73%

EXHIBIT 27.2 Pricing tool showing late cash vanilla option

- If CCY1 rates are above CCY2 rates, the swap points between the standard delivery date and the late delivery date will be negative. In this case, the CCY1 call option on forward will be cheaper than the European vanilla because the payoff calculated using the forward to the late delivery date will be lower than the payoff calculated using spot at maturity.

- If CCY1 rates are below CCY2 rates, the swap points between the standard delivery date and the late delivery date will be positive. In this case the CCY1 call option on forward will be more expensive than the European vanilla because the payoff calculated using the forward to the late delivery date will be higher than the payoff calculated using spot at maturity.

The option on forward price can be approximated using a 1yr vanilla option with a strike adjusted by the negative of the swap points between the standard delivery date and the late delivery date. For example, if the swap points between August 18, 2015 and August 18, 2016 are −125, the price can be approximated using a 1yr vanilla option with the strike moved *higher* by 1.25. Note that this causes the option

Contract Details	Leg 1	Leg 2
Currency Pair	USD/JPY	USD/JPY
Horizon	Thu 14-Aug-2014	Thu 14-Aug-2014
Spot Date	Mon 18-Aug-2014	Mon 18-Aug-2014
Strategy	Vanilla	Option on Forward
Call/Put	USD Call/JPY Put	USD Call/JPY Put
Maturity	1Y	1Y
Expiry Date	Fri 14-Aug-2015	Fri 14-Aug-2015
Delivery Date	Tue 18-Aug-2015	**Thu 18-Aug-2016**
Cut	NY	NY
Strike	103.00	103.00
Notional Currency	USD	USD

Market Data		
Spot	102.50	102.50
Swap Points	-40	-165
Forward	102.10	100.85
Deposit (USD)	0.30%	0.65%
Deposit (JPY)	0.00%	0.00%
ATM Volatility	8.05%	8.05%
Pricing Volatility	**8.05%**	**8.05%**

Outputs		
Output Currency	USD	USD
Mid Price	2.75%	2.23%

EXHIBIT 27.3   Pricing tool showing option on forward

to be priced at a (slightly) different implied volatility than the standard European vanilla.

The effects of swap points are included in leg 2 of the pricing tool mid-price shown in Exhibit 27.3.

Prices within Exhibit 27.3 are calculated using a pricing model that assumes interest rates are static so the effects of stochastic interest rates must be additionally factored in. The most important effect will come from correlations between spot and both interest rates, which must be considered with reference to the option payoff. This CCY1 call option pays out with a higher spot. Therefore, for example, if there is a positive correlation between spot and CCY1 interest rates, when the option pays out, the swap points will have moved more negative. This effect will make the quoted price lower than the static interest rate price generated by the pricing model.

Late-Delivery Vanilla Options

The late-delivery vanilla option in Exhibit 27.1 could, at maturity, be exercised against a fix. But rather than being cash settled on the standard delivery date as usual

(August 18, 2015), the option physically delivers into a forward at the strike settling on the late delivery date (August 18, 2016).

The key element in this **late-delivery** option is **non-optimal exercise** compared to the option on forward. The late-delivery option is exercised if spot at maturity is above the strike and it is expired if spot at maturity is below the strike. It could therefore be constructed in a pricing tool using a discrete barrier on the expiry date that knocks out below the strike and pays out a forward to the late delivery date.

If interest rates are all statically zero, the price of the late-delivery option would be the same as the standard European vanilla option and the late cash option because the expiry decision would be optimal (since spot = forward). However, as soon as interest rates are non-zero, exercise becomes non-optimal.

If swap points between the standard delivery date and the late delivery date are negative (i.e., CCY1 rates > CCY2 rates) and spot at maturity is above the strike, exercising a call option into the forward at the strike level in the future may result in negative P&L.

Example: On August 14, 2015, USD/JPY spot is 103.25. Therefore, the option exercises into a long forward at 103.00 for August 18, 2016. The forward points are negative and the prevailing forward outright to August 18, 2016 is 102.00. Buying the August 18, 2016 forward at 103.00 leads to negative P&L.

If swap points between the standard delivery date and the late delivery date are positive (i.e., CCY1 rates < CCY2 rates) and spot at maturity is below the strike, not exercising a call option into the forward at the strike level in the future may result in positive P&L being missed.

Example: On August 14, 2015, USD/JPY spot is 102.75. Therefore, the option expires. However, the forward points are positive and the forward outright to August 18, 2016 is 104.00. Buying the August 18, 2016, forward at 103.00 would have lead to positive P&L, which has not been realized due to the exercise decision mechanism.

The pricing reduction from this non-optimal exercise is shown leg 2 of Exhibit 27.4.

This price is calculated assuming interest rates are static so the effects of stochastic interest rates must be additionally factored in. For example, higher interest rate volatility will reduce the quoted price of the late-delivery vanilla because it increases the chances of non-optimal exercise.

American Vanilla Options

European vanilla options can be exercised by the option holder *only* at the exact option expiry date and cut time. American vanilla options can be exercised by the option holder *at any time* up to the option expiry date and cut time.

American vanilla options are rarely traded in the OTC FX derivatives market, where the vast majority of vanilla options are traded European-style. If early exercise

Contract Details	Leg 1	Leg 2
Currency Pair	USD/JPY	USD/JPY
Horizon	Thu 14-Aug-2014	Thu 14-Aug-2014
Spot Date	Mon 18-Aug-2014	Mon 18-Aug-2014
Strategy	Vanilla	Late Delivery Vanilla
Call/Put	USD Call/JPY Put	USD Call/JPY Put
Maturity	1Y	1Y
Expiry Date	Fri 14-Aug-2015	Fri 14-Aug-2015
Delivery Date	Tue 18-Aug-2015	**Thu 18-Aug-2016**
Cut	NY	NY
Strike	103.00	103.00
Notional Currency	USD	USD
Market Data		
Spot	102.50	102.50
Swap Points	-40	-165
Forward	102.10	100.85
Deposit (USD)	0.30%	0.65%
Deposit (JPY)	0.00%	0.00%
ATM Volatility	8.05%	8.05%
Pricing Volatility	**8.05%**	**8.05%**
Outputs		
Output Currency	**USD**	**USD**
Mid Price	**2.75%**	**1.90%**

EXHIBIT 27.4   Pricing tool showing late delivery vanilla

is required, it is possible to unwind a European vanilla and trade spot to get the same net position change as early exercising the American option. However, American vanilla options are often standard products on exchanges, for example, the Chicago Mercantile Exchange (CME).

No exact closed-form solutions exist for pricing American vanillas and hence they are more complicated to accurately value. Ideally, since they are path dependent, the full interest rate curve, full ATM curve, and potentially even stochastic interest rates should be taken into account within pricing. Several well-established closed-form approximations do exist but they rely on fairly restrictive simplifying assumptions.

American vanilla options contain *more optionality* than the equivalent European vanilla options. Therefore, American vanillas are always at least as expensive as the equivalent European vanilla, with the value difference increasing with longer time to expiry.

The early exercise feature of an American vanilla should be activated *when the value lost from holding the option (mainly due to the forward drift) is more than the value of the remaining optionality*.

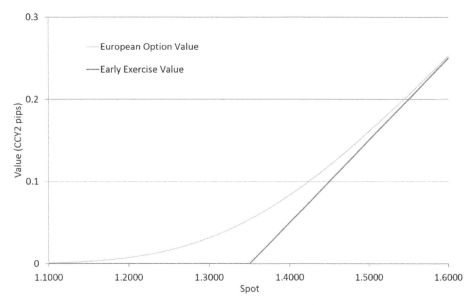

EXHIBIT 27.5 European option value versus early exercise value: zero interest rates

Consider the value of a 1yr European CCY1 call/CCY2 put vanilla option versus the equivalent early exercise value. The zero interest rate case is shown in Exhibit 27.5.

With zero interest rates and hence no forward drift or discounting, the European option value is always above the early exercise value. Therefore, it is always optimal to keep the optionality rather than early exercise.

A higher CCY2 interest rate case is shown in Exhibit 27.6. The European option value is again above the early exercise value at all spots, plus this it is further over than the zero interest rate case due to the forward drift. Recall that the forward to time T (F_t) is given by:

$$F_T = Se^{(rCCY2-rCCY1).T}$$

Higher CCY2 interest rates ($rCCY2 > rCCY1$) leads to a forward that is above spot. This leads to an expected call option payoff calculated off the higher forward that is always larger than the early exercise value calculated off spot. Therefore, it is always optimal to keep the optionality and hence benefit from the forward drift rather than early exercise.

Higher CCY1 interest rate cases are shown in Exhibits 27.7 and 27.8. Higher CCY1 interest rates ($rCCY1 > rCCY2$) leads to a forward that is below spot. This leads to an expected call option payoff calculated off the lower forward, which can be lower than the early exercise value calculated off spot.

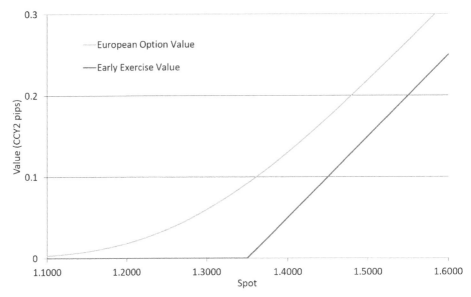

EXHIBIT 27.6   European option value versus early exercise value: rCCY1 = 0%/rCCY2 = 5%

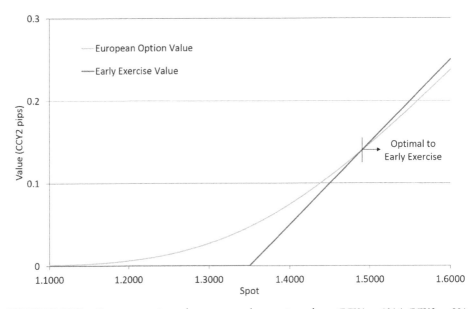

EXHIBIT 27.7   European option value versus early exercise value: rCCY1 = 1%/rCCY2 = 0%

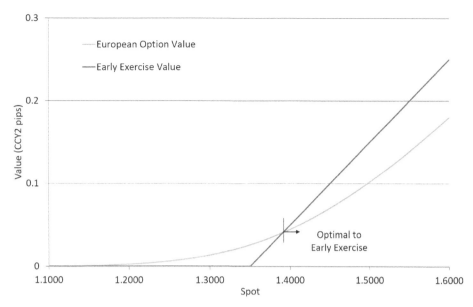

EXHIBIT 27.8 European option value versus early exercise value: rCCY1 = 5%/rCCY2 = 0%

At in-the-money spots beyond a certain level, the European option value is below the early exercise value due to the forward drift. At these spot levels it is optimal to early exercise the American vanilla option.

These examples reveal some important rules:

- The early exercise feature of American vanillas only has value when the *payoff is a call on the higher yielding currency* (i.e., the currency with higher interest rates).

When the payoff is a CCY1 call, the early exercise feature only has value when CCY1 interest rates are higher than CCY2 interest rates. When the vanilla payoff is not a call on the higher yielding currency, in a static interest rate world, the pricing and Greeks on an American vanilla will be identical to the equivalent European vanilla.

- If it exists, the optimal early exercise level moves closer to the strike the higher the interest rate differential.

This occurs because more value is lost from the forward drift at higher interest rate differential.

- When long an American vanilla, the European vanilla price versus early exercise value difference must be monitored.

Beyond a certain spot level it is optimal to early exercise the American vanilla. This occurs when spot is in-the-money versus the payoff and the forward drift will cause more value to decay away over than is remaining in time value. If this optimal exercise point is not monitored, early exercise optionality has been paid for and then not used; roughly equivalent to throwing money away.

For a client, when the early exercise decision is based on some external trigger rather than on the value of the early exercise optionality, it is usually preferable to trade the standard European vanilla option. However, in currency pairs with limited spot market liquidity, the ability to avoid crossing two option spreads (original deal plus unwind) plus the spot market spread may save money.

American Vanilla Pricing and Greeks

Comparing American and European vanillas in the CCY1 call and higher CCY1 interest rates case demonstrates how early exercise impacts trading risk. Price profiles are shown in Exhibit 27.9.

As mentioned, the American vanilla is always more expensive than the equivalent European vanilla. The value of the early exercise optionality (the difference between the lines in Exhibit 27.9) becomes a significant part of the total option value when spot is deep in-the-money.

Delta profiles are shown in Exhibit 27.10. The American vanilla delta picks up more sharply with a higher spot. Beyond the optimal early exercise point, the delta on the American vanilla becomes 100%, equivalent to exercising the vanilla into spot.

Gamma profiles are shown in Exhibit 27.11. The sharper delta pickup generates increased gamma exposure on the American vanilla with spot higher. Beyond the

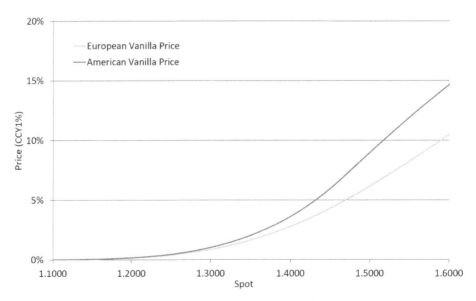

EXHIBIT 27.9   1yr 1.3650 EUR call/USD put American vanilla versus European vanilla price

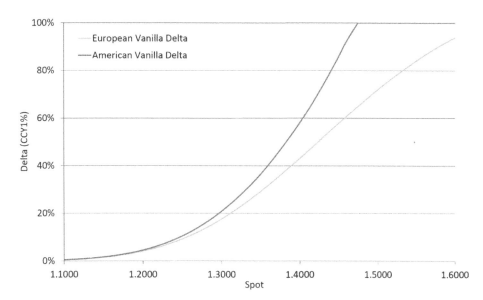

EXHIBIT 27.10 1yr 1.3650 EUR call/USD put American vanilla versus European vanilla delta

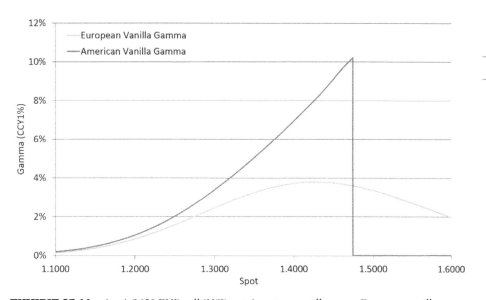

EXHIBIT 27.11 1yr 1.3650 EUR call/USD put American vanilla versus European vanilla gamma

optimal early exercise point, gamma becomes zero as it is assumed the vanilla will be exercised into spot.

Vega profiles are shown in Exhibit 27.12. Once again, Greeks are curtailed beyond the optimal early exercise point as optionality disappears. At in-the-money spot levels, vega risks on American vanillas move forward to tenors prior to the

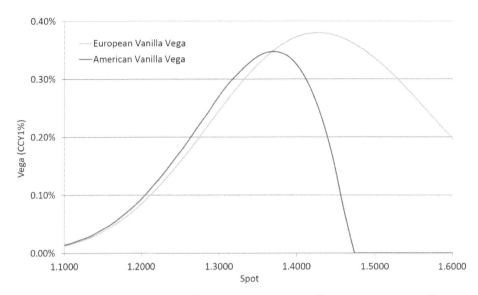

EXHIBIT 27.12 1yr 1.3650 EUR call/USD put American vanilla versus European vanilla vega

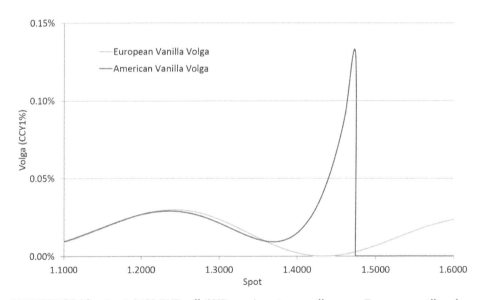

EXHIBIT 27.13 1yr 1.3650 EUR call/USD put American vanilla versus European vanilla volga

option expiry, whereas for European vanillas the vega risks are always to expiry. This is key for risk management; To properly assess the trading risk on American vanillas, bucketed vega exposures must be used.

The volga and vanna exposures are significantly larger on an American vanilla option with spot near the optimal early exercise point as shown in Exhibits 27.13 and 27.14.

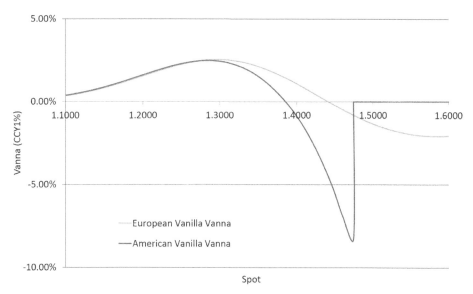

EXHIBIT 27.14 1yr 1.3650 EUR call/USD put American vanilla versus European vanilla vanna

American Vanilla Pricing

When pricing American vanilla options, traders must understand what methodology is being used to price the option in order to understand which effects are being taken into account and which are being ignored.

At shorter tenors (e.g., under 3mth), where the early exercise optionality has little value, it may be sufficient to price the European vanilla using the volatility smile, and then add in a constant volatility American-style versus European-style price difference.

At longer tenors, stochastic interest rates must be taken into account. If spot and interest rates move in a correlated manner, that will significantly impact the price of American vanilla options. Consider the case where the vanilla option payoff is a CCY1 call but CCY2 interest rates are currently higher than CCY1 interest rates. In the basic analysis, this means that the price will be that of the European vanilla, but the interest rate differential may flip over time, giving the early exercise feature value. This effect is quantified by a stochastic interest rate model.

Finally, the bid–offer spread on American vanillas is generally slightly wider than the equivalent European vanilla (particularly in longer tenors) due to the additional risk management and monitoring they require.

■ Self-Quanto Vanilla Options

The standard European vanilla option payoff is generated in CCY2 terms, and at maturity it can be converted back to CCY1 terms at the prevailing spot. Self-quanto options have their payout converted back into CCY1 at a fixed rate (usually the strike) rather than at spot. Call and put payoffs react differently to this adjustment and therefore they must be examined separately.

Vanilla CCY1 Call Options

For a CCY1 call option, the European vanilla payoff has a CCY2 P&L at maturity:

$$Notional_{CCY1}.max(S_T - K, \ 0) = Notional_{CCY1}.(S_T - K)^+ = Payout_{CCY2}$$

The payout can be converted from CCY2 to CCY1 using spot at maturity so:

$$Notional_{CCY1}.\left(\frac{S_T - K}{S_T}\right)^+ = Payout_{CCY1}$$

In the standard self-quanto case, rather than dividing by S_T to get back to CCY1 terms, the payout is divided by K:

$$Notional_{CCY1}.\left(\frac{S_T - K}{K}\right)^+ = Self\text{-}Quanto \ Payout_{CCY1}$$

$$Notional_{CCY1}.\left(\frac{S_T - K}{K}\right)^+.S_T = Self\text{-}Quanto \ Payout_{CCY2}$$

If spot is in-the-money at maturity on the CCY1 call, then $S_T > K$, which implies the self-quanto payout is larger than the regular vanilla payout and hence:

$$P_{CCY1 \ Call \ Self\text{-}Quanto} > P_{CCY1 \ Call \ Vanilla}$$

Exhibit 27.15 shows the payoff at maturity of long 1.3500 EUR call/USD put European and self-quanto vanilla options in EUR1m notional. An intuitive way to think about the self-quanto is that buying a self-quanto CCY1 call can be replicated by buying the CCY1 call European vanilla with same strike *plus buying* a strip of CCY1 call vanillas above the strike to the same maturity. This strip of options, with notionals far smaller than the self-quanto notional, is visualized in Exhibit 27.16.

Therefore, the self-quanto CCY1 call is longer topside vega compared to the European vanilla as shown in Exhibit 27.17.

Vanilla CCY1 Put Options

For a CCY1 put European vanilla option, again, the natural vanilla payoff has CCY2 P&L at maturity:

$$Notional_{CCY1}.max(K - S_T, 0) = Notional_{CCY1}.(K - S_T)^+ = Payout_{CCY2}$$

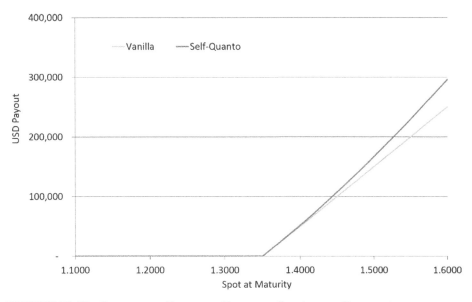

EXHIBIT 27.15　European vanilla versus self-quanto call option payoff at maturity

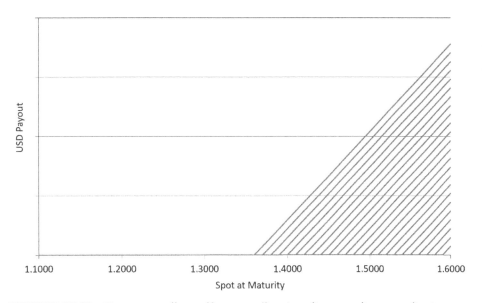

EXHIBIT 27.16　European vanilla to self-quanto call option adjustment discrete replication

The payout can be converted from CCY2 to CCY1 using spot at maturity so:

$$Notional_{CCY1} \cdot \left(\frac{K - S_T}{S_T} \right)^{+} = Payout_{CCY1}$$

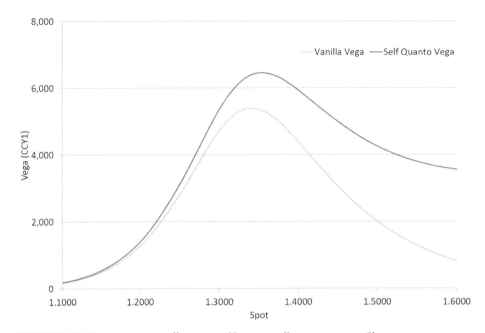

EXHIBIT 27.17 European vanilla versus self-quanto call option vega profile

In the standard self-quanto case, rather than dividing by S_T to get back to CCY1 terms, the payout is divided by K:

$$Notional_{CCY1} \cdot \left(\frac{K - S_T}{K} \right)^+ = Self\text{-}Quanto\ Payout_{CCY1}$$

$$Notional_{CCY1} \cdot \left(\frac{K - S_T}{K} \right)^+ \cdot S_T = Self\text{-}Quanto\ Payout_{CCY2}$$

If spot is in-the-money at maturity on the CCY1 put, then $S_T < K$, which implies the self-quanto payout is smaller than the regular vanilla payout and hence:

$$P_{CCY1\ Put\ Self\text{-}Quanto} < P_{CCY1\ Put\ Vanilla}$$

Exhibit 27.18 shows the payout at maturity of long 1.3500 EUR put/USD call European and self-quanto vanilla options in EUR1m notional.

Buying a CCY1 put self-quanto can be replicated by buying the CCY1 put European vanilla with same strike *plus selling* a strip of CCY1 put vanillas below the strike to the same maturity. Therefore, the self-quanto CCY1 put is shorter downside vega compared to the European vanilla as shown in Exhibit 27.19.

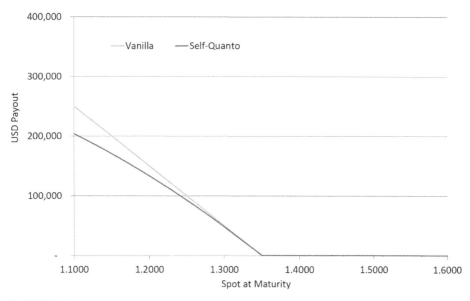

EXHIBIT 27.18   European vanilla versus self-quanto put option payoff at maturity

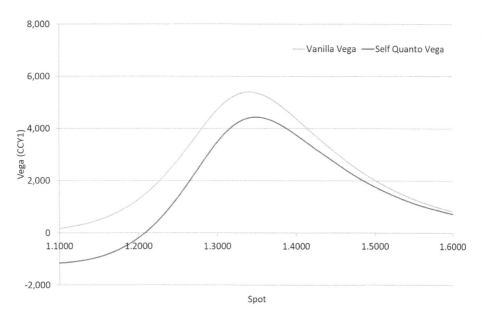

EXHIBIT 27.19   European vanilla versus self-quanto put option vega profile

Self-Quanto Bid–Offer Spread

For a self-quanto CCY1 call, the replication suggests that it should be quoted wider than the equivalent European vanilla option because there is compounding vega risk from the additional strip of CCY1 calls. However, care must be taken to look at risks beyond just ATM vega; There may be significant optionality in the wings, particularly in high skew currency pairs which should be accounted for within the bid-offer spread.

For a self-quanto CCY1 put, the replication suggests that it should be quoted tighter than the equivalent vanilla option because there is less vega risk due to the offsetting strip of CCY1 puts.

CHAPTER 28

Accrual and Target Redemption Options

Accrual options and target redemption options are both popular within the FX derivatives market. Accrual features and target redemption features are typically added to a forward contract or a strip of forward contracts in order to improve the transaction rate for the client.

◼ Accrual Options

The key characteristic of accrual options is that the notional, rather than being static, builds up (accrues) over time. Accrual options have a fixing schedule and the rate of accrual depends on where spot fixes compared to the **accrual barriers** within the structure. There are two main types of accrual barrier:

1. *European*: If spot goes through the barrier, accrual stops with what has been accrued retained, but if spot later comes back inside the barrier, accrual restarts.
2. *American Keep*: If spot *ever* goes through the barrier, accrual stops, but what has been accrued prior to that point is retained.

Range Accrual Options

The simplest accrual product is a **range accrual**, which pays out an accrued notional at expiry. Range accrual prices are quoted in payout currency % terms, like touch options or European digital options.

Following are some typical European double barrier range accrual contract details:

Example: European Double Barrier Range Accrual

Currency pair: USD/JPY
Tenor: 1yr
Spot: 102.50
Notional: USD1m
Fixings: 250 daily fixings (USD and JPY holidays excluded)
Fixing Source: ECB37
Down European accrual barrier: 100.00
Up European accrual barrier: 110.00

For products with fixings it is vital to specify the fixing source, confirm which holiday calendars are used to generate the fixing schedule, and agree the fixing schedule itself with the client prior to quoting a price.

Within the example range accrual, the notional is split between the fixings (usually equally), that is, USD1m/250 = USD4k per fixing. Therefore, for every fixing in the schedule where spot is between the accrual barriers, USD4k is added onto the cash payout at maturity.

These are *European* accrual barriers, so if spot goes outside the range (either between fixings or it fixes outside the range) and then later fixes within the range again, the notional continues to accrue. A typical European range accrual structure is shown in Exhibit 28.1.

Therefore, within a European range accrual:

$$\text{Cash payout at expiry} = \textit{Notional} \times \frac{n}{N}$$

where n is the number of times spot fixes within the European accrual barriers and N is the total number of fixes in the fixing schedule.

If there is just one fixing at expiry, the option becomes a European digital range that pays out the full notional if spot is within the range at expiry. Extending this idea further, **European range accruals** can be perfectly replicated by a strip of European digital ranges expiring at each fixing within the range accrual, each with

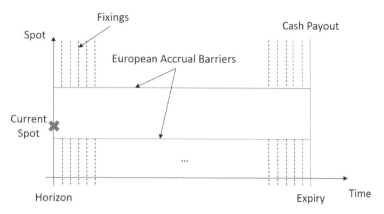

EXHIBIT 28.1   European range accrual structure

their [Notional $\times \left(\frac{1}{N}\right)$] cash payout late-delivered to the range accrual delivery date. As seen in Chapter 21, the vega profile from a long European digital range is long vega in the wings (want spot to move back into the range) and short vega between the barriers (don't want spot to move) and this same profile also applies to European range accruals:

- If spot is between the European range accrual barriers, more payout will be accrued if spot stops moving; hence short vega.

- If spot is outside the European range accrual barriers, spot needs to move into the range again in order to start accruing; hence long vega.

Exhibit 28.2 shows the long wing vega profile from a long European range accrual. Recall from Chapter 18 that contracts with long wing vega profiles usually have positive TV adjustments.

The fact that European range accruals can be replicated with a strip of European digital ranges demonstrates two important features of European range accruals. First, accrual option pricing must take the full ATM term structure into account because there is vega exposure to every date within the fixing schedule, not just to the expiry date. Second, any well-calibrated smile pricing model will correctly incorporate the impact of the volatility smile into the product. Therefore, the simplest and quickest available smile pricing model (often local volatility) can be used.

American keep range accruals stop accruing and all accrued notional is kept if spot ever goes through an American keep accrual barrier. Therefore, the European range accrual will be more expensive than the American keep range accrual with the same barriers. In turn, the American keep range accrual will be more expensive than a no-touch option in the full notional with the same barriers because the entire no-touch notional is effectively lost if a barrier level trades.

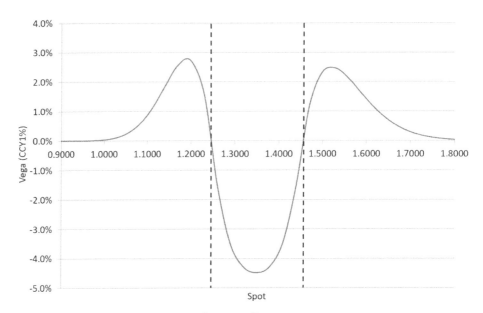

EXHIBIT 28.2   European range accrual vega profile

An American keep range accrual can be replicated with a strip of double no-touches with their cash payouts late-delivered to the range accrual delivery date. Therefore, the vega profile of a long American keep range accrual looks similar to a long double-no-touch option, with no vega beyond the barriers as shown in Exhibit 28.3. Again, the vega profile is long wings and will usually have a positive TV adjustment.

Importantly, the process of stripping barrier or digital risk from a single date into multiple dates reduces trading risk because it is not possible to gain or lose the entire notional on a single date. For this reason, the bid–offer spread on a range accrual is usually tighter than the bid–offer spread on the equivalent European digital range or double-no-touch option in the total notional.

The stripping process also reduces model risk on accrual options because the stripped contract has different exposures at each fixing and this is similar in some sense to taking an average. American keep accrual options with many fixings often give similar valuations under different models and therefore the simplest and quickest available smile pricing model (often local volatility) can often be used.

Accrual Forwards

The most popular accrual products are **accrual forwards**. These products contain a forward payout at maturity with the notional determined by how spot moves.

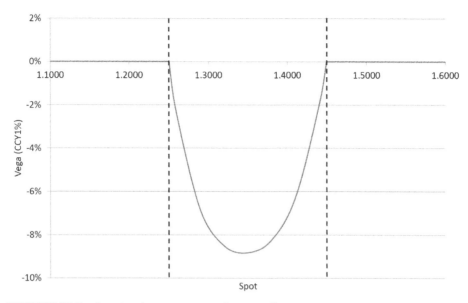

EXHIBIT 28.3 American keep range accrual vega profile

There are many variations, but the most popular is a **double accrual forward**. The notional accrues:

- 1× (notional/number of fixings) for each spot fix in an area where the payoff is positive for the client at maturity

- 2× (notional/number of fixings) for each spot fix in an area where the payoff is negative for the client at maturity

Therefore, the product can accrue up to double the notional if spot fixes in the 2× accrual area at every fix. The different accrual multiples generate value for the client and hence the forward rate is moved in the client's favor, meaning that the client transacts for zero premium.

The risk from a simple accrual forward can be decomposed into two range accruals with the same accrual barriers. For example, a long EUR/USD accrual forward can be replicated using:

- Long EUR range accrual in the accrual forward EUR notional.

- Short USD range accrual in the appropriate notional (using CCY2 notional = CCY1 notional × strike).

As before, a simple smile pricing model can be used for European accrual forwards and is often sufficient for pricing American keep accrual forwards with many fixings.

Following are some typical American keep double accrual forward contract details:

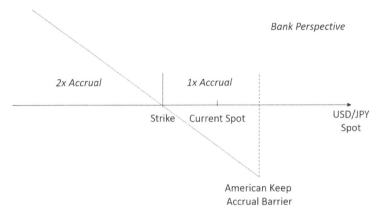

Bank Perspective

2x Accrual | 1x Accrual

Strike   Current Spot

USD/JPY
Spot

American Keep
Accrual Barrier

EXHIBIT 28.4   American keep double accrual forward structure

	Example: American Keep Double Accrual Forward	

Currency pair: USD/JPY
Tenor: 1yr
Spot: 102.30
Forward: 102.05
Notional: USD1m
Direction: Bank sells USD/JPY, Client buys USD/JPY
Strike: 98.80
Accrual forward barrier: 106.00
Accrual multiple below strike: 2×
Accrual multiple between strike and barrier: 1×

By capping the upside with the American keep accrual barrier and making the downside worse with 2× accrual below the strike the client buys USD/JPY in 1yr forward at 98.80 rather than at 102.05 for zero premium. This is shown in Exhibit 28.4.

The vega risk on this American keep double accrual forward is similar to an American knock-out option, with a vega peak around the strike. This is shown in Exhibit 28.5.

These products are almost always long vega from the trading desk perspective. Traders describe the risks on accrual forwards as "vanilla," meaning the vega and gamma are well-behaved over time. In addition, there are no large digital risks to hedge due to the payout depending on a strip of fixings. Therefore the bid–offer spread on accrual forwards with European or American keep barriers is often just derived from the vega spread.

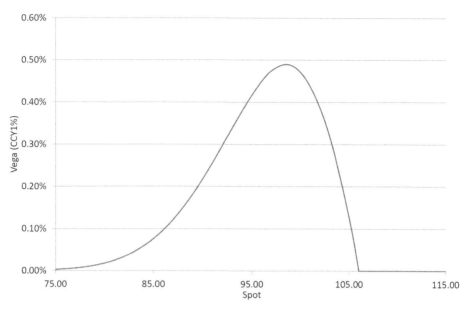

EXHIBIT 28.5 Double accrual forward with American keep barriers vega (trading desk perspective)

■ Target Redemption Options

The key characteristic of a target redemption option is that the option payoff depends in some way on a quantity that counts up to a *target* over time. Within a typical target redemption product, the client enters into a strip of forwards (or similar, e.g., leveraged forwards) with rates better than the forward outrights. In the standard target redemption forward (TARF) variation, the client's gains count up and the whole structure expires once a target is reached. The client's losses do not count toward the target.

There are many TARF variations, often based around differences in behavior when the target is reached or exceeded. Plus there are variations based on the payoff (e.g., a TARF EKI features a European knock-in payoff or a TARF Box features a digital range payoff). Another variation is a Count TARF in which the target is not based on the accumulated gain, but on the number of times that the client receives a positive gain. In general, the risk management of these different variations is usually fairly similar except for their behavior at fixings, particularly when the target is close to being breached.

Example: EUR/USD 1yr TARF with monthly fixings. Spot is at 1.2770 and the 1yr forward is 1.2800. At each fixing, the client buys EUR against USD at the strike 1.2290 (well below the forward) provided the USD30,000 target profit has not been reached. Once the USD30,000 target profit is reached, the structure terminates. At each fixing, the client buys either:

- EUR300k against USD at 1.2290 if EUR/USD spot fixes at or above the strike

  or

- EUR600k against USD at 1.2290 if EUR/USD spot fixes below the strike

The accumulated positive gain is calculated by summing the client's gains at each fixing. Within this trade, client gains occur above the strike and client losses occur below the strike, plus note that the trade has *leverage*: 2X notional is transacted below the strike.

Vega Risk

Exhibit 28.6 shows the bucketed vega exposures from the example trade at various spot levels from the trading desk perspective. The maximum total vega is usually located around the strike, especially if there is leverage in the trade:

- In the spot direction where the client has losses (and hence the target is less likely to be reached), the vega reduces like the equivalent vanilla structure.

- In the spot direction where the client has gains (and hence the target is more likely to be reached), vega converges to sharply and the vega risk moves to closer maturities.

Looking at the vega exposures at each spot level in Exhibit 28.6:

- 1.1750 spot: The bucketed vega profile looks similar to a strip of leveraged forwards, which has the same vega exposures as a strip of vanilla options in the unmatched notionals (see Chapter 8)—exactly what the structure would become if the target feature was removed.

Tenor\Spot	1.1750	1.2260	1.2770	1.3280	1.3790
1W	-	-	-	-	-
1M	14	48	217	100	-
2M	253	898	3,882	1,872	-
3M	580	1,972	3,856	180	-
4M	1,179	3,048	1,766	79	-
5M	1,411	2,573	872	33	-
6M	3,458	4,247	1,161	55	-
9M	5,966	5,390	1,229	52	-
1Y	3,165	2,388	552	26	-
Total Vega (USD)	16,025	20,564	13,535	2,398	-

EXHIBIT 28.6 Target redemption vega exposures

- 1.2260 spot: Spot is closest to the strike (1.2290) and hence optionality (vega) is maximized.

- 1.2770 spot (current spot): The client is accumulating gains and therefore the structure will more likely knock out early. Overall vega and stopping time has reduced and there is increased vega at closer maturities.

- 1.3280 spot: The structure will likely knock out soon, so the vega move into closer tenors is even more exaggerated. The vega is bucketed mainly in the 2mth tenor, which suggests that the stopping time on the trade is around two months.

- 1.3790 spot: The structure will knock out at the first fixing and therefore has minimal exposure to implied volatility.

Exhibit 28.7 shows the vega chart of the TARF compared to the equivalent leveraged forward structure. The presence of the target reduces the stopping time of the structure and decreases the vega, particularly at higher spots where the structure will terminate more quickly.

Exhibit 28.8 shows a vega chart of the TARF with different targets. With a higher target, the vega on the TARF increases and the chance of knocking out decreases.

Delta and Gamma Risk

The spot ladder from the EUR/USD TARF from the trading desk perspective is shown in Exhibit 28.9.

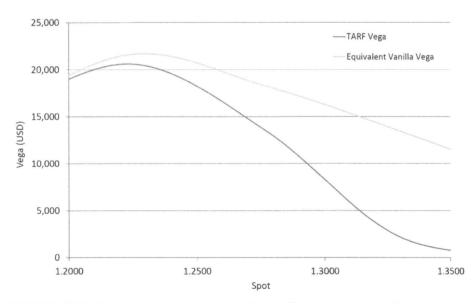

EXHIBIT 28.7 Target redemption versus equivalent vanilla structure vega profiles

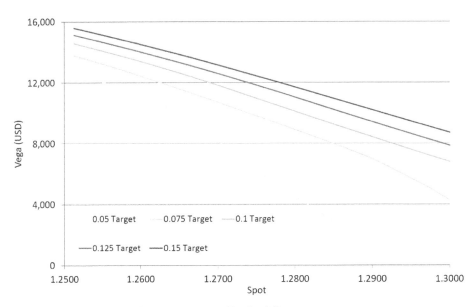

EXHIBIT 28.8   Target redemption vega profiles for different targets

Spot	P&L (USD)	Delta (EUR)	Gamma (EUR)	Weighted Vega (USD)	Vega (USD)
1.3407	-73,388	-79,747	292,246	148	108
1.3024	-43,107	-1,269,164	458,974	6,049	8,209
1.2922	-28,430	-1,609,267	445,352	7,334	10,309
1.2871	-19,739	-1,771,020	410,659	7,936	11,390
1.2820	-10,265	-1,935,447	394,415	8,503	12,467
1.2769	**0**	**-2,088,980**	**359,749**	**9,031**	**13,540**
1.2717	11,042	-2,236,907	385,827	9,544	14,608
1.2666	22,876	-2,394,641	398,602	10,006	15,625
1.2615	35,502	-2,556,814	406,360	10,410	16,565
1.2513	63,265	-2,881,144	392,283	11,031	18,183
1.2130	202,724	-4,512,695	454,251	11,440	20,417

EXHIBIT 28.9   Target redemption spot ladder

The trade is long gamma for the trading desk because from the trading desk perspective the trade gains more value with spot lower than it loses with spot higher due to the target. Thinking about the delta exposure on the trade confirms this:

- If spot goes lower, the deal will get more and more in-the-money for the bank until the delta eventually becomes the leveraged notional and the trading risk becomes equivalent to a strip of forwards.

- If spot goes higher, eventually the delta position on the trade goes to zero as the deal is deep in-the-money for the client and the bank has no more to lose due to the target being reached.

Target Redemption Fixing Risk

Aside from the standard gamma and vega trading risks, the main risk management challenges on TARFs come from the fixings. At inception, the example EUR/USD trade will knock out at the first fixing if spot fixes at 1.3290 or above, paying the client the $(1.3290 - 1.2290) \times 300k$ USD = 30k USD target. Suppose instead spot fixes at 1.2790 at the first fix, hence generating USD15k profit. The deal will then knock out at the second fixing if spot fixes at or above 1.2790 again. Before the first fixing there was no explicit digital risk at the second fixing. However, after the first fixing, it becomes known that the future value of the remaining fixings will be lost if spot fixes above 1.2790 at the second fixing. Therefore, the trade develops digital risk at 1.2790 at the second fixing.

The more frequently fixings occur within a structure, the more digital risks must be risk managed. These digital risks will be particularly large if the termination level is close to the strike, so if spot fixes on one side of the strike, the option will knock out, while if spot fixes on the other side of the strike, it will have a far longer time to maturity. Large digital risk is also generated by strike changes within the contract details of the trade. For example, if the remaining strikes all move to a new level after the next fixing, the difference in option value between the option staying alive or expiring at the next fixing will be large.

The crystallization of digital risk at the next fixing can also cause delta changes. These delta gaps at fixings require careful monitoring and management within the TARF deal population.

Target Redemption Pricing

Target redemption options are conceptually similar to accrual options: Both have fixing schedules, and in some sense target redemptions knock out on *time* while accruals knock out on *spot*. The similarity extends to the pricing: Both products have minimal model risk. This can be confirmed by pricing the TARF using various smile pricing models; different models will often give similar valuations.

Traders describe the risks on target redemption forwards as "vanilla," meaning that the vega and gamma are generally well-behaved through time. As noted, the major risk management challenges come from the fixings. It is therefore important that these potential digital risks at fixings are taken into account within the bid–offer spread as well as the usual vega-based spreading.

CHAPTER 29

Asian Options

The key characteristic of Asian options is that some element of their payoff is based on an *average*. The most common Asian option variations have a single average that is used in place of either the spot or the strike at maturity within a vanilla payoff. The average is either calculated from spot fixings that occur regularly between the horizon and expiry date as shown in Exhibit 29.1, or the fixings can be over a subsection of the period as shown in Exhibit 29.2.

Fixings can be taken at different sample frequencies, for example, daily, weekly, or monthly. Plus note that Asian options are always *cash-settled* at maturity.

Average Rate Options

Within an average rate option, the *spot* at expiry within a standard vanilla payoff is replaced with an average of fixings:

$$Payoff_{Average\ Rate\ Call} = (AV - K)^+$$
$$Payoff_{Average\ Rate\ Put} = (K - AV)^+$$

where AV is an average of spot fixings.

EXHIBIT 29.1 Example single average fixing schedule A

EXHIBIT 29.2   Example single average fixing schedule B

The following are example average rate option contract details:

Example: Average Rate Option with 12 monthly spot fixings

Currency pair: EUR/GBP
Tenor: 1yr
Spot: 0.8725
Forward: 0.8785
Notional: EUR100m
Direction: EUR put/GBP call
Strike: 0.8250

The average rate option (0.24 EUR%) is significantly cheaper than the equivalent European vanilla (0.91 EUR%). The realized spot action in Exhibit 29.3 shows why this is the case.

Spot moves sharply lower but the average moves lower far more slowly and hence the average rate put option has a lower payoff at maturity than the equivalent vanilla put option. In general, the volatility of the average of spot fixings will be lower than the volatility of spot itself.

The price profile of the average rate option compared to the equivalent European vanilla shown in Exhibit 29.4 confirms that the average rate option is cheaper than the equivalent European vanilla option.

For ATM strikes it is the case that (approximately):

$$Vega_{AverageRate} = \frac{Vega_{Vanilla}}{\sqrt{3}} = 0.6 \times Vega_{Vanilla}$$

as demonstrated in Exhibit 29.5.

Exhibit 29.6 shows the initial vega profiles from the average rate option and the equivalent European vanilla option. The full story of this average rate vega profile is more complicated than simply lower vega exposure. There are fixings throughout the life of the option and therefore the payoff depends not just on spot at maturity

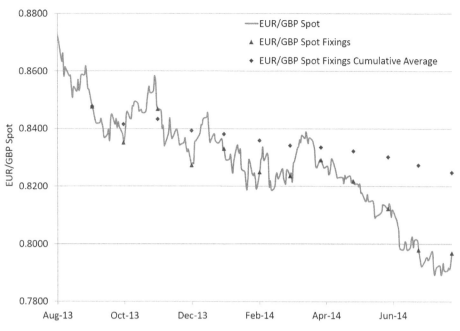

EXHIBIT 29.3   EUR/GBP realized spot, fixings, and the cumulative average

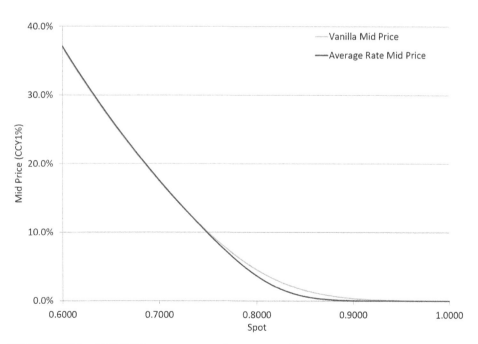

EXHIBIT 29.4   EUR/GBP average rate option versus vanilla option price

Contract Details	Leg 1	Leg 2
Currency Pair	EUR/GBP	EUR/GBP
Horizon	Fri 08-Aug-2014	Fri 08-Aug-2014
Spot Date	Tue 12-Aug-2014	Tue 12-Aug-2014
Strategy	Vanilla	Average Rate
Call/Put	EUR Call/USD Put	EUR Call/USD Put
Maturity	1Y	1Y
Expiry Date	Mon 10-Aug-2015	Mon 10-Aug-2015
Delivery Date	Wed 12-Aug-2015	Wed 12-Aug-2015
Cut	NY	NY
Strike	0.8015 (ATM)	0.8015 (ATM)
Notional Currency	EUR	EUR
Average Type		Arithmetic
Fixing Schedule		Daily (255 fixings)

Market Data		
Spot	0.7975	0.7975
Swap Points	60	60
Forward	0.8035	0.8035
Deposit (EUR)	0.10%	0.10%
Deposit (USD)	0.80%	0.80%
ATM Volatility	6.90%	6.90%
Smile Volatility	6.90%	

Outputs		
Output Currency	EUR	EUR
TV		1.52%
TV Adjustment		-0.20%
Mid Price	2.86%	1.32%
Vega	0.40%	0.23%

EXHIBIT 29.5   EUR/GBP average rate option in pricing tool

but on the path it takes. Put another way, Asian options have *path dependence*. This path dependence causes average rate options to have vega exposures to dates on which fixings occur. For example, a EUR/GBP 1yr ATM average rate option and a European vanilla option in EUR100m notional have the bucketed vega exposures shown in Exhibit 29.7.

This process of moving optionality toward the horizon leads to the increased initial gamma exposures within the average rate option shown in Exhibit 29.8. Increased gamma can also be seen in Exhibit 29.4 where the average rate option has more curvature in the price profile.

As time passes and the fixings set, the exposures on the average rate option decrease. Exhibit 29.9 shows vega profiles after six monthly fixings within the average rate option.

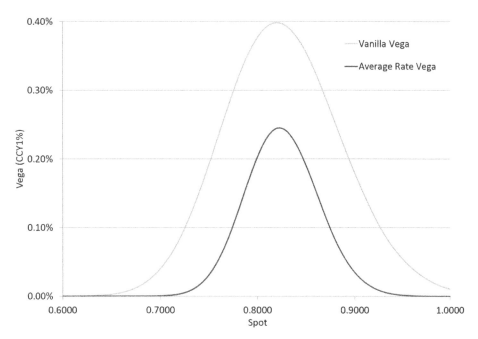

EXHIBIT 29.6   EUR/GBP average rate option versus equivalent vanilla vega profile

Tenor	Vanilla Vega (EUR)	Average Rate Vega (EUR)
1W	-	4
2W	-	217
1M	-	8,823
2M	-	14,550
3M	-	21,267
4M	-	24,053
5M	-	26,563
6M	-	52,406
9M	-	75,953
1Y	398,275	18,001
Total Vega (EUR)	**398,275**	**241,837**

EXHIBIT 29.7   EUR/GBP average rate option versus equivalent vanilla bucketed vega profile

The vega has reduced on both options but it has reduced far more on the average rate option. When pricing average rate options, as a sense check, the reduced vega exposure leads to smaller TV adjustments than the zeta of the equivalent vanilla option. A local volatility model is often sufficient for pricing average rate options.

The gamma on the vanilla option increases closer to expiry as expected but the gamma on the average rate decreases over its life as shown in Exhibit 29.10.

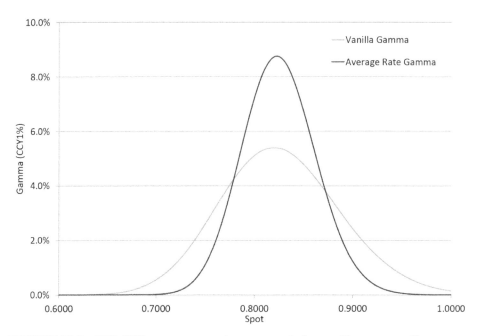

EXHIBIT 29.8   EUR/GBP average rate option versus equivalent vanilla gamma profile

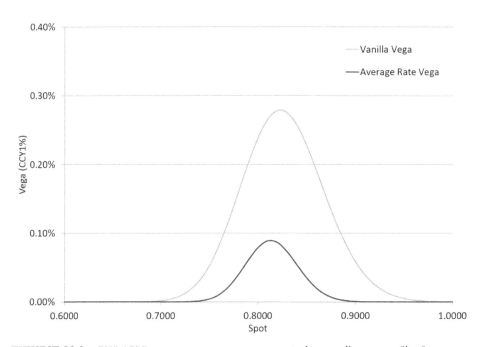

EXHIBIT 29.9   EUR/GBP average rate option versus equivalent vanilla vega profile after six monthly fixings

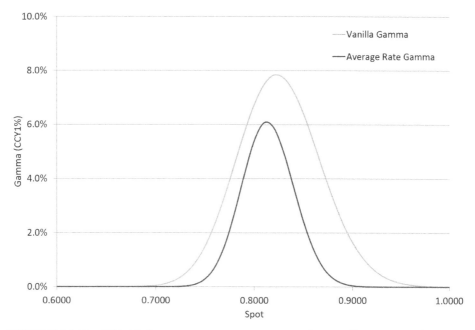

EXHIBIT 29.10 EUR/GBP average rate option versus equivalent vanilla gamma profile after six monthly fixings

Before any fixings have occurred, the average rate will be most sensitive to changes in spot because all future fixings are impacted by spot moves. However, as time passes and fixings occur, spot moves will have a smaller and smaller impact on the payoff and therefore exposures reduce.

Toward the end of the fixings, average rate options have virtually no gamma risk because so much of the average has already been determined. At the final fixing itself, there will be a delta jump at the spot level at which the resulting average goes through the strike. The size of this delta jump is the average rate option notional divided by the number of fixings: very small if the average rate option has daily fixings. For this reason, average rate options are often used to reduce strike pin risk at expiry by, for example, setting daily fixings for the last week of the option.

Average rate options are easier to risk manage than the equivalent European vanilla options due to reduced risk at expiry and generally reduced Greek exposures. Therefore, an average rate option is often quoted with a tighter premium bid–offer spread than the equivalent vanilla option.

Another feature of Exhibits 29.9 and 29.10 is the average rate vega and gamma peak exposures moving to lower spot levels. The reason for this is that maximum optionality occurs when the expected future value of the underlying (in this case,

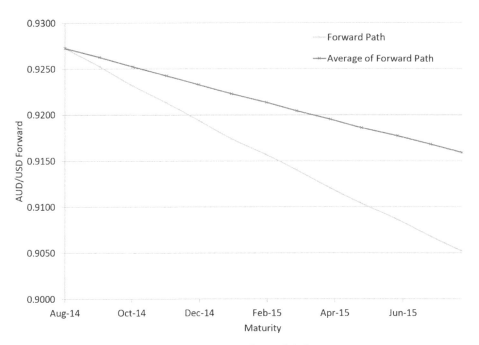

EXHIBIT 29.11   AUD/USD average rate option forward drift

the average) is at the strike. After six months, the six completed fixings have an average of 0.8360 compared with a prevailing spot of 0.8250. Therefore, for the expected average at maturity to be equal to the strike (also 0.8250), spot must be around 0.8140; hence the average rate peak exposures are pulled to lower spot levels.

Understanding forward drift within average rate options is also important. Consider the drift on a 1yr AUD/USD option, along with an average derived purely from the drift, as shown in Exhibit 29.11.

The averaging curtails the forward drift. If the forward drift were linear, the averaging would cut the drift in half. This effect is particularly relevant in high-interest-rate-differential currency pairs at longer tenors.

In practice, averages within Asian options can be constructed in two different ways and it is important that traders appreciate that this difference exists. The **arithmetic average** is the simplest form of average: the sum of the observations divided by the number of observations:

$$Average_{Arithmetic} = \frac{\sum_{i=1}^{n} S_i}{n}$$

The arithmetic average payoff is naturally quoted in CCY2 per CCY1 terms. For a CCY1 call arithmetic average rate option:

$$Payoff_{CCY2} = Notional_{CCY1} \cdot (Average_{Arithmetic} - K)^+$$

The **harmonic average** uses the arithmetic average of the inverse observations:

$$Average_{Inverse} = \frac{1}{n} \sum_{i=1}^{n} \frac{1}{S_i}$$

For a harmonic average payoff, the reciprocal of this inverse average is used within a CCY1 notional option payoff. For a CCY1 call harmonic average rate option:

$$Payoff_{CCY2} = Notional_{CCY1} \cdot \left(\frac{1}{Average_{Inverse}} - K \right)^+$$

These variations basically come down to either calculating the average of the fixings in standard terms and then inverting the average or taking the inverse of the fixings and then calculating the average. These may seem like irrelevant differences but such flexibility is required in order to provide precise payoffs for clients that exactly match their FX flows.

Average Strike Options

Within an average strike option, the *strike* within the standard vanilla payoff is replaced with an average of fixings:

$$Payoff_{Average\ Strike\ Call} = (S_T - AV)^+$$
$$Payoff_{Average\ Strike\ Put} = (AV - S_T)^+$$

where AV is an average of fixings and S_T is spot at maturity.

The following are example average strike option contract details:

Example: Average Strike Option with 12 monthly spot fixings

Currency pair: EUR/GBP
Tenor: 1yr
Spot: 0.8725
Forward: 0.8785
Notional: EUR100m
Direction: EUR put/GBP call

Again, the average option (1.85 EUR%) is cheaper than the equivalent European vanilla option (2.85 EUR%) with strike set to the average of the forward path. This occurs because within an average strike put option:

- As spot moves lower, the expected strike level moves lower and therefore the average strike CCY1 put payoff decreases relative to the equivalent vanilla option.
- As spot moves higher, the expected payoff from the put option decreases.

Whereas within an average strike call option:

- As spot moves lower, the expected payoff from the call option decreases.
- As spot moves higher, the expected strike level moves higher and therefore the average strike CCY1 call payoff decreases relative to the equivalent vanilla option.

Before any fixings have occurred, the vega profile from an average strike option is flat because the (expected) strike moves with spot. As fixings occur, the strike starts to be known, although the averaging keeps the strike closer to spot as spot moves. This in turn keeps the wings of the vega profile higher than the equivalent European vanilla option as shown in Exhibit 29.12.

The gamma profile from the average strike option starts at zero before any fixings have occurred, and gradually builds up over time. After the last fixing, when the strike level is known, the gamma (and all other Greek exposures) of the average

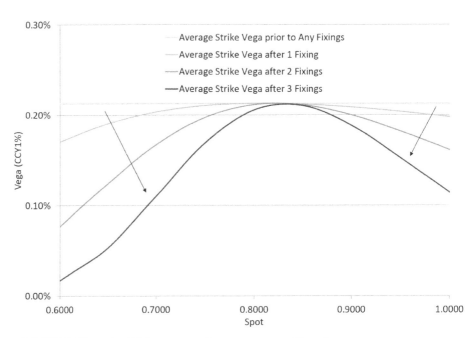

EXHIBIT 29.12   EUR/GBP average strike option vega profile as fixings occur

strike option will be exactly equal to the regular vanilla to the expiry date. However, the fact that the strike is not exactly known until the final fixing makes precise pre-hedging of the strike risk impossible.

In general, average strike options will be quoted with a bid–offer spread roughly equal to the equivalent European vanilla. Like average rate options, smile risks on average strike options are usually subdued compared to the equivalent vanilla option and a local volatility model is often sufficient for pricing.

Double Average Rate Options

Within a double average rate option, both the strike and the spot within the standard European vanilla payoff are replaced with averages of fixings:

$$Payoff_{Double\ Average\ Rate} = (AV1 - AV2)^+$$

where $AV1$ and $AV2$ are averages of fixings. This is shown in Exhibit 29.13. Note that these fixing periods may overlap.

The following are example double average rate option contract details:

Example: Double Average Rate Option

Description: "Spot" fixings ($AV1$) daily for the last three months and "strike" fixings ($AV2$) daily for the first three months
Currency pair: EUR/GBP
Tenor: 1yr
Spot: 0.8725
Forward: 0.8785
Notional: EUR100m
Payoff: EUR call/GBP put, i.e., $(AV1 - AV2)^+$

Within this trade, the "strike" is determined first, then "spot." Exhibit 29.14 shows the bucketed vega exposures from the trade.

EXHIBIT 29.13   Example double average fixing schedule

Tenor	Double Average Rate Vega (EUR)
1W	-
2W	-1,461
1M	-8,612
2M	-31,331
3M	-37,582
4M	-
5M	-
6M	-
9M	218,750
1Y	181,416
Total Vega (EUR)	**321,180**

EXHIBIT 29.14   Double average rate option bucketed vega profile

While the strike is fixing during the first three months of the trade, vega is short, because if spot doesn't move, that keeps the strike average close to spot, hence maximizing the optionality. Once the strike has fixed, the trade is long vega because increasing implied volatility moves the spot average as far as possible from the strike.

So many possible products can be created within the double average framework it is hard to generalize, but TV adjustments on double average rates are often small because the double averaging subdues the Greeks even more than the single average variations.

CHAPTER 30

Multi-Asset Options

When the payoff from an FX derivatives contract is based on more than one currency pair it is described as a **multi-asset option**. Having multiple currency pairs within an option structure adds extra dimensions and can significantly increase risk management complexity.

Multi-Asset Trading Risks

Standard Greek exposures are not sufficient for managing multi-asset risk. Single values for delta, gamma, and vega make little sense when the exposures in a given currency pair depend not just on changes in that currency pair but on *all* the currency pairs within the structure.

It is therefore vital for a trader to understand the methodology used to calculate exposures on multi-asset products within their pricing and risk management systems. If standard Greek exposures are used to risk manage multi-asset options, they certainly rely on strict assumptions about how the underlying assets move together. This can lead to big risk management shocks when the assumptions break down.

Correlations between spot log returns are key parameters within the multi-asset framework. When pricing the two-currency-pair case, for intuition it is often useful to consider how the option payoff is impacted by perfectly positively correlated spots, perfectly negatively correlated spots, and spots with zero correlation. For multi-asset options with more than two currency pairs, correlations are often viewed within a matrix. For example, the following three-asset correlation matrix shows a 25% correlation between asset 1 and asset 2:

$$\begin{bmatrix} 100\% & \mathbf{25\%} & 75\% \\ \mathbf{25\%} & 100\% & 30\% \\ 75\% & 30\% & 100\% \end{bmatrix}$$

Within risk management it is common to flex the correlation matrix and observe how the option price is impacted. However, this flexing process is often easier said than done. The correlation matrix must always be "valid," meaning *positive semi-definite* in mathematical terms. This prevents correlation matrices where, for example, assets 1 and 2 are 100% correlated, and assets 1 and 3 are 100% correlated, but assets 2 and 3 are not correlated:

$$\begin{bmatrix} 100\% & 100\% & 100\% \\ 100\% & 100\% & 0\% \\ 100\% & 0\% & 100\% \end{bmatrix}$$

There are also issues around instantaneous correlation versus terminal correlation to worry about. The best material on these issues exists in Riccardo Rebonato's book *Volatility and Correlation: The Perfect Hedger and the Fox* (John Wiley & Sons, 2nd Edition, 2004).

Unlike Equities, where there is no notion of cross-stocks, in FX there are tradable volatility surfaces in major currency pairs *and* cross currency pairs. Recalling the ATM volatility triangle framework from Chapter 16, it is therefore possible to view multi-asset risk in vega terms across all relevant currency pairs. Alternatively, cross-volatility risk can be viewed as exposure to correlation between major pairs.

Recall also from Chapter 16 that correlations are quoted between two currency pairs such that the common currency is CCY1 or CCY2 in both cases. If the market convention pair ordering has the common currency as CCY1 in one pair and CCY2 in the other pair, the negative of the correlation must be used within calculations.

Pricing models for multi-asset options are not as well-established as single-asset pricing models. Certainly there is no equivalent to the mixed volatility model. Local and stochastic correlation models have been developed, plus the notion of a correlation smile has been explored, but this is an area in which quants continue to apply their considerable brain power.

Since multi-asset pricing models are generally less sophisticated, scenario analysis becomes a relatively more important risk management tool for trading multi-asset positions. Market data is flexed in different ways and the resultant P&Ls are used to identify the major risks in the position. For example, if USD rates rise by 1% and implied volatilities all drop by 1%, what P&L is generated?

Another complicating factor within multi-asset options is that the fixes used to determine spot at maturity in different currency pairs may be sampled at different times of the day. Additional bid–offer spread should be charged in cases where this issue may arise.

Finally, traders often actively write-off risk (see Chapter 15) and use shadow barriers (see Chapter 25) to simplify multi-asset risk management.

Multi Asset Bid–Offer Spreading

Two standard approaches exist for calculating bid–offer spreads on multi-asset options. The first approach can be thought of as **confidence interval spreading**. Correlations are flexed up and down to generate a change in option value. By assessing the variability of historical correlation an appropriate correlation flex is determined. As a rough rule of thumb, in G10 pairs for medium tenors (1mth to 1yr), correlation flexes around 10% to 15% are often appropriate. This is a neat and convenient method, plus it gives a good intuitive feel for the risk in the trade. However, it does not take into account the liquidity of the currency pairs within the product and will generate too much spread in some cases and not enough in others. It must also be understood that short-dated correlations are much less stable than long-dated correlations and $\frac{\partial price}{\partial correlation}$ is generally lower for short-dated options. Therefore, correlation must be flexed more on contracts with shorter maturities.

The second approach can be thought of as **replication spreading**. Vega exposures are calculated in all major and cross currency pairs, multiplied by the ATM volatility bid–offer spread in each pair and then summed to get a total bid–offer spread. This approach is appealing because it uses real implied volatility bid–offer spreads but it will usually overestimate bid–offer spread because it does not give any discount for offsetting risk.

A combination of these approaches can also be used, with replication spreading used in major currency pairs and confidence-interval spreading applied in cross-currency pairs.

Basket Options

Basket options contain a number of currency pairs with a common currency between them. Spot moves in the basket pairs are normalized and averaged to create a *basket spot* move. At maturity, the basket spot is compared to a basket strike and a cash settlement is generated based on a basket vanilla or basket digital payoff.

The following formula can be used to calculate the basket spot. Each currency pair within the basket must be quoted such that CCY1 is the common currency. This may mean, for example, flipping AUD/USD into USD/AUD terms:

$$S_{t,basket} = \sum_{i=1}^{n} \omega_i \frac{S_{0,i}}{S_{t,i}}$$

where there are n currency pairs in the basket, $S_{t,i}$ is the spot at time t in currency pair i, and therefore $S_{0,i}$ is the inception spot in currency pair i. Weights ω_i sum to 1 and are almost always set to $\frac{1}{n}$ but the flexibility exists to offer different variations.

The process of constructing a basket is similar to constructing a financial index. The most well-known FX basket is BRIC, which contains the currencies of Brazil, Russia, India, and China.

Within this framework, the basket spot starts at 1 and therefore basket strikes are often quoted as a percentage (e.g., 100%). A basket call payoff at maturity is:

$$Payoff_{Basket\ Call} = Notional_{CommonCCY} \cdot max(S_{T,\ basket} - K_{T,\ basket}, 0)$$

It is also possible to construct an "inverted" or "self-quanto" basket by flipping the formula used to calculate the basket spot:

$$S_{t,basket} = \sum_{i=1}^{n} \omega_i \frac{S_{t,i}}{S_{0,i}}$$

And flipping the payoff at maturity:

$$Payoff_{Basket\ Call} = Notional_{CommonCCY} \cdot max(K_{T,\ basket} - S_{T,\ basket}, 0)$$

Inverted basket payoffs are often preferred by clients because they are cheaper than the standard case.

Example: 1yr EUR/GBP/AUD basket call versus USD with 100% strike. The basket has common currency USD in which the notional is specified and the cash payout at expiry is calculated. Exhibit 30.1 shows realized returns from the individual spot rates plus the basket spot. As with the Asian options seen in Chapter 29, the averaging within the basket reduces the basket spot volatility compared to the component spot volatility.

Like a regular vanilla option, the value of the basket is dependent on the basket forward (i.e., some average of the component forward drift) and the basket spot volatility. The volatility of the basket spot compared to the component spots depends on the correlations between the currency pairs in the basket. If all component spots were 100% correlated, the basket spot would be as volatile as an average of the component spot volatilities. However, as the correlations between pairs move lower than 100%, the basket volatility reduces. Consider a stylized two-pair basket where the spots move in equal and opposite directions; the basket spot would be static.

As noted in Chapter 16, higher correlation between major currency pairs implies lower cross-volatility. Basket options are long vega in the major currency pairs and long correlation between the major currency pairs, hence short vega in the cross-currency pairs.

Basket options are usually quoted with a tighter bid–offer spread than the cumulative spread resulting from vega risk in all major and cross currency pairs within the basket, since the vega risks offset.

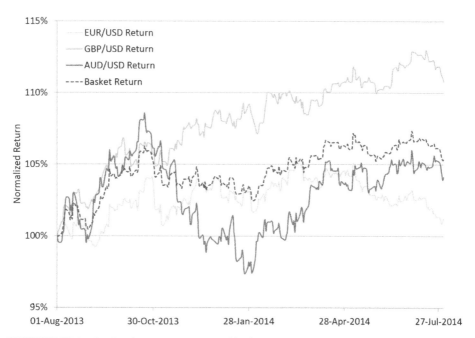

EXHIBIT 30.1 Realized component spot and basket spot returns

Baskets sound complex but in most cases the averaging effect significantly reduces their trading risks. A copula (see Chapter 12) approach can be used to take the volatility surface into account and this generally captures the majority of exposures to the volatility surface. Basket options are commonly traded as an investment product and they are attractive because the basket is usually cheaper than buying the individual vanilla options.

One variation in which the risk management becomes more challenging is a **basket digital**. If the basket spot is near the basket digital level at expiry, this can be difficult to manage because all spots within the basket impact the payoff, so it is not possible to accurately hedge the digital risk with a standard European digital contract.

Dual Digital Options

Dual digital options are combinations of two European digital options in separate currency pairs but to the same expiry date. The dual digital pays out if both digitals are in-the-money at expiry. For example, a dual digital might payout USD1m if EUR/USD is above 1.3000 *and* GBP/USD is below 1.6000 at expiry. At inception, if EUR/USD spot is at 1.3000 and GBP/USD spot is at 1.6000 (the digital levels) and there was no significant drift or discounting, each individual digital will cost around 50%. The price of the dual digital then depends on the *correlation* between EUR/USD and GBP/USD spots.

In a stylized world, if EUR/USD and GBP/USD spots move in a perfectly positively correlated manner, the dual digital will be valued at 0%. There would be no chance for the product to payout since that requires EUR/USD higher *and* GBP/USD lower. Alternatively, if EUR/USD and GBP/USD spots move in a perfectly negatively correlated manner, the dual digital will be valued at 50% because there is a half chance of EUR/USD higher (and GBP/USD lower) triggering the payout. If there is 0% correlation between the spots, the dual digital will be valued at 25%. The relationship between correlation and dual digital TV is shown in Exhibit 30.2.

Exhibit 30.2 shows how this dual digital has a significant short correlation exposure. Recall again the link between correlation and cross volatility: *correlation higher = cross-volatility lower*. This is demonstrated in Exhibit 30.3, which confirms that this dual digital option has a long exposure to the cross (i.e., EUR/GBP) volatility.

Dual digital options can be difficult to risk manage because of the implicit *leverage* within the product. Consider a dual digital product where each digital option has an individual TV of 50% and the dual digital TV is 25%. If a highly correlated spot jump occurs due to an external event in the common currency, each individual digital TV jumps to 80% and the dual digital TV jumps to 64%. This pickup in value from 25%

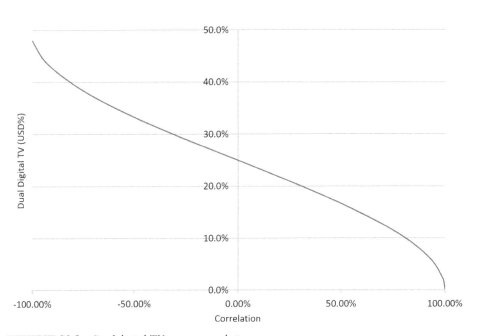

EXHIBIT 30.2 Dual digital TV versus correlation

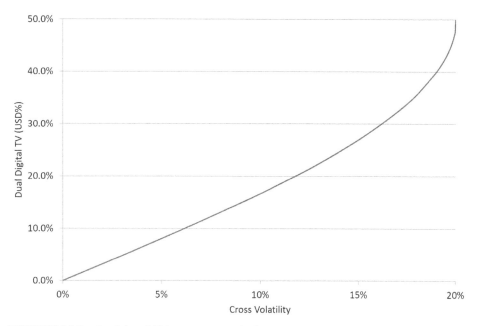

EXHIBIT 30.3   Dual digital TV versus cross volatility

to 64% is difficult to hedge using vanilla options. The risk management challenge from this issue increases for e.g. a triple digital contract.

Trading Risks

The dual digital product pays out if both digitals are in-the-money at maturity. Therefore, the main exposures within the product change depending on relatively how in-the-money each digital is.

If one digital is far in-the-money and the second is at-the-money, the primary trading risk transfers onto the at-the-money digital and the risks will be similar to a standard digital option. Intuitively, one digital is likely to be in-the-money at maturity, hence it is less important than the digital payout which is in the balance. In this case, trading risk is mainly concentrated in one currency pair rather than being dependent on how the currency pairs are moving together.

If one digital is far out-of-the-money and the second is at-the-money, the primary trading risk transfers onto the out-of-the-money digital. Intuitively, to get the payout it is most important that the spot within the out-of-the-money digital currency pair moves in-the-money. Again, trading risk is mainly concentrated in one currency pair rather than being dependent on how the currency pairs are moving together.

If both individual digitals have roughly the same value, the risk is mainly concentrated on how spots in the two currency pairs are moving together (i.e., their correlation).

Vega Risk

Going back to the EUR/USD and GBP/USD dual digital example, consider the vega exposure in EUR/USD with a variable GBP/USD digital level. If the GBP/USD digital level starts very high, with a certain payout, the EUR/USD digital will have a familiar vega profile similar to a risk reversal. Then, as the GBP/USD digital level moves lower, the EUR/USD vega profile moves lower as shown in Exhibit 30.4.

Ponder this for a moment: With the GBP/USD digital level at-the-money-spot, at 1.6000, if EUR/USD implied volatility goes lower, that increases the chance of payout and hence the option value, but why? Intuitively, simply having a less volatile EUR/USD spot does not increase the chance of a payout.

This exposure results from assumptions made within the vega calculation. All implied volatilities within the system are kept constant except for the one that is being flexed. Therefore, EUR/USD volatility does not impact the EUR/GBP cross-volatility and instead correlation is updated to maintain a valid volatility triangle. In this case, lower EUR/USD volatility results in lower EUR/USD versus GBP/USD correlation and therefore a higher price. Within this dual digital contract the main exposure is to correlation, but that correlation exposure is being represented as EUR/USD vega.

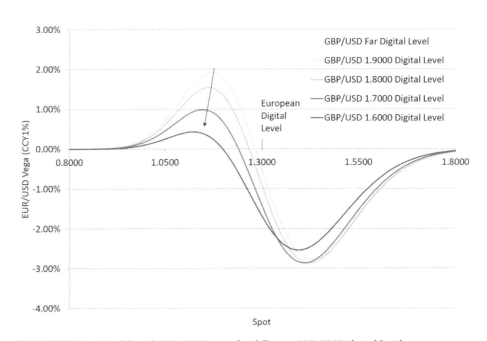

EXHIBIT 30.4 Dual digital EUR/USD vega for different GBP/USD digital levels

Correlation also impacts the GBP/USD vega exposure in the same way. Again, for an at-the-money-spot EUR/USD digital the GBP/USD vega becomes negative at current spot. This is shown in Exhibit 30.5.

These examples show why, when risk managing multi-asset options, it is vital to understand what assumptions are used to calculate Greek exposures. Within this example, the exposures calculated are:

■ Short EUR/USD vega (with all other implied volatilities held constant but correlation moving)

■ Short GBP/USD vega (with all other implied volatilities held constant but correlation moving)

■ Long EUR/GBP cross vega (with all other implied volatilities held constant but correlation moving)

But using a different calculation methodology it would be possible to view the same risk as:

■ Flat EUR/USD vega (with correlation and the other major volatility held constant but cross-volatility moving)

■ Flat GBP/USD vega (with correlation and the other major volatility held constant but cross-volatility moving)

■ Short EUR/USD versus GBP/USD correlation exposure

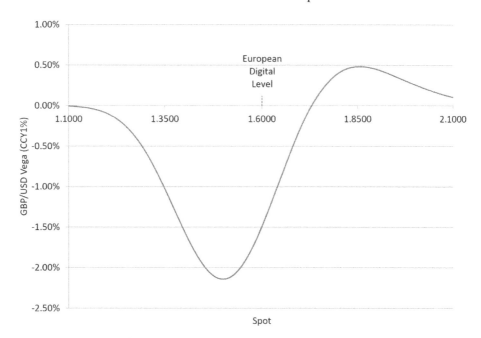

EXHIBIT 30.5 Dual digital GBP/USD vega profile

The second formulation is arguably a more intuitive way to view the risks on the trade. It also makes it easier to assess the smile risk in each major currency pair using a vega versus spot chart or vanna exposures.

Best-of and Worst-of Options

Rainbow options have payoffs generated across multiple currency pairs. At maturity, the payoff of the rainbow option is some function of ranked vanilla payoffs. In FX derivatives, best-of (pays out the maximum payoff) and worst-of (pays out the minimum payoff) options are by far the most commonly traded rainbow options. Each payoff has the same expiry date and there must be a common currency between the pairs, Payoffs can be calls or puts and the common currency can be CCY1 or CCY2 in the pair. On the expiry date, only the best- or worst-performing option is exercised and like a normal vanilla option it will only be exercised if it is in-the-money.

In symbols, for options in n currency pairs:

$$Payoff_{Best-of} = max(payoff_1, payoff_2, \ldots, payoff_n)$$

$$Payoff_{Worst-of} = min(payout_1, payout_2, \ldots, payoff_n)$$

If the common currency is CCY1 in currency pair i: $payoff_i = \frac{S_{T,i} - K}{S_{T,i}}$

If the common currency is CCY2 in currency pair i: $payoff_i = \frac{S_{T,i} - K}{K}$

where the spot at maturity in currency pair i is denoted $S_{T,i}$.

The best-of payout can be reduced where the worst-of cannot:

$$Payoff_{Best-of} = max\left(max\left(\frac{S_{T,1} - K_1}{S_{T,1}}, 0\right), max\left(\frac{S_{T,2} - K_2}{S_{T,2}}, 0\right), \ldots\right)$$

$$= max\left(\frac{S_{T,1} - K_1}{S_{T,1}}, \frac{S_{T,2} - K_2}{S_{T,2}}, \ldots, 0\right)$$

$$Payoff_{Worst-of} = min\left(max\left(\frac{S_{T,1} - K_1}{S_{T,1}}, 0\right), max\left(\frac{S_{T,2} - K_2}{S_{T,2}}, 0\right), \ldots\right)$$

The following pricing identities give intuitive bounds on best-of and worst-of option prices:

- $Price_{Worst-of} \leq Price_{Best-of}$
- $Price_{Best-of} \geq$ any single vanilla option price

- $Price_{Worst-of} \leq$ any single vanilla option price

- $Price_{Best-of} \leq$ sum of all vanilla option prices

Plus, if only two currency pairs are included within the structure:

- $Price_{Best-of} + Price_{Worst-of} =$ sum of the two vanilla option prices

Worst-of options are often a lot cheaper than the equivalent vanilla options. This makes them attractive to institutional investors (particularly hedge funds) with strong directional spot views over multiple currency pairs.

Trading Risks

At different times during the life of a best-of or worst-of option, the main exposure could be to correlation between currency pairs or it could be to implied volatility in one major currency pair. The split between the two types of risk depends on how certain it is which option (if any) will be exercised. If the vanilla options within the rainbow option have similar values, correlation risk is maximized. If one of the vanilla options has a value significantly larger (for best-of) or smaller (for worst-of) than the rest, it becomes clearer which vanilla the trade will become, correlation risk reduces, and vega risk in that currency pair increases.

When pricing a worst-of contract it can be instructive to remove each currency pair in turn and compare the new TVs. This approach shows a trader where the discount within the price is coming from and it is particularly applicable if payouts are deep in-the-money. This technique can also be used when risk managing a short worst-of position: When a particular spot is in-the-money versus the strike, it can often be moved deep in-the-money at very little cost because it has a low probability of being the lowest payout. Moving the strike such that spot is deep in-the-money effectively removes that pair from the worst-of and hence reduces potential future correlation risk.

In general, it is important not to over-hedge best-of and worst-of options. The dynamics of these products mean that their risk profiles change dramatically and keep changing over their life. Initial hedges will almost certainly need to be unwound or rebalanced.

Vega Risk

Example 1: Best-of EUR put/USD call and GBP put/USD call option. In this example, the major pairs are EUR/USD and GBP/USD and the cross-pair is EUR/GBP. This option is long vega in the major pairs since option buyers always like increasing volatility plus the best-of has more value if the two major spots move in opposite directions. Therefore the best-of is long vega in the cross-pair since short correlation exposure implies long cross-vega.

Example 2: Worst-of EUR put/USD call and GBP put/USD call option. This option is long vega in the major pairs since, again, option buyers like increasing volatility. However, this time the worst-of has more value if the two major spots move in the same direction. Therefore the worst-of is short vega in the cross-pair since long correlation implies short cross-vega.

As in the dual digital case, care must be taken to understand the methodology used to calculate vega: What is held constant and what moves within the calculation?

Delta Risk

Delta exposures on best-of and worst-of options need to be treated with caution. The calculation often assumes that each major currency pair moves in isolation. For example, for a worst-of in EUR/USD and AUD/USD, the AUD/USD delta can be calculated assuming AUD/USD moves by itself, EUR/USD does not move, and hence EUR/AUD takes all the strain. This has little chance of being how the spots actually move and hence single-delta numbers have little chance of being correct for risk management purposes.

In practice, a move in one currency pair impacts the delta in other currency pairs. In this example, as EUR/USD moves, the AUD/USD delta will change. Delta exposures in best-of and worst-of options are multidimensional and should therefore be viewed as such.

Payout Direction Risk

One of the key aspects of best-of and worst-of options is the different risks that occur if the option pays out in the same call/put direction on the common currency or it does not.

Consider a simplified two-pair case where the payout on the common currency is the same in both pairs (i.e., EUR put/*USD call* and AUD put/*USD call*). Exhibit 30.6 shows the TV versus correlation profiles; higher correlation leads to a higher worst-of price and a lower best-of price.

Exhibit 30.7 shows the relationship between cross-volatility and TV. The linear relationship implies zero second-order $\frac{\partial price}{\partial crossvol}$ (cross-volga) exposure within this option.

Now consider a simplified two-pair case where the payoff direction on the common currency is different (e.g., EUR put/*USD call* and AUD call/USD *put*). The TV versus correlation relationship is similar to the same payoff direction case as shown in Exhibit 30.8. Again, higher correlation implies a higher worst-of price and a lower best-of price.

Exhibit 30.9 shows the relationship between cross-volatility and TV when the payoff direction on the common currency is different. The relationship is different from the same payoff direction case; it is *no longer linear*, implying a second derivative $\frac{\partial price}{\partial crossvol}$ (i.e., cross-volga) exposure. This leads to increased risk

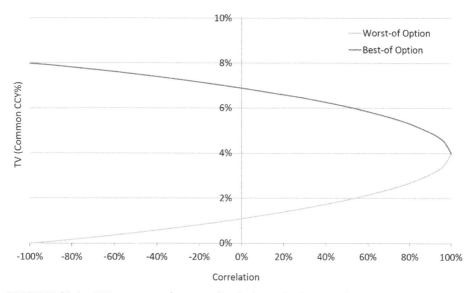

EXHIBIT 30.6 TV versus correlation profiles for best-of and worst-of options: Same payoff direction on common currency

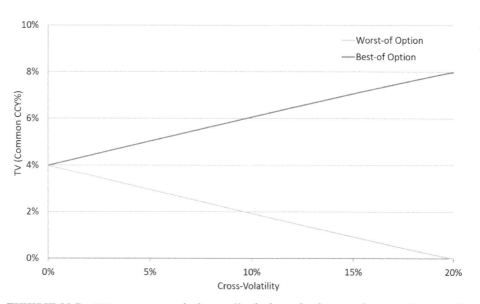

EXHIBIT 30.7 TV versus cross-volatility profiles for best-of and worst-of options: Same payoff direction on common currency

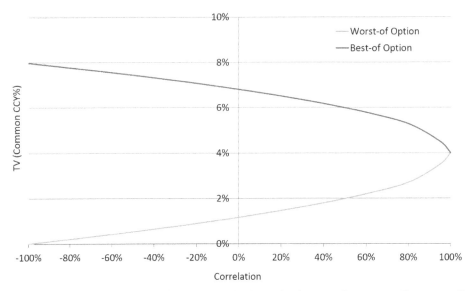

EXHIBIT 30.8 TV versus correlation profiles for best-of and worst-of options: Different payoff direction on common currency

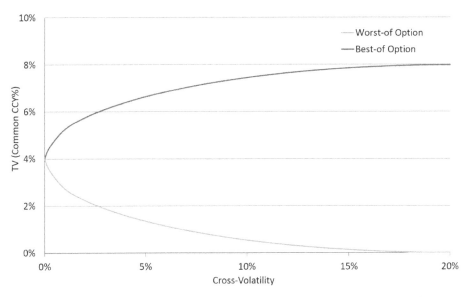

EXHIBIT 30.9 TV versus cross-volatility profiles for best-of and worst-of options: Different payoff direction on common currency

management challenges plus the different payoff directions on the common currency usually cause the option to have a low valuation and hence the trade has increased leverage that will be difficult to hedge using vanilla options.

In general, this cross-volga exposure causes worst-of options with different payoff direction on the common currency to trade more over TV than trades with the same payoff direction on the common currency. If no sophisticated stochastic correlation pricing models are available to value the cross-volga exposure, it can be estimated using a simple method that is analogous to the old-school "alpha" method for pricing double-no-touch options: Flex the cross-volatility up and down a fixed amount and find the average TV to put an approximate value on the second-order exposure.

Switching Hedge

Finally, it is interesting to consider a "switching hedge" strategy for best-of or worst-of options. For best-of options, buy the most expensive single vanilla initially and switch it into another currency pair when the most expensive vanilla changes (costing money at each switch). At expiry, this strategy will have the best vanilla payoff as required.

For worst-of options, buy the least expensive single vanilla initially and switch it into another currency pair when the least expensive vanilla changes (earning money at each switch). At expiry, this strategy will have the worst vanilla payoff as required.

These strategies give intuition as to why worst-of options are cheap and best-of options are expensive. It also shows why the risks are more difficult to manage when vanilla values are similar because more switches would be required within the switching hedge.

■ Quanto Options

Within quanto options, the option payoff is denominated in a third currency, rather than CCY1 or CCY2 within the currency pair. Therefore, these products are sometimes called **third currency quanto** options to distinguish them from self-quanto options (see Chapter 27).

Example: 1yr EUR/USD EUR call/USD put 1.3500 option that pays out at maturity in GBP. To calculate the payoff, a GBP% payoff must be calculated. This is typically achieved by calculating, for example,

$$Notional_{GBP} \cdot max \left(\frac{S_T - K}{QF}, 0 \right)$$

where QF is called a quanto-factor and is usually equal to the strike (K).

Quanto options are most often used as investment products where clients require their payout in a specific currency. From a risk management perspective, third-currency quanto options are slightly more complex than regular vanillas due to the third-currency element.

Within a Black-Scholes framework, quanto options are priced by adjusting the drift and applying discounting in the quanto currency. Specifically, the standard stochastic differential equation:

$$\frac{dS_t}{S_t} = (rCCY2 - rCCY1)dt + \sigma dW_t$$

becomes:

$$\frac{dS_t}{S_t} = (rCCY2 - rCCY1 - \rho.\sigma_1.\sigma_2)dt + \sigma_1 dW_t$$

where σ_1 is the volatility of CCY1/CCY2, σ_2 is the volatility of CCY3/CCY2, and ρ is the correlation between CCY1/CCY2 and CCY3/CCY2. The quanto forward therefore shifts such that:

$$F_{quanto} = F.e^{-\rho.\sigma_1.\sigma_2}$$

Therefore, when pricing the example EUR/USD quanto into GBP call option:

- If the correlation is zero or GBP/USD has zero volatility, the only pricing difference between the quanto option and the regular European option will come from the quanto currency discounting.

- If EUR/USD and GBP/USD are positively correlated, the quanto forward moves relatively lower and the price of a quanto call option is lower in the quanto currency (GBP) than the regular European vanilla call option is in USD.

- If EUR/USD and GBP/USD are negatively correlated, the quanto forward moves relatively higher and the price of the quanto call option is higher in the quanto currency (GBP) than the regular European vanilla call option is in USD.

It is possible for any option payoff to be quantoed into a third currency. The forward adjustment and discounting are the main adjustments within the pricing, but in currency pairs with significant skew or wings the volatility surface should also be taken into account using, for example, a quanto local volatility model. Once quanto options are booked into the trading position, they rarely cause any significant pricing or risk management issues unless their notionals are very large. The correlation risk on quanto options is small relative to the risks on dual digital or worst-of options.

CHAPTER 31

Miscellaneous Options

Exotic FX derivative option types not yet examined include "volatility" products like volatility swaps, variance swaps, and forward volatility agreements, plus forward start options, and compound options.

Volatility and Variance Swaps

In FX derivatives:

- A **volatility (vol) swap** is a forward contract on the realized volatility of spot over an agreed period.

- A **variance (var) swap** is a forward contract on the realized variance of spot over an agreed period.

Most commonly, daily spot fixings are used to determine realized volatility and variance. Mathematically, for daily spot fixings, realized variance (V) is calculated using this formula:

$$V = \frac{252}{N} \times \sum_{i=1}^{N} a_i^{\,2}$$

where a_i are spot log returns, that is, $a_i = \ln\left(\frac{S_i}{S_{i-1}}\right)$, S_i is spot fixing number i, and in total there are N log returns.

The mean return is usually not included in the realized variance formula and usually this will not significantly impact the result. However, clients sometimes request it and it is important to check whether it is required. If the mean return is added, the calculation becomes:

$$V = \frac{252}{N} \times \sum_{i=1}^{N}(a_i^2 - \bar{a})$$

where $\bar{a}$ is the mean of the log returns.

In a vol swap, the strike is quoted in volatility terms and the notional is effectively a vega amount:

$$Payoff_{volswap} = Notional_{vol} \cdot (\sqrt{V} - K_{vol})$$

In a var swap, the strike is quoted in volatility-squared terms and the notional is a cash amount per volatility point squared:

$$Payoff_{varswap} = Notional_{var} \cdot (V - K_{vol}^2)$$

The variance notional is usually linked to vega with this formula:

$$Notional_{var} = \frac{Notional_{vol}}{2.K_{vol}}$$

This formula ensures that if realized volatility is 1 percent away from the volatility strike at maturity, the variance swap payoff is approximately equal to the volatility swap payoff. When volatility swaps and variance swaps are quoted for institutional clients, a two-way volatility or variance strike is quoted for zero upfront payment. When traders talk about the vol swap or var swap "price", this is what they mean.

The classic quantitative research document on vol swaps and var swaps is a Goldman Sachs paper by Demeterfi, Derman, Kamal, and Zou from 1999 entitled "*More Than You Ever Wanted to Know about Volatility Swaps.*" The document highlights how variance swaps are theoretically the more natural product because, in a Black-Scholes world (specifically, no spot jumps plus deterministic interest rates), the variance swap payoff can be perfectly replicated by a contract that pays out a **log contract** at expiry, which in turn can be replicated using a portfolio of vanilla options to the same expiry date.

Volatility swap and variance swap payoffs are shown in Exhibit 31.1 for USD10k vega and a 12% strike. The volatility swap payoff is linear in realized volatility, as expected, while the variance swap payoff is convex in realized volatility, i.e., above the volatility strike the variance swap gains more than the volatility swap, whereas below the volatility strike the variance swap loses less than the volatility swap. Therefore, in a given currency pair and tenor, the rate quoted on the variance swap

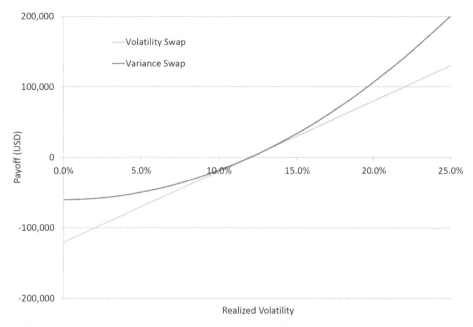

EXHIBIT 31.1   Volatility swap and variance swap payoffs

will be higher than the equivalent rate quoted on the volatility swap. Tracking the vol swap versus var swap strike difference can be used to price volatility swaps, or this "convexity adjustment" can be valued by modeling volatility itself.

Vol swaps and var swaps are attractive products for clients because they give a pure payoff based on realized volatility or variance. As has been observed, ATM vanilla options do not give pure exposures because as spot moves, forwards move, or time passes their exposures change.

Variance swaps are a popular product in the equity derivatives market but they are relatively less popular in FX. In FX, both volatility and variance swaps are traded in the interbank broker market but in volumes which are a fraction of vanilla option volumes.

Volatility Swap Greeks

In terms of risk management, the important thing about the volatility swap is that throughout its life, as fixings occur, more is fixed and less is still to be determined. This makes the payoff less sensitive to changes in market data (like Asian options), and hence exposures generally reduce over time.

Prior to any fixings, as spot moves, the value of the vol swap remains constant. This is shown in Exhibit 31.2.

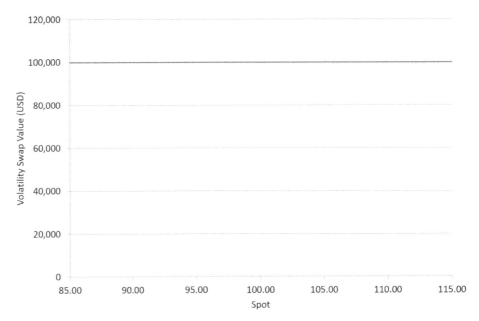

EXHIBIT 31.2   Volatility swap value prior to any fixings

After spot fixes, as spot then moves away from each fixing, either higher or lower, realized volatility increases and hence the volatility swap value increases as the log return increases. This is shown in Exhibit 31.3.

Note that this payoff is similar to being long an overnight ATM option; value rises the further spot moves from the strike.

The value profile in Exhibit 31.3 implies a delta position that starts at zero at the fixing, then moves longer with spot higher and shorter with spot lower. The delta profile is shown in Exhibit 31.4.

Put another way, the product is long gamma with the peak gamma at the previous fixing as shown in Exhibit 31.5.

The shape of the gamma profile remains approximately unchanged at each fixing except that it moves such that the peak gamma is at the previous fixing.

It is important to dwell for a moment on how these exposures work in practice. As each fixing occurs, the exposures reset. This causes a delta jump at each fixing that will be particularly large if spot is far from the previous fixing. These delta jumps make the gamma exposure harder to trade than the gamma on a standard vanilla option. Plus, at each fixing, gamma jumps back to the peak value.

Before any fixings have been made, the vega of a vol swap is a positive constant across all spot values. When the first fixing occurs, the trade has a reference point and the vega stays unchanged at the fixing rate but moves lower in the wings.

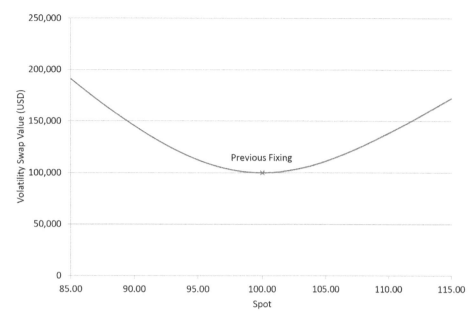

EXHIBIT 31.3   Volatility swap value after fixing

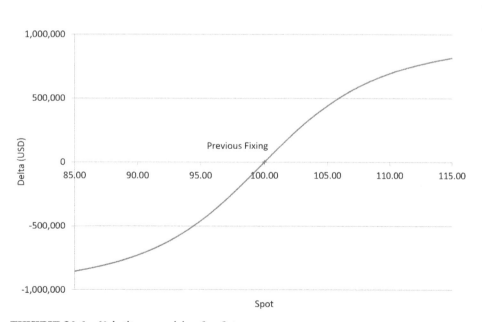

EXHIBIT 31.4   Volatility swap delta after fixing

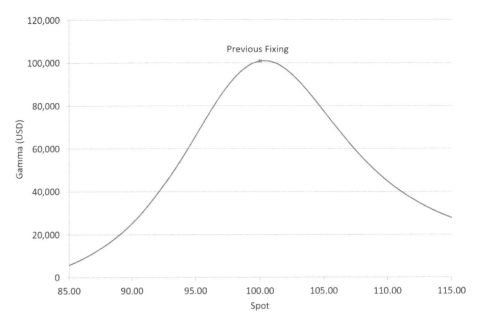

EXHIBIT 31.5   Volatility swap gamma after fixing

Volatility swaps contain a type of optionality similar to an overnight ATM straddle: If spot moves either higher or lower from the previous fixing, realized volatility increases. In the wings, further away from this "optionality," vega reduces.

The peak vega reduces at a linear rate over time as more fixings occur. Note that the vega profile shown in Exhibit 31.6 is symmetric because all fixings are set to 100.00.

Vol swap vega is also impacted by the level of implied volatility: At higher implied volatility, the distribution widens and vega is higher in the wings after each fixing. At lower implied volatility, the distribution tightens and vega is lower in the wings after each fixing. This is shown in Exhibit 31.7.

Again, it is important to understand how vega evolves in practice. When the volatility swap fixes, vega resets to the peak of the profile, but this vega peak is at a lower level than the peak at the previous fixing. This is one reason why volatility swaps are popular with clients; vega does not permanently reduce as spot moves away from a fixed strike. In a vol swap, it is as if the "strike" keeps resetting back to the ATM at each fixing.

Volatility swaps have no tradable vanna or volga exposures since the position resets the vega position at each fixing. Plus volatility swaps have minimal interest rate exposures, apart from discounting and some minor second-order effects.

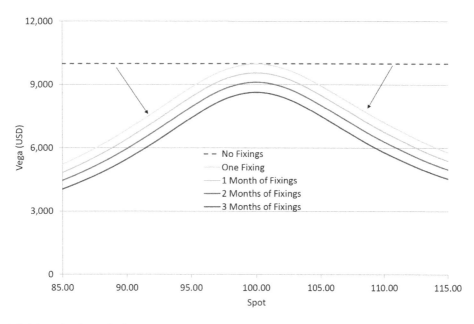

EXHIBIT 31.6   Volatility swap vega over time

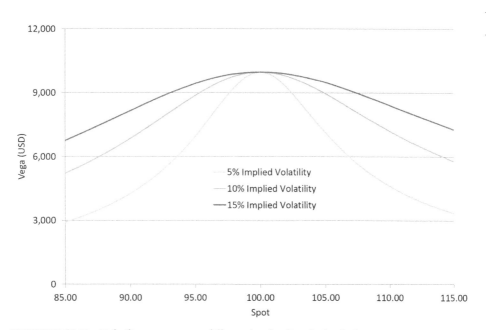

EXHIBIT 31.7   Volatility swap vega at different levels of implied volatility

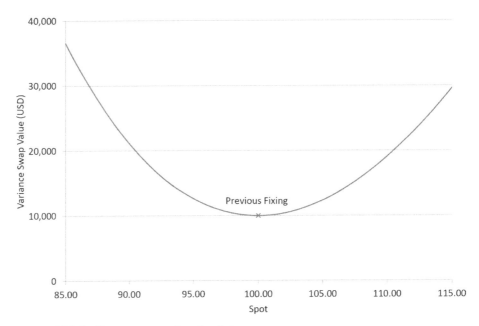

EXHIBIT 31.8 Variance swap value after fixing

Variance Swap Greeks

As with volatility swaps, variance swap value is constant and static over all spot values prior to any fixings occurring. Then, as spot moves away from each fixing, realized variance increases and hence variance swap value increases. This is shown in Exhibit 31.8.

Within a variance swap, delta moves linearly with spot as shown in Exhibit 31.9. This implies a constant gamma exposure that also stays approximately constant as time passes. These are important results:

- Variance swaps can be replicated with a so called "log contract".

- Variance swaps have constant gamma over all spots.

- The log contract generates a constant gamma exposure over all spots.

In a similar way, vega on a variance swap is constant over all spots and decays away regularly over time as fixings occur. This is shown in Exhibit 31.10.

The vega on a variance swap is linear in implied volatility, which implies a constant long volga exposure over all spots. This is shown in Exhibit 31.11.

Constant gamma and vega profiles over spot are sometimes called "strikeless gamma" or "strikeless vega."

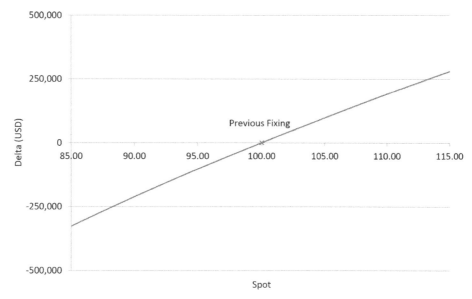

EXHIBIT 31.9   Variance swap delta after fixing

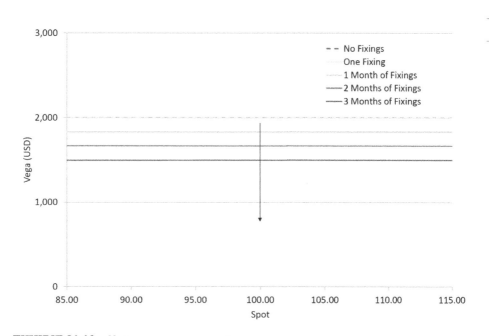

EXHIBIT 31.10   Variance swap vega over time

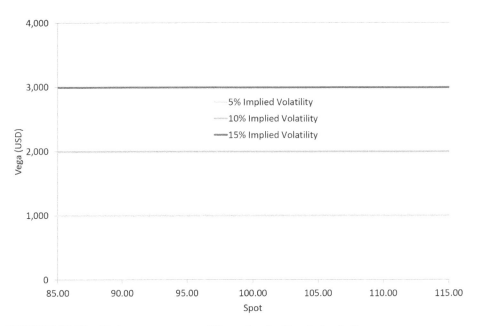

EXHIBIT 31.11 Variance swap vega at different levels of implied volatility

Volatility Swap Pricing

In a theoretical Black-Scholes world, the volatility swap price is almost exactly equivalent to the ATM volatility to the same tenor. However, the volatility swap rate is additionally impacted by the number of fixings within the calculation. The standard multiplier used within interbank trades is 252, as quoted in the formulas at the start of the chapter. The holiday calendar most often used for vol swaps is WMR, which has fewer holiday days than the USD and therefore more fixings so it is common to see the quoted rate pulled lower by this effect.

Another important point to be aware of when quoting volatility swaps and variance swaps is the *payout currency*. The quoted volatility strikes for CCY1 versus CCY2 payouts can be quite different so it is important to confirm which payout currency the client requires. Particularly large valuation differences occur when there is a large skew in the volatility surface. For example, in a currency pair with a large downside risk reversal, higher volatility on downside strikes implies spot has an increased chance of moving further to the downside. With spot lower, CCY2 becomes relatively more valuable than CCY1, so a volatility or variance swap with CCY2 payout will be worth more than the equivalent contract with CCY1 payout.

There is a big difference between pricing vol swaps in liquid G10 currency pairs versus pricing them in managed emerging market currency pairs. In liquid

G10 currency pairs, pricing models can be used to generate reference points: Local volatility gives an approximate upper bound for the quoted vol strike and stochastic volatility gives an approximate lower bound for the quoted vol strike. This counterintuitive result occurs because both models (if well-calibrated) have the same variance and since local volatility has a lower vol-of-vol the expectation of the volatility will be higher. A well-calibrated mixed vol model often gives a good indication for short-dated volatility swaps while at longer tenors the effect of stochastic interest rates should additionally be quantified. In practice, traders often track the differential between their models and the interbank broker market prices over time and quote reflecting this adjustment.

In managed emerging market currency pairs it is important to remember that the volatility swap pays out on the realized *spot volatility*, not the realized forward volatility, so forward volatility must be stripped out of the ATM volatility when pricing a vol swap. This effect can be assessed by calculating historic realized spot volatility using daily fixings and comparing it to the ATM volatility.

It is also important to understand the spot dynamic in the currency pair. This allows a trader to assess the expected spot distribution: Does the central bank intervene in the spot market? Is the fixing an average or a point-in-time fix? How will this impact realized volatility? What else might cause spot to jump?

Volatility swaps and variance swaps need special attention in emerging market currency pairs because the vega stays with spot as it moves. If the emerging market exchange rate jumps and implied volatility spikes, this can cause far larger P&L swings for these products than vanilla options with equivalent vega.

In practice, wing vanilla options are often used to hedge a volatility swap vega profile. Specifically, 10 delta strangles usually hedge vega over a wide enough spot range. However, over time this hedge must be rebalanced as gamma exposure increases if spot moves close to one of the hedge strikes. Plus, if spot jumps a long way through the strikes, the hedge will no longer work.

Variance Swap Pricing

Variance swaps can be perfectly replicated with vanillas to the variance swap expiry date. Specifically, the replication involves transacting a strip of vanilla options that pays out a *log contract* at maturity. The log contract replication sets up vanilla notionals such that they are inversely proportional to the strike squared. Example notionals are shown in Exhibit 31.12.

By trading strikes with these wide gaps between them (10 figures), the accuracy of the replication reduces toward expiry. A perfect replication providing constant gamma exposure over all spots would require vanilla options to be traded at all possible strikes between zero and infinity. (No, that isn't actually possible.)

EXHIBIT 31.12	Log Contract Vanilla Replication	
Strike (K)	Strike^2	Notional (CCY1)
60.00	3,600	2,777,778
70.00	4,900	2,040,816
80.00	6,400	1,562,500
90.00	8,100	1,234,568
100.00	10,000	1,000,000
110.00	12,100	826,446
120.00	14,400	694,444
130.00	16,900	591,716
140.00	19,600	510,204

From a pricing point of view, since the replication involves buying very low delta strikes, it is vital to consider whether the wings of the volatility smile match the market for very low delta options, particularly to the downside since this is where the notionals rise within the replication. At this point, theory meets reality with a bump. The replication method assumes large amounts of low-premium wing options can be traded at midmarket. As mentioned in Chapter 15, in practice, traders are reluctant to sell large amounts of low-premium options due to the leverage in the product. Therefore, the market offer for these strikes is usually higher than the model offer, which in turn causes the market price for variance swaps to be above the theoretical model value.

Transacting a strip of vanilla options will approximately hedge the vega profile from a variance swap, although if spot jumps a long way, the hedge will no longer work. Variance swaps are more dangerous than volatility swaps in this regard because the payoff is based on volatility squared. Therefore, no practically attainable vanilla hedge will provide protection from a short variance swap contract if spot moves far enough. For this reason restrictions are sometimes added to the variance swap contract, e.g., knock-out barriers or maximum daily moves. These considerations are particularly applicable in pegged currency pairs where an exchange rate de-pegging could generate big P&Ls on variance swap contracts.

Forward Volatility Agreements

Forward volatility agreements (FVAs) are another commonly traded volatility product. They are quoted as a forward implied volatility between two expiry dates. At the first expiry date, a spot fixing is taken from an agreed source and the option then becomes an ATM with a fixed strike (calculated from the spot fix) to the final expiry date. Most commonly the dates are specified in terms of market tenors.

EXHIBIT 31.13 FVA dates structure

For example, Exhibit 31.13 shows a "three-month-in-six-month" FVA that turns into a 3mth ATM in six months' time.

Forward vol agreements are closely linked to forward implied volatility, a variance-based calculation given in Chapter 11:

$$\sigma_{12} = \sqrt{\frac{\sigma_2^2 \cdot t_2 - \sigma_1^2 \cdot t_1}{t_2 - t_1}}$$

where σ_{12} is the forward ATM implied volatility between the first and second expiry dates, σ_1 is the ATM implied volatility to the first expiry date at time t_1, and σ_2 is the ATM implied volatility to the second expiry date at time t_2.

The vega exposure from an FVA is flat over different spots until the contract fixes, at which point it becomes a standard ATM vanilla to the final expiry date. This is shown in Exhibit 31.14.

An important point is that the vega exposure is to *forward* ATM implied volatility and there are therefore vega exposures to *both* expiry dates within the contract. For a long FVA position, the vega exposure will be short to the first expiry date and long to the final expiry date. Looking at the forward implied volatility calculation:

■ Lower ATM volatility at the first expiry date (σ_1) increases the forward implied volatility.

■ Higher ATM volatility at the second expiry date (σ_2) increases the forward implied volatility.

Usually, the ATM curve rises at longer tenors due to interest rate volatility but there is no exposure to interest rates (except discounting) on an FVA until it fixes, only forward implied vol exposure. Therefore, on long-dated FVAs, interest rate volatility should be stripped out of the pricing. Put another way, an FVA volatility curve (if such a thing existed) should be much flatter than the equivalent ATM curve.

This overlaps with trader intuition about how attractive an FVA contract is to buy or sell. If the ATM curve is upward sloping, the forward implied volatility will be high and the FVA contract will often be more attractive to sell.

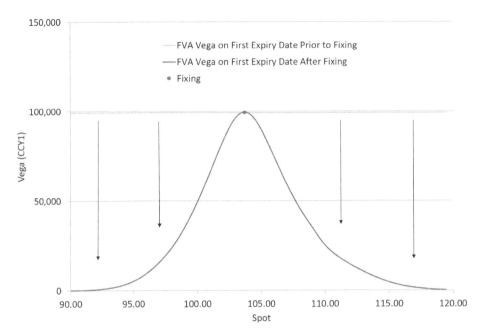

EXHIBIT 31.14   FVA vega profile change at first fixing

The pricing of an FVA depends mainly on the forward implied volatility within the volatility surface. Therefore, it is preferable that within the pricing model used, volatility itself is random. Local volatility is therefore not a good model choice because (local) volatility is deterministic within the model.

Finally, consider possible vanilla hedges for an FVA. If only the net vega position to the final expiry date is hedged, there will be a significant exposure to the shape of the ATM curve left unhedged. A better hedge for a long FVA would be to buy some 10 delta strangles to the first expiry date and sell some 25 delta strangles to the final expiry date. Notionals should be configured such that the hedge gives matching forward volatility exposures and outright volatility exposure. Although again, over time, the hedge accuracy will reduce and may need to be rebalanced.

Forward Start Options

Forward start options (also called *cliquets*) are like FVAs in that their structure relies on two expiry dates in the future. Again, these dates can be specified in terms of actual dates or market tenors. A diagram of the dates is shown in Exhibit 31.15.

At the first expiry date, rather than settling into an ATM like an FVA, the forward start option can settle into a wider range of options to the final expiry date. The options are most commonly European vanillas but they can also be European digital, European barrier, or American barrier options. Strikes and/or barriers on these

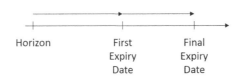

EXHIBIT 31.15 Forward start option dates structure

options are set with reference to a spot fixing taken on the first expiry date. The strike or barrier levels can generated in one of two ways:

1. Strike or barrier level = spot fix on first expiry date + constant
2. Strike or barrier level = spot fix on first expiry date × constant

Example: EUR/USD forward start EUR Put/USD Call vanilla from January 23, 2015, into June 23, 2015, with strike set at the ECB fixing × 95%.

The forward start vega exposure is similar to the FVA in that it remains flat until the moment spot fixes on the first expiry date, at which point the option becomes a standard FX derivatives product (e.g., a vanilla option or a barrier option). However, note that the vega may not be at the peak when it fixes. In the case of the EUR/USD forward start example, as spot fixes, the vega position jumps from being flat to having a large vanna/skew exposure from the long downside vanilla as shown in Exhibit 31.16.

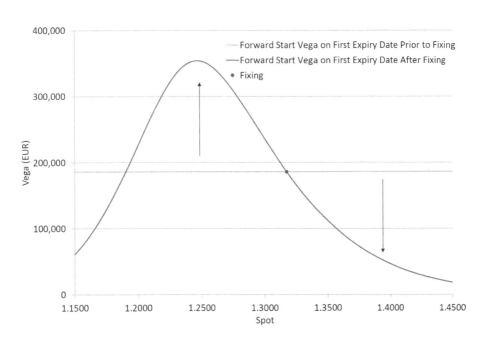

EXHIBIT 31.16 Forward start vega profile

Like an FVA, there are vega exposures to both the first expiry date and the final expiry date but the volatility smile now plays a more important role in the pricing. In the EUR/USD forward start example, pricing will depend on the future expectation of implied volatility for a strike equal to spot × 95%.

Therefore, as well as the full term structure of ATM volatility and interest rates, the forward smile is a key consideration. Different pricing models calibrated to the same vanilla surface produce very different forward smile dynamics. Viewing the forward smile generated by the model enables an opinion on the forward start option price.

■ Compound Options

The compound option product is an *option on an option*. Therefore compound options have two expiry dates: a decision date and a final expiry date. These dates can be specified in terms of actual dates or market tenors. A diagram of these dates is shown in Exhibit 31.17.

At the first expiry date (sometimes called the decision date), the owner of the compound option has either the right to buy or the right to sell a specific vanilla option to the final expiry date at a pre-agreed price (sometimes called the compound strike).

Compounds are either a call (the right to buy) or a put (the right to sell) the vanilla option to the final expiry date. In turn, the underlying vanilla option can be either a call or a put. Compound options are therefore described in terms of their call and put directions:

- *Call on a call*: the right to buy a vanilla CCY1 call option

- *Call on a put*: the right to buy a vanilla CCY1 put option

- *Put on a call*: the right to sell a vanilla CCY1 call option

- *Put on a put*: the right to sell a vanilla CCY1 put option

Clients trade compound options because they lock in the price of the vanilla while deferring the decision to trade. This is appropriate if the underlying vanilla option is a hedge for an uncertain cash flow. Compounds are generally far cheaper than the

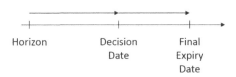

EXHIBIT 31.17 Compound option dates structure

equivalent outright vanilla option, although the premium for the underlying vanilla option also must be paid at the decision date.

Example: USD/JPY 3mth compound call option on a 3mth 100.00 strike USD Put/JPY Call option at 0.30 USD%. Therefore, in three months the owner of the compound option decides whether to exercise the compound optionality. Exercising the compound involves paying 0.30 USD% for the 3mth option to the final expiry date. The compound should be exercised if the market price of the vanilla to the final expiry date is higher than 0.30 USD%, otherwise the compound should be expired.

Note that the decision on whether to exercise or expire the compound is based on spot, interest rates, and implied volatility market data for the final expiry date. The consequence of this is that the exercise point *moves in spot space*.

Compound owners have long vega exposures to both the decision date and the final expiry date because there is optionality at both dates. The peak vega on the decision date is around the spot level at which the option will either be expired or exercised—the center of the optionality. The vega to the final expiry date will have its peak at the strike as usual but that exposure will be weighted by the probability of the compound being exercised on the decision date.

Exhibit 31.18 shows the vega profiles from the above USD/JPY compound option.

The relative vega exposures between the two dates depend on the probability of compound exercise. For example, if the compound strike on a compound call is 0%,

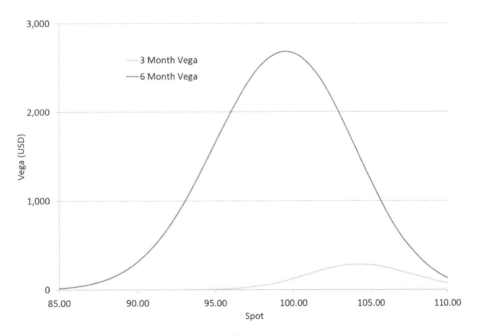

EXHIBIT 31.18   Compound option vega profile

the compound should always be exercised (bought at zero). The vega profile will therefore simply be that of a vanilla to the final expiry date. As the premium strike rises, the total price of the compound plus the final vanilla must always be more expensive than the vanilla option to the final expiry date because the compound contains additional optionality.

Compound option pricing depends on the forward volatility smile and forward interest rates. Like forward start options, as many of these elements as possible should be taken into account when pricing.

Finally, a more general version of a compound is an **option on strategy**, which is the right to buy or the right to sell a portfolio of (usually) vanilla options.

These are the books that I get the most from, in terms of either entertainment or information, ordered in increasing quantitative content.

Reminiscences of a Stock Operator by Edwin Lefevre (John Wiley & Sons, Abridged Edition, 2004)

A classic story about the ups and downs of trading written in the early twentieth century. Amazingly, most of the wisdom still holds true today. There's a hardcover version available that features lovely period artwork.

Where Are the Customer's Yachts? by Fred Schwed Jr. (John Wiley & Sons, 1ˢᵗ Edition, 2006)

A cynical description of how Wall Street operates based around the 1929 Crash. When so much material written and presented about finance and financial markets is completely humorless, this is a cracking read. The parts on options are particularly interesting, written as they are before the development of the Black-Scholes model. It is fascinating to consider how the derivatives market developed even without a consistent way of pricing volatility.

Volatility Trading by Euan Sinclair (John Wiley & Sons, 2008)

Explains how buyside (i.e., hedge funds) trade volatility with a nice balance of practical and technical material. The approach is centered on picking individual trades, managing them through to maturity, and tracking their P&L rather than risk managing a portfolio of options. For a derivatives trader at a bank it is interesting to see how hedge funds assess value and manage their risk; many of the techniques are applicable to market-makers, too.

Dynamic Hedging by Nassim Taleb (John Wiley & Sons, 1st Edition, 1996)

A stunning book: years ahead of its time when it was published. It successfully combines technical details with the experience and thrill of trading. Much of the analysis style used in this book comes directly from this material. It can be hard going for new joiners, but once you are familiar with derivatives the book is packed full of wisdom and verve.

Paul Wilmott on Quantitative Finance by Paul Wilmott (John Wiley & Sons, 2nd Edition, 2006)

A comprehensive introduction to quantitative finance from one of the key figures in the industry. Covers a massive range of topics from a quantitative perspective but without losing sight of the real-world application.

Options, Futures, and Other Derivatives by John C. Hull (Prentice Hall, 6th Edition, 2005)

A favorite for students and junior traders. This is a good book for learning the basics of financial products across all asset classes. Written with clarity, good worked examples, and nicely pitched mathematical content. Plus it is often updated to cover new financial products.

The Complete Guide to Option Pricing Formulas by Espen Gaarder Haug (McGraw-Hill Professional, 2nd Edition, 2007)

Does what it says on the cover: a book containing options formulas covering a massive variety of payoffs. A fantastic achievement that every quant-centric trader will have on their desk as a reference.

Financial Calculus by Martin Baxter and Andrew Rennie (Cambridge University Press, 1st Edition, 1996)

A gem of a book: If you want to understand the mathematical framework underpinning Black-Scholes, this is the place to start. Leads you by the hand through Itō Calculus, Martingales, and finally Black-Scholes.

The Volatility Surface: A Practitioner's Guide by Jim Gatheral (John Wiley & Sons, 1st Edition, 2006)

An ideal book for understanding how the volatility surface is modeled in practice. Written by a quant whose volatility smile models have been adopted throughout the industry. Probably more useful for quants than traders, but given the complexity of the material it is still accessible.

This book is accompanied by a companion website at www.wiley.com/go /FXtraderschool (wiley15).

Readers will find the following completed practicals, which correspond to the practicals in this book:

- Practical A: Building a Trading Simulator in Excel
- Practical B: Building a Numerical Integration Option Pricer in Excel
- Practical C: Building a Black-Scholes Option Pricer in Excel
- Practical D: Generating Tenor Dates in Excel
- Practical E: Constructing an ATM Curve in Excel
- Practical F: Constructing a Volatility Smile in Excel
- Practical G: Generating a Probability Density Function from Option Prices in Excel
- Practical H: Building a Monte Carlo Option Pricer in Excel

Asian options, 396, 527–538
    average rate options, 527–535
    average strike options, 535–537
    double average rate options,
      537–538
Ask, *see* Offer(s)
ATM, *see* At-the-money
ATM calendar spreads:
    price making, 132
    trading exposures, 132
    vanilla, 132
ATM curve, 103–106
    construction of, 171–191
      adding weights, 199–204
      core ATM curve, 172–179
      events and holidays, 188–189
      in Excel, 193–204
      and FX derivatives market
       pricing, 182–184
      implied volatility patterns over a
       week, 182
      intraday variance patterns, 187
      New York cut vs. Tokyo cut
       pricing, 185–187
      overnight ATM on a Friday,
       184–185
      pricing same-day options,
       190–191
      for short-dates, 180–191
      using a model, 178–179,
       197–199
      using interpolation, 172–178,
       193–197
      variance, 171–172
      weekday variance patterns,
       189–190
    in market instrument analysis,
      344–346
    seasonality, 346
    slope, 354–356
    theta and roll down, 271, 272
    weighted changes in, 154
ATM gamma, 272
ATM position:
    defined, 138
    trading, 152–155
ATM volatility and correlation
      framework, 313–321
    ATM volatility triangles, 313–319
    cross-currency positions
      management, 321
    dephased vega, 319–320
ATM volatility triangles, 313–319
At-the-money (ATM). *See also* ATM
      curve
    forward implied volatility, 171–172
    implied volatilities of, 103–105
    market conventions, 118–120
    vega exposures, 209–211
    and volatility smile, 205
    volatility spreads, 113–114
    zero-delta straddles, 122
Average rate options, 396, 527–535
Average strike options, 535–537
Axe, 468

B

Bank trading desks, 39–40. *See also*
      Interbank broker market
    client types, 40–41
    structure, 41–44
      internal trading, 43–44
      sales desks, 42–43
      support functions, 43
Barrier delta gap (touch options),
      429–430

One-touch (OT) options, (*Continued*)
variations, 434–436
CCY1 vs. CCY2 payout,
434–435
pay-at-maturity vs. pay-at-
touch, 435–436
O/N options, *see* Overnight options
Optionality of contracts, 79
Option on forward, 498–500
Option on strategy, 572
Option orders, 303–304
Option payoff, in Excel numerical
integration option pricer, 72–75
Option premium:
conversions for vanilla FX
derivatives, 163–164
and delta, 265
vanilla calls, 12
and variance, 180–181
Option price:
generating probability density
functions from, 253–259
in numerical integration option
pricer, 72–75
Option pricers (Excel):
Black-Scholes option pricer, 91–101
generate first-order Greeks,
98–100
plot exposures, 100–101
set up simple option pricer,
91–96
set up VBA pricing function,
96–98
Monte Carlo option pricer,
485–496
extensions, 496
multi-asset simulation, 494–496
pricing barrier options, 492–493

set up multiple payoffs, 490–492
set up simulation, 485–487
set up vanilla option payoff and
Monte Carlo loop, 487–490
numerical integration option pricer,
69–75
set up option payoff and calculate
option price, 72–75
set up terminal spot distribution,
69–72
testing, 75
Option values:
terminal spot distributions in
calculating, 65–66
vanilla FX derivatives, 77–82
Order book, 20
OTC (over-the-counter) market, 39,
294
OT options, *see* One-touch options
Out-of-the-money (OTM), 17
Overnight (O/N) options:
ATM on a Friday, 184–185
expiry and delivery dates, 162
vanilla trading, 296–299
Over-the-counter (OTC) market, 39,
294

P

''Paid'' offers, 23
Parallel ATM shift, 106
Partially exercised options, 151
Path dependence, in pricing exotic FX
derivatives, 373
Path-dependent options, in SDE,
59–60
Pay-at-maturity one-touch options, 436
Pay-at-touch one-touch
options, 436

593

Smile gamma effect, 272–273
Smile position, 272
Smile pricing models, 375
    jump diffusion, 383–384
    local volatility, 380–382
    mixed volatility, 382–383
    stochastic volatility, 377–380
Smile volatility roll, theta, 271
Smoothing barriers, 466
Sovereigns, 41
Speed of transactions, in FX derivatives
        market, 293–294
Spot (spot rate), 3–6, 11
Spot dates, 3, 161–162
Spot delta, *see* Delta
Spot dynamic, 469
Spot firm orders, 303
Spot jumps, 245, 246
Spot ladder, 138
Spot market:
    limited open hours, 469–470
    speed of transactions, 3
Spot rate (spot), 3–6, 11
Spot volatility, forward volatility vs.,
        470–471
Spread(s):
    ATM calendar:
        price making, 132
        trading exposures, 132
        vanilla, 132
    bet, 410
    bid–offer, 22–23
        European barrier options, 418
        European digital options, 405
        exotic FX derivatives, 462–463
        front-window barrier options,
        477–478
        multi-asset options, 541

one-touch options, 434
    self-quanto vanilla options, 514
    vanilla, 113–116
call/put:
    price making, 134
    vanilla, 132–134
confidence interval spreading, 541
defined, 304
horizontal, 132
positive, 307–308
replication spreading, 541
vanilla trading:
    positive, 307–308
    quoting, 304–305
vertical, 134
Spread contracts, *see* Risk reversal (RR)
Spread price:
    call/put, 134
    risk reversals, 130
Standardized language, 8–9
Stick strike analysis, 351
Sticky delta, 276
Sticky strike, 276
Stochastic interest rate pricing models,
        384–385
Stochastic local volatility models, 382
Stochastic Volatility Inspired (SVI), 232
Stochastic volatility pricing models,
        377–380
Stop-loss orders, 22, 429
Stopping time, in pricing exotic FX
        derivatives, 370–371
Straddles:
    long ATM, interest rate risk,
        291–292
    price making, 122
    trading exposures, 124
    vanilla, 121–124

Printed and bound by CPI Group (UK) Ltd, Croydon, CR0 4YY

23/04/2025

14661015-0004